THE HANDBOOK OF EMPLOYEE BENEFITS

SEVENTH EDITION

THE HANDBOOK OF EMPLOYEE BENEFITS

Health and Group Benefits

Jerry S. Rosenbloom, Ph.D.

Editor

McGraw Hill

New York Chicago San Francisco
Lisbon London Madrid Mexico City
Milan New Delhi San Juan Seoul
Singapore Sydney Toronto

The McGraw-Hill Companies

1 2 3 4 5 6 7 8 9 10 QFR/QFR 1 6 5 4 3 2 1

ISBN 978-0-07-174598-7
MHID 0-07-174598-X

e-ISBN 978-0-07-176309-7
e-MHID 0-07-176309-0

Library of Congress Cataloging-in-Publication Data

The handbook of employee benefits : health and group benefits/edited by Jerry S. Rosenbloom. — 7th ed.
p. cm.
ISBN 978-0-07-174598-7 (alk. paper)
1. Employee fringe benefits—United States. 2. Employee fringe benefits—Law and legislation—United States. 3. Employee fringe benefits—Taxation—Law and legislation—United States. I. Rosenbloom, Jerry S.
HD4928.N62U6353 2011
658.3'250973—dc22

2010052511

This book is printed on acid-free paper.

To Lynn, Debra, Heather and Amy

BRIEF CONTENTS

CONTENTS

PART TWO

MEDICAL AND OTHER HEALTH BENEFITS 55

Chapter 4

Health Plan Evolution 57

Chapter 5

Health Care Cost Containment: Demand-Side Approaches 115

Chapter 6

Managing and Measuring Care Management Intervention Programs 141

PREFACE

Much has taken place in the employee benefits field since the publication of the sixth edition of *The Handbook of Employee Benefits* in 2005. The seventh edition has been modified and updated to reflect major new pieces of legislation, dramatic changes in health care delivery, as demonstrated by the enactment in 2010 of the Patient Protection and Affordable Care Act as amended by the Health Care and Reconciliation Act, and the development and implementation of many new employee benefit concepts. This edition of the *Handbook* recognizes these changes and concentrates on the health and group benefits side of employee benefits.

The chapters that remain from the previous edition have been updated to incorporate legislative and other changes in the field, and several have been expanded to include new topic areas. Chapters have been added covering new and emerging areas in employee benefits. These new chapters include Health Care Cost Containment: Demand-Side Approaches; Managing and Measuring Care Management Intervention Programs; Pharmacy Benefits; Medicare Part D Prescription Drug Benefits; Funding Health Benefits: Self-Funded Arrangements and Captive Insurance Arrangements; Employee Benefit Plans for Small Companies; and Multiemployer Plans.

These changes reemphasize the basic premise that employee benefits can no longer be considered "fringe benefits" but must be regarded as an integral and extremely important component of an individual's financial security. A recent Bureau of Labor Statistics report on employee benefits indicates that, on average, employee benefits account for over 30 percent of a worker's total compensation. In light of the ever-increasing importance of benefit plans, those dealing with them must be well versed in the objectives, design, costing, funding, implementation, and administration of such plans.

While *The Handbook of Employee Benefits* is intended for students in the benefits field and for professionals as a handy reference, it can serve as a valuable tool for anyone with an interest in the field in general or in a specific employee benefit topic. The *Handbook* can be used as a reference work for benefit professionals or as a textbook for college courses, and for professional education and company training programs. Each chapter of the *Handbook* stands alone and is complete in itself. While this produces some overlap in certain areas, in many cases it eliminates the need to refer to other chapters while providing important reinforcement of difficult concepts.

The chapters of the *Handbook* are structured into eight parts, each covering a major component of the employee benefit planning process:

Part One: The Environment of Employee Benefit Plans

Part Two: Medical and Other Health Benefits

Part Three: Life Insurance Benefits

Part Four: Work/Life Benefits

Part Five: Social Insurance Programs

Part Six: Employee Benefit Plan Administration

Part Seven: Group and Health Benefit Plan Financial Management

Part Eight: Employee Benefit Plan Issues

The *Handbook* consists of 34 chapters written by distinguished authorities—academics, actuaries, attorneys, consultants, human resources professionals, and other benefit experts—covering all areas of the health and group benefits field. Their practical experience and breadth of knowledge provide insightful coverage of the employee benefits mechanism, and the examples and case studies presented throughout the *Handbook* illustrate the concepts presented.

In such a massive project, many people provided invaluable assistance, and it would be impossible to mention them all here. Special thanks must be extended, however, to the authors of the individual chapters for the outstanding coverage of their subject areas in a comprehensive and readable manner. Appreciation also must go to Diana Krigelman, who has been involved in the previous six editions and has spent many hours on all aspects of this manuscript. I would like to extend a grateful thanks to Fina Maniaci and Dennis F. Mahoney, who work with me in the Certified Employee Benefit Specialist (CEBS) Program, for their dedicated work in reviewing the entire manuscript and their many helpful comments. Thanks are also due to Diane Luedtke, who provided valuable guidance and insight throughout the manuscript development process.

In a work of this magnitude, it is almost inevitable that some mistakes may have escaped the eyes of the many reviewers of the manuscript. For these oversights I accept full responsibility and ask the reader's indulgence.

Jerry S. Rosenbloom

CONTRIBUTING AUTHORS

Stuart H. Alden, FSA, MAAA, FCA, Director of Actuarial Practice, Towers Watson

Mark S. Allen, Vice President of Global Benefits, TE Connectivity Ltd.. E-mail: mark.s.allen@te.com

Everett T. Allen, Jr., Vice President and Principal, Towers Perrin (deceased)

Mark A. Andruss, Vice President, Assurant Employee Benefits. E-mail: mark.andruss@assurant.com

David Blumenstein, Senior Vice President and National Director, Multiemployer Consulting, The Segal Company. E-mail: dblumenstein@segalco.com

Tony R. Broomhead, FIA, ASA, Director, International Consulting Group, Towers Watson. E-mail: tony.broomhead@towerswatson.com

John F. Burton, Jr., Professor, School of Management and Labor Relations, Rutgers: The State University of New Jersey. E-mail: jfburtonjr@aol.com (www.workerscompresources.com)

Amy L. Cavanaugh, CPC, QPA, QKA

Alan P. Cleveland, Esq., Sheenan, Phinney, Bass & Green. E-mail: acleveland@sheehan.com

Susan Conant, FLMI, CEBS, Senior Associate, Education & Training Division, LOMA

Ann Costello, Ph.D., Associate Professor, Department of Economics, Finance, and Insurance, Barney School of Business, University of Hartford. E-mail: acostello@hartford.edu

Craig J. Davidson, CEBS, Principal, Davidson Marketing Group, LLC; Lecturer, University of Wisconsin, Milwaukee. E-mail: craigd@davidsonmarketing.com

Ian Duncan, FSA, FIA, FCIA, MAAA, President, Solucia Consulting, a SCIOinspire Company. E-mail: iduncan@soluciaconsulting.com

G. Victor Hallman III, Ph.D., J.D., CPCU, CLU, Lecturer in Financial and Estate Planning, Department of Insurance and Risk Management, The Wharton School, University of Pennsylvania

David Harvey, Sales Associate, International Foundation of Employee Benefit Plans. E-mail: davidh@ifebp.org

Ronald L. Huling, PRM Consulting. E-mail: ron.huling@prmconsulting.com

Edward Jones, Ph.D., Executive Vice President Value Options

Dagmar King

Robert T. LeClair, Ph.D., Associate Professor, Finance Department, College of Commerce and Finance, Villanova University. E-mail: leclairr@msn.com

Diane Luedtke, FSA, CLU, Principal and Consulting Actuary, Navigator Benefit Solutions, LLC. E-mail: d.luedtke@navben.us

Timothy Luedtke, FSA, MAAA, CFA, Principal and Consulting Actuary, Navigator Benefit Solutions, LLC. E-mail: t.luedtke@navben.us

Dennis F. Mahoney, MS, CEBS, CFP®, Director, Wharton Executive Education, Certified Employee Benefit Specialist (CEBS) Program, The Wharton School, University of Pennsylvania. E-mail: mahoneyd@wharton.upenn.edu

Serafina Maniaci, MS, CEBS, Certified Employee Benefit Specialist (CEBS) Program, The Wharton School, University of Pennsylvania

William J. Mayer, MD, MPH, Vice President, Chief Quality Officer, Bronson Healthcare Group. E-mail: williamjmayer@gmail.com

Ann McClanathan

Jan McFarland, Director of LTC Marketing & Communications, John Hancock Financial Services. E-mail: jmcfarland@jhancock.com

Robert J. Myers, LLD, FSA, Professor Emeritus, Temple University, Chief Actuary, Social Security Administration, 1947–1970; Deputy Commissioner, Social Security Administration, 1981–1982; and Executive Director, National Commission on Social Security Reform, 1982–1983 (deceased)

Richard Ostuw, FSA, Towers Watson

William H. Rabel, Ph.D., FLMI, CLU, John & Mary Louise Loftis Bickley Endowed Teaching Chair in Insurance & Financial Services, The University of Alabama

John S. Roberts, CLU, President and CEO, Assurant Employee Benefits. E-mail: john.roberts@assurant.com

Jerry S. Rosenbloom, Ph.D., CLU, CPCU, Frederick H. Ecker Emeritus Professor of Insurance and Risk Management, Department of Insurance and Risk Management; and Academic Director, Certified Employee Benefit Specialist (CEBS) Program, The Wharton School, University of Pennsylvania

Craig S. Stern, PharmD, MBA, President, ProPharma Pharmaceutical Consultants, Inc. E-mail: craig.stern@propharmaconsultants.com (www.ProPharmaConsultants.com)

Gary K. Stone, Ph.D., CLU, ChFC, Executive Vice President, The American College (retired). E-mail: stoneg@msu.edu

Richard L. Tewksbury, Jr., CLU, TRION Group. E-mail: rtewksbury@trion.com

Ronald L. Woodmansee, CLU, CEBS, MSFS, Woodmansee & Co. E-mail: woody@woodmanseeandco.com

PART ONE

The Environment of Employee Benefit Plans

In the United States employee benefits constitute a major component of an employee's financial and economic security. Such benefits have gone from being considered "fringe" benefits to constituting as much as 35 percent or more of an employee's compensation. This being the case, it is easy to see why these benefits and the plans under which they are provided are a major concern of employers and employees alike.

Individuals responsible for the design, pricing, selling, and administration of employee benefits carry a broad range of responsibilities, and the role of the benefits professional has changed rapidly and radically in the past 25 years. During that period, the number of employee benefits has virtually exploded, with expansion occurring in many of the more traditional benefits and with the addition of totally new forms of benefits. The passage of the Patient Protection and Affordable Care Act (PPACA) raised many new questions and issues for all those involved in every aspect of employee benefit plans.

Part One of the *Handbook* is concerned with the environment in which employee benefit plans are designed and operated. Chapter 1 considers many important design issues. Chapter 2 extends the discussion of employee benefit plan design concepts by looking at the functional approach to designing and evaluating employee benefits. The functional approach provides a framework for various strategies used to consider benefits on a risk-by-risk basis and as a part of total compensation. Chapter 3 considers some of the risk and insurance concepts inherent in many approaches to employee benefit planning and lays the foundation for many of the concepts used throughout the *Handbook*.

CHAPTER 1

The Environment of Employee Benefit Plans

Jerry S. Rosenbloom

In the United States, employee benefits are an extremely important part of an employee's financial security. Once considered to be "fringe" benefits because of their relatively small magnitude, this cannot be said today of employee benefits, which may account for over 35 percent of an individual's total compensation. In many firms, that percentage is even higher. Furthermore, many new types of employee benefits have come onto the scene in recent years as employers compete for a talented workforce, and benefits have become much more of a strategic consideration for many firms. Moreover, with the passage of the Patient Protection and Affordable Care Act (PPACA) on March 23, 2010, many new questions for employee benefit plans, particularly in the health care area, have and will continue to emerge. To ensure that both employers and employees utilize employee benefit plans in the most effective manner requires a thorough knowledge of all aspects of benefit plan design, funding, and administration, including communications.

This chapter gives the necessary background for the rest of the volume by outlining what employee benefits are, the reasons for their growth, what they are intended to achieve from both the employer and employee perspectives, and what makes such plans work.

EMPLOYEE BENEFITS DEFINED

Employee benefits are a part of almost every employee's total compensation—that is, "all forms of financial returns and tangible services and benefits employees receive as part of an employment relationship."[1]

Broad View of Employee Benefits

Many definitions of employee benefits exist, ranging from the broadest to the most narrow. In the broad view, employee benefits are virtually any form of compensation other than direct wages[2] and might be defined broadly to include the following:

1. Employer's share of legally required payments (Social Security and Medicare, unemployment insurance, and workers' compensation benefits)
2. Payments for time not worked (e.g., paid rest periods, paid sick leave, paid vacations, holidays, parental leave, and the like)
3. Employer's share of medical and medically related payments
4. Employer's share of retirement and savings plan payments
5. Miscellaneous benefit payments (including employee discounts, severance pay, educational expenditures, and child care, among others)

Table 1-1 illustrates the relative importance of employer costs for benefits as a percentage of payroll for civilian workers, private industry, and state and local government. As the table indicates, employee benefits are intertwined with almost every facet of an individual's economic and financial security.

A More Limited View of Employee Benefits

The broad view of employee benefits encompasses both legally mandated benefits such as Social Security and other governmental programs and private plans, while the narrow view can be summarized as "any type of plan sponsored or initiated unilaterally or jointly by employers and employees in providing benefits that stem from the employment relationship that are not underwritten by or paid for directly by government."[3]

---

1. George T. Milkovich, Jerry M. Newman and B. Gerhart, *Compensation*, 10th ed., New York, NY: McGraw-Hill Irwin, 2011, p. 10.
2. Jerry S. Rosenbloom and G. Victor Hallman, *Employee Benefit Planning*, 3rd ed., Englewood Cliffs, NJ: Prentice Hall, 1991, pp. 2–3.
3. Martha Remey Yohalem, "Employee Benefit Plans—1975," *Social Security Bulletin*, Vol. 40, No. 11, November 1977, p. 19.

TABLE 1-1

Relative Importance (%) of Employer Costs for Employee Compensation, December 2010

Compensation Component	Civilian Workers	Private Industry	State and Local Government
Wages and salaries	69.7	70.8	65.6
Benefits	30.3	29.2	34.4
Paid leave	7.0	6.8	7.5
Supplemental pay	2.3	2.7	0.8
Insurance	8.8	8.0	11.9
Health benefits	8.4	7.5	11.6
Retirement and savings	4.5	3.5	8.1
Defined benefit	2.7	1.5	7.3
Defined contribution	1.8	2.0	0.8
Legally required	7.8	8.2	6.0

Source: Bureau of Labor Statistics, "Employer Costs for Employee Compensation, December 2010," news release, March 9, 2011, p. 3.

This narrow definition of employee benefits will be the one primarily used in the *Handbook*. This is not in any way meant to imply that legally required benefits are unimportant. On the contrary, these benefits are extremely important and must be considered in employee benefit plan design and in integrating private employee benefit plans with the benefits provided by governmental bodies. This interrelationship is stressed throughout the book. In addition to benefits provided through government bodies and those provided through the employment relationship, benefits provided by an individual for his or her own welfare or that of his or her dependents are also described when appropriate. This so-called tripod or three-legged stool of economic security underlies the foundation of individual and family financial security.

REASONS FOR THE GROWTH OF EMPLOYEE BENEFIT PLANS

Numerous reasons exist for the evolution of employee benefit plans from a fringe benefit to a major component of financial security today. They stem from external forces as well as the desire of employers and employees to achieve certain goals and objectives.

Business Reasons

A multitude of business reasons explain why employee benefit plans were established and why they have expanded greatly. Employers want to attract and retain capable employees. Having employee benefit plans in place helps to serve this objective. Also, in many cases, an employer's competition has certain benefit plans, and it is necessary to have equal or better plans to attract and retain employees. Moreover, employers hope that corporate efficiency, productivity, and improved employee morale will be fostered by good benefit plans. Concerns for employees' welfare and social objectives have also encouraged employers to provide benefits.

Collective Bargaining

Through the collective bargaining process, labor unions have had a major impact on the growth of employee benefit plans. The Labor Management Relations Act (LMRA), which is administered by the National Labor Relations Board (NLRB), requires good-faith collective bargaining over wages, hours, and other terms and conditions of employment. A notable event occurred in 1948 when the NLRB ruled that the meaning of the term wages includes a pension plan, and this position was upheld in the landmark case of *Inland Steel Co.* v. *National Labor Relations Board* in the same year. Shortly thereafter, in 1949, the good-faith bargaining requirements were held to include a group health and accident plan (*W.W. Cross & Co.* v. *National Labor Relations Board*). As a result of these two decisions, it was clearly established that the LMRA provisions applied to both retirement and welfare benefit plans, and their subsequent growth has been substantial.

The LMRA, or Taft-Hartley Act, as it is commonly known, has also played significant roles in the development of employee benefit plans. Along with the Internal Revenue Code (IRC), it established the distinction between retirement benefits and welfare benefits such as life and health insurance. Additionally, the statute sets forth the basic regulatory framework under which both of these major categories of benefits are to be jointly administered with the collective bargaining process. As such, it is the legislative basis on which jointly trusteed benefit plans are founded. (See Chapter 33.)

Favorable Tax Legislation

Over the years, the tax laws have favored employee benefit plans. Such preferential tax legislation has greatly encouraged the development of employee benefit plans as well as helping to shape their design, because many plans seek to maximize the tax advantages or lessen the tax consequences of various employee benefit plans. The main tax benefits of employee benefit plans are as follows: (1) most contributions to employee benefit plans by employers are deductible as long as they are reasonable business expenses; (2) contributions from employers within certain limits on behalf of employees generally are not considered income to employees; and (3) on certain types of retirement and capital accumulation plans, assets set aside to fund such plans accumulate tax-free until distributed. Some additional tax benefits may be available when such distributions are made. All in all, favorable tax legislation has had a great impact on the development and expansion of employee benefit plans.

Efficiency of the Employee Benefits Approach

Following the Industrial Revolution, the aggregation of employees and employers in cities and in business firms made it possible for the employee benefits concept to flourish by covering many employees under one contract. The simplicity and convenience of providing coverage to people through their place of employment made sense from many standpoints. Employee benefits providers and suppliers, such as insurance companies, banks, and various types of health care coverage providers, all found the marketing of such benefits through the employer to be a cost-effective and administratively efficient channel of distribution.

Other Factors

Many other factors have contributed to the growth of employee benefit plans. One such factor was the imposition of limitations on the size of wage increases granted during World War II and the Korean War. While wages were frozen, employee benefits were not. As a result, compensation of employees could effectively be increased by provision of larger benefits. The result was a major expansion of employee benefits during these two periods.

Some have argued that various legislative actions over the years have encouraged employee benefit plans not only through providing favorable tax treatment but also by the government's "moral suasion" that, if such benefit plans were not established voluntarily by employers and employees, additional governmental programs might result. With the enactment of health care reform through the PPACA legislation, many questions have arisen concerning this concept. Also, allowing employee benefits to be integrated with governmental benefits has enhanced the private employee benefit approach by taking into consideration benefits provided by governmental plans in benefit plan design.

Development of the group approach to certain employee benefits has helped expand the employee benefit mechanism. The techniques utilized in the group selection process made it possible for employers to provide benefits that previously could only be provided on an individual basis with coverage often determined by individual medical selection.

GROUP TECHNIQUE

The group technique enables insurance programs such as life insurance and health insurance, to name only two, to be written as employee benefit plans.[4] Unlike individual insurance, group insurance is based on a view of the group rather than the individual as the unit to be insured. Usually, individual insurance eligibility requirements are not required for group insurance written under an employee benefit plan.[5] The concepts that make the group technique work are all designed to prevent "adverse selection"—that is, to reduce the possibility that less-healthy individuals may join a group or be a larger percentage of a group than anticipated because of the availability of insurance or other benefits.

Characteristics of the group technique of providing employee benefits include some or all of the following:[6]

1. *Only certain groups eligible.* While most groups qualify, this requirement is intended to make sure that the obtaining of insurance is incidental to the group seeking coverage. Thus, a group should not be formed solely for the purpose of obtaining insurance.
2. *Steady flow of lives through the group.* The theory behind this concept is that younger individuals should come into the group

4. See Chapter 14 for additional discussion of the "group mechanism" to providing employee benefits.
5. A discussion of the insurance technique and how and why it works is presented in Chapter 3.
6. See Jerry S. Rosenbloom and G. Victor Hallman, *Employee Benefit Planning*, 3rd ed., Englewood Cliffs, NJ: Prentice Hall, 1991, pp. 15–20.

while older individuals leave it, thus maintaining a fairly constant mortality or morbidity ratio in the group. If the group does not maintain this "flow through the group" and the average age of the group increases substantially, costs could increase dramatically.

3. *Minimum number of persons in a group.* A minimum number of persons, typically 10, must be in a group to be eligible for group benefits. However, this requirement has been liberalized to the point where two or three individuals in a group may obtain coverage. This minimum-number provision is designed to prevent less healthy lives from being a major part of the group and to spread the expenses of the benefits plan over a larger number of individuals.[7]
4. *A minimum portion of the group must participate.* Typically, in group life and health insurance plans, if the plan is noncontributory (solely paid for by the employer), 100 percent of eligible employees must be covered. If the plan is contributory (employer and employee share the cost), 75 percent of the employees must participate. The rationale for this provision is also to reduce adverse selection and spread the expense of administration.[8]
5. *Eligibility requirements.* Frequently, eligibility requirements are imposed under group plans for the purpose, once again, of preventing adverse selection. An employee must be actively at work on the first day of eligibility. The employer may have a period of time, called the eligibility period, before the employee may participate in the benefit plan. Certain benefit plans may require an elimination or waiting period to elapse before an employee receives a benefit for which he or she is eligible. Also, if employees do not join when eligible and want to enroll at a later date, some form of medical information may be required.
6. *Maximum limits for any one person.* In certain cases, maximum limits on the amount of life or health benefits may be imposed to prevent the possibility of excessive amounts of coverage for any particular unhealthy individual.
7. *Automatic determination of benefits.* To prevent unhealthy lives in a group from obtaining an extremely large amount of a

7. Ibid.
8. Ibid.

particular benefit or benefits, coverage is determined for all individuals in the group on an automatic basis. This basis may be determined by an employee's salary, service, or position, it may be a flat amount for all employees, or it may be a combination of these factors.

8. *A central and efficient administrative agency.* To keep expenses to a minimum and to handle the mechanics of the benefit plan, a central and efficient administrative agency is necessary for the successful operation of an employee benefit plan. An employer is an almost ideal administrator because it maintains the payroll and other employee information necessary in meeting tax and record-keeping requirements.[9]

Over the years, many of the requirements just described have been liberalized as providers of employee benefits have gained experience in handling group employee benefits, and because of the competitive environment. Nevertheless, the basic group selection technique is important in understanding why employee benefits can work on a group basis and how any problems that exist might be corrected.

OVERALL EMPLOYEE BENEFIT CONCERNS

As previously noted, because employee benefits provide such an important dimension of financial security in our society, some overall questions need to be asked to evaluate any existing or newly created employee benefit plan. While later chapters in this *Handbook* analyze benefit design, cost, funding, administration, and communication issues, some principles permeate all these areas and need brief mention early in this text.[10]

What are the Employer and Employee Objectives in Establishing the Plan?

The design of any employee benefit plan must start with the objectives for the benefit plan from the standpoint of both employer and employee.

9. Ibid.
10. Some of the ideas presented here are based on Jerry S. Rosenbloom and G. Victor Hallman, *Employee Benefit Planning*, 3rd ed., Englewood Cliffs, NJ: Prentice Hall, 1991, Chapter 23. For a more detailed analysis, consult this publication.

What Benefits Should Be Provided Under the Plan?

There should be clearly stated reasons or objectives for the type of benefits to be provided. Benefits provided both under governmental programs and through purchase by employees should be considered.

Who Should Be Covered Under the Benefit Plan?

Should only full-time employees be covered? What about retirees or dependents? What about survivors of deceased employees? These and a host of similar questions must be carefully evaluated. Of course, some of these issues depend on regulatory and legislative rules and regulations.

Should Employees Have Benefit Options?

This question has become more assumed greater prominence for employee benefit plans because of the changing workforce. Additionally, with the growth of flexible benefits or cafeteria plans, employee choice continues to increase. Even in nonflexible benefit plan situations, should some choices may be given?

How Should the Benefit Plan Be Financed?

Several important questions need to be answered in determining the approach to funding an employee benefit plan. Should financing be entirely provided by the employer (a noncontributory approach) or on some shared basis by the employer and employee (a contributory approach)? If on a contributory basis, what percentage should each bear?

What funding method should be used? A wide range of possibilities exists, from a total insurance program to total self-funding, with many options in between. Even when one of these options is selected, further questions still remain concerning the specific funding instrument to be used. The cost of providing benefits has become a major area of concern for both employers and employees. Many methods of trying to contain employee benefit costs are discussed throughout this *Handbook*.

How Should the Benefit Plan Be Administered?

Should the firm itself administer the plan? Should an insurance carrier or other benefit plan provider handle the administration? Should some external organization such as a third-party administrator (TPA) do this work? Once the decision has been made, the specific entity must be selected.

How Should the Benefit Plan Be Communicated?

The best employee benefit plan in existence may not achieve any of its desired objectives if it is improperly communicated to all affected parties. The communication of employee benefit plans has become increasingly important in recent years with the increased employee choice in several benefit areas and increased reporting and disclosure requirements. Effective communication and education regarding what benefit plans will and will not do is essential if employees are to rely on such plans to provide part of their financial security at all stages of their lives. Technology has provided many new options in this area. (See Chapter 27.)

Future of Employee Benefits

With the spate of legislation affecting certain aspects of employee benefit plans, the varying needs of today's diverse workforce, and the outsourcing of many benefit functions, some benefit experts believe there may be more changes than ever before. While certain new approaches and techniques may be utilized, employee benefit plans are woven into the fabric of our society in such a way that the basic character or importance of such plans will not be altered. With pressures to contain health care costs and with retirement costs ever increasing, greater efficiencies in the benefits approach, more tailoring to individual needs in the growth of flexible benefits or cafeteria compensation plans, and other refinements will drive the employee benefits mechanism. While it seems certain that employee benefits will not grow as rapidly as they have in the past, their place is secure and there will continue to be a demand for people who are knowledgeable about all aspects of the design, funding, administration, and communication of employee benefits. Professionals in this area will make such plans more effective while helping to provide economic security for society at large.

CHAPTER 2

Functional Approach to Designing and Evaluating Employee Benefits

G. Victor Hallman III

This chapter deals with the functional approach toward analyzing an existing employee benefit program and evaluating the need for new or modified employee benefits. The functional approach can be defined as an organized system for classifying and analyzing the risks and needs of active employees, their dependents, and various other categories of persons into logical categories of exposures to loss and employee needs. These exposures and needs may include health care (medical, dental, and other) expenses, losses resulting from death, losses caused by short- and long-term disabilities, retirement income needs, other capital accumulation needs, needs arising out of short- and long-term unemployment, custodial care (long-term care) needs, dependent care assistance needs, and other employee needs.

THE FUNCTIONAL APPROACH IN CONCEPT

As indicated above, the functional approach is the application of a systematic method of analysis to an employer's total employee benefits program. It analyzes the employer's program as a coordinated whole in terms of its ability to meet employees' (and others') needs and to manage loss exposures within the employer's overall compensation goals and cost parameters. This approach can be useful in overall employee benefit plan design, in evaluating proposals for new or revised benefits, for evaluation of cost-saving proposals, and in effective communication of an employer's total benefits program to its employees. It can be seen that the functional approach, which is essentially a planning approach, fits logically with the total compensation philosophy, as explained later in this chapter.

The functional approach to employee benefits is not really a new concept. In 1967, George C. Foust outlined the approach in the American Management Association book, *The Total Approach to Employee Benefits*.[1] Similarly, Robert M. McCaffery in his pioneering 1972 work, *Managing the Employee Benefits Program*, stated:

> The "package" or total approach to employee benefits is simply the purposeful management of an integrated program. Rather than continually reacting to current fads, outside pressures, and salesmen's pitches, the contemporary businessman relies on fundamental principles of management in developing, organizing, directing, and evaluating systems of employee benefits for his organization.[2]

The functional approach represents such systematic management of the employee benefits function.

NEED FOR THE FUNCTIONAL APPROACH

The functional approach is needed in planning, designing, and administering employee benefits for several reasons.

First, in most instances, employee benefits are a very significant element of the total compensation of employees. Benefits have become an important part of the work rewards provided by employers to their employees. They also generally are a very tax-effective way of compensating employees. Therefore, it is important to employees, and hence to their employers, that this increasingly important element of compensation be planned and organized to be as effective as possible in meeting employee needs.

Second, employee benefits generally represent a large item of labor cost for employers. Therefore, effective planning and hence avoidance of waste in providing benefits can be an important cost-control measure for employers.

1. George C. Foust, Jr., "The Total Approach Concept," in *The Total Approach to Employee Benefits*, ed. Arthur J. Deric, New York: American Management Association, 1967, Chapter 1.
2. Robert M. McCaffery, *Managing the Employee Benefits Program*, New York: American Management Association, 1972, p. 17. There is also a revised (1983) edition of this book. These farsighted concepts are developed further by McCaffery in Chapter 2, "Planning a Total Program," of Robert M. McCaffery, *Employee Benefit Programs: A Total Compensation Perspective*, 2nd ed., Boston: PWS–KENT Publishing Company, 1992.

Third, in the past, employee benefits may have been adopted by employers on a piecemeal basis without being coordinated with existing benefit programs, as suggested by the McCaffery quote above. Thus, it is often fruitful to apply the functional approach in reviewing existing employee benefit plans or proposed changes in plans to determine where overlapping benefits may exist and costs can be saved, and where gaps in benefits may exist and new benefits or revised benefits may be in order.

Fourth, because of new benefits and coverages, changes in the tax laws, changes in the regulatory environment, a challenging economic climate, and other developments in recent years, it is important to have a systematic approach to planning benefits to keep them current, cost effective, and in compliance with regulatory requirements.

The last point can be illustrated by the enactment of the Patient Protection and Affordable Care Act (PPACA) as amended by the Health Care and Reconciliation Act. This extensive law shows the demands that may be placed on the benefit plans of private employers to help solve perceived social problems. Among many other provisions that become effective at various times, this sweeping new law starting in 2014 will assess a shared responsibility payment (a nondeductible penalty) on larger employers (those with an average of 50 or more full-time employees) who do not offer their full-time employees and the employees' dependents the opportunity to enroll in an eligible employer-provided health care plan providing minimum essential coverage and who have at least one of their full-time employees enrolled in a state Health Insurance Exchange with a premium tax credit or cost-sharing reduction for the employee(s). A shared responsibility payment may even be due from larger employers who do offer minimum essential coverage for their full-time employees and their dependents if the employer has one or more full-time employees enrolled in a state Health Insurance Exchange with a premium tax credit or cost-sharing reduction for the employee(s). In addition, such employers who offer minimum essential coverage to their employees and pay any portion of the costs of such coverage must provide and pay for free choice vouchers to employees who do not elect to participate in the employer's plan and who meet certain required contributions and household income limits (i.e., generally employees whose required contributions are "too large" a percentage of their household incomes). Moreover, the PPACA, starting in 2010, imposes some important coverage and reporting requirements on group health care plans and individual coverage. Further, starting in 2018, employers are required to calculate and report the excise tax due on high-coverage (so-called "Cadillac") employer-sponsored health care plans to the coverage providers and the Treasury Secretary (the IRS). Coverage providers include insurers for insured group health care plans and plan administrators for self-insured plans and some other plans. This excise tax of 40 percent of any excess benefit (which is the amount the employer's cost for coverage exceeds a statutory threshold amount) may well cause employers to keep their cost of health care coverage at or below the threshold amounts. On the other hand, smaller employers (those with 25 or fewer full-time employees with average compensation of $50,000 or less) may be eligible for tax credits for the premiums they pay toward health coverage for their employees. Clearly, complying with these regulatory requirements will be a substantial issue for employers for many years.

Finally, a given employee benefit or program, such as a pension plan, often provides benefits relating to several separate employee needs or loss exposures. Therefore, an employer's benefit plan needs to be analyzed according to the functional approach so its various benefit programs can be integrated properly with each other.

CONSISTENCY WITH AN EMPLOYER'S TOTAL COMPENSATION PHILOSOPHY

In designing the total compensation package, an employer should seek to balance the various elements of its compensation system, including basic cash wages and salary, current incentive compensation (current cash bonuses and company stock bonuses), longer-term incentive plans (including stock-based and performance-based plans), and so-called employee benefits, to help meet the needs and desires of the employees on the one hand and the employer's basic compensation philosophy and objectives on the other. Thus, it is clear that the functional approach to planning and designing an employee benefit plan must remain consistent with the employer's total compensation philosophy. A particular employer, therefore, may not cover a certain employee desire for benefits, or may cover it in a rather spartan manner, not because the desire is not recognized but because the employer's total compensation philosophy calls for a relatively low level of employee benefits or, perhaps, benefits oriented in a different direction.

Employers may adopt different business policies regarding the general compensation of their employees. For example, many employers want to compensate their employees at a level in line with that generally prevailing in their industry or community, or both. They do not wish to be much above or below average compensation levels. The employee benefit programs of such employers also frequently follow this general philosophy.

Other employers may follow a high-compensation philosophy (including employee benefits) with the goal of attracting higher levels of management, technical, and general employee talent. This may be particularly true in industries where the need for a highly skilled workforce is great. On the other hand, there may be employers that follow a low-compensation policy, feeling that, for them, the resultant lower payroll costs more than outweigh the resulting higher employee turnover and lower skill level of their workforce. An employer with this kind of philosophy may want to adopt more modest employee benefit programs.

Type of industry and employer characteristics also will have an impact on an employer's total compensation philosophy and on the design of its employee benefit plan. Table 2-1 is a grid presented by one employee benefit consulting firm showing the relationship between type of organization, working climate, and compensation mix.

Thus, a larger well-established employer in a mature industry, a financial institution, or a nonprofit organization may take a relatively liberal

TABLE 2-1

Organizational Style and Compensation Mix

		Reward Management Components			
		Cash		Noncash	
Type of Organization	Working Climate	Base Salary	Short-Term Incentives	Level	Characteristics
Mature industrial	Balanced	Medium	Medium	Medium	Balanced
Developing industrial	Growth, creativity	Medium	High	Low	Short-term oriented
Conservative financial	Security	Low	Low	High	Long-term, security-oriented
Nonprofit	Societal impact, personal fulfillment	Low	None	Low to medium	Long-term, security-oriented
Sales	Growth, freedom to act	Low	High	Low	Short-term oriented

Source: Hay-Huggins, member of the Hay Group.

approach toward meeting the benefits needs and desires of its employees. But developing industrial firms, high-tech companies, and other growth companies, which may have considerable current needs for capital and seek a highly skilled and motivated workforce, may seek to rely more heavily on short-term oriented incentive types of compensation. Further, industries that are highly competitive, subject to cyclical fluctuations, or perhaps in a currently depressed state may not be willing to add to their relatively fixed labor costs by adopting or liberalizing employee benefits, even if there may be a functional need for them. In fact, such firms may seek to cut back on their employee benefit commitments when possible. However, even in these situations, firms should attempt to allocate their available compensation dollars in as consistent and logical a manner as possible to meet the needs and goals of their employees as well as their own corporate compensation objectives. In fact, the functional approach may be even more appropriate in such cases, because their resources for compensating employees are relatively scarce.

Another area of employer philosophy that affects the functional approach and how it is actually applied is whether the employer tends to follow a compensation/service-oriented benefit philosophy or a benefit- or needs-oriented philosophy. Employers having a compensation/service-oriented philosophy tend to relate employee benefits primarily to compensation or service, or both, in designing their employee benefit plans (of course, remaining consistent with any nondiscrimination rules). Thus, the level of benefits would tend to be tied in with compensation level, and eligibility for benefits may be conditioned directly or indirectly on salary level. For example, separate benefit plans may be provided for salaried and for hourly rated employees, with more generous benefits being made available to the former group. Further, some types of benefits may be available only to certain higher-paid employees or executives. In addition, such employers tend to emphasize service with the employer in determining benefit levels and eligibility for benefits. The theory of this approach is that employee benefits generally should be aimed at rewarding the longer-service employees who have shown a commitment to the employer. The benefit- or needs-oriented philosophy, on the other hand, tends to focus primarily on the needs of employees and their dependents, rather than on compensation and service.

In practice, the design of employee benefit plans tends to be a compromise between these two philosophies. On one side, certain kinds of employee benefits, such as medical expense benefits, tend to be primarily benefit- or needs-oriented. On the other side, benefits such as group life insurance and pensions customarily are compensation oriented, at least for nonunion employees. Thus, this distinction in philosophy really is one of degree. However, the extent to which eligibility for benefits, participation requirements, and levels of employee benefits reflect compensation or service, or both, may affect the extent to which the needs of employees or certain categories of employees will be met by an employee benefit plan.

APPLICATION OF THE FUNCTIONAL APPROACH

While the functional approach to planning employee benefits has been actively discussed since the early 1960s, no clearly developed procedure or technique exists for the application of this approach to individual benefit plans. However, based on the underlying concept and the way it is applied in practice, here are the logical steps in applying the functional approach to employee benefit plan design, revision, or review. For convenience of presentation, these steps can be listed as follows:

1. Classify employee (and dependent) needs or objectives in logical functional categories.
2. Classify the categories of persons (e.g., employees, some former employees, and dependents) the employer may want to protect, at least to some extent, through its employee benefit plan.
3. Analyze the benefits presently available under the plan in terms of the functional categories of needs or objectives, in terms of the categories of persons the employer may want to benefit, and in terms of regulatory requirements and possibly mandated coverages.
4. Determine any gaps in benefits or overlapping benefits, or both, provided from all sources under the employer's employee benefit plan and from other benefit plans in terms of the functional categories of needs and the persons to be protected.
5. Consider recommendations for changes in the employer's present employee benefit plan to meet any gaps in benefits and to correct any overlapping benefits, including possible use of the flexible benefits (cafeteria plan) approach.
6. Estimate the costs or savings from each of the recommendations made in step 5.
7. Evaluate alternative methods of financing or securing the benefits recommended above, as well as the employee benefit plan's existing benefits.

8. Consider other cost-saving techniques in connection with the recommended benefits or existing benefits (i.e., plan cost-containment strategies).
9. Decide upon the appropriate benefits, methods of financing, and sources of benefits as a result of the preceding analysis.
10. Implement the changes.
11. Communicate benefit changes to employees.
12. Periodically reevaluate the employee benefit plan.

Each of these steps is considered in greater detail below. Naturally, it must be recognized in applying this process to a particular employee benefit plan that some of these steps may be combined with others and some will be taken implicitly. However, each step represents a logical decision point or consideration in the design or revision of an employee benefit plan.

Classify Employee and Dependent Needs in Functional Categories

The needs and exposures to loss of employees and their dependents can be classified in a variety of ways, some being more complete than others. The following classification appears to cover most of the commonly accepted needs and exposures to loss that may be covered under an employee benefit plan:

1. Medical expenses incurred by active employees, by their dependents, by retired (or certain otherwise terminated, suspended, or temporarily not in service) employees or former employees, and by their dependents
2. Losses due to employees' disability (short-term and long-term)
3. Losses resulting from active employees' deaths, from their dependents' deaths, and from the deaths of retired (or certain otherwise terminated, suspended, or temporarily not in service) employees or former employees
4. Retirement needs of employees and their dependents
5. Capital accumulation needs or goals (short-term and long-term)
6. Needs arising from unemployment or from temporary termination or suspension of employment
7. Needs for financial counseling, retirement counseling, and other counseling services

8. Losses resulting from property and liability exposures and the like
9. Needs for dependent care assistance (e.g., child-care or elder-care services)
10. Needs for educational assistance for employees themselves or for employees' dependents, or for both
11. Needs for custodial-care expenses (long-term care) for employees or their dependents or for retired employees or their dependents
12. Other employee benefit needs or goals (such as a desire to participate in corporate stock plans or other longer-term incentive programs)

Naturally, a given functional analysis often does not encompass all these needs, goals, or loss exposures. The above classification is intended to be more exhaustive than frequently is included in a functional analysis. The history of employee benefit planning since the end of World War II generally has been one of expanding the areas of employees' (and others') needs for which employers provide benefits of various kinds. However, in recent years, increasing attention has been paid to containing the costs to the employer of benefit plans. The functional approach can also be used to evaluate cost-containment measures.

Table 2-2 provides an illustration of the functional approach, using the employee benefit plan of a large corporation and the functional categories used by that corporation. Note that the employee needs, goals, and exposures to loss are shown on the left-hand margin of the grid, while the components of this corporation's employee benefit plan are shown across the top of the grid. This arrangement shows how each benefit plan applies to each of these employee needs, goals, or loss exposures. Any gaps or duplications in coverage (or need for further information) can be seen more easily through this systematic process of analysis.

Classify by Categories the Persons the Employer May Want to Protect

This step basically involves the issues of who should be protected by an employee benefit plan, for what benefits, for what time period, and under what conditions. These issues have become increasingly important in employee benefit planning as the scope of employee benefit plans has increased not only in terms of the benefits provided but also in terms of

TABLE 2-2

Illustration of Functional Approach to Employee Benefit Planning

Employee Needs, Goals, or Exposures to Loss	Health Care Plan	Basic Salary Continuation Plan	Extended Salary Continuation Plan	Long-Term Disability Plan	Basic Life Insurance Plan
Medical expenses	Choice among 3 types of plans (health maintenance organization, preferred provider organization and point of service options) with different levels of employee contributions and cost-sharing. Dental, hearing, and vision care also covered.				
Disability losses	Coverage continues while employee receives disability benefits under company plans.	Full salary for up to 30 days of absence each year for illness or injury.	After the basic allowance is exhausted, employee's full salary less offsetting benefits is maintained up to a maximum of 25 months depending on length of service.	After extended plan ends, 75% of base monthly pay less offsetting benefits for up to 25 months; then, a voluntary payroll deduction LTD benefit of 50% of salary.	Coverage continues while employee receives disability benefits under company plans.
In case of death	Dependent coverage continues for 4 months plus an additional period depending upon employee service, at the employer's expense. Thereafter, the plan meets COBRA requirements.	Coverage terminates.	Coverage terminates.	Coverage terminates.	Provides beneficiary with a benefit of $3,000.
Retirement	Modified plans may be continued for life during retirement on a contributory basis.	Coverage terminates.	Coverage terminates.	Coverage terminates.	$3,000 coverage continues after retirement for as long as employee lives.
Capital accumulation					
Dependent care assistance					

TABLE 2-2

Primary Life Insurance Plan	Travel Accident Plan	Savings Plan	Employees' Stock Purchase Plan	Pension Plan
Coverage continues while employee receives disability benefits under company plans.	Pays a benefit of up to 3 times employee's annual base pay if disability involves an accidental dismemberment while traveling on company business.	Contributions are discontinued when long-term disability benefits begin. Participation may continue unless employee becomes permanently and totally disabled or until formal retirement. Withdrawals are permitted.	Employee receiving disability benefits may suspend any payments being made to the plan for a period not to exceed 6 months or a specified date in the offering.	Participation continues while employee receives company disability benefits; service credits accumulate until end of extended disability period or up to 3 months.
Provides beneficiary with a benefit of 3 times employee's current annual base pay (offset by pension plan,s preretirement survivor benefit). Employee also has the option to purchase additional life insurance at favorable group rates, up to 3 times current base pay.	Pays beneficiary a lump-sum benefit of 3 times employee's annual base pay if death is the result of an accident while traveling on company business.	Beneficiary receives the amount credited to employee's account.	Payment is made of any amount being accumulated during a 'purchase period' with interest.	Active employees: preretirement survivors benefit for vested employees' spouses if employees die before retirement; no cost to employee; coordinated with primary life insurance plan. Retired employees: retiree may elect pension option to provide benefits to beneficiary upon retiree's death, subject to QJSA rules.
Continues after retirement with the amount and duration of coverage depending on the option employee chooses.	Coverage terminates.	Employee may receive the balance in the plan account upon retirement under various payout options.	Stock purchased under plan available at and before retirement; retirees not eligible for future offerings.	Defined benefit plan integrated with Social Security pays regular benefit at 65, with alternatives for early retirement before age 65.
		Employees may contribute up to 16% of pay or up to the tax law limit (with permitted catch-up contributions) for Sec. 401 (k) plans before-tax per year. Employer matches 50% of contributions, up to 6% of pay. Six investment options available. Withdrawals permitted on termination of employment or in service in special cases. Plan loans available subject to tax law requirements.	Employees can purchase company stock in amounts based on salary up to tax law maximum at 85% of stock price at either the beginning or the end of any purchase period; payment in installments by payroll deduction.	

(continued)

TABLE 2-2 (continued)

Employee Needs, Goals, or Exposures to Loss	Social Security	Workers' Compensation	Supplemental Workers' Compensation	Flexible Spending Accounts (FSAs)
Medical expenses		Pays if illness or injury is job- related under the workers' compensation laws.		Allows employees to set aside before- tax up to $2,500 per year for tax- eligible health care expenses.
Disability losses	Pays after 5 months of continuous total disability when approved by Social Security.	Pays if disability is job-related under the workers' compensation laws.	Increases disability income if employee receives workers' compensation benefits.	
In case of death	Pays a lump- sum death benefit and monthly survivor income to spouse and children.	Pays if death is job-related under the workers' compensation laws.	Coverage terminates.	
Retirement	Pays unreduced retirement benefits at full-benefit retirement age or reduced benefits as early as age 62. In addition, health care expenses may be covered under Medicare.	Coverage terminates in accordance with the workers, compensation laws.	Coverage terminates.	
Capital accumulation				Allows employees to set aside before- tax up to $5,000 per year for tax- eligible child or other dependent care.
Dependent care assistance				

continuing to protect employees or former employees once the formal employment relationship has ended and in terms of protecting dependents of employees in a variety of circumstances. It is a logical part of the functional approach because the needs, goals, and loss exposures of employees imply consideration not only of the kinds of benefits to be provided but also of the persons to be protected and when they will be protected. Thus, in designing its employee benefit plan, the employer should consider how the various functional categories of needs and goals will be met for different categories of persons under a variety of circumstances.

In this type of analysis, the following are among the categories of persons whom the employer may want to consider protecting under its employee benefit plan—under at least some circumstances and for at least some benefits:

1. Active full-time employees
2. Dependents of active full-time employees
3. Retired former employees
4. Dependents of retired former employees
5. Disabled employees and their dependents
6. Surviving dependents of deceased employees
7. Terminated employees and their dependents
8. Employees (and their dependents) who are temporarily separated from the employer's service, such as during layoffs, leaves of absence, military duty, strikes, and so forth
9. Other than full-time active employees (e.g., part-time employees, directors, and so forth)

The employer basically must decide how far to extend its employee benefit program, and for what kinds of benefits, to persons who are not active full-time employees (in some cases, it may be required to do this). This represents a significant issue in employee benefit planning both in terms of adequacy of employee protection and cost for the employer. Some extensions of benefits, such as provision of medical expense benefits to retirees and perhaps their dependents (retiree medical benefits), and continuation of group term life insurance (normally in reduced amounts) on retirees' lives, can be quite expensive. The importance of this issue has been heightened for employers by the adoption by the Financial Accounting Standards Board (FASB) of Financial Accounting Standard (FAS) 106—Employers' Accounting for

Postretirement Benefits Other Than Pensions. FAS 106 generally requires employers to recognize during covered employees' periods of service the accrued benefit cost of these post-retirement benefits (the net periodic post-retirement benefit cost) as a current business expense, and to recognize the liabilities for and any plan assets funding these benefits for balance-sheet purposes.

The extent to which employers may want to extend coverage of their benefit plans to one or more of these categories of persons varies with employer philosophy, cost constraints, funding and accounting considerations, union negotiations, and employee benefit practices in the particular industry and geographic area involved. Such extensions also vary considerably among the different kinds of benefits. Regulatory requirements also must be observed.

For example, medical expense benefits may be extended to active employees, various categories of dependents of active employees, retired former employees, dependents of retired former employees, surviving spouses and other dependents of deceased retired former employees, disabled employees, dependents of disabled employees, and surviving dependents of deceased active employees. Further, medical expense coverage must be made available for specified periods under the terms of the Consolidated Omnibus Budget Reconciliation Act of 1985 (COBRA), as amended, for terminated employees, certain dependents of terminated employees, certain dependents of active employees who no longer meet the definition of an eligible dependent under the regular employee benefit plan, certain dependents of deceased employees, and in certain other situations. There are also other mandated extensions of medical benefits.

Group term life insurance, on the other hand, may be provided to active full-time employees, disabled employees who meet the definition of disability under the plan, and retired employees in reduced amounts. Also, some plans provide dependent group life insurance to eligible dependents of active employees.

Another factor to consider in this analysis is to what extent, and on what contribution basis, certain employee benefits will be provided to or continued for various categories of persons. Benefits may be provided or continued without contribution by the employee or covered person in full or in reduced amounts. Or, the benefits could be provided or continued with contribution to the cost by the employee or covered person in full or on a reduced basis. Finally, benefits may be provided or continued to covered persons on an elective basis at the covered person's own cost.

Analyze Benefits Presently Available

The next step in the functional approach is to analyze the benefits, terms of coverage, and plan participation by employees in terms of how well the existing or proposed employee benefit plan meets employee needs and goals in the various functional categories for those classes of persons the employer wants to protect or benefit. This step involves measuring the employee benefit plan against the objectives and coverage criteria set up for it under the functional approach just outlined.

Types of Benefits

A common application of the functional approach to employee benefit planning is to outline the different types of benefits under an employee benefit plan that apply to each of the categories of employee needs and goals. This may be done in the form of a grid as shown in Table 2-2.

Levels of Benefits

In a similar fashion, the levels of benefits under the various components of the employee benefit plan can be determined or shown, or both, for each of the categories of needs or goals.

To supplement this analysis, it may be helpful to use benefit illustrations to depict or illustrate the levels of benefits that would be provided under the various components of the employee benefit plan or proposed plan in the event of certain contingencies and using certain assumptions. For example, it might be assumed an employee with certain earnings and using certain salary projections will retire at age 65 with 30 years of service with the employer. This employee's total retirement income then may be estimated from various components of the employer's employee benefit plan as well as from Social Security as of the assumed retirement date. This can be expressed as a percentage of the employee's estimated final pay, which often is referred to as the employee's retirement income "replacement ratio." The employee benefits used in such an analysis may include only the employer's pension plan and Social Security, but it would be more logical to include all potential sources of retirement income available through the employee benefit plan, such as a pension plan, profit-sharing plan, thrift or savings plan, supplemental executive retirement plans, and perhaps other kinds of plans or benefits intended primarily to provide capital accumulation or stock-purchase benefits. Naturally, assumptions must be made for a variety of factors if all these sources of retirement income are considered. Also, different assumptions as to employee earnings, year of retirement, final pay, years of service, and so forth may be used to test the adequacy of retirement income for employees.

The same kind of analysis can be made for disability benefits from all sources under the employee benefit plan. When the analysis of disability benefits is made, it may be found that excessive benefits will be paid under certain conditions and for certain durations of disability, while inadequate benefits will be paid under other conditions. Thus, better coordination of disability benefits may be called for in making recommendations for changes in the plan.

This approach may also prove fruitful for other employee loss exposures, such as death, medical expenses at various levels and under various conditions, long-term care (custodial care), and so forth. Finally, the adequacy of benefit levels can be tested for different categories of persons the employer may want to protect.

Another interesting kind of analysis in terms of benefit levels is to estimate the potential for capital accumulation available to employees under the components of an employee benefit plan designed primarily for this purpose. These may include, for example, profit-sharing plans, thrift or savings plans, stock-purchase plans, stock options, restricted stock, employee stock ownership plans (ESOPs), other stock-based performance plans, and so forth. Employees often are pleasantly surprised to learn how much capital can be accumulated under such plans over a period, even using relatively conservative investment assumptions.

In evaluating levels of benefits and benefit adequacy, consideration also may be given to optional benefits that may be available to employees under the employee benefit plan. Such options may involve the opportunity for employees to purchase coverage or additional levels of coverage beyond a basic level of benefits. Through such optional benefits, the employer in effect is giving employees the opportunity at a given cost to themselves to make their total benefits more adequate in certain specific areas. As an example, the life insurance plan shown in Table 2-2 allows eligible employees to purchase additional life insurance at favorable group rates up to three times their base pay over and above the employer-provided benefit of three times annual base pay (subject to certain individual underwriting requirements). Another such area of optional benefits exists when employers allow employees to purchase long-term care (LTC) insurance for themselves or specified dependents on an employee-pay-all group basis.

Of course, an employer may extend the idea of optional benefits or employee choice-making even further by adopting a flexible benefits (cafeteria compensation) program as part of its employee benefit plan. This idea is discussed again below with regard to "Flexibility Available to Employees."

Probationary Periods

In assessing how well an existing employee benefit plan meets the needs and loss exposures of employees and certain other individuals, it is also helpful to analyze the probationary periods required for the various types of benefits contained in the plan. Such probationary periods, or the length of service otherwise-eligible employees must have with the employer before they become eligible to participate in the various types of benefits, will have an effect on the plan's protection for employees, their dependents, and possibly others, as well as on plan costs for the employer. The longer the probationary period required, the greater the exposure of employees and others to a loss not covered by the plan. But, many employers believe only employees with certain minimum periods of service, and hence demonstrable connection with the employer, should be eligible for at least certain types of benefits.

Probationary periods by their nature create gaps in coverage for newly hired or newly eligible employees and their dependents. Thus, probationary periods should be analyzed as part of the functional approach to determine whether the resulting gaps in coverage are appropriate and consistent with the employer's objectives and the employees' needs.

It seems desirable that the use of probationary periods in an employee benefit plan should be based on a reasonably consistent employer philosophy. One possible philosophy in this regard is to divide employee benefits into "protection-oriented" benefits and "accumulation-oriented" benefits. Protection-oriented benefits would consist of medical expense benefits, life insurance benefits, short- and long-term disability benefits, and so forth. These benefits protect employees and their dependents against serious loss exposures that, if they were to occur, could spell immediate financial disaster for the employees or their dependents, or both. For such benefits, where the need/protection orientation is great, there might be no probationary period, or a relatively short one. The rationale for this would be that the need for immediate coverage would override the traditional reasons for using probationary periods or longer probationary periods.

Accumulation-oriented benefits, such as pension plans, profit-sharing plans, savings or thrift plans, stock-bonus plans, stock-purchase plans, and so forth, could involve relatively long probationary periods if desired by the employer and could be subject to legal requirements. The theory might be that these kinds of benefits should be a reward for relatively long service with the employer. Also, an employee who stayed with the employer would have a relatively long time in which to accumulate such benefits, and thus longer probationary periods would not really place such longer-service employees at any serious disadvantage or risk.

Of course, cost control may provide another rationale for longer probationary periods, depending on the employer's compensation philosophy.

Eligibility Requirements

Requirements for eligibility for benefits, including definitions of covered persons, obviously affect those who may benefit from or be protected by various employee benefits. In this area, for example, the employer, or the employer and the union or unions with whom the employer negotiates, should consider such issues as

1. Which dependents of active employees (and perhaps dependents of retired former employees, disabled employees, and deceased employees—see 2, 3, 4, and 5 below) should (or must) be covered for medical expense benefits?
2. Should retirees (and perhaps their spouses and other dependents) continue to be covered, and if so, for what benefits?
3. Should survivors of deceased active employees continue to be covered, and if so, for what benefits and for how long?
4. Should survivors of retired former employees continue to be covered, and if so, for what benefits?
5. Should employees or former employees on disability (and perhaps their dependents) continue to be covered, and, if so, for what benefits, for how long, and under what conditions?
6. Should (or must) coverage be extended to employees during layoffs, leaves of absence, strikes, and other temporary interruptions of employment, and if so, for what benefits, for how long, and under what conditions?
7. Should coverage be limited to full-time employees (or employees meeting ERISA and PPACA requirements) or should coverage, or some coverage, be extended to part-time employees as well?
8. What coverage should (or must) be continued or made available to persons (or for the dependents of such persons) after termination of employment with the employer and on what basis?

The resolution of some of these issues depends in part on statutory or other legal requirements, insurance company underwriting rules, collective bargaining agreements, and similar factors. However, the philosophy or rationale of the employer, or the employer and union, concerning the employee benefit program will have a substantial impact on how some of these coverage and eligibility issues are resolved. At the heart of many of these issues is the basic question of how far an employer (or union) should feel obligated to go, either legally or morally—or possibly can afford to go—in meeting the various needs and loss exposures of its employees, their dependents, and persons who once were employees or dependents of employees but who now have various other relationships or no relationship with the employer.

Employee Contribution Requirements

If certain employee benefits under an employer's employee benefit plan are contributory (i.e., the employees or possibly their surviving dependents must contribute to the cost of the benefit), this will have an impact on employee participation and hence on how well the plan meets the needs of the employee group as a whole. This really represents a trade-off: between the financing (cost) and other advantages of a contributory plan—and the loss of employee participation in the plan, which results from requiring employee contributions, assuming employee participation in the contributory plan is voluntary. Thus, an employer, and union if the plan is negotiated, may have to decide whether a particular employee benefit will be noncontributory or contributory, and, if it is to be contributory, how much the employees will have to contribute toward the cost of the plan. Further, if the plan is contributory, the employer (or employer and union) will have to decide whether participation will be voluntary or mandatory as a condition of employment. Making a contributory plan mandatory solves the employee participation problem, but it may create serious employee relations and morale problems. Therefore, most employers do not have mandatory contributory plans. Still another possibility is for employers simply to make the coverage available to employees (usually on a more favorable basis than they could purchase it individually) on an employee-pay-all basis.

In the context of this cost/employee participation trade-off, one approach that can help planners strike an agreeable balance is to rank employee benefits in terms of the relative degree to which the employer feels that all employees and their dependents should be protected, and hence what benefits should the plan aim for 100 percent participation, compared with benefits for which such a high level of participation is not deemed essential. This same kind of analysis might also be helpful in determining the level of employee contribution if it is decided to have the plan be contributory. Another factor bearing on this decision is whether other benefits in the employer's overall plan may also be available to meet the same functional need. For example, employee benefit plans frequently contain a number of kinds of benefits intended to help provide retirement income for employees. Still another factor to consider is the extent to which employees or their dependents, or both, may have similar benefits available to them elsewhere. Those employees or dependents who have an alternative source of similar benefits may opt not to participate if the plan is made contributory, thereby helping to avoid duplication of benefits. An example of this is the availability of multiple plans of medical expense benefits when both a husband and wife are employed outside the home.

There is a tendency toward providing employees with alternative benefits or levels of benefits, with varying degrees of employee contributions (if any) required. In any event, as part of its benefit planning system, it will be helpful for an employer to make a benefit-by-benefit analysis, within the context of its total benefit and compensation philosophy, to evaluate the desirability of any employee (and possibly dependent) contributions to the cost of the various employee benefits or levels of benefits.

Of course, to the extent that voluntary salary reduction (normally before tax) is part of a flexible benefits (cafeteria compensation) plan, the covered employees themselves really are making the decision as to the level of their contributions (through salary reduction) to pay for the benefits they select within the scope of the plan. To this degree, the decision-making regarding contributions into these plans is at least partly shifted to the covered employees, depending on the benefit options they select.

Flexibility Available to Employees

The degree to which employees have flexibility in making such choices as to whether they will participate in a given employee benefit; the amounts of additional coverage they may wish to purchase; the opportunity to select from among two or more alternative plans of benefits; and even the opportunity to structure their own benefit program, as under a flexible benefits (cafeteria compensation) approach, clearly has an impact on the extent to which employees may tailor an employee benefit plan to meet their own needs and goals within the functional categories described above. In fact, it may be argued that the more flexibility employees have, the more likely it is that the benefit program they select will meet their individual needs and goals. It thus can be argued, on the one hand, that flexibility in employee benefit plan design should facilitate the goals of the functional approach. On the other hand, it can also be argued that allowing too much employee flexibility works against the functional approach, because employees may misperceive or not understand their and their families' needs and hence leave some important needs uncovered. This concern is often addressed by limiting the choices of employees or by specifying a core of benefits that are not subject to employee choice.

A distinct trend exists toward giving employees more flexibility in the structuring of their own benefits. As just discussed, this trend probably buttresses the functional approach, in that it may be presumed that rational employees will opt for those benefits and coverages that will best meet their individual needs and goals.

Actual Employee Participation in Benefit Plans

It was noted above that, under the functional approach, an employer may analyze the types of benefits provided to employees and their dependents according to the various functional categories. The employer may also estimate or project benefit levels for the benefits in the different categories under certain assumptions and given certain contingencies or events. However, these analyses and estimates of benefits and benefit levels may not completely show how well certain employee benefits actually reach a given employee group. Therefore, an employer may also want to calculate the actual participation ratios for its employees and their dependents for given employee benefits. These ratios can be calculated in terms of the employees (and their dependents) actually participating in the plan as a ratio of total full-time employees, as a ratio of total eligible employees, or both.

A given employee benefit plan may have many beneficial features, and may even be quite liberal in some respects; but if the ratio of employee participation is low, the particular benefit may not be meeting the employer's objectives in terms of its total compensation system.

Of course, if a given employee benefit is noncontributory, and if its eligibility requirements are reasonably liberal, all the eligible employees will be covered and, probably, a reasonably high percentage of total employees will also be covered. However, when employee benefit plans are contributory, or are optional benefits under a flexible benefits plan, and/or eligibility requirements are tighter, participation ratios may drop significantly. When this is the case, an employer may wish to evaluate the reason(s) for the low participation and what steps, if any, it might take to increase participation in the particular plan or plans.

Determine Gaps in Benefits and Any Overlapping Benefits

From the preceding steps, it is possible to more effectively analyze any gaps in the employer's present employee benefit plan. These gaps may exist in terms of the benefits available from all sources to meet various categories of employee needs and goals, in terms of the projected levels of benefits for those needs, in terms of coverage of the various categories of persons the employer may want to protect, and finally in terms of the actual participation of employees in the various components of the employee benefit plan. In a similar fashion, the employer will want to determine any overlapping benefits that presently may be provided from all sources in its employee benefit plan to meet certain categories of needs.

Consider Recommendations for Changes in Present Plan

As a result of the functional approach described here, the employer may consider various recommendations or alternative recommendations for changes in its present employee benefit plan not only to eliminate gaps in benefits or persons covered but also to avoid any overlap in benefits. Part of this step also may involve consideration of adopting or modifying an existing flexible benefits (cafeteria compensation) plan to meet employee needs. Essentially, this step involves the consideration of alternatives, which is implicit in any decision-making system.

Estimate Costs (or Savings) for Each Recommendation

The cost or savings estimate is an important step before any recommendation for improvements, reductions, or changes in an employee benefit plan can be adopted. These estimates are based upon certain assumptions and may be expressed in terms of ranges of possible cost (or savings) results. An employer will normally have certain overall cost constraints on its employee benefit planning. Therefore, recommended improvements or changes in the plan may have to be assigned certain priorities in terms of which benefits the employer can afford to adopt.

Evaluate Alternative Methods of Financing Benefits

This step involves the evaluation of how recommended changes in benefits or existing benefits, or both, should be financed or secured. While this may not strictly involve the functional analysis of benefits in relation to needs, it is an essential step in analyzing any employee benefit plan.

Consider Cost-Saving or Cost-Containment Techniques

At this point, the employer should also consider cost-saving techniques concerning its employee benefits. These may involve changes in benefit plan design, elimination or reduction of certain benefits, adoption or modification of a flexible benefits (cafeteria compensation) approach, use of alternative methods of financing certain benefits, use of managed care approaches for medical benefits, use of utilization review for medical expense benefits, use of disability management and rehabilitation, adoption of wellness and similar programs, changes in insurers or servicing organizations, changes in investment policies or advisors, the decision to self-fund or retain certain benefits, and other similar techniques. Again, while consideration of such techniques may not be directly involved in the functional analysis of an employee benefit plan, it is a logical step in the planning process once such a functional analysis is begun.

Decide on Appropriate Benefits and Financing Methods

Once the preceding analysis is complete, the employer, or employer and union, is in a position to decide on the particular benefit recommendations it wants to adopt or bargain for. The employer may also decide on appropriate financing methods. This is essentially the selection of the best alternative or alternatives in the decision-making process.

Implement Any Changes

This step involves the implementation of the changes or recommendations decided on above. It is the implementation phase of the decision-making process.

Communicate Benefit Changes to Employees

The effective communication of employee benefits and changes in such benefits is a vital element in the overall success of any employee benefit plan. It is often a neglected element. An employer may go to a great deal of time, trouble, and expense in making improvements in its employee benefit plan, but all this effort and cost may not be as effective as it could be in terms of good employee relations and meeting the employer's total compensation policies if the improvements are not effectively communicated to employees.

Many employers periodically communicate to employees the current overall status and value of their employee benefits. Frequently, this is done annually. Such a communication concerning the status and total value of an employee's benefits may be accomplished, at least in part, by using categories of benefits similar to those classified in the functional approach described above. See Chapter 27 for a more detailed discussion of employee benefits communications.

Periodically Reevaluate the Plan

Employee benefit planning is a task that is never complete. Concepts of employee needs, the benefits available to meet those needs, how those benefits should be made available to employees, and regulatory requirements are constantly changing. Therefore, the employee benefit plan must be constantly reevaluated and updated to change with them.

CHAPTER 3

Risk Concepts and Employee Benefit Planning

Gary K. Stone

RISK AND EMPLOYEE BENEFITS

The concept of risk is fundamental in any discussion of employee benefit planning.

Definition of Risk

For our purposes, risk will mean *uncertainty* with respect to possible *loss*. In other words, it is the inability to determine a future loss and to figure out how expensive it will be should the loss take place. For example, individuals have very little ability to know when they will die, or become ill, disabled, or unemployed. All the typical potential losses associated with employee benefits are "risks" from the standpoint of the individual. *Loss* is meant to convey any decrease in value suffered. A hospital bill associated with an illness could result in a loss, because it would cause a decrease in the value of assets held by a person.

Peril and Hazard Distinguished from Risk

The concept of risk is different from the concepts of peril and hazard, but the three have an interrelationship. Peril and hazard are insurance terms used primarily in property and liability insurance but also in life and health insurance. They also have considerable application in employee benefit planning.

A peril is defined as the cause of personal or property loss, destruction, or damage. Common perils involving property are fires, floods, earthquakes, thefts, and burglaries. These same perils can also cause personal harm. Other perils that cause personal losses are illnesses, bodily injuries, and death. A number of insurance policies are identified by the perils covered. Life insurance and health policies normally do not name the perils but usually cover all perils associated with those policies. Actually, they were originally called death insurance policies and accident and sickness policies, but their names were changed for euphemistic and marketing reasons.

A hazard is a condition that either increases the probability that a peril will occur or increases the severity of the loss when a peril occurs. The three basic types of hazards are designated as physical hazards, moral hazards, and morale hazards.

Physical hazards are physical conditions that fit within the definition of hazard. In the workplace, there can be numerous physical hazards. The presence of flammable materials or hazardous waste, the absence of fire-extinguishing equipment or first-aid kits, machines without appropriate safety devices, and faulty heating and air-conditioning units are examples of physical hazards.

Unfortunately, some employees qualify as moral hazards. A moral hazard occurs when an individual intentionally causes a loss or increases its severity. The category includes those who steal from the employer, purposely damage employer property, file fraudulent medical claims, abuse sick leave and personal time off, or file false overtime and expense statements.

Morale hazards exist when people act with carelessness or indifference. Some individuals appear to be accident- or disaster-prone and, as such, are morale hazards. On the other hand, specific morale hazards include failing to lock rooms, vaults, or areas from which valuable items are stolen; forgetting to notify the employer of faulty materials that ultimately cause personal injuries to a handler; or ignoring the fact that a number of employees all experience the same symptoms of physical discomfort, which ultimately can be traced to a job-related cause. An important problem in the benefits area that can be considered a morale hazard is employees or medical providers scheduling unnecessary medical tests or prescribing unneeded medications. This is a source of increasing cost in the medical benefits area. Note the distinction between moral and morale hazard. This distinction is not made in some areas of study. For instance, many economists use the term moral hazard to describe morale hazard.

Types of Risk

Risk can be classified into many categories depending upon the use of the term. For the purposes of this chapter, a simple classification is used. Risk is divided into two types or classes: (1) pure risk and (2) speculative risk.

Pure risk is risk in which only two alternatives are possible: Either (1) the risk will *not* happen (no financial loss) or (2) it *will* happen and a financial loss takes place. Nothing positive can result from a pure risk. An example is illness. The best thing that can happen is that a person does not become ill. If a person does become ill, a negative result takes place. Many examples of pure risk are available. The risks of loss from fire, automobile accidents, illness, unemployment, disability, theft of property, and earthquake are all pure risks. Many of the risks covered by employee benefits fall into this classification. Pure risks for the most part can be insured.

Speculative risk inserts another possibility not existing in pure risk. The additional alternative is the possibility of a gain. Speculative risks then would have three potential outcomes: (1) a loss, (2) no loss, and (3) a gain. Examples of speculative risk are the purchase of a share of common stock, acquiring a new business venture, or gambling. The emphasis of this chapter is on pure risk, rather than on speculative risk.

Pure Risk

Pure risk can be subclassified depending upon the type of financial loss. The three classifications of pure risk are

1. Personal risk
2. Property risk
3. Legal liability risk

The most important classification of pure risk from an employee benefit standpoint is personal risk. Personal risks can result in losses that have a direct impact on an individual's life or health. Many risks involving employee benefit plans fall into the category of personal risk. Death, illness, accidents, unemployment, and old age are all considered to be personal risks. This type of risk can be measured with some degree of accuracy. It is difficult to be precise, but by estimating potential lost income from a particular risk and the medical and other costs associated with it, one can approximate the potential loss. With that information, one can estimate needed protection and seek insurance or whatever other risk-handling measure is appropriate.

Property risks are the uncertainties (possible losses) that decrease the value of one's real or personal property. Fire, flood, earthquake, wind, theft, and automobile collisions are examples of types of property risk. The home, furniture, cars, and jewelry would be the types of property subject to possible loss. Legal liability risk is the uncertainty of a loss a loss resulting from negligent actions of a person that result in injury to another person. It stems from lawsuits by an injured party seeking damages from a negligent party. Common sources of legal liability would be negligent behavior associated with automobiles, one's home or business, the sale of products, or professional misconduct (malpractice). A serious difficulty connected with liability risk is that it has an unlimited potential loss. The dollar impact of this risk is a function of the seriousness of the negligence and the status of the parties involved. Malpractice awards against physicians or awards resulting from automobile accidents are examples in which potential losses can extend into the millions of dollars.

As noted above, employee benefit plans deal substantially with personal risks. The magnitude of life insurance, medical expense, disability income, retirement, and other personal risk-oriented benefit plans reflects this. However, property and liability risk coverage also can be found in a number of benefit plans. For example, homeowner's insurance, automobile insurance, group legal services, and financial planning services are all examples of property and liability risk coverages available in some employee benefit plans. Nevertheless, there is a considerably greater emphasis on personal risk coverages.

Methods of Handling Risk

There are several methods of handling risk. Although the main focus of this chapter is on the use of some type of insurance method to handle the risks associated with benefit plans, it should be recognized that other alternatives are available and are used. The primary risk-handling alternatives are

1. Avoidance
2. Control
3. Retention
4. Transfer
5. Insurance

Avoidance

Avoidance is a perfect device for handling risk. It means one does not acquire the risk to begin with and hence would not be subject to the risk. For example, if a person does not want the risk associated with driving automobiles, he or she won't drive a car. The problem with avoidance is that many times one cannot help but have the risk (the nondriver as a pedestrian or passenger is still exposed to the risk of other persons' driving), or one does not want to avoid it. For risks covered by employee benefits, it is almost impossible to use the avoidance technique. How does one avoid the risk of death or illness? The point is that one is unable to avoid some risks. Attention, then, must be focused on the other alternatives.

Control

Control is a mechanism by which one attempts either to prevent or reduce the probability of a loss taking place or to reduce the severity of the loss after it has taken place. Many examples of control devices exist. Smoke detectors, fire-resistant building materials, seat belts, air bags, crash-resistant bumpers on automobiles, nonsmoking office buildings, physical examinations, and proper diets would be considered control devices.

Employee benefit plans can use control in conjunction with other risk-handling techniques, such as insurance. Any procedure used to reduce or prevent accidents, illnesses, or premature death would help in lowering the cost of most benefit plans. It is not unusual for employers to adopt accident-prevention programs, wellness programs, a smoke-free environment at work, and other programs with the intent of lowering workers' compensation and other employee benefit costs as well as improving employees' health and welfare.

Retention

Retention means that the risk is assumed and paid for by the person suffering the loss or taking responsibility for the loss. Assumption or retention can be used with losses that are small in terms of their financial impact on a person or company. The cost of insurance or some other risk-handling device could be higher than paying for such losses when they happen, and some losses can be handled more efficiently simply by doing that. For example, assume you have an old automobile worth $600. Collision insurance with a typical deductible of $250 would give you only a $350 recovery upon a total loss. In other words, the cost of the insurance plus the deductible could be higher than the value of the loss. In such cases, it may be more economical to retain the risk than to insure it. One has to be careful with retention, in that it should be used only with the types of loss that will not cause a financial disaster. Retaining or assuming risks with high severity potential can result in financial catastrophe. It should not be assumed that because a loss is unlikely to happen (low probability), it could or should be retained. The crucial factor is the financial result (severity), if it does take place. A fire that destroys one's home is unlikely, but it is devastating if it happens.

Retention can be a useful tool in handling employee benefit plans. An employer (insured) might decide to retain its short-term disability income loss exposure because it knows that the short-term disability period will not exceed 26 weeks. Another use of retention can be found in the administration of benefit plans. Employers can take over many of the administrative duties of the insurance company. Payroll deduction, claims administration, answering questions from plan members, and filing of forms can sometimes be done more efficiently by the insured than the insurance company, and by carrying out these functions itself, an employer may be able to lower its direct dollar outlay. However, this form of retention should be examined carefully before being adopted, because the administrative burden and other negative factors may outweigh any potential savings.

Transfer

Transfer is a concept in which one switches or shifts the financial burden of risk to another party. Two forms of transfer are usually recognized: (1) insurance, which is covered in the next section of this chapter, and (2) noninsurance transfers, which can take place in many different forms. Noninsurance transfers would be transferring losses to a third party that is not a licensed insurance company. For example, a landlord may require new tenants to pay extra money up front as a security deposit for potential damage to the premises. This would be a form of noninsurance transfer. The landlord would be transferring his or her possible loss to the tenant. Another example involves travel agents. A client may want to travel to the Middle East during a time of potential military conflict. The travel agent suggests avoiding the area. The client insists upon taking the trip, so the travel agent has the client sign a form waiving legal claims against the travel agent for dissatisfaction with a trip that the travel agent has not recommended. The hope is that, if a lawsuit develops, the travel agent can assert that the traveler took the responsibility for the burden of any loss upon himself or herself.

Employee benefit plans use transfer extensively often in the form of insurance contracts. Nevertheless, noninsurance transfers may also occur. For instance, the large-scale transformation of the private retirement plan system from a defined benefit to a defined contribution structure has resulted in the transfer of risk from plan sponsors to individual participants.

Insurance

Insurance is a common method of financing employee benefits. The definition of insurance varies depending upon whether one is looking at insurance from an economic, legal, social, or mathematical viewpoint. However, for purposes of this chapter, the following definition of insurance will be used.

> Insurance is the pooling of fortuitous losses by transfer of such risks to insurers who agree to indemnify insureds for such losses, to provide other pecuniary benefits on their occurrence, or to render services connected with the risk.[1]

From the standpoint of an employee benefit plan, insurance would be a mechanism in which the insured (employer/employee) would pay money (premiums) into a fund (insurance company). Upon the occurrence of a loss, reimbursement would be provided to the person suffering the loss. Thus, the risk has been reduced or eliminated for the insured, and all the individuals who paid into the fund share the resulting loss.

Insurance is but one method by which an employee benefit plan may be financed. Large benefit plans may rely on insurance, self-funding, and various combinations of the two. However, many small- to medium-size firms rely almost exclusively on the insurance mechanism.

Before continuing with the discussion of insurance, it is important to clarify the difference between insurance and gambling. Since both insurance and gambling have a relationship to risk, they are sometimes viewed erroneously as essentially the same. However, there are several important features of insurance that distinguish it from gambling. First, insurance is a mechanism for handling an existing risk; whereas gambling creates a

1. George E. Rejda. *Principles of Risk Management and Insurance*, 10th ed., Boston, MA: Pearson Education, Inc., 2008, p. 19.

risk where one did not previously exist. Second, the risk created by gambling is a speculative risk; whereas insurance deals with pure risks. Third, gambling involves a gain for one party, the winner, at the expense of another, the loser, whereas insurance is based on a mutual sharing of any losses that occur. Fourth, the loser in a gambling transaction remains in that negative situation, whereas an insured who suffers a loss is financially restored in whole or in part to his or her original situation. Obviously, the insurance-gambling discussion is more appropriate to individual rather than to group insurance, but the comparison also has some applicability to the group mechanism.

Additionally, the use of insurance to make the victims of losses whole reflects the principle of indemnification on which insurance is structured. An insured is indemnified if a covered loss occurs. That is, he or she is placed somewhat in the same situation that existed prior to the loss (e.g., by reimbursement for damaged property or medical bills, disability income, and the like).

Summary of Risk-Handling Alternatives

It is possible to use a number of alternatives in the design of employee benefit plans. One or more of the alternatives in some combination is common. The one alternative that is mutually exclusive of the others is avoidance. If you avoid the risk, you are not subjected to potential losses, so no need exists for insurance, loss control, or any other risk-handling technique. The remaining alternatives, however, could be used in combination.

Assume a typical medical benefit plan for a firm's employees. The firm might purchase a medical insurance plan with a deductible of $1,000 per year per covered member. The plan is insured, and so transfer has been used. In addition, someone must pay the $1,000 deductible, so there is retention or assumption of part of the risk. Further, assume that the firm is interested in keeping the cost of medical benefits down. It may initiate a number of control devices, such as a smoke-free work environment and an accident-prevention program to aid the effort. Thus, a number of the risk-handling alternatives are used together.

Another example of benefit plan risk-handling alternatives involves long-term care. Long-term care insurance has had a slow growth in the private sector. Recently, there has been an increase in the popularity of this insurance, but the fact remains that most families remain uninsured for long-term care. The high cost of this insurance, restrictive underwriting, tax issues, and the lack of public understanding of the problem have all contributed to this fact. The cost of long-term care insurance directly increases with age, the amount of the daily benefit, and the shorter the length of the elimination period. Often, families put off the decision on this type of protection until later in life, when the cost has increased considerably.

Although the need for long-term care cannot be completely avoided, serious thought must be given how to handle this risk. Likely techniques could be insurance (transfer), proper health care and living conditions (control), and finding a way to pay for the loss out of savings or income (retention). Retention may be the only available risk-handling technique, but employees and families must seriously consider how to prevent a catastrophic loss to the family. Accumulated liquid assets may be adequate to pay this loss, but this is a sizable sum. Insurance, Medicaid planning, planning with potential caregivers, and increased savings amounts are a few of the areas that one needs to analyze to determine what is best for the family in the solution to the problem. Employers are taking an increasing role in helping employees understand and cope with the problem. Insurance and long-term care planning are examples of help provided by the employer. The Community Living Assistance Services and Support (CLASS) Act may assist employees by facilitating payroll deduction and allowing for broader coverage on a guaranteed-issue basis. Although passage of this Act represented a positive public policy initiative, the extent to which this legislation covers the risk exposure will take time to assess.

What factors should be considered in deciding upon the "best" method of handling the risk of a particular benefit plan? In general, one should consider the most economical from a financial standpoint, but with proper consideration given to employee welfare. What is being suggested is that there is nothing wrong with opting for the lowest-cost alternative, as long as proper consideration is given to the nonfinancial aspects of the employees' welfare. Failing to put a guard on a machine to prevent injury is generally unacceptable, even if it might cost less to let the accident take place. Firms must consider employee welfare and mandatory requirements set forth by the state and federal government in evaluating the alternatives for handling risk.

INSURANCE AND INSURABLE RISK

Insurance is one of the most popular methods of funding employee benefit plans, but, as explained in later chapters of this *Handbook*, many other options exist. The advantages and disadvantages of using insurance in the design of a benefit plan are discussed in the next section.

Advantages of Insurance

A number of reasons account for why insurance can be used effectively in an employee benefit plan. One advantage is that there may be a known premium (cost) that is set in advance by the insurance company. The employer may have better control over its budget with a known premium, because any high shock losses would be the problem of the insurance company and not the insured. Having an outside administrator also can be an advantage to the employer. The employer does not have to get involved in disputes involving employees over coverage of the plan, because these would be handled by the insurance company. Employers may prefer insurance to some other form of funding in order to obtain the financial backing of an outside financial institution. This, of course, depends upon the financial strength of the insurance company selected, and care should go into this choice. Insurance companies are often leaders in the area of loss control and may help in the design and implementation of systems designed to control costs for the employer. A final advantage is that it may be more economical for an employer to use insurance rather than other alternatives. The insurance company may be more efficient and able to do the job at a lower total cost.

Disadvantages of Insurance

Insurance is not always the preferred method of funding employee benefit plans. A number of costs are involved that must be considered. Insurance companies charge administrative expenses that are added to the premium (or loaded) to compensate for their overhead expenses. Home office costs, licensing costs, commissions, taxes, loss-adjustment expenses, and the like all must go into the loading. One must realize that the premium covers not only direct losses but also the insurance company's overhead. The amount may vary from a small percent of the premium (e.g., 2 percent to 5 percent) to potentially a very high amount (25 percent or more) depending on the type of contract involved. Another potential disadvantage is that employer satisfaction is directly affected by the insurer's ability to handle claims and solve problems. Slow payment or restrictive claim practices can have an adverse effect on employees.

Whether something is an advantage or disadvantage often depends upon the specific insurance company involved. It is important to use care in the selection of an insurer. Discussing the merits of the insurer with other clients and carefully analyzing the carrier's financial stability are critical elements in the selection process.

Characteristics of an Insurable Risk

It often is said that anything can be insured if one is willing to pay the premium required. Insurance companies, however, normally will insure a risk only if it meets certain minimum standards. These standards or prerequisites are needed for an insurer to manage the insurance company in a sound financial manner. Without suitable risks, an insurance company can find itself in serious financial trouble. An insurance company is subject to the same problems as any other business—inadequate capitalization, a weak investment portfolio, or poor management. Insurance companies have the additional problem of insuring risks that could result in catastrophic losses.

The following is a list of the characteristics of a risk that are desired in order for it to be considered an "insurable risk":

1. There should be a large number of homogeneous risks (exposure units).
2. The loss should be verifiable and measurable.
3. The loss should not be catastrophic in nature.
4. The chance of loss should be subject to calculation.
5. The premium should be reasonable or economically feasible.
6. The loss should be accidental from the standpoint of the insured.

It should be noted that this list is what is considered ideal from the standpoint of the insurance company. Most risks are not perfect in all aspects, and insurance companies have to weigh all aspects of a risk to determine if, overall, it meets the criteria of an insurable risk.

Large Number of Homogeneous Risks

The insurance company must be able to calculate the number of losses it will incur from the total number of risks it insures. Assume that a life insurance company has just been formed and it is to insure its first two people. Each wants $100,000 of life insurance. In order to calculate a premium, the company needs to know the chance of dying for each of the two people. Without this information, the company will have no idea of whether these people will live or die during the policy period. Should both die during this period, $200,000 would be needed for the claims. If neither dies, the company would need nothing for the claims. The conclusion one reaches is that the premium should be somewhere between $0 and $200,000. This information is not very helpful, and the insurance company could not insure the risk based on it. What is needed is a large number of similar risks so that statistics can be developed to determine an accurate probability of loss for each risk being evaluated. Insurance is based on the *law of large* numbers, which means that the greater the number of exposures, the more closely will the actual results approach the probable results that are expected from an infinite number of exposures. For example, life insurance companies have accumulated information based on the large number of lives that have been insured over the years that enables them to develop mortality tables reflecting the expected mortality for a given type of risk. Life, medical, dental, and disability risks all require large numbers of cases to determine proper premium rates.

Employee benefit plans may or may not have the numbers needed to accurately determine loss expectations. This would depend upon the specific plan. Those plans with large numbers of homogeneous risks can be experience rated. This means the premiums will be calculated with the data from the plan experience itself. Smaller plans would not have an adequate number of risks, and other alternatives would be needed. For example, small plans can be combined with other small plans to get creditable statistics, or insurance companies might ignore small-plan statistics and rely on loss statistics developed independently of the plan.

Loss Should Be Verifiable and Measurable

It is important that an insurance company be able to verify a loss so as to determine the actual financial loss involved. Certain risks pose no problem in determining if a loss has taken place. Examples would be fire and windstorm losses with a home or a collision loss with one's automobile. Furthermore, the financial value of these losses can be determined accurately by the use of appraisals and other forms of valuation. Other types of risks are harder to evaluate. An example is a claim for theft of money from a home. Did the theft take place? Did the person have any money at home to be stolen? With risks that are difficult to evaluate, the insurance company has to take other precautions to protect itself from false and inflated claims.

Employee benefits are subject to the same types of problems. Death claims and retirement benefit claims generally are the easiest in which to determine whether a loss has taken place or not. Once a death claim has been verified, the amount of loss is normally the face value of the insurance contract. Few problems result from death claims. The same is true of retirement benefits. Assuming the age of the retiree can be verified, the benefit promised by the plan will be paid. At the other extreme are disability income claims. In some situations, an insurer might be uncertain as to whether a valid claim exists or not. Some disability losses, such as back injuries, are very difficult to determine. Is the insured actually disabled or not? Still other employee benefit losses may fall between these two extremes. Medical and dental losses can fall into this category. Several methods are available to prevent cases where employee benefit loss is difficult to verify or measure. Policy provisions, benefit maximums, waiting periods, alternate medical verification, required second opinion on certain surgical procedures, and hospital-stay monitoring are a few of the provisions that help limit these situations.

Loss Should Not Be Catastrophic in Nature

A serious problem occurs when a large percentage of the risks insured can be lost from the same event. Assume a fire insurance company insured all of its risks in one geographic location. A serious fire could result in catastrophic losses to the company. This did happen in the early history of fire insurance. Fires in London, Chicago, Baltimore, and San Francisco resulted in insurance company bankruptcies and loss of confidence in the industry. It became obvious that a geographic spread of the risks insured was essential, because a concentration of losses from one event could seriously impair or even bankrupt a company. Cases exist in which it is almost impossible to obtain a spread of the risks. In such cases, insurance becomes difficult or impossible to obtain. Flood and unemployment losses are examples. Unemployment can cover wide geographic areas, and a geographic spread would not help prevent a catastrophic loss. The same could be true for flood losses. The federal or state government might insure this type of risk, but it would be necessary for it to subsidize the premium rates to make them affordable.

Employee benefits are seldom subject to problems relating to inability to get a geographic spread of the risk. Benefit plans often insure life risks, hospital and dental risks, and disability income losses. For the most part, these types of risks are not subject to catastrophic loss due to geographic location, but examples can be imagined in which catastrophic losses might exist. The possibility of a plant explosion or a poison gas leak causing a large number of deaths or medical losses, or a concentration of certain diseases because of the exposure to certain elements that are indigenous to a specific employee group theoretically exist. Usually, however, this is not an important consideration in underwriting typical benefit plans. Policy limitations, reinsurance, and restrictions on groups insured can all be used to minimize the problem to the extent it exists.

Chance of Loss Should Be Subject to Calculation

For an insurance company to be able to calculate a premium that is reasonable to the insured and that represents the losses of a particular risk, certain information is essential. Data on both the frequency of losses and the severity of the losses must be available to determine the loss portion of the premium. This often is referred to as the pure premium portion of the premium. Essential to the pure premium calculation would be a large number of homogeneous exposure units, as already discussed. If an employer is large enough, the plan losses alone could be used to determine the pure premium portion. The meaning of "large" depends upon the type of risk involved. At least several hundred employees would probably be needed for full reliance upon the data.

Premium Should Be Reasonable or Economically Feasible

For an employee benefit plan to be acceptable to an employer and to employees, the plan must have a premium that is considered reasonable relative to the risk being insured; that is, the insured must be able to pay the premium. An insurance company's expenses not related to the losses covered by the pure premium must be added to that premium to obtain the total premium. The expense portion may be referred to as the loading associated with the risk. The "pure premium" plus the "loading" would make up the total premium to be paid by the plan. Employees who pay a part or all of the premium (participating plan) will not participate if they can obtain a lower premium in an individual insurance plan or if they can be insured through a spouse's plan at a lower cost, and the employer will be unable or unwilling to pay the premium if the rate is not reasonable.

Why would a premium be noncompetitive? This could happen for any number of reasons. For example, a plan could be populated by a high number of older employees. The resulting rate may mean that the younger employees can find lower-cost insurance outside of the plan. The younger employees are unwilling to subsidize the rates for the older employees. Also, the employer may not want to pay the needed premiums. Other reasons for noncompetitive plans could be poor loss experience from a high number of sick and disabled in a plan, or a plan having specific benefits that have resulted in high loss payout. For example, a plan may provide unlimited benefits for drug- or alcohol-related sickness, and the plan member makeup may have resulted in heavy payout for these problems. The bottom line is that the resulting loss experience has made the plan noncompetitive. It is not unusual for an employee group initially to pay a rate that is considered reasonable only to have the plan premiums become unreasonable over time. Failure to keep the average age of the members in the plan low or a higher incidence of illness could be the reason.

The employer must keep track of the factors contributing to premium increases. Inflation related to medical benefits has in recent years resulted in plan costs increasing beyond the regular cost-of-living index. This is particularly true with plans covering prescription drugs. The cost of this coverage has dramatically increased over the past 15–20 years. Constant review of benefits, benefit levels, employees covered by the plan, and competitive rates for alternative plans must take place. It has become common for plans to move away from "first dollar" medical benefits and to incorporate deductibles, waiting periods, and other cost-saving features. An obvious factor to review is the cost of alternative plans. Would it be financially sound to use an alternative insurance plan or an alternative method of delivering the benefits, such as a health maintenance organization (HMO) or a preferred provider organization (PPO)?

Loss Should Be Accidental from the Standpoint of the Insured

The insurance company does not want to pay for a loss if it is intentionally caused by the insured. This can be a serious problem in most forms of insurance. Arson and fake automobile accidents in property and liability insurance would be examples. In the life and health insurance area, false life and health claims, excess or overuse of drugs and medical tests could fall into this category. This type of problem can be reduced or eliminated by the use of policy provisions or by restricting the available plans or benefits made available to employees. The push toward "consumer-directed" health plans is partially an attempt to encourage employees to become more selective and aware of the importance of cost control in benefit selection.

Insurable Risk Summary

Insurance companies consider providing insurance to employee benefit plans if they meet the minimum standards of an insurable risk. Benefit plans in general fit the minimum standards as set forth above. Such plans would include life insurance, medical and dental insurance, disability income, and retirement programs. Policy provisions, benefit restrictions, and reinsurance can be used to help alleviate problems to the extent they exist. Life insurance is probably the best example of a plan that meets all the desirable standards of an insurable risk. Disability income, although normally insurable, creates more of a problem from an insurability standpoint. Although not a common employee benefit, excess unemployment insurance would be a benefit that borders on being uninsurable.

Handling Adverse Selection

Adverse selection is the phenomenon in the insurance mechanism whereby individuals who have higher-than-average potentially insurable risks "select against" the insurer. That is, those with greater probabilities of loss, and who therefore need insurance more than the average insured, attempt to obtain the coverage. For example, people who need hospitalization or surgical coverage seek to purchase medical insurance, those who own property subject to possible loss by fire or flood attempt to obtain some form of property insurance, and individuals who own valuable jewelry or objects of art want to purchase appropriate coverage for those items. This tendency can result in a disproportionate number of insureds who experience losses that are greater than those anticipated. Thus, the actual losses can be greater than the expected losses. Because adverse selection is of concern to insurers for both individual and group contracts, certain safeguards generally are used in each case to prevent it from happening.

Under a block of individual insurance contracts, the desirable situation for an insurance company is to have a spread of risks throughout a range of acceptable insureds. The so-called spread ideally will include some risks that are higher and some that are lower than the average risk within the range. Insurers attempt to control adverse selection by the use of sophisticated underwriting methods used to select and classify applicants for insurance and by supportive policy provisions, such as suicide clauses in life insurance policies and the exclusion of certain types of losses under homeowners policies.

The management of adverse selection under group insurance contracts necessarily is different from the approach used in individual insurance. Group insurance is based on the group as a unit and, typically, individual insurance eligibility requirements are not used for the group insurance underwriting used in employee benefit plans. As an alternative, the group technique itself is used to control the problem of adverse selection. The characteristics of the group technique are covered in Chapter 1 of this

Handbook in the discussion of the factors that have contributed to the development of employee benefits, and again in Chapter 14 in the context of its application to group life insurance contracts.

Self-Funding/Self-Insurance

Self-funding, or self-insurance, is a common method of providing financing for employee benefit plans. Essentially, this means that the organization is retaining the risk. It is important to realize, however, that many of the activities performed by the insurance company under an insured plan still have to be done. The identical problems associated with insurable risks for an insurance company exist for the firm that is self-funding or self-insuring. Therefore, the characteristics of an ideally insurable risk would be just as important for those firms that use self-funding as they are for an insurance company. The mechanism used for funding is not directly related to the question of whether a risk is a good one to include in the benefit plan. One should realize that generally only large firms with many employees would be able to meet all the characteristics of the ideally insurable risk. It is not uncommon to find that firms that say they self-fund or self-insure have, in fact, some arrangement with an insurance company or companies to insure part or all of a particular benefit. Many firms use insurance to provide backup coverage for catastrophic losses or coverage for losses the firm feels cannot be self-funded. The self-funded or self-insured plan has most of the characteristics found in the definition of insurance and has many of the same problems.

SUMMARY

Risk may be defined as uncertainty with respect to future loss or decrease in financial value. Risk can be classified as either pure or speculative. The difference between the two types is that speculative risk has the possibility of gain associated with it as well as loss. Pure risk, on the other hand, involves only the possibility of loss. Insurance is designed to handle pure risk but not speculative risk. Most employee benefit plans involve pure risk, so it is not uncommon to find these plans funded with insurance.

Pure risk can be classified as personal, property, and legal liability risk. Personal risk was the focus of this chapter and would include any loss suffered directly to a person, such as death, disability, illness, unemployment, or old age. Many risk-handling methods are used to solve the problems connected with the uncertainty of risk. Avoidance, retention, control, noninsurance transfer, and insurance are typical methods. Employee benefit plans often use a combination of methods, such as control, retention, and insurance.

Insurance is a mechanism by which one's risk (uncertainty) can be handled by transferring the risk to a third party, most often an insurance company. Although insurance is a popular risk-handling device, it is not appropriate for all risks. Insurance companies prefer that the risk have certain characteristics. The risk must have a large number of similar exposure units, the loss should be able to be verified and measured, the risk should not be subject to catastrophic loss, the chance of loss should be subject to calculation, the premium should be reasonable, and the loss should be accidental from the standpoint of the insured. Fortunately, most employee benefit plans cover insurable risks; thus, insurance is a feasible solution. Life risks conform to these conditions from a desirable-risk standpoint, while unemployment risks generally fail to conform to these conditions as insurable risks for private insurance companies.

The functional approach to planning employee benefits (Chapter 2) considers the factors discussed in this chapter. Risk alternatives, characteristics of insurable risks, and types of risk are all important concepts in developing an employee benefit plan, and failure to consider these factors could result in eventual failure of the plan itself.

PART TWO

Medical and Other Health Benefits

In this part, the critically important topic of medical benefits and issues is explored. Of prime importance in any discussion of medical benefits is the subject of cost containment—a topic so important today that it is referred to, either explicitly or implicitly, in all the chapters in this section.

Part Two opens with a discussion of the basic designs and strategic consideration of health plans in Chapter 4. The next three chapters all deal in one way or another with recent ways of dealing with health care cost containment. Chapter 5 covers demand-side approaches to cost containment, Chapter 6 deals with managing and measuring care management intervention programs, and Chapter 7 examines consumer-driven health care plans. The focus of Chapter 8 is behavioral health care benefits, and Chapter 9 describes how to evaluate the quality of health care provided by plans—quality has tremendous impact on both treatment outcomes and plan costs.

The next four chapters expand the coverage of health benefits to four specific benefits. Chapter 10 discusses the problem of high prescription drug costs and plan designs found to curtail plan cost increases. Dental benefits, which are much valued by employees and require only a modest employer investment, are covered in Chapter 11. Long-term care insurance is the topic of Chapter 12. Finally, completing this series of chapters, Chapter 13 deals with disability income benefits.

CHAPTER 4

Health Plan Evolution

Dennis F. Mahoney

Medical plans are an important benefit to the employees who receive them. In fact, several surveys[1] regarding the value that employees place on their respective employee benefit offerings universally rate health coverage as by far the most important benefit component to the majority of employees. This is particularly the case in more recent times as individuals have seen the cost of medical care significantly escalate, often outpacing the general level of price inflation for other goods and services. Even in times of relatively little inflation or in times of moderate deflation, the price of medical care seems to rise. Medical bills for those who do not have adequate health protection can mean depletion of family resources and ultimately financial ruin. Of those individuals and families whose financial circumstances have necessitated filing for bankruptcy, a significant number have identified health expenses and the loss of adequate medical coverage as a major contributing factor leading to the bankruptcy filing.[2]

Medical plans have changed considerably since first introduced as an employee benefit. While today's plans are considerably different from those offered in the past, we seem poised at the current time for yet another iterative step in the development of health plans. This impending

1. For instance, see Mercer Workplace Survey: 2010 results at www.mercer.com/articles/workplacesurvey 2010.
2. David U. Himmelstein, Elizabeth Warren, Deborah Thome and Steffie Woolhandler, "Illness and Injury as contributors to bankruptcy," *Health Affairs* (February 2005), pp. 1377–1387.

transformation of existing health plans is related to major health care reform legislation enacted in 2010 with passage of two laws: the Patient Protection and Affordable Health Care Act (PPACA), amended by the Health Care and Reconciliation Act of 2010. These combined laws make major revisions in the rules relating to employment-based plans. Beginning in 2014, these laws require that individuals obtain health coverage for themselves and their dependents. In preparing for mandated individual health coverage, major changes are occurring for insured and self-funded employer-based plans. Some of these preparatory changes commenced as early as plan years beginning after September 23, 2010.

THE EARLY ORIGINS OF MEDICAL PLANS

The early medical plans were either prepaid service plans providing a set allowance for hospitalization/medical services or traditional indemnity-type plans providing cash reimbursement for specific covered services. These approaches to medical insurance have become far less popular among employers in the present era because of the inability to manage costs and the failure to place a value on the health care received. Although traditional prepayment and indemnity designs may still be found on a very limited basis in employee benefit plans and as choices in some flexible benefit programs, medical care increasingly moved to managed care programs during the 1980s and 1990s. In more recent times, consumer-driven health plan designs have been added to the menu of health plan alternatives. Consumer driven health plan designs have not assumed a majority market share position in terms of plan participants seeking health coverage through the private health system. Managed care designs, inclusive of preferred provider organizations (PPOs), health maintenance organizations (HMOs), point-of-service (POS) programs, and consumer driven health plans (CDHPs), as a group predominate in the current landscape of private health plan offerings. These plans have replaced the traditional indemnity plans of yesteryear. However, even managed care plans and consumer driven health plan designs have faced significant rate increases and cost challenges. Employers continue to review their plan designs in search of better values.[3]

This chapter describes the early, traditional fee-for-service prepayment and indemnity plan structures and chronicles the evolving plan configurations that have led to today's predominant managed care programs. As alluded

3. Managed care plans and consumer driven health plans can involve a great variety of alternate designs.

to earlier, it appears these plans will again undergo significant transformation as the requirements of health care reform move from theory into practice. It is useful to understand that actual benefits and coverage levels varied widely among plans prior to the roll out of health reform. Since health reform established the concept of "minimum essential health coverage," it was likely that more standardization would occur in plan design. It is useful to have a rather comprehensive understanding of the benefits commonly provided through conventional plans. In the case of traditional indemnity programs, it is also helpful to understand which benefits were provided under the various component parts of the plan. The exact level of benefits was contractually defined by the insurer or plan sponsor, and the benefits described throughout this chapter are representative of benefits commonly provided. In addition to describing the evolutionary development of health plans and a preview of expected post health care reform plan features, the chapter also discusses issues in developing a health care strategy and describes common provider reimbursement approaches. Developing a health care strategy and determining the methodology for provider reimbursement are particularly important issues when the health care environment is in flux and as plan designs emerge from the actual implementation of legislated health care reforms. Other chapters in this *Handbook* cover in greater detail various types of managed care delivery systems, how to assess quality in health care, and specific approaches to controlling health care costs.

THE EVOLUTION OF HOSPITAL/MEDICAL PLAN DESIGNS

Hospital medical plans have evolved over the years.

Prepayment Service and Indemnity Plans

Because the primary distinction between original prepayment and insured indemnity products was whether the benefit coverages were stipulated as a set level of benefits or an indemnified dollar amount to cover a certain amount of benefit, these two types of plans are described together.

Hospitalization Coverage: The Early Days

Insurance that covered hospital stays was traditionally obtainable as a stand-alone product separate from insurance for medical services. Although medical benefit insurance has evolved into a more comprehensive product that covers hospital stays, physician services, and other medical expenses, it is still useful to examine the separate components.

The Blue Cross/Blue Shield organizations played a dominant role in the emergence of these early plans, setting up separate entities to handle hospital insurance and medical care insurance. Their hospital insurance products were configured as prepayment plans in which benefits were set in terms of allowable days of hospitalization. These plans emerged in the early 1930s. They contracted with hospitals and reimbursed them directly for patient lengths of stay. The Blue Cross organizations provided insurance to all policy seekers under their own charter. Insurance companies entered the marketplace soon thereafter but provided a hospital-day benefit that was based on a fixed dollar figure, which was the amount for which the insurance company indemnified the subscriber. This dollar figure was calculated based on the expected cost of the hospitalization. While the Blue Cross organizations were nonprofit entities, the insurance companies were for-profit organizations, were not community rated, and were not open to all those seeking coverage.

The early hospitalization plans were configured as first-dollar plans, in which benefits were paid from the first dollar of expense incurred, and the subscriber did not incur any expense with the hospitalization. This first-dollar coverage was in keeping with the model of a prepayment plan and was doable because the cost and utilization patterns for medical care were quite different from what they are today. Many of these plans, particularly the Blue Cross plans, were underwritten by community rating, an insurance approach whereby a uniform rate is used for all subscribers or insureds within a given geographical area.

Hospitalization Benefits: Further Development

The hospitalization portion of the pre-health-care-reform (2010) plans generally has covered all services, supplies, and procedures provided and billed through a hospital. These included the following:

- Inpatient room and board. This benefit usually covered hospital charges for a semiprivate room and board and other necessary services and supplies.
- Emergency care for services obtained at a hospital emergency room.
- Intensive and specialty care.
- Maternity and required associated newborn care for a set number of days or a stipulated dollar amount.

- X-ray, diagnostic testing, and laboratory expenses when the insured was hospital-confined or when these services were performed by a hospital on either an inpatient or outpatient basis.
- Skilled nursing facility care. A plan would pay for confinement in a skilled nursing facility if it met prescribed requirements. Usually, there was a daily limitation either on a yearly basis or per confinement. Historically, a hospital stay of at least three consecutive days immediately prior to confinement was required to trigger allowance for skilled nursing facility care. Many plans have eliminated this prior hospitalization requirement.
- Radiation and chemotherapy. This benefit typically covered materials and their preparation, as well as use of hospital facilities.
- Inpatient mental and nervous care.
- Inpatient drug and alcohol substance abuse care.
- Physical, inhalation, and cardiac therapy.
- Home health care. This benefit was provided for a specific number of visits per year by physicians, nurses, and home health aides. Care usually had to be under a treatment plan supervised by a home health agency.
- Hospice care. This benefit was provided when the subscriber's attending physician certified that the subscriber had a terminal illness with a limited medical prognosis, in many plans six months or less. This type of care allowed the subscriber to receive care primarily at home, to help relieve pain and provide comfort rather than curing the patient. Hospice care typically allowed for admission into a hospice facility, and benefits would usually be provided until the earlier of either a patient's death or discharge from a hospice.
- Respite care. Coupled with hospice care, this benefit allowed the terminal patient short-term inpatient care in a skilled nursing facility or member hospice when it was necessary to relieve primary caregivers in the patient's home. An example of this benefit might be an allowance of seven days every six months.

Under a major medical plan (described below) when allowances for hospitalization services were exceeded by a plan participant, the excess charges typically flowed to the major medical component of the plan where the plan reimbursed the participant after he or she paid the applicable deductible and coinsurance amounts.

Medical/Service Coverage: The Early Days

Just as Blue Cross provided hospital insurance coverage, Blue Shield provided for insured medical care, including physician and other health care provider expenses. Similar to Blue Cross, the Blue Shield plans were service-type plans, which provided a limit on the services covered rather than a strict dollar indemnification. Blue Shield plans followed the creation of the Blue Cross hospitalization plans. The insurance companies that followed Blue Shield into the marketplace provided indemnification to the subscriber up to certain dollar amounts for covered medical services.

Medical/Service Benefits: Further Development

The medical/service benefits paralleled the benefits provided under the earlier medical/service plans. The medical/surgical portion of these plans covered most services of health care practitioners. Their fees were reimbursed either on a scheduled fee basis or on a "reasonable and customary (R&C) basis." A scheduled fee basis provided a maximum allowance for itemized procedures in terms of either a flat dollar amount or a unit value per procedure, which was then multiplied by a conversion dollar amount. The reasonable and customary basis was reimbursement based on the individual practitioner's customary charge for the procedure and the charges made by peer physicians in the given geographic area. Typically, "reasonable and customary" covered the equivalent of the full charge of 75 percent to 90 percent of all physicians within a geographic region. The plan then reimbursed the lesser of the individual practitioner's charge or the reasonable and customary fee. The advantage to a medical/surgical plan that paid on an R&C basis was that, unlike a scheduled fee plan, it was not necessary to amend the medical plan to account for medical inflation. However, in times of dramatic medical inflation, an insurer might not update the reasonable and customary database as frequently to exercise some restraint on price escalation.

The following services were typically covered in the medical/surgical insurance component:

- Surgeons
- Anesthesiologists
- Nurses and other surgical assistants
- Service fees associated with inpatient medical care

- Second surgical opinions
- X-ray, diagnostic, and laboratory expense benefits made in a doctor's office or by an independent laboratory
- Skilled nursing care
- Obstetricians and pediatricians associated with prenatal, delivery, and postnatal care
- Inpatient intensive care and concurrent care in a hospital
- Allergy testing
- Transplant services
- The administration of radiation and chemotherapy
- Inpatient physical therapy
- Immunizations for children

An insurer could contract with physicians and other health care practitioners to establish fees for services. This agreement with physicians was common practice in the past with Blue Shield plans. With these plans, in agreeing to be a "participating doctor," the physician would agree to accept as payment in full, Blue Shield's usual, customary, and reasonable (UCR) fee. Thus, the doctor agreed that he or she would not balance bill the plan participant an additional amount if the doctor's fee was higher than the fee assigned by Blue Shield. The benefit that the doctor received for being a participating provider with Blue Shield was that she or he would be paid directly and would not have to seek collection from the individual patient. Most physicians were participating providers with Blue Shield.

If, on the other hand, the plan participant were to receive medical services from a "nonparticipating" doctor, the basic component of the plan might reimburse the participant a dollar amount that was less than the doctor's charge. In this case, the participant could often submit the excess billed amount to the supplemental major medical portion of the plan and receive a second level of reimbursement after paying the required deductible and coinsurance amounts required on the major medical insurance component of the plan.

As managed care organizations have become the predominant health plan providers, they have been able to exert greater influence over physician fee arrangements.

Major Medical Coverage: The Early Days

The third component that was joined with hospitalization and medical service to comprise traditional plans was supplemental major medical insurance. Major medical insurance was characterized by high limits of coverage; it was not typically written as first-dollar coverage but involved reasonable up-front deductibles and coinsurance. Two of the earliest attempts at health care cost containment—deductibles and coinsurance amounts—were two distinct methods of cost sharing with plan participants. The deductible was and is an amount of eligible covered medical expense that the insured subscriber must incur before the plan pays benefits. The rationale for a deductible is to lower plan costs. Coinsurance is another means by which plan participants share in the cost of their medical care. After an insured participant exceeds his or her deductible, the plan reimburses at less than 100 percent. This cost-sharing device ensures that the insured participant has a financial stake in the cost of medical care. The major medical insurance policy was written as "all-except" coverage rather than as "named peril" coverage, which specifically identified the services that were covered. Major medical coverage included a widely defined array of medical expenses, and named those services or medical items that were either limited in or precluded from coverage. A major medical policy could also be issued as a stand-alone policy, which was prevalent when this type of coverage was first introduced.

Major Medical Benefits: Further Development

The supplemental major medical portion of plans covered eligible expenses that may not have been covered in full or that were specifically excluded from either the basic hospitalization or the basic medical/surgical portions of the plan. Typically, these charges included the following:

- Excess hospitalization charges if the limit for services or a dollar amount on the hospitalization portion of the plan was exceeded
- Excess medical/surgical expenses experienced in receiving medical services from a "nonparticipating" doctor (if the plan was a Blue Cross/Blue Shield Plan)
- Diagnostic home and office visits
- Ambulance service
- Durable medical and surgical equipment
- Blood transfusions
- Oxygen and its administration

- Prescription drugs not used in a hospital or outpatient facility
- Prosthetics and orthotics
- Skilled nursing facility care in excess of the basic benefit allowance
- Outpatient mental and nervous care
- Outpatient drug and alcohol/substance-abuse care

These expenses were generally reimbursed after the participant paid an annual deductible in a major medical plan. He or she was then responsible for the relevant coinsurance amount. A plan may have required a deductible of $500 worth of eligible major medical type expenses per person before the plan began to reimburse. A typical level of coinsurance required by the participant was 20 percent. Therefore, under this type of arrangement, the plan would begin to reimburse at 80 percent after the deductible was satisfied. Typically, the plan reimbursed at 100 percent after an individual incurred a certain amount of coinsurance. For instance, the plan may have reimbursed at 80 percent for the first $10,000 of expenses and then picked up at 100 percent above the $10,000 threshold after the individual had paid $2,000 worth of co-payments out of pocket. The rationale for eliminating the coinsurance after a certain level and establishing an out-of-pocket maximum payment by the subscriber was the recognition that even requiring a coinsurance amount of 20 percent can cause extreme financial hardship in the event of a catastrophic illness.

Major medical plans had some lifetime maximum cap on eligible benefit charges after which the plan ceased reimbursing the participant. For instance, an individual might have been subject to a $1 million lifetime plan maximum, meaning that the plan would no longer cover expenses if the individual incurred eligible major medical expenses in excess of this limit.

The Patient Protection and Affordable Care Act (PPACA), as amended by the Health Care and Education Reconciliation Act of 2010, sought to protect individuals from losing their health coverage in the event of adverse illness. One method to achieve this goal was to prohibit the imposition of *lifetime* dollar limits on health benefits. PPACA prohibited lifetime dollar limits on "essential health benefits" for plan years beginning on or after September 23, 2010. Plans were permitted to impose "restricted" *annual* dollar limits on essential health benefits until the 2014 plan year. However, beginning in 2014, even restricted *annual* dollar limits were prohibited.

The rules regarding lifetime and annual dollar limits only applied to "essential health benefits." Plans could continue to impose lifetime dollar limits on benefits that were not considered to be "essential." Under PPACA, at a minimum, "essential benefits" included

- Ambulatory patient services
- Emergency services
- Hospitalization
- Maternity and newborn care
- Mental health and substance-use disorders, including behavioral health treatment
- Prescription drugs
- Rehabilitative and habilitative services and devices
- Laboratory services
- Preventative and wellness services and chronic disease management
- Pediatric services, including oral and vision care

It should be noted that "essential health benefits" are the types of benefits that must be provided through the Health Exchanges when they are established in 2014; they are not at present mandates for employer plans. Employer plans (as of 2011) needed only to be concerned about these benefits in connection with lifetime and annual dollar limits. Until the Department of Labor (DOL) determined benefits typically covered by employers via survey, a "good faith effort" to comply with the term "essential benefits" was permissible.

Comprehensive Plans: The Early Days

It is not hard to imagine the change in design of medical plans that occurred as the economics of medical care, utilization patterns, and technological enhancements increased the cost of the prepayment and traditional indemnity plans. Comprehensive medical plans were an adaptation of the major medical approach. Essentially, the structural approach of up-front deductibles and coinsurance was applied not only to supplemental medical services but also to hospitalization and basic medical services. What was a supplemental insurance approach to items not covered in the base medical plan became the mode of providing all medical insurance. The cost of medical insurance was decreased for two primary reasons. First, plan participants were cost sharing each time medical expenses were incurred through the up-front deductible and coinsurance. Second, because plan participants were required to pay a portion of medical costs when incurring services, they were given a financial incentive to be better health care consumers, unlike with first-dollar coverage, where there was no incentive to curb unnecessary utilization or choose less costly care. Comprehensive plans tended to be easier to communicate to plan participants, because there was no need to explain different component parts of a plan, which benefits were in each component, and which benefits were subject to deductibles and coinsurance.

Cost Control Features of Comprehensive Plans

Because many comprehensive plans were designed with cost savings as a primary objective, they had other cost-controlling features. Some of these features were applied later to other plan designs when organizations wanted to restrain the cost escalation in these programs. Some of the cost-controlling features included requiring second surgical opinions, full coverage for certain diagnostic tests, preadmission certification requirements for hospitalizations, utilization reviews by the insurer or a third-party administrator, and enhanced reimbursements if procedures were performed at an outpatient facility.

These plan features were intended to control costs and reduce unnecessary care. A plan sometimes exempted certain items such as second surgical opinions and diagnostic testing from the deductible and coinsurance provisions, and either required or encouraged their use. The belief was that second surgical opinions could decrease unnecessary surgical procedures, and diagnostic tests could result in early detection of certain medical conditions that were more cost effectively treatable if identified early. Preadmission certification required either plan participants or the admitting hospital to check with a specialist at the insurer or the plan sponsor before admitting an individual for treatment. The intent was to allow insurers to review provider decisions as to the cost-effectiveness and necessity of the treatment before hospitalization and to intervene if necessary. Utilization review involved an examination of medical patterns to determine whether plan participants or certain health care providers seemed to be outside average utilization ranges or expected practice patterns. Utilization review was concurrent, prospective, or retrospective. Enhanced reimbursements or waiving of deductibles and co-payments would occur if certain procedures were performed on an outpatient basis. The belief here was that a financial incentive would encourage plan participants to opt for a less costly outpatient treatment rather than a more costly treatment involving hospital inpatient care.

Comprehensive Plan Benefits: Further Development

The cost-control features just described are mainstream in comprehensive plans if offered today. These plans would subject virtually all expenses to a deductible and then reimburse an amount that excludes the coinsurance the participant must pay. However, certain benefits might be paid at 100 percent if they are viewed as contributing to a more economical means of accessing medical services, primarily as an alternative to inpatient hospital care. Also, as with major medical programs, most comprehensive plans had a maximum out-of-pocket payment, after which the plan would reimburse 100 percent of the UCR fee. Special daily limitations and annual maximum and lifetime caps also applied. (As was indicated and summarized above, PPACA severely limited annual and lifetime caps on "essential benefits.") A typical plan with a 20 percent coinsurance amount might have had benefits configured in the following way:

Benefits Paid at 80 Percent of the Insurer's Established UCR Fee (Subject to Deductible)

- Inpatient days room and board (preadmission certification required for admission)
- Maternity and newborn care
- Administration of radiation and chemotherapy
- Inpatient surgical services
- Physician office visits
- Chiropractic care
- Anesthesia
- Outpatient hospitalization services
- Emergency accident and medical emergency expenses
- Prescription drugs
- Private duty nursing
- Preadmission hospital testing
- Skilled nursing facility care
- Hospice care

- Respite care
- Physical and respiratory therapy

Benefits Paid at 100 Percent of the Insurer's Established UCR Fee (Not Subject to Deductible)

- Outpatient diagnostic tests, X-rays, and laboratory examinations
- Outpatient surgery or procedures performed at an ambulatory care facility, doctor's office, or surgi-center
- Home health care
- Second surgical opinions for specific medical procedures (it should be noted that many plans no longer required second surgical opinions, but had a concurrent utilization review procedure that served the same purpose)

In obtaining medical services from a Blue Cross/Blue Shield Comprehensive Plan, it could still be beneficial to seek services from the "participating" doctors, because a "nonparticipating" provider could charge an amount in excess of the insurer's UCR fee schedule. This could result in a plan participant having to pay more than 20 percent coinsurance because the plan would reimburse based upon the UCR fee.

It is unlikely that an employer would have offered a comprehensive major medical plan as a stand-alone plan once health reimbursement accounts (HRAs) and health savings accounts (HSAs) became available. If the comprehensive-type approach to a medical plan was desired, generally it would make more sense for the employer to offer a consumer driven health plan (CDHP) (described below), where a tax-advantaged reimbursement account would be combined with a high deductible health plan (HDHP). In essence, the enhancement of a tax-advantaged reimbursement account generally made comprehensive plans obsolete and CDHPs more state of the art.

MANAGED CARE PLAN DESIGNS: THE PREDOMINANT STRUCTURES

Managed care delivery systems go beyond the cost-control features detailed above and attempt to control costs through active ongoing health care management. Health care management can entail many different aspects. Some of the more common managed care delivery systems are detailed below.

Health Maintenance Organizations

The introduction of the health maintenance organization (HMO) was seen by many as the first real attempt at managed health care. An HMO differs from traditional approaches to health care in that it stresses wellness and preventive care. The HMO's intent is to maintain the participant's health, and therefore its orientation is toward health maintenance rather than treatment of illness only. Accordingly, HMOs provide richer preventive benefits, such as wellness programs, health screenings, and immunizations. Also, the financial incentives and cost controls are structured differently. Whereas comprehensive and major medical programs have up-front cost sharing to discourage "excess" medical utilization, HMOs usually have no up-front costs or charge only modest copayments for routine physician visits. Theoretically, HMOs control plan costs by maintaining health, managing care more cost-effectively, and controlling specialist referral. Most HMOs assign a primary care physician (PCP) to the plan participant. This PCP is charged with providing routine medical care to the subscriber and serves as a "gatekeeper," steering the subscriber to appropriate and cost-effective care should referral to specialists be required.

HMOs can take a variety of forms. The *individual practice association (IPA) model* is one in which an HMO contracts with individual physicians or associations of individual physicians to provide services to the health plan's subscribers. A *group model* is one where the HMO purchases services from an independent multispecialty group of physicians. A *network model* HMO is similar to the group model, but more than one multispecialty group practice provides services to members. Yet another variation in organizational design and service delivery is the *staff model* HMO. Here, rather than the HMO contracting with independent physicians or multispecialty groups, the physicians are full-time, bona fide employees of the HMO that pays their salaries. As many HMOs have grown, the clear distinction between individual practice model, group model, network model, and staff model has become somewhat blurred. The dramatic and ongoing growth of various health systems has meant the aggregation and merging of these disparate models.

HMO Benefits

As mentioned earlier, most managed care providers offer broader health care coverage especially in the areas of wellness and preventive care.

Often, a fundamental difference is the manner in which one accesses the delivery of care. At the time of initial enrollment in the plan, the subscriber and his or her dependents select a PCP who is responsible as the primary caregiver for most routine medical care. This PCP is the person to make referrals and provide authorization for specialty care when needed. Different managed care organizations have different approaches to the process by which specialty care referrals can occur. For instance, some managed care companies publish a listing of specialists in the network and leave a referral to the discretion of the PCP. Other companies have this function centralized and require the assignment of specialty authorizations to a centralized unit that ensures steerage to the most cost-effective specialty providers. This centralized approach to specialty care can be beneficial in ensuring that serious illnesses are directed to a "center of excellence," a provider known to have unique procedures or competence in treating certain types of injury or illnesses.

Wellness and preventive care benefits are key coverages that HMOs (and other managed care plans) provide that traditional plans have not provided. Expenses for these services historically have not been covered in the traditional fee-for-service type of plan. They include

- Routine physical examinations
- Preventive screenings and diagnostic tests for early detection of certain diseases
- Prenatal and well-baby care
- Immunizations for prevention of diseases (particularly for children)
- Vision and dental checkups
- Allowances for health club memberships

Because of the growing understanding of the benefits of preventive care, some states had enacted legislation requiring all health plans to offer certain benefits, such as childhood immunizations and screenings for diseases that would clearly benefit from early detection. Hence, some of the distinctions between plan models in terms of benefits offered have been blurred as preventive measures have been added to the traditional insurance plans.

Employers who maintained group health plans on March 23, 2010 were able to maintain "grandfathered" plans that are not subject to some of the PPACA provisions. A "grandfathered" plan is any group health plan or health insurance coverage in which an individual was enrolled on the date of PPACA's enactment. Employer-sponsored grandfathered plans may continue to add family members and new employees. Grandfathered plans only need to implement some of the insurance market reforms. Nongrandfathered plans must adhere to all of the insurance market reforms as they become effective.

PPACA required nongrandfathered group health plans to provide certain preventive items and services without cost sharing for plan years beginning on or after September 23, 2010. The regulations prohibited the imposition of cost sharing (including copayments, coinsurance, or deductibles) in connection with four broad categories:

- Items or services with an "A" or "B" rating in the current recommendations of the United States Preventive Services Task Force ("USPSTF")
- Immunizations for routine use as recommended by the Advisory Committee on Immunization Practices of the Centers for Disease Control and Prevention
- Preventive care and screenings for infants, children and adolescents provided for in the guidelines supported by the Health Resources and Services Administration (HRSA)
- Preventive care and screening for women provided for in guidelines supported by the HRSA

A group health plan is not required to provide coverage after the recommendation or guideline is no longer described by the regulations, and a group plan is required to cover only those preventive services that are recommended at least one year prior to the start of the plan year. Under certain exceptions, cost sharing may be permitted.

Preferred Provider Organizations

A preferred provider organization (PPO) is formed when a group of medical providers such as hospitals and doctors contract with employers, insurance companies, or other plan sponsors to provide various medical services. The medical providers usually offer discounted pricing because of the volume of business received from the contracting organizations. The medical providers are often reimbursed on a fee-for-service basis, but the fees are lower than in a traditional plan because of the negotiated discounts.

PPOs have emerged as the predominant managed care plan structure presently. Approximately 58 percent of plan participants receive their health benefits through a PPO arrangement. A comparison of other plan structures would show HMOs with approximately 19 percent of covered participants, POS programs (described below) with 8 percent, consumer-driven health programs with 13 percent, and traditional indemnity plans with a scant 1 percent.[4]

Preferred Provider Organization Benefits

The PPO health benefit option is best understood as a configuration of benefit design features offered through a contracted network (its major distinction from indemnity options) that can be assembled in many different ways. It may be assembled in a fully customized fashion by a self-funded employer or offered by an insurance carrier that develops network-based products that are sold to customers on an insured basis. Many self-insured employers rely on a third-party administrator (TPA) to assemble the package of services needed to launch a PPO offering, including renting access to a preferred provider network, selecting the kind of medical/utilization management to be used with the benefits, and claims processing. (In some instances, the administrator may be an insurance company providing administrative services only, or ASO, instead of bearing risk.) Insurance carriers engage in similar decision-making steps in product development, although some or all of the components are already in place in their organizations.[5]

Benefits provided through a preferred provider organization vary depending on the capabilities of the providers in the organization and the overall size of the PPO. A PPO could be the only source of medical care for an employee group, or the PPO may be one choice among several medical plans the employer offers. Alternatively, a PPO may provide the in-network benefit for a point of service plan, described below.

The PPO, as its proponents argue, can be whatever a purchaser wants it to be—if the purchaser is self-insured. The standard HMO products being sold may have more comprehensive benefits than an employer wishes to offer. In a PPO option, the component parts can be acquired separately from different vendors and assembled in a highly customized fashion. The benefit design can be built up or brought down from an a la carte menu, and

4. Kaiser/Health Research and Educational Trust Survey of Employer-Sponsored Health Benefits, 1999–2010.
5. Robert E. Hurley, Bradley C. Strunk, and Justin S. White, "The Puzzling Popularity of the PPO," *Health Affairs*, March/April 2004, p. 58.

varied combinations of cost-sharing provisions can be selected. The design can afford considerable transparency to consumers, who are advised of what is covered and not covered, which providers are in or out of a network, and what the differential level of coverage will be based on the site of service. For small employers that offer a single benefit design, a PPO option can enable workers to choose a narrow or a broad network, differentiated by coinsurance levels.[6]

Point-of-Service Programs

Another type of managed care program is the point-of-service (POS) program. This managed care product is somewhat of a cross between an HMO and the comprehensive major medical plan. Essentially, the plan sponsor contracts either with a number of health care providers or with a managed care company to provide cost-effective medical care through a preferred provider organization of health care providers. Plan participants are free to use the network of preferred providers when they need health care. Alternatively, the plan participants can decide to utilize other medical providers who are not included in the network. However, if the participant uses out-of-network providers, he or she incurs additional expense in the form of greater deductibles and copayments. It is at the point of service that the plan participant is making the decision whether to remain in network and receive a higher level of coverage or to select a medical provider who is out of network and be personally responsible for a larger share of the cost for this care. The POS program can be an attractive delivery system for participants who do not want to be restricted to receiving medical care only from network providers yet would still like to receive the same coverage and wellness benefits provided through a managed care system. This system of health care delivery suits some medical providers who are willing to join the PPO and provide medical services for discounted fees but are unwilling to assume the financial risks of HMO participation, where a monthly fee is often paid to the doctor for each member regardless of the frequency of visits and the care provided. However, the particular financial arrangement and whether service providers bear any financial risk can be determined in various ways. These points are discussed later in this chapter.

6. Ibid., pp. 62–63.

POS Plan Benefits

The POS plan is a hybrid of sorts, offering managed care case-management features and health maintenance approaches to medical care within the network but allowing plan participants the added flexibility of going outside the network if they are willing to bear a larger share of the cost for such flexibility. The extent to which subscribers are either penalized for going outside the network or rewarded for staying within it can be determined by the deductible and coinsurance levels that are set. An organization could have varying reasons for setting the deductible and coinsurance levels either low or high. Also, these coinsurance levels can vary for various types of medical services. For instance, if the network of medical providers is not particularly well developed in certain specialty areas, such as pediatrics, a company would find it difficult to penalize employees for not utilizing an in-network benefit. Another example could be that, for certain types of medical services (e.g., psychiatric benefits), a company may perceive it as intrusive to require use of an in-network benefit. This may be particularly true if the POS plan is newly installed and would result in disruption of ongoing treatment. As medical plans migrated from traditional indemnity plans to managed care structures, some organizations had used POS plans as a means to transition from an indemnity plan to a PPO or another form of managed care. In this situation, deductibles and coinsurance would typically be initially set slightly lower than in the traditional indemnity plan for employee relations reasons and then later increased as utilization grew in the managed care environment and employees became more comfortable with using in-network providers.

Integrated Health Systems

As the managed care delivery structures continued to grow, what started out as HMOs or PPOs were evolving into larger health systems that may have included a managed care company, various physician and multispecialty practices, as well as entire hospitals and ancillary service providers. The preceding discussion of health care delivery structures is not meant to provide strict classifications into which each health plan must be distinctly assigned. Rather, it is hoped this characterization will be helpful in understanding basic differences between existing health care delivery systems and a starting point for understanding the relative merits of alternative designs. An employer's health plan should be configured matching the plan sponsor's objectives and assisting in meeting total compensation and human resource objectives.

Consumer Driven Health Plans

Close to the turn of the millennium, a new type of health plan design was created—the consumer driven (directed) health plan (CDHP). Though these plans could involve a variety of different features, there were certain common attributes that characterized them. CDHPs, as first conceived, involved linking a high-deductible supplemental major medical plan with a savings account that would be used to pay either discretionary medical costs or certain charges before the deductible was reached. (Recall the observation earlier in this chapter that virtually all comprehensive major medical plans would have evolved into CDHPs, since it would make sense to add the tax-advantaged savings account to such a plan.) Decisions involving the spending of funds in the savings account were made by the plan participant. There would often be a deductible gap before the high-deductible supplemental major medical plan would cover expenses. The rationale for the CDHP model was that the plan provided a financial incentive to the plan participant to selectively choose medical care in a cost-efficient manner, and thus to be a good health care consumer. If the consumer-driven health plan was designed well, patient behavior was changed. This was and is of particular consequence to the plan's economics if patients requiring chronic and acute care, those who are responsible for high-volume discretionary expenditures, change their behavior.

Under a typical CDHP, as first introduced, a plan participant would receive some employer contribution, say $1,000 to $2,000, deposited into a health reimbursement account (HRA). When the funds in the HRA were exhausted, the participant would need to pay certain medical costs out of pocket before receiving insured health coverage under the high-deductible supplemental major medical plan.

The early CDHPs utilized HRAs as consumer-managed, side savings health care accounts. Promoters of consumer driven health plans sought tax guidance from the Internal Revenue Service (IRS), and the IRS responded that these accounts would be considered employer-provided health benefits exempt from income and employment tax and deductible as an employer business expense. It is noteworthy that HRAs were created by regulatory guidance rather than by statute. In order to qualify as an HRA, these accounts needed to be funded solely by employer contribution, they needed to be used to reimburse employees for medical care as defined by Section 213(d) of the Internal Revenue Code (IRC), and medical expenses needed to be incurred by the employee or the employee's spouse or dependents as defined in Section 152 of the IRC. The HRAs provided reimbursements up to a maximum amount, but the IRS ruled that any unused portion of the maximum dollar amount remaining at the end of a coverage period could be rolled over and increase the maximum reimbursement amount in subsequent coverage periods.

> The true viability of the consumer-directed health care model was ensured on June 26, 2002. That was the day the Internal Revenue Service issued guidelines approving the right of HRA owners to carry over unused amounts from year to year. This ruling may have been the most important change in health care in 25 years.[7]

The significance of this ruling was that it introduced a savings element into health plans, allowing capital accumulation and investment possibilities so that participants could advance fund future medical care.

Not long after the introduction of the HRA, another type of consumer-managed health care account was created. The Medicare Prescription Drug, Improvement and Modernization Act of 2003 allowed for the use of health savings accounts (HSAs) beginning in 2004. HSAs were similar to HRAs in that they allowed unused account balances to be carried forward into future years. Only individuals covered by a high-deductible insurance plan were permitted to establish an HSA. An innovative feature of the HSA was the wide latitude in funding source. An HSA can be funded by employer contribution, or using employee pretax money, or by an individual making a tax-deductible contribution. Another innovative feature was the account ownership characteristic. The accounts were the property of the individual, were nonforfeitable, and could be rolled over from one employer to another and from one account to another. The alternate funding sources for an HSA allowed for a variety of plan design approaches involving employer contribution, employee contribution, or both. Also, the fact that an individual or an employer could establish an HSA allowed its creation apart from the employer as long as the individual was a participant in a high-deductible health plan.

Beyond the basics of a consumer-managed health care account linked to a supplemental major medical plan, what did CDHPs offer? Some designing these plans saw a much wider array of consumer choice embedded in these plans. In keeping with the spirit of consumerism, many saw

7. Ronald E. Bachman, "Consumer-Driven Health Care: The Future Is Now," *Benefits Quarterly*, Vol. 20, No. 2, Second Quarter 2004, p. 18.

the inclusion of consumer education as integral to the success of the plan and the receptiveness of employees to these plans.

> Most consumer-driven plans are designed in several ways to encourage employees to be better health consumers. First, these plans offer the participant much more information about health choices, including providers, treatments and facilities. These plans may offer far more choice in services. Some allow the participant to "build" his or her own plan, literally choosing the deductible, copay, health providers and benefits covered. Consumer-driven plans frequently offer quality measures and evaluations of various health providers. They may offer health coaches for general health issues or designated specialist coaches for chronic conditions and disease management.[8]

Some practitioners were forecasting several stages in the development of CDHPs.[9] Under this evolutionary schema, second-generation CDHPs would involve employers funding the consumer-managed health account in creative ways with rewards, discounts, or other incentives when employees made behavioral changes. Looking further into the future, CDHP theorists envisioned optimizing the relationship between health care costs and employee performance.

> An important component of this strategy is the health risk appraisal. Profiling employees in areas such as stress can lead to an understanding of what health or workplace modifications are needed to lower costs and improve performance.[10]
>
> Future-generation CDHPs will emphasize personalization. Under this scenario, decision support systems will link each person with a personalized health care electronic support system providing real-time feedback on health status, lifestyle and health concerns.[11]

Although the future alone will determine the realization of these prognostications, it is clear that the plethora of innovative features comprising CDHPs is likely to expand into many new and exciting areas. See Chapter 7 for a complete discussion of CDHPs.

8. Martha Priddy Patterson, "Defined Contribution Health Plan to Consumer Driven Health Benefits: Evolution and Experience," *Benefits Quarterly*, Vol. 20, No. 2, Second Quarter 2004, p. 50.
9. Ronald E. Bachman, "Consumer-Driven Health Care: The Future Is Now," *Benefits Quarterly*, Vol. 20, No. 2, Second Quarter 2004, pp. 20–22.
10. Ibid., p. 21.
11. Ibid., pp. 21–22.

Special Provisions

Special provisions and limitations had historically applied to mental illness and substance abuse (drug or alcohol treatment) benefits.

Mental Health and Substance Abuse Benefits

Special provisions and limitations were a very common plan design feature. In 1993 for example, 97 percent of participants in medium and large private establishment health plans were eligible for some level of outpatient mental health services, while only 3 percent had the same benefits as those for other illnesses.[12] Similarly, while 98 percent of full-time participants in medium and large private establishment medical plans in 1993 were covered for inpatient detoxification for alcohol and drug abuse treatment, 28 percent and 29 percent, respectively, had the same level of coverage for these illnesses as they had for other illnesses.[13] However, on September 26, 1996, the Mental Health Parity Act (MHPA) was signed into law. The MHPA required that annual or lifetime limits on mental health benefits be no lower than the dollar limits for medical and surgical benefits offered by the group health plan. The MHPA applied to group health plans for plan years beginning on or after January 1, 1998 and contained a "sunset" provision providing that the parity requirements did not apply to benefits received on or after September 30, 2001. These parity requirements were subsequently extended. The MHPA originally did not apply to benefits for substance abuse or chemical dependency. Subsequently the Mental Health Parity and Addiction Equity Act (MHPAEA) of 2008 was enacted. The clarifying regulations related to this act were issued in 2010. The MHPAEA broadened the MHPA parity rules as to limits for mental health benefits, and amended them to extend to substance-use disorder benefits as well.

In the past, substance-abuse benefits were not separately delineated in many plans but were covered under mental and nervous benefits. However, because new treatment approaches had been developed and because the federal government and some states had enacted legislation mandating minimum levels of treatment for mental and nervous benefits, more plans separated these benefits into distinct and separate categories. Most plans in the past had limitations on both mental/nervous and drug/alcohol benefits that resulted in greater cost sharing by the participant.

12. Cecelia Silverman, Michael Anzick, Sarah Boyce, Sharyn Campbell, Ken McDonnell, Annmarie Reilly, and Sarah Snider, in *EBRI Databook on Employee Benefits*, 3rd ed., ed. Carolyn Pemberton and Deborah Holmes, Washington, DC: Education and Research Fund, 1995, p. 328.

13. Ibid., p. 328.

There were two common forms of limitations on these benefits. The first was to set the coinsurance at a higher level, say 50 percent in a 20 percent reimbursement plan, and establish an annual maximum for this benefit, such as $1,500. Additionally, a different lifetime maximum applied to this benefit, say $10,000. A second form of limitation was to set a maximum number of outpatient visits per year, such as 20 visits, with a maximum covered charge, such as $50. Similarly, with inpatient coverage on the basic hospitalization portion of the plan, it was common to have a lifetime cap on this specific type of care and a maximum number of days allowable per plan year or calendar year. Since the MHPA prohibited specific dollar limitations for mental and nervous benefits different from other medical and surgical benefits offered by the plan, many plans eliminated such provisions but kept limitations in terms of days of treatment and outpatient visits. Some plans had used this same approach for substance-abuse benefits, although dollar limitations were still permissible until the MHPAEA was passed in 2008. Since PPACA prohibited annual and lifetime limits on "essential benefits" and included mental health and substance-use disorders, including behavioral health treatments, in the category of essential benefits; subsequent clarifying regulations related to PPACA will likely impact these benefits as well.

When issued in 2010, the regulations implementing MHPAEA were more expansive than anticipated, and prohibited group health plans that provide medical and surgical benefits and mental health or substance-use disorder benefits from applying "financial requirements" or "treatment limits" that were more restrictive than the "predominant" financial requirement or treatment limit that applied to "substantially all" medical and surgical benefits.

"Carve Out" and Separate Management of Costly Expense Items

Many organizations have "carved out" prescription drug benefits from their plans and were managing those benefits on a separate basis. This was because prescription drugs had been among the fastest growing cost components in many medical plans. The emergence of drug management firms provided opportunities for cost savings through pharmacy networks, mail-order discount programs, inclusion of generic drug substitutes, drug formulary management, prescription utilization review, and disease management programs. Mental health and substance-abuse benefits also had been carved out and were separately managed by many medical plans as discussed above.

VARIATIONS IN PLAN DESIGN

The preceding descriptions of benefit provisions were intended to acquaint the reader with standard types of medical plans and how the development of new plan types evolved from the types of structures that preceded them. The reader should be aware that there is wide latitude in design alternatives within the frameworks described.

Accordingly, a plan sponsor could use this flexibility in designing plans that best suited the organization's objectives. The sponsor should consider designs that balance human resource and organization goals with administrative, communication, and funding realities.

As of this writing (2011), it is rather early to prognosticate on all of the impacts of PPACA and its clarifying regulations on the next generation of health plan designs and their administrative processes. Nevertheless, even at this early juncture, certain emergent themes can be anticipated. Some of these expected effects include

- A move towards standardization of certain benefits. This effect emanates from (1) insurance market reforms mandated by the federal government, (2) expected regulatory guidelines on minimum essential coverage, and (3) the need to conduct future actuarial determinations that will assess whether plans comply with the 60% contribution affordability measure.
- A continuing exodus from employer-provided health care for early retirees. This effect is expected, since early retirees will have access to coverage through health exchanges. The establishment of a "temporary reinsurance" program by the Department of Health and Human Services to combat this effect points to its occurrence.
- A diminished role for flexible spending accounts (FSAs) in underwriting certain health care expenses. This effect is a direct consequence of the stipulation that employee salary reduction contributions to health FSAs be limited to $2,500 per year, beginning in 2013.
- A more conservative contribution approach to health savings accounts (HSAs). Like the preceding effect, the imposition of an additional tax on distributions from an HSA that are not used for qualified medical expenses will make these accounts less appealing. Beginning in 2011, this tax is increased from 10 percent to 20 percent.

- Greater reliance on outsourcing services in administering health plans. This effect is all but certain, given additional administrative requirements in the realms of disclosure, actuarial determinations, and business transactions with health exchanges.
- The curtailment of health plan offerings by certain employers. Given the additional complexity of health plan administration and the possibility for employees to secure affordable health insurance through state exchanges, some employers will opt to pay the penalty tax and avoid the endeavor of plan sponsorship.

UNDERWRITING AND FUNDING APPROACHES

Health care cost control has become of paramount importance as the cost of medical care has increased.[14] Medical costs are a significant expense and a risk exposure that can have a substantial impact on an organization's overall compensation costs and operating results. In light of this, it is not surprising that many organizations have looked to innovative financial arrangements at the same time they restructure benefit design and health care delivery.

Community Rating

The early prepayment plans offered by the Blue Cross and Blue Shield organizations were offered as community-rated products. Under this financing approach, all insureds in a given geographic area paid a uniform rate. Because the Blue Cross and Blue Shield organizations were chartered with the intention of providing insurance to all those seeking coverage and because they negotiated contractual reimbursement arrangements with providers, this method of underwriting was possible in the early years when costs were lower and the Blue Cross/Blue Shield plans were the principal underwriter of medical care. HMOs at their inception also used community rating and, in order to be qualified under the Health Maintenance Organization Act of 1973, were required to adhere to specific rules regarding it. These requirements were relaxed with the 1988 amendments to the

14. This section provides an overview of certain underwriting and funding approaches. See Appendix 4.1 for a detailed analysis of techniques used in both price management and utilization management to control medical plan costs. Additionally, Appendix 4.2 provides information on vision care and hearing care plans.

Health Maintenance Organization Act. Community rating is still used for individual subscribers and for smaller group contracts. However, community rating is much less popular in the group insurance market, where larger organizations prefer to be experience rated rather than be rated with other organizations, which potentially have less-favorable risks.

Adjusted Community Rating

At times, an insurer will offer a plan sponsor insurance rates that have been calculated using adjusted community rates. The baseline claims data used to establish these rates are the claims and utilization patterns in the community at large. However, based on certain favorable characteristics of the plan sponsor's own past claims data, the insurer is willing to offer more beneficial rates, which have been approved by the state's insurance department and the insurer's underwriting department, for a client that exhibits favorable claims characteristics.

EXPERIENCE RATING

An organization that is willing to proactively manage its health care costs through benefit plan redesign and innovative delivery of care will seek to capture the cost savings generated by these actions. An experience-rated plan uses recent claims and utilization data of a particular organization to establish the appropriate insurance rates for a future time period. If an organization has had a history of favorable claims experience, the experience-rated insurance product may offer substantial cost advantages over an underwriting approach that uses aggregate community claims experience to establish insurance rates.

Cost-Plus and Self-Insured Approaches

An organization of sufficient size may finance its health care benefits using a cost-plus or self-insured approach. Under such a scenario, the organization will pay for the actual claims of its group, along with an administrative charge to an insurer or third-party administrator who handles claims processing. Such an agreement is often called an administrative services only (ASO) agreement. Under this type of arrangement, it is important to understand provider reimbursement methods. For instance, are hospital daily room costs based on actual charges or a discounted amount below charges? Will the hospital be paid for each day a patient is hospitalized, or will the hospital be paid for a fixed number of days commensurate with the expected length of stay usually associated with the medical condition and its course of treatment? This latter approach would give the hospital an incentive to ensure that patient lengths of stay are in line with practice norms.

Stop-Loss Insurance

If an organization utilizes a cost-plus or self-insured method of financing, it may choose to limit its potential aggregate medical claims exposure by purchasing insurance that would make payment if claims exceeded a certain predetermined amount for the entire group. This insurance coverage for capping the total claims experience of the group is known as aggregate stop loss. A firm might also limit its liability using specific stop loss. Specific stop loss sets a limit on the amount that a plan sponsor will pay for an individual case. If a catastrophic medical case occurs, the employer will only be responsible for paying covered medical costs on that individual case up to the stop-loss amount.

Because the insurer is assuming risk for excess claims, the contractual document will clearly define when the insurer assumes the risk. It is extremely important when contracting for stop-loss protection to carefully analyze terms and conditions to ensure that the intentions for protecting against loss are matched by the insurer's policy. For instance, the period for claims coverage could be specified on the basis either of when a claim is incurred or of when a claim is paid. It is also important to ensure that definitions for coverable expenses in the employer's health plan match coverages in the stop-loss agreement. Medical plans and stop-loss coverage typically exclude medical care that is deemed experimental in nature. Do both documents have the same definition of experimental medical care? Other issues to examine would be whether specific subscribers undergoing treatment are excluded from the stop-loss coverage and how the run-out of claims payments going beyond the stop-loss coverage period are handled.

PROVIDER REIMBURSEMENT APPROACHES

Provider reimbursement approaches include fee-for service, capitation, and health care purchasing cooperatives and coalitions.

Fee-for-Service

Under this payment method, health care providers charge separately each time services for care are rendered. This is a common reimbursement method under traditional indemnity plans. Providers commonly set their own charge and are paid accordingly. Sometimes, insurers negotiate a fee schedule that establishes the maximum amount the plan will pay for any given medical procedure or service. Fee-for-service has been the most common provider reimbursement approach for the traditional prepayment, indemnity, and comprehensive plan designs. Preferred provider options may pay a fee for services, but this fee typically would be a negotiated and discounted fee.

Capitation

Under capitation, providers are paid a set amount (generally monthly for primary care providers (PCPs)) for each plan participant, regardless of the number of visits or services provided.

Capitation payment methods are used extensively by HMOs. This form of payment shifts some risk to the medical provider, who accepts the capitation amount, assuming the increased enrollment will level out the risks. Some plans reimburse PCPs and certain specialists using capitation, and have a fee schedule for other medical specialists.

Other Provider Reimbursement Approaches

Some employers have banded together into purchasing cooperatives to have greater health care buying power in the marketplace. Such an arrangement is used to gain favorable pricing from medical providers because of the large volume of business that can be supplied. This means of purchasing health care can be particularly attractive to a small employer who would not be able to procure the same discount on services that a large employer could. In some ways, the insurance company or managed care provider plays this role for smaller groups. However, the emergence of health care purchasing cooperatives provides another alternative for employers to negotiate pricing with medical providers.

DEVELOPING A HEALTH CARE STRATEGY

Developing a health care strategy for providing employee health and medical care benefits can be viewed as a program for managing risk exposures on a variety of levels. In its most elementary form, managing this risk involves a three-pronged strategy. First, the organization sponsoring the plan must decide what mode of health care delivery system will be used. Second, the organization must decide on the benefits that will be provided through the selected system. Third, the plan sponsor must decide what contractual, financial, or payment arrangement will be negotiated with insurers or providers of medical care. Negotiation of the financial arrangement also includes what level of risk is assumed by the plan sponsor and whether certain types or levels of risk will be shifted to a third party such as an insurer or the providers of the medical care itself. Increasingly, plan sponsors shift some of this risk to ensure that medical providers have a stake in providing cost-effective and quality care. All three of these macro decisions involve many other tiers of decisions at the micro level, which can have a profound impact on the levels of risk assumed and the financial costs assumed by the plan sponsor. With the advent of health care reform, additional risks have been entered into the system, since plan sponsors may be subject to providing subsidies or vouchers (see subsequent discussion in this chapter) to some of their employees and/or will be subject to certain excise taxes.

Designing the Plan and Delivery System

The plan sponsor is not only selecting one of the delivery systems discussed previously, but also has latitude to select various plan designs offered by alternate delivery systems or to include plan-specific provisions or procedures particular to the employer group. Unless federal or state law requires certain benefits, an employer quite often has flexibility to design its own schedule of benefits, assuming it is of sufficient size to gain this degree of customization by an insurer or managed care company. At times, even state insurance law is not an immovable constraint, because certain administrative service financing arrangements exempt plans from state insurance mandates. Limitations on specific coverages, uses of deductibles or copayments, and the systems for case management and precertification can profoundly impact both risk exposure and cost. The delivery system and plan design, its oversight, and financial incentives also can have behavioral impacts on plan participants influencing the utilization of health care services.

With the passage of major health care reform legislation in 2010, a new era began in structuring health benefit programs. Additional regulation at the federal level immediately impacted plan design decisions. For example, this is evident in the previously described distinction between grandfathered and nongrandfathered plans. PPACA also distinguished between large and small employer plans. The Act included a tax credit for small employers that purchased health insurance for their employees when the employer

- Has fewer than 25 full-time equivalent employees
- Pays average annual wages under $50,000
- Contributes a uniform percentage of at least 50 percent of the total premium cost

The full credit is available to employers with ten or fewer full-time equivalent employees and average annual wages of less than $25,000, and begins phasing out over those amounts. (Beginning in 2014, the credit is available only for qualified health plan coverage purchased through a health exchange, and employers may only receive the credit for a maximum of two consecutive years.)

Various insurance market reforms mandated by PPACA placed constraints on plan sponsor design decisions. For instance, six months after enactment, group health plans and health insurers were not allowed to

- Impose lifetime or annual limits on essential benefits (subject to certain exceptions).
- Rescind coverage unless there was fraud or misrepresentation by the enrollee.
- Drop coverage for adult children on their parents' coverage, regardless of the adult child's student or marital status, until the adult child turns 26 years old.
- Impose preexisting condition exclusions on enrollees under age 19.

Self-Administration, Third-Party Administrators, and Unbundled Services

The decision to purchase an assembled delivery system from an insurer or managed care company or to directly contract with providers is generally dependent on employer size and the geographic concentrations of an organization's employees. When an employer is of sufficient size, it might want to deal directly with medical providers and eliminate the costs associated with the intermediary insurer. Even if an employer does not want to assume the burden of self-administration, it is not necessary to purchase all medical care management services through a single provider. An employer can decide to unbundle specific services that might be more effectively performed by separate entities or purchase an integrated set of services or programs through one provider. Moving specific, specialized functions to third-party vendors with special expertise in one area can sometimes address certain goals. At the very least, an employer should understand the costs of these services if they are left bundled with the insurer and review claims and other reports to evaluate the services' effectiveness and contributions to cost control.

Under PPACA, by 2014, certain employers' employees gain access to health insurance through health exchanges. PPACA requires each state to establish one or more health exchanges in which small employers and individuals can purchase health insurance. Initially, only small employers have access to purchase group health insurance through an exchange. However, by 2017, states may permit large employers to purchase group health coverage through their exchanges. States have the right to define "small" and "large" employers before 2016, though small employers generally will not exceed 100 employees. Lawful United States' residents (except incarcerated individuals) generally can access individual health coverage through an exchange in a state in which they live.

Use of Multiple Plan Offerings and Single or Multiple Administrators

Medical care delivery systems and benefit design are not an "all-or-nothing" decision for many large employers. Though some employers place their entire block of business with a single insurer or managed care company, many other employers have configured a variety of health plan alternatives and give employees the choice of selecting the health plan that best meets their individual needs. This can be accomplished through a simple choice of medical plan options or through a flexible benefit plan. In large part because of limited dollars available to expand benefit programs and a recognition that a diverse workforce may have varying benefit needs, flexible benefit programs proliferated in the 1980s. In a flex plan, employees are allocated a set amount generally in the form of credits or dollars from the employer, which they can "spend" to select the benefits and plan options of their choice or receive those credits in the form of cash if not spent on benefits. Nevertheless, many managed care companies and insurers offer employers an array of multiple plan designs. Price concessions are often offered if an employer agrees to place the entire block of business with a single administrative entity. An employer must balance the price concessions it will receive and assess the effectiveness of the administrative entity at managing health care costs against the loss of competition that occurs when multiple plan offerings through various administrators are eliminated.

Pricing Plan Options and Designing Employer Subsidies

Regardless of whether multiple administrators or a single administrator are used for separate plan offerings, the plan sponsor must look at the pricing of plan options and make decisions regarding the form and amount of employer subsidy provided to employees. An employer offering a flexible benefit program may price various plan options at prevailing market rates, assign all employees an equal credit amount, and allow them to spend the credits as they prefer. Other employers provide a direct subsidy to their medical plans and only show employees the remaining employee costs they will be required to pay. Some employers subsidize family contracts to a greater extent than single coverage. The employer must also decide how to relate the subsidy to each medical plan option. Plan pricing will affect employee selection patterns. Premiums are impacted by the level of deductibles and co-payments that have been included in the front-end plan design. Accordingly, an employer can determine whether plan costs and certain benefits are being borne by those utilizing those particular benefits or are being spread over the employee group at large.

More transparency and analysis on pricing plan options emerged in the wake of PPACA's passage. The Act imposed penalties, effective 2014, on employers with an average of 50 or more employees who

- Offer inadequate or unaffordable minimum essential coverage or do not offer minimum essential coverage; or
- Have at least one full-time employee who qualifies for federal premium assistance for coverage through an exchange

The penalty varies depending on whether the employer fails to offer minimum essential coverage or offers inadequate or unaffordable minimum essential coverage. Effective 2018, employers who provide health benefits deemed to be too generous will also be assessed penalties. An employer sponsoring a so-called "Cadillac" group health plan is required to pay a 40 percent excise tax on the excess value of the coverage.

The Effects of Multiple Plan Offerings on Employee Selection Patterns and Pricing

The offering of multiple benefit offerings can create an exodus of favorable risks from existing offerings and result in price escalations for those who choose to stay with a previously offered plan. In some cases, the offering of a new plan at favorable pricing can cause such dramatic migration out of a plan that the remaining plan will experience a price spiral that causes termination of the plan. This was particularly true in the mid-1980s for many employers who offered traditional indemnity plans. The offering of either a less expensive comprehensive plan or an HMO resulted in those employees with low utilization for major services migrating to the less costly plans, seeking to reduce their expenditures on monthly health care premiums. With this loss of favorable risks, the indemnity plan retained less favorable risks with higher utilization patterns. Because there was a smaller pool of favorable risks in the plan over which to spread plan costs, the premiums charged to those who remained increased. This increase in plan costs resulted in another wave of more favorable risks choosing to leave the plan rather than bear the increased costs of the plan. Again costs increased, giving further incentive for favorable risks to migrate from the plan. Ultimately, a cost spiral like this will cause a plan to become prohibitively expensive and result in its demise.

As the provisions of PPACA are phased in, employers will need to be vigilant regarding the effects that alternative access to coverage through health exchanges have on their employee selection patterns and pricing. Effective 2014, employers that pay for any portion of health coverage and offer minimum essential coverage are required to supply "free choice vouchers" to qualified employees to purchase qualified health coverage through an exchange. A qualified employee eligible for free choice vouchers has the following characteristics:

- His or her required contribution for minimum essential coverage through the employer's plan exceed 8 percent but is less than 9.8 percent of the employee's annual household income.

- His or her household income does not exceed 400 percent of the federal poverty level.
- He or she does not participate in an employer-sponsored health plan.

The value of the free choice voucher is the most generous amount that the employer would have contributed under the firm's plan for self-only coverage or, if relevant, family coverage. Employers are required to pay this sum to an exchange. Subsequently, the exchange credits the amount towards the monthly premium for the plan selected by the employee. When the free choice voucher amount exceeds the exchange plan premium, the difference is refunded to the employee and is subject to taxation. Employers may deduct the amount paid in vouchers and are not assessed the employer mandate penalty for employees receiving vouchers.

Designing the Underwriting and Financial Arrangements

As indicated in the discussion of alternative financing techniques, an employer can dramatically alter the financial arrangement of its medical benefits program by determining the amount of risk it will accept. The strategic issue is to select a financial arrangement that controls costs and allows management to assume the level of risk that it believes appropriate for its employee group. The financial arrangement selected can have a behavioral impact on both the providers managing care and the insurer or administrator responsible for management of the plan. Increasingly, employers have explored arrangements that shift more risk to health care providers and that promote incentives to provide quality care. Much research is being done on measuring quality of care and developing information systems that can be used to evaluate cost and quality of care.

The financial strategy for a medical benefits program will have multiple tiers. This is particularly true if multiple plan options are available and employees choose between plan offerings. Plan pricing and plan offerings can alter enrollment patterns and affect the effectiveness of a given financial arrangement or risk-management strategy.

Determining cost-effective medical providers and health plans is not an easy exercise. Certain plans will attract employees from certain demographic and geographic constituencies because of plan benefits or the convenience of provider locations. Health care costs are directly correlated with age, in that older individuals tend to need more care and need to access more extensive and thus more expensive care. Likewise, there can be regional differences in the cost of medical care. Sometimes, base premium costs or allocated costs per participant are not the best indicator of cost-effective medical care. Analyzing plan costs by adjusting for demographic, geographic, and other variables in the plan population is the best way to evaluate the cost efficiency.

Measuring Performance and Managing the Plan

A final attribute of health care strategy is to create a system of monitoring and measuring the attainment of plan objectives. It is also important to have a system of controls that ensures that the plan is being effectively managed. A well-developed plan design is of little use if a third-party administrator is unable to administer the design as it was intended. A system for auditing plan results, ensuring quality outcomes, and reporting utilization is necessary. For this reason, any delegation of responsibilities for health plan management should involve negotiation on the management reporting responsibilities of the administrator and the performance standards it is expected to achieve. Assigning financial penalties or providing rewards associated with these performance standards can be very effective. For instance, with a traditional insured product, a plan sponsor can require claims payment within a certain number of days for a percent of the claims. With a managed care provider operating a staff model HMO, reporting could be required on the telephone systems for contacting PCPs. There could be performance criteria on the amount of time it takes to reach a physician by phone, and scheduling standards for the amount of time between the initial call and an available appointment.

SUMMARY AND CONCLUSIONS

There are many different approaches to providing medical benefits to plan participants. Some of these approaches are less popular today because of various trends in medical care, particularly the need to provide a delivery system that controls costs and provides appropriate care. Nevertheless, it is important to understand the different models for providing medical benefits and the historical context out of which these plan designs have emerged. In the present day, the passage of PPACA dramatically affects all aspects of benefit plan design, providing new opportunities and introducing new risks. PPACA alters the environmental context for health plans, providing radical, transformational change.

The plan structure, delivery system, and employer subsidy chosen can have important implications on the plan selection decisions of employees and the choices they make in procuring individual medical care for themselves and their families. These choices will determine the effectiveness of the plan in meeting human resource and budget objectives. The financial arrangements to insure the plan or pay for care are also critical. The plan sponsor must decide how to insure the plan and how to pay providers, and then must negotiate price. Any financial arrangement involves a decision on what amount of risk will be retained by the employer and what amount of risk will be transferred to another party—whether an insurer, third-party administrator (TPA), managed care company, or medical provider. Structuring the financial arrangement properly can drive the incentives that promote effective cost and quality management of medical care. Development of a health care strategy involves not only strategic decisions at the macro level, but also a series of micro decisions that together should ensure the plan meets its goals and objectives. Any plan design, delivery system, and financial arrangement that is configured to manage this risk and meet organizational objectives is of little consequence unless the program is effectively executed and managed at all levels and from multiple vantage points. It is precisely the challenge to create and effectively manage a plan from the multitude of possible configurations in the realms of plan design, health care delivery systems, and financial arrangements that makes medical care benefits management an exciting area in which to work.

BIBLIOGRAPHY

Association of Private Pension and Welfare Plans (APPWP), *Health Notes*, September 15, 2000.

Bachman, Ronald E., "Consumer-Driven Health Care: The Future Is Now," *Benefits Quarterly*, Vol. 20, No. 2, Second Quarter 2004, pp. 15–22.

Cheiron, "Healthcare Reform: The New Paradigm for America's Healthcare Financing," *Cheiron Advisory*, Vol. 7, No. 3, Summer 2010.

Commerce Clearing House Editorial Staff, *2010 Tax Legislation: Patient Protection and Affordable Care Health Care Reconciliation, HIRE, and Other Recent Tax Acts: Law, Explanation and Analysis*. Chicago, IL: CCH, 2010.

Department of Labor, *General Facts on Women & Job Based Health Benefits*, April 2000.

Department of the Treasury, Department of Health and Human Services, Department of Labor, *Fact Sheet: The Mental Health Parity and Addiction Equity Act of 2008 (MHPAEA)*, February 2010.

Geisel, Jerry, "Health Plan Inflation Held to 8% in 1993," *Business Insurance*, February 14, 1994, p. 1.

Goldsmith, Jeff C., Michael J. Goran, and John G. Nackel, "Managed Care Comes of Age," *Healthcare Forum Journal*, September/October 1995, pp. 14–24.

Groom Law Group, "New Interim Final Regulations on Mental Health Parity and Addiction Equity Act of 2008," *Groom Law Group Memorandum to Clients*, February 15, 2010.

Hancock, Daniel, Johnson & Nagle PC, "Health Reform Impact on Employer-Sponsored Health Plans," *HDJN Client Advisory*," June 25, 2010.

Herzfeld, Jeff, "Optimizing the Value of a Pharmacy Benefit Management Plan," *Managing Employee Health Benefits*, Vol. 3, No. 10, Fall 1995, pp. 32–34.

Hewitt Associates, *Employer Reaction to Health Care Reform: Grandfathered Status Survey*, August 2010.

Hewitt Associates, *Employers to Face Double Digit Health-care cost Increases for Third Consecutive Year*, October 23, 2000.

Hurley, Robert E., Bradley C. Strunk, and Justin S. White, "The Puzzling Popularity of the PPO," *Health Affairs*, March/April 2004, pp. 56–68.

Kaiser Family Foundation and Health Research and Educational Trust, "Exhibit 5.1: Distribution of Health Plan Enrollment for Covered Workers, by Plan Type, 1999–2010," *Employer Health Benefits 2010 Annual Survey*, Health Care Marketplace Project, September 15, 2010.

KPMG Peat Marwick, "Health Benefits in 1995," *Benefits Spectrum*, October 1995.

Mayer, Jack, "Consumer-Driven Health Plans: Design Features to Promote Quality Improvement," *Benefits Quarterly*, Vol. 20, No. 2, Second Quarter 2004, pp. 23–31.

Miani, Jennifer M. and Susan M. Szafranski, "New Guidance Regarding PPACA Preventive Health Care Requirements," *Day Pitney LLP Client Letter*, July 27, 2010.

National Association of Insurance Commissioners & The Center for Insurance Policy and Research, "Health Care Reform Frequently Asked Questions

(FAQ)," *NAIC Website: Special Section: Health Insurance Reform*, www.naic.org/index_health_reform_section.htm.

O'Leary, James S., "The Evolving Role of Pharmacy Benefits Management Firms in a Managed Care Environment," *Benefits Quarterly*, Vol. 11, No. 3, Third Quarter 1995, pp. 24–33.

Ostuw, Richard, "Engaging Employees in Health Care Can Contain Costs and Improve Quality," *Benefits Quarterly*, Vol. 20, No. 2, Second Quarter 2004, pp. 38–42.

Patterson, Belknap, Webb & Tyler LLP, "Navigating National Health Care Reform: What Every Employer Should Know," *Employee Benefits and Executive Compensation Alert*, April 2010.

Patterson, Martha Priddy, "Defined Contribution Health Plan to Consumer Driven Health Benefits: Evolution and Experience," *Benefits Quarterly*, Vol. 20, No. 2, Second Quarter 2004, pp. 49–59.

Pemberton, Carolyn and Deborah Holmes, eds., *EBRI Databook on Employee Benefits*, 3rd ed., Washington, DC: Education and Research Fund, 1995.

Reiff, Michael and L. Kenneth Sperling, "Measuring the Savings from Managed Care: Experience at Citibank," *Benefits Quarterly*, Vol. 11, No. 2, Second Quarter 1995, pp. 9–15.

Tinnes, Christy, Brigen Winters, and Christine Keller, "Preparing for Health Care Reform: A Chronological Guide for Employers," Practical Law Publishing Limited and Practical Law Company, Inc., 2010, usld.practicallaw.com/6-502-1419.

Troutman Sanders LLP, "Health Care Reform: Plan Design Requirements, Summary of Pay-or-Play Provisions, Mandatory Coverage Provisions, and Summary of Penalties," Summer 2010.

APPENDIX 4.1

HEALTH CARE COST EQUATION

To understand the potential impact of managed care alternatives on the costs of medical care, it is important to understand the basic health care cost equation: Cost = Price × Use, where *Price* is the average cost per unit of health services delivered, and *Use* (or utilization) represents the average number of units of health services.

Effective managed care strategies must address both portions of the cost equation: *price* management, which is a function of network development and provider reimbursement strategy; and *utilization* management, which is a function of medical management capabilities and quality controls employed by the managed care company.

ELEMENTS OF PRICE MANAGEMENT

Provider reimbursement methodology is the cornerstone of price management. It must cover broad provider service categories, and it must be actively managed, with regular review and renegotiation. Those health plans that fail to take advantage of negotiated pricing will bear greater and greater cost shifting from governmental and other managed care plans.

Hospital Reimbursement Strategies

Hospital reimbursement strategies are most important, since facility expenses account for, on average, more than a third of total health care expenditures. Common strategies include the following:

1. *Straight discount (percentage off)* is simply a negotiated percentage (e.g., 15 percent) off billed charges with no risk sharing by the provider. Managed care companies disfavor

This appendix was written by Philip D. Pierce and previously appeared as a portion of Chapter 7 in the 6th edition of *The Handbook of Employee Benefits*. The author gratefully acknowledges its use here.

straight discounts because they do not protect expenses against general medical inflation; hospitals can still increase their prices, while the managed care company can only take the same discount off higher and higher costs. Furthermore, this method does little to control increased utilization of hospital services.

2. *Diagnostic (diagnosis) related group (DRG)* pays a prenegotiated amount to the hospital for the total cost of treatment, for each of about 520 specific "diagnoses." DRGs became increasingly common after they were universally adopted for Medicare reimbursements in 1984. With DRGs, the hospital has an incentive to manage utilization of services, by being put at some financial risk to effectively manage length of stay and intensity of services per admission. However, since the number of admissions is not limited, hospitals could discharge patients early and readmit them. Stop-loss arrangements are often set up to protect the hospital from catastrophic cases. Additional problems with DRGs include negotiating an appropriate pricing level for the various DRG categories, which requires significant claims data; artificially high charges can occur if the base is determined before utilization has been aggressively managed. The additional administrative burden of assigning a DRG number requires advanced billing and claims adjudication software to avoid "DRG creep" whereby a hospital raises the classification of an illness in order to receive a higher amount. Periodic claim audits are critical to assure actual treatment matches the assigned DRG for the hospital confinement.
3. *Case rates* are flat negotiated reimbursements for a specific type of service (e.g., outpatient surgery rates or obstetric (OB) case rates), rather than for all services related to a specific diagnosis. With this arrangement, the hospital is at risk for managing cost as well as increases in cost for services, but not for managing the actual number of services provided.
4. *Per diem* entails a prenegotiated fixed daily rate, usually set up in broad categories, such as medical/surgical, delivery, intensive care, and so on. Per diem allows the managed care company to share some risk with the hospitals and gives the hospital an incentive to effectively manage cost per day.

However, in contrast to DRG reimbursement, the hospital is paid for each day of care and thus has no incentive to control admission rates or the average length of stay (ALOS) per admission.

5. *Global rates* pay a specific fee for a major episode of care. They are broader than DRG reimbursement because the negotiated fee includes all professional, ancillary, anesthesia, and facility fees associated with the episode of care, so one payment is made for all services rendered (usually to the facility). Under global rates, the hospital is at risk for effectively managing all health costs related to the negotiated episodes as well as increases in the cost of these services. These arrangements are typically restricted to high-cost, catastrophic types of care, such as organ transplants, or where larger integrated health systems already have wholly owned facility and professional services.

It is not uncommon for health maintenance organizations (HMOs) to engage in multiple reimbursement arrangements with various hospitals and other inpatient facilities.

Physician Reimbursement Strategies

Physician reimbursement strategies largely depend on the type of managed care plan, discussed in detail below. Physicians costs are influenced two ways in a managed care environment:

1. *Nonrisk-sharing arrangements*, which focus only on negotiating unit prices and then employ specific utilization management procedures, such as detailed medical treatment protocols coupled with advanced information measurement systems, which intend to intervene, monitor, and influence physician practice.
2. *Risk-sharing arrangements* that give providers financial incentives to control patient utilization.

Most managed care programs rely on both of these strategies, depending on the readiness and sophistication of the local provider community. But it is the physician reimbursement strategy that provides the basic structure in controlling costs.

NonRisk Sharing Arrangements

In traditional plans, and even in managed indemnity and many preferred provider organization (PPO) plans, fee-for-service is the standard reimbursement method for nonfacility health care providers, such as physicians. While discounts are sometimes applied to fees, fee-for-service does not directly control utilization.

1. *Fee-for-service—Reasonable and Customary (R&C) or Usual, Customary, and Reasonable (UCR)* utilizes a schedule of maximum allowable (or "prevailing") fees for covered services within a particular geographic area. The prevailing R&C fee is typically set at the most frequently occurring charge within a particular range. Physicians are paid the lesser of billed charges or the prevailing R&C fee. This is the way traditional plans have operated for years, and most patients do not even realize a prevailing fee schedule is being used unless the provider "balance-bills" the patient for any excess over the prevailing fee. Since this arrangement reimburses the provider for each service, there is no specific incentive for providers to effectively manage utilization. R&C reimbursement is common with indemnity and managed indemnity plans, since it requires no established contract with providers.
2. *Fee-for-service—Fee Schedule* reimburses physicians based on negotiated rates (e.g., using a relative value scale). The physician is reimbursed the lesser of billed charges or the negotiated maximum, which is usually based on the current procedural terminology (CPT) code. The entire fee schedule is subject to a relative value scale (RVS), which takes into account the physician's type of specialty and location. Like the R&C method, this arrangement reimburses the physician for each service, resulting in little incentive to manage utilization. These fee schedules are common in PPOs, in which a negotiated contract sets the fee schedule in advance with contracted physicians. Participating physicians agree to accept the scheduled fee as payment in full and they agree not to balance bill for any additional charges above the scheduled fee, although they are allowed to bill for allowed copays, deductibles, and coinsurance portions that the plan requires of the member. It is crucial that the managed care company provide monitoring and review of physician utilization patterns in order to avoid unnecessary expenses.

3. *Resource-based relative value scale (RBRVS)* is a variation of RVS under which the relative value assigned to a procedural code is derived from the components of physician work units (including time and skill), practice expense units, and malpractice expense units, with the intent of reimbursing according to comparable costs of doing business, not according to specialty. Medicare adopted this approach in 1992.

Risk-Sharing Arrangements

Risk sharing is best suited for stronger-form managed care plans, such as HMO and point-of-service (POS) plans, since these models rely on the primary care physician (PCP) as the central control point for member health care delivery. The PCP is best positioned to monitor a member's care and to control benefit utilization. Furthermore, integrated delivery systems (e.g., group practices, individual practice associations (IPAs), and physicians hospital organizations (PHOs)) have shown interest in risk-sharing models because they have the administrative systems to monitor broad levels of member care and can better assume the risks associated with such financial incentives.

The risk-sharing model has to be flexible enough to adapt to local market conditions and to grow and change over time. An effective risk-sharing model should generally include the following conditions:

1. A PCP in place for each member to serve as the entry point for referral and hospital care
2. Risk pools that include about 10 to 12 PCPs per pool, in order to aggregate claims experience
3. A given PCP that has a minimum concentration of membership (e.g., 150 to 200 members) in order to make the revenue flow significant enough to be "at risk"
4. Risk sharing within group and IPA HMO models that takes a variety of forms depending on the following conditions:
   a. Receptivity of the provider community
   b. Membership leverage by the managed care company among its participating providers
   c. Sophistication of the provider group and the managed care company

Types of risk-sharing models include

1. *Case management fee*, where the managed care company pays the PCP a set fee per member for overall case management

services. This fee is paid in addition to charges for medical services rendered. It is intended to compensate physicians for the added work of acting as case manager for their membership, but this approach is typically not favored by managed care companies. Many companies feel PCPs should *already* serve as overall case managers for their membership and should not receive additional compensation. Furthermore, case management fees alone do not provide an effective vehicle to influence specific physician behavior.

2. *Physician incentive/bonus* rewards positive performance in specific measurable categories, such as financial results (e.g., average monthly costs per member), quality assurance compliance, and member satisfaction survey results. Results are shared with providers on a regular basis to improve effectiveness of performance-based incentives. Some advantages of using bonus plans are that they are relatively easy to develop and establish, and can be administered in conjunction with other risk arrangements. Concerns include whether bonus payments are large enough to outweigh gains from potential plan over utilization and whether comparative systems need to be developed to measure performance among PCPs.
3. *Fee-for-service with a "withhold"* reduces provider reimbursement by a withheld amount (e.g., 15 percent) at the time the claim is adjudicated, and this withhold is placed in specially assigned risk pools. Cumulative withholds are either returned or retained each year based on the results of the risk pool compared with expected results. Typically, catastrophic claim costs are not charged against the selected risk pool so that they do not unfairly influence the results of the risk pool. Some advantages of the withhold arrangement are that it is relatively easy to develop and administer, and it encourages PCPs to deliver services within its practices rather than refer to other specialists, which helps control utilization. Concerns include the following: (1) there is the possibility of overutilization of physician services to increase revenue in order to offset the withhold; (2) the plan can be "nickeled and dimed" on PCP services; and (3) providers often perceive withholds as part of their discounts and do not put serious effort into adjusting performance to regain the withholds. Effective use of withhold arrangements requires critical information system tools, physician profiling data systems to monitor performance criteria,

a limit on the number of specific fees for office visits, and regular communication with PCPs, so they can properly manage their practices.

4. *Capitation for defined services* provides a fixed monthly payment for each member selecting a PCP, as compared with payment for each service delivered by that physician. It is critical to define exactly what services are to be covered in that capitation payment so that a physician knows what level of care is being covered through the reimbursement.

   PCP services typically include the following:

   a. Office visits, including routine examinations and well-baby care
   b. Immunizations and therapeutic injections
   c. Inpatient visits while the member is confined in a hospital or other facility
   d. A specific list of routine laboratory and diagnostic services (e.g., EKGs)
   e. A specific list of routine office procedures (e.g., minor surgical procedures)

   To supplement the capitation for defined services, the managed care company may also pay the PCP an additional fee-for-service reimbursement for after-hour and emergency treatment to avoid the higher cost of sending the member to the emergency room.

   Capitation rates are usually age- and sex-specific (e.g., with different rates for adult versus child, or male versus female) to recognize differences in the member population. It is possible to capitate most types of providers or groupings of providers (e.g., hospitals, IPAs, PHOs, laboratories, and drug vendors), provided there are clear definitions of the services to be provided and the expectations of the provider. Advantages of capitation for defined services are that it rewards prudent utilization of services (PCPs "keep" excess capitation payments above their actual costs of delivering care) and that it eliminates claims processing for low-cost, routine, high-volume services.

   Concerns about capitation models include the following: (1) it can be more difficult to recruit physicians if they are not willing to accept capitated services and (2) it can be difficult to collect accurate and relevant encounter (claims) data because physicians have no incentive to complete paperwork. Effective audit systems must be established to ensure that services contracted under the capitation agreement are not also submitted and reimbursed as under fee-for-service; physicians must have sufficient financial strength to assume the risk inherent in capitation; and the managed care organization must closely monitor the practice to make sure PCPs are delivering appropriate care, rather than simply referring care to other providers (for which the managed care organization pays additional fees). Thus, critical tools for implementing capitation for defined services include a clear and workable definition of capitated services, monitoring reports to identify inappropriate referrals, systems support to give PCPs information necessary to manage their budgets, and quality screens to protect against underutilization.

5. *Capitation with a withhold* is the same as capitation for defined services, except that a portion of the capitation payment is withheld as a tool to reduce PCP "triaging" (i.e., making too many referrals) to other providers. The withhold is returned at the end of the fiscal year, depending on PCP performance. The key advantage is that the PCP has a financial stake in properly managing referral care. The same concerns about capitation exist, and recruiting primary care physicians who will accept this model is tricky.
6. *Capitation for complete services* capitates the PCP for all services rendered to a member, including referrals to specialists and hospital services. The capitation payments are used to establish a PCP budget, against which the costs for all services are charged. The PCP has a stake in managing the total care for assigned members. However, unless PCPs are careful, a string of catastrophic cases can be financially devastating (usually protected against by some type of stop-loss coverage).
7. *Budgeted capitation* sets up a pool, which is funded directly from premiums, for a group of PCPs. Claims are charged directly against the budgeted pool during the fiscal year; if the pool runs dry, no further monies are paid out for services, but excess monies in the pool at the end of the fiscal period can be available as surplus and shared with providers. Advantages of budgeted capitation include those noted above for other methods of capitation, plus the added feature that medical expenses

cannot exceed premiums collected. However, an added concern is that the PCP's average member costs vary by plan group and the PCP has no control over them.

8. *Salaried physicians* are employed by staff model HMOs. Like capitation models, a key advantage is that the supposed financial incentives for overutilization are removed, and, more importantly, this "vertically integrated" approach to health care delivery allows for efficiencies not possible in other types of arrangements. However, it is crucial that the appropriate "corporate" goals and policies be developed and broadly communicated to give staff providers direction on utilization and quality.

ELEMENTS OF UTILIZATION MANAGEMENT

While price management is the first step in managing the health care cost equation, some regard it as a "one-time" savings once the plan sponsor gains discounts. This is not entirely correct, since continuing price management is crucial to controlling ongoing costs. However, the long-term cost advantage of managed care rests in its ability to reduce the rate of increase of utilization. The rate declines with stronger and stronger forms of managed care, thereby, ideally, reducing the number of units of unnecessary health care services delivered. Reducing that number is the principal function of medical utilization management (UM).

Primary Utilization Management

Primary UM programs can be found in all forms of managed care and they are often the principal controls in managed indemnity and PPO plans. These programs have generally focused on controlling hospital confinements, through reducing the number of admissions and/or reducing the average length of stay. The following programs are typically included:

1. *Precertification* reviews the medical necessity of inpatient care and identifies potential case management opportunities prior to admission.
2. *Concurrent review* monitors patient care during hospital confinements with the intent of managing the length of stay by identifying alternate settings that can provide less costly care.

3. *Discharge planning* assesses whether additional services are needed following discharge and prepares the patient's transfer to less costly alternate settings for treatment (e.g., a skilled nursing facility or home health care).
4. *Large case management* provides a continuous process of identifying members with high risk for problems associated with complex, high-cost health care needs and of assessing opportunities to improve the coordination of care.

Primary UM programs are typically handled by telephone (e.g., a toll-free help line) to the managed care company's central member services offices, although selected cases may be supplemented with local on-site review, either through clinical representatives of the managed care company or through contracted medical professionals.

Expanded Utilization Management

Expanded utilization management programs are more commonly included with stronger forms of managed care, such as POS and HMO plans, although they are increasingly available with PPO plans on a stand-alone basis. Some programs are fairly sophisticated, combining protocol-based telephonic intervention services with more intensive clinical analysis of specific treatments of care. Because of the nature of HMO and POS plans, many of these advanced UM programs are initiated by the PCP and are ideally transparent to the member. Provider compliance with the requirements of these programs is essential to managing care. Elements of these programs often include the following:

1. *Referral management* is the primary UM technique differentiating HMO and POS plans from PPO plans. It requires members to access care through their PCPs, who then manage referrals to specialists within the provider network. Properly handled, referral management, also known as the "gatekeeper" approach, ensures that high quality care is delivered in the most cost-effective setting possible by coordinating care through one source (the PCP) and eliminating unnecessary or inappropriate care.
2. *Outpatient precertification* requires prior authorization from the managed care company for certain outpatient surgical and medical procedures, with the intent being to reduce unnecessary, inappropriate, and potentially harmful procedures.

3. *On-site concurrent review* complements telephone-based concurrent review in basic UM services by placing clinically trained nurses at hospitals and other inpatient facilities to review the necessity of continued confinements, proposed tests, and procedures.
4. *Centers of excellence* include a network of designated, nationally recognized medical facilities that perform selected, highly sophisticated, and high-cost procedures (e.g., organ transplants, open-heart surgery, and advanced forms of cancer treatment). The managed care organization typically negotiates preferred rates with the centers.
5. *Prenatal advisory services* (also called prenatal planning and maternity management services) help identify women who may be at risk for delivering low-birth-weight, preterm, or unhealthy babies and provides education and counseling on proper prenatal care.

Most managed care companies use sophisticated protocols and medical guidelines to develop and administer their UM programs. Whether their operations are centrally based or located in local member service centers, today's UM programs are highly automated and integrated with the claims payment systems, so that there are minimal delays in the handling of member claims after UM procedures have been approved. Similarly, the managed care company will usually provide toll-free numbers for both members and providers and extended customer service hours to decrease the "hassle factor" often associated with having to preauthorize confinements, referrals, or outpatient procedures.

APPENDIX 4.2
VISION CARE AND HEARING CARE PLANS

VISION CARE

Most of us would rank vision as a very important, if not the most important, of our senses. Yet vision care is often neglected. Eye disease, treatment, and surgery are traditionally covered under hospital, surgical, major medical, and comprehensive medical policies. However, most of these plans exclude routine vision examination and eyewear from coverage. Separate (freestanding) vision plans cover services such as routine examinations and materials (products) such as lenses, frames, and contact lenses. In a purist sense, some do not consider this coverage insurance, because of the absence of illness or disease. Nevertheless, the need for appropriate vision care is real, as about 60 percent of the adult population in North America wears corrective eyewear. A routine vision examination not only confirms whether prescription eyewear is necessary but may detect unrelated problems such as diabetes and high blood pressure. Aside from the obvious medical benefits to employees, vision care plans have the potential of reducing accidents and increasing productivity—factors that are of major importance to the employer. Vision care is often compared to dental care because of its frequently elective and predictable nature. However, despite general reductions in employee benefit programs, some—though not many—employers are adding or continuing to provide vision care benefits.

Providers

There are three types of vision care professionals:

1. *Ophthalmologists* are medical doctors (MDs) specializing in the total care of the eye, including diagnosis, treatment of eye diseases, and surgery. Many perform eye examinations and

This appendix is based on sections from Chapter 11 of the 5th edition of the *Handbook of Employee Benefits*, written by Eugene J. Ziurys, Jr. The author gratefully acknowledges its use here.

prescribe corrective lenses. Some also dispense corrective eyewear. An ophthalmologist typically completes four years of premedical training, another four years of medical school, and subsequent internship and residency.

2. *Optometrists* are doctors of optometry (ODs) and are licensed to examine, diagnose, treat, and manage diseases and disorders of the visual system, the eye, and associated structures as well as diagnose related systemic conditions. They are trained to detect eye disease and/or symptoms requiring the attention of ophthalmologists. In addition to performing vision examinations and prescribing lenses, most optometrists dispense glasses and contact lenses. An optometrist typically completes undergraduate work and is graduated from a college of optometry.
3. *Opticians* fit, adjust, and dispense eyewear (lenses, frames, and contact lenses) prescribed by ophthalmologists and optometrists. They are eyewear retailers and provide advice on which lenses and frames are most appropriate. Many grind and fabricate eyewear, verify the finished products, and repair and replace various ophthalmic devices. Optician certification, licensure, and registration vary by state, as do training and apprenticeship.

Covered Benefits

Covered benefits include vision examination, lenses, and frames.

Vision Examination

A thorough examination includes a history of general health, vision complaints, and an external and internal eye examination. Other services may include various ocular tests, usually including, but not limited to, coordination of eye movements, tonometry, depth perception (for children), and refraction testing for distance and near vision. In addition to the possible need for corrective eyewear, the examination could detect cataracts, glaucoma, diabetes, and brain tumors. Some plans allow an examination at 12- or 24-month intervals, and it is up to the employee to arrange for eyewear if needed. Health maintenance organizations (HMOs) often feature "exam-only" plans.

Lenses

The lens is the heart of sight-corrective material. Single-vision lenses are the most widely used, with multivision lenses (bifocal or trifocal) also being dispensed in large quantities. Plastic has replaced glass as the predominant lens material, and a wide array of lenses, such as oversized, photochromic, and tinted, are available. Most plans consider these "cosmetic extras" and outside normal plan limits. Many plans do provide benefits for contact lenses even though they are likely to be worn for cosmetic rather than for medical reasons.

Many dispensers have an in-house laboratory for grinding and fabrication of the more routinely prescribed eyewear, while others use full service laboratories.

Frames

The cosmetic element is much more obvious in the area of frames than in lenses. Frames are increasingly being selected for cosmetic purposes and at times are part of a fashion wardrobe. The cost can run into hundreds of dollars for plastic or metal frames of almost limitless sizes, shapes, and colors. Herein lies a dilemma for the payor. The frame is a must, but how does one avoid paying for fashion while giving a fair reimbursement for utility? Certain plans make allowances up to a specified dollar figure, while others approve a limited selection; for example, $100 frames each for men, women, and children.

Plan Design

Plan design include frequency limits, schedule-of-benefits approach, and preferred provider networks.

Frequency Limits

To control unnecessary use and keep administrative costs down, plans use a time limit (frequency) with which a participant may utilize a benefit plan for covered expenses. Examples of frequencies allowed by four plans are noted in Table A4.2-1.

Schedule-of-Benefits Approach

This type of plan has maximum allowances for each service and material and a limit on the frequency of use. Examples are shown in Table A4.2-2. A typical schedule pays the lesser of the claimed or schedule maximum.

TABLE A4.2-1

Examples of Frequencies with Which Participants May Access Benefits

Month Intervals				
	Plan 1	Plan 2	Plan 3	Plan 4
Examinations	24	12	12	12
Lenses	24	24	12	12
Frames	24	24	24	12

Schedules can be national or regional, based on a geographic percentage of usual, customary, and reasonable (UCR) charges.

Advantages of a schedule-of-benefits plan are that it is easy to understand, it has no restriction on the choice of provider, and it encourages the thrifty employee to shop around. The employer is cognizant of premium outlay, as the schedule ceiling does not change with inflation, and administration is simplified for the insurer or administrator because the frequencies and caps are determined in advance.

TABLE A4.2-2

Examples of Maximum Allowances for Vision Care Plans

Service/Material	Maximum Allowed ($)
Examination	50
Lenses (pair)	
Single-vision	60
Bifocal	90
Trifocal	110
Lenticular	140
Contacts (elective)	100
Frames	60

Preferred Provider Networks

Preferred provider plans steer employees to a network of participating providers that have agreed to provide certain services for a negotiated fee. Employees who use a provider in the network may have many of the plan benefits covered 100 percent or pay only a minimum copayment, usually from $5 to $20. There is no claim form for the employee. An employee simply shows an identification card, which can be subject to confirmation at the provider's place of business, or the employee can mail a request for vision services and materials to the administrator and receive a benefit form stating which benefits are available and for what length of time, and the extent of the copayment.

Providers are solicited by the insurer or administrator with the expectation of increased patient volume. In return, the provider agrees to reimbursement of discounted material costs plus dispensing fees. Some plans also mandate the use of specific laboratories. Various quality control measures are inserted into these plans, and peer review is common. In some plans, participating providers can charge the regular retail price for oversized or tinted lenses and for designer frames, while others call for reduced charges for these extras.

Most plans allow reimbursement even when a participating provider is not utilized. In these instances, the employee must pay the provider's charge and file a claim. Reimbursement is based on a schedule or UCR determination. When a nonnetwork provider is used, the employee's out-of-pocket expense is almost always greater than it would be with a participating provider. Figure A4.2-3 illustrates a sample plan.

These plans usually follow a medical plan pattern, with a percentile of the charges in a given area prevailing. A higher figure is allowed for examination and lenses, and less for lenses of a cosmetic nature. Inflation is shared with the employee, with a percentage of coinsurance applied with the medical reimbursement. A separate means of administration is unnecessary.

Vision Benefits in Flexible Benefit Plans

Flex plans increasingly include ancillary benefits, including vision care. They enable an employee to choose among various coverages, taking into account factors such as overall health, spouse coverage, and specific family needs. Although the design of these plans varies, employers sometimes allocate a certain number of "flex credits" to each employee, who then uses these to "purchase" benefits. Each employee chooses the benefits that best

FIGURE A4.2-3

Preferred Provider Network Sample Plan

	In-Network	Out-of-Network (Program Allowance)
Exam (every 12 months)	100%	$32
Frames (every 12 months)	100%	$24
	(up to $60 retail value)	
Lenses (every 12 months)	100%	$24 single vision
		$36 bifocal
		$46 trifocal
		$72 aphakic/lenticular
Contact lenses (every 12 months in lieu of glasses)		
Prescription and fitting	100%	$20 daily wear
		$30 extended wear
Standard	100%	$48
Specialty	100%	$48
	(up to $75 retail value)	
Vision Care Options*	10% discount	Not covered
(such as tints, contact lens solution)		

*These allowances and discounts are only available at the point of purchase.

fit his or her needs. Once the employer allocation has been used, the employee may purchase additional benefits at his or her own cost. They place vision care in competition with other coverages.

Flexible Spending Accounts

If not covered under a medical plan or a freestanding plan, eligible vision care expenses often are covered by some type of spending account. Under a flexible spending account (FSA) arrangement, the employee may reduce income and Social Security taxes by funding benefits such as vision care with pretax dollars. At the beginning of the plan year, employees can designate a certain amount of money (up to a maximum) to be deducted from salary, thereby reducing the base upon which taxes are paid. The employer holds the money and "reimburses" the employee upon verification of covered expenses. (See Chapter 25 for a complete discussion of flex plans and FSAs.) Alternatively, vision care expenses are eligible for reimbursement under a health savings account (HSA) or a health reimbursement account (HRA) if an employee participates in such plans.

Occupational Safety and Health Administration

Occupational Safety and Health Administration (OSHA) requires employers to provide protective eyewear to employees in positions exposing them to the danger of eye injury. These "safety glass" programs are usually outside the normal health benefit package.

HEARING CARE

A majority of benefit packages do not contain this coverage. The aging population, coupled with a noisy contemporary society, contributes to hearing loss and impairment, and it is estimated that more than 10 percent of the population is affected. Despite the generally acknowledged increase in the number of hearing-impaired persons and the substantially improved technology of hearing-aid instruments available, many would rather continue with this impairment than bear the stigma of wearing a hearing aid in public.

Coverage

Surgical procedures affecting the ear are normally covered in standard medical policies. Beyond this, some HMOs and major medical and comprehensive policies include hearing aids. However, more complete coverage is afforded by plans designed specifically to cover hearing care.

Hearing Care Benefits

A common benefit package includes an 80 percent reimbursement of services and materials up to a ceiling of \$300 to \$600. The frequency of benefit availability is usually every 36 months. The following items are often covered:

- Otologic examination (by a physician or surgeon)
- Audiometric examination (by an audiologist)
- Hearing instrument (including evaluation, ear mold fitting, and follow-up visits)

Preferred provider plans in which access to a panel would result in discounts for audiologist fees as well as hearing-aid instruments are also available. Several administrators have developed service plans in which copayments apply when participating providers are utilized. Material costs can be reimbursed on a cost-plus dispensing-fee basis. However, identical procedures vary in different geographic areas and even within specific metropolitan areas.

As with vision care expenses, an FSA is a convenient vehicle through which to budget for hearing care expenses in the absence of employee benefit coverage.

CHAPTER 5

Health Care Cost Containment: Demand-Side Approaches

David Harvey

Historically, the path to managing health care costs has been paved with various forms of cost shifting. Health maintenance organization (HMO) plans introduced the primary care physician (PCP) or gatekeeper concept as well as referral requirements for treatment by a specialist. In preferred provider organization (PPO) plan designs, the form of cost-shifting initiatives can involve increasing deductibles and copayments for both office visits and prescription drug charges. In general, most plan designs have adopted a variety of provider contracts and fee schedules with hospitals and physicians, moving away from first-dollar coverage. Finally, as employer premiums have increased, so have employee contributions.

These employer cost-shifting efforts may be viewed by employees as having compromised the value of their health and welfare benefit programs, whose original objective, theoretically at least, was to recruit, retain, and motivate employees. This view is understandable in that many employees have little, if any, health care utilization, and as such do not understand the reason for the reduction in plan benefits or the increase in payroll contributions. Figure 5-1 reports health care plan claim distribution by dollar amount and illustrates that the vast majority of health care plan expenditures occur within a relatively small minority of the total covered population.

With this in mind, perhaps the answer to cost containment may not lie in large-scale benefit plan changes but rather in smaller, more focused

FIGURE 5-1

The High Concentration Of U.S. Health Care Expenditures: Percent of Total Health Care Expenses Incurred by Different Percentiles of U.S. Population, 2002

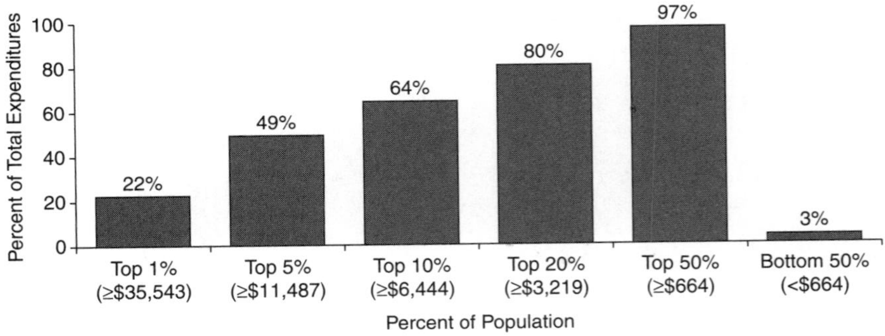

Note: Figures in parentheses are expenses per person

Source: L. J. Conwell and J. W. Cohen, "Characteristics of people with high medical expenses in the U.S. civilian noninstitutionalized population, 2002," *Statistical Brief*, No. 73, March 2005, Rockville, MD: Agency for Healthcare Research and Quality.

initiatives targeting the two highest cost categories of plan participants: the chronically ill and the emerging chronically ill.

Many plan sponsors are indeed exploring ways to address the health care costs of these two categories of plan participants, and in so doing the possibility of reducing or tempering the need for large-scale plan changes emerges.

This chapter examines the various mechanisms that exist and are evolving to address health care costs in the chronically ill and the emerging chronically ill. Essentially, the new mechanisms represent a more targeted approach as opposed to the large-scale plan changes that can be viewed more as blanket initiatives covering all plan participants. The chapter begins with a review of longstanding wellness programs and then covers disease management. Finally, it introduces the newest demand-side entrant to cost containment, value-based benefit design (VBBD). It also discusses predictive modeling.

BACKGROUND

Already high health care costs continue to rise at a much greater rate than the rate of inflation measured by the change in the consumer price index (CPI). Figure 5-2 shows health care claims by diagnosis category, and Figure 5-3 (page 118) shows that behavior is the primary determinant of health status.

FIGURE 5-2

Sick Patients Often Go without Diagnosis or Treatment in the United States: Prevalence, Diagnosis, and Treatment for Selected Disease Categories

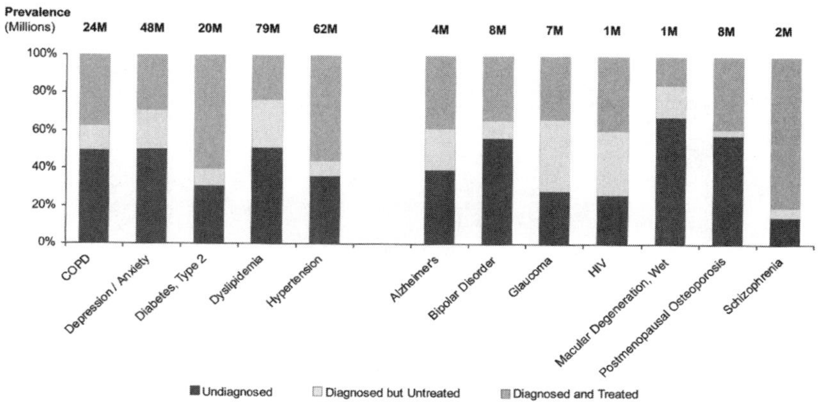

Source: Pfizer internal analysis, completed March 2006, based on the following references: Decision Resources, Datamonitor, Mattson-Jack, NHANES, Cogent, JAMA, DDC Consumer Prevalence Survey, Synovate HIV Therapy Monitor, Verispan, National Osteoporosis Risk Assessment, Centers for Disease Control, Pfizer Outcomes Research.

Many health care analysts see much of the claims experience within a plan largely related to lifestyle or behavior, and notwithstanding the efforts of many people at wellness and lifestyle management, overall the general population still smokes too much, eats the wrong foods, and does not adequately exercise.

Moreover the trend is not positive. Figure 5-4, from a Centers for Disease Control (CDC) presentation,[1] looks at the percentage of body mass index (BMI) in the United States from 1985 through 2008. BMI is a measure of an individual's weight in relation to height. A BMI of 30 or higher is considered obese, and the data clearly show an emerging epidemic in obesity occurring in the United States.

WELLNESS PROGRAMS

As with many aspects of employee benefits today, there exist a wide variety of wellness programs. The trend is away from merely placing wellness posters in the company lunchroom and toward programming that has shown quantifiable results.

1. "Vital Signs: State Specific Obesity Prevalance Among Adults–United States, 2009," Centers for Disease Control and Prevention, August 2010.

F I G U R E 5-3

Behavior–The Primary Cost Driver: Determinants of Health Status

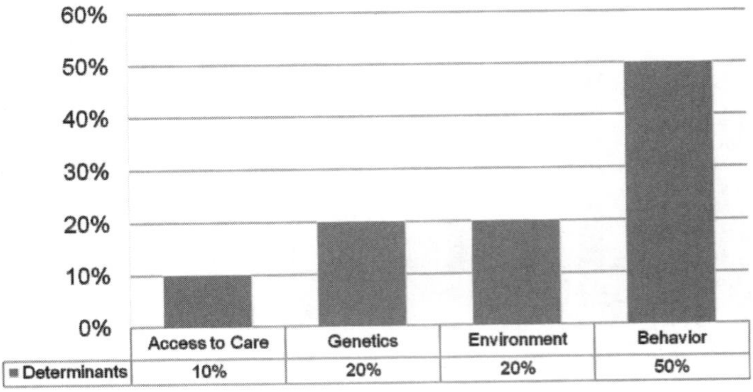

Source: IFTF and Centers for Disease Control and Prevention, *Health and Healthcare 2010*, January 2000.

Many of the plan designs of the original HMOs in the 1970s included incentives for routine physical examinations as well as a number of wellness-related benefits. Preferred provider organization plans added their own ideas, which included not only plan design initiatives but also a number of communication and awareness efforts such as payroll stuffers and posters

F I G U R E 5-4

Obesity* Trends Among U.S. Adults

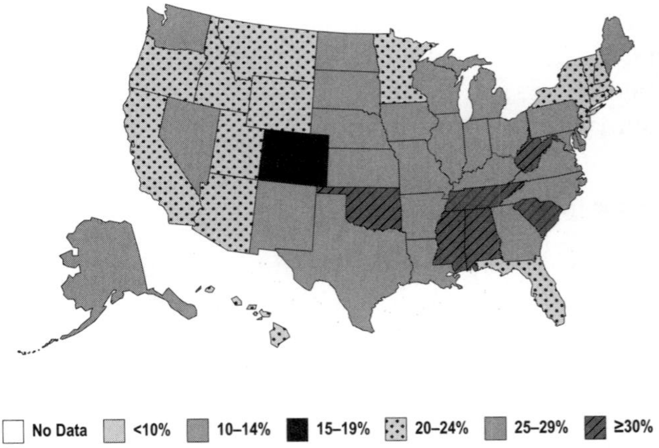

*Defined as BMI ≥ 30, or ~30 lb overweight for a 5 ft 4 in. person

Source: Behavioral Risk Factor Surveillance System (BRFSS), Prevalence and Trends Data, 2008.

for the lunchroom. These communication pieces addressed a variety of wellness topics such as smoking cessation, weight control, blood pressure monitoring, and diabetes awareness.

The Health Insurance Portability and Accountability Act (HIPAA) wellness program final regulations, effective for plan years after July 1, 2007, provided plan sponsors and health plans with definitive guidance on what comprises a HIPAA-compliant wellness program. Essentially, the regulations divide wellness programs into two types of programs: participation-only and standards-based. A participation-only program can offer a reward or incentive for merely participating in a healthier-lifestyle or smoking cessation program without regard to the outcome or impact of the program. Standards-based programs contain five specific conditions that must be met to comply with the HIPAA regulations. Briefly, they are as follows:

1. The reward cannot exceed 20 percent of the cost of employee-only coverage. The Patient Protection and Affordable Care Act of 2010 increases the reward to 30 percent, and potentially 50 percent, in 2014.
2. The wellness program must promote better health or disease prevention.
3. Annual qualification for the program must be provided to the plan participants.
4. The reward must be available to all similarly situated individuals; and, alternative standards or waivers must be made available.
5. There must be full disclosure of the terms of the program, and the availability of alternative standards or waivers.

As a byproduct of the HIPAA regulations, many wellness providers and plan sponsors began to adopt standards-based programs. More recently, standards-based programs go well beyond prior era approaches, and many programs now incorporate a health risk assessment, coupled with a biometric screening, blood test, and urinalysis.

Many of the programs have a "report card" that contains a numeric score based on the inputs from the assessment, biometric screening, and laboratory tests and is confidentially provided to each participant. For example, a score of 70 or above is considered passing and one below 70 is considered in need of improvement or failing. In many plans, the incentive to the participant with a passing score is a reduced monthly contribution amount, consistent with the allowance in the HIPAA regulations, for participation in the health plan. For those whose score is less than 70, there are wellness programs that incorporate readily attainable goals to help them improve their score. For example, over a 12-month period, they can gain a 5-point increase in their score by participating in a smoking-cessation or exercise program, lowering their blood pressure, or completing an online wellness course.

With this approach, the plan participants have an economic incentive to not only participate in the program, but also continually strive to upgrade their score. As annual qualification is a required element under the HIPAA regulations, participants repeat the wellness program each year and continue to receive a reduced monthly health plan contribution rate. Individuals electing not to participate in the wellness program or whose score of less than 70 did not improve are charged a higher monthly contribution amount. The higher monthly participant plan contribution rate is set at a level to provide an incentive for appropriate wellness, without being financially burdensome. The goal is to provide an economic incentive to those plan participants with risk factors to "modify" their behavior, thereby reducing the likelihood of their becoming a part of the chronic or emerging chronic population.

A key component to programs of this nature is communication. In addition to senior management support, communication is critical to assure participants in the wellness program of the medical confidentiality of the information. Participants are reminded that the only data reported back to the plan sponsor is information relating to those individuals who did or did not participate in the program. There is no reporting of any individually identifiable data.

DISEASE MANAGEMENT

Disease management programs represent the next step in the participant engagement process. Historically disease management focused on a limited number of chronic conditions diagnoses such as

- Diabetes
- Congestive heart failure (CHF)
- Coronary artery disease (CAD)
- Chronic obstructive pulmonary disease (COPD)
- Asthma

Following these earlier approaches, disease management has been expanded to include hypertension, depression and mental health, chronic

TABLE 5-1

Costs and Utilization of Various Types of Claims

Type of Claim/Occurrence	Cost (%)	Utilization (%)
General/routine care	5.8	58.1
Functional impairment	14.6	5.5
Chronic	47.7	34.8
Acute/serious	24.7	1.5
Trauma	7.2	0.1

back pain, high-risk maternity, and oncology.[2] Chronic diseases such as these tend not only to be costly but also to require a significant amount of physician-patient interaction in their management.

According to Towers Perrin, chronic conditions account for the majority of the health care costs in a plan (Table 5-1). Moreover, the survey indicates that of the claims in the "acute/serious" category, more than half are preventable.[3]

Additionally, the target population for disease management programs is a moving one. Studies show that only 12 to 18 percent of the high-cost population in year one remain in the high-cost category in the second and subsequent years.[4]

As noted researcher Dee Eddington of the University of Michigan stated at a health care conference:

1. Risks flow toward high risk, and costs toward high cost if left unchecked.
2. Keeping healthy people healthy is a critical health management strategy.[5]

Simply put, disease management is an outreach program to those plan participants with chronic conditions to assist them in their management of

2. Lydell C. Bridgeford, "Disease," *Employee Benefit News*, January 2009, p. 26.
3. Michael B. Garrett, "Evaluating and Improving Disease Management Programs," *Compensation and Benefits Review*, Vol. 38, September/October 2006, p. 53.
4. "Change the Facts: Seven Keys to Greater Change: Best Practices for Employer Health Programs," *Healthways*, February 2010, p. 5.
5. Ibid., p. 2.

those conditions. On the surface, this seems like a relatively simple initiative, but often patients with chronic conditions do not do well with care or self-management programs, and patients who do not comply with the programs often not only incur costly health care expenses but also have a diminished quality of life.

Many patients lack care coordination as a result of multiple medical providers and physicians. As such, one would expect that patients with chronic diseases and their physicians would welcome the engagement and intervention offered by a disease management program. However, a 2009 survey of 700 U.S. companies indicated that fewer than 40 percent of the eligible individuals enrolled in wellness programs and fewer than 15 percent in chronic disease management programs.[6] Research by the Disease Management Association of America (DMAA) showed that 70 percent of the disease management providers believe that physicians view disease management programs as intrusive, and 41 percent believe that physicians are unlikely to encourage patients to participate in a disease management program.[7]

How is it that patients with chronic diseases or conditions choose to forgo the prescription drug regimens or treatment protocols outlined by their physicians? As research has shown, this is a complicated issue and there are a variety of reasons that patients deviate from prescription drug regimens and treatment protocols. Compounding the issue is that the physician usually is not aware or does not have any mechanism to determine compliance with such regimens and protocols. A behavioral theory called hyperbolic discounting suggests that individuals have a tendency to select a reward that occurs sooner but is smaller than a reward that is larger but occurs later in time. Said differently, a reward, such as better health that occurs quickly, is preferred over an "optimized health outcome" that occurs over a long period of time. The obvious dilemma is that many chronic diseases are lifestyle related and hence develop over a lifetime. As such, achieving an optimized health outcome for chronic patients can be difficult, as reconciling the behaviors that brought about the chronic condition in the first place do not occur over a short period of time. Perhaps this is a contributing factor that helps to explain why as many as 50 percent of the individuals with physician-prescribed medications fail to conform to the prescription regimen.[8]

6. Ibid., p. 4.
7. Lydell C. Bridgeford, "Disease," *Employee Benefit News*, January 2009, p. 26.
8. "Change the Facts: Seven Keys to Greater Change: Best Practices for Employer Health Programs," *Healthways*, February 2010, p. 4.

Recent studies have indicated that disease management is as much a process of helping to manage a patient's care and wellbeing as it is in engaging the patient in the disease management program. The key to maximizing participation in a program seems to be the incentives that are offered by the plan sponsor to the participants. Recently, the Center for Health Research reviewed incentives for disease management programs and best practices and found

1. Incentives and disincentives can be effective in improving participation and behavior change at least in the short term. Examples of incentives would include a value-based benefit design (described in-depth later in the chapter); cash contributions into a health savings account (HSA), health reimbursement account (HRA), or flexible spending account (FSA); cash bonuses; paid time off; gift cards; or a gift catalog. Disincentives would include increases in plan copayments or a reduction in benefits or salary. Not surprisingly, the incentives are much more effective than disincentives, and cash-based incentives appear to be the most popular.
2. Incentive programs can prevent attrition in a disease management program.
3. Incentives are most effective when provided on an ongoing basis.
4. Disease management programs can improve outcomes with incentives that are of appropriate value, are well structured and communicated, and for which the value or amount of the incentive reflects the action or effort required of the plan participant.[9]

In the 2010 Health Care Cost Survey published by Towers Perrin, high-performing employers utilize the following communications initiatives to engage plan participants:

1. Tailor the message and communication program to the specific audience. This would include an understanding of the demographic factors of the plan participants such as age, income, and education.
2. Acknowledge privacy concerns.
3. Maximize engagement with multiple touch points to the targeted population over time.
4. Demonstrate senior management support.

9. Ibid.

5. Monitor and address individual changes in the disease management program.[10]

Finally, a new tool has become available to measure participation engagement in a disease management program—namely, the Patient Activation Measure (PAM). The PAM is a short survey that assesses an individual's knowledge, skill, and confidence in managing his or her disease or condition. The results from the survey are then used by a health coach or disease management nurse to identify and overcome barriers to behavioral change. As such, when incorporated with motivational interviewing techniques, the chronic patient can be given a series of small, incremental steps that are comfortable, that will result in greater participation over an extended period of time, and that will ultimately improve his or her health and ability to deal with the chronic condition.[11]

Evaluating a Disease Management Program

Evaluating the effectiveness of a disease management program can be challenging. As with the early days of precertification and utilization review programs, the "savings" from a program can sometimes be difficult to quantify. Nonetheless, measurements for evaluating a disease management program include

1. Clinical outcomes, such as the percentage of patients with diabetes who have seen a reduction in their hemoglobin A1c or patients with depression who have maintained their pharmaceutical regimen over an 18-month period.
2. Utilization outcomes, which measure reductions in the number of services for health care interactions with providers.
3. Financial outcomes, which are usually expressed as return on investment (ROI) or direct cost savings.
4. Humanistic factors, which include the quality of life of the patient and the retention rate of participation in the disease management program.[12]

---

10. Ibid.
11. Christobel E. Selecky, "Reversing the High Cost of Chronic Illness with Activated Employees," *Benefits and Compensation Digest*, June 2009, p. 13.
12. Michael B. Garrett, "Evaluating and Improving Disease Management Programs," *Compensation and Benefits Review*, Vol. 38, September/October 2006, p. 52.

In addition, a robust disease management program should utilize nurses or health coaches who are trained in evidence-based guidelines. The importance of data integration between the health plan pharmacy data and demographic information cannot be overstated. The plan sponsor should have a good understanding of the participation and engagement strategies of the disease management vendor and how the vendor will respond to entities or subgroups with different demographic characteristics. Finally, understanding the criteria for determining outcomes, measurements, and ROI is vital in articulating the value and efficacy of a disease management program.

VALUE-BASED BENEFIT DESIGN

One of the developing and more interesting approaches to managing health care costs is the concept of value-based benefit design. VBBD has at its core, the concept that health care plans pay for "value" and not simply for services received. The VBBD concept is sometimes referred to as value-based insurance design (VBID). VBBD may also include incentives to promote the use of high-performing health care providers. Value-based purchasing, another strategy used to pay based on quality, differs from VBBD in that it is a supply-side approach and reimburses providers on the basis of value. In a white paper entitled "Aligning Incentives and Systems: Promoting Synergy Between Value-Based Insurance Design and the Patient-Centered Medical Home," the authors state:

> The motivation of VBID is that the current across-the-board benefit designs do not acknowledge that medical services differ in the amount of health (or value) gained per dollar spent. VBID is clinically nuanced, meaning that employers, usually through health plans, consciously identify health care treatments and services most likely to improve health and change benefit design to influence the use of those services. The basic premise of a clinically nuanced design is that when barriers to high-value medical services are kept low, more health is achieved at any price point.[13]

VBBD is based on three principles:

1. Value equals the clinical benefit achieved for the money spent.
2. Health care services differ in the health benefits they produce.

13. A. Mark Fendrick, Bruce Sherman, and Dennis White, *Aligning Incentives and Systems: Promoting Value-Based Insurance Design and the Patient-Centered Medical Home*, 2010, p. 2.

3. The value of health care services depends upon the individual who receives them.[14]

By definition, VBBD uses incentives, rewards, and/or reductions in cost or contribution to encourage the plan participants to

1. Use "high-value" health care services, including certain prescription drugs and preventive services
2. Adopt healthy lifestyles, such as smoking cessation or increased physical activity.[15]

As Figure 5-5 illustrates, the adherence and fill rate for prescription drugs goes down as the cost to the plan participant is increased. From a purely underwriting perspective, the increase in prescription drug copayments achieves the desired result in reducing health care costs. However, within the framework of a VBBD, the reduction in the compliance and fill

FIGURE 5-5

Increased Out-of-Pocket Costs May Reduce Adherence: Percentage Change in Days of Medication Supplied for Selected Medication Classes When Copays Were Doubled

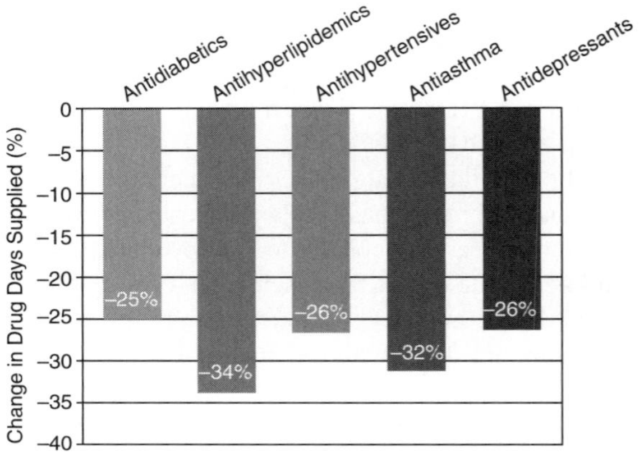

Source: Adapted from D. P. Goldman et al., "Pharmacy benefits and the use of drugs by the chronically ill," *JAMA*, Vol. 291, No. 19, 2004, pp. 2344–2350.

14. Ibid., p. 3.
15. Margaret Houy, *Health Plan Capabilities to Support Value Based Benefit Design*, Washington, DC: National Business Coalition on Health, January 2009, p. 5.

rate is undesirable for chronic patients, as the cost "reduction" produced by increasing prescription drug copayments is offset by health care cost increases in other more expensive areas such as unnecessary hospitalizations and the emergence of comorbidities. Hence, a VBBD recognizes it is more prudent in terms of value to offer chronic patients necessary medications with little or no copayment, so that the cost to the participant is not a barrier to consumption and adherence to a prescription protocol.

Approaches

There are a variety of approaches in VBBD programs. As discussed in the "Implementation" section below, there is no single best approach in VBBD programs, as ultimately the approach adopted and implemented is a function of each plan sponsor's unique circumstances, corporate culture, and budget. The common denominator with the different approaches is that plan participants are encouraged to be better stewards in managing their chronic or emerging chronic conditions as well as to utilize preventive services to avoid or minimize further illness or disease.

One approach would allow plan participants to access and utilize high-value health care services with little or no copayment or coinsurance for certain diagnoses or procedures. Examples might include mammography screening for women over age 40, cholesterol testing regardless of the age of the patient, and waiving copayments for all statin drugs that have been proven to lower cholesterol.[16] In addition, the cost of any procedures, treatments, or medications relating to diabetes, elevated blood pressure, or cholesterol could be covered at reduced or no deductible, copayments, or coinsurance. Many health plans already have this type of a VBBD approach with the inclusion of wellness benefits in a health plan. Wellness or routine-physical expenses are often covered without deductible or copayment, and encourage the early diagnosis and treatment of diseases that might otherwise go undetected. One final note about wellness or routine-physical benefits concerns the matter of provider coding. While many benefit plans will include a wellness or routine-physical benefit, there is often confusion and misunderstanding with the benefit, the plan participant, and the provider. Too often, plan participants do not make their health care provider aware of the presence of the wellness or routine-physical benefit. Moreover, many

16. A. Mark Fendrick, *Value-Based Insurance Design Landscape Digest*, Reston, VA: National Pharmaceutical Council, July 2009, p. 7.

health care providers do not use the proper common procedure terminology (CPT) coding for wellness or routine physicals so that the appropriate benefit level or copayment can be properly applied. For example, a major employer has been unable to implement different copayments for preventive services versus diagnostic services because of the CPT coding issue.[17]

Another approach would be to reduce or waive copayments or deductibles for chronic or high-risk patients. An example might be patients with depression or emotional disorders for whom maintenance of their prescription drug regimen is necessary to maintain their emotional well-being as well as minimizing physician visits and hospitalizations. This type of approach often requires a robust disease management program and communications program as well as an equally robust predictive modeling program described later in this chapter. A variation on this approach would couple the benefit with the participant's active involvement in a disease management program. "Active involvement" means that the participant is engaged and actively participating in the disease management program and is compliant with the program's efforts. This approach provides for reduced or waived copayments to high-risk participants similar to the above approach. Many advocates of VBBD feel that this may be the most effective approach.[18] As previously noted, many health care expenses are linked to behaviors. Behaviors, particularly lifestyle behaviors, have been learned by the plan participant over an extended period of time. Conversely, as behaviors have been learned, they can also be unlearned or modified with appropriate incentives and reinforcement—hence the term "modifiable risk factors." By way of example, a deposit can be made in a plan participant's health savings account or health reimbursement account each time an objective, established by the disease management organization, is attained by the plan participant. Not surprisingly, one of the best methods to assure compliance with the disease management program is to initially set modest and easily obtainable goals for the plan participant. Upon attainment of each new goal, the plan participant receives positive reinforcement with the change in behavior, not only in the form of better health and reinforcement from the disease management company but also in the form of a financial reward in the HSA or HRA. Incentives can vary widely,

17. Margaret Houy, *Value-Based Design: A Purchaser Guide*, Washington, DC: National Business Coalition on Health, January 2009, p. 10.

18. Ibid., p. 5.

as can the tasks, goals, or challenges of the plan participant. Additional examples might include maintaining compliance with a pharmaceutical regimen, completing on-line wellness classes, attending a weight reduction program, or completing a health risk assessment. The issue is not so much the specific task or the attainment of the goal, but rather the modification and elimination of behaviors (smoking, overeating, prescription drug noncompliance, and the like) that may have evolved over a lifetime and cannot be changed overnight. One final example of the impact of using a disease management participation approach is the Asheville Project, wherein free medications and testing supplies were provided for patients with diabetes who participated in a variety of education sessions on the disease.[19]

Implementation

The adoption of a VBBD should not be made in a vacuum, but rather should be the final step of an analysis that confirms the wisdom and appropriateness of the approach. This process is no different from the adoption of countless other offerings, approaches and initiatives that exist within the employee benefits landscape today.

The starting point is with data on the current population as it relates to demographics, claims history, major diagnostic categories, diagnosis trends, utilization data, prescription drug and wellness information (such as biometric data), health risk assessments, and detailed claims analysis. This type of analysis requires a robust tool to consolidate and coordinate all of this disparate information into a usable framework. The consolidation and integration of data from a variety of vendors and resources may be the biggest challenge in adopting or initiating a VBBD.[20] Once the data has been compiled in a usable format, the opportunities and solutions become not only much more identifiable, but also much more quantifiable in terms of their potential savings.[21] Absent a clear understanding of the existing cost and utilization anomalies, it may be difficult to quantify the efficacy of adopting a VBBD. As a VBBD program is generally thought of as a type

---

19. A. Mark Fendrick, *Value-Based Insurance Design Landscape Digest*, Reston, VA: National Pharmaceutical Council, July 2009, p. 7.
20. Margaret Houy, *Value-Based Design: A Purchaser Guide*, Washington, DC: National Business Coalition on Health, January 2009, p. 9.
21. Ibid.

of targeted approach to managing health care costs, a plan sponsor must have a clear understanding of the objective:

> The bedrock of an effective VBBD initiative is data collection and analysis designed to identify the areas of greatest opportunity for the purchaser. The best practice is to integrate data from multiple sources to create as complete an employer profile of risks and opportunities as possible.[22]

The second step in the introduction of a VBBD program is analysis. Having theoretically compiled all the data into a usable form, the process of analysis can begin to target areas of opportunity within the benefit program. The analysis might focus on locations, specific populations, or diagnosis trends. Whatever the focus, the analysis phase is one in which the aggregated, compiled, and scrubbed data (in which claims outliers are removed so that trends can be more easily identified) is the beginning point in determining which of the various approaches outlined above might yield the highest returns.

The third step in the process is the selection of the VBBD approach to be deployed. At this point, the data can be modeled along with the approach selected to quantify the financial impact of the adopted approach. While every organization is different, many plan sponsors will initially adopt a modest VBBD approach. A modest VBBD approach might be simply reducing or eliminating copayments for certain prescription drugs or office visits or for supplies for plan participants with diabetes. Plan sponsors may initially be reluctant to adopt a VBBD approach that requires, for example, disease management participation.

The remaining steps in the implementation process are no different than with any other health and welfare plan initiative:

1. Communications: the plan participants need to know the "who/what/when/where/why" information about the VBBD and the specific approach selected.
2. Education: initial and ongoing education and information about the VBBD program. Plan sponsors that target a specific condition, such as diabetes, can tailor their communications and education accordingly. Again, the key here is repetition and reinforcement of desired behavior change with the plan participant. The desired behavior change might be weight loss, maintaining a pharmaceutical regimen, diet, exercise, wellness, or program participation.

22. Ibid.

3. Decision support tools: provide for a telephonic or on-line health coach that provides support, encouragement, and mentoring of the plan participant, as well as a variety of on-line education programs to again reinforce the behavior changes or drug compliance with the plan participant.
4. Evaluation: establish a timetable to review the data and to determine if the quantifiable goals established at the outset of the adoption of the VBBD program are being attained. The data analysis outlined above in the implementation process is not an isolated event but rather an ongoing process to not only quantify the approach being deployed, but also monitor new or developing opportunities for health care improvement and VBBD plan enhancements.

Concerns in Adopting a VBBD

The following are common concerns of which to be aware when adopting a VBBD:

1. Costs and utilization are likely to initially increase—plan sponsors are likely to see an increase in costs and utilization with the adoption of a VBBD. Therefore, it is important to carefully set timetables, expectations, and financial goals and to maintain a long-term focus. Again, it should be remembered that the drivers and consumption patterns of the plan participants that are yielding the current-day utilization did not evolve overnight. As a result, the behavior and consumption changes that will occur with VBBD will not yield an overnight success. The adoption and implementation of VBBD is a long-term solution to a long-term problem. With that in mind, plan sponsors initially should expect to see an increase in both utilization and consumption of health care services for the programs targeted in the VBBD.
2. Data collection and aggregation is challenging—perhaps one of the biggest challenges in adopting a VBBD is compiling and aggregating the data at the outset. Given the multiplicity of vendors and locations in which many plan sponsors operate, compiling information from a variety of vendors into a usable and understandable format that allows for detailed analysis can be very challenging.

3. Plan sponsors may be concerned about the issue of fairness in offering a welfare plan that has a category of plan participant eligible to receive a better benefit, and the importance of communication cannot be overemphasized in responding to this concern. Plan sponsors have a variety of communication and education tools available as a resource for plan participants on the importance of health care cost management and proper benefit plan utilization. Moreover, survey data has recently indicated that employees have not reacted adversely to a VBBD that may otherwise be perceived as favoring a particular type of employee.[23]

VBBD and Consumer-Driven Health Plans

Consumer-driven health plans (CDHPs) have the following common characteristics:

1. High deductible health plan (HDHP)—generally a PPO-type plan design in which health plan costs, including those of prescription drugs, are borne by the plan participant subject to a calendar-year deductible. Usually the minimum deductible is $1,200 per individual or $2,400 per family. Typically, however, HDHPs allow for routine physical benefits at no deductible.
2. Health savings account or health reimbursement arrangement—An account-based arrangement that is funded by the employee, the employer, or both that provides for payment of health care expenses below the deductible amount, as well as the coinsurance amount above the deductible.

The basic premise behind a CDHP is that the consumer is "engaged" in the health care consumption-and-utilization equation by virtue of the presence of the HDHP as well as the extent to which the funds in the HSA or HRA are available for use or may "roll over" from one year to the next. Hence, it is the plan participants' responsibility to spend their health care dollars wisely and to determine those services that provide the greatest "value."

The "value" of a VBBD is embedded within the plan design itself. Health care services that provide the greatest value are determined by the

23. Ibid., p. 15.

plan sponsor based upon analysis and evaluation of utilization and consumption patterns from a variety of data inputs. As such, a plan driven by VBBD principles with its many data inputs and an understanding of the most efficacious treatment alternatives, may make the VBBD a better alternative for the plan participant than a standard CDHP. Additionally, a VBBD approach does not have the potential risk that plan participants may forego needed health care as in a standard CDHP. Rather, the VBBD participant has an incentive to seek "value-based" health care. The studies and information in the Introduction to this chapter underscore the extent to which increasing deductibles and copayments reduces utilization and consumption yet may also lead to the participant potentially foregoing needed health care services.

A study by the Employee Benefit Research Institute (EBRI) illustrates the impact of prescription drug adherence for CDHP enrollees, and concludes that, while overall use of brand name prescription drugs fell and generic drug use increased, "... overall use of prescription drugs among CDHP enrollees with certain chronic conditions fell, or did not increase when enrollees met their deductible."[24]

If the goal of a health plan is to manage the chronic patient population and to "engage" the emerging chronic population, the adoption of VBBD features within a plan may be more successful than a CDHP alone in meeting this goal. While the discussion here contrasts the merits of a standard CDHP plan with a VBBD approach, employers and insurance carriers can, and are likely to, incorporate various value-based design strategies and features into existing plans, including CDHPs. As various VBBD strategies are proven effective, they are likely to become more prevalent within the whole array of plan structures which are available to employers.

Does this mean that CDHPs are not a viable alternative in today's employee benefits landscape? This is hardly the case. A closer examination of the demographics of CDHP enrollees might provide valuable insight into the applicability of a standard CDHP or one containing VBBD features.

Finally, it should be noted that both VBBDs and CDHPs generally have integrated disease management programs. The disease management programs will have outreach initiatives to engage the participant as well as

24. Paul Fronstin, *What Do We Really Know About Consumer-Driven Health Plans?*, Washington, DC: Employee Benefit Research Institute, August 2010, p. 23.

health care providers and family members in the management of the patient's condition and prescription drug regimen, as well as identification and intervention with the emerging-chronic plan population.

Early Adopters

The following are examples of organizations that have adopted a VBBD. It is interesting to note not only the results to date but also that the organizations that have adopted a VBBD range from municipalities to large multinational employers with both union and nonunion workers. Those organizations that are early adopters do not necessarily fall into a specific demographic, but rather reflect the willingness of an organization to undertake a new approach to health care cost management.

1. *Dell.* Dell has more than 27,000 employees insured among three different health plans, with employees in every state in the United States. The VBBD initiatives deployed include
   a. Reduced copayments for generic medications for certain conditions.
   b. Diabetic medications and supplies at reduced or zero copayments.
   c. Smoking cessation agents with zero copayments.
   d. Incentives for completing a health risk assessment. A financial incentive is included not only for completing the assessment, but also for enrolling and completing an on-line wellness program.

   Within 12 months of the introduction, 19,100 participants have completed the health risk assessment. Of this population, 14,900 are eligible for health coaching, of which 7,897 (53 percent) have enrolled in the coaching program.[25]
2. *City of Springfield, Oregon.* The City of Springfield employs 430 individuals, with a total of 1,100 plan participants. The city offers both PPO and HMO plan designs to their nonunion and union workforce. The VBBD emphasis of this municipality was with diabetes. The city randomly selected plan participants with type 1 or type 2 diabetes to participate in either the "control"

25. Margaret Houy, *Value-Based Design: A Purchaser Guide*, Washington, DC: National Business Coalition on Health, January 2009, p. 22.

group or the "intervention" group. The control group received a variety of printed education materials, while the intervention group received personal counseling with pharmacy experts to encourage diabetes medication adherence, regular physician visits, and diet and exercise programs. The results showed a 30 percent reduction in sick leave for the intervention group as well as a 50 percent reduction in hemoglobin A1c.[26]

3. *The Asheville Project.* In March 1997, the City of Asheville, North Carolina, along with community pharmacists, physicians, nurses, dieticians, and the local hospital, launched what has become known as the "Asheville Project." While the original focus of the project was diabetes, the project has since been expanded to now include patients with asthma. Additionally, the North Carolina Center for Pharmaceutical Care (NCCPC) was also involved in this project. It was the belief of the NCCPC that the nature of diabetes is such that it requires a significant amount of disease management and monitoring by the patient. The monitoring of blood glucose levels, insulin injections, and managing food intake are but a few of the components in managing diabetes. As such, the role of the NCCPC was underscored by the fact that pharmacists understand diabetes medication therapy and are five times more likely than any other health care professional to see patients with diabetes. The Asheville Project involved a coordinated effort between plan participants in the City of Asheville's employee benefit program as well as the participants' physicians. Each participant in the project was matched with a pharmacist within the city. The pharmacists met with their assigned patients on an appointment basis and established initial baseline information, needs assessments, and goals for each patient. Within 14 months of the program being established, the number of patients with a normal range of hemoglobin A1c increased from 33 percent to 67 percent. Additionally, health care costs were reduced, and the number of sick days was decreased significantly, as was the number of short-term disability insurance claims.[27]

26. Ibid.
27. "The Asheville Project: A Special Report," Supplement to *Pharmacy Times*, October 1998.

4. *Gulfstream Corporation.* As an aerospace manufacturer, Gulfstream Corporation has over 9,000 employees, with more than 21,000 covered plan participants. Gulfstream deployed a number of VBBD initiatives, including
   a. A health risk assessment, including a biometric screening offered on-site
   b. Zero-dollar copayment for generic drugs for asthma, diabetes, heart disease, cholesterol, and hypertension
   c. Incentives to use quality-based physicians

   Over a four-year period, Gulfstream experienced a health care costs trend decrease of 3.4 percent per year. Additionally, claims data analysis showed significant reductions in the number of amputations, heart attacks, strokes and overall health costs of patients with diabetes. Women who obtained regular mammograms experienced a reduced rate of mastectomies. Moreover, pharmaceutical costs were reduced, and a 98.4 percent generic substitution rate was achieved.[28]
5. *IBM.* IBM has more than 130,000 U.S.-based employees, with a total number of plan participants in excess of 500,000. In addition to financial incentives for completion of a health risk assessment, IBM also offers a smoking cessation program and a disease management program that is integrated into a total health management initiative. Finally, personal health management is incorporated into job expectations, with senior management involvement. Since the inception of the program, IBM has experienced premiums that range from 6 percent to 15 percent lower than those of similarly situated organizations, as well as reductions in hospital admissions, emergency room visits, and pharmacy expenses.[29]
6. *Pitney Bowes.* With more than 22,000 employees, and three national health plans, Pitney Bowes offers preventive care at little or no co-payment to the plan participant. In addition, the prescription drug benefit is based upon a coinsurance arrangement in which Tier One is at 10 percent, Tier Two is at 30 percent, and Tier Three is at 55 percent. Out-of-pocket limits

28. Margaret Houy, *Value-Based Design: A Purchaser Guide*, Washington, DC: National Business Coalition on Health, January 2009, p. 23.
29. Ibid.

exist for the prescription drug benefits. Certain brand name drug medications for chronic conditions (asthma, diabetes, and blood pressure) have been moved to Tier One. In addition, any plan participant having a cardiac event receives statins and diabetes medication at no cost. Finally, the completion of a health risk assessment results in a contribution by Pitney Bowes to the participant's health savings account.[30]

PREDICTIVE MODELING

Managing health care costs involves a careful review of data to determine the best approaches in plan design, medical management, provider networks, and a host of other managed care initiatives. The fundamental weakness in data analysis is that the data is always of a historical nature, similar to the forensic process of determining the cause of a fire after the building has already burned down.

But what if there existed a mechanism by which it were possible to determine which participant populations or demographic groups were in need of health management intervention *before* health plan, sickness, and disability expenses were incurred? Predictive modeling can be used to identify and intervene with the potentially emerging chronic element of an enrolled population. In addition to identifying the emerging chronically ill, predictive modeling can also be used to develop health care cost management techniques for the existing chronically ill participant population to maximize patient satisfaction and quality of life as well as reducing or eliminating unnecessary health care costs.

Simply put, predictive modeling is a statistical tool that takes into consideration data or information from a variety of disparate and seemingly unrelated sources to identify trends, populations, and areas of health care cost management. Some of the "unrelated" sources of information would include pharmacy data, demographic information, claims data, wellness information, and biometrics. There are a number of providers of predictive modeling and often their analytics will fall into the categories of risk grouping, statistical models or artificial intelligence (AI).[31] This grouping utilizes analytical models with a variety of data inputs, such as gender, date of birth, and pharmacy data, which when run through a series of

30. Ibid., p. 24.
31. Chris Silva, "What's in the Cards?" *Employee Benefit News*, April 1, 2008, p. 22.

algorithms yields actionable data. Statistical models can also be used to benchmark an existing plan population or demographic against established standards and norms to again determine areas of benefit plan management or focus. Finally, AI can be used to fill in any gaps or voids in data to not only determine areas of benefit plan management but also predict the most effective form of plan management that will achieve the desired cost management objective, given the enrolled population and human behavior tendencies. Joel Brill, Chief Medical Officer at Predictive Health, stated, "The purpose of predictive modeling is to identify the patient who is at risk for incurring higher health care costs in the next 12 to 18 months, or who is at risk for hospitalization, but does not otherwise know that they are at risk for such."[32]

Some of the principles of predictive modeling include a focus on the entire plan participant population and addressing the entire health care continuum, emphasizing long-term behavior change, supporting benefit plan designs with strong communication and incentives, and creating data-driven programs tailored to individual risk, health status, and learning.[33]

An example of the usefulness of predictive modeling is with a plan sponsor with a high male population. Often young to middle-aged males lack a primary care physician and do not establish a physician relationship until the onset of symptoms. Such is often the case with hypertension. In many cases, hypertension is an under-diagnosed condition that can lead to a heart attack or stroke later in life. Predictive modeling can be used to examine an existing population with the diagnosis or tendencies (height/weight, and the like) for hypertension against what might otherwise be considered normative levels of hypertension within a plan. The data may indicate that the plan sponsor consider a health fair for hypertension screening and education. Moreover, predictive modeling can be used to identify disease conditions that impact the greatest number of plan participants and be most effective in terms of cost, productivity, lost work days, and treatment program.[34]

From an insurance company perspective, predictive modeling can be used to review initial and renewal underwriting determinations, measure the impact of disease management programs, and identify cost drivers. As

32. Ibid.
33. Chris Silva, "Employers Investigating Predictive Models to Cut Health Care Costs," *Employee Benefit News*, February 2009, p. 38.
34. Ned Cooper, "Workforce Demographic Analytics Yield Health Care Savings," *Employment Relations Today*, Vol. 36, October 2009, p. 15.

such, predictive modeling is not just an initiative for large groups but also applies to the small-group market. Predictive modeling can be used to determine loss ratio targets for blocks of small-group insurance, taking into consideration the medical information provided at the time of initial enrollment. Likewise, to review rate filings and future premium needs, predictive modeling can be used to analyze small group health plans by delivery model (HMO, PPO, or POS), as well as provider network composition and payment methodologies.

The connection between the discussion of VBBD and predictive modeling is best described using a case study involving a diabetes management program. Predictive modeling and data analysis indicated that nearly half of the diabetic population was not following the appropriate pharmacy treatment regimen, thereby exposing the plan to unnecessary health care costs as well as exposing the plan participants to avoidable and undesirable health risks such as the loss of an extremity or sight. The role of predictive modeling went beyond that of simply diabetes management in that it indicated that the plan sponsor should eliminate co-pays for pharmaceuticals to treat diabetes as well as those to treat hypertension and depression.[35]

Health care cost containment initiatives no longer have as their sole focus plan participants with chronic health conditions. In the new millennium, predictive modeling has been shown to be a powerful analytical tool to improve not only the health care, quality of life, and health care costs of the chronic patient population, but also those of the "emerging chronic" population before the health care costs are incurred. Essentially, therefore, the focus of predictive modeling is not one of analyzing what caused the barn to catch fire, but rather to prevent the barn from burning in the first place.

CONCLUSION

While a significant portion of this chapter has focused on value-based benefit design, it is important to remember that all of the initiatives outlined can work alone or together. Employers and plan sponsors may want to consider adopting a wellness program, a disease management program, or a VBBD. While each initiative has the ability to stand alone, the plan sponsor may find powerful synergies in combining programs. All of the parts must be coordinated and integrated for the combination of programs to be fully effective.

---

35. Ibid.

Lifestyle and health care consumption patterns generally evolve over an extended period of time. Correspondingly, altering the modifiable risk factors and health care consumption patterns of the chronic and emerging chronic plan population is not a short-term, quick-fix process. Yet the encouraging news is that, as lifestyle and health care consumption patterns are learned, so too can they be unlearned. The role of the disease management program is one in which data are taken from a variety of inputs and resources to not only identify those plan participants in the chronic and emerging chronic plan population but also to engage them on a regular, frequent and consistent basis to better manage their health or conditions or to alter and change their lifestyles and health care consumption patterns. The level of engagement must be frequent and provide enough ongoing touch points with the chronic and emerging chronic plan participants so as to provide a path for behavior change. A VBBD program, in and of itself, may not be sufficient to engage the plan participant to bring about the desired changes in lifestyle or health care consumption. The role of the disease management program is therefore one of outreach that engages, encourages, supports, and coordinates the health care consumption and utilization of the chronic and emerging chronic plan population.

CHAPTER 6

Managing and Measuring Care Management Intervention Programs

Ian Duncan

BACKGROUND

Early insurance approaches to the financing of health care focused on hospital reimbursement and were characterized by two key assumptions. The first assumption was that providers would exercise reasonable professional judgment in the provision of services to patients. The second assumption was that patients would tend to be conservative regarding their use of services (since these services often involved both discomfort and uncertain outcomes).

In this model, the insurance company's role was limited to "traditional" insurance functions, such as underwriting and pricing, verification of insurance eligibility, and claim payment. Cost was restrained through the above means, as well as through traditional insurance product features such as deductibles and coinsurance. Intervention in actual medical services—either with the patient or the provider—was unthinkable in this era.

Over time, the traditional insurance model failed to contain costs and was replaced by a more interventionist model in which the entity financing the services began to try to influence the demand for and access to medical resources and services. The "insurance" model gave way to the "managed care" model.

Since managed care became commonplace in the United States in the mid-1980s, managed care organizations (MCOs) have tried a multitude of methods to influence the resource consumption behavior of health care providers and patients. Early managed care models focused on physicians and hospitals, using a variety of administrative, regulatory, or legal tactics. These included a formal peer review process to reduce unnecessary hospital admissions and inappropriately long hospital stays, a formal regulatory and planning process aimed at gradually reducing the number of unneeded hospital beds, and a reimbursement mechanism (diagnostic related groups, DRGs) that limited the number of days above a norm for which a hospital was reimbursed. Other tactics included a requirement that physicians obtain approval for hospital admissions prior to admitting a patient (preauthorization, utilization review, concurrent review), as well as various contracting models with "preferred providers." Because of consumer and provider reaction to the service denials that resulted from preauthorization, managed care plans began to seek other solutions to contain rapidly increasing costs: programs that aim to manage care directly either through the member or the member's provider(s).

More recent solutions aim to include both the patient and the provider in the process, while responding to complaints about the intrusiveness of some interventions. For example, "disease management," a set of interventions focused on individuals with one or more chronic conditions, has become a major initiative of many health plans and employers. With the passage of the Patient Protection and Affordable Care Act (PPACA) in March 2010, a number of the "traditional" risk management techniques will be outlawed. In the new, post-reform environment, medical management techniques that have been developed over the last 20 years will become even more important to health insurers.

One way of classifying intervention programs is to identify the target of the intervention, as in Table 6-1.

There is little controversy over the clinical benefits of care management intervention. The financial value is more controversial. Unlike insurance models that could be implemented through underwriting and claims payment systems, managed care models tend to be relatively costly, since they are patient focused, employ many skilled professionals, and require a supporting infrastructure. The care management industry has had difficulties convincing purchasers of services that their interventions produce more in savings than the cost of the programs themselves (a positive return on investment, ROI). Apparently exaggerated claims that are made for outcomes from some programs, sometimes scientifically dubious measurement methodologies and recent lack of demonstrated financial success in well-publicized pilots such as the Medicare Health Support initiative do not help make the case for the

TABLE 6-1

Types of Medical Management Interventions

Care Coordination:	Condition Management:	Provider Management:
Focus on the System	**Focus on the Patient**	**Focus on the Provider**
■ Intensive case management ■ Behavioral health case management ■ Discharge planning ■ In-hospital care coordination ■ Concurrent review	■ Chronic condition (disease) management ■ Specialty case management (e.g., maternity, behavioral) ■ Population/wellness and risk factor management	■ Concurrent review ■ Treatment management ■ Provider profiling ■ Preauthorization ■ Pay-for-performance ■ Medical home

economic value of interventions. Historically, the assessment of outcomes and savings has been the responsibility of the clinical professions. The increasing importance and costs of these programs and the skepticism about their results has resulted in increasing interest in them by chief financial officers, who are increasingly seeking more objective financial information.

TYPES OF CARE MANAGEMENT INTERVENTIONS

As the following list makes clear, care management programs have evolved from their inception as a requirement of prior authorization of certain procedures. The following are some intervention programs commonly encountered in health plans and self-insured employers:

1. Preauthorization review
2. Concurrent review
3. Case management
4. Demand management
5. Disease management
6. Medical homes
7. Pharmacy benefits management
8. Specialty case management
9. Population health management and wellness

Care Management Definitions

These interventions are briefly defined as follows:

1. Preauthorization (also called "prior authorization") requires a physician or hospital to obtain approval from a managed care organization prior to performing a diagnostic procedure or surgical intervention on a health plan member. As medical practice adapts to accommodate the requirements of preauthorization, some procedures will be eliminated from the list and be replaced by new treatments. A related intervention, second surgical opinion, was popular in the 1980s but fell largely into disuse as medical practice accommodated many of its requirements. This intervention has, however, enjoyed a minor comeback in limited situations targeted at "preference sensitive conditions," or diagnoses for which surgery is recommended. Where an alternative, less-invasive therapy is also possible, a health plan may sometimes require its members to explore the alternative treatment before approving surgery.
2. Concurrent review requires monitoring a health plan member's care while he or she is still receiving care in an acute hospital or nursing home. This process is most commonly performed by a nurse, who may review a hospitalized patient's medical record to collect information and discuss the case with the responsible clinician via telephone. As the provision of services within the hospital has become more complex and multidisciplinary, services may be coordinated by a physician located in the hospital (but paid by a health plan), called a "hospitalist." The hospitalist's function is to coordinate the different disciplines directed to an individual patient, eliminating overlaps or gaps in care and ensuring better outcomes and lower cost. Another intervention provided for hospitalized patients, either in the hospital or very shortly after discharge, is discharge planning, which aims to avoid readmissions for patients who have inadequate care or support after discharge.
3. Case management is typically performed by a health care professional who coordinates the care of a patient with a serious disease or illness (such as a stroke, multiple sclerosis, AIDS, some cancers, or lupus erythematosus). The complexity of diseases that involve a case manager usually results in medical

care that involves multiple medical specialties, institutions, a wide array of possible diagnostic and therapeutic tools, and a significant social or community-based welfare element. Case management is similar, in some respects, to disease management, with one key difference: case managers often have the authority to approve extra-contractual benefits for members.

4. Demand management refers to certain passive forms of informational intervention, often provided by clinical staff over the telephone. Demand management includes widely offered services such as nurse advice lines. Unlike disease management and case management, demand management addresses episodic, often acute, occurrences. One objective of these services is "triage" or the process of determining, on the telephone, whether a medical condition or event requires immediate intervention, such as an emergency room visit. Another type of nurse-information line, shared decision making, provides education for patients facing a significant medical decision (e.g., major surgery), aiming to provide the patient with information on alternatives to surgery, coaching in questions to ask the medical provider, and a framework for informed decision making. We classify these interventions as "passive" because, unlike case management or disease management (for example), the contact with the intervention is initiated by the patient rather than the care manager.
5. Disease management has gained substantial prominence in managed care organizations, as evidenced by the formation of the Disease Management Association of America (DMAA) now renamed the Care Continuum Alliance or CCA. The focus is on chronic conditions because certain characteristics of chronic diseases make them suitable for clinical intervention:
   a. Once contracted, the disease remains with the patient for the rest of the patient's life.
   b. The disease is often manageable with a combination of pharmaceutical therapy and lifestyle change.
   c. Patients frequently require education, support and encouragement to adhere to the prescribed treatment regimen.
   d. Data analysis has improved to such an extent that patients with "gaps in care," or evidence of nonadherence to

best-practice standards of care may be easily identified and contacted by a health care professional.

e. The average cost of a chronic patient's care is sufficiently high to warrant the expenditure of additional resources to manage the condition.

As defined by the CCA (to which most providers and many purchasers belong) disease management is a system of coordinated health care interventions and communications for populations with conditions in which patient self-care efforts are significant. It

- Supports the physician or practitioner/patient relationship and plan of care
- Emphasizes prevention of exacerbations and complications utilizing evidence-based practice guidelines and patient empowerment strategies
- Evaluates clinical, humanistic and economic outcomes on an ongoing basis with the goal of improving overall health

Traditionally, disease management has focused on the "big five" chronic diseases: asthma, chronic obstructive pulmonary disease (COPD), congestive heart failure (CHF), coronary artery disease (CAD), and diabetes. Initially, disease management focused on single diseases, and some vendors still specialize in managing a single disease. However, over time, the industry has moved more towards a "whole person" model in which all of a patient's diseases (and, in many cases, lifestyle risk factors) are managed by a disease management program.

6. Medical homes are the central offices in which a primary care physician coordinates all aspects of a patient's care, including the types of services obtained from a disease management program (e.g., identification of gaps in care, coaching, and outreach). As disease management began to assume a larger role in the care of chronically ill patients, many clinicians questioned the role and efficacy of remote (often telephonic) intervention that replaced the regular course of treatment delivered by the patient's physician. Disease management clearly provides benefits and services to the patient that many providers were not equipped to provide. The medical home initiative recognizes that a patient should have a medical home.

7. Pharmacy benefit management is a set of intervention programs targeted at the outpatient prescription drug utilization of insured patients. Pharmaceutical benefits tend to reimburse claims for drugs for which a national drug code (NDC) is assigned, in contrast to certain high-cost drugs that are reimbursed as part of the medical benefit, for which a different set of codes is used (often G codes). These benefits are often managed by a separate organization, the specialty pharmacy manager (see below). Pharmacy benefits management encompasses a number of different interventions, often delivered at the point of dispensing by a pharmacist, including the following:

a. Generic substitution: substitution of a less expensive (but therapeutically equivalent) generic drug for a more expensive brand name drug.

b. Step therapy: beginning the patient's treatment with a cheaper therapeutic equivalent and switching to more expensive alternatives if required.

c. Pill splitting: this technique takes advantage of the similarity in pricing between larger and smaller doses of the same drug. Considerable savings may be realized by "splitting" a larger-dose tablet.

d. Preauthorization: a physician may be required to obtain authorization before prescribing certain drugs.

e. Quantity and dosage limits: because prescriptions are often filled on a regular basis, it is possible to limit the number or volume of a particular drug dispensed at any one refill.

8. Specialty case management is performed by a care manager who has expertise in a particular area (such as mental health, organ transplantation, oncology, or biological or injectable drug therapy) and to whom the managed care organization has assigned primary responsibility for coordinating the care of a patient. The primary purpose of the specialty pharmacy management program is to leverage improved drug discounts while improving the clinical quality of care for members requiring specialty drugs, as well as, in some cases where the same drug may be administered at more than one site, to steer patients to a less expensive site of administration.

9. Population health management is a broad term that covers a number of different types of programs and interventions. Unlike disease management, the focus is not on patients with a particular disease, with the objective of prevention, but on the majority of health plan members who have no manageable diseases but who show evidence of other forms of risk that may predispose them to disease (e.g., smoking or obesity). A broader approach is used in which the entire membership in a health plan is evaluated, often using self-reported data called health risk assessments. Other statistical tools, such as predictive modeling, may be used to identify potential high-cost patients who can benefit from some kind of "softer" intervention. These programs, also known as wellness programs, are delivered via many different media, including telephonic, Internet, mail, and, most recently, smart-phones. Wellness, health promotion, and disease prevention have been defined as "a set of organized activities and systematic interventions, offered through corporations/worksites, managed care organizations, and governmental/community agencies, whose primary purposes are to provide health education, identify modifiable health risks, and influence health behavior changes."[1]

The workplace has become an important focus of the drive for behavioral changes necessary for a healthier lifestyle that bring benefits to the individual, the employer, and the wider community. Workplace wellness programs primarily focus upon common modifiable health risks that have been shown to increase health expenditures, such as obesity, consumption of tobacco and alcohol, stress, a sedentary lifestyle, depression, high blood pressure, high blood glucose levels, risky sexual behavior, and the failure to use seat belts in vehicles. The current generation of worksite programs, characterized as health and productivity management,[2] are multifaceted, integrating health promotion and disease prevention with demand and disease management programs. The evolution of worksite programs has led some employers to provide worksite clinics (initially for occupational medical conditions, but expanded to include common primary care services

1. M. Mulvihill, "The definition and core practices of wellness," *Journal of Employee Assistance*, Fourth Quarter 2003, pp. 13–15.
2. R. Goetzel and R. Ozminkowski, "Health and productivity management: emerging opportunities for health promotion professionals in the 21st century." *American Journal of Health Promotion*, Vol. 14, No. 5, 2000, pp. 211–214.

and even on-site pharmacy services) and fitness centers. Worksite programs will always have one drawback over other types of delivery (e.g., nurse telephonic outreach), because only the employee is present at the worksite, and employees rarely represent more than 50 percent of the entire employer-covered population.

RETURN ON INVESTMENT IN INTERVENTION PROGRAMS

A number of authors have conducted surveys and meta-analyses of the financial results of some of the different care management interventions listed above. The metric used most frequently to assess financial outcomes from programs is the annualized rate of return on investment in the program (usually referred to as ROI)[3] or savings from the program divided by the program cost.

In other financial applications, rate of return is generally expressed on a net basis (i.e., as the difference between savings and cost). In care management applications, it is traditional to express the rate of return in gross terms, that is, including the cost. It is important that the user of this information clearly define and understand the basis of the calculation. Table 6-2 presents a summary prepared in 2006 of a large number of different care management programs that had reported a financial savings or ROI at that time.

ECONOMICS OF CARE MANAGEMENT

In order to understand the potential financial effect of interventions on care, as well as its analysis, it is important to understand the economics of care management. Program savings are the difference between reduced health care resource use, often caused by a reduction in hospital admissions or days, or diversion to a less intense or less expensive place of service, and the cost of the interventions. Because intervention programs employ clinical professionals, they can often be costly, particularly if they are offered to a large population. Often a care management program or group of programs may be one of the largest initiatives undertaken by a health plan, comparable in scale, for example, to the cost of a new claims payment system. Some health plans have actively marketed programs to employers in

3. See Appendix 6.1 for a mathematical discussion.

TABLE 6-2

Care Management Financial Results from the Published Literature

Intervention	Total No. of Studies	Major Findings
Preauthorization/ utilization review (UR)	9	Early studies show admission and bed-day reductions from UR in the range of 10–15%. Recent international studies of data not subject to managed care show considerable opportunity for utilization reduction. Early gains were not maintained as medical management models changed; there is also evidence of increased outpatient utilization due to inpatient UR. More recently, these reductions are in the range of 2–3%; savings are estimated at between $25 and $74 per member per year; we estimate an ROI of 4.60 based on a reported intervention cost of $16 per member for this study.
Concurrent review	5	Early gains due to concurrent review were not maintained as medical practice patterns changed. Current evidence shows that concurrent review can reduce bed-days by 2–3%. One study in a hospital setting showed an ROI of 0.9 (savings < cost of review).
Case management (sometimes called intensive case management) (CM or ICM)	22	Reported results are variable (depending on target condition and program). Evidence exists of clinical improvement and reduction in utilization due to CM, particularly for heart disease. A survey of CM financial outcomes for diabetes found no valid studies. ROIs in the range of 2–6 times have been reported.
Demand management	6	Evidence exists that demand management reduces unnecessary physician and ER visits. Financial results indicate ROIs of 1.37 and 3.86.
Disease management	52	For one population (multi-disease) program that reported per-member per-month (PMPM) savings, gross savings are estimated at approximately $1.45 PMPM. For programs that report ROI, the range is 1.2–6.4. Highest savings are reported for heart diseases. Moderate savings are reported in diabetes and mixed results (in some cases no savings) for asthma. A recent study using a randomized control showed no discernible savings.

TABLE 6-2

Specialty case management	5	Relatively few studies. Prevalence of members with target conditions makes them a poor candidate for randomized control trials. Evidence shows support for financial outcomes in mental health and some high-cost diseases, such as renal diseases.
Population management (PM)	8	Evidence has been reported of dollar savings within population-wide programs. One study reported an ROI of 5.0. Studies of programs to intervene within entire chronic condition subpopulations report measurable PMPM savings.
Wellness	*	Due to the broader-based nature of wellness interventions, findings on the effectiveness of health promotion and wellness programs are more conjectural. Industry literature indicates ROIs of, say, 1.5, 3, or even higher with the return from some well-designed comprehensive programs at $3 to $8 per dollar invested, within 5 years following program initiation. The beneficial effect on reduced absence has been demonstrated to increase this return.
TOTAL	107	

Source: Ian Duncan, *Managing and Evaluating Healthcare Intervention Programs*, Winsted, CT: Actex Publications, 2008.
*See Duncan (2008), Chapter 14.

return for an add-on fee, but, for the most part, the cost of a program(s) is incurred as part of a plan's general and administrative (G&A) expense, soon to be subject to the limits imposed by the PPACA. An often overlooked feature of disease and population management programs is that, in addition to their clinical aspects, they can also represent a very large direct marketing exercise—the average prevalence of the "big five" chronic diseases in a commercial population, counting members with multiple conditions once, is 5 percent to 10 percent (depending on the specific definition of disease used). For members without a manageable condition, as many as 60 percent of members will have one or more risk factors. Medicare and Medicaid populations have higher prevalences of these conditions.

Financially, care management programs produce their savings by identifying members who are at risk of high-cost events (often hospital admissions) over the medium to long term (6 to 24 months), intervening with those members and their physicians, and changing the member's behavior (increasing the member's compliance with best-practice care, ceasing smoking, etc.). Increased self-care and compliance with treatment protocols and healthy lifestyle will reduce future high-cost events. To reduce the cost of personalized interventions, some programs have attempted to leverage lower-cost media such as mail or Internet communication, but without the same effectiveness in terms of either participation or behavior change.

Not every high-risk member is equally likely to be "manageable" by a program. Why is this? First, many conditions and risk factors are not amenable to management, and, second, some members will have so small a probability of an event that the expenditure of resources on their management will not be economic. For a large number of members, the cost of managing the member will be higher than the potential savings from reduced utilization (particularly if the employer provides a participation incentive). Although predictive modeling techniques are important for identifying members who are likely to experience high cost, an equally important use of these techniques is in program planning. Application of a predictive model allows us to rank members by the likelihood that the member will have an expensive event (hospital admission or emergency room visit, for example). Irrespective of the specific risk factor, the distribution of the population at risk will usually follow a pattern such as that in Figure 6-1. As we increase the penetration into a population, so the predicted frequency of the targeted event decreases.

We can combine the event frequency with a cost per event and rank member cost levels by predicted frequency. We can then construct a financial ROI model by incorporating variables such as likely behavior change, likelihood of enrolling in a program, and cost of intervention to estimate the likely savings at each level of penetration into the population.

FIGURE 6-1

Population Risk Ranking

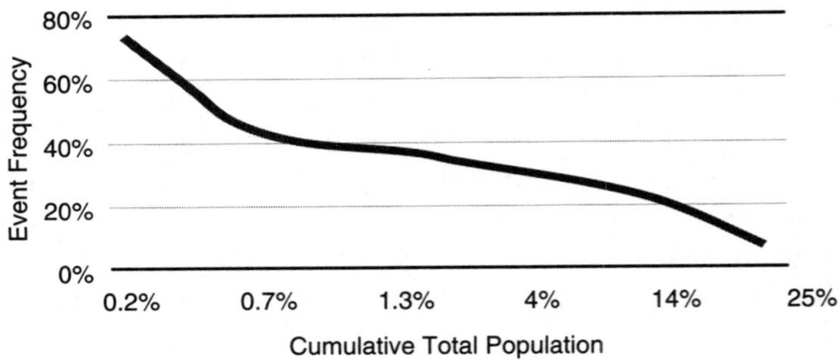

FIGURE 6-2

Relationship between Program Cost and Savings for Different Levels of Program Intervention

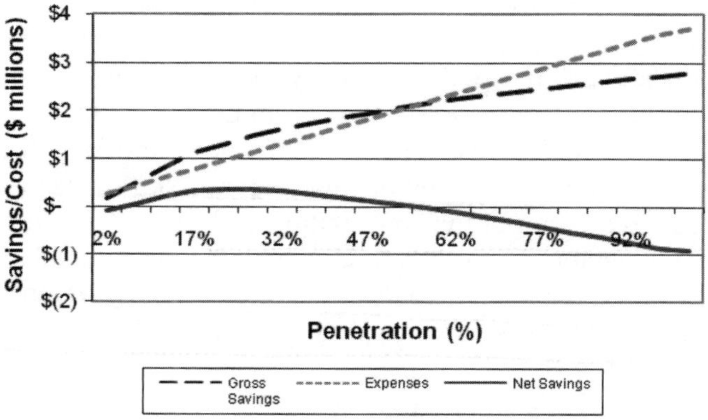

The cost of the program rises progressively with penetration, as illustrated in Figure 6-2.

One conclusion from this analysis is that there is no such thing as "the" return on investment from a program. ROI is a useful concept for planning a program, because it can help a purchaser determine the size of program that he or she wants to sponsor ("penetration"). As Figure 6-2 shows, ROI will differ at different levels of penetration; as does net savings. Maximum ROI and maximum net savings are seldom achieved at the same penetration level. Actual savings and outcomes will depend on many different factors, including random events that will be difficult for a purchaser to control. Purchasers often require guarantees as a condition of implementing a program, whereby the risk of the uncertain outcome is transferred to the vendor. Sometimes this risk is priced into the cost of a program, sometimes not.

PLANNING AN INTERVENTION PROGRAM USING THE VALUE CHAIN

Value chain analysis,[4] developed by Professor Michael Porter of Harvard University, is a useful tool in planning and managing care management

4. See M. Porter, *Competitive Advantage: Creating and Sustaining Superior Performance*, New York: Free Press, 1985 and J. F. Fitzgerald et al., "A case manager intervention to reduce readmissions," *Archives of Internal Medicine*, Vol. 154, No. 15, 1994, pp. 1721–1729.

programs. Breaking the disease management process into its strategic components is a useful exercise for several reasons:

1. Care management is a collection of different activities that call on expertise from different industries or backgrounds (e.g., information systems, analytics, consumer marketing, health education, behavioral psychology, clinical medicine, and pharmaceutical therapy). A program may combine these activities in different ways and different quantities. Program assessments are focused on total program outcomes, not on the effectiveness of or the contribution to the outcomes of the component parts. A value chain analysis provides a framework for analyzing the effectiveness or value of the different components, and how well they work as an integrated product.
2. The different combinations of components make care management a good candidate for "dose response"[5] analysis. For example, what components, in what quantities, applied to which patients (members), add the most value to the final outcome? However, in order to do so, an analytical structure is necessary so that components of the "dose" and "response" may be identified. The care management industry has been slow to adopt consistent definitions of the components of care management that will allow different vendors and approaches to be compared.
3. The evolution of the disease management industry over the approximately 20 years of its existence has been one of rather large and sudden swings. In the 1990s, the disease management industry was dominated by in-house programs or those offered by pharmaceutical companies. In the early 2000s, the industry experienced a rapid shift from in-house to outsourced programs as commercial insurers, employers, and state Medicaid plans all demanded programs, and recognized that the components necessary to build a successful program were beyond the capabilities of the typical payer. So great was the growth that the cost of disease management services in a typical health plan

5. The dose response relationship describes the change in effect on an organism caused by differing levels of exposure (or dose) to a stressor (usually a drug, but may also be an intervention such as disease management). Studying dose response and developing dose response models in drug therapy is central to determining appropriate and safe dosage. In disease management, studying dose response helps determine what aspects of the program are effective, with which patients, and in what volume.

became (in some plans), for a while, the largest single outsourcing cost faced by the plan. Between 2000 and 2006, it was unusual to find a large payer that performed its own disease management in house. Use of a single outsourced vendor by a payer, however, resulted in the payer purchasing the vendor's "bundle" of components whether or not the vendor was providing these in the appropriate quantity or mix and whether or not the vendor provided "best of breed" services for each component. Service providers did not report in a way that enabled a purchaser to determine whether all components were equally efficient, and, if appropriate, to substitute a different service model or even a different provider for specific services. While this model was successful for some program sponsors, it did not contribute to transparency and understanding of the importance of individual components and elements of the program value chain. The result was that, by about 2006, plans that had previously outsourced their programs began to look very carefully at the value that the programs were delivering, and many plans began once again to provide some or all of the components of their programs in house.

4. The bundling of outsourced disease management components makes it difficult to compare performance between vendors, or to study the "dose response" effect of using different configurations of components. Occasionally, a vendor will publish results in this area, such as Health Dialog's analysis of its "Deeper Dive" program, but these analyses are rare. Attempts to standardize, or at least define, the components of a disease management program in order to be able to make comparisons between programs or vendors have met with little success in the industry, although, as the industry matures, these attempts may be more frequent.

As we apply the value chain concept to care management, we deconstruct the process into six components, each of which triggers the next component. These components are illustrated in Figure 6-3. In addition, typically there are a number of support services (information systems, human resources, and the like) without which an entity cannot operate.

Whether a program operates in house or is outsourced, a program sponsor will need to understand the detailed components of the program and be able to benchmark its own (or its vendor's) performance for each component. Typically, vendor reporting has focused on the end results (ROI or clinical outcomes). The value chain helps the program sponsor

FIGURE 6-3

Components of the Care Management Value Chain

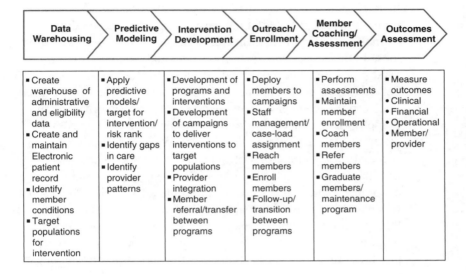

Data Warehousing	Predictive Modeling	Intervention Development	Outreach/ Enrollment	Member Coaching/ Assessment	Outcomes Assessment
▪ Create warehouse of administrative and eligibility data ▪ Create and maintain Electronic patient record ▪ Identify member conditions ▪ Target populations for intervention	▪ Apply predictive models/ target for intervention/ risk rank ▪ Identify gaps in care ▪ Identify provider patterns	▪ Development of programs and interventions ▪ Development of campaigns to deliver interventions to target populations ▪ Provider integration ▪ Member referral/transfer between programs	▪ Deploy members to campaigns ▪ Staff management/ case-load assignment ▪ Reach members ▪ Enroll members ▪ Follow-up/ transition between programs	▪ Perform assessments ▪ Maintain member enrollment ▪ Coach members ▪ Refer members ▪ Graduate members/ maintenance program	▪ Measure outcomes • Clinical • Financial • Operational • Member/ provider

understand the contribution of individual components to this end result, and to be able to develop reporting that identifies shortcomings.

MEASURING CARE MANAGEMENT SAVINGS OUTCOMES

There is no single, agreed-on methodology for measuring financial savings in the industry. However, in the course of performing or evaluating a care management study, it is important to understand the following common actuarial issues that may impact the results.

Evaluating the Savings of a Program

Three issues should be considered when evaluating financial outcomes of a program:

1. Has the measurement been performed according to a valid methodology?
2. How has that methodology been applied in practice? In other words, what assumptions, adjustments and calculation processes have been used to prepare the results?

3. Are the results arithmetically correct? Have data processing, arithmetic, or calculation errors been made in the preparation of results?

Before we discuss evaluation of savings calculations, we define two terms that are important in this area: *causality* and *methodology.*

Causality

Causality is an important concept in both scientific and commercial studies of disease management outcomes. Just because savings are associated with a program does not necessarily mean that these savings are the result of the program. Attributing causality to an intervention program is a difficult problem, and one that has not been much studied in the field of care management outcomes. Research to date has been focused on attempts to obtain an accurate estimate of savings no matter the source. Because of the difficulties inherent in proving causality, commercial purchasers of care management programs usually are satisfied with a weaker standard of proof—"demonstration" of savings—rather than proof of causality.

What is a "Methodology"?

Methodology is a term frequently used but rarely defined in outcomes studies. The definition of a methodology is "a body of methods, rules and postulates employed by a discipline: a particular procedure or set of procedures" (*Merriam-Webster Unabridged Dictionary Online*). What distinguishes a methodology from a calculation technique, however, is the fact that a methodology stands alone and can be implemented alone. A technique (such as an adjustment for age or for trend) does not stand on its own but is rather an input to a methodology.

Principles of Measurement Design: What Constitutes a Valid Methodology?

Evaluation of a methodology is a different problem than the evaluation of the results of an analysis. The former is a question of conformance to evaluation principles, while in the latter case we evaluate whether or not the author's hypothesis is rejected.

Whether designing an analysis from scratch, or evaluating a published study, the same principles determine whether a methodology is likely to be judged acceptable.

- Use a reference population. Any outcome's measurement requires a reference population against which to evaluate the statistic of interest. The reference population could be an equivalent (but different) population, or even the same population measured at a different point in time, with suitable adjustment.

- Ensure equivalence. To ensure validity in outcomes measurement, the reference population's measures should be equivalent to those of the intervention population.
- Use consistent statistics. The comparison needs to measure the same statistic, the same way, in the reference and intervention populations.[6]
- Avoid irrelevant and potentially confounding data. At its most extreme, this may imply measurement only of what the program is charged with managing. The average disease management program, for example, is usually only responsible for a limited subset of conditions, claims, and patients, not the entire health plan population or even all claims of the chronic population.
- Control the exposure. Assign each member to appropriate measurement categories for each month of exposure.
- Reconcile the results. The data going into an evaluation should be controlled (i.e., reconciled to a valid or published source). The outcomes, too, should be reconciled to a valid source and should be plausible. An example often cited, implausible savings outcomes, consists of studies that show all or almost all of the cost incurred in an asthmatic population being reduced by a disease management program. We shall discuss the importance of plausibility in more detail later.

In addition to the requirement for scientific rigor that may be necessary for an academic paper, commercial purchasers of care management are likely to have additional requirements:

- The methodology must be one that a purchaser (or its consultant) is familiar with, or at least can grasp readily, and that should be perceived in the marketplace as sound.
- The methodology must be documented in sufficient detail for another practitioner to replicate the analysis, and, if required, allow the client to be able to replicate the savings

6. For example, if the measured statistic is claims per member per month, this measurement should be performed the same way in both the baseline and intervention period, including identification of members, number of months of run-out, etc.

estimates themselves (or at least major components of the calculation).

- The results of the application of the methodology must be consistent with the client's savings expectations and be plausible overall.
- The application should lead to stable results over time and between clients, with differences between different studies and clients that can be explained.
- The methodology must be practical, that is, it must be possible to implement it cost-effectively, without significant commitment of resources relative to the potential benefit being measured.

Issues in Outcomes Evaluations

We discuss here some issues that are frequently encountered in program evaluations.

Regression to the Mean

Many before-and-after evaluations that use the patient as the unit of measurement (so-called "prepost" or "patient as their own control" designs) ignore the phenomenon that the outcomes of patients in period $t + 1$ (evaluation or measurement period) are very often influenced by the patient's state in the prior period t. Specifically, a high percentage of high-cost patients in period t are no longer high-cost in period $t + 1$.

The graph in Figure 6-4 illustrates the phenomenon of regression to the mean at the level of the individual member.

Depending on when this individual's experience begins to be tracked for the purpose of measurement, regression to the mean may be observed in the claims data. For example, if the identifying event for a disease management program is the hospitalization claim that occurred in Quarter 3, and this claim is included in costs before the start of the program, comparison with post-intervention experience will show lower cost. The reduced cost may incorrectly be attributed to the program, when, in fact, the cost reduction is the result of the natural course of the individual's illness, recovery and claims experience. This phenomenon is illustrated in Figure 6-5 (page 161). In this example, an individual member is identified (through claims) and enrolled in a program. The experience before the member's enrollment (the enrollment is indicated by the vertical line) is included in the "Pre" experience; the experience after enrollment is included in the "Post" experience.

FIGURE 6-4

Regression to the Mean at the Level of the Individual Member

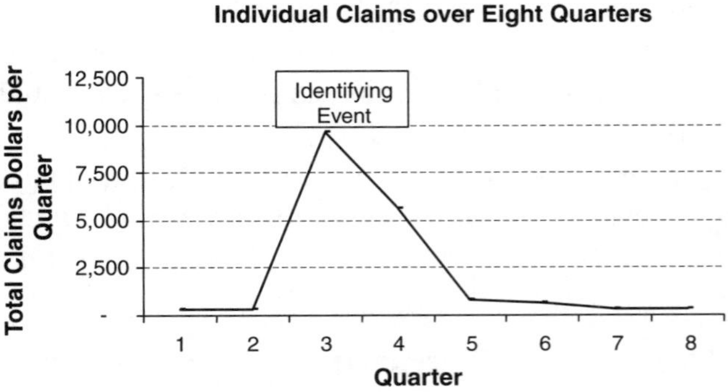

It is often assumed that, because individual-member-level regression (as illustrated above) is present, the entire population experience will exhibit the same phenomenon. This is not necessarily the case, however. Many studies are performed on a population basis without adjustment for regression to the mean, based on the observation that the distribution of increases and decreases in costs is random in a large group. A group of individuals all identified at the same time through a sentinel event (e.g., a hospitalization) will exhibit regression to the mean; an entire population, consisting of members identified at different times or stages of disease may or may not exhibit regression. Some of this effect is illustrated in Table A6.1-1 in Appendix 6.1.

A related issue is that of duration of illness. In a perfect world, we would know when every member first becomes chronic and could track members by durational cohort. In reality, we can only measure duration since first identification in the population (given that identification takes place through claims). Because utilization and cost increase with duration of illness, some actuaries make a durational adjustment in the calculation to allow for changes in the mix of duration of illness over time, adjusting if there is a change in that mix.

Establishing Uniform Risk Measure for Comparability

Below, we list some specific risk factors that must be considered in any measurement calculation and which should be reported in order to ensure

FIGURE 6-5

Regression to the Mean at the Level of the Individual Member "Pre" and "Post" Program Enrollment

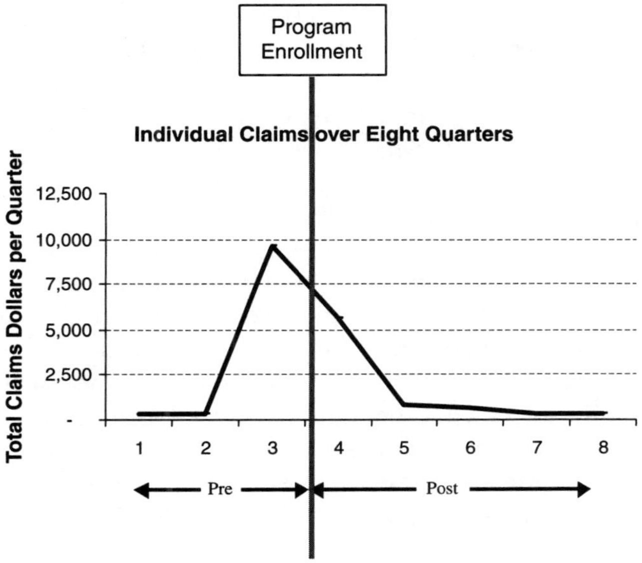

comparability and reproducibility of results. In any study, various characteristics of the reference and intervention groups must be evaluated, so that the effect of the intervention on outcomes can be properly assessed. Statistical techniques (beyond the scope of this chapter) may be used to adjust for differences, if needed. At the least, information should be given regarding the risk factor and its potential effect. The eight variables listed below are referred to by economists and epidemiologists as "confounding variables." Benefits managers may know them as "risk factors," and may be accustomed to allowing for them in pricing or underwriting health insurance coverage.

1. Demographic variables
2. Exclusionary conditions that exclude certain members
3. Exclusionary conditions that exclude certain claims
4. Persistency
5. Disease and risk factor prevalence and risk classification
6. Severity of illness
7. Contactability
8. Operational Issues

Patient Selection Bias

If evaluation of a program is performed other than through a randomized trial, there is always a potential problem of selection bias. Authors are divided about whether it is possible to adjust for bias. One of the most common sources of bias in evaluation is a study design that limits evaluations to those members who enroll in a voluntary program, and compares them with those who do not enroll. By definition, those members who elect to enroll in a voluntary program must represent a different risk profile those members who do not elect to enroll—at the very least, they demonstrate a difference in their readiness to change behavior.

Members may drop out of a follow-up study for a number of reasons, and are another example of self-selection: voluntary exit, termination from the health plan, transfer to a different group or product, or death. These factors can affect the outcomes. Within the enrolled group, the follow-up with different members is also potentially anti-selective; some patients will stay in a telephonic intervention program for the prescribed duration, while others will drop out because they are feeling better or for other reasons. Program sponsors should be aware that there is no consistent definition within the industry of participation in and graduation from a program, which makes comparisons between different programs more challenging.

AN ACTUARIAL METHODOLOGY FOR ASSESSING SAVINGS

A method that is prevalent in the disease management industry, and which has application to other programs, is an "adjusted historical control" methodology. We call this an "actuarial" methodology because it uses trend to adjust an historic period's experience and compares it with that of the intervention period. An example of an application of this methodology is provided below.

Example of a Savings Calculation

In this example, we apply the data assembled in Table 6-3. The calculation is shown in Table 6-4. The avoided admissions (equal to measured period admissions less baseline period admissions) are multiplied by an average cost per admission to generate overall dollar savings. The average cost per admission may be observed directly from the nonchronic population in the measurement period, or may be estimated by trending forward an average

TABLE 6-3

Basic Data Used in the Calculation

	Baseline Period	Measurement Period
Period	1/1/2008–12/31/2008	1/1/2009–12/31/2009
Average total population	150,000	150,000
Average chronic population	50,000	50,000
Chronic member months	600,000	600,000
Chronic population inpatient admissions	30,000	28,800
Chronic population inpatient admissions per 1000 per year	600.0	576.0
Cost per admission	$7,500	$8,000
Utilization (admission) trend (derived from an external source, e.g., the "nonchronic" population)	—	5.3%

cost per admission from the baseline period, using a suitable admission unit cost trend.

Once the calculation has been completed, the savings are validated and reconciled to the underlying cost. To test the reasonability of the result, compare the calculated savings with the underlying cost of the population. Assuming that the underlying cost of a Medicare population ranges between $6,000 and $8,000 per member per year, for 150,000 members,

TABLE 6-4

Example of a Savings Calculation

Estimated Savings due to Averted Admissions =		
Baseline Admissions/1,000 × Utilization Trend		600.0 × 1.053 = 631.8
Minus:	Actual Admissions/1,000/year	576.0
Equals:	Reduced Admissions/1,000/year	55.8
Multiplied by:	Actual member years in measurement period/1000	50.0
Equals:	Total reduced admissions	2,790.0
Multiplied by:	Trended unit cost/admission	$8,000
Equals:	Estimated Savings due to Averted Admissions	$22,320,000

the total population cost will be $900,000,000 to $1.2 billion. While estimated savings of $22.3 million from a program in the chronic population may seem high in absolute terms, relative to the total cost of the Medicare population, the savings represent 1.9 percent to 2.5 percent, which is consistent with results from other studies of this type.

Plausibility, a method that is widely used as a check on the results of a savings calculation, is discussed later in the chapter.

The Importance of Trend

The importance of trend in the calculation should be obvious from the above example. A small change in the measured (or assumed) trend can have a significant effect on the estimated savings. Trend is the rate of increase in per-member per-month cost, or the difference between year two and year one costs per member per month, divided by year-one cost per member per month. Trend may be defined on a calendar-year or on any 12-month basis, and, with appropriate adjustment, may be annualized to a 12-month period.

A study that compares observed trends in commercial chronic and nonchronic populations by Bachler, Duncan, and Juster[7] found that, under some chronic identification methodologies, a "migration bias" may be present that results in lower trend being observed in the chronic population than either the nonchronic population or the overall population. Therefore, adjustment of historical observed claims per member per month by nonchronic or population savings could result in an upward bias in the estimated savings. The authors found that one way to avoid this bias is to retroactively identify the chronic population (i.e., all members who ever meet the chronic criteria are included in the chronic population from the beginning of the study). Other potential corrections identified by the authors are the application of requalification (i.e., members who do not continue to meet qualifying criteria on an annual basis are eliminated from the chronic population) and a risk score adjustment.

Size of Population and Credibility

As programs have been applied to conditions with smaller prevalence, and to smaller employer populations, the issue of population and credibility of

7. R. Bachler, I. Duncan, and I. Juster, "A comparative analysis of chronic and nonchronic insured commercial member cost-trends," *North American Actuarial Journal*, Vol. 10, No. 4, 2006, pp. 76–89.

outcomes has become more prominent. A paper by Farah and others[8] provides guidance in terms of the credibility of the outcomes of different size populations. Only the largest employer populations are of a sufficient size that their financial results can be considered credible without adjustment. Financial results of smaller employers are unlikely to be credible, but if utilization outcomes are measured, results of smaller employer populations may be credible. Appendix 6.1 contains examples of relative group size requirements for financial and utilization credibility.

Validation of Savings Calculations

In addition to the obvious validation of the data by tying claims and membership to a reliable source, the actuary may wish to review utilization data to ensure that these are trending in line with the calculated savings. For example, because disease management achieves its effect through reductions in hospitalizations and specialist visits, while increasing drug and primary care provider utilization, changes in utilization measures should be consistent with this pattern. A related technique that has achieved prominence is the use of plausibility analysis. This technique essentially tracks changes in utilization between the pre- and post-period of a program, comparing the measured (dollar) savings with the savings implied by reduction in utilization.

Plausibility analysis requires the calculation of the following statistic (the plausibility factor) for the entire health plan:

$$1 - \frac{\text{Disease-specific admissions}/1{,}000\ \text{(program year)}}{\text{Disease-specific admissions}/1{,}000\ \text{(baseline year)}}$$

A small positive value of the plausibility statistic implies that there has been an overall reduction in admissions. This reduction should be consistent with the claimed (dollar) savings from the program. We can apply this technique to the data in Table 6-4.

$$\text{Plausibility factor} = \left(1 - \frac{576}{600}\right) = 0.04$$

If a vendor had claimed savings of $22.3 million without supporting evidence, a quick calculation of the plausibility factor would demonstrate that indeed a positive reduction in admissions had occurred.

8. J.R. Farah et al., "Random fluctuations and validity in measuring disease. management effectiveness for small populations," *Population Health Management*, Vol. 11, No. 6, 2008, pp. 307–316.

The use and the limitations of utilization-based measures, however, need to be clearly understood. Plausibility factors, being utilization based, are a special case of the more general example of causality demonstration using changes in utilization. They deserve closer scrutiny, however, because they are being promoted, and are becoming accepted, as demonstrating validity. However, the factors themselves have never been subjected to the type of scrutiny that has been applied to calculation methodologies.

Use of Plausibility Factors

The theory of plausibility factors use is that they independently validate the measured financial results of a savings calculation by demonstrating that utilization is reduced by the intervention, consistent with the financial measurement. Plausibility factors generally are utilization rates per 1,000 of the overall population for hospital admissions and emergency room visits for the primary diagnoses that are targeted by the program. The proposed interpretation of the plausibility measures is that if the savings calculation results in positive savings but the utilization-based measures do not, the savings are not validated. Rather than reconciling the two contradictory results, the plausibility factors are so dispositive that their results always trump any other outcomes calculation.

How Valid Is the Utilization-based Calculation?

In order to be a valid test of the outcomes of a savings calculation, utilization-based measures must be calculated on the same basis as the savings. With plausibility factors, this is not the case. The plausibility factors are a poor validator for the following reasons:

1. In a disease management evaluation, the measurement population is carefully constructed to consist of members with sufficient eligibility to be enrolled and managed by the program and to exclude members and conditions that may confound the calculation. As calculated, the plausibility factors bear only a tenuous relationship to the population being managed and measured. Their use implicitly assumes comparability between populations, but this comparability is not demonstrated.

2. Because they apply to admissions and ER visits for primary diagnoses only, plausibility factors represent a very small percentage of all admissions and costs for chronic patients. For example, within a commercial population, these admissions and ER visits only account for 3 percent of the total claims costs for members with diabetes and the admissions only account for approximately 7 percent of inpatient spend. Even a very successful program that avoided 25 percent of diabetes admissions could never demonstrate enough savings to justify program costs under this methodology. Therefore, by definition, purchasers must be assuming that the program beneficially affects other utilization measures of the population. So failure to demonstrate reduction in the direct utilization measures does not necessarily imply lack of success with other types of utilization.
3. Plausibility factors do not take account of the risk profile of a population. For example, it is entirely possible that from one year to the next a new group of relatively high-risk members may replace a relatively low-risk group, increasing the measured chronic admission rate per 1,000.
4. The plausibility factors take no account of volatility in admission rates.
5. The plausibility factors, unlike the underlying adjusted historical control methodology, take no account of underlying trends in the population. While admission trends are low (lower than overall trend), they are still nonzero. To understand this point, consider Table 6-5, which reports the actual discharges per 1,000 for selected chronic conditions for Medicare patients between 1998 and 2007. Over the nine-year period, the average trend in admissions for all chronic conditions except renal failure and syncope is negative. Trends in individual years deviated from the average, increasing in the early part of the 21st century, indicating the volatility in admission rates per 1,000.

Figure 6-6 illustrates the important point that the underlying discharge trend present in the population (which may well be negative) will need to be taken into consideration in plausibility analysis. However, much as the program sponsor may wish to avoid the issue of trend, as with the adjusted historical control method, plausibility analysis requires consideration of and adjustment for trend.

TABLE 6-5

Medicare Discharges per 1,000 by Condition

(DRG)	294	316	096	088	132–144	141–142
Year	Diabetes	Renal Failure	Bronchitis and Asthma	COPD	Heart	Syncope
1998	2.214	2.455	1.597	10.254	17.954	3.283
1999	2.187	2.566	1.773	10.617	17.738	3.367
2000	2.280	2.768	1.470	9.925	18.744	3.608
2001	2.458	3.001	1.352	10.047	19.949	3.915
2002	2.516	3.174	1.428	10.275	19.682	4.089
2003	2.450	3.984	1.385	10.335	18.706	4.259
2004	2.425	4.498	1.276	9.564	19.320	4.230
2006*	2.267	5.632	1.217	8.878	15.976	4.001
2007†	2.172	6.105	1.128	8.295	15.270	n/a
Annualized Trend	–0.2%	10.7%	–3.8%	–2.3%	–1.8%	2.5%

Source: Medicare and Medicaid Statistical Supplements, various years. Available at www.CMS.gov.

* 2005 data are not available.

† In 2007, a major redefinition of DRGs was introduced, resulting in post-2007 discharges being inconsistent with the earlier series. Results for 2007 are based on the reported (nine-month) data for this year. Annualized trends are calculated based on the change between initial and final years.

IMPLICATIONS FOR THE FUTURE

The evolution of care management programs and their likely future under health care reform suggests more, rather than fewer, potential interventions and programs. In the "new world" of managed care, benefits professionals cannot work alone, and need to become much better educated in a number of different subjects, including epidemiology, statistics, and clinical topics. The traditional focus of benefits management has been on health care services (hospital, prescription drugs, physician, etc.). The change in focus from services to members and their conditions is shifting attention to the conditions that drive service utilization.

FIGURE 6-6

Trends in Selected Discharges per 1,000 in Medicare Patients

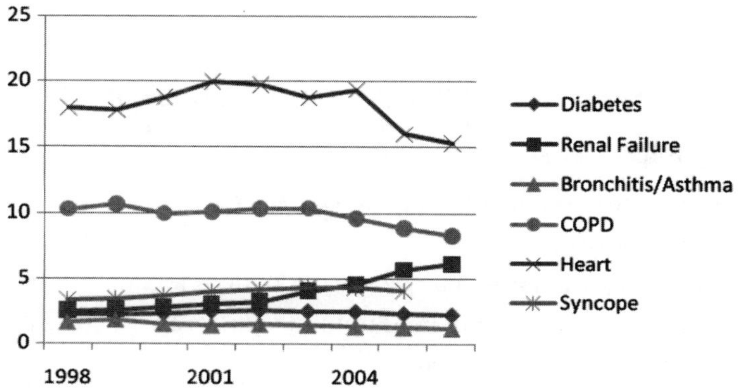

It is also clear that the new world of benefits management will require application of techniques that are well accepted in other areas but that are new to health-benefits management, including risk adjustment, direct marketing, behavior change and outcomes measurement.

APPENDIX 6.1

TECHNICAL ASPECTS

DEFINITION OF RETURN ON INVESTMENT

Define the following quantities:

Rate of return on investment (ROI) = R

Internal rate of return = i

Evaluation period = n (may be greater than or less than 1 year)

Savings attributable to the program in year $t = S_t$

Cost of the program attributable to year $t = C_t$

Both costs and benefits are measured during a measurement period, although the two periods need not be of the same duration (start-up costs, for example, are typically incurred prior to the beginning of enrollment and well before the emergence of savings from interventions). Because costs are incurred differently in different time periods, costs may be "annualized" and, for example, start-up costs amortized over the life of the program.

Mathematically, the rate of return on investment (R) is defined as follows:

$$R = \frac{\sum_1^n S_t/(1+i)^t}{\sum C_t/(1+i)^t}$$

When the period of measurement is not one year, adjustments should be made to the formula. This expression applies equally when $t < 1$, although the validity of results becomes increasingly less reliable for shorter durations. More usually, ROI is calculated for one year only and the expression becomes:

$$R = S/C$$

REGRESSION TO THE MEAN

In Table A6.1-1, 82.6 percent of Year 1 low-cost members remain in the same category in Year 2, with approximately the same average cost. Regression to the mean is illustrated by the migration of the 1.8 percent of members who were high cost in Year 1: 11 percent of these members are

TABLE A6.1-1

Migration Between Risk Levels

Baseline Year		Subsequent Year		
Baseline Year Cost Group	**Baseline Percentage Membership**	**Low: <$2,000**	**Moderate: $2,000–$24,999**	**High: ≥$25,000**
Low: <$2,000	69.5%	57.4%	11.7%	0.4%
Moderate: $2,000–$24,999	28.7%	9.9%	17.7%	1.1%
High: ≥$25,000	1.8%	0.2%	0.9%	0.6%
TOTAL	100.0%	67.6%	30.3%	2.2%

Source: Solucia Consulting data; Baseline year 2005.

low cost in Year 2, 50 percent migrate to the moderate-cost group, and only one-third remain high cost. Overall, the proportion of low-cost members falls slightly (to 67.6 percent from 69.5 percent), while the proportion of moderate- and high-cost members rises. This analysis represents a closed cohort; if we were to allow for members to terminate and be replaced by new entrants who are more likely to be low cost, the distribution of costs would show even less variation from year to year. In summary, the phenomenon of regression to the mean is real, and should be considered in evaluating a study, but simply because it may be observed at the individual member level does not mean that it necessarily is present in an entire population.

DEFINITION OF HEALTH CARE TREND

Trend from period t to period $t + 1$ is defined as follows:

$$\text{Trend} = \frac{\text{Pmpm}_{t+1} - \text{Pmpm}_t}{\text{Pmpm}_t}$$

$$\text{Pmpm}_t = \frac{\sum_{j=1}^{12} \sum_{i=1}^{n_j} C_{ij}}{\sum_{j=1}^{12} n_j}$$

where

Pmpm_t is the monthly per member per month health care cost

C_{ij} is the claims (or utilization, or other statistic being measured) of the *i*th member in the *j*th month

n_j is the number of members enrolled in the *j*th month

EXAMPLES OF CREDIBILITY OF OUTCOMES OF DIFFERENT SIZE POPULATIONS AND EXPECTED LEVELS OF SAVINGS

Figure A6.1-1 plots outcomes confidence levels, in terms of standard deviations (SDs) from the mean, versus population size.

FIGURE A6.1-1

Outcomes Confidence Levels for Different Size Populations (Utilization)

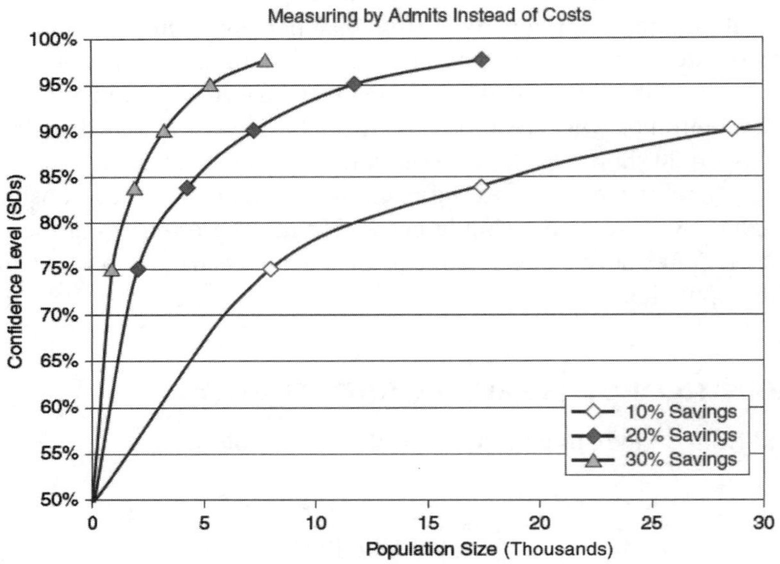

CHAPTER 7

Consumer-Driven Health Plans

Diane S. Luedtke

Many public and private employers are embracing consumer-driven health plans (CDHPs) in the continuing quest for better ways to control spiraling health plan costs. CDHPs add a new dimension to the health care cost equation. Traditional managed care programs focus on the provider or supply side of health care, relying on discounted provider networks and care management intervention programs. Consumer-driven plans recognize the value of engaging the health care consumer to further contain costs. By incorporating the consumer into the equation, consumer-driven plans attack cost and utilization problems from both the provider/supply and the patient/demand sides.

CDHPs operate on the premise that individuals will become better health care consumers if given the proper information tools and financial incentives. Individuals who have a greater financial stake in health care decisions will consider more carefully whether the care is needed and shop more judiciously for that care. The concept is consistent with the belief that employees must take some measure of personal responsibility in maintaining a healthy lifestyle and become more engaged consumers of health care.

The typical CDHP includes a high-deductible health insurance plan and an individually controlled health account, in the form of either a health

This chapter is partly based on the chapter titled "Consumer-Driven Health Care" in the 6th Edition of *The Handbook of Employee Benefits*, authored by Martha Priddy Patterson.

savings account (HSA) or a health reimbursement arrangement (HRA). Pairing a high-deductible plan with an individually controlled account encourages financially responsible decisions. CDHPs using HRAs were offered beginning in 2001. HSA-based plans followed in 2004.

In addition to financial incentives, consumer-driven plans typically provide information and decision-making tools regarding health care cost and quality, thereby empowering employees to make informed health care decisions. Cost transparency, quality information, and online decision tools are vital to the success of consumer-driven health care.

Since their introduction, CDHPs have experienced substantial growth. As more employers have adopted CDHPs, sufficient experience has emerged to draw some conclusions about the success of CDHPs in fulfilling their promise to better manage health care costs and change consumer behavior.

WHY CONSUMER-DRIVEN HEALTH CARE?

Health care now accounts for more than one-sixth of the U.S. economy.[1] Yet, the purchaser often has little regard for or understanding of its costs, and relatively minimal financial responsibility. The typical health care consumer is unlikely to question the price or consider the value of the services received, making it unnecessary for health care providers to compete on price and quality the way most other industries do. Many health-policy economists and other experts believe this disconnect between the users of health care and those who pay for that care is a key contributor to the overutilization of health care services and rising health care costs. They point out, as seen in Figure 7-1, that in the early 1970s, individuals paid almost 35 percent of health care costs and health care as a percentage of gross domestic product (GDP) was about 6 percent. By 2008, individuals paid only about 12 percent of costs and health care represented almost 16 percent of GDP. In fact, as consumer out-of-pocket spending consistently decreased over time, health care costs consistently increased.

Private health insurance and other private funds currently pay for 40 percent of health care expenses, most of which is covered by employers. Medicare and Medicaid and other state and local programs pay for 48 percent, leaving individuals paying for the remaining 12 percent of

1. CMS, *National Health Expenditure Data*, 2010.

FIGURE 7-1

Total Health Care Spend as Percentage of GDP versus Consumer Out-of-Pocket Spend as Percentage of Total

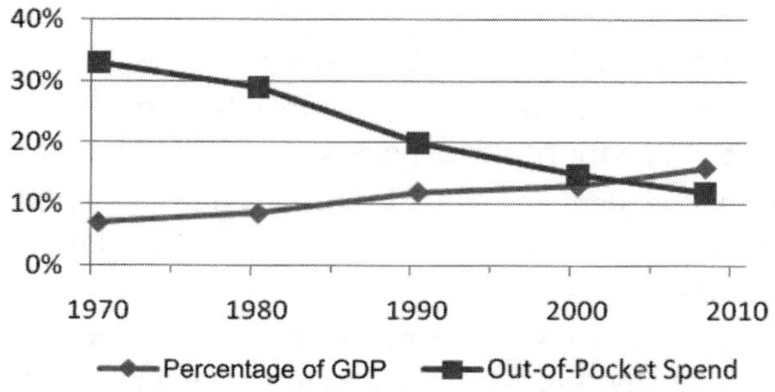

Source: CMS, National Health Expenditure Data, 2010.

health care costs.[2] Consumer-driven health care proponents argue that until individuals pay for these costs more directly, there is little impetus for individuals to be actively involved in cost decisions or for the health care industry to control costs.

Consumer-driven health care gives consumers a greater stake in the health care cost equation and empowers them to make informed decisions. But will individuals actually take responsibility and make the effort to drive their health decisions? The experiences with smoking and drunk driving in the past few decades suggest that publicity along with a change in social mores actually can achieve better individual health behavior. Public information campaigns driven by determined individuals as well as organizations considerably reduced smoking and its resulting diseases and reduced drunk driving and its deaths and injuries. These campaigns certainly did not end these health hazards, nor did they lead to a net reduction in health costs, but they did reduce the hazards and slowed the rate of cost increases.

Proponents assert that as health care consumers become financially responsible for more of the real cost of health care services and receive more information on treatments available, possible outcomes, and the quality of the health care provider, they will be empowered and motivated to purchase more efficient and effective health care. The changes in consumer behavior will then reduce both demand and long-term health expense.

2. Ibid.

KEY COMPONENTS

CDHPs must engage and inform individuals on the issues of health care costs by providing information on cost, quality, and outcomes, thereby challenging the notion that more expensive health care is better care. CDHPs come in various forms, with most typically including the following elements:

- A high-deductible health plan (HDHP)
- An individual health account that may be carried over from year to year to pay for health expenses not covered by the HDHP
- Information sources and tools both to educate the individual on health issues and to find the highest quality health care providers at the lowest cost
- A communications program to enhance employee understanding of the plan and to encourage consumerism and healthy behaviors
- A conveniently accessible health "coach" or "consultant" to help plan participants obtain and use existing health information, answer questions about the individual's health issues, and provide guidance on use, choice, and interaction with health care providers
- In cases of serious chronic conditions or illnesses, a proactive medical professional who may contact the patient on a regular basis and act as liaison and coordinator among the patient and his or her medical providers

To date, most consumer-driven health care plan participants are in employer-sponsored health-benefit programs. The critical features of these plans are designed to educate employees as to the true cost of medical services and their role in managing health care spending. The plan designs have built-in incentives to give the employee freedom in medical purchasing decisions and hold the employee more financially responsible for those decisions. But, importantly, these plans provide clinical and financial information enabling employees to be true health care consumers and to shop for the best "deal." While not unique to CDHPs, most also provide proactive clinical management and coaching to optimize provider efficiencies and courses of treatment.

PLAN DESIGN BASICS

CDHPs typically combine a high-deductible health plan with one of two types of individually controlled accounts that can be used to pay

FIGURE 7-2

Sample CDHP Plan Design

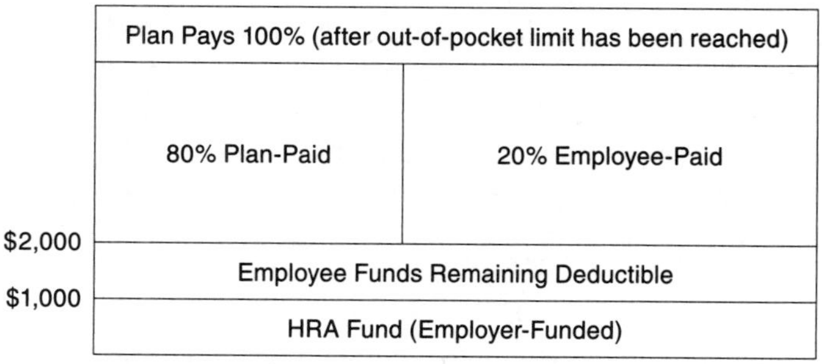

deductibles and other costs not covered by the high-deductible plan: a health savings account may involve both employee and employer contributions; a health reimbursement arrangement allows only employer contributions. These accounts are discussed in detail later in the chapter.

The basic plan structure provides first-dollar coverage through either an HRA or an HSA fund. The employee then bears full responsibility for the difference between the fund amount and the deductible. Once the deductible has been reached, the plan coinsurance and copayments apply. Figure 7-2 illustrates a sample HRA plan design. In the simplified example, the deductible is $2,000 and the employer contributes $1,000 to the employee's HRA fund. Once the HRA fund has been exhausted with payment of the first $1,000 of the deductible, the employee pays the next $1,000 of medical costs until the deductible is reached. Thereafter, the employee is responsible for 20 percent of costs until the out-of-pocket limit is reached. Typically, deductibles, fund contributions, coinsurance, and copayments would differ for single versus family coverage and in-network versus out-of-network services.

An HSA plan would have the same basic structure as the sample HRA plan. However, the HSA fund could include both employer and employee contributions. And, since unused HSA funds are carried over into future years, the total fund balance could grow to exceed the deductible over time.

CDHPs have no specific or legally required features. Neither the Employee Retirement Income Security Act (ERISA) nor federal tax law regulates these plans directly. However, federal law does define precisely how the tax-favored individual health savings accounts common to the

CDHPs must be structured.[3] Federal law also specifies minimum deductibles and maximum out-of-pocket limits for the high-deductible health plans that must accompany one of these individual health savings accounts if the accounts are to receive available tax benefits.[4]

Consumer-driven plans can be fully insured or self-insured. Likewise, there are no restrictions on the type of underlying plan. It could be a preferred provider organization (PPO) plan, a point-of-service (POS) plan, or even a health maintenance organization (HMO). There are many variations in plan design in the marketplace, especially among self-insured and HRA-based plans.

INDIVIDUALLY CONTROLLED HEALTH ACCOUNTS

A key element of consumer-driven health care includes a "personal account" under the control of the individual. This account can be used for health care expenses, including copayments, deductibles, health care items, or services not covered by the plan. These accounts can be structured in several ways and go by various names. However, to take full advantage of favorable tax treatment, most of these accounts will fall under one of three legally recognized accounts:

- Health flexible spending accounts or arrangements (FSAs)
- HRAs
- HSAs

Each of these accounts provides tax-advantaged reimbursement for qualified medical expenses as defined in Section 213(d) of the Internal Revenue Code. However, the Patient Protection and Affordable Care Act (PPACA) prohibits reimbursement for over-the-counter drugs, unless the drug is a prescribed drug or is insulin, in taxable years beginning after December 31, 2010. Each also provides some degree of employee control over health care spending decisions. Yet, each has distinctive benefits, features, and restrictions. While more than one type of account may be desirable to optimize

3. See IRC Sec. 223; Notices 2004–50, 2004–23, and 2004–25; Rev. Proc. 2004–22, Rev. Rul. 2004–38, and DOL FAB 2004 –1 (guidance on health savings accounts, created in the Medicare Modernization Act); and IRS Notice 2002–45 and Revenue Ruling 2002–41 (providing regulatory authorization of and establishing rules for health reimbursement arrangements).

4. IRC Sec. 223(c)(2).

benefits and tax advantages, there are rules governing the use of multiple accounts.[5]

As defined earlier, a CDHP involves an HDHP coupled with either an HRA or an HSA. However, an employee may be eligible for, and enrolled in, more than one type of account. The rules provide:

- An employee covered by a HDHP and either a health FSA or an HRA generally cannot make contributions, or have employer contributions made on their behalf, to an HSA. However, an employee can make contributions to an HSA while covered under an HDHP and a "limited purpose" FSA. Limited purpose FSAs cover expenses not otherwise covered by the plan, such as dental or vision care.
- An HRA participant may also have a general purpose FSA, although both accounts cannot be used for the same claim. The employer establishes the priority, which is outlined in the plan document.

Cafeteria Plan Health FSAs

Health FSAs have been popular since the 1980s and usually operate as part of a "cafeteria plan," as defined under the federal tax code, and so named because these plans allow an employer to offer employees a selection of various benefits. Health FSAs are funded on a pretax basis, usually through salary reduction. Amounts contributed to FSAs are not subject to Federal Insurance Contributions Act (FICA) or Federal Unemployment Tax Act (FUTA) taxes, adding another level of savings for the employer and the employee. The employee, however, may be ambivalent about the impact the FICA exemption has on future Social Security benefits. The big drawback with FSAs is the "use-it-or-lose-it" rule. Health FSAs do not allow unused balances to carry over from year to year. However, plans may permit a grace period of up to two and one-half months after the end of the plan year for remaining balances to be utilized.[6] The plan is not permitted to refund any unused balances left in the account. This "use-it-or-lose-it" feature of FSAs has long been recognized—and criticized—as punishing the "thrifty" employee and encouraging unnecessary health care spending.

5. *Health Savings Accounts and Other Tax-Favored Health Plans.* IRS Publication 969.
6. IRC Sec. 125(d)(12) and Treas. Reg. Sec. 1.125-2T Q&A 1(b), Prop. Reg. 125–1, Q&A-7.

Health Reimbursement Arrangements

A few employers began offering HRAs in 2001. By early 2002, the Internal Revenue Service (IRS) and its parent agency, the U.S. Department of Treasury, were besieged with insurance companies seeking guidance on the tax treatment of a high-deductible health insurance product that would be coupled with an annually funded health care account in which the unused balances could be carried over from year to year. These plans and accounts met with a sympathetic view. And as health care costs began to escalate again after a few years of relatively modest growth, the accounts seemed to make sense.

The IRS ruled that HRAs paid for solely by the employer and permitting unused amounts to be carried over from year to year would qualify as health benefits exempt from federal income taxes and employment taxes. But the IRS specifically prohibits the use of employee contributions. Contributions cannot be funded through employee salary deferrals under a cafeteria plan. HRAs are notional accounts, meaning they normally are not funded. Claims are paid as incurred, providing an attractive cash flow advantage to the employer.

HRAs can be used to pay for unreimbursed qualified medical expenses, as defined in Section 213(d) of the Internal Revenue Code. However, an employer may limit what expenses are eligible under the HRA. For example, an employer could restrict HRA reimbursements to include only those expenses eligible under the employer's medical plan. Alternatively, the employer could elect to allow HRA use for services not normally covered by the plan, such as dental and vision. The employer may also permit payment of Consolidated Omnibus Budget Reconciliation Act (COBRA) or retiree health care plan premiums from balances remaining at termination or retirement.

HRAs offered proponents of consumer-driven health care plans an opportunity to move forward. Yet these accounts had the considerable disadvantage of allowing only claim payments from employer dollars and did not provide any tax advantages to prefund health care expenses. Employees who needed more tax-favored money to pay out-of-pocket expenses could not supplement the employer account with pretax dollars.

Health Savings Accounts

Consumer-driven health care proponents were finally able to convince Congress that an account funded by employers or employees or both on essentially a tax-free basis could truly provide a boost to consumer-driven health care and increase participants' active involvement, because the participant would see the account as "my money," not the employer's. In 2003, as part of the Medicare Modernization Act (MMA), Congress adopted HSAs, and the first plans became available in 2004. The IRS moved quickly to provide additional guidance on their usage.

Health savings accounts are largely an extension of Archer Medical Savings Accounts (MSAs) that were first passed by Congress in 1997. MSAs could be offered only to small employers (fewer than 50 employees) and permitted balances to be carried forward from year to year if coupled with a high-deductible health insurance policy. No other health coverage could be offered by the employer. These accounts were not allowed to be established after 2007 and have essentially been replaced by HSAs.

When compared with an HRA or a traditional health care flexible spending account offered under a cafeteria plan, HSAs offer much more flexibility in funding and encourage participant savings for future medical expenses. An HSA provides triple tax savings: tax deductible contributions, tax-free interest on investment earnings, and tax-free distributions for qualified medical expenses.

HSA accounts are fully owned by the employee and have the advantage of portability. The employee has unfettered access to the funds, even for nonmedical purposes. However, distributions for reasons other than qualified medical expenses are subject to income tax as well as an additional 20 percent tax penalty.[7] Claim substantiation requirements differ for HSAs compared to HRAs and FSAs. Under HRAs and FSAs, medical expenses must be substantiated to the HRA or FSA administrator for reimbursement. HSA reimbursements may be made without submitting proof that the costs were incurred, but substantiation is required in case of audit.

Immediate employee ownership and access to funds for nonmedical purposes, while very attractive to employees, may make some employers reluctant to contribute to the account. Yet, employer contributions to the HSA are a good enticement for employees to enroll in an HSA-qualified plan. Unlike HRAs and health FSAs, which can be coupled with any type of health plan or can stand alone as the only employer health benefit, an HSA can be used only if it is coupled with a high-deductible plan that meets specific criteria as outlined in Table 7-1 below.

Table 7-1 compares the features of HSAs, HRAs, and the long-established health FSAs.

7. The penalty was increased from 10% to 20% effective January 1, 2011 as part of the PPACA.

TABLE 7-1

Comparison of Health Care Accounts

	Health Savings Account (HSA)	Health Reimbursement Arrangement (HRA)	Flexible Spending Account (FSA)
	Eligibility Requirements		
Who can set up an account	Individuals and employees covered by a qualified HDHP and no other health insurance, except specifically listed coverages. Cannot be enrolled in Medicare or claimed as a dependent on another's tax return.	Only employers.	Only employers.
	Health Plan Requirements		
Accompanying health plan requirements	HDHP must meet federal requirements. ■ Minimum deductible* $1,200—Self-only coverage $2,400—Family coverage ■ Maximum out-of-pocket* $5,950—Self-only coverage $11,900—Family coverage *2011 amounts; adjusted annually for inflation.	None. May be used with any type of health plan or as a stand-alone account.	None.
	Funding		
Who can contribute	Employers and employees.	Only employers.	Employers and employees.
Contribution limits	2011 limits, adjusted annually: $3,050—Self-only coverage $6,150—Family coverage Age 55 or older annual catch-up contribution for 2009 or later: $1,000.	No federal income tax law limits. Employers usually set limits	No required limits through 2012, although employer may impose limits. Beginning in 2013: $2,500 limit (indexed).
Carryover of unused balances	Yes. No annual or lifetime limits on the amount that can be carried over or accumulated.	Yes, subject to limits set by employer.	No.
Portability	Yes. Employees can keep their HSAs when they leave or change jobs.	No	No.

TABLE 7-1

	Health Savings Account (HSA)	Health Reimbursement Arrangement (HRA)	Flexible Spending Account (FSA)
Permissible Reimbursements			
Qualified medical expenses	Unreimbursed "qualified medical expenses," as defined in Section 213(d) of IRC (excluding over-the-counter drugs unless the drug is a prescribed drug or is insulin).	Same as HSAs.	Same as HSAs.
Health insurance premiums	HSAs generally may not pay health insurance premiums on a tax-favored basis, except under specific circumstances: ■ Any health plan coverage while receiving federal or state unemployment benefits ■ COBRA continuation coverage ■ Medicare premiums and out-of-pocket expenses	Yes.	No.
Long-term care insurance premiums	Yes.	Yes.	No.
Long-term care services	Yes.	No.	No.
Tax Treatment			
Employer contributions	Subject to funding limits, contributions are excludable from gross income and not subject to FICA or FUTA.	Excludable from gross income and not subject to FICA or FUTA.	Same as HSAs.
Individual contributions	Subject to funding limits, contributions are deductible even if the individual does not itemize deductions.	Employees cannot contribute to HRAs.	Employee contributions to health FSAs generally are made on a pretax, salary-reduction basis and are not subject to FICA.
Earnings on accounts	Earnings generally are not taxable, but may be subject to the IRC §511 unrelated business income tax rules.	Employers generally maintain HRAs as notional accounts, so there are no earnings.	Same as HRAs.

(continued)

TABLE 7-1 (continued)

	Health Savings Account (HSA)	Health Reimbursement Arrangement (HRA)	Flexible Spending Account (FSA)
Distributions	No income tax on medical reimbursements or on timely distributions of excess contributions. All other distributions are subject to federal income tax plus a 20% penalty tax, but no penalty tax is applied to distributions after the account beneficiary becomes Medicare-eligible or disabled, or dies.	Only to reimburse qualified medical expenses.	Only to reimburse qualified medical expenses.
Employer Compliance Issues			
ERISA	HSAs are generally not ERISA plans where employer involvement with the HSA is limited, per DOL Field Assistance Bulletins 2004-1 and 2006-02.	HRAs sponsored by employers subject to ERISA generally are ERISA plans.	Same as HRAs.
Nondiscrimination rules	HSA contributions made through a cafeteria plan are subject to cafeteria-plan nondiscrimination rules. Otherwise, employer HSA contributions must be comparable for similarly situated participants.	Subject to the general nondiscrimination requirements for self-insured medical expense reimbursement plans.	Subject to both the general nondiscrimination requirements for self-insured medical expense reimbursement plans and to cafeteria-plan nondiscrimination rules.
COBRA health continuation	Not subject to COBRA.	COBRA continuation coverage rules apply.	Same as HRAs.
Trust requirement	HSA assets must be held in a trust or custodial account.	No trust required.	Same as HRAs.

OTHER PLAN DESIGN CONSIDERATIONS

Individual employer plans vary greatly. The plan designs generally reflect the company size, benefit objectives, and strategy. The most successful plan designs achieve health care cost management while improving employee health and quality of care. Higher deductibles and larger accounts generate greater consumer engagement. In addition to establishing the basic parameters of the high-deductible plan and selecting an account type, other important plan design decisions include the following:

- Preventive care coverage
- Whether the CDHP is a full replacement plan or an option
- Employer contribution strategy
- HRA carryovers

Preventive Care

Preventive care is a critical piece of consumer-driven health care. An obvious and important premise of consumer-driven health care is that staying healthy is always cheaper—in both direct and indirect costs—than treating illness. Consequently, most CDHPs offer an initial health screening or physical at no, or very low, cost. If potential health issues are found, the plan may assign a "health coach" at that time. This coach, usually a nurse practitioner, will map out a suggested course of action. Depending on the nature of the health issue, this could range from a simple list of suggested health changes, such as weight reduction, change of diet, or more exercise, to immediate referral to a treating physician if the screening information suggests serious health issues. Immunizations, routine annual physicals or tests, and well-mother and well-baby visits are also a part of preventive care.

While this was previously a plan sponsor decision, the Patient Protection and Affordable Care Act (PPACA) now requires qualified health insurance plans to cover a broad list of recommended preventive services without cost sharing. However, this requirement does not apply to "grandfathered plans."[8]

Full Replacement versus Option

CDHPs are often offered as an option alongside one or more other health plans, especially by large employers. Initially, this has the advantage of making the employees comfortable with consumer-driven health care. Over time, enrollment may increase as the consumer-driven plan gains employee acceptance, or an employer may transition to offering a CDHP as the only

8. A "grandfathered plan" is generally a health plan that was in existence on March 23, 2010, and that has not made any changes that would result in a loss of grandfathered status.

available plan. Alternatively, an employer may introduce the CDHP as a full replacement plan. This approach is more common among small employers than large employers. However, adopting total replacement is increasingly common among large employers. The advantage to having a CDHP as the only medical plan is that it minimizes adverse selection and maximizes potential cost savings. The drawback is employee resistance to change.

Employer Contribution Strategy

Properly set employer contribution levels are vital to a consumer-driven program's success. This key component reflects employer objectives and affects employee acceptance, participation, and behavior. First, an employer must decide how much to contribute to the individual health fund. An important consideration is the relationship between the employer fund contribution and the deductible. Generally, employer account contributions will fund only a portion of the deductible, thus encouraging greater consumerism. The fund contribution may be set as a flat dollar amount or a percent of the deductible. Frequently, an employer will use part of the premium savings from introducing the high-deductible plan to fund the individual employee accounts. In the case of HSAs, employer contributions are optional and the accounts may be funded only by the employees. However, employer contributions to the fund provide a stronger enticement to participate.

Employer-established employee contribution levels will influence enrollment, especially in a choice environment. When employees have a choice between a CDHP and other non-CDHP plans, care must be taken in aligning the options. The potential for adverse selection exists whenever employees are given choices. Even though the CDHP may have a lower premium than other options, total plan costs may not be lower if only the best risks select that option. Employers often set CDHP contributions such that they compare favorably with other options. And, as with employee premium contributions and deductibles, employer fund contributions are often tiered by family status.

HRA Carryovers

An employer may permit the carryover of unused HRA balances to later years. The employer also has discretion over the amount that may be carried over. The "use-it-or-lose-it rule" of FSAs does not apply to HRAs. Former employees, including retirees, may be allowed continued access to unused balances. However, employers are not permitted to refund any part of the remaining balance to current or former employees. The funds may be used only to reimburse qualified medical expenses.

Despite the flexibility granted the employer in this element of plan design, permitting carryovers is generally a desirable feature. It is consistent with the key tenets of consumerism and strengthens the financial incentive to spend more carefully. It further differentiates HRAs from traditional FSAs, which encourage year-end spending to avoid losing unused balances.

PRICE AND QUALITY TRANSPARENCY

Information-based decisions help create good outcomes. Greater consumer involvement necessitates detailed and understandable health information about provider quality, costs, treatments, and best medical practices. The tools provided to evaluate cost and quality must be easy to use. Information technology and increasing transparency initiatives, aimed at making publicly available provider price and quality-of-care data, make gathering and managing medical information far easier than it was in the past. Employees often can access this information via their company's Website. Easier access and greater availability encourage plan members to actually use the information when they need it.

Various studies have been conducted to examine how available cost and quality data impacts consumer behavior. One such study was commissioned by the Department of Health and Human Services.[9] The study assessed the extent to which consumers use cost and quality information to find the highest-value provider, a key component of CDHPs. The analysis has two key findings. First, the study found that women and older, sicker individuals were more likely to use the information. Second, use of the information had the effect of lowering expenditures. Both total expenditures and out-of-pocket medical spending were reduced, while out-of-pocket pharmacy costs were not reduced. The authors conclude, "Although the results are quite early, they show promise and suggest that additional information on price and quality can indeed be processed by consumers to serve their interests in gaining more value from their health insurance benefits."[10]

---

9. Stephen Parente and Roger Feldman, *Continuation of Research on Consumer Directed Health Plans: Does Access to Transparent Provider and Cost Information Affect Health care cost and Utilization of Preventive Services?*, Office of Health Policy, ASPE (2008), Department of Health and Human Services, December 15, 2008.
10. Ibid.

COMMUNICATIONS AND INFORMATION

With the number of working pieces involved in consumer-driven health care and the potential for confusion, a key component of a successful CDHP is an effective employee communication and education program. Employers and their advisers will need to discipline themselves to forgo overly complicated plan designs that seek to maximize every tax advantage, in order to keep the plan understandable and user-friendly for the majority of their employees. Communications programs, important in any employee benefit context, are especially critical for consumer-driven plans.

A successful CDHP requires that the employee not only understand the mechanics of the plan, but also be empowered to make informed and cost-effective personal health care decisions. CDHPs hold employees more accountable for their own health and health care expenditures. Consequently, most plans offer some form of a health coach to help employees navigate the health care system. The "coach" may be an assigned individual, especially in cases of chronic or severe illnesses, or simply a toll-free number staffed by health professionals to answer general questions. The coach's services may range from providing a list of specialists in the member's area to suggesting a list of questions to take along to the annual physical. Information about the plan, its covered benefits, and required procedures can also be available electronically at all times and from various portals.

The most effective communication and education campaigns reach out to employees early and often. While the initial communications are critical to employee acceptance and understanding, ongoing communications are important to achieving and sustaining the behavior changes needed to make CDHP cost savings objectives possible.

POPULARITY AND GROWTH

Consumer-driven plans have shown significant growth in a relatively short period of time. Since their inception, CDHPs have grown steadily in both the percentage of firms offering the plans and total enrollment. Fifteen percent of firms offered a CDHP in 2010, and 13 percent of covered workers participated in one of these plans.[11] And, as the number of HSA account holders has grown, so have total HSA assets. Appendix 7.1 provides details on CDHP offer rates, enrollment figures, and assets and account balances.

11. Kaiser Family Foundation, *Employer Health Benefits 2010 Annual Survey*, pp. 144, 147.

EXPERIENCE AND EFFECTIVENESS

Debate has grown as more employers are turning to CDHPs as a way to restrain health care costs.[12] Proponents of consumer-driven health plans claim that benefit costs will be lowered if participants are given the proper financial incentives and information tools to become better health care consumers. Critics contend consumer-driven plans are simply high-deductible plans that shift cost to employees. They argue that while these plans may lower costs, it is because they are selected by healthier individuals. And, further, they question whether savings are at the expense of foregoing necessary care. Proponents respond that this criticism overlooks the intrinsic value of the account feature and its ability to induce greater employee engagement and financial responsibility. Questions regarding cost and quality of care are important ones for employers considering CDHPs. Many employers now have several years of CDHP experience, especially with HRAs, which were offered first. "Given this experience and the potential role of CDHPs as health care reforms are implemented, there is interest in the health status of those selecting HRAs and how these plans affect enrollees' health care spending and utilization compared with traditional plans."[13] Finally, enough data has emerged to draw some conclusions.

Numerous studies tout the positive results of CDHP experience. While it is easy to find published and advertised results, deciphering which studies are credible and reliable can be complicated. Many studies have been developed by market participants, who may be biased toward illustrating success of the plans. To address this issue, the American Academy of Actuaries commissioned a work group to perform a comprehensive review of several experience studies. From their independent analysis, the group selected those studies they considered best in terms of study design, methodology, detail and relevance. All studies selected accounted for selection bias or the impact of health status on the CDHP. The selected studies examined actual multiyear experience covering hundreds of thousands of plan members.[14] The studies meeting their selection criteria include the following:

- Making an Impact—Aetna Health Fund (2008)
- CIGNA Choice Fund: Two Year Experience Study, 2005–2006 (March 2008)

---

12. Diane Luedtke, "Cutting Costs, Not Care," *Navigator Benefit Solutions LLC, The Actuarial View*, June 2009, presented some of these findings.
13. Government Accountability Office (GAO), *Consumer-Directed Health Plans: Health Status, Spending and Utilization of Enrollees in Plans Based on Health Reimbursement Arrangements*, July 2010, page 2.
14. American Academy of Actuaries, *Emerging Data on Consumer-Driven Health Plans*, May 2009.

- UnitedHealth: Uniprise—2008 CDHP Results Discussion (March 2008)

In 2010, the Government Accountability Office (GAO) published results of a comprehensive review it performed on 31 CDHP studies published between 2003 and 2009.[15] Of these, eight studies met the GAO criteria of examining health care spending and addressing selection bias. The GAO also analyzed experience results for two large employers, one public and one private. Each of these employers offered an HRA as a health insurance option.

Cost and Trend Results

Key findings of the American Academy of Actuaries' analysis are as follows:

- All studies showed a favorable effect on first-year costs under a CDHP. Plan trends ranged from –4 to –15 percent. When compared with trend rates of 8 to 9 percent experienced under traditional plans, total first-year savings could be as high as 12 to 20 percent.
- Subsequent year savings showed trend rates 3 to 5 percent lower than traditional PPO plans.
- The findings alleviated concerns that employers are using CDHPs as a mechanism to shift more cost to employees. Most employers choose CDHPs for their potential utilization savings rather than their cost-shifting potential.

More recent updates to the Aetna[16] and CIGNA[17] studies reinforce these findings.

The GAO reported favorable cost results for the two employers it analyzed.[18] Spending and utilization generally increased by a smaller amount or decreased for HRA enrollees compared with those in traditional PPO plans. For the large public employer, average annual spending for HRA enrollees increased $478, or 10 percent, from the two-year period before HRA introduction to the five-year period after, compared with an increase of $879, or 7 percent, for the PPO group. The higher percentage increase for

15. Government Accountability Office (GAO), *Consumer-Directed Health Plans: Health Status, Spending and Utilization of Enrollees in Plans Based on Health Reimbursement Arrangements*, July 2010.
16. Sixth Annual Aetna Health Fund Study, 2010.
17. CIGNA Choice Fund Experience Study, 2009.
18. GAO, *Consumer-Directed Health Plans: Health Status, Spending and Utilization of Enrollees in Plans Based on Health Reimbursement Arrangements*, July 2010, pp. 13–19.

the HRA was attributed to the lower base spending compared with the PPO. The smaller dollar increase for the HRA group was driven by decreased spending for prescription drugs and by smaller increases in average annual utilization of services compared with the PPO group. The large private employer also showed smaller average annual spending increases for the HRA enrollees compared with the PPO group. This was attributed to smaller increases in spending for physician office visits and decreases in spending for emergency room visits, as well as more favorable average annual utilization changes.

Of the eight published studies that examined total or medical spending and controlled for differences in health status or other characteristics of enrollees, the GAO found that seven of them reported lower spending among CDHP enrollees as compared with traditional plans.[19] However, it should be noted that three of the studies were published by CIGNA and were each one-year updates of experience.

The very favorable results shown in these studies are not always borne out at the individual employer level. One of the most difficult challenges is controlling for the effect of differences in health status of participants in different plans. Actual results depend upon many factors, including such things as plan design, the impact of large claims, group demographics, whether the CDHP is the only plan, the employer contribution strategy, and how well employees understand the plan.

Consumer Behavior and Quality of Care

The American Academy of Actuaries study also assessed the impact on consumer behavior and the effect on quality of care, and reached the following conclusions:

- *Necessary care.* All studies demonstrated that CDHP participants did not forego necessary care. In fact, they received the same or higher levels of care as those in traditional plans.
- *Preventive care.* All of the studies showed significantly higher use of preventive services for CDHP participants. Reasons for this included the practice of most plans of providing preventive care at no charge and increased messaging to participants.
- *Recommended chronic care.* The three studies reported that participants received the same (Aetna) or higher (CIGNA and UnitedHealth) levels of care compared with traditional plan

19. Ibid, pp. 19–20.

participants for chronic conditions such as diabetes and hypertension.

- *Prescription drug utilization.* Aetna noted greater use of generic drugs by CDHP members. CIGNA showed higher drug utilization but lower costs per prescription, indicating greater usage of generics among the CDHP population. CIGNA also found both higher prescription costs and utilization for second-year CDHP participants compared with traditional plan members. Since total medical costs were lower, this may mean that they are substituting drug therapies for more costly treatments. Similarly, UnitedHealth showed higher prescription trend rates for the CDHP.

The more recent Aetna and CIGNA studies both show that CDHP members are more engaged consumers and are much more likely to use online consumer tools and information. The GAO study confirmed a higher use of preventive services for CDHP members.

CONCLUSION

In the final analysis, consumer-driven health plans reflect a return to basic insurance principles. Insurance is meant to protect against individual losses that are not expected by the individual, yet could cause financial hardship if they occur. Coverage of predictable or controllable claims often results in an indifference to loss. Insurance plan designs that distance the individual from the cost of services create unnecessary utilization, as well as excessive administrative costs.

CDHPs were developed with these principles in mind. They protect against a broad range of catastrophic medical expenses, while recognizing that the insured could often afford to pay minor medical costs without the use of insurance. These policies have the advantage of protecting against potentially devastating financial losses, while reducing over-utilization and small claims, for which administrative costs are relatively high. The individual health accounts included with CDHPs further engage the consumer and encourage individuals to seek more cost-effective care. They also maintain the advantage of paying for some out-of-pocket costs on a tax-favored basis. On balance, consumer-driven health care is not a silver bullet for rampaging health costs, yet it has demonstrated success at controlling costs. And many employers have embraced the CDHP as a viable health care cost management strategy.

APPENDIX 7.1

CONSUMER-DRIVEN HEALTH PLANS: POPULARITY AND GROWTH

OFFER RATES

The broad-based Kaiser Family Foundation/Health Research and Educational Trust (KFF/HRET) 2010 Annual Survey of Employer Health Benefits shows 15 percent of employers offering a CDHP in 2010, up from 7 percent in 2006.[20] Similarly, Mercer's 2010 national survey of health plans found that CDHPs are offered by 16 percent of employers.[21] Other key findings include:

- The larger the employer, the more likely a CDHP is to be offered. The Mercer survey showed that CDHPs were offered by 23 percent of employers with 500 or more employees and 51 percent of firms with 20,000 employees or more.[22] The KFF survey found that 34 percent of firms with 1,000 or more employees offered a CDHP, compared with 21 percent of firms with 200 to 999 employees and 15 percent of firms with 3 to 199 employees.[23]
- HSA plans are the more popular offering and have grown faster than HRA plans: 12 percent of firms offering health benefits in 2010 offered an HSA-qualified plan, contrasted with just 4 percent offering HRA-based plans.[24] Greater HSA popularity stems from the permissibility of both employer and employee contributions to the fund, as well as the account portability.

20. Kaiser Family Foundation, *Employer Health Benefits 2010 Annual Survey*, p. 144. The KFF/HRET survey covers over 2,000 employers of all sizes, including both public and private employers.
21. Mercer's *National Survey of Employer-Sponsored Health Plans 2010*. The survey covered almost 3,000 employers with 10 or more employees, in both public and private organizations.
22. Ibid.
23. Kaiser Family Foundation, *Employer Health Benefits 2010 Annual Survey*, p. 145.
24. Ibid, p. 144.

ENROLLMENT

Enrollment figures show less variation between HRA and HSA plans than do offer rates. The KFF survey reported:

- Thirteen percent of covered workers were enrolled in a consumer-driven health plan in 2010, with 7 percent participating in an HRA and 6 percent in an HSA plan.[25]
- Enrollment rates varied by company size: 16 percent of covered workers in small firms enrolled in a CDHP, compared with 12 percent in large firms.[26]

Even though large firms are more likely to offer CDHPs than small firms, overall enrollment rates for large firms have been lower because large firms generally have more medical plans to choose from. However, this difference is narrowing as more large employers are transitioning to full replacement CDHPs.

America's Health Insurance Plans (AHIP) conducts an annual census to determine the number of people covered by HSA-based CDHPs.[27] Virtually all private health insurance carriers in the HSA/HDHP market participate in the census. Among their findings for 2010 were the following:

- Ten million people had HSA/HDHP coverage, up from 8 million in 2009 and 6 million in 2008.
- Of those enrolled, 8 million had group coverage and 2 million were covered under individual plans.
- Of those with group coverage, 3 million were in the small-group market and 5 million in the large-group market.

CDHP enrollees tend to be younger and higher-income and to exhibit healthier behaviors than the average traditional plan enrollee. Over time, as more employees enroll in CDHPs, these differences generally lessen.

25. Ibid, p. 147.
26. Ibid, p. 148.
27. America's Health Insurance Plans Center for Policy and Research, *2010 Annual Census*, May 2010. Figures reported are based on people enrolled in HSA/HDHPs. While all of these are eligible to set up an HSA, some may not have done so. The census does not include HRAs.

ASSETS AND ACCOUNT BALANCES

As more people open HSA accounts and as individual account balances increase over time, HSA assets have shown considerable growth. By one estimate, total HSA balances were estimated to be $6.75 billion as of early 2009.[28] Average account balances grew by 13 percent between January 2008 and January 2009 to $1,561.[29] A 2009 survey conducted by the Employee Benefit Research Institute (EBRI) yielded similar results. According to EBRI, total HSA and HRA assets increased from $5.7 billion in 2008 to $7.1 billion in 2009, up from just $835 million in 2006.[30] Since HRAs tend to be notional accounts, and not funded, it can be assumed most of these assets are HSAs. Average account balances increased from $696 in 2006 to $1,419 in 2009.[31] The increasing HSA assets have presented a growth opportunity for many financial institutions.

28. *Processing Health Savings Accounts: Paths to Success*, Report Published by Celent, January 12, 2009.
29. *HSA Benchmarking Analysis: Market Trends and Economics 2009*, Report Published by Celent, June 29, 2009.
30. Paul Fronstin, "Health Savings Accounts and Health Reimbursement Arrangements: Assets, Account Balances, and Rollovers, 2006–2009," *EBRI Issue Brief*, No. 343, June 2010, p. 5.
31. Ibid.

CHAPTER 8

Understanding Behavioral Health Care Benefits

Edward Jones

Ann McClanathan

Dagmar King

Diane S. Luedtke

BEHAVIORAL HEALTH CARE

The term "behavioral health care" refers to mental health and substance abuse services provided by behavioral health specialists. Behavioral health care benefits are subject to the general forces of managed care while also facing unique issues and challenges of their own. In recent years, there has been a heightened focus on behavioral health care benefits because they are a key contributor to increased employee productivity and lower medical costs. Of an estimated 301 million Americans with health insurance,[1] 78 percent have some type of behavioral health care coverage.[2]

Mental Illnesses and Other Behavioral Disorders

The most severe mental illnesses such as schizophrenia, bipolar disorder, and major depressive disorder are generally considered biologically based disorders that affect the brain, profoundly disrupting a person's thinking, feeling, mood, ability to relate to others, and capacity for coping with the demands of life. They cannot be overcome through "will power" and are not related to a person's character or intelligence. Nonbiologically based

1. United States Census Bureau, 2009 American Community Survey, www.census.gov.
2. Bureau of Labor Statistics, National Compensation Survey 2008, Table 26.

mental disorders can also severely impact an individual's functioning. Early identification and treatment is of vital importance; according to Dr. Thomas Insel, Director of the National Institute of Mental Health, between 70 and 80 percent of individuals suffering from depression experience significant reduction of symptoms and improved quality of life through psychotherapy and/or medication.[3]

Mental disorders can loosely be categorized into the following categories:

1. Adjustment disorders (e.g., situational stress)
2. Anxiety disorders (e.g., panic disorder)
3. Childhood disorders (e.g., autism)
4. Eating disorders (e.g., anorexia)
5. Mood disorders (e.g., major depressive disorder)
6. Cognitive disorders (e.g., dementia)
7. Personality disorders (e.g., antisocial personality disorder)
8. Psychotic disorders (e.g., schizophrenia)
9. Substance-related disorders (e.g., alcohol or drug dependence)

The most serious and disabling conditions such as major depression, schizophrenia, bipolar disorder, panic disorders, and obsessive compulsive disorders affect about 6 percent of adults in the United States.[4] Just over 20 percent of children, either currently or at some point in their lives, have had a seriously debilitating mental disorder.[5]

The Need for Behavioral Health Care Benefits

Behavioral disorders can have a devastating impact on affected individuals, their families, and society. Mental illness is a leading cause of disability. To illustrate, one nationwide study found that 2.4 billion disability days resulted from physical conditions, and 1.3 billion disability days from mental conditions.[6] It is also well-documented that alcohol consumption

3. Dr. Thomas Insel, Director of the National Institute of Mental Health, CNN Interview, January 15, 2004.
4. National Institute of Mental Health, 2010, www.nimh.nih.gov/statistics.
5. Ibid.
6. Merikangas KR. Ames M, Cui L, Stang PE, Ustun TB, von Korff M, Kessler, RC. The impact of comorbidity of mental and physical conditions on role disability in the US adult population. *Archives of General Psychiatry*, Oct 2007; VOL 64(10).

accounts for a large percentage of industrial injuries and fatalities, and worker stress has been shown to greatly increase absences. Given these alarming statistics, it stands to reason that health care benefit purchasers gain from providing their workforces with relatively inexpensive mental health, chemical dependency, and employee assistance programs (EAPs) that cover the full spectrum of behavioral care needs. Unfortunately, behavioral health care benefits are often the least understood and, until the 2010 effective date of the Mental Health Parity and Addiction Equity Act of 2008, the most poorly compensated of all the possible components of a health care benefits package.

Common Misperceptions

Most people are unaware of the possible inadequacy of behavioral health benefits found in insurance plans, since it is falsely assumed that mental health and chemical dependency treatment needs are fully covered under medical plans, and in addition, that employee assistance programs fill in the gaps. Unfortunately, these are common misconceptions. The mandated behavioral benefits in a medical plan are limited to emergency assessment and crisis coverage. Mental health "parity" riders—legislatively mandated add-ons to medical benefit plans—are limited in the scope of disorders they cover. Employee assistance programs focus on workplace productivity and offer only a limited number of visits for emotional counseling. To fully understand behavioral health care benefits and the multitude of ways they are structured, it helps to take a brief look at the growth of the behavioral health care industry.

HISTORY AND INDUSTRY OVERVIEW

Today, behavioral health plans are widely adopted, but that was not always the case.

The Early Years

Prior to the 1940s, treatment for mental disorders was usually only provided in state mental hospitals. After World War II, general hospitals opened onsite psychiatric clinics and added psychiatrists to their staffs, which prompted commercial insurance carriers to include hospitalization coverage for mental illness. Initially, this coverage provided the same level of benefits as for nonpsychiatric benefits. Soon, however, insurers placed limits on outpatient mental health care because treatment often continued for indefinite lengths of time, and there was much subjectivity surrounding mental disorders and treatment methods.[7]

Growth of Managed Care

The Health Maintenance Organization (HMO) Act of 1973 promoted and set minimum standards for health maintenance organizations and required managed care plans to include an outpatient mental health benefit consisting of 20 visits annually for emergency assessment and crisis intervention.[8] While HMOs proliferated in the 1980s as a response to rapidly rising health care costs, their coverage for mental illness was extremely limited and differed significantly from coverage for physical illness. Hospital coverage was restricted to 30–45 days per mental illness, or 30 or 60 days per year. For medical illnesses, the number of days was usually unlimited. And for outpatient services—care received in the outpatient department of a hospital or in a clinician's office—coverage limitations were dramatically lower for mental health treatment than for medical treatment. The most common limitations for mental health outpatient treatment were a maximum dollar limit of $1,000 per year and a maximum reimbursement per visit ranging from $25 to $40. Coinsurance rates also varied dramatically between medical and mental coverage.[7]

The Behavioral Health Care Carve-Out

The limitations of HMO coverage for mental health disorders led to the development of behavioral health care "carve-outs." A behavioral health care carve-out is a program that separates—or "carves out"—mental health and chemical dependency services from the medical plan and provides them separately, usually under a separate contract and from a separate company known as a managed behavioral health care organization (MBHO). MBHOs offer mental health and chemical dependency plans that fill the coverage gaps in medical plans—many MBHOs also offer employee assistance programs. They are able to offer enriched, flexible, and affordable behavioral health care benefits along with sophisticated administrative,

7. Allan P. Blostin, "Mental Health Benefits Financed by Employers," Vol. 110, No. 7, July 1987.
8. Tom Trabin and Michael A. Freeman, *Managed Behavioral Healthcare History, Models, Strategic Challenges and Future Course*, 1995.

operational and care management capabilities. MBHOs focus on matching appropriate levels of specialists and treatment settings with the behavioral treatment needs of members to most cost-effectively provide care and maximize treatment effectiveness. Behavioral health care carve-outs have the potential to produce significant savings because (1) they are usually managed by firms that specialize in behavioral health treatment; (2) they allow large, self-funded employers to offer the same behavioral health benefits across all health plans offered; and (3) they allow a health plan to minimize adverse selection, which may occur in a choice environment when employees who utilize high levels of behavioral treatment opt for the medical plan with the most generous benefits.

Growth of the Employee Assistance Program

An employee assistance program is a confidential resource for information and referral to emotional counseling, covering such matters as relationship issues, family conflicts, job-related stress, alcohol abuse, drug addiction, financial hardships, and other personal problems. The first EAPs arose in the 1950s and focused on early intervention for alcohol and drug abuse. Since the 1970s, EAPs have evolved into an industry of their own. In the mid-1980s, EAPs began diversifying their services to include a wide range of work/life services along with human resource support, and the EAP is now considered a low-cost, high-return tool for enhancing workplace productivity.

PSYCHOTROPIC MEDICATION MANAGEMENT

Psychotropic medications—drugs that affect psychic function, behavior, or experience—are part of the medical benefit and are generally administered by companies contracting with health plans called pharmacy benefit managers (PBMs). Psychotropic medications account for a significant part of the overall cost of health care because of the chronic nature of many mental illnesses, but a fractionalized system currently exists that prevents optimum management of these medications. Although behavioral specialists contracting with MBHOs routinely prescribe psychotropic medication to their patients, many psychotropic medications (primarily antidepressants) are prescribed by family physicians, internists, and pediatricians, who have little training in mental health issues.

Because MBHOs do not manage the prescription drug benefit but bear the responsibility for managing the behavioral care for their members, they are often unaware if psychotropic medications prescribed to their members are of the appropriate types and dosages, or if there are appropriate interventions during treatment to ensure their members are medication-compliant. Even if the "silos"—MBHOs, health plans, PBMs, primary care physicians, and behavioral specialists—are bridged through coordination-of-care protocols, the situation is further complicated by the Health Insurance Portability and Accountability Act (HIPAA) privacy legislation, which adds another layer of difficulty in sharing prescription information.

MENTAL HEALTH PARITY

Mental health parity—equal insurance benefits for mental and medical disorders—is, in part, the result of years of work by groups such as the National Alliance for the Mentally Ill, government advocates, and thousands of other supporters to erase the stigma society attaches to mental illness—to bring it out of the dark shadows and acknowledge it as a disease as painful and often as life-threatening as physical illnesses.

The Mental Health Parity Act of 1996

The Mental Health Parity Act of 1996 (MHPA) was signed into law on September 26, 1996 and took effect January 1, 1998. This federal law is subject to concurrent jurisdiction by the Departments of Labor (DOL), the Treasury, and Health and Human Services, and prevents group health plans, insurance companies, and HMOs from placing lower annual or lifetime dollar limits on mental health benefits than on medical and surgical benefits offered under the plan.

The MHPA applies only to groups that offer mental health benefits and have more than 50 workers. However, the law does not require them to include mental health benefits in their benefit packages. MPHA does not apply to small groups or health insurance coverage in the individual market and it does not address substance abuse or chemical dependency treatment. The law does, however, allow for limits on inpatient days, prescription drugs, outpatient visits, and raising deductibles, which, in fact, has the effect of subjecting benefits to dollar limits. The United States General Accounting Office in May 2000 found that 87 percent of complying health plans evaded the spirit of the law by using day and visit limits to maintain unequal benefit levels for mental versus medical disorders.

The Mental Health Parity and Addiction Equity Act of 2008

The Mental Health Parity and Addiction Equity Act of 2008 (MHPAEA) continues and expands on MHPA, which required parity only in aggregate lifetime or annual dollar limits and did not extend to substance use disorder benefits. MHPAEA requires parity in the coverage of mental health or substance use disorder (MH/SUD) benefits as compared with medical/surgical benefits in group plans. MHPAEA, effective for plan years beginning after October 3, 2009, applies to both self-insured and fully insured group health plans with more than 50 employees.

MHPAEA prevents plans from imposing financial requirements and treatment limitations applicable to MH/SUD, which are more restrictive than the "predominant"[9] financial requirements or treatment limitations that apply to "substantially all"[10] medical/surgical benefits. Financial requirements include deductibles, copayments, coinsurance, and out-of-pocket maximums. The law addresses both quantitative and nonquantitative treatment limitations. Quantitative treatment limitations refer to limits on the frequency of treatment, number of visits, or days of coverage, or similar limits on the scope or duration of treatment. Nonquantitative treatment limitations are those that are not expressed numerically, such as medical management standards, formulary design, and methods for determining usual, customary, and reasonable amounts.

The parity requirements apply to six classifications of benefits:

1. Inpatient in-network
2. Inpatient out-of-network
3. Outpatient in-network
4. Outpatient out-of-network
5. Emergency care
6. Prescription drugs

The "substantially all/predominant" test must be applied separately to each classification. If a plan provides MH/SUD benefits in any classification of benefits, then it must provide MH/SUD benefits in all classifications of benefits in which medical/surgical benefits are provided.

- MH/SUD benefits may not be subject to any separate cost-sharing requirements or treatment limits that apply only to such

9. "Predominant" means more than one-half.
10. "Substantially all" means at least two-thirds.

benefits. All cumulative financial requirements must integrate both MH/SUD and medical/surgical benefits. An example of a cumulative financial requirement is a deductible which must be satisfied before a plan will start paying benefits.

- MPHEA includes two new disclosure requirements for group health plans. First, the criteria for medical necessity determinations made under a plan with respect to MH/SUD benefits must be made available to any current or potential participant, beneficiary, or contracting provider upon request. Second, the reason for any denial of reimbursement or payment for services with respect to MH/SUD benefits must be made available upon request. A plan subject to ERISA can satisfy this requirement by following the ERISA claim denial procedures for group health plans.
- MHPAEA does not require group plans to include mental health and substance abuse benefits in their plans. Rather, if a plan provides both medical/surgical and mental health/substance abuse benefits, it must comply with the parity provisions. State laws, however, may require inclusion of certain mental health and substance abuse conditions and benefits.
- MPHAEA provides a cost exemption to the parity requirements. A group health plan may apply for an exemption if compliance with the parity requirements causes its plan costs to increase by more than 2 percent in the first year or 1 percent in subsequent years. The requirements, as clarified by the Department of Labor (DOL),[11] are cumbersome and the cost exemption is only available in alternating years. In practice, very few plans are expected to take advantage of this exemption.

As shown in Figure 8-1, many firms have made changes to their mental health benefits in response to MHPAEA.

Patient Protection and Affordable Care Act of 2010

- The Patient Protection and Affordable Care Act of 2010 (PPACA) broadly affects health care plans. Two points are worth noting

11. Department of Labor, *FAQs About Affordable Care Act Implementation Part V and Mental Health Parity Implementation*, December 22, 2010.

FIGURE 8-1

Percentage of Firms With More Than 50 Workers Reporting the Following as a Result of the 2008 Mental Health Parity and Addiction Equity Act, 2010

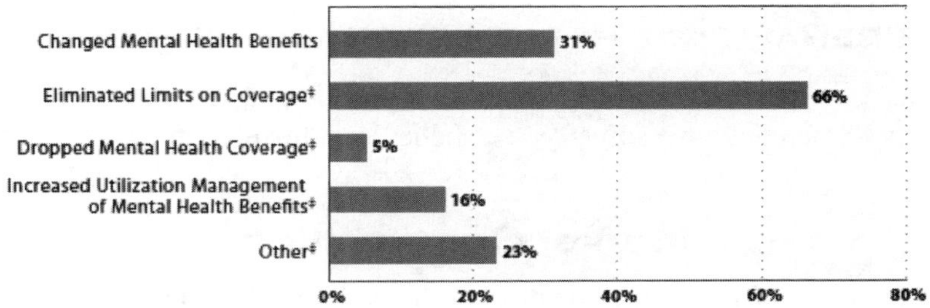

‡Among firms reporting they made changes to the mental health benefits they offer as a result of the Mental Health Parity and Addiction Equity Act of 2008.
Source: Kaiser/HRET Survey of Employer-Sponsored Health Benefits, 2010.

regarding its interface with MHPAEA. First, the Department of Labor clarified the small employer exemption under MPHAEA.[12] The DOL noted that although there were changes to the definition of small employer for other purposes under PPACA, group health plans that are subject to Employee Retirement Income Security Act (ERISA) and the Internal Revenue Code are exempt from the MPHAEA requirements if they have 50 or fewer employees, regardless of any state insurance law definition of small employer.

- Second, PPACA prohibits group health plans from placing annual or lifetime limits on essential health benefits.[13] Mental health and substance use disorder benefits are considered essential health benefits. The ban on lifetime limits for essential health benefits is effective for plan years beginning on or after September 23, 2010. The lifetime limit rules do not prohibit a plan from excluding all benefits for a condition, although other state or federal rules may apply. Plans may not impose annual limits on

12. Ibid.
13. PPACA defines essential health benefits to include at least the following: ambulatory patient services, emergency services, hospitalization, maternity and newborn care, mental health and substance use disorder services, prescription drugs, rehabilitative services, laboratory services, preventive and wellness services and chronic disease management, and pediatric services.

essential health benefits for plan years beginning on or after January 1, 2014. Restricted annual limits are permitted prior to the 2014 effective date.

THE BEHAVIORAL HEALTH CARE MARKET TODAY

Of an estimated 301 million Americans with health insurance, approximately 78 percent have some type of behavioral health care coverage.

Market Composition

The majority of behavioral health care benefits sold in the United States are purchased by large groups that buy comprehensive health care and other insurance benefits for their covered members. Purchasing groups for behavioral health carve-outs include self-funded and other large employers, health plans, union trust and Taft-Hartley trust funds, school districts and educational coalitions, state and county mental health agencies supported by public funds, and the government's Federal Employees Health Benefits Program (FEHBP). The smaller the group the more likely it is that behavioral benefits are sold as an integrated part of a general health plan, which may or may not have a specialty MBHO provide the behavioral benefit.

The Sales Environment

Behavioral benefits are sold through multiple channels. Large brokerage and consulting firms often serve as the go-between for behavioral benefit purchasers, helping them locate and negotiate insurance contracts. A broker or consultant may also be an agent for an MBHO, delivering policies and collecting premiums. Brokers generally work on commission, consultants on a fixed retainer. In addition, most large MBHOs employ sales forces that sell directly to purchasers or through brokers and consultants and generally are compensated on a combined base salary and commission pay structure. Since many MBHOs are subsidiaries of health plans, health plan sales forces also sell behavioral benefits as part of the plans they offer.

Changing Market Landscape

As with other segments of the managed care industry, MBHOs rapidly evolved in response to payer, member, legislative, and market demands.

During the 1990s, MBHOs went through a period of consolidation, using mergers, joint ventures, and other strategies to attract investors and capital. Four factors have been cited as drivers of behavioral health care mergers and acquisitions:[14]

1. Payers were demanding greater capital reserves to pay providers more quickly and cover risk adequately.
2. Greater investment was required in management information systems to meet accountability and accreditation requirements.
3. Premium and capitation payments were stagnant, meaning that managed care companies were not seeing increases in revenues through existing business.
4. The costs involved in developing public procurement bids, especially for statewide contracts, could be large.

Merger and Acquisition Activity

Approximately three-quarters of the market was controlled by the 10 largest companies, with three companies comprising a little more than half of the market according to 2002 data. In large part, this was a result of merger and acquisition activity. Magellan Behavioral Health, a publicly traded MBHO with 69 million members, dominated the market, capturing 30.3 percent of total enrollment as of 2002. In addition to Magellan's acquisitions, MBHO merger and acquisition activity throughout the 1990s was rampant. During the early years of the 21st century, merger and acquisition activity briefly slowed down, but it will likely persist because of continuing price pressures and economy-of-scale issues.

BEHAVIORAL HEALTH CARE BENEFIT PLANS

Typical Plan Features

According to the Substance Abuse Mental Health Services Administration (SAMHSA), the vast majority of employer-sponsored plans cover inpatient and outpatient mental health treatment services. They cover intermediate mental health treatment services such as residential treatment and partial (or day) hospitalization and intensive outpatient services, which can include

14. American Federation of State, County and Municipal Employers, AFL-CIO, AFSCME Public Policy, 1998.

psychosocial rehabilitation, case management, and wraparound services for children (developing treatment plans for children that involve their families). Many plans also include a parity benefit—often called a "severe mental illness" benefit—that specifies which disorders are covered under their state parity law. A well-designed benefit package should cover a wide range of clinically effective services and treatments while incorporating financial incentives to substitute lower-cost alternatives for higher-cost alternatives when it is clinically appropriate to do so.

ERISA

The Employee Retirement Income Security Act of 1974 regulates the majority of private pension and welfare group benefit plans in the United States. The provisions of ERISA prevent states from regulating multistate employers on the provisions of their health benefits. Most notably, this affects the 9.5 million federal employees enrolled in the Federal Employee Health Benefit Plan (FEHBP). It also affects many large self-insured employers and union trust groups.

HIPAA

The Health Insurance Portability and Accountability Act (HIPAA) applies to all health insurance plans, including MBHOs. It allows employees to continue their health insurance coverage from one group to another. HIPAA's nondiscrimination provisions prohibit a group health plan or insurance company from denying an individual eligibility for benefits or from charging an individual a higher premium based on a health factor, including health status, medical condition (both physical and mental illnesses), claims experience, receipt of health care, medical history, genetic information, evidence of insurability, and disability. HIPAA also may serve to reduce health care fraud and abuse and protect privacy and is projected to significantly reduce the 29 cents of every health care dollar spent today on administration. The HIPAA Administration Simplification component consists of three areas:

- *Data standards* enforce standards for the electronic transmission of health care information.
- *Security* protects confidential and private information through sound and uniform security practices.
- *Privacy* maintains confidentiality of member information.

Because behavioral stigma still prevails, HIPAA plays a particularly important part in protecting sensitive patient information gathered during behavioral treatment.

BEHAVIORAL HEALTH CARE BENEFIT PLAN DESIGNS

Behavioral health care benefit plan designs are closely aligned with medical plan designs. As with medical plans, behavioral benefit plans are predominantly network-based (HMO, POS, or PPO), and only rarely nonnetwork-based (indemnity). A large employer or purchasing group often will customize a behavioral health care carve-out plan to provide a standard plan design to all members regardless of their medical coverage. This greatly facilitates plan administration, but insurance and utilization review laws and third-party administrator licenses vary from state to state, complicating behavioral plan administration. To fully understand behavioral health care benefit plan design, it is essential to first understand funding arrangements.

Fully Insured Arrangements

In a fully insured funding arrangement, often called "full risk" or "risk-based," MBHOs assume the financial risk for providing behavioral services, paying the claims submitted by providers for behavioral services rendered. Financial risk falls on the MBHO. When service utilization and corresponding claims costs exceed expected levels, the MBHO absorbs those increased costs. Purchasers pay MBHOs a predetermined, fixed (usually monthly) premium for assuming financial risk for behavioral treatment costs. On average, a monthly premium for a fully insured, full-risk behavioral plan, excluding an EAP, ranges between 3 and 6 percent of a medical plan's premium, although rates can vary depending upon a group's utilization experience, number of members, geographic location, benefit plan, and state parity laws. The two primary cost drivers for a fully insured funding arrangement are group utilization rates and unit costs for practitioner and facility care.

A variation of a fully insured funding arrangement is a shared-risk arrangement, in which purchasers agree to assume financial risk for claims payment up to a certain amount. Premiums are based on projected claims costs. If claims exceed a prespecified amount, the MBHO assumes those claims costs or a percentage of those costs. If claims come in below the targeted amount, the balance can be shared by the MBHO and client or refunded to the client. There are many iterations of these shared agreements.

Administrative Services Only

Under an administrative-services-only (ASO) arrangement, an MBHO, for a fee, will handle medical management, utilization review, benefit, and other administrative functions, such as claims payment (although some ASO contracts do not include claims payment). Often called a "self-funded" or "self-insured" arrangement, the purchaser assumes the financial risk for the health care costs for its members. Self-funded plans may also be administered by independent organizations called third-party administrators (TPAs), which often provide administrative and medical management services in addition to claims processing. The larger the group, the more likely it is to self-fund, because the financial risk is spread across more employees and its budget is large enough to absorb the risk. Self-funded groups typically have stop-loss insurance, which protects them from catastrophic losses.

A key advantage of an ASO arrangement is that employers can offer the same benefit to employees working in different states. Because ERISA exempts self-funded health plans from compliance with state laws and regulations, employers that self-fund can avoid individual state regulations such as diverse state mental health parity laws. Self-funded employers may also be able to save money because they can limit the risk pool to their own employees, avoid state taxes on insurance company premium revenues, and have complete control over benefit packages. In addition, some employers may self-fund to access claims data, allowing them to understand the true costs of their health care plans and tailor their plans accordingly. Table 8-1 outlines benefit plan design and funding arrangement options.

TABLE 8-1

Behavioral Health Care Benefit Plan Funding Arrangements

Benefit Plan Design	Funding Arrangement
▪ Network Providers (HMO, PPO, POS) ▪ Nonnetwork Providers (Indemnity)	▪ Fully Insured ▪ Shared-risk ▪ Administrative Services Only (ASO) – Network Management – Claims Payment

EMPLOYEE ASSISTANCE PROGRAMS

An employee assistance program is a confidential, short-term counseling service to assist employees and their family members with personal problems that negatively affect their job performance. These programs vary considerably in design and scope, and are offered by MBHOs, stand-alone EAP companies, and work/life companies. EAPs originally focused on substance abuse problems, but most today take a comprehensive approach to support members with a range of employee and family issues. Some include proactive prevention and health and wellness programs, and may even be linked to the health plan and MBHO benefit structure. While most EAPs offer a wide range of services, they generally refer members to other professionals or agencies that can offer additional or extended help in particular areas. EAPs also provide human resource support through management consultation, on-site employee and employer seminars, and critical incident stress management after catastrophic workplace events. Eighty-two percent of large employers and 24 percent of small employers offer an EAP.[15] Table 8-2 shows the benefits offered by a typical EAP.

TABLE 8-2

Typical Employee Assistance Program Benefit Summary

24-hour toll-free access to the EAP
Confidential services
Available to all household and dependent family members
Unlimited calls
Five face-to-face counseling sessions (per incident) with EAP provider
Child and elder care referral services
Legal assistance and referral
Financial counseling and debt management
Alternative medicine referral
Concierge services

15. Mercer, National Survey of Employer-Sponsored Health Plans, 2008.

Basic EAP Types

Basic EAPs types are EAP counselors and work/life benefits.

EAP

Full-service EAPs offer a predetermined number of face-to-face counseling visits, generally from three to eight per year (sometimes per incident). EAP counselors are community-based, licensed mental health professionals that contract with an MBHO or stand-alone EAP company. In addition to counseling visits, which are free to EAP members, the full-service EAP includes a full array of work/life referral services (referrals are free, but services incur costs), free information resources (Web-based and hard-copy books, pamphlets, and videotapes), as well as management consultation services.

Work/Life Benefits

A stepped-down version of the full-service EAP described above includes all EAP services except for the face-to-face counseling visits; these are often replaced with telephonic or Web-based access to EAP counselors.

Advantages of an EAP

EAPs offer easy access to timely problem resolution, and utilization tends to be high because accessing employee assistance carries less stigma than accessing behavioral health care benefits. An EAP is also a proven cost-management tool because of its focus on early resolution and its high utilization. Studies have shown that, after implementing an EAP, a plan can expect savings in the form of fewer and less expensive medical claims and reduced mental health and substance abuse costs. Successful EAP implementation relies on maintaining continuing visibility, and so EAP providers generally distribute a stream of regular communications to their EAP members, including onsite posters, newsletters, premium items, special mailings, and email blasts.

HOW BEHAVIORAL HEALTH BENEFITS WORK TOGETHER

An effective behavioral health program should include an integrated mental health/chemical dependency benefit that includes inpatient and outpatient services as well as an EAP. This combination of relatively low-cost benefits provides a "safety net" for the wide range of behavioral disorders suffered by a worker population and its dependents. But a behavioral program's effectiveness relies on (1) employee and employer awareness of the program's services and value, (2) appropriate use of the benefits, and (3) how well the behavioral vendor and its network providers prevent and manage costly disorders.

Even when people access their behavioral benefits by calling for a referral, the "presenting symptom"—such as the need for divorce counseling—is often the tip of the iceberg.

A typical example is "Jim"—recently divorced, he is having excessive difficulty adjusting to the situation. Jim calls his MBHO and is asked a series of questions to ensure he receives a referral to appropriate services. Jim is referred to a specialist in marriage and family therapy (MFT). After an initial assessment, the therapist determines that his patient is experiencing adjustment disorder with depressed mood. As therapy progresses, additional factors come to light. The therapist finds out that the primary reason for the marital breakup was financial: apparently Jim had been—and still is—abusing cocaine and was depleting the couple's bank account to support his habit. The therapist calls the MBHO, and the licensed professional who takes the call refers Jim into an intensive outpatient chemical dependency treatment program. The MBHO case manager also recommends that Jim use his EAP benefit for financial counseling. Fortunately, Jim had access to a full behavioral program, because each one of his behavioral benefits was essential to a successful recovery.

Even seemingly obvious EAP situations, such as a need for referral to child care, can turn into a need for more extensive mental health benefits. Often individuals will begin EAP counseling for this type of situation only to run out of visits. Take a look at how this can occur:

"Mary," a production worker in a large manufacturing plant, is divorced and the mother of two children, ages three and six. She is living paycheck to paycheck and works from 7:30 a.m. to 4:30 p.m. Monday through Friday. She has her child care down to a "science." Before work, she drops off her three-year-old at a day-care facility near her house, and then swings by school to drop off her six-year-old. Mary enjoys a reputation as a loyal, dependable, and productive worker. Suddenly, Mary begins coming into work late, she is frequently absent, and the quality of her work slips. When her supervisor confronts her, she breaks down in tears, confessing that her three-year-old has a recurring illness and the day-care center will not watch her. Mary has been relying on the goodwill of neighbors, which is often sporadic. The supervisor recommends that Mary contact her EAP for a referral to a child care facility that takes sick children, which she does. But her childcare issues are only the tip of the iceberg. Because Mary is an hourly employee and has missed work, her income has fallen and she is behind on her rent and other bills. In addition, the new childcare facility is expensive and adds to her financial problems, compounding her stress. She contacts her EAP, receives a referral to consumer credit counseling, and also makes an appointment for emotional counseling because she is deeply concerned about both her daughter and her job. She forges a bond with her counselor and begins making progress.

BEHAVIORAL HEALTH PROVIDERS

The behavioral health providers should be in a specialty network, have credentials, and meet the group's needs.

The Specialty Network

A behavioral specialty network must cover a wide range of behavioral treatment needs and levels of care. A typical behavioral health specialty network includes individual (solo) practitioners and multispecialty group practices consisting of clinical psychologists (PhDs, PsyDs, EdDs), social workers (LCSWs, LISWs, ACSWs, MSWs, CISWs), masters-level therapists (MPSYs, MFTs, MFCCs, LMFTs, LPCs), psychiatric nurses (ANRPs, RNs), and psychiatrists. A network may also include medical doctors who specialize in addictionology, and developmental behavioral pediatricians (DBPs) to improve access for children with special needs.

In addition to behavioral specialists, the network includes inpatient facilities and programs that accommodate the broad spectrum of treatment needs. Acute inpatient facilities are designated for the most acute treatment needs, meaning individuals who are unable to care for themselves in some way and may be suicidal or homicidal. Partial hospital programs (sometimes called day treatment) offer intensive treatment during the day, but patients return home overnight. Finally, intensive outpatient programs are designed for patients who need more intensive treatment than weekly outpatient therapy provides, but they require fewer hours each day than partial or day facilities provide. Each program or facility may specialize in a certain age group (adult, geriatric, adolescent, child), while some programs focus on mental illnesses only, others on chemical dependency, and a few specialize in co-occurring disorders. MBHOs employ specific criteria to authorize facility-based care and treatment programs for their members, and licensed care managers provide oversight to ensure treatment plans and lengths of stay are appropriate.

Provider Qualification: The Credentialing Process

MBHOs perform primary source verification of practitioners' credentials before they are accepted to practice in their network and serve their members. Areas of scrutiny include investigation into a provider's education, board certification, background and work history, liability insurance and malpractice coverage, practice information (addresses, hours, and facility description), population, language and treatment specialties, and hospital admitting privileges. MBHOs conduct recredentialing—typically every two to three years—to ensure that providers maintain quality standards.

Meeting Group Needs: Customized Networks

MBHOs often custom-build behavioral provider networks to meet a group's diverse geographic, cultural, language, and specialty needs, as well as member preferences. Standards for member access and availability of services are designed to ensure that members have a choice of providers—outpatient practitioners, inpatient facilities, and specialized treatment programs—across the continuum of care, within an acceptable travel distance, and with appropriate clinical subspecialties. Most MBHOs forge alliances with community-based mental health and substance abuse treatment providers both to provide covered services and as referral sources for noncovered services, and they develop these linkages based on the particular needs of the membership being served. Rural areas often have a limited number and diversity of practitioners and facilities. Consequently, Medicaid-supported community mental health centers often dominate as the de facto service provider for a wide range of treatment needs. To increase access to treatment in rural areas, MBHOs may at times work with Medicaid-supported providers to establish these centers as referral options for their members. In addition, MBHOs are beginning to consider telephonic or Web-based psychiatry to serve rural populations that do not have access to local professionals.

BEHAVIORAL PROVIDER PAYMENT ARRANGEMENTS

Behavioral provider payment arrangements include a fee for service, capitation, and per diem and case rates.

Fee for Service

The most widely used payment arrangement today is fee for service. A fee-for-service (FFS) arrangement means that there is payment for individual services at an established contract rate, which is often negotiated and discounted based on the promise of a large volume of services. The length and intensity of behavioral services are managed by an MBHO through various utilization and quality control mechanisms.

Capitation

Capitation is a fixed payment, usually calculated on a per member per month basis, for the delivery of a defined range of behavioral services to a defined member population. Financial risk is assumed by the provider, and the provider's profit is contingent on expending less money on caring for the capitated population than is received in capitation fees. Organized group practitioners are more likely to handle capitation arrangements than are solo practitioners.

Per Diem and Case Rates

The most common payment arrangements for facilities and organized programs are per diem and case rates. A per diem rate is a negotiated and contracted daily rate for all services provided while a patient is in an inpatient program. A case rate, essentially a capitated arrangement for individual cases, is no longer common except in chemical dependency treatment, where an MBHO may contract with a treatment facility or program to pay a flat fee for the treatment episode.

CARE MANAGEMENT AND COST CONTROL

Care management and cost control include items such as care access, predictive modeling and assessment, performance measurement, outcomes management, and coordination of care.

Care Access

MBHOs traditionally require preauthorization to access treatment. MBHOs generally operate their own customer service centers, and when a member calls for a referral, an intake specialist asks the member a series of questions to establish the reason for the call, assess risk, acuity, specialty needs, and member preference. After listening to the caller's concerns and explaining the nature of the caller's benefits, the intake specialist separates routine from urgent and emergency situations. More than 80 percent of incoming calls are generally for routine referrals; industry standards dictate that members receiving routine referrals must be seen by a provider within 10 business days. If a member's needs are urgent, an appointment is arranged within 48 hours, although the more stringent standard of 24 hours is adopted for some contracts. If an individual requires immediate, emergency services (e.g., he or she is suicidal or homicidal), referral is generally made to a hospital or inpatient facility if an immediate appointment is not available with a network practitioner. Most MBHOs employ a dedicated team of licensed crisis care managers, who are specially trained in emergency protocol, active listening, diffusing, and referral. Ambulance services and/or police may also be involved in diffusing hostile situations and transferring an individual to psychiatric facilities.

Predictive Modeling and Risk Assessment

High-service utilizers—generally individuals with severe and persistent mental illnesses such as schizophrenia and major recurrent depression—represent a small percentage of overall service users but account for a disproportionate, higher percentage of treatment resources and claims costs. MBHOs analyze claims and treatment data to identify high-risk members who have a history of high utilization and repeated hospitalizations. Predictive modeling techniques provide the ability to forecast who those high-risk, potentially high-cost members are, and intervene in time to avoid preventable treatment costs. The degree of risk can be identified and members stratified accordingly, so care management resources can be applied most effectively and efficiently. MBHO care management resources tend to be in short supply, so it pays to use those limited resources to deliver the best clinical and economic value to both the member and the payer.

Performance Measurement

MBHOs typically measure provider network performance through a number of variables, which include accessibility, utilization, and adequacy and appropriateness of treatment. Traditionally, these performance data are collected after the fact through provider assessment reports and claims data. Today, however, some MBHOs are collecting member-reported and provider-reported data earlier on in the process to guide timely treatment interventions that can avert unnecessary emergency hospitalizations and contribute to more effective treatment outcomes. Profiling provider performance on clinical outcomes is an important step forward in the performance measurement arena.

Case Management

Case management is a term that refers to oversight of an MBHO member's treatment to ensure it is appropriate. Case managers employed by the MBHO coordinate the member's care in collaboration with treating providers, facilities, and community resources, and often work with members and their families to ensure they continue to receive the appropriate level of care for their fluctuating needs. This ensures a cost-effective course of treatment in an appropriate setting. Potentially high service utilizers are identified so case managers can focus on those individuals with the greatest needs to ensure they continually receive appropriate treatment levels. Most MBHOs use an escalating series of models or protocols based on the patient's level of acuity and chronicity, which determine how frequently case managers monitor treatment. Case management goals are crisis stabilization, prevention of long-term disability, and reduced reliance on hospital care by facilitating patient engagement in outpatient treatment and community resources.

Utilization Review and Management

Utilization review is an activity that determines the medical necessity and appropriateness of treatment being provided, and is performed at various times, including at the point of care (prospective review), during care (concurrent review), and after treatment (retrospective review). While MBHOs generally perform this function, self-funded employers and health plans may purchase this service from stand-alone utilization review organizations. MBHOs utilize written criteria based on clinical evidence to guide the evaluation of the medical necessity, appropriateness, and efficiency of mental health and chemical dependency services.

Outcomes Management

MBHOs have developed tools to assess treatment effectiveness and quantify outcomes, bringing technology, data, and increased objectivity to a field once dominated by subjective assessment. The measurement of outcomes concurrent with the treatment process is the most powerful approach to outcomes management because feedback to clinicians can shape care as it is being delivered. The objectives of outcomes management are to identify risks early so treatment interventions contribute to more positive outcomes, as well as prevent emergencies and unnecessary hospitalizations.

Coordination of Care

Behavioral disorders often coexist with each other (e.g., depression and substance abuse), and with medical disorders (e.g., depression and chronic heart disease). An individual may be seeing his or her primary care doctor for treatment of a physical disorder and a behavioral specialist for treatment of a mental disorder. Coordination of medical and behavioral health care services results in improved treatment outcomes for patients. When coordination of care does not take place, there are increased risks, such as repeated or unnecessary testing and adverse drug reactions. A consumer in today's complex health care environment is faced with a mind-boggling array of organizations, programs, services, and providers, each of which can play a vital role in his or her care and successful recovery. Patients benefit from an interconnected series of care coordination protocols between behavioral health specialists, primary care/medical doctors, medical plans, MBHOs, pharmacy benefit managers, and community affiliates. Health care accrediting and regulatory bodies are pressing the managed care industry to integrate behavioral care into medical delivery systems. Even though progress has been made, much work is needed to create a truly integrated health care system.

Depression Disease Management Programs

Depression is a mental illness that often goes unnoticed, and it co-occurs with many physical illnesses, such as diabetes and heart disease. It is increasingly a focus of disease management initiatives because of its chronic nature and large economic impact. MBHO depression disease management programs support the clinician–patient relationship and plan of care, and emphasize prevention of disease-related exacerbations and complications using evidence-based guidelines and patient empowerment tools. These programs require coordination among health plans, physicians, pharmacists, and patients. Disease management can improve patient outcomes and quality of life while potentially reducing overall health care costs.

Substance Abuse Relapse Programs

Addiction to alcohol and other drugs is a chronic condition, characterized by relapses. Therefore, the prevention of relapse is one of the critical elements in successful treatment. Standard chemical dependency treatment was once a 28-day inpatient treatment program. Since detoxification on an outpatient basis is more often recommended today, only persons with severe withdrawal and other medical complications now require hospitalization. Most substance abuse treatment experts today consider intensive outpatient treatment more effective for most patients in treating chemical dependency. Outpatient programs encourage individuals to remain sober while confronting their day-to-day living situations. In addition, most MBHOs today offer after-care programs to their members who complete a course of chemical dependency treatment. The programs are aimed at preventing relapse and often include telephonic support and self-help tools.

MBHO ACCREDITATION

Managed behavioral health organizations may be accredited by the National Committee for Quality Assurance, the Utilization Review Accreditation Commission (URAC), and The Joint Commission.

National Committee for Quality Assurance

The National Committee for Quality Assurance (NCQA) is the nation's largest accrediting body for HMOs. It released accreditation standards for its Managed Behavioral Health Accreditation Program in January 1997 and began accepting MBHO accreditation applications in February 1997. An MBHO must demonstrate that it meets several quality standards, including standards covering access and triage to ensure that patients can see appropriate clinicians in a timely manner. Behavioral health standards also cover such areas as network adequacy, and they require that an MBHO demonstrate well-established lines of communication between members' primary care physicians and their behavioral health practitioners. The highest level of NCQA MBHO accreditation is "full," which is effective for a three-year period. That is followed by a one-year accreditation level, and finally a provisional accreditation level, after which NCQA will review the plan to see if it qualifies for a higher level.

URAC

URAC was originally incorporated under the name "Utilization Review Accreditation Commission"; however, that name was shortened to just the acronym "URAC" in 1996 when it began accrediting organizations such as health plans and preferred provider organizations. URAC offers 15 accreditation programs, the most common for MBHOs being Core Accreditation and Health Utilization Management Accreditation. Core Accreditation standards are the foundation of URAC accreditation, and include organizational structure, staff qualifications, training and management, oversight of delegated activities, quality management, and consumer protection. URAC Health Utilization Management Accreditation standards ensure that MBHOs follow clinically sound utilization management processes, respect patients' and providers' rights, maintain confidentiality, give payers reasonable guidelines, and are compatible with the 2002 U.S. Department of Labor claims regulations.

Joint Commission

The Joint Commission (TJC) originated as the accrediting body for hospitals, but TJC has been active in behavioral health care accreditation since 1972. It started offering specialized accreditation services to managed behavioral health plans and integrated delivery systems in 1994. To be eligible for a TJC accreditation survey, a behavioral health plan or integrated system must provide for health care services to a defined population of individuals, offer comprehensive and/or specialty services, and have both a centralized, integrated structure and contract with, or manage, actual care delivery sites, which include practitioner offices and/or components that deliver care.

FUTURE DEVELOPMENTS IN BEHAVIORAL HEALTH CARE

While many Americans need mental health treatment, only about 36 percent of American adults with mental disorders are receiving treatment.[16]

16. Wang PS, Lane M, Olfson M, Pincus HA, Wells KB, Kessler RC. Twelve month use of mental health services in the United States. *Archives of General Psychiatry*, 2005 Jun;62(6):629–640.

Some of the reasons for this are cost, lack of insurance, stigma, and not understanding what behavioral insurance covers. Although the stigma associated with mental health care is fading, some individuals are still concerned that employers, coworkers, or friends will think less of them for seeing a therapist. Others are skeptical that therapy is effective and actually solves problems. And some people simply cannot find, or do not know how to find, a therapist who works well with them.

The costs for not accessing needed behavioral treatment are many. Depression can complicate a patient's recovery from a major illness. Patients with chronic or serious mental illnesses who do not have appropriate outpatient care can bounce in and out of inpatient facilities, while families and patients suffer from poor outcomes and mounting insurance bills. Finally, lack of care can lead to the most serious outcome possible: death of the patient through suicide.

Broadening Care Access

Radical new approaches to reaching those in need of mental health care are needed—and fortunately, are either in development or in use already. They include the following:

- Proactive disease management programs that operate on several fronts: working with employers to reach out to employees through the workplace, and with health plans to identify patients taking psychotropic medications who need additional support; and reaching out to patients with other diseases such as diabetes or cardiac conditions who may also suffer from mental illness.
- Outreach to people who want treatment but do not know how to access it or to find a therapist who is best for them. One's choice of a psychotherapist is primarily impacted by a physician's recommendation, the health plan network, and the location of the clinician's office. Offering information about clinicians online, even identifying those within a network with specializations or a track record of producing the best outcomes, can help people make more informed choices. Just as health plans publish physician "report cards" to educate consumers, so psychotherapist report cards might help people choose the best therapist for their needs.
- New ways of delivering therapy that are more accessible and cost effective. For example, patients with mild to moderate levels of

distress can benefit from a "coach" who offers counseling over the telephone or via the Internet. The Internet can also play an important role in promoting compliance with treatment, and augment other treatment offerings.

Productivity

One of the challenges facing managed behavioral health care organizations is the ability to demonstrate to purchasers that the benefits they deliver result in increased workplace productivity. Studies of this type are usually collaborative efforts between an employer group and MBHO, and results are often skewed by nuances of the individual group. In 2003, PacifiCare Behavioral Health, a leading national managed behavioral health care organization, reported the results of a four-year study of nearly 20,000 of its members in behavioral treatment representing multiple employer groups and health plans across the country. By measuring the degree of work impairment through a patient survey tool administered in clinicians' offices at the beginning and at multiple points during psychotherapy, the MBHO was able to track patient improvement. Five questions on the survey assessed degrees of work impairment. The MBHO found that 31 percent of people accessing behavioral services met criteria for being work-impaired—meaning their day-to-day functioning was impaired. After only three weeks of treatment, the percentage of work-impaired patients dropped to 18 percent, and after nine weeks, it dropped to 15 percent. Generally, patients who still appear work-impaired after a few months of treatment are those with chronic behavioral health conditions that need more intensive services with careful monitoring and typically are enrolled in a disease management program.

CONCLUSION

If an employer knew how many of its employees accessing its behavioral health benefits were work-impaired, that employer would undoubtedly see treatment as a worthwhile investment if many of those starting treatment work-impaired are able to return to nonimpaired status. Absenteeism and presenteeism (working, but not functioning at full capacity) in the workforce caused by depression and substance use disorders are responsible for huge losses each year for U.S. employers. If these costs can be reduced substantially with treatment, then behavioral health care services would rank as one of the most worthwhile investments an organization's management can make.

CHAPTER 9

Health Care Quality: Are We Getting Our Money's Worth?

William J. Mayer

Employers have a number of reasons for offering medical benefits to their employees. Perhaps most important is the objective of attracting and retaining employees.[1] More than 75 percent of small businesses offering medical benefits indicate that they think the provision of these benefits is "the right thing to do."[2] As employers have turned to managed care organizations (MCOs)—preferred provider organizations (PPOs), health maintenance organizations (HMOs) and point-of-service (POS) plans—and consumer-driven health care plans to help control the cost of these benefits, many have recognized the need to address issues of quality of care to ensure that their medical benefit plans serve the purposes for which they were designed. Major reports from the Institute of Medicine have focused the attention of employers, health professionals, and the public at large on serious deficiencies in the quality of health care in the United States and

1. Stanton M.,"Employer-Sponsored Health Insurance: Trends in Cost and Access." *Research in Action, Agency for Healthcare Research and Quality*, No. 17. September 2004.
2. P. Fronstin, R. Helman, and M. Greenwald, "Small Employers and Health Benefits: Findings from the 2002 Small Employer Health Benefits Survey," *EBRI Issue Brief*, No. 253, January 2003, pp. 1–21.

recommended steps for its improvement.[3] The risk for employers is that they will continue spending vast resources to provide a health care benefit that is not valued by current and/or prospective employees and that fails to maintain the health and productivity of the workforce.

Despite the obvious importance of this value equation in health care purchasing, as in all other purchasing, many employers, employees, and families do not explicitly factor quality of care into their health care purchasing decisions. There may be many reasons for this apparent paradox. Some individuals may be skeptical of their own or their employer's ability to define and measure quality of care. Some may be intimidated in their dealings with health professionals because of a lack of technical knowledge of health care. Some may view managed care organizations as contract and claims administrators, assuming that MCOs have little or no impact on quality of care.

This chapter describes further why it is important for employers to focus on quality of care in purchasing health care. It offers a definition of quality and discusses what we know about how to improve it. The chapter also presents suggestions for improving quality through changes in consumer and employer purchasing behavior, including practical approaches to evaluating the quality of MCOs, with options based on resources available for evaluation. Recommendations are offered for setting quality performance standards and performance guarantees for managed care contracting. And, finally, additional resources are suggested for those who wish to pursue efforts to improve the quality of their health care purchases. This chapter is intended to help the reader better appreciate the importance of quality of care in health care purchasing, gain a higher level of confidence in his or her ability to evaluate and improve quality of care, and become aware of resources available to further pursue the subject.

IS QUALITY OF CARE IMPORTANT?

Quality of health care is an important issue for employer and employee purchasers for a number of reasons. First, there are widespread documented errors in the delivery of health care services. Second, there is substantial evidence for extensive overuse and underuse of various health care services. Third, poor quality of care erodes the value of health care purchases. And,

3. (a) L. Kohn, J. Corrigan, and M. Donaldson, eds., Institute of Medicine, Committee on Quality of Health Care in America, *To Err is Human: Building a Safer Health System*, Washington, DC: National Academy Press, 2000. (b) J. Corrigan et al., eds., Institute of Medicine, Committee on Quality of Health Care in America, *Crossing the Quality Chasm: A New Health System for the 21st Century*, Washington, DC: National Academy Press, 2001.

finally, lack of attention to quality of care can have negative consequences for an employer in employee relations and relationships with providers and others in the local business community. Each of these reasons is discussed in this chapter.

Errors in the Delivery of Health Care Services

Two decades ago, the Harvard Medical Practice Study found that injuries caused by medical management occurred in 3.7 percent of hospital admissions in New York State. Among these injuries were drug complications, wound infections, and technical complications. Fully 27.6 percent of these injuries were the result of negligence, and 13.6 percent of the injuries led to death.[4] Extrapolating these results to all U.S. hospital admissions, as many as 98,000 Americans may have died because of errors during their hospitalization in a single year.[5]

The Institute of Medicine focused attention on the impact of errors in medicine through the work of its Quality of Health Care in America Project. Its first published report—*To Err is Human: Building a Safer Health System*—notes: "More people die in a given year as a result of medical errors than from motor vehicle accidents (43,458), breast cancer (42,297), or AIDS (16,516)."[6] The group estimated that preventable adverse events resulted in total national costs of between $17 billion and $29 billion, over one-half of which are direct health care costs. More recently it has been reported that health care-associated infections affect 1.7 million hospitalizations each year, with hospital-acquired sepsis resulting in a mortality rate of 19.5 percent and $32,900 in additional costs per patient.[7] A study commissioned by the Society of Actuaries estimated that medical errors and the problems they can cause, such as bedsores, infections, and device complications, cost the U.S. economy almost $20 billion in 2008.[8] As sobering as these numbers are, they almost certainly underestimate the

4. T. Brennan et al., "Incidence of Adverse Events and Negligence in Hospitalized Patients: Results of the Harvard Medical Practice Study I," *New England Journal of Medicine*, Vol. 324, 1991, pp. 370–376.
5. American Hospital Association, *Hospital Statistics*, Chicago, 1999.
6. L. Kohn, J. Corrigan, and M. Donaldson, eds., Institute of Medicine, Committee on Quality of Health Care in America, To Err is Human: Building a Safer Health System, Washington, DC: National Academy Press, 2000.
7. M. Eber et al., "Clinical and Economic Outcomes Attributable to Health Care-Associated Sepsis and Pneumonia," *Archives of Internal Medicine*, Vol. 170, No. 4, 2010, pp. 347–353.
8. J. Shreve et al., "The Economic Measurement of Medical Errors," Schaumburg, IL: Society ofActuaries, June 2010, www.soa.org/research/research-projects/health/research-econ-measurement.aspx.

impact of medical errors due to their focus on the hospital inpatient setting. A recent study of outpatient internal medicine physician visits using standardized patients found that error-free care was provided in less than 40 percent of complicated encounters.[9]

Clearly, medical errors have a significant negative impact on employer health care costs, as well as employee health outcomes and productivity. These findings raise the question of what employers and individuals can do to help minimize the likelihood and the impact of medical errors in the health care services they purchase and receive—a question to be taken up later in this chapter.

Overuse of Health Care Services

Investigators have long noted dramatic geographic variations in the use of health care services, without apparent differences in the health of the populations being served. For example, one study showed that Medicare hospitalization rates were 60 percent higher in Boston than in New Haven, yet Medicare mortality rates did not differ between the two cities.[10] A study of Medicare end-of-life spending found that beneficiaries in higher-spending regions of the United States received approximately 60 percent more care than beneficiaries in lower-spending regions, without finding consistent differences between these groups in quality of care or access to care.[11] Recently, total hip replacement surgery rates among Medicare beneficiaries were found to vary by 300 percent from low-use regions to high-use regions.[12]

There is a large and growing body of research on the extent of medical care that is inappropriate or unnecessary. Studies of appropriateness of care have found that as much as 32 percent of selected procedures are inappropriate.[13] An excellent example of research supporting this estimate is the series of studies commissioned by the State of New York Cardiac

9. S. Weiner et al., "Contextual Errors and Failures in Individualized Patient Care: A Multicenter Study," *Annals of Internal Medicine*, Vol. 153, No. 2, 2010, pp. 69–75.
10. E. Fisher et al., "Hospital Readmission Rates for Cohorts of Medicare Beneficiaries in Boston and New Haven," *New England Journal of Medicine*, Vol. 331, 1994, pp. 989–995.
11. E.S. Fisher et al., "The implications of Regional Variations in Medicare Spending. Part 1: The Content, Quality, and Accessibility of Care," *Annals of Internal Medicine*, Vol. 138, 2003, pp. 273–287.
12. E. Fisher et al., "Trends and Regional Variation in Hip, Knee, and Shoulder Replacement," Dartmouth Atlas Surgery Report, Dartmouth, NH: The Dartmouth Institute for Health Policy and Clinical Practice, April 6, 2010, www.dartmouthatlas.org/downloads/reports/Joint_Replacement_0410.pdf.
13. R.H. Brook and M.E. Vaiana, *Appropriateness of Care: A Chart Book*, Washington, DC: National Health Policy Forum, 1989.

Advisory Committee on the appropriateness of various cardiac procedures in New York State. Evaluation of coronary angiographies (inserting a catheter into coronary arteries and injecting contrast material) found that 20 percent were of uncertain appropriateness and 4 percent were clearly inappropriate.[14] When percutaneous transluminal coronary angioplasty (PTCA) (using a balloon catheter to open blood flow through a coronary artery) was evaluated, 38 percent were of uncertain appropriateness and 4 percent were clearly inappropriate. At some hospitals, as many as 57 percent of PTCAs were either inappropriate or of uncertain appropriateness.[15] In a companion study, inappropriate and uncertain use of coronary artery bypass graft surgery was found to be 2.4 percent and 7 percent, respectively. Though these rates may appear relatively low, they have significant health implications, given that the average mortality rate for patients undergoing surgery in the study was 2 percent and the complication rate was 17 percent.[16] A study of CT and MRI scans ordered by primary care physicians in the outpatient setting found more than one in four was not considered appropriate.[17] A recent commentary in the *Journal of the American Medical Association*, *JAMA*, described a "perfect storm" of overutilization due to both physician and patient factors from financial incentives, to medical malpractice, to direct-to-consumer marketing.[18]

These are but a few examples of research suggesting that inappropriate and unnecessary medical care has substantial negative consequences both for employee health and the cost of health care.

Underuse of Health Care Services

Another deficiency identified in health care quality is the failure to apply services known to be beneficial in improving health. In a study of patients hospitalized for acute myocardial infarction (heart attack), Marciniak and

14. S.J. Bernstein et al., "The Appropriateness of Use of Coronary Angiography in New York State," *JAMA*, Vol. 269, 1993, pp. 766–769.
15. L.H. Hilborne et al., "The Appropriateness of Percutaneous Transluminal Coronary Angioplasty in New York State," *JAMA*, Vol. 269, 1993, pp. 761–765.
16. L.L. Leape et al., "The Appropriateness of Use of Coronary Artery Bypass Graft Surgery in New York State," *JAMA*, Vol. 269, 1993, pp. 753–760.
17. B. Lehnert and R. Bree, "Analysis of Appropriateness of Outpatient CT and MRI Referred from Primary Care Clinics at an Academic Medical Center: How Critical Is the Need for Improved Decision Support?" *Journal of the American College of Radiology*, Vol. 7, 2010, pp. 192–197.
18. E. Emanuel and V. Fuchs, "The Perfect Storm of Overutilization," *JAMA*, Vol. 299, 2008, pp. 2789–2791.

colleagues found that between 11 percent and 68 percent of patients nationwide did not receive particular standard treatments for this condition, despite being "ideal candidates" for therapies.[19] An earlier study found that internists and family physicians were less knowledgeable about, and less inclined to practice, state-of-the-art advances in treatment of acute myocardial infarction than were cardiologists.[20]

Similarly, a study of patients with diabetes treated in primary care offices found that between 55 percent and 84 percent of these patients did not receive optimal services recommended for their condition according to national guidelines in use. Optimal use of services varied by location of practice by as much as 238 percent.[21] A study of 439 indicators of quality of care for 30 conditions and preventive care among a random sample of adults in 12 U.S. metropolitan areas found that only 54.9 percent received recommended care. Quality of care varied by medical condition, from a high of 78.7 percent of recommended care received for senile cataract to a low of 10.5 percent of recommended care for alcohol dependence.[22] A study of the quality of outpatient care provided to children found similar rates of underutilization of health services. Overall, pediatric patients received only 46.5 percent of indicated care. Almost one in three children did not receive indicated care for acute conditions, while 59 percent of children did not receive indicated preventive care.[23]

Some studies suggest that physicians are more likely to underuse health care services when treating women, particularly black women. Research by Roger and colleagues found that women with unstable angina (chest pain from blockages in arteries supplying blood to heart muscle) were 27 percent less likely to undergo noninvasive cardiac tests, and a startling 72 percent less likely to receive invasive cardiac procedures.[24] Even

19. T. Marciniak et al., "Improving the Quality of Care for Medicare Patients With Acute Myocardial Infarction: Results From the Cooperative Cardiovascular Project," *JAMA*, Vol. 279, 1998, pp. 1351–1357.

20. J.Z. Ayanian et al., "Knowledge and Practices of Generalist and Specialist Physicians Regarding Drug Therapy for Acute Myocardial Infarction," *New England Journal of Medicine*, Vol. 331, 1994, pp. 1136–1142.

21. J.P. Weiner et al., "Variation in Office-Based Quality: A Claims-Based Profile of Care Provided to Medicare Patients with Diabetes," *JAMA*, Vol. 273, 1995, pp. 1503–1508.

22. E.A. McGlynn et al., "The Quality of Health Care Delivered to Adults in the United States," *New England Journal of Medicine*, Vol. 348, 2003, pp. 2635–2645.

23. R. Mangione-Smith et al., "The Quality of Ambulatory Care Delivered to Children in the United States," *New England Journal of Medicine*, Vol. 357, 2007, pp. 1515–1523.

24. V. Roger et al., "Sex Differences in Evaluation and Outcome of Unstable Angina," *JAMA*, Vol. 283, 2000, pp. 646–652. See also D. Mark, "Sex Bias in Cardiovascular Care: Should Women Be Treated More Like Men?" *JAMA*, Vol. 283, 2000, pp. 659–661.

within Medicare managed care health plans, black plan members were found to receive poorer quality of care than white plan members, specifically for eye examinations for patients with diabetes, for beta-blocker use after heart attack, and for follow up to hospitalization for mental illness.[25]

There is also evidence to suggest that underuse varies by type of health plan. For example, a study found that Medicare patients with joint pain who were enrolled in HMOs reported less improvement in symptoms than similar fee-for-service Medicare beneficiaries.[26] Yet, other research suggests no significant difference between quality of care in HMO and fee-for-service environments in such areas as hypertension and diabetes.[27]

Failure to apply services known to be beneficial in improving health is a substantial and widespread problem. Clearly, this type of quality problem has negative implications for employee health and productivity. The implications for cost of care are more variable, because some of the underused services may result in a net increase in direct medical care costs, despite being effective in preventing negative and costly health outcomes. Nevertheless, in purchasing health care for ourselves or for employees, these are services we would want to receive as part of state-of-the-art quality in health care delivery. Whether one looks at quality from the perspective of individual providers, practices, or health plans, these landmark studies shed new light on deficiencies in quality of care, and suggest how appropriate to health care is the maxim "Let the buyer beware."

Employee, Provider, and Community Relations

When medical benefits decisions are made without substantive consideration of quality of care, employees can take away the message that their health and well-being are not valued by their employer. This message can undermine one of the key objectives of offering medical benefits: to promote the recruitment and retention of employees. Incorporating quality assurance and continuous quality improvement (CQI) processes into medical benefits decisions, and effectively communicating these processes to

25. E.C. Schneider, A.M. Zaslavsky, and A.M. Epstein, "Racial Disparities in the Quality of Care for Enrollees in Medicare Managed Care," *JAMA*, Vol. 287, 2002, pp. 1288–1294.
26. D.G. Clement et al., "Access and Outcomes of Elderly Patients Enrolled in Managed Care," *JAMA*, Vol. 271, 1994, pp. 1487–1492.
27. S. Greenfield et al., "Outcomes of Patients with Hypertension and Non Insulin Dependent Diabetes Mellitus Treated by Different Symptoms and Specialties. Results from the Medical Outcomes Study," *JAMA*, Vol. 274, 1995, pp. 1436–1444.

employees, can help avoid the employee relations pitfall of employee dissatisfaction with their medical benefits.

Disillusioned providers also can undermine the extent to which employees value their medical benefits. Employee opinion may be influenced by negative assessments from physicians about the quality of an employer's health plan. In addition, physician performance may be adversely affected by a poor-quality health plan, with consequences for employee health and productivity.

Failing to demonstrate a commitment to quality assurance (QA) and CQI in health care decisions can leave employers vulnerable to the charge of neglecting corporate social responsibility as well. This can have obvious negative implications for community relations.

Value of Medical Care Expenditures

The value of health care services can be defined as the health benefit per dollar spent.[28] Chassin and the National Roundtable on Health Care Quality observed that errors in the delivery of health care services, as well as overuse of services, can reduce the value of health care services by both decreasing the numerator and increasing the denominator of this equation. Conversely, by reducing errors and overuse, the value of health care services can be increased. (The impact of underuse on value is more variable, as it tends to move the numerator and denominator in the same direction.) Most businesses would not view as prudent the practice of purchasing from suppliers based upon price alone. When viewing health plans and providers as you would view other suppliers to your business, considerations of quality and service, as well as cost, become essential components of the value equation.

DEFINING QUALITY

Brook has defined health care quality as consisting of three components: appropriateness, excellence, and satisfaction.[29] Quality care is care that is appropriate given the current state of the art in medicine. It is also care that is excellent in its execution and that produces a high degree of patient satisfaction.

---

28. M. Chassin et al., "The Urgent Need to Improve Health Care Quality," *JAMA*, Vol. 280, 1998, pp. 1000–1005.
29. R.H. Brook, "Define and Review the Purpose of Guidelines," Presentation at Measuring Performance and Implementing Improvement Conference, April 27, 1995, Chicago.

One of the positive, and in this author's view essential, attributes of this definition is the fact that it is measurable. The literature cited above on cardiac services in New York State provides examples of how appropriateness can be quantified. Excellence in execution can be measured in terms of both the processes and outcomes of care. Examples of process measures of excellence might include transfusion rates in coronary artery bypass surgery. Outcome measures might include operative mortality or complication rates for this type of surgery.

In the area of patient satisfaction, there is well over a decade of research demonstrating that this component of quality of care also can be measured in ways that are reliable and valid. Resources to assist in evaluating these elements of quality will be provided later in this chapter.

EVALUATING QUALITY

Let us assume that an employer is convinced of the importance and feasibility of considering quality in health care purchasing. How should it go about assessing quality or promoting employee evaluation of quality, whether at the level of the physician, hospital, ancillary services provider, or health plan?

Physician Quality

Most assessments of physician quality begin with the physician's training, experience, and professional certifications. The literature on the link between these factors and quality is limited. Nevertheless, these characteristics can serve as a starting point for evaluating a physician's level of knowledge and skills, which we might postulate would be related to the appropriateness and excellence of his or her practices. In addition, a review of physician credentials might reveal that small proportion of physicians for whom glaring quality-of-care problems have been identified. Characteristics to consider in this assessment include the following:

- Current unrestricted license to practice in your state
- Current unrestricted license to dispense prescription drugs from the state and the Federal Drug Enforcement Administration
- Certification by a specialty board recognized by the American Board of Medical Specialties
- Current active, unrestricted hospital staff privileges

The last of these criteria may not apply to physicians who choose not to see patients in a hospital setting. It may be difficult, however, to determine if a physician's privileges were dropped as a result of his or her own choice or because of a quality-driven decision by the hospital. The advantages of using a physician with hospital privileges include having continuity of both inpatient and outpatient care and having the benefit of the hospital's QA and/or CQI program apply to your physician. This latter benefit includes hospital access to the National Practitioner Data Bank, a national database on physician quality problems that is not accessible to the public.[30]

Conspicuously absent from the above list is malpractice experience. There are questions about the extent to which malpractice experience is a reflection of physician quality.[31] On the other hand, research indicates that any history of malpractice claims, paid or unpaid, is associated with an increased likelihood of future claims.[32] Therefore, it may be worth evaluating a physician's malpractice claim history, if only to reduce your risk of being involved in a future malpractice claim. Medical malpractice claims closed within the past five years in 17 states, including California, Florida, New York, and Texas, can be found through the "Background Check" tab available from HealthGrades under find-a-doctor search at www.healthgrades.com. Additional malpractice claim information on individual physicians may be available from the court clerk in the jurisdiction(s) where the physician has practiced.

A physician's credentials can be evaluated directly by employees, by benefit managers, or by health plans. The following are some of the resources for employees and benefit managers to consider in conducting such an evaluation:

- American Board of Medical Specialties (www.abms.org)
- American Medical Association (www.ama-assn.org)
- HealthGrades (www.healthgrades.com)
- Federation of State Medical Boards (www.docinfo.org)

30. S.L. Horner, "The Health Care Quality Improvement Act of 1986: Its History, Provisions, Applications and Implications," *American Journal of Law and Medicine*, Vol. 16, 1990, pp. 455–498.
31. U.S. Congress, Office of Technology Assessment, *The Quality of Medical Care: Information for Consumers*, OTA-H-386, Washington, DC: U.S. Government Printing Office, 1988.
32. R.R. Bovbjerg and K.R. Petronis, "The Relationship Between Physicians' Malpractice Claims History and Later Claims: Does the Past Predict the Future?" *JAMA*, Vol. 272, 1994, pp. 1421–1426.

The state physician licensing board is a good place to look for answers to questions about the state licensing status of individual physicians. Most states have such information available online. A review of information available from state licensing boards has been assembled by Public Citizen Health Research Group and can be found at www.citizen. org/hrg. Physician sanctions and disciplinary actions by state licensing boards for all 50 states can also be found through the "Background Check" tab available from HealthGrades under find-a-doctor search at www.healthgrades.com.

The quality-related issues described above pertain to all physicians, regardless of their specialty. When assessing physician quality as it relates to specific diagnoses or conditions, additional factors should be considered. For example, physicians being evaluated for their quality in performing a particular surgical procedure should be asked such questions as these:

- What kind of advanced training and/or certification has the physician had in performing the procedure?
- What is the annual volume of the procedure performed by the physician?
- What are the complication and mortality rates for the procedure as performed by the physician?
- What is the success rate for the procedure as performed by the physician?
- What is the average length of hospital stay for the procedure?
- What is the average length of disability following the procedure?

The applicability of these and other questions will vary by specialty, condition, and procedure. Generally speaking, however, the quality of a physician's performance, as in the example of percutaneous transluminal coronary angioplasty described above, is related to the frequency with which he or she performs the procedure. For some conditions and procedures, there may be regional or national research centers or centers of excellence. Helpful resources in learning about such centers, and obtaining consumer information about various health issues include the following:

- National Cancer Institute, Cancer Information Service (Tel. 800-4-CANCER)
- American Cancer Society local affiliates (see local phone book)
- American Heart Association local affiliates (see local phone book)

- American Lung Association local affiliates (see local phone book)
- National Institute of Mental Health (Tel. 800-421-4211)

The National Committee for Quality Assurance (NCQA), in collaboration with the American Heart Association, American Stroke Association, and American Diabetes Association, has developed programs to recognize physicians demonstrating that they provide high-quality care for patients with selected common chronic conditions, including diabetes mellitus, cardiac conditions, and stroke. Information about these programs and a database of recognized physicians is available at www.bridgestoexcellence.org. The NCQA is promoting use of Bridges To Excellence recognition by employers and health plans to select and reward physicians.

Another important aspect of the quality of primary care physicians is the responsibility they take for providing for all the health care needs of their patients. This responsibility has been formalized in the concept of a patient-centered medical home (PCMH). The American College of Physicians, American Academy of Family Physicians, American Academy of Pediatrics, and American Osteopathic Association have jointly defined the medical home as a model of care where each patient has an ongoing relationship with a personal physician who leads a team that takes collective responsibility for patient care. The physician-led care team is responsible for providing all the patient's health care needs and, when needed, arranges for appropriate care with other qualified physicians. Functional elements of a PCMH include enhanced access and communication, patient tracking, care management, electronic prescribing, test and referral tracking, and performance reporting and improvement. The PCMH is founded upon research demonstrating the benefits to quality of primary care and the Chronic Care Model.[33] NCQA has established a program to recognize primary care physician practices as medical homes: Physician Practice Connections–Patient-Centered Medical Home. NCQA has been working with national and regional health plans to promote the PCMH concept and encourage its adoption by physicians through the use of incentive payments.[34] Ask your primary care physician if he or she has been recognized as a PCMH through a health plan or NCQA.

33. MacColl Institute for Healthcare Innovation, 2010, www.improvingchroniccare.org.
34. National Committee for Quality Assurance, "Physician Practice Connections–Patient-Centered Medical Home," www.ncqa.org/tabid/631/Default.aspx.

If your physician participates in any managed care programs, he or she may receive periodic performance report cards from the MCO and may be willing to share the results with you. Some of these results may be published. For example, the Pacific Business Group on Health has published performance data on medical groups that make up California health plans (though the data are not broken out by individual physician).

Physician report card data are publicly available for selected locations and specialties. For example, the Pennsylvania Health care cost Containment Council has published heart attack mortality data for physician groups.[35] More recently, the Society of Thoracic Surgery has made available comparative data on clinical quality for 221 cardiac surgical groups from 42 states in Consumer Reports and at www.sts.org. The data identifies groups as above average, average, or below average for quality of treatment, complication and survival rates.[36]

While "report cards" on physicians promise to be increasingly available, they should be interpreted with caution. A number of potential pitfalls with such reports have been identified. For example, multiple physicians may participate in a patient's care, making it difficult to assign primary responsibility for the patient's outcome to any one physician or medical group.[37] In a study of physician report cards for diabetes care, Hofer and colleagues found that they were unable to reliably detect true practice differences among physicians at three practice sites. They also found that physicians could easily "game" the reporting system by avoiding or deselecting patients with high prior cost or with poor adherence or poor response to treatment.[38]

Another public source of information about physician quality is patients. A growing number of organizations publish patient-reported ratings of physician quality. While these ratings are based upon patient perceptions only, they present a vitally important aspect of physician quality. HealthGrades offers such patient ratings information at www.healthgrades.com, as does Angie's List at www.angieslist.com. A 2010 study identified 33 physician-rating Web sites offering 190 reviews on 27 percent of 300

35. *Focus on Heart Attack in Pennsylvania in Western Pennsylvania*, Harrisburg, PA: Pennsylvania Health Care Cost Containment Council, June 1996.

36. T. Ferris and D. Torchiana, "Public Release of Clinical Outcomes Data—Online CABG Report Cards." *New England Journal of Medicine*, Vol. 363, 2010, pp. 1593–1595.

37. J. Jollis and P. Romano, "Pennsylvania's Focus on Heart Attack—Grading the Scorecard," *New England Journal of Medicine*, Vol. 338, 1998, pp. 983–987.

38. T. Hofer et al., "The Unreliability of Individual Physician 'Report Cards' for Assessing the Costs and Quality of Care of a Chronic Disease," *JAMA*, Vol. 281, 1999, pp. 2098–2105.

randomly chosen Boston physicians.[39] While these Web sites appear to address a minority of physicians with relatively few patient raters today, they are likely to become more robust in their coverage and inputs with the continued growth of social networking on the web.

An influential force for improving physician-specific quality data is the Centers for Medicare and Medicaid Services' (CMS) Physician Quality Reporting Initiative (PQRI). Under the 2006 Tax Relief and Health Care Act (TRHCA), CMS created an incentive payment for eligible health professionals who report data on standard quality measures for outpatient services provided to Medicare Part B beneficiaries.[40] PQRI quality measures include vaccinations, screening mammograms, diabetes management, and body mass index (BMI) screening and follow up, to name a few. Eligible professionals who satisfactorily report these quality measures for 2010, for example, earn an incentive payment of 2 percent of their total estimated Medicare Part B allowed charges during the same reporting period. CMS periodically sends eligible professionals feedback reports on their performance. Beginning in 2015, failure to report PQRI measures will result in reductions in payments to eligible professionals under the Patient Protection and Affordable Care Act of 2010 (PPACA). While these data are not yet public, the PPACA requires an Independent Payment Advisory Board to produce an annual report on quality of care, including regional comparisons of provider practice patterns and costs.[41]

Finally, there is a large body of research suggesting that physician–patient communication is related to the quality and outcome of care. Perhaps the best way to evaluate a physician's communication skills is to do so firsthand, scheduling an office visit to get to know a physician you may not already be familiar with. If you make such a visit, it may be helpful to prepare both general questions and questions particular to your circumstances in advance of your appointment.

Investigating even this minimum set of criteria for physician quality care requires a significant investment of time and resources. And such assessments should be repeated periodically to ensure that there has been no change in physician status. The extensive nature of this undertaking points to one advantage of purchasing medical care from a health plan that

39. T. Lagu et al., "Patients' Evaluations of Health Care Providers in the Era of Social Networking: An Analysis of Physician-Rating Websites," *Journal of General Internal Medicine*, Vol. 25, 2010, pp. 942–946.

40. Centers for Medicare and Medicaid Services, 2010, www.cms.gov/pqri/.

41. The Henry J. Kaiser Family Foundation, "Summary of Key Changes to Medicare in 2010 Health Reform Law, 2010," www.kff.org/healthreform/7948.cfm.

includes a network of providers. The various aspects of physician quality described above and others can be consistently and rigorously assessed by the plan on an ongoing basis, with associated economies of scale.

Hospital Quality

Some of the same approaches to quality assessment described for physicians can be applied to hospitals. A useful starting place for assessing a hospital's quality is its accreditation. Accreditations to look for include the following:

- Current, unrestricted license from the state
- Current, unrestricted, nonprobationary accreditation from the Centers for Medicare and Medicaid Services for participation in Medicare and Medicaid
- Current, unrestricted, nonprobationary accreditation from the Joint Commission

The Joint Commission has an extensive process for assessing hospital quality with unannounced on-site surveys.[42] Beginning January 1, 1995, the Joint Commission made available summaries of the results of its new surveys.[43] These summaries, however, are brief and offer only general information. In addition, the Joint Commission's surveys were at one time criticized by the Inspector General of the U.S. Department of Health and Human Services (DHHS) as "unlikely to detect patterns, systems, or incidents of substandard care."[44] Among the improvements implemented by the Joint Commission in an effort to address these concerns are the inclusion of outcomes measures in its review process, such as acute myocardial infarction, congestive heart failure, and complications of surgery.

General information on hospital facilities, personnel, and services are published annually by the American Hospital Association.[45] This

42. *1995 Accreditation Manual for Hospitals*, Oakbrook Terrace, IL: Joint Commission on Accreditation of Healthcare Organizations, 1994.

43. For information on whether a survey summary is available for a particular hospital, contact the Joint Commission at 630-792-5800. If your hospital has not undergone a survey since January 1, 1995, you can contact the hospital administration and request a summary of its most recent survey.

44. HHS Inspector General Reports on The External Review of Hospital Quality, OEI-01-97-00050; -00051; -00052, and -00053.

45. *AHA Guide, 2011 Edition*, Schaumberg, IL: American Hospital Association, 2010, www.ahadata.com/ahadata/html/AHAGuide.html.

information can sometimes be helpful in making inferences about quality for particular conditions or procedures. For example, if you are having a high-risk delivery, you may wish to choose a hospital that has an advanced-level nursery, including a dedicated neonatal intensive care unit. One variable to consider in assessing hospital quality is whether it is a major teaching hospital (defined as more than 0.097 teaching residents per hospital bed set up and staffed for patient care). Such hospitals have been found to have a lower risk of death than other hospitals, when evaluated for mortality due to hip fracture, stroke, coronary heart disease, and congestive heart failure.[46] A review of 23 studies comparing quality of care in teaching hospitals as compared with nonteaching hospitals found better performance in teaching hospitals over a range of locations, conditions, and populations.[47]

The Leapfrog Group is an organization of large purchasers of health care that strives to create big leaps in health care safety, quality and value. The group gathers data voluntarily reported by hospitals on standards of safety, quality, and value. Ratings of hospital conformance to Leapfrog standards are published on their Web site at www.leapfroggroup.org.

The Centers for Medicare & Medicaid Services makes data publicly available on hospital performance through its Medicare Provider Analysis and Review (MEDPAR) files. In some states (e.g., Pennsylvania and New York), data are publicly available on hospital performance for specific conditions and procedures.[48] These data can include the volume of cases, outcomes (mortality and complication rates), average length of stay, and average cost per case. HealthGrades is an organization that analyzes and reports hospital quality rating information at www.healthgrades.com. The HealthGrades quality rating system relies on publicly available Medicare data and a statistical model for risk adjustment to assess hospital mortality and complications by diagnosis and procedure. A study of the ability of HealthGrades ratings to discriminate between individual hospitals in the processes and outcomes of their care was published by a team of researchers at Yale University. They found that HealthGrades ratings could accurately identify groups of hospitals that performed better in quality than

46. D. Taylor, D. Whellan, and F. Sloan, "Effects of Admission to a Teaching Hospital on the Cost and Quality of Care for Medicare Beneficiaries," *New England Journal of Medicine*, Vol. 340, 1999, pp. 293–299.

47. J. Kupersmith, "Quality of Care in Teaching Hospitals: A Literature Review," *Academic Medicine*, Vol. 80, 2005, pp. 458–466.

48. (a) *A Consumer Guide to Coronary Artery Bypass Graft Surgery*, Harrisburg, PA: Pennsylvania Health Care Cost Containment Council, 1991. (b) *Hospital Effectiveness Report*, Harrisburg, PA: Pennsylvania Health care cost Containment Council, 1994.

other hospital groups. HealthGrades ratings did poorly, however, when it came to discriminating between two individual hospitals on their processes of care or mortality performance.[49]

CMS also makes hospital quality data available on its Web site at www.hospitalcompare.hhs.gov. These data include the following:

1. Process-of-care quality measures such as timely use of antibiotics for all surgery patients, and control of blood sugar and prevention of blood clots for selected surgery patients
2. Outcome-of-care measures such as death rate for pneumonia patients and readmission rate for heart attack patients
3. Use of medical imaging such as overuse of outpatient combination (double) CT scans of the chest or abdomen when a single scan may be more appropriate
4. Survey of patients' hospital experiences and ratings of quality
5. Medicare payment and volume data by condition and procedure

The Commonwealth Fund has further analyzed these measures to permit comparisons of performance for one or more hospitals to national and state averages and top 1 percent, 10 percent, or 25 percent of hospitals. This information can be found at their Web site at www.whynotthebest.org.

Whether or not data are publicly available for the condition or procedure of interest to a particular patient, he or she may wish to consider approaching the hospital administration directly with the following questions:

- What is the hospital's volume of admissions for the condition or procedure of interest?
- What is the mortality or complication rate for the condition or procedure as performed at the hospital?
- What is the success rate for the treatment or procedure at the hospital?
- What is the average length of stay for the condition or procedure?
- Does the hospital participate in any managed care networks (e.g., HMO, PPO, or POS plans)?
- Has the hospital been designated as a center of excellence for the condition or procedure by a health plan?

---

49. H.M. Krumholz et al., "Evaluation of a Consumer-Oriented Internet Health Care Report Card: The Risk of Quality Ratings Based on Mortality Data," *JAMA*, Vol. 287, 2002, pp. 1277–1287.

The final question will apply to only a small number of conditions, procedures, and hospitals. Nevertheless, one can find designated regional and national centers of excellence for high-risk, high-cost conditions and procedures, such as organ transplantation, open-heart surgery, and burns. The National Institutes of Health also designates research centers for selected conditions. One might postulate that these centers are more likely to provide quality care for these conditions because of their successful research programs.

The question pertaining to volume of patients admitted for a particular condition or procedure can be extremely useful as a surrogate measure of quality. More than 20 years of research and dozens of published studies have linked better outcomes to hospitals and doctors delivering higher volumes of particular health care services.[50] Research has confirmed the link of high volume to better outcomes in acute myocardial infarction (hospitals with more than 6.3 Medicare patients with acute myocardial infarction per week on average), major cancer surgery (hospitals with more than one Medicare patient per year on average for a given procedure), and carotid endarterectomy, i.e., surgery removing blockages from the carotid arteries to prevent stroke (hospitals with more than 62 Medicare patients undergoing the procedure per year).[51] Yet, volume is not a perfect surrogate for quality. A study of coronary artery bypass surgery in 164 hospitals found that higher-volume surgeons and hospitals had lower mortality and readmission rates. Low-volume hospitals that consistently provided patients with proven elements of care, however, had mortality and readmission rates no different than high-volume hospitals.[52]

Additional resources to consider when evaluating hospital quality include the following:

- American Hospital Association, Chicago (www.aha.org)
- Centers for Medicare & Medicaid Services, Baltimore, MD (www.cms.hhs.gov)
- The Joint Commission, Oakbrook Terrace, IL (www.jointcommission.org)

---

50. E. Hannan, "The Relation Between Volume and Outcome in Health Care," *New England Journal of Medicine*, Vol. 340, 1999, pp. 1677–1679.
51. (a) Op. cit., D. Thieman et al., 1999. (b) C. Begg et al., "Impact of Hospital Volume on Operative Mortality for Major Cancer Surgery," *JAMA*, Vol. 280, 1998, pp. 1747–1751. (c) R.D. Cebul, et al., "Indications, Outcomes, and Provider Volumes for Carotid Endarterectomy," *JAMA*, Vol. 279, 1998, pp. 1282–1287.
52. A. Auerbach et al., "Shop for Quality or Volume? Volume, Quality, and Outcomes of Coronary Artery Bypass Surgery," *Annals of Internal Medicine*, Vol. 150, 2009, pp. 696–704.

Assessing hospital quality, both initially and on an ongoing basis, can be a labor-intensive process. As in the case of physician quality assessment, this kind of assessment and more should be obtainable with economies of scale through a quality health plan offering a provider network (see below).

Managed Care Organization Quality

One of the great potential advantages of purchasing health care through a managed care organization is the cost-effective ongoing quality assurance and continuous quality improvement that these plans can provide. Research has demonstrated the contribution of health plans to variations in quality of care.[53] The question for the employer or purchaser of an MCO is how to evaluate the quality and the contribution of its supplier's QA/CQI programs. One approach to this question is to look for accreditation by an independent organization that has evaluated the quality of the MCO. Today, the major accrediting organization for MCOs is the National Committee for Quality Assurance (NCQA).

The NCQA has reviewed a majority of MCOs in the United States.[54] Its accreditation process involves a review of MCO quality-related systems, including quality improvement, processes for reviewing and authorizing medical care, quality of provider network, and members' rights and responsibilities.[55] Documentation of these processes provided by the MCO are analyzed, and a site survey is conducted involving both physician and administrative reviewers.

In addition to its process-oriented assessments, the NCQA has developed the Healthcare Effectiveness Data and Information Set (HEDIS) to help standardize the measurement and reporting of health-plan performance. Higher performance on HEDIS measures has been linked to better physical and mental health outcomes in health-plan enrollees with

53. D. Thiemann, et al., *The Association Between Hospital Volume and Survival After Acute Myocardial Infarction in Elderly Patients*," New England Journal of Medicine, Vol. 340, 1999, pp. 1640–1648; J. Ross, et al., *Hospital Volume and 30-Dau Mortality for Three Common Medical Conditions*, New England Journal of Medicine, Vol. 362, 2010, pp. 1110–1118.

54. www.ncqa.org, February 2005.

55. National Committee for Quality Assurance, *2011 Standards and Guidelines for the Accreditation of Health Plans*, Washington, DC: NCQA, August 2011, www.ncqa.org/publications.

diabetes.[56] HEDIS measures have become the basis of performance measures produced by many health plans and purchasing coalitions.[57] HEDIS has measures applicable to commercial, Medicaid, and Medicare plans. In the area of effectiveness of care, the measures include such items as breast cancer screening, controlling high blood pressure, and follow-up after hospitalization for mental illness. In the area of access and availability of care, measures include getting needed care and getting care quickly. In the area of satisfaction, HEDIS incorporates the Consumer Assessment of Health Plans (CAHPS) instrument—a reliable and valid survey and reporting kit developed by a consortium of the Harvard Medical School, the RAND Corporation, and the Research Triangle Institute under the sponsorship of the Agency for Health Care Policy and Research.[58] Based upon these reviews, and MCO performance on HEDIS and CAHPS, the MCO is granted one of the following levels of accreditation status:[59]

- *Excellent*—Demonstrated performance that meets or exceeds NCQA requirements for consumer protection and quality improvement (QI), and HEDIS results among the highest scoring plans nationally or regionally
- *Commendable*—demonstrated performance that meets or exceeds NCQA requirements for consumer protection and QI
- *Accredited*—performance meeting most of NCQA's requirements for consumer protection and QI
- *Provisional*—compliance with some, but not all, of NCQA's consumer protection and QI requirements
- *Denied*—failure to meet NCQA requirements for consumer protection and QI requirements

The performance of health plans can be compared using accreditation level and HEDIS measures. Individual plan performance and performance benchmarks can be accessed through NCQA's Health Plan Report Cards and Quality Compass program (see www.ncqa.org). Report cards include ratings of health-plan performance on access and service, qualified providers, staying healthy, getting better, and living with illness. NCQA

56. J. Harman et al., "Association of Health Plans' Healthcare Effectiveness Data and Information Set (HEDIS) Performance with Outcomes of Enrollees with Diabetes," *Medical Care*, Vol. 48, 2010, pp. 217–223.

57. National Committee on Quality Assurance, *HEDIS 2005*, Washington, DC: NCQA, 2004.

58. www.ahrq.gov, February 2005.

59. National Committee for Quality Assurance, *Standards for the Accreditation of MCOs*, Washington, DC: NCQA, 2004/2005, www.ncqa.org/publications.

has also created an economic model for projecting the comparative performance of health plans. The Quality Dividend Calculator projects cost savings that an individual employer can expect from choosing a high-quality MCO. Projections are based upon how health care quality as measured by HEDIS reduces absenteeism and increases productivity among employees. The calculator is also available through the NCQA Web site. It should be noted that not all health plans collect and publish HEDIS data, and although NCQA audits HEDIS data, the data are collected and analyzed by the health plans themselves, with the potential for bias that is inherent in this approach.

In assessing health-plan quality of care, it would be worthwhile to ask the following questions of health plan administrators:

- Has your MCO applied for accreditation from the NCQA?
- If so, when was your most recent review, and what category of accreditation did your MCO receive?
- Will the MCO provide a summary of the findings of the accreditation process?

A list of health plans reviewed by NCQA for accreditation is available online at www.ncqa.org. While reviewing the results of these accreditation processes can be informative, the accreditation organizations explicitly warn that they do not warranty any third parties (e.g., employers) regarding the quality of care of an MCO. In addition, many MCOs have not yet undergone accreditation. Therefore, whenever an employer or employee is purchasing MCO services, it would be advisable to do some additional evaluation, including contacting your state departments of insurance and/or public health, reviewing some minimal documentation related to MCO quality, and making a site visit.

State governments generally have some regulatory authority over MCOs operating within their borders. This regulatory authority may reside with the department of public health, the department of insurance, or some combination of these. A call to one or both of these agencies in your state, asking for information about the status of a particular MCO, can be informative. If the MCO of interest is an HMO, you may want to ask for a copy of the HMO's annual report, which must be filed with the state department of insurance.

Requesting and reviewing the following information from the MCO also can be helpful:

- Credentialing criteria and processes for network physicians, hospitals, and ancillary providers (e.g., laboratory, X-ray, and home health agencies): Do these criteria and processes include those mentioned above under physician and hospital quality? Are provider credentials verified by the MCO, or do they accept a provider's self-report? How frequently are providers recredentialed? Does the recredentialing process include routine, systematic consideration of member complaints, member satisfaction, and other quality indicators?

- A copy of the most recent quality assurance, quality management, or CQI plan and annual report (individual provider and patient identifiers can be removed to protect confidentiality): Does the plan include reliable and valid measures and standards of appropriateness of care, excellence in care, and satisfaction with care as described above? Are providers educated about these measures and standards? Are performance measures documented and routinely fed back to providers? Is meaningful reinforcement and support provided for performance improvement? Are there credible, specific documented examples of performance improvement over the preceding year?
- Routine provider quality profiles (i.e., sample reports on provider performance routinely analyzed by the MCO): How reliable, valid, and useful to quality improvement are the data contained in the reports? To what extent has the quality performance monitoring described in the quality assurance plan been incorporated into MCO reporting systems?
- Reimbursement formula for physicians in the MCO: Are there substantial financial incentives for physicians to withhold necessary care? Conversely, are there substantial financial incentives for physicians to provide quality care? (It has been this author's observation that MCOs providing such financial incentives are more likely to have reliable and valid measures of physician quality and systems for monitoring and feedback of these measures.)
- Preventive care programs offered and participation rates: What preventive care programs does the MCO offer, at what location, and with what frequency? What member cost sharing, if any, is required? What are the participation and success rates for these programs?
- Plan-wide measures of quality: Will the MCO provide the most recent report of performance using HEDIS measures? Did it use survey instruments recommended in HEDIS for assessing

member satisfaction and health status? If not, how did it ensure the reliability and validity of the instruments? What were the response rates to these surveys?

An additional step that can be immensely helpful in assessing the quality of an MCO is to conduct a brief site visit to "kick the tires." In this author's experience, it is not uncommon to come away from such a visit with an entirely different assessment of MCO quality than is conveyed in written material from the organization. Consultants with some knowledge of managed care can be helpful but are not necessary. For a site visit to be most helpful, the following guidelines are recommended:

- Allow four to eight hours for the visit.
- Try to limit the time devoted to marketing and formal presentations.
- Arrange to meet key staff, including the medical director and the heads of member services, quality assurance, utilization management, and finance. What is their relevant training and experience? Are they credible and involved? What is their level of commitment?
- Devote the most time on site to direct observation and questioning of MCO operations staff, and listening to staff on the telephone in member services, claims administration, and utilization management. What is their relevant training and experience? What is their level of commitment? What is the quality of their customer service? Do they document members' complaints, concerns, and questions, and follow up? Do you see signs of a pervasive CQI program with posted performance standards and measures?
- Discuss quality-related information provided prior to the site visit (see above). What are the processes for collection and quality control of data? What were the most successful improvement initiatives in the preceding year? Review minutes of the most recent quality assurance committee meetings.
- Assess the philosophy of the MCO. Is it a good fit with your own and that of your organization? Is the MCO interested in you as a customer, your quality concerns, and your business needs?

Patient, member, and/or physician confidentiality should not be a barrier to conducting a site visit as long as reviewers are willing to sign confidentiality agreements.

For larger employers, all of the above elements can be incorporated into a formal competitive bid process involving multiple MCOs. A nationwide health plan evaluation program has been produced by the National Business Coalition on Health and endorsed by Bridges To Excellence and the Leapfrog Group. This program—eValue8—is a collaborative effort by employer coalitions around the nation to share data comparing health plan performance. More information about this program can be found at www.nbch.org.

Other resources to consider when evaluating MCO quality include the following:

- National Committee for Quality Assurance (NCQA), Washington, DC (www.ncqa.org)
- America's Health Insurance Plans (AHIP), Washington, DC (www.ahip.org)
- Institute for Health Care Improvement (IHI), Roxbury, MA (www.ihi.org)
- Centers for Medicare & Medicaid Services, Baltimore, MD (www.cms.hhs.gov)
- Agency for Healthcare Research and Quality (AHRQ), Rockville, MD (www.ahrq.gov)

Evaluating MCO quality, like physician and hospital quality assessment, can be a time-consuming process. Yet, this may be a relatively small investment of time when weighed against the resources spent by employer and employee on health care and the risks posed by the purchase of poor-quality health care.

IMPROVING QUALITY

Conceptually, approaches to improving quality of health care fall into two major categories: provider or supply-side approaches and patient/consumer or demand-side approaches.

Supply-Side Approaches

The resources required to significantly change provider behavior, whether at the level of the physician, hospital, or MCO, make it unlikely that relatively small purchasers of health care (e.g., individuals and small businesses) acting alone will be successful in driving this approach to quality improvement. By banding together in purchasing or policy making, however, a supply-side quality improvement agenda can be advanced. Business coalitions on health care have proliferated throughout the United States, most with a focus on controlling costs.[60] Many, however, are also addressing issues of quality of care with some effect.

Larger businesses and health care purchasing cooperatives have the ability to influence quality of care through their managed care purchasing decisions and contracting. By increasing the numbers of covered lives at stake in a managed care bid process, large employers and purchasing cooperatives can generally enhance the responsiveness of MCOs to comparative evaluations of quality. This can help ensure the selection of an MCO with superior quality.

Ensuring that an MCO will maintain or improve quality of care, however, may require the purchaser to take additional steps.

When contracting with an MCO, the following approaches to promoting CQI are recommended:

- Identify key deficiencies in the MCO's QA/CQI and stipulate that they be remedied in a specified reasonable period. Failure to remedy deficiencies in the agreed-upon period should result in financial penalties to the MCO. In a self-insured, administrative-services-only arrangement, this penalty may be a significant portion of the MCO's administrative fee (e.g., 10 percent). In a fully insured arrangement, the penalty may be cost sharing by the MCO in noninsured, employer health-related costs (e.g., worksite health promotion or disease prevention).
- Specify reliable and valid measures to be used to track MCO quality over the life of the contract. Ideally, these will be measures already tracked by the MCO (e.g., HEDIS measures) and will include appropriateness of care, excellence of care, and satisfaction. It may be necessary to stipulate that the MCO adopt new measures, or to hire an independent organization to do the MCO quality measurement.
- Require periodic reporting of the above quality measures and track the MCO's performance. Arrange to meet with key MCO staff to review the reports. Financial penalties and rewards should be specified in the contract for failing to meet or exceeding agreed-upon targets for improved performance, respectively.

60. *National Business Coalition on Health, Health Care Data and Quality: The Role of the Business Coalition*, Washington, DC: National Business Coalition on Health, 1995.

By monitoring MCO performance in routine reports, providing feedback in periodic meetings, and reinforcing CQI with financial rewards and penalties, employers can continue to enhance the value of their health care expenditures over the life of an MCO contract. This approach has been taken by the Pacific Business Group on Health in negotiating more than two dozen performance guarantees with 13 California HMOs. Of more than $8 million at risk for meeting performance targets, nearly $2 million was refunded for sub-par performance. Eight of 13 plans missed their targets in the area of childhood immunization. Most plans met or exceeded their targets in such areas as satisfaction, cesarean section rates, mammography, Pap smear, and prenatal care.[61]

On a nationwide basis, the National Business Coalition on Health eValue8 program has engaged 13 employer coalitions in a collaborative effort to evaluate and improve quality of care provided by 72 health plans.[62] For information on business coalition activity in your area, contact the National Business Coalition on Health at www.nbch.org.

Large employers and purchasing coalitions can also use quality data to selectively contract with providers. A survey of business coalitions found that 35 percent directly contract with providers, and 20 percent contract with "centers of excellence" for high-cost and/or high-risk conditions or procedures.[63] An example of a provider taking the lead with this approach is ProvenCare offered by the Geisinger Clinic. For a fixed fee, the Clinic offers all services (e.g., physician, hospital, home health, emergency care, and diagnostic testing) related to coronary artery bypass (CAB) surgery from preadmission screening to post-discharge care for up to 90 days following surgery.[64] Any care required for complications, including readmissions and reoperations, is included at no additional charge. To assure that these additional costs are avoided, Geisinger has identified 40 proven elements of CAB surgery care recommended by the American College of Cardiology and American Heart Association and implemented processes to deliver them reliably to patients. This approach to bundled payment has the potential to better align incentives for physicians and hospitals to

61. H. Schauffler, C. Brown, and A. Milstein, "Raising the Bar: The Use of Performance Guarantees By the Pacific Business Group on Health," *Health Affairs*, Vol. 18, 1999, pp. 134–142.

62. *eValue8 2009: Measuring Progress Toward Value-Based Purchasing*, Washington, DC: National Business Coalition on Health, 2009.

63. I. Fraser et al., "The Pursuit of Quality by Business Coalitions: A National Survey," *Health Affairs*, Vol. 18, 1999, pp. 158–165.

64. D. Kamerow, "Great Health Care, Guaranteed," *BMJ*, Vol. 334, 2007, p. 1086.

collaborate in promoting evidence-based, high-quality, cost-effective care for selected procedures and episodes of illness. Based upon promising early results from this and other examples, the Patient Protection and Affordable Care Act of 2010 calls for further funding of demonstrations of bundled payment.[65]

Providing feedback on hospital and medical staff performance, with encouragement to initiate quality improvement activities, can also produce significant results. This approach was applied by Medicare in its Cooperative Cardiovascular Project, yielding improvements in the use of state-of-the-art care for acute myocardial infarction and reducing mortality for this condition.[66]

Another model for improving both quality and cost efficiency is contracting with an accountable care organization (ACO). These are organizations, incorporated or "virtual," made up of physicians, hospitals and others with

1. The ability to provide and manage the continuum of care across different settings (e.g., outpatient care, hospital care, home health)
2. The capability of prospectively planning budgets and resource needs
3. Large enough size to support comprehensive, valid, and reliable performance measurement[67]

The Patient Protection and Affordable Care Act of 2010 calls for a Medicare ACO pilot program. This program will contract with ACOs to be accountable for the overall care of their Medicare patients, offer adequate numbers of primary care providers, promote evidence-based medicine, report on quality and costs and coordinate care. The Act calls for three-year ACO contracts with ACOs having the potential to receive a share of the savings they produce.[68]

Whether contracting with MCOs, providers or ACOs, one tool used to promote quality improvement has been performance incentives, or

65. The Henry J. Kaiser Family Foundation, "Summary of Key Changes to Medicare in 2010 Health Reform Law, 2010," www.kff.org/healthreform/7948.cfm.
66. T. Marciniak et al., "Improving the Quality of Care for Medicare Patients With Acute Myocardial Infarction: Results From the Cooperative Cardiovascular Project," *JAMA*, Vol. 279, 1998, pp. 1351–1357.
67. M. Merlis, "Accountable Care Organizations," *Health Affairs Health Policy Brief*, July 27, 2010.
68. The Henry J. Kaiser Family Foundation, "Summary of Key Changes to Medicare in 2010 Health Reform Law, 2010," www.kff.org/healthreform/7948.cfm.

so-called "pay-for-performance" programs. Research on the effectiveness of these programs in improving quality is limited, though studies to date have been generally positive.[69] The impact of pay for performance was also demonstrated in the Medicare Physician Group Practice Demonstration, the first pay-for-performance initiative under the Medicare program. Under the program, physician groups received performance payments of up to 80 percent of the savings they produced by achieving cost and quality goals. All ten participating multispecialty physician groups achieved benchmark or target performance on at least 28 of 32 quality measures over a three-year period. Five of the ten groups received $25.3 million in performance payments for improving both quality and cost-efficiency of care.[70]

Even as these programs have proliferated and generated some positive results, questions have arisen about their effectiveness. In a study of CMS pay for performance for acute myocardial infarction, there was no significant difference found between incented and non-incented hospitals in treatment quality or mortality.[71] Another cautionary note with pay for performance is the finding that removing incentives can result in declines in quality.[72]

Apart from issues of effectiveness of pay-for performance, the Society of General Internal Medicine has raised ethical concerns about the practice. These concerns include lack of proven safety and benefit for patients, inadequate definitions of quality, and the potential for adverse effects on physicians, patients, and society. They make recommendations for safeguards to protect vulnerable populations and prevent unintended consequences, such as protections for physicians serving vulnerable patients and before and after monitoring of program impact.[73] Also weighing in with pay-for-performance recommendations are the American Medical Association, the American College of Physicians, and the Joint Commission. These recommendations may provide helpful guidance to employers,

69. L. Peterson et al., "Does Pay-For-Performance Improve Quality of Care?" *Annals of Internal Medicine*, Vol. 145, 2006, pp. 265–272.

70. Center for Medicare & Medicaid Services, "Medicare Physician Group Practice Demonstration," www.cms.gov/DemoProjectsEvalRpts/downloads/PGP_Fact_Sheet.pdf.

71. S. Glickman et al., "Pay for Performance, Quality of Care, and Outcomes in Acute Myocardial Infarction," *JAMA*, Vol. 297, 2007, pp. 2373–2380.

72. H. Lester et al., "The Impact of Removing Financial Incentives from Clinical Quality Indicators: Longitudinal Analysis of Four Kaiser Permanente Indicators," *BMJ*, Vol. 340, 2010, c1898.

73. J. Wharam et al., "High Quality Care and Ethical Pay-for-Performance: A Society of General Internal Medicine Policy Analysis," *Journal of General Internal Medicine*, Vol. 24, 2009, pp. 854–859.

health plans, ACOs, and others in the continued development of pay-for-performance programs.

Demand-Side Approaches

A time-honored approach to modifying consumer demand for health care is through health-plan design. Health plans have long used the approach of increased cost sharing in the form of copayments and deductibles as a means of reducing consumption of unnecessary and inappropriate care. This can contribute to improved quality of care by avoiding the negative health impact of care that does not offer significant health benefits. Unfortunately, cost sharing can also reduce the use of health care products and services that produce a significant positive impact on health, such as immunizations, well-child visits, and medications to control high blood pressure and diabetes.[74] The conflicting effects of generalized cost sharing on quality have been cast in high relief with the adoption of high-deductible health plans. These plans have annual deductibles of at least $1,200 for individuals and $2,400 for a family if they are linked to a health savings account (HSA.). HSAs permit consumers and employers to set aside funds tax-free to cover deductibles and other expenses. Balances in the account can be built up year after year and can be taken by employees when they leave their jobs. In the most recent employer health benefits survey by the Kaiser Family Foundation and Health Research and Educational Trust, 13 percent of all employers offered high-deductible health plans in 2009.[75] Among employers with 1000 or more employees, more than one-third offered such plans. Passage of the Patient Protection and Affordable Care Act of 2010 has raised questions about whether high-deductible plans will be able to compete in health insurance exchanges mandated by the Act. This has created uncertainty about the future of these plans.[76]

A more selective approach to the use of plan design to improve quality has recently been gaining adherents—value-based insurance design (VBID). VBID increases and reduces cost sharing to reflect the value of the services and products being purchased. Services and products with evidence of a high clinical benefit have reduced or no cost sharing, while those with little or no demonstrated clinical benefit have higher cost-sharing requirements.

74. The Rand Corporation, 2010, www.rand.org/health/projects/hie/.
75. The Henry J. Kaiser Foundation, 2010, ehbs.kff.org/.
76. M. Andrews, "High-Deductible Health-Insurance Plans Grow More Attractive to Employers," *The Washington Post*, June 22, 2010.

There is some evidence to suggest that VBID plans can enhance quality of care and improve outcomes while controlling health care costs.[77] Some VBIDs, such as the medical benefit plan at Active Health Management, have focused on reducing or eliminating co-payments for drugs used to treat serious chronic conditions (e.g., diabetes mellitus, high blood pressure, and asthma).[78] Others, such as Evraz Oregon Steel, use both "carrots" and "sticks." Their plan offers free care for diabetes and depression, for example, while charging substantial deductibles and co-payments for procedures that are frequently overused (e.g., total hip replacement and coronary artery stents).[79] Whether these plans will produce their desired effects on quality and cost remains to be seen. Nevertheless, we are likely to see increased adoption of the principles of VBID. The Patient Protection and Affordable Care Act of 2010 allows for guidelines to include VBID in plans offered through health insurance exchanges.[80]

Other demand-side approaches to improving quality of care can be considered under the broad heading of "demand management." Demand management has been defined as "the support of individuals so that they may make rational health and medical decisions based on a consideration of benefits and risks."[81] Viewed in this way, traditional health promotion and disease prevention can be regarded as quality-of-care-related demand management. Much of the attention received by demand management has been directed at controlling utilization and cost of health care.[82] Yet, there is intuitive appeal to the concept of modifying consumer behavior to improve quality of care. There is also some research evidence to suggest such an approach can be effective.

It has long been apparent that providing preventive services is an important element of quality health care. The U.S. Preventive Services Task Force, a panel of medical and health experts appointed by DHHS, has published guidelines that have set the standard for quality in preventive

77. M. Chernew et al., "Evidence that value-based insurance can be effective," *Health Affairs*, Vol. 29, 2010, pp. 530–536.

78. Ibid.

79. J. Appleby, "Carrot-and-Stick Health Plans Aim to Cut Costs," *KHN: Kaiser Health News*, March 11, 2010.

80. University of Michigan Health System, UMHS Newsroom, April 1, 2010, www.sph.umich.edu/vbidcenter/.

81. D.M. Vickery and W.D. Lynch, "Demand Management: Enabling Patients to Use Medical Care Appropriately," *Journal of Occupational and Environmental Medicine*, Vol. 27, 1995, pp. 551–557.

82. J.F. Fires et al., "Reducing Health Care Costs by Reducing the Need and Demand for Medical Services," *New England Journal of Medicine*, Vol. 329, 1993, pp. 321–325.

care since 1989.[83] Since that time, the NCQA has incorporated measures of delivery of selected preventive services into its HEDIS measures of MCO performance. Clearly, employers can improve the quality of care received by their employees by increasing employee demand for these preventive services.

Research also suggests that consumer-directed decision support, in the form of interactive video, can be effective in improving the appropriateness of medical treatment. This approach, referred to as shared decision-making programs, has produced dramatic changes in patient preferences for treatment of benign prostatic hypertrophy (BPH), (benign enlargement of the prostate gland). Patients with BPH participating in early shared decision-making programs showed a 44 to 60 percent reduction in surgery rates, opting more frequently for "watchful waiting" as an alternative.[84] These results suggest the tremendous potential for targeted and well-designed demand management programs to improve quality. For more information on shared decision-making programs contact The Center for Informed Choice at the Dartmouth Institute at tdi.dartmouth.edu/centers/informed-choice/.

Another approach attempting to modify consumer care-seeking behavior has been the dissemination of information about provider quality. This approach has been used by the Minnesota Health Data Institute, the Cleveland Health Quality Choice program, the Pennsylvania Health care cost Containment Council, and others. Schneider and Epstein studied the impact of this approach, as implemented by the Pennsylvania Health care cost Containment Council in its Consumer Guide to Coronary Artery Bypass Graft (CABG) surgery. The Guide provided CABG mortality ratings of all cardiac surgeons and hospitals in the state. A telephone survey of patients who had undergone CABG in one of four hospitals included in the Guide revealed that only 12 percent of patients were aware of the Guide, and fewer than 1 percent knew the correct rating of their surgeon or hospital and reported that it had a moderate or major impact on their selection of provider.[85] The authors concluded: "Efforts to aid patient decision-making with performance reports are unlikely to succeed without a tailored and intensive program for dissemination and patient education."

83. U.S. Preventive Services Task Force, *Guide to Clinical Preventive Services*, Washington, DC: U.S. Government Printing Office, 1989.
84. J.F. Kasper et al., "Developing Shared Decision-Making Programs to Improve the Quality of Health Care," *Quality Review Bulletin*, Vol. 18, 1992, pp. 183–190.
85. E. Schneider and A. Epstein, "Use of Public Performance Reports: A Survey of Patients Undergoing Cardiac Surgery," *JAMA*, Vol. 279, 1998, pp. 1638–1642.

Despite the proliferation of physician report cards, there are few studies indicating that they influence consumer behavior. In a survey of employees in firms participating in the Minneapolis-based Buyers Health Care Action Group, health care consumers reported they were using employer-provided information on satisfaction and service quality for physicians.[86] Another survey of individuals with employer-sponsored health benefits reported that patients remain largely passive consumers of physician services.[87]

More general approaches to demand management have produced suggestive, though less well-documented, results. One such approach is telephonic nurse counseling. These services offer telephone access to nurses to discuss health issues in general and answer clinical questions in particular. Vendors of these services purport to be effective in reducing costs and improving appropriateness of health care, and they appear to have convinced a growing number of employers and health plans.

Telephonic nurse case management is also being targeted to patients with specific medical conditions, such as congestive heart failure, diabetes, and asthma. A variety of organizations offer this type of service, including pharmacy benefit management firms, MCOs, hospitals, and others. This approach appears to hold promise for improving compliance with state-of-the-art treatment through improved self-care and patient–provider communication.

The explosive growth of the Internet and its widespread use in the arena of health, suggests that it may be a medium that can contribute to health care quality improvement. Yet, its growth and use have raised a number of new quality-related issues. One study of Internet-derived information on clinical questions found the following:

- Eighty-nine percent of retrieved pages were not applicable to the question that prompted the search.
- Fewer than 1 percent of pages consisted of original research or systematic reviews.
- 69 percent of pages did not indicate an author.
- Only 1 percent of pages provided information on financial or other conflicts of interest.

86. J. Schultz et al., "Do Employees Use Report Cards to Assess Health Care Provider Systems?" *Health Services Research*, Vol. 36, 2001, pp. 509–530.
87. K.M. Harris, "How do Patients Choose Physicians? Evidence from a National Survey of Enrollees in Employment-Related Health Plans," *Health Services Research*, Vol. 38, 2003, pp. 711–732.

- Fewer than 18 percent of pages gave the date they were posted or most recently updated.[88]

While the Internet represents a tool with great promise for health care quality improvement, consumers, purchasers, and providers should employ the same rigor in evaluating its application as we do for other quality improvement interventions. The U.S. Department of Health and Human Services, Agency for Health Care Research and Quality has useful resources for consumer decision making about health care quality. These resources and Internet links can be found at www.ahcpr.gov.

Demand management represents a wide variety of concepts and products with potential application to quality improvement. The most cost-effective of these are likely to be focused on well-defined, measurable target behaviors, and to include education and skill building, monitoring, and reinforcement of target behaviors. Effective integration of such demand-management programs with supply-management programs will likely bring about the greatest impact on quality improvement.

CONCLUSION

Quality is an essential component of the value equation in health care purchasing. There are a number of reasons employers and employees should make efforts to evaluate and improve health care quality, including errors in the delivery of health care services; overuse and underuse of health care services; employee, provider, and community relations; and the potential to improve the value of health care expenditures. Quality of care can be defined and measured. Furthermore, these measures can be used to evaluate the quality of physicians, hospitals, other providers, and MCOs. Through both supply and demand management, employers, in particular, have the potential to improve quality of care. Supply management opportunities include the use of employer coalitions; purchasing cooperatives; and contractual provider, MCO, and ACO performance incentives. Opportunities for quality improvement through demand management include value-based insurance design, health promotion and disease prevention, shared decision-making programs, dissemination of quality information, telephonic nurse counseling, and telephonic disease management. The most effective strategies to improve quality will likely involve combinations of these approaches.

88. W. Hersh, P. Gorman, and L. Sacherek, "Applicability and Quality of Information for Answering Clinical Questions on the Web," *JAMA*, Vol. 280, 1998, pp. 1307–1308.

CHAPTER 10

Pharmacy Benefits

Craig S. Stern

This chapter focuses on prescription medications used in the ambulatory environment. It discusses the elements of a pharmacy benefit, the role of pharmacy benefit managers, and the role of pharmacy in workers' compensation.

Historically, pharmacy benefits were packaged with vision and dental plans to complement medical benefits and were sold as "riders" to be added to the major medical package for an additional premium. However, prescription drugs differ from vision and dental care in that the latter are frequently elective and predictable in nature, whereas prescription drugs may be predictable for many chronic conditions but are infrequently elective. Before the 1970s, drug prices lagged behind the consumer price index (CPI). In the 1980s, drug prices soared, outpacing the overall CPI and its medical component. As prescription drug price inflation rose, due in part to the introduction of new medications and increased outpatient drug therapy, the pharmacy (or prescription drug) benefit was unbundled from the major medical benefit. The rise in the cost of prescription medications caused individual patients and health plans to look to the global market for relief. However, even though the cost of medications in other countries is often lower than in the United States, the global market did not provide a viable option for purchasing all drugs required in a prescription drug plan. As a result, prescription drug benefit programs have followed designs that are focused on decreasing overall drug price inflation relative to the medical CPI.[1]

PRESCRIPTION DRUG PLANS

As already mentioned, until the late 1980s, the term prescription drug plan was most often used to describe a prescription drug benefit within a health plan member's major medical coverage or a separate benefit sold as a "rider" to the major medical package. Under such a program, plan members would submit receipts to a claims administrator or insurance company and would be reimbursed for prescription drugs in the same manner as for medical expenses. These programs did not offer the plan sponsor any discounts or control over the use of prescription drugs.

The newer prescription drug plans usually are "carved out" from the medical benefit and are typically administered by a pharmacy benefits manager (PBM) or third-party administrator (TPA). These plans offer payers discounts off normal pharmacy charges, electronic claims administration according to benefit requirements, and utilization reports. They also offer programs to reduce costs through mail service and the Internet, and rebates from manufacturers for volume purchasing. In an effort to differentiate their offerings, PBMs provide various value-added programs for drug and disease management.

Varieties of prescription drug plans are available, but all usually include the following elements:

- Member eligibility cards
- Online claim adjudication
- Tiered copays or deductibles and coinsurance
- Pharmacy networks providing discounts for branded medications
- Maximum allowable cost (MAC) pricing for generics
- Mail service
- Formularies and/or preferred drug lists
- Prior authorizations for certain high-cost medications
- Therapeutic interchange or switching.

1. Taken from Craig S. Stern, "The History, Philosophy, and Principles of Pharmacy Benefits," *Journal of Managed Care Pharmacy*, Vol. 5, No. 6, 1999, pp. 525–531.

Pharmacy Benefit Design and Management

Prescription medication plans originate through many sources—private and public and for-profit and not-for-profit. Not-for-profit medical carriers such as Blue Cross Blue Shield organizations and for-profit insurance companies can offer prescription drug programs. Plan sponsors also may "go direct" to a PBM.

Until recently, only large organizations such as self-funded companies, managed health care organizations, such as health maintenance organizations (HMOs), and trust funds had the requisite number of members (typically more than 2,000) to be considered by PBMs for discounts and program development. However, with the growth of coalitions, companies with fewer than 2,000 employees usually can find a way to enjoy the benefits of a prescription drug program. Some smaller employers should be cautious when totally self-funding the risk of prescription drugs, as one catastrophic case could be too large an expenditure for them to bear. Reinsurance typically is available through numerous stop-loss carriers.

When designing and managing a pharmacy benefit plan, an employer has several options. Employers and other payers can (1) manage the benefit and adjudicate claims internally; (2) outsource the benefit management to a health plan, PBM, or TPA; or (3) contract directly with pharmacies and adjudicate claims internally. Although no hard and fast rule applies, payers covering fewer than 15,000 members usually do not retain the management of the pharmacy benefit in house, although some large employers do so in the belief that they can negotiate better terms with pharmacies and pharmaceutical manufacturers than can PBMs.

The Prescription Drug Card Program

A prescription drug card program provides its participants with prescription medications from a participating pharmacy at a prenegotiated discount rate. The covered employee presents his or her prescription to the participating pharmacy. The pharmacist uses an online computer network to get answers to a number of questions, such as whether the drug is covered by the plan, whether the individual is eligible for the medication, and whether any limitations are associated with the medication before filling the prescription. The employee typically pays a fixed copayment, and the payer is billed at a prenegotiated discount rate.

Covered Drugs

Generally, this type of program covers only prescription drugs that treat an illness or injury, subject to applicable limits and copayments. Common plan exclusions are medications used for smoking cessation, hair loss, obesity, and cosmetic conditions (e.g., Chantix™ for smoking cessation or Retin-A™ for facial wrinkles).

Exclusions

Biotechnology medications are a special class in benefit designs. When these medications can be self-injected, they are frequently covered under the pharmacy benefit. When a health care professional must administer them, they are usually covered under the medical benefit and billed under a "J" Code or other Healthcare Common Procedure Coding System (HCPCS) code. Many plans are placing these drugs under the pharmacy benefit in order to apply managed care tools for control of utilization and cost. The pharmacy benefit allows for more discounted pricing, formulary management, edits, and physician profiling for managing the use of these medications.

Contraceptive prescription drugs are sometimes a special class. Most prescription drug plans cover prescribed contraceptives. Insured plans may have a rider that allows a plan sponsor to opt for coverage of contraceptives. Multiple court rulings have required plans to cover contraceptives, even in plans for religious organizations, but this trend is starting to be reversed. In March 2007, the Court of Appeals for the Eighth Circuit ruled that Union Pacific Railroad was not in violation of the Pregnancy Discrimination Act because it did not cover any contraception for women or for men.[2]

A common excluded class is so-called lifestyle drugs—the term applied to prescription products that do not necessarily cure illness but can be used to improve daily life by boosting psychological attitudes, energy levels, sexual performance, and body image. Common examples are Viagra™, testosterone supplements for women to improve sexual desire, and Rogaine™ to counter hair loss. Lifestyle drugs have occasioned a debate over what should be covered in health care insurance and over the essential nature of insurance. Conditions treated by these drugs are not subject to actuarial risk analysis, and as a result, they frequently are excluded from pharmacy benefit plans.

2. *In re* Union Pacific R.R. Empl. Practices Litig. 479 F.3d 936 (8th Cir. 2007).

Over-the-counter (OTC) medications also are a common exclusion. Very few plans cover OTC medications. A few plans cover some OTC medications, such as insulin, needles and syringes, prenatal vitamins, and diabetic devices and test strips. Some plans have experimented with covering OTC medications that are lower in cost, but equally effective as their prescribed counterparts, for the treatment of allergies or female yeast infections. Very few plans have covered alternative medications (e.g., herbals, nutraceuticals, or vitamins) as part of their alternative options for health care maintenance and prevention services. As an overall trend, however, OTC medications generally have not been adopted as plan benefits.

Of note is that although prescription drug card programs are convenient, they may encourage drug overuse because the member does not pay out of pocket for the prescription and wait for reimbursement. Sponsors of prescription drug card programs should conduct periodic audits to ensure that the PBM and its retail network of pharmacies are processing only legitimate claims. Today, the majority of the plans offer a prescription drug card program.

The Patient Protection and Affordable Care Act of 2010 (PPACA)

The PPACA enacted several changes of note. It made further changes to the flexible spending account (FSA), health reimbursement arrangement (HRA), and health spending account (HSA) with regard to OTC products. Effective January 1, 2011, medical FSA, HRA and HSA funds may no longer be used to purchase OTC drugs and medicines (other than insulin) without a directive form from a medical provider. If an OTC drug or medicine is required to treat a specific medical condition, reimbursement can be done by submitting a certification of medical necessity. Some examples are

- Allergy and sinus medicines
- Antibiotic products
- Baby rash ointments and creams
- Cough, cold, and flu medicines
- Pain relief medicines
- Gastrointestinal aids
- Sleep aids and sedatives
- Stomach remedies

The law does not apply to eligible OTC medical supplies. OTC medical supplies that are not drugs or medicines still can be purchased with a benefit card, or a claim may be submitted for reimbursement. These items include

- Band-aids
- Contact lens solution
- Health monitors (e.g., blood pressure)
- Ophthalmic products
- Supports and braces[3]

Coverage Disclosure Considerations

Insured managed pharmacy plans provide full disclosure of the medications they do or do not cover by publishing formulary listings. PBMs and insured programs may publish the medication categories that are not covered or are not preferred on a formulary. Plan sponsors should carefully review all elements of the plan to be certain that they are aware of any specific drugs that the plan or PBM does not cover. Current member utilization should be compared with the drug coverage available in each plan or PBM considered.

The plan design is driven by the employer's benefit. Employers should stipulate their plan design in detail, including all excluded categories, and review the plan design documents with the PBM. If the employer is purchasing a PBM's plan design, then the plan sponsor should also carefully review contract terms to ensure the availability of data, full audit rights by auditors of the employer's choice, and complete definitions of included drugs and drug categories.

The Roles of Capitation and Risk Sharing in Pharmacy Benefit Management

Capitation involves an agreement between a payer and a PBM to provide prescription benefits for a predetermined amount per participant, regardless of the cost of the prescriptions actually dispensed. In the early 1990s, some plan sponsors and PBMs explored capitation as a method of ensuring that their incentives were aligned. Payers wanted the PBMs to "manage"

3. http://www.benefitresource.com/uploads/file/ppt_page_otc_05_2010.pdf.

the benefit cost beyond expense reduction. The major PBMs could not determine a cost-equitable capitation formula, and most capitation arrangements were never realized. The major concern was that PBMs could not control physician prescribing to an extent that would make the plan profitable. As a result, few of these arrangements were ever successful.

Some plans have found better success with a "risk sharing" arrangement in which the PBM and plan sponsor share accountability for the pharmacy benefit costs. Risk sharing better aligns goals and incentives and avoids many of the pitfalls seen in either pure capitation or fee-for-service arrangements. However, these agreements have been limited by the ability to measure actual expense reduction beyond that provided by claim administration and to attribute any successes to the plan benefit or to PBM programs.

Cost Considerations

The Agency on Healthcare Research and Quality (AHRQ) published spending data for medications prescribed in outpatient settings from 1997 through 2007 identifying that drug spending increased from $72 billion in 1997 to $232 billion in 2007.

The overwhelming majority of increases in expenditures on prescription drugs are attributable to the increased volume, mix, and availability of products, as well as cost increases passed on by the pharmaceutical industry.

In 2009, drug-price inflation for branded products was the single most important factor driving up cost per unit according to the Express Scripts Annual Report. This significant growth in cost particularly affects the drug therapy classes that have limited generic availability, including specialty drugs and antiviral medications. Inflation was 11.5 percent for biotech drugs compared with 9.1 percent for traditional-therapy branded medications.

Direct-to-consumer (DTC) advertising also has increased the demand for many drugs. A Harvard University study funded by the Kaiser Foundation found that for every $1 spent on DTC advertising, manufacturers reap $4.20 in sales. Recent evidence indicates that DTC advertising is less effective in current media, so it is being redirected to the Internet and other distribution channels in order to have a greater impact on the general public.

Demographics are driving up prescription medication costs as the population ages. However, more and more new drug therapies are targeting the "young old" population, individuals in the 40–60 age group, in an effort to prevent certain diseases, such as hyperlipidemia and hypertension, from progressing and increasing the chances of heart disease and stroke later in life.

In some cases, prescription drugs are a substitute for other forms of health care. More appropriate utilization of prescription drugs can potentially lower total health care expenditures and improve the quality of care. For example, by taking the right medicine, an asthmatic patient might be able to avoid emergency room visits and hospitalizations. H2 antagonists, such as Tagamet™ and Zantac™, have virtually eliminated painful and invasive ulcer surgery that was common a few years ago. On the other hand, many more patients now take proton pump inhibitors (PPIs) such as Nexium™ and Prilosec™, which were originally developed for severe gastric bleeding problems, but are now used for common heartburn. Medication can offer an effective and less invasive method of treatment, and, as a result, more patients are being treated with it and thus expanding the potential for inclusion in the therapeutic category in terms of sales of the medication.

Today, prescription drugs represent 10 to 25 percent of an employer's overall health care benefit costs. Therefore, prescription drug costs are a significant area to target for better outcomes and lower costs. Selecting a marginal PBM or not knowing how to optimize the services a PBM offers can cost a health plan sponsor considerable money. New therapeutic categories and complicated plan designs have increased the need for competent prescription drug benefit managers.

Prescription Drug Trends

Prescription drugs typically account for approximately 8 to 11 percent of the total health care dollar. Many plans have set target pharmacy benefit limits to no more than 20 percent of major medical plan costs; but the pharmacy benefit trend was between 11 and 18 percent nationally for the last half of the 1990s.

Pharmacy benefit expense is driven by increases in raw drug costs, plan member utilization, new entrants into the drug market, introduction of new biotechnology drugs, and the branded drug mix.

According to the Centers for Medicare and Medicaid Services (CMS), by 2011, drug spending is projected to accelerate 5.6 percent, corresponding to an increase in use that is due to a projected improving economic climate. Prescription drug spending growth is expected to halt in 2012 and 2013 as many top-selling brand names lose patent protection, although this may not be enough to offset the spending on biotechnology drugs. After that, it is anticipated to accelerate through 2019, reaching 7.7 percent, with increases in drug prices expected to account for about half of this growth.

Biotechnology drug spending follows a separate trend line. Trend reports vary depending on the agency reporting the numbers, but recent data from the Segal Health Plan Cost Trend Survey shows the 2010 trend rate for biotech drugs is expected to be 17.8 percent, nearly equal to the 2009 trend rate (18.1 percent). According to Express Scripts, spending for biotechnology drugs grew to 19.5 percent in 2009, primarily due to increased cost per unit and a greater prevalence of use. The top three biotechnology classes are inflammatory conditions, multiple sclerosis, and cancer.

Differences in trends reported by different sources are based on the varying constituents of each source's book of business. Therefore, it is necessary for each purchaser to review multiple sources and compare the benchmark book of business with their own to derive a reasonable benchmark for trend for their company or industry.

Copayments

For purposes of definition, Copayments (copays) are flat amounts paid by members for individual prescriptions. The 2009–2010 Takeda Prescription Drug Benefit Report indicates increasing copayments in 2009 for one PBM (Express Scripts):

- Average generic retail copay was $9.96.
- Preferred branded drugs average copay was $25.19.
- Nonpreferred branded drugs average copay was $42.95.

The major increase is in three-tier plans—that is, the lowest tier for generics, the next higher for preferred brands, and the highest tier for nonpreferred or nonformulary brands. Again, according to the 2009–2010 Takeda Prescription Drug Benefit Report, a total of 86.9 percent of respondents using a formulary have it structured with multiple tiers.

In 2008, the average copay decreased $0.29 to $12.82. The decrease in copayments was attributed to an increase in the use of generic medications. The breakdown for trends in average copay changes for the period from 2007 through 2008 were as follows:

- Generic drugs increased $0.37 to $7.82.
- Brand drugs increased $1.21 to $22.69
- Specialty drugs increased $2.98 to $44.04

Note that the above data reflect only one PBM's book of business and may not be applicable to all types of payers.

Copayment is more common than coinsurance for prescription drugs. Coinsurance is the percentage of the cost paid by a plan member, as opposed to copay, which is a flat amount. The 2008 Mercer survey reported that 27 percent of large employers and 62 percent of those with at least 20,000 employees require coinsurance for at least one medication class. On the other hand, according to the 2006 Mercer survey, only 14 percent of prescription drug plans required coinsurance and 9 percent had coinsurance for mail order. The 2008 United Benefit Advisors (UBA) prompt patients to obtain and take higher doses less prompt patients to obtain and take higher doses less survey stated that 79.5 percent of plans provide copayment only and 1.9 percent offer only coinsurance, with the balance using a combination. This should be compared with the 2006 UBA survey, where less than 1 percent of all employers required coinsurance for all prescription drugs purchased at retail, but 9 percent had some combination of coinsurance and copays. The Kaiser Family Foundation Employer Health Benefits Report of 2008 lists that, on average, 79 percent of employees covered in a plan with three-tier cost sharing have copayments only, while 11 percent have coinsurance only. This is an increase in coinsurance and a decrease in copayments when compared with the Kaiser Family Foundation Employer Health Benefits Report of 2007, in which it reported that, on average, 8 percent of employers use coinsurance and 84 percent use copayments.

Prior Authorization Programs

A prior authorization (PA) program restricts coverage under the plan of certain drugs based on the patient's conditions and maximizes the outcome of the medication. Under this program, the physician must call into the entity that is administering the PA program (typically the PBM or health plan). The physician answers questions about the patient's condition and, based on the information, the drug will either be covered under the plan or not. Many drugs that are subject to PA programs have monthly costs that range from $250 to $2,000 a month. Some drugs also have quantity limits in addition to a PA requirement.

Very few studies have been conducted to determine the overall effectiveness of PA programs. Yet health plans, PBMs, and TPAs claim that PA programs are very effective both at controlling costs and at ensuring quality. A study of five Medicaid PA programs commissioned by the Kaiser Foundation concluded that PA programs were more effective and less controversial when developed with local provider input. Since most PA programs are developed by health plans or PBMs that are far removed from local input, it is necessary for plan sponsors to require evidence of the effectiveness and return on investment (ROI) of these programs.

Quantity Limits

Quantity limits (QLs) are predefined maximal quantities for specific medications. QLs restrict the number of dosage units (e.g., tablets or capsules) that can be dispensed for a 30-, 60-, or 90-day supply of a prescription. QLs were originally established to ensure that certain medications could not be abused or overused. At the same time, they help to improve compliance with medication therapy. Instead of taking a lower strength of a drug more frequently, QLs prompt patients to obtain and take higher doses less frequently. For example, instead of taking 5 mg of a drug twice a day, a patient takes 10 mg once a day. These programs not only improve compliance, they also lower costs.

Some drugs have both a PA requirement and a QL. One of the more famous drugs in this category is Viagra™. Most plans in which it is not excluded altogether require a PA for Viagra™ and limit the coverage to six tablets per month.

Drug Usage versus Overall Costs

Proper drug usage may reduce other costs, but the evidence is equivocal. According to an article in the *American Journal of Industrial Medicine*, employees using sedating antihistamines purchased over the counter to treat allergic rhinitis (hay fever) have a significantly higher risk of injury than employees taking prescribed nonsedating antihistamines. In addition to adding to workers' compensation costs, the sedating antihistamines contributed to lower productivity.

Nonetheless, most plan sponsors have experienced increased costs in both medical and pharmacy programs. For this reason, it has been difficult to determine just how much proper drug usage has affected the medical health care trend. Many new "dot com" companies were formed in the early 2000s to merge pharmacy and medical data in an effort to answer questions concerning the effect of medical care spending as it applies to proper drug usage. A significant factor in not being able to tie drug use to medical spending is that diagnosis codes are not required for prescription drug claim adjudication. Because of this limitation, drug use must be inferred based on common uses rather than the specific disease that the drug is prescribed to treat.

What is the motivation for an employer to have a separate prescription drug plan rather than combining medical and prescription drug coverage? There are a number of reasons for having separate plans, all of which are motivated by cost management:

- Under the indemnity plan, there are typically no discounts for prescription drug coverage. Plan sponsors may pay as much as 10 percent above the average wholesale price rather than 15 percent below it.
- Medical claims processors often do not require detailed receipts for prescription drugs and therefore cannot review the prescriptions for coverage as effectively as the PBMs' online claims processing environment.
- Because detailed information is not entered into medical claims processing systems, limited data are available in report format for reviewing drug trends.
- Rebates and other cost-savings programs, which are available in prescription benefit plans, are not available through medical claims processors.

Some employers may wish to avoid a freestanding drug plan in favor of covering medication under a major medical or comprehensive health plan so as to manage the entire medical benefit. Carving the pharmacy benefit out of the major medical benefit may lead to micromanagement of the pharmacy portion, leading to losses for the medical portion. For example, excluding certain medications could lead to increased emergency medical visits or physician encounters. This problem is magnified when no alignment exists between the medical encounter and pharmacy claims databases that would allow for oversight of cost or utilization shifts.

Pharmacy Benefits—Cost Factors

What factors influence the cost of the prescription benefit? The cost of a prescription benefit depends on a variety of factors. First, the demographics (age and gender) of the population drive the disease mix that is being treated. Second, benefits, copays, and formulary design drive what is covered in the plan. Third, drug cost and the mix of branded products covered by the benefit drive the cost of drugs. Drug mix is a factor of the preferred drug list, or the restrictiveness of the formulary. Rebates may mitigate some branded drug cost, particularly if 100 percent of the rebates are being returned to the plan. Preferred drugs may actually cost more on a monthly basis in terms of the cost of the discounted ingredient costs, but, after rebates, the "net" costs of the preferred drugs should always be less than those of the nonpreferred drugs within a therapeutic category unless the agent (a particular drug) is clinically superior. Fourth, the utilization (number) of prescriptions used by the members is the multiplier of drug cost. Fifth, the costs charged by the PBM and the PBM's ability to gain profit from retail and mail order discounts, rebates, and other programs should provide offsetting discounts to the cost of the program. PBMs can increase costs, however, if all earned fees and discounts are not returned to the plan sponsor. Sixth, other factors influencing the cost of a prescription drug plan are fraud (by pharmacies, patients, or physicians) and prescription misuse. Seventh, the ability of the plan to manage costs has a definite impact on the cost of the benefit. Tightly managed plans always yield lower costs on a patient-by-patient basis than those of nonmanaged plans. As a result, union plans, which may be restricted by labor agreements, may have higher costs than nonbargained plans.

Pharmacy Benefits—Mail Service

A mail service component in a prescription drug plan allows patients to obtain prescription drugs by mail. Mail service prescriptions typically are used for chronic conditions that require maintenance medications for long periods of time, such as high blood pressure, asthma, or diabetes. Typically, 70 percent of all prescriptions fall under the category of maintenance medications. This service may save patients time and money. It typically allows a greater quantity and lower out-of-pocket expenses compared with retails sales. Mail service pharmacies (MSPs) are staffed by a full complement of pharmacists and technicians, who ensure quality control and a high level of service. Mail service typically can save as much as 10 percent of the cost of traditionally delivered prescription drugs. In addition, most PBMs offer a toll-free customer service line (some with up to 24-hour coverage) to answer enrollees' questions about their prescription drugs. Prescriptions by mail also typically include newsletters or brochures about the specific diseases or conditions for which the medications were prescribed.

A mail service pharmacy is a revenue producer for a PBM, but it may not save money for the payer if copays are not structured appropriately. Studies have shown that the ratio of copays for mail to retail prescriptions must be at least 2.7:1 for the mail service to save money for the payer. Payers should analyze their costs to ensure that benefit designs do not inhibit the cost savings available from mail service.

Mail Service versus Retail Pharmacy

How do MSP programs compare with retail pharmacies filling maintenance prescriptions? A constant battle rages between retail pharmacies and MSPs over maintenance prescription business. Since the inception of mail service, retail pharmacies have fought to have MSPs regulated by each state similar to retail outlet stores. MSPs have fought state regulation as being onerous because they do business in all states. The utilization of MSPs varies, as reported by the Sanofi-Aventis 2009 Pharmacy Benefit Summary. The report states that in 2008, 83 percent of HMOs and 6.3 percent of preferred provider organizations (PPOs) utilize MSPs. The battle has heated up over mandatory mail service in PBM contracts. Several of the largest pharmacy chains, which also have mail service subsidiaries, announced that they will not sign new PBM contracts that stipulate mandatory mail service from captive MSPs owned by the PBMs. These retail chains have promised discounts equal to those offered by the MSPs so that patients can receive their 60- or 90-day maintenance medications from their local pharmacies.

MSPs offer a lower cost of dispensing and quality control through automation that is uncommon in retail pharmacy. Many of the larger chain pharmacies, the Veterans Administration, and some multiclinic pharmacies are using mail service to provide maintenance medications to their retail outlets with 24-hour turnaround times. This fulfillment practice has helped to mitigate some of the problems of pharmacist shortages and to reduce costs for retail pharmacies.

Are prescriptions by mail safe? Error rates in MSPs are at least no worse than or, in most instances, below those of most retail pharmacies. A handful of leading PBMs offer state-of-the-art technology designed to improve efficiency and ensure safety. Among the techniques used to ensure safety are radio-controlled totes, a conveyor system that routes prescriptions to various stations, and intensive quality-control programs that ensure that prescriptions are filled efficiently and accurately. Another key to the quality and safety measures in MSPs is an imaging application that shows pharmacists on the computer screen the NDC number and the "image" of what the prescribed drug must look like. By carefully comparing the ready-to-ship product with the image on the screen, the pharmacist can confirm the content and thus ensure accuracy during filling operations.

Mail Service Utilization in Pharmacy Benefits

Are MSP programs over- or underused? Typically, MSPs are underused because enrollees are not familiar with a plan's mail service benefit or are not sure how to access the service. Some patients with chronic conditions (e.g., asthma) are fearful of not receiving their medications in time. However, studies indicate that once enrollees are introduced to the convenience, simplicity, and safety of an MSP program, most express a high level of satisfaction with the plan. Industry analysts and the managed care pharmacy industry expect the mail service industry to experience tremendous growth in the next few years. They believe that, as millions of aging baby boomers begin to need more prescriptions, they will want to take advantage of the convenience offered by mail service. Yet, competition exists. Of particular note is the rise of 90-day point-of-service (POS) plans offered by retail pharmacy networks that provide competition to the mail service as they offer convenience, access, and comparable costs.

Are there studies on the effectiveness of MSPs? In the mid-1980s and early 1990s, the savings from MSPs were greater than they are at present. Nonetheless, the Pharmaceutical Care Management Association (PCMA), which represents the PBM industry, cites numerous studies that conclude that managed care MSPs reduce overall prescription costs while maintaining and even improving quality. A Mercer study concluded that MSPs reduce a plan sponsor's total gross costs, despite minor increases in the use of their prescription drug program. The Boston Consulting Group obtained similar results. It found that "at the unit-cost level, [mail service pharmacy] plans offered savings of 30 to 35 percent on maintenance drugs over card and [major medical] plans." A study by FIND/SVP observed a 26 percent difference in cost between a mail order prescription and a prescription reimbursed through a standard major medical plan.

In 2004, a 90-day POS competitive option was offered by many managed health care plans and some PBMs. The 90-day POS option offered retail network discounts of 16 to 18 percent off the average wholesale price (AWP), with dispensing fees of $0 or $1. Pricing guarantees also contain the "lower of" usual and customary (U&C) language and maximum allowable cost (MAC) pricing. MAC and U&C pricing make the overall effective rate close to average wholesale price less 18 percent, with no dispensing fee. Mail service discounts have not kept up with these changes in discounts in retail, therefore making the MSP not as financially beneficial as in the past. The increase in utilization is heightened when combined with therapeutic interchange programs (TIPs), which may switch maintenance medications that patients have been used to receiving in the retail program. A recent court decision against Medco Health Services has provided new rules preventing PBMs from switching medications without the patient's and his or her physician's consent, as well as the disclosure of any financial relationships that the PBM has with pharmaceutical manufacturers. (TIPs are discussed in greater detail later in the chapter.) Each plan should review its specific discounts and copay arrangements to determine if mail order is truly a cost-effective arrangement.

Selecting a Mail Service Option

How does a health care purchaser know if an MSP is right for its population? MSPs are developed for any health care purchaser whose population uses maintenance medications. MSPs offer convenience for beneficiaries and may offer cost savings to plan sponsors. Good MSPs should also offer programs that add value for the sponsor and patient. The programs may include toll-free counseling with pharmacists, drug information mailed with every prescription, and health and wellness information as part of disease management programs.

Some plans offer incentives to use their mail order program. Some health plans have lower copays for mail order drugs; other plans offer a larger supply of the medication for the same copay; and still others offer larger supplies for lower copays. The backlash against managed care has had an effect on mail order programs. For example, a 1997 Missouri law bars HMOs from using benefit incentives to favor mail order drugs. Plan sponsors should structure copays to approximate the additional discounts obtained through the mail order program so that there is not a financial loss to the plan sponsor when members use the mail service program. Generally, copays should be at least 2.5 to 2.7 times the retail copays to obtain this balance.

According to the Takeda 2009–2010 Prescription Drug Benefit report, the 2009 mail service copayments were as follows:

- Average generic copay was $20.23.
- Preferred branded drugs average copay was $51.70.
- Nonpreferred branded drugs average copay was $88.04.

Pharmacy Benefits—Cost Management Concepts

Many techniques are available to manage pharmacy costs. It is important to understand that although PBMs can offer programs and services to aid in managing prescription drugs, it is ultimately the responsibility of the plan sponsor to direct the PBM, design the plan coverage, and implement the programs that meet the plan's spending targets. The following is a list of techniques typically used by plan sponsors to control pharmacy costs:

1. Review the design of the pharmacy benefit and how it fits into the overall medical program. With flat dollar copayments that may not have increased in several years, many plans are subsidizing the cost of the pharmacy benefit by as much as 95 percent.
2. Analyze experience to identify areas needing better management. Typically, ulcer and depression therapy are the two most frequently dispensed medications. Ensure that a program is developed to help employees use those drugs properly.
3. Use the following pharmacy management tools and techniques:
   a. Reduce the pharmacy network to the smallest size without compromising access; in addition, offer pharmacy incentive programs aimed at additional reimbursement for increases in generic substitution and formulary compliance to decrease cost trends.
   b. Offer mail service or 90-day retail POS prescriptions as a convenient option to members, rather than making mail service prescriptions a requirement, and make the copayments per day's supply equal in retail pharmacies and mail order pharmacies.
   c. Adopt a plan design that encourages generic drug substitution (where patients have to pay the difference between the cost of brand medication and the generic drug if the patient or the physician requires a brand).
   d. Use a formulary that is designed to promote cost-effective and clinical therapeutic drugs coupled with a rebate program that passes on 100 percent of the rebates to the plan sponsor.
   e. Practice utilization management that targets high-cost users and intervenes with physicians and patients to ensure quality outcomes.
   f. Offer physician profiling that highlights high-cost physicians with low-acuity patients coupled with an incentive program to dispense appropriate medications.

g. Utilize health management programs designed to educate patients about alternatives to high-cost therapies.

h. Communicate cost trends to plan members to help them become better consumers.

4. Anticipate the financial impact of new drugs and therapies and set policies and procedures for the new drugs before they are released.

Pharmacoeconomics

Pharmacoeconomic research can be used to determine the cost-effectiveness of pharmaceuticals, to design formularies, disease management programs, and pharmacy benefit programs. Such research can show plan sponsors which prescription drugs provide optimal therapeutic and cost values, with the goal of decreasing overall health care costs. For example, research may demonstrate that using a relatively expensive medication may be justified given its ability to decrease surgical treatment. Pharmacoeconomic research may result in a decrease or an increase in actual prescription drug expenses, but it can contribute to a decrease in overall health care cost trends. It can also use trends as a predictive tool to determine which patients are most likely to be high-cost patients in the future.

Pharmacy Benefits–Utilization Management Concepts

Drug utilization review (DUR) programs are designed to ensure that patients are taking medications that are appropriate for a particular condition and that will yield the optimum outcome. Three types of DUR programs are available: concurrent, retrospective, and prospective. Concurrent DUR occurs at the point of service (the pharmacy) and flags potential overuse based on clinical monitoring criteria or "edits" that have been programmed into the PBM's systems. These edits (referred to as "hard edits" because the claim will not be adjudicated until they are cleared) are for too-soon refills, duplicate claims, drugs requiring prior authorization, or quantity limits. These edits help eliminate overuse and abuse. Soft edits are also sent back to the pharmacist warning of drug–drug interactions. However, many pharmacists do not act on these edits because of the time needed to reach the patient and physician, and pharmacies are not routinely compensated for these cognitive services. In addition, in an effort to increase productivity, some retail chain pharmacy systems actually block these edits so that they are not viewable by pharmacists and technicians.

In retrospective DUR programs (pharmacy case management), pharmacists or nurses review patient profiles to determine if patients are complying with their drug therapy or to suggest alternative therapies to their physicians that may be better or more cost effective. PBMs have been reluctant to offer these types of programs because PBMs are paid to fill rather than not fill prescriptions by plan sponsors (and drug manufacturers). Many PBMs refer to their therapeutic switching programs as retrospective DUR. However, therapeutic switching programs are aimed more at substituting one drug for another rather than determining if the therapy is appropriate.

Prospective DUR refers to educating physicians and patients about drugs or drug therapy. With the exception of a limited few, PBMs have not been successful at these programs or in cost justifying the return on investment. Many prospective DUR programs are funded by drug manufacturers.

Pharmacy Benefits—Formularies and Pharmacy and Therapeutics Committees

In practice, a formulary is a list of drugs preferred by a health plan or PBM. A formulary is designed by a process of evaluation and analysis that is usually under the auspices of a pharmacy and therapeutics (P&T) committee. A P&T committee is composed of physicians, pharmacists, and nurses, who may be complemented by pharmacoeconomists, ethicists, the lay public, and plan administration. The P&T committee has the responsibility for evaluating all available evidence to choose medications to treat the conditions indigenous in the insured population. These deliberations consider all clinical and pharmacologic considerations first. Once the comparative effectiveness and safety of medications has been evaluated, economic considerations are reviewed to determine the most cost-effective medications of the clinically effective choices. The Academy of Managed Care Pharmacy (AMCP) has developed a standard format for drug dossiers to be submitted for P&T submission (see www.amcp.org). The development of a standard format is an evolutionary step in improving P&T deliberations, in ensuring that all available information is available for analysis, and that economic considerations are exhaustive and specific to the insured population.

If the P&T committee has determined that drugs within a therapeutic class are equally effective, a formulary selects drugs within the category that are most cost effective based on a combination of average wholesale price and rebates that manufacturers are willing to give to the PBM or plan. Although generic drugs may be listed on the formulary as preferred, formulary development typically centers on brand products. Some PBMs contract with generic manufacturers for rebates, although generally this practice is uncommon. It is critical for plan sponsors to ensure that they receive all earned rebates whether for brand or generic drugs.

When plan sponsors purchase formularies developed by health plans, PBMs, or TPAs, it is important for them to know who the representatives are on a PBM's formulary. Information should be available to the plan sponsor as to the composition of the P&T committee, their employers, and any relationships with pharmaceutical manufacturers in order to evaluate biases that these individuals may have toward any drug manufacturer.

Open, Preferred, and Closed Formularies

Open formularies allow plan enrollees any covered prescription drug prescribed for them. Open formularies traditionally have been quite popular with physicians and patients, who perceive them as offering freedom of choice. Since most physicians are primarily familiar with only the handful of prescription medications they use most often, open formularies—which typically include hundreds of possible medications and several options per category—give physicians and patients the chance to make better-informed choices. In an open formulary environment, the list of preferred drugs is distributed to patients and physicians for informational purposes only.

Preferred formularies have become quite popular in the last several years. They encourage patients to use the preferred or formulary drugs in return for a reduced copayment. For example, generic drugs may require a $5 copayment, preferred brands a $10 copayment, and nonpreferred drugs a $25 copayment—referred to as three-tier copayments. Although not as popular with patients and physicians as an open formulary, most patients and their physicians can find effective drugs on the preferred listing.

Closed formularies often meet with resistance from plan enrollees. They simply mean that the plan will not cover the nonformulary drug. Closed formularies are typically found in hospital settings and tightly managed HMO programs—employers normally do not use this type of formulary.

Open and preferred formularies are more prevalent in self-funded plans, and, as just mentioned, closed formularies are more frequently used in tightly managed HMOs. The use of formularies is growing because formularies, particularly preferred formularies, are very effective at moving patients to lower-cost drugs and maximizing rebate potentials.

Advantages and Disadvantages of Formularies

The primary advantage to introducing formularies is to reduce costs and to encourage patients to use the most effective medication within a therapeutic class. Formularies also help educate patients and physicians about cost-effective alternatives to expensive brand medication. PBMs have a great deal of influence over the development and management of formularies. Plan sponsors frequently defer to the formularies developed by the PBM's P&T committee, the drug experts whose decisions are based on safety, efficacy, utilization, prescribing patterns, and cost. Plan sponsors need to review the policies and decisions of the P&T committee to ensure that they meet the specifications of the plan's benefit.

One of the primary drawbacks to formularies is the constant communication to physicians and patients that is necessary regarding the current list of preferred products. Formularies differ depending on the health plan, PBM, or TPA that developed and maintains them. There also may be multiple formularies within each health plan, PBM, or TPA for different clients, such that not a single source exists that references "all preferred products." Therefore, when a PBM changes its formulary and does not communicate those changes to members, members may become dissatisfied because their copayment may differ from what they had expected. Members and physicians may also resent having to limit selection within the therapeutic class in order to obtain the lowest copayment option.

Which drugs typically are excluded from formularies? It is important when answering this question not to confuse benefit coverage with formulary coverage. Typically, certain types of drugs are completely excluded from benefit coverage, including drugs used for cosmetic purposes, OTC products, and drugs classified as experimental by the Food and Drug Administration (FDA). In addition, products such as vaccines and other injectables may be covered under a medical benefit rather than a separate prescription benefit. Formularies may overlap benefit coverage, depending on the type of formulary being used. In a preferred formulary, drug products not listed on the formulary may still be considered a covered benefit, perhaps with a higher share of the cost borne by the beneficiary. In a closed formulary, drug products not listed typically are not part of the benefit coverage, and if a physician prescribes a nonformulary product, the beneficiary would be responsible for the entire cost of the medication.

How Do Health Plans and PBMs Get Physicians to Support a Formulary?

Patients continue to look primarily to their personal physicians to recommend prescription drugs. With the plethora of formularies in the community, physicians frequently treat patients covered by 12 to 15 formularies or more on a daily basis. The task of remembering all these formularies is clearly beyond the ability of any health care professional. As a result, health plans, PBMs, and plan sponsors provide paper and electronic copies of their formularies for physician use. In actuality, physicians remember drug formulary coverage for the most frequently seen patient populations, and they expect pharmacies to contact them if they prescribe medications that are not on specific formularies. The advent of personal digital assistants (PDAs) has allowed formularies to be downloaded to these mobile products. Plan sponsors should evaluate the companies that perform these services to ensure that they are not unduly influenced by mass media marketing campaigns or pharmaceutical manufacturers.

The physician can help to enlighten a patient about a change in prescription drugs recommended by a PBM, or the physician can choose not to communicate appropriately and possibly instill fear and bewilderment in a patient when drugs are changed; therefore, it is imperative that health plans, PBMs, and TPAs place a great deal of emphasis on developing a cooperative relationship with physicians.

Some PBMs are particularly effective in communicating to physicians. The major publicly held PBMs have pharmacists across the United States whose primary responsibility is to meet with physicians to explain the formulary and review specific changes for specific patients that would result in increased use of preferred products.

Typically, a number of alternative prescription drug products are available to treat a particular health condition and are grouped together in a therapeutic class. For example, Tagamet™, Zantac™, Pepcid™, and Axid™ are all drugs used to treat gastric ulcers or heartburn. Each of those products has a different chemical composition but the same therapeutic effect in the body.

Therapeutic interchange programs (TIPs), sometimes called "therapeutic switching programs" are documented procedures for substituting one therapeutically equivalent product for another, with the goal of a more cost-effective medical outcome through physician support of formularies.

The protocols are generally developed by a multidisciplinary group of physicians, pharmacists, and nurses.

Under a TIP, pharmacists contact prescribers to discuss more cost-effective therapeutic alternatives. Often, the TIP is combined with visits from pharmacists and educational seminars.

TIPs have been open to criticism and controversy. In order for TIPs to have credibility, the programs must be based on evidence-based medicine, and there must be full disclosure of financial relationships affecting the choices of medications.

When properly developed, executed, and communicated to physicians and patients, TIPs can be quite successful, and some PBMs have achieved close to a 90 percent success rate in moving patients to lower-cost therapies through their use.

Do Formularies Usurp the Role of Physicians in Prescribing Medicines?

Physicians, pharmacists, and PBMs must work together to provide a prescription drug program to plan sponsors that yields optimal results. A well-managed formulary does not dictate what drugs a physician can and cannot prescribe. Instead, the PBM works with the physician to help educate him or her about the myriad prescription drug options available and the cost associated with each. For example, the difference in cost between the lowest- and highest-cost branded medications in the same therapeutic category may be 50 percent or more. The question to be asked is whether a 50 percent clinical improvement exists between the lowest-cost brand and the more expensive therapeutically equivalent drug. Often, physicians are unaware of this cost. Giving physicians all the facts about a particular prescription medication helps them make reasonable and appropriate prescription decisions for their patients. In addition, many formularies will encourage physicians to return to previous medications if desired results are not being achieved with a newly suggested drug.

Formulary Controversies

Formularies typically meet with resistance because plan sponsors, enrollees, and physicians mistakenly believe that they are being asked to sacrifice therapeutic efficacy in order for the plan sponsor to save money.

Recent consolidations in the PBM industry have also caused concern among consumer advocates, physicians, and the pharmaceutical industry in general. The Federal Trade Commission has voiced strong concern over alleged improprieties by drug manufacturers, which involve promoting the manufacturer's brands on the formularies of PBMs. Plan sponsors and formulary development panels should ensure that specific drugs included on formularies are balanced, keeping the needs of enrollees and the goals of the plan sponsor in mind.

The Effect of New Drugs on Formularies

In the first half of 2009, the Food and Drug Administration (FDA) approved 34 new drugs and biologic agents. Many of the new drugs treat illnesses that could require lengthy hospital stays or that were previously untreatable. Some of the newly released drugs are simply targeted to take market share away from a leader such as Nexium™, which is used to treat gastrointestinal diseases. Drugs considered breakthrough drugs should be included on a formulary to provide quality patient care and possibly control costs. Drugs added to formularies should clearly benefit the covered population. Formularies should be reviewed at least quarterly to ensure that new drugs are properly placed on or off the preferred list.

Are There Ways to Manage Costs Even Without a Closed Formulary?

Formularies are only one tool in the management toolbox. At best, formularies may save about 15 percent in drug costs. Other cost-management methods, discussed in this chapter, include

- Network management, better discounts with retail and mail order programs, and monitoring performance to avoid fraud and abuse
- Designing plans that meet the objectives of the overall benefit program
- Quantity limits and maximum dollar limits on all prescriptions
- Step-therapy programs to ensure that prescribing complies with national guidelines for treatment of particular diseases
- Prospective review of new drugs and early policy determination
- Clinical management through a thorough pharmacy case management program

- Other DUR programs, such as concurrent and prospective programs
- Quality data management that provides early intervention reporting

Pharmacy Benefits–Disease State Management Concepts

Disease state management (DSM) programs were developed to measure and manage all health care outcomes and costs associated with a particular disease across the entire continuum of health care delivery. The top five DSM categories include asthma, depression, diabetes, high blood pressure, and high cholesterol. Costs associated with treating and managing these diseases include physician visits, emergency room visits, hospitalization, laboratory expenses, and pharmacy expenses. In the pharmacy expense area, for example, DSM programs may indicate that increasing expenses for drug therapy helps to decrease emergency room visits, resulting in an overall decrease in health care costs. Disease management programs became one of the most popular health plan design options of the 1990s, and, according to the 2009–2010 Takeda Prescription Drug Benefit Report, 69 percent of employers offer them.

Two types of DSM programs are offered: the medical model and the therapy-directed model. The medical model consists of call centers staffed by nurses and their assistants to triage patients to appropriate levels of care. These centers follow up on patients with select diseases to ensure that the patients are scheduling physician appointments, receiving appropriate tests and procedures, and understand the importance of taking their medications. The therapy-directed model is directed by PBMs, pharmaceutical manufacturers, health plans, and disease management companies. These entities foster improved compliance with medication therapy, patient education, and testing for outcomes of care. Critics argue that neither model has any standardized methods to judge success and ROI.

In the last five years, DSM programs have come under careful review by some plan sponsors. Critics have argued that these programs are thinly veiled "advertisements" from the drug manufacturers (as in information distributed to patients of mail order firms) rather than actively managed DSM programs. In addition, most PBM DSM programs have a financial interest in increasing consumption of low-cost prescription drugs that treat, for example, asthma and diabetes, rather than high-cost prescription drugs that treat depression, pain, or ulcers, for example.

Critics of DSM programs also argue that the DSM targeted diseases are "low-hanging fruit," in that their treatment can be easily improved with compliance and education programs to properly use medications. They argue that the benefits of these programs are front loaded, in that the benefits are achieved with initial interventions, and further clinical improvements and cost reductions are marginal, or at best, incremental.

PCS Health Systems (now CVS/Caremark) reported that after introducing an information program aimed at physicians and patients, emergency room usage declined 58 percent for asthma and 27 percent for diabetes. Inpatient hospital costs for asthma also declined 38 percent, but costs for diabetes only declined 1 percent. Other PBMs have had more difficulty in proving the value of information-only programs.

Although disease management holds promise, it is important to ensure that the program does more than simply target prescription drugs to treat the disease. To function optimally, disease management should focus on the full spectrum of treatment options available to treat the disease and not just on prescription drugs.

Do Disease Management Programs Decrease Prescription Drug Costs?

Employers and health plans are working with PBMs to introduce programs that will help manage health care costs related to a disease by optimizing the use of pharmaceuticals available. DSM programs offered through PBMs may increase, decrease, or have no effect on prescription benefit costs. The important measure of a DSM program is its effect on total costs related to the disease.

Medication compliance programs are an ideal way to help patients get the most benefit from the medication prescribed for them. It is estimated that $100 billion in annual health care costs can be attributed to patients seeking care in emergency rooms, physicians' offices, and operating rooms as a result of not taking prescribed medication or of taking it improperly. In addition, working directly with physicians, PBMs can provide pharmacoeconomic information to physicians that can assist them in prescribing cost-effective medications.

Evaluating a DSM Program

The May/June 1997 issue of the *Journal of Managed Care Pharmacy* suggested the following evaluation tools:

1. Health care, not therapeutics, should be emphasized.
2. Provider network support must be available.
3. Programs should include member education and motivation elements.
4. The delivery system should be integrated.
5. There should be a clearly defined system for organization and management.
6. There should be well-defined contractual criteria, including performance criteria.
7. A program for information management should be included.
8. There should be a well-defined program for measuring outcomes.
9. The economic impact must be well defined.
10. Any risk sharing should be based upon an actual risk assessment.
11. There should be a clear understanding of whether the program is a strategic partnership or a service offering.
12. There should be a clear evaluation of the total quality management (TQM) impact as an expectation or added value.
13. There must be performance audits and service guarantees, if applicable.

Pharmacy Benefits–Quality Management and Oversight

Evidence-based medicine (EBM) is an approach to medical decision making that emphasizes scientific evidence and statistical methods for evaluating outcomes and risk of treatments. EBM is at the center of formulary development, DUR, and comparative evaluations of cost-effective therapies. EBM is the response to the enormous volume of information available for diagnosis and treatment of disease. It is also a response to arrive at objective decisions in the face of mass media advertising, direct-to-consumer advertising of drugs, and the promotions of pharmaceutical and device manufacturers. EBM requires standard data submissions and statistical evaluations to ensure that all medical decisions are supported by objective information.

Identification of Duplicate Prescriptions

Pharmacies submit prescription claims electronically at the time the prescription is filled. A PBM's data center, or central clearinghouse, compares the submitted prescription with the patient's prescription profile. If a duplicate prescription exists, the pharmacy is notified immediately before the prescription is dispensed. Duplicates are generally defined as a drug dispensed to the same patient on the same day in the same therapeutic drug category.

It is fairly easy to track duplicate claims, since PBMs use some of the most advanced and sophisticated software programs available. Software programs are available that identify the same drug dispensed to the same member by the same pharmacy. Concerns come into play when a generic of the originally dispensed brand-name drug is dispensed by multiple pharmacies.

With the support of retail pharmacists, duplicate dispensing can be prevented, and prescription abusers can be stopped.

Error Detection

As part of the DUR process conducted by health plans, PBMs, and TPAs on behalf of their clients, a variety of clinical monitoring criteria or "edits" are applied to each submitted claim. An example would be a drug–drug interaction edit. If a potential harmful drug–drug interaction exists, the pharmacy is notified online. Identifying these potential problems is very important: between 10 and 25 percent of all hospitalizations are estimated to be due to drug therapy problems. Some PBMs may provide clients with reports documenting the number of edits that were executed on behalf of these clients. The reports are helpful in identifying physicians who might not be properly reviewing a patient's history before prescribing medications.

Electronic Data Interchange Reviews of Prescriptions

In today's environment, approximately 99 percent of all prescriptions paid by plan sponsors are processed electronically. The pharmacy enters vital patient and prescription information into the computer and transmits the information to a data center typically operated by a PBM. The PBM applies a variety of criteria in evaluating the prescription submitted, including determination of whether the drug is covered, at what price the pharmacy will be reimbursed, and if there are any limits or edits for the prescription. Information is transmitted back to the pharmacy that allows the pharmacist to fill the prescription or that informs the pharmacist of a potential conflict.

In order to allow for verification, prescription validation, and fraud detection, the National Association of Boards of Pharmacy (NABP) and the National Council for Prescription Drug Programs designed codes to be used in electronic data interchange (EDI). The American National Standards Institute (ANSI) establishes codes so that electronic data transmissions can be standardized and easily understood across many data platforms and also establishes codes for the National Association of Boards of Pharmacy. The National Council for Prescription Drug Programs (NCPDP) assigns an ID number to all licensed pharmacies in the United States and territories as well as the National Provider Identifier (NPI) number mandated by the Health Insurance Portability and Accountability Act of 1996, which is required of all pharmacies submitting claims.

Point of Dispensing or Point of Sale

Point of dispensing allows doctors to dispense certain drugs from their offices. This is common in workers' compensation insurance programs. The drugs dispensed are the most frequently prescribed medications that can be conveniently stocked. They are also usually medications to treat acute symptomatology rather than chronic conditions.

Typically, a computer provides the physician access to a variety of information, allowing the doctor to check for allergies, duplicate therapies, and drug interactions, while verifying that the product is on the formulary. Very few physicians have this capability. Currently, there is debate in the industry as to who will pay for the physicians to adjudicate the claim electronically. Physicians want to be paid for this service because retail pharmacies are paid a dispensing fee for doing the same thing. Plan sponsors believe it is the duty of the physician to research a conflict before prescribing the medication. PBMs and drug manufacturers have so far been unwilling to fund this activity.

A complication to oversight of prescription drugs over broad geographic areas is the fact that health plan and PBM enrollees may go anywhere to have their prescriptions filled. Typically, to receive coverage, employees participating in a prescription drug program must have their prescriptions filled by a network pharmacy, except in emergencies. However, some plan sponsors will pay for prescriptions filled outside the network but may reduce reimbursement up to what would have been paid had the member gone to a participating pharmacy. Pharmacies join networks and provide services at reduced rates in exchange for volume business. It is up to the PBM to design a network that meets the needs of enrollees and is convenient and acceptable. A tight network of pharmacy providers allows PBMs to control costs and quality effectively.

Quality Measurement of a Prescription Drug Plan

In addition to cost savings, plan sponsors should work with their PBMs to develop specific, attainable goals for prescription drug plans. One goal might be the reduction in the utilization of prescription anti-inflammatory medications and the increased use of therapeutically equivalent OTC medications that plan sponsors may want to consider covering in limited quantities. An increased focus on enrollee educational programs such as programs on exercise and smoking cessation, which can help diminish dependence on prescription drugs, might be another goal. Employers and other health plan sponsors should become actively involved in all elements of the pharmacy benefit to ensure optimal results.

Prescription drug plan satisfaction rates are another valid measure of the quality of services offered by a PBM. However, surveys of satisfaction rates can be quite subjective. The results can depend on variables such as wording of questions, recent changes in benefits design, and how often prescription benefits are used. This is not to say that plan sponsors should not expect their PBMs to provide customer satisfaction surveys as a measure of quality service; however, it may be best to develop customized questionnaires specifically tailored to the needs of the plan sponsor and to update them periodically as the plan matures. In most cases, satisfaction rates increase as enrollees become familiar with the parameters of their plan. If the satisfaction rates do not rise, benefit administrators should discuss ways to improve the level of satisfaction with their PBMs.

The Pharmacy Benefit Management Institute (PBMI) publishes an annual survey of the satisfaction of plan sponsors regarding their PBMs. Typically, the largest PBMs are evaluated by their clients. Results of the surveys can be viewed on PBMI's Web site, www.pbmi.com. Overall satisfaction has declined in the industry according to the latest survey results. As PBMs and their plan sponsors mature, and as prescription drug costs increase, there has been more discontent in the industry.

Pharmacy Benefits–HIPAA Impact

The Health Insurance Portability and Accountability Act of 1996 (HIPAA) requires plan sponsors to fully disclose entities that retain information regarding a covered member's prescription drug data. This requirement extends to the PBM and any subsidiaries or subcontractors of the plan or PBM. Patients must be better informed as to what entities may review their personal prescription drug information and be better informed as to how such data are being used.

How does HIPAA change the interaction of pharmacies with their patients? Pharmacies must provide private counseling areas to protect the privacy of their customers. In addition, pharmacies are requiring signature logs to ensure that customers are informed of their rights and consent to the services that the pharmacy provides. In some cases, message boards in pharmacies have changed to remove patient names and display only numbers for customer pick up of their prescriptions. When pharmacists are unfamiliar with patients, they also are requiring patient approvals for family or friends to pick up their prescriptions. In some cases, physicians are refusing to refill prescriptions without seeing their patients first. There are also concerns among pharmacists and physicians that patient-specific data violates HIPAA guidelines, even when such data are used for payment, or organizational case management, disease management, and utilization review.

All of the above are sources for member complaints and customer service problems. Plan sponsors should ensure that health plans, PBMs, and TPAs are adequately communicating with their pharmacy networks to minimize HIPAA-related privacy concerns.

Pharmacy Benefit Managers

A pharmacy benefit manager is an entity that administers managed pharmacy programs. It is defined as an application of programs, services, and techniques designed to control costs associated with the delivery of pharmaceutical care by

1. Streamlining and improving the prescribing and dispensing process through online and real-time claims adjudication

2. Maintaining a retail network of pharmacies and a mail order option that in turn offer discounts off the cost of prescription drugs and potentially monitor the performance of the network
3. Offering limited DUR online at the point of sale or dispensing
4. Providing data and reporting regarding drug use
5. Controlling the cost of prescriptions dispensed through clinical and financial programs, such as formulary development and rebate contracting with drug manufacturers

Estimates of the current number of enrollees in some type of pharmacy program—whether managed or simply a claim processing or prescription card service—is at least 130 million and now higher due to the addition of Medicare Part D patients. Some analysts believe these numbers are inflated. One point is clear: within the past decade, the number of people utilizing PBMs has increased significantly.

According to CNN Money, the three largest PBMs in 2009 were Medco Health Solutions, Caremark (acquired by CVS in 2007), and Express Scripts. These three PBMs manage drug benefits for more than 200 million Americans—an estimated 95 percent of those who have prescription drug coverage. The market has remained largely unchanged. According to *Business Insurance*, the largest PBMs, ranked by 2008 revenues from unbundled PBM services, were Medco Health Solutions, CVS/Caremark, Express Scripts, Inc., RxSolutions (now United Health Care), and Catalyst Rx.

PBM Portfolio of Services

PBMs offer a standard portfolio of services and a variety of value-added options to differentiate themselves in the marketplace. A standard portfolio of services is common to all PBMs and includes

- Claim processing
- Account management and support for plan design alternatives, trend analysis, and general advice regarding prescription drugs
- A retail network of pharmacies for the purchase of medication at discounts
- Dispensing mail order prescriptions
- Communication to patients regarding program use
- Formulary development and rebate administration

- Some drug utilization management, including prospective, concurrent, and retrospective review programs
- Reporting of drug utilization and industry trends
- Some educational components for patients and physicians

PBM Charges for Services

PBM prices can vary dramatically by region, age of enrollees, type of industry covered by the plan, overall health of beneficiaries, size of the group that is being covered, and, most specifically, by the elements the plan sponsor wants to include. PBM administrative and prescription costs combined can range from $25 to $35 per member per month to $60 to $70 per member per month for a plan with few controls, older members, and low copayments. PBM administrative fees typically are 3 or 4 percent of total prescription plan costs.

PBMs charge claims processing fees to the plan for such services as account management, standard report delivery, and claims processing. These charges range from 15 to 75 cents per claim. The largest (also known as "jumbo") clients pay nothing for the administrative claims processing fee, while the smallest clients usually pay 45 cents or more per claim. A pricing scheme composed of a combination of discounts off the average wholesale price and a dispensing fee are paid to retail pharmacies or the mail order firm for the actual medication. These discounts are shown in Table 10-1.

In some cases, PBMs take the difference between what is charged to the client and what is reimbursed to the pharmacy. Therefore, the rates

TABLE 10-1

Common PBM Pricing Guarantees

Retail network brand drugs	12–16% off average wholesale price plus a $1–3 dispensing fee
Retail network generic drugs	MAC plus a $0–3 dispensing fee
Mail order brand drugs	20–25% off average wholesale price plus a $0–1 dispensing fee
Mail order generic drugs	50–65% off average wholesale price or MAC plus a $0–1 dispensing fee

shown in the table are typically what are charged to clients. Actual reimbursement rates to pharmacies may differ by 1 to 2 percentage points. The margin made by chain drug stores can range from 5 percent and up for brand drugs to 25 percent for generic drugs, since chain pharmacies purchase prescription drugs in bulk and often obtain discounts from wholesalers.

PBM Compensation

PBMs may generate profits in many ways. The typical revenue streams are through claim administration fees, mail service, and rebates. The following is a more extensive list of potential PBM revenue streams:

- Charging payers an administrative fee per transaction based on the number of prescriptions or employees
- Retaining rebate administrative fees negotiated with manufacturers
- Filling mail service prescriptions from their wholly owned mail order pharmacies
- Providing disease management, education, and value-added programs negotiated with pharmaceutical manufacturers
- Securing discounts through a contracted network of pharmacies or through direct purchasing when the PBM owns its mail service pharmacy
- Retaining the pharmacy spread
- Retaining the spread in MAC list payments for generics that is greater than what is paid to the network pharmacies
- Reducing payments to pharmacies based on certain package sizes, regardless of the package size dispensed

Pharmacy Spread

The difference between the amount the PBM collects from the payer and the amount the PBM pays the pharmacy is called the pharmacy spread. Pharmacy spreads are a revenue source for PBMs and are frequently not stipulated in the payer contract. Payers should ask a PBM they are considering whether a spread exists, and how that will influence the performance of the PBM's network. Payers may choose between PBMs based on those retaining a spread and those that do not.

Zero-Balance Billing

Some PBMs allow pharmacies to collect the entire copay even when the cost of the drug is less than the copay. This is called zero-balance billing. PBMs have used zero-balance billing to extract greater discounts from pharmacies for their clients. When the pharmacy keeps the entire copay, the payer does not lose, but the plan member will pay more. Payers should question PBMs as to whether zero-balance billing occurs, and whether that is consistent with their benefit philosophy.

Rebates

A rebate is an agreement between a PBM and a drug manufacturer to secure significant reductions in the cost of prescription drugs. Some of the savings are passed along to employers. Over the past 10 years, rebates have grown from 1 to 2 percent of a payer's total drug expenses to 6 to 9 percent of the total. The growth in rebates paid to payers has paralleled the rise of pharmacy benefit inflation and the advent of multitiered copay designs.

In some cases for specific drugs, rebates can account for up to 50 percent off the cost of the prescription medication. In the past, manufacturers would discount solely based on utilization; however, today manufacturers require an increase in market share before giving discounts.

With rebates, drug manufacturers reward PBMs that are able to encourage a significant percentage of enrollees to switch to the company's key products. At the end of a predetermined period, typically on a quarterly basis, the PBM and the manufacturer review utilization. If the goals agreed upon were met, the PBM receives a rebate that varies from 5 percent to 50 percent and can be as high as about 50 percent of the cost of the drug. In some cases, the savings are passed on to the PBM's client. Rebates are becoming increasingly more controversial because many plan sponsors are led to believe that they are receiving almost all of the rebate payments, when in reality, some plan sponsors receive only a small portion. Further, critics argue that rebates bias drug selection while the plan sponsor still pays more than it would for a generic or a lower-cost therapeutic alternative.

Components of rebate contracts include administrative fees, access rebates, and market share rebates. Administrative fees are almost always retained by the PBM and average 2 to 4 percent of the average wholesale price cost of the drug under contract. Access rebates are minimum amounts paid by the manufacturer for placement on the formulary. Access rebates are about 5 percent of the average-wholesale-price cost of the drug. Additional rebates, or market share rebates, are paid to the PBM if the market share of one drug within the therapeutic category reaches or exceeds the contract threshold. Market share rebates are usually based on the formulary-driven claims payments to pharmacies and belong to plan sponsors.

Many PBMs do not allow disclosure of these rebate arrangements, because they fear that if plan sponsors understand these arrangements, they will demand more of the rebate monies and therefore reduce the profitability of the PBM.

What Is the Role of Rebates in Lowering Drug Costs?

Rebates are payments to health plans, PBMs, TPAs, and payers for volume purchasing of medications within therapeutic categories that reach target market share. Rebates, which are paid to clients from PBMs, are based on drug manufacturer payments to the PBM. Rebates typically range from $1 per prescription for open formularies, $2 per prescription for preferred formularies, and $3 per prescription for closed formularies; however, a wide variation occurs, depending on contracts and class of trade. Rebates have been a controversial issue in the industry, since PBMs have been reluctant to discuss the details of these arrangements with their clients or provide any information as to the accuracy of the billing and collection process. PBMs have frequently been criticized in the media for secretive deals with drug manufacturers where they retain, in some cases, as much as 50 percent of the total dollars paid by drug manufacturers rather than passing these savings on to clients.

Almost all PBMs offer new members enrollment materials that detail how to obtain retail and mail order prescriptions, how to obtain an ID card, and other basic information such as the difference between brand drugs and generic drugs. These materials may be included in the base claims processing fee or can be purchased for an additional per-piece fee.

Many PBMs distribute monthly newsletters to enrollees offering information on specific health problems such as asthma or diabetes. The plan should review these communications to make sure they meet the plan's standards. A number of PBMs now allow members to order prescriptions on their Web sites, which are linked to medical information sites.

Few PBMs, however, offer true educational information regarding drug therapies for either physicians or members. Most PBMs defer to the patient's physician.

Choosing a Pharmacy Benefit Manager

The primary question a plan sponsor should ask a PBM is "How can you make my prescription drug benefit better meet the needs of my enrollees in a cost-effective manner?" The most important element in selecting a PBM is the ability of the PBM to meet the unique needs of the plan sponsor. For example, if a plan sponsor wants a PBM to handle all administrative responsibility for the plan, it needs a plan that is simple, easy to understand, does not require the sponsor to review formularies and drug trends, and provides excellent member service that will not give rise to "complaints" from members. A more sophisticated plan sponsor may want extensive reporting, full disclosure of rebate contract terms (so that a customized formulary can be developed), and carved-out traditional PBM services such as retail network management that it can retain in house.

Every plan sponsor must develop its own list of objectives before soliciting proposals from PBMs. Through a short interview process, the plan sponsor may first determine which type and level of services it considers most important. Then, the plan sponsor may solicit formal proposals from only those PBMs that meet its list of needs.

Cost is a major factor; however, claims administration that is consistent with the plan benefit designs, service delivery, administrative oversight, and transparency of pricing also are critical. The following specific questions should also be asked:

1. What are the options and pricing of the network of providers that the PBM offers? What support does the PBM provide for customizing the network (adding and deleting pharmacies that are important to the plan)? Does the PBM reimburse pharmacies at a rate different from what it charges to the plan?
2. Does the PBM own the mail order program? If not, how does the subcontractual relationship work between the two organizations? How are mail order claims monitored for accuracy and timeliness?
3. Are price guarantees backed by unrestricted audits by the plan sponsor?
4. Are service and performance offerings backed by guarantees and significant financial penalties?
5. What kind of reports does the PBM offer?
6. What types of DUR edits are performed routinely? Can these edits be customized? Are the DUR edits limited to too-soon

refills, prior authorization, quantity limits, and duplicate claims, or are pharmacists notified of DUR alerts (drug–drug interactions) during the dispensing process so that the prescription may be changed if needed.

7. Are DUR edits based on criteria that are measurable in the claims detail supporting the invoices? Is the edit performance backed by a return on investment (ROI) that can be independently verified in the claims?
8. How does the PBM work with physicians to educate and modify prescribing patterns?
9. What types of educational programs are offered to patients?
10. If the PBM offers disease management programs, how are the programs designed? Do they emphasize more than prescription drugs? How are the programs funded?
11. What types of ancillary services are provided? Are claims processed in house?
12. What drugs are preferred by the PBM? Can a client make changes to the preferred list? Are there therapeutic switching programs in mail order or retail edits to flag preferred drugs? Who are the representatives on the PBM's pharmaceutical and therapeutics committee? What are their affiliations? Do these members accept grant money from drug manufacturers?
13. What are the results of these programs? Does the PBM track savings and the return on investment of programs offered?

Part of the due diligence in selecting a PBM is the questioning of a PBM's current clients. A plan sponsor that is considering purchasing the services of a PBM should ask the PBM's current clients the following questions:

- Are the PBM's reports delivered in a timely manner? Are reports available online and in real time using both standard and ad hoc query systems?
- Do the reports provide the type of information needed to improve management of the prescription benefit?
- What type of customer service does the PBM offer? Are enrollees treated courteously, and are their questions answered promptly?

- Do enrollees experience difficulty in getting prescriptions filled because of technical problems, such as computer system downtime?
- What is the PBM's reputation with physicians and pharmacies?
- What kind of therapeutic interchange protocol program does the PBM use?
- What kind of cost savings has the PBM produced for its clients?
- How has the PBM enhanced its clients' prescription benefit programs?
- How did the implementation process proceed?

PBMs versus PBAs

PBMs offer prescription adjudication, knowledge of prescription administration in various jurisdictions, enrollment cards, quality oversight of prescriptions through DUR and clinical edits, and further cost control through cost-effective formularies. In addition, they offer the ability to screen all prescriptions against the applicable diagnoses of plan participants. Rebates are offered as cost offsets. These services are common and generally undifferentiated across the industry.

In contrast, pharmacy benefit administrators (PBAs) focus on prescription administration. Most offer a discounted pharmacy network, formularies, DUR edits that can be applied at the time of prescription adjudication, enrollment cards, and screening of prescriptions to ensure that they are within the scope of the participants' diagnoses. They emphasize "transparency" in adjudicating prescriptions such that the payer knows the actual cost of the prescription from the pharmacy, and actual rebates earned and collected.

Aside from transparency issues, the payer will have to decide on how much support they require—a PBM provides all services, while a PBA may require more of the payer's time and input. Both will require the payer to continue usual oversight functions, such as accounts-payable review of invoices, quarterly (or more frequent) review of progress, and final judgments on prior authorizations. The key question for the payer is whether the additional services offered by the PBM provide sufficient value to the organization to be worth the additional cost premium over the PBA expense.[4]

4. Craig S. Stern, "Worker's Compensation Pharmacy Vendor Contracts," *Healthcare Savings Chronicle*, Vol. 5, No. 4, April 2007.

Potential Conflicts of Interest

Many PBMs are either owned by or have historical relationships with large drug chains or pharmaceutical manufacturers. In addition, smaller PBMs may be owned by chains or independent pharmacy consortiums. The ownership of PBMs should be scrutinized to ensure that the best discounts and oversight of owned pharmacies are available to the payer. In some cases, a plan funds claims for retail pharmacies from the PBM. In this situation, it is advisable to have controls, such as an external audit firm, in place to ensure proper controls for funding transfers.

Other relationships between PBMs and pharmaceutical firms can be of concern to plan sponsors as well. Many PBMs have contractual relationships with drug manufacturers for rebates. Based on these relationships, a PBM's advice concerning medications must be taken with caution.

Other PBMs are owned by managed care organizations, and the controls implemented with HMOs could be too severe for some employers or Taft-Hartley Funds.

Employers should carefully review the PBMs that they are considering before making their final selection. Biases regarding preferential treatment of certain products or of certain pharmacies can cost plans more than the potential savings gained through volume discounts.

PBM Reporting

Perhaps the single most important report a PBM can provide is a review of utilization. The information in a utilization review can be broken down in whatever manner the sponsor prefers—by region, sex, age, and so forth; however, some PBMs provide utilization in one report, claims data in another, and reports from different regions covered by the plan sponsor in yet another. For a complete analysis of the PBM's activity, it is preferable to have one integrated report that provides an overview of all elements of the pharmacy program; the reports should be available semimonthly, quarterly, and annually. Reports can be used to identify and manage trends, as well as to answer specific questions. Additionally, they are of critical importance in the day-to-day management of a successful PBM program. Many PBMs now offer the plan sponsor the ability to query data in a variety of ways, using the PBM's ad hoc reporting tool. These report query systems allow each plan sponsor to develop its own customized reports.

PBMs with Nationwide Service

Employees who are members of a PBM are required to have their prescriptions filled by a network pharmacy (except in emergencies) in order to receive benefits. If the plan sponsor and its enrollees are located in one area, a nationwide network may not be necessary. On the other hand, nationwide service can be beneficial for large employers with employees in multiple locations, employees (and retirees) who travel frequently, or employees who are frequently transferred.

Pharmacies join networks and provide services at reduced rates in exchange for volume business. A tight network of pharmacy providers allows a PBM to better control costs and quality. A PBM should design a network that meets the needs of enrollees and offers convenience, although obviously not every pharmacy can be in a network. The strategy of developing tightly controlled networks of pharmacies is somewhat limited by legislative action in many states. More than 20 states have adopted "any willing provider" (AWP) laws, which require PBMs and plan sponsors to allow any pharmacy that meets the PBM's maximum reimbursement rate to participate in its network. In essence, these requirements make it easier for PBMs and plan sponsors to eliminate pharmacies or pharmacy chains that are unwilling to participate at a desired targeted discount rate.

Pharmacy Issues in Workers' Compensation Insurance

The existence of different rules of coverage and payment of claims within each of the states' jurisdictions adds a level of complexity to the administration of workers' compensation claims that is not common in group health.

To lower the cost of prescription drugs, pharmacy vendors (PBMs and PBAs) have traditionally offered a discounted network of pharmacies. The pharmacy vendor acts as a "middle man" to adjudicate prescriptions and to ensure that the prescriptions are paid only for eligible injured workers and that pharmacy prescriptions are within the scope of the injury. Constant concerns have been, and continue to be, "first fills" for prescriptions before eligibility is verified, the adjudication of prescriptions dispensed by physicians, and prescriptions repriced and aggregated for payment by third-party payers.

Traditional PBMs and pharmacy benefit administrators (PBAs) are expanding the service offering through enrollment cards, online claim administration, prospective DUR, formularies when applicable, screening for prescriptions within the scope of the injury, and enhanced reporting. The result is that workers' compensation is becoming a commodity offering that is a subspecialty of the mainstream vendors. The following discussion provides an inventory of offerings that should be used when choosing vendors and their experience with workers' compensation.[5]

What are the key questions that should be asked of a PBM or PBA when deciding on the right vendor to adjudicate workers' compensation prescriptions? When reviewing requests for proposals (RFPs), contracts, or even evaluating current services, the following issues should be considered as part of contract negotiations:

1. Knowledge of workers' compensation:
   a. Experience with workers' compensation
   b. Experience with adjudicating claims in various jurisdictions
   c. Compliance with Sarbanes-Oxley disclosures
2. Pricing questions:
   a. Pricing language regarding "lesser of," and the impact of average wholesale price discounts, maximum allowable charge, state fee schedules, and usual and customary pricing
   b. Management of third-party prescriptions
3. Claim administration questions:
   a. Management of physician-dispensed prescriptions
   b. Management of customized formularies when allowed
   c. Management of prescriptions to ensure that they are within the scope of the injury
4. Service portfolio, delivery, and guarantees:
   a. Management of eligibility
   b. Prescription administration policies and procedures that comply with claim management
   c. Provision of service and performance guarantees
   d. Audit policies consistent with the workers' compensation carrier and Sarbanes-Oxley requirements

5. Ibid.

More than ever, workers' compensation now has the opportunity to look more closely at quality issues and has greater clinical edit oversight with the expansion of vendor offerings for workers' compensation in the prescription payment arena. With greater offerings come choice, vendor price competition, and expansion of offerings. It is crucial, however, that the pharmacy expense is viewed as one component within the context of the entire claim review. This can only help workers' compensation to improve over time.[6]

CONCLUSION

Pharmacy benefit design and management grew out of the need to supply a broad range of therapies to multiple patient populations. Because of the needs of the various populations, drug therapies expanded to fill therapy gaps. As a result, from the beginning, there was a conflict between desires and resources. The financial resources necessary to support prescription drug benefits continue to increase such that all management techniques are based on cost control. However, the introduction of new therapies, particularly biotechnology agents and the new testing techniques required for their management, will stretch cost control techniques to their limits. Future therapies and testing will require more aggressive utilization management based on demonstrated benefits and evidence-based criteria. In the final examination, though, medication therapy will continue to be based on delivering the maximal therapeutic benefit, at the minimum acceptable risk, and at an affordable cost.

6. Ibid.

APPENDIX 10.1
DEFINITIONS

Since a prescription drug plan is based on medications, it is necessary to understand the different types of medications.

BRAND NAME MEDICATIONS

A *brand name medication*, also known as "pioneer" or "branded" medication, is made by one manufacturer under a patent issued by the United States Patent Office. The manufacturer of the branded medication has a 20-year exclusive patent during which no other manufacturer is allowed to produce the exact same product. Examples of brand name medications include Lipitor™, Exubera™, and Humira™.

GENERIC MEDICATIONS

A *generic medication*, or *multisource medication*, is a medication produced by multiple manufacturers. Generic products are allowed to be marketed after the brand-name medication loses patent protection. Generic manufacturers vie to be the first one on the market, as they are given a 180-day exclusivity period to regain development costs. After the exclusivity period, any manufacturer may apply for a license to market a generic version of the pioneer product. Pricing discounts, which are typically 10 to 15 percent during the exclusivity period, become 50 to 70 percent or more after that time.

Multisource Medications

Multisource simply means that multiple manufacturers produce the same medication. Some payers refer to a multisource medication as the first generic on the market after the pioneering brand-name medication loses patent protection. Within the industry, the terms "generic medication" and "multisource medication" are used interchangeably.

AUTHORIZED GENERICS

Authorized generics are considered brand drugs under a generic label. Put simply, a brand drug manufacturer supplies its drug to a generic firm and allows the firm to market the product under a different label for royalties. Brand companies can also create their own companies or subsidiaries to manufacture these authorized generics. By taking either route, these authorized generics can compete with the first generic drug maker during their 180-day exclusivity period. The implications of such actions create a price war that reduces the price of both generics in the 180-day period, thereby reducing the market share and profitability for the generic manufacturer.

BRANDED GENERICS

Branded generics also play a role in drug plans. *Branded generics* are brand-name drugs that contain the same active ingredient as the original branded drug but can act somewhat differently in the body because they contain slightly different compounds. Traditional generics do not have to pass the rigorous testing process of branded drugs, but branded generics do need to win Food and Drug Administration approval. Makers of branded generics do not infringe on patent protections. Traditional generics do not appear on the market until after patents expire. Branded generics appear on the market sooner and cost more than traditional generics, but less than the original brand name drug. PBMs usually treat branded generics as brand-name drugs, but branded generics are likely to win a spot on a formulary and push the original drug to nonformulary status.

APPENDIX 10.2
PHARMACEUTICAL PRICING

The logical consequence of brand, generic, specialty, and other categories of medications is that there are various pricing mechanisms applied for each type of medication. Essentially, pharmaceutical pricing is based on the supply chain where manufacturers sell to wholesalers and distributors who, in turn, sell to pharmacies, hospitals, physicians, and other end users. The various prices involved in the supply chain are detailed below. Health plan pricing is commonly based on the average wholesale price, but a recent court case that was decided against the publishers of the AWP has changed the marketplace to favor contracts based on wholesale acquisition cost (WAC). WAC pricing contracts are expected to replace AWP-based contracts in 2011 and 2012 agreements.

AVERAGE WHOLESALE PRICE

The AWP of a medication is the price assigned by the drug manufacturer. This price is used as a reference price for all discounts paid to pharmacies and PBMs. PBM contracts usually refer to the price that will be paid to pharmacies as a discount off the average wholesale price for a branded medication. It is important to understand that the average wholesale price may have no direct relationship to the actual cost of providing the medication. However, public and private contracts include the AWP as a reference for pricing guarantees.

The WAC is the list price for wholesalers, distributors and other direct accounts before any rebates, discounts, allowances or other price concessions that might be offered by the supplier of the product. The WAC is what the wholesaler buys the drugs for from the manufacturer.

> In the USA, the wholesaler industry is a concentrated market dominated by five firms. Wholesalers act as distributors, buying pharmaceuticals from manufacturers at the average manufacturer price, (which is equal to the WAC), and then selling them on to pharmacies using a "cost-plus" approach (plus a mark-up percentage) or a "list less" (less a discount percentage) approach.[7]

7. www.doh.gov.uk/generics/oxera_report_a7.htm

On March 17, 2009, the United States District Court in Massachusetts entered the Final Order and Judgment approving a class action settlement in two cases—one involving First DataBank (FDB) and one involving Medi-Span. FDB is the most widely used publisher of prescription drug prices in the United States and Medi-Span is a provider of electronic drug data to health care professionals. Beginning September 26, 2009, the AWP of over 400 brand name drugs will decrease as a result of these two lawsuits.

New England Carpenters Health Benefits Fund, et al. v. First DataBank, Inc. and McKession Corp.

In 2005, a class-action lawsuit was brought against FDB and McKesson Corporation by New England Carpenters Health Benefits Fund, et al., a third-party payor class. McKesson Corp. is one of the largest pharmaceutical distributors in the nation. The plantiffs accused FDB and McKesson Corp. of artificially inflating the AWP of over four hundred brand name drugs by 5 percent for drugs purchased from August 1, 2001 through March 15, 2005. The lawsuit alleged that the defendants inflated the AWP while keeping the WAC the same so that large retail chains and other pharmacies, many of whom were customers of McKesson, received larger profits on those drugs. As a result, many drug purchasers were overpaying for these drugs. These mark-ups were not noticed for many years because the derivation of WAC and AWP is not subject to regulatory review.

District Council 37 Health & Security Plan v. Medi-Span, a division of Wolters Kluwer Health, Inc.

There was a related lawsuit against Medi-Span which published its AWP for prescription drugs based on data provided to it by FDB from December 2001 to April 2004. As a result, the lawsuit claims that the AWP published by Medi-Span was also illicitly inflated.

Independent of the settlement, FDB and Medi-Span have voluntarily offered to discontinue publishing AWP data within the next two years. Both companies will continue to publish other drug pricing data information to facilitate the establishment of a drug pricing benchmark. A source of concern throughout the industry is that there is no standard to take the place of using AWP as a pricing benchmark.[8]

MAXIMUM ALLOWABLE COST

The maximum allowable cost of a generic medication places a ceiling on the reimbursement for generics. The genesis of the MAC concept is in the federal Medicaid program. CMS publishes a federal upper limit (FUL) price for all generic medications paid in the Medicare and Medicaid programs. Unfortunately, not all therapeutic categories of medications are covered on the FUL, nor is it updated as frequently as manufacturers change prices. As a result, health plans, PBMs, and TPAs developed their own MAC lists to cover all generic medications. Since generics are made by many manufacturers, several options are used for pricing the MAC. It may be the average cost of all manufacturers' average wholesale prices, or the lowest average wholesale price, or a formula for arriving at an aggregate average wholesale price discount for the entire MAC list. Most plans offer payers a MAC list that will deliver a 50 percent or more discount off the average wholesale price. As a reference price for generics, the MAC is referred to in PBM contracts, but it may or may not apply to all generic claims. The MAC may be quoted as an "average" or as a range of discounts.

AVERAGE MANUFACTURER PRICE

The average manufacturer price (AMP) is the "average price paid to the manufacturer by wholesalers for drugs distributed to the retail pharmacy class of trade, after deducting customary prompt payment discounts."[9] The AMP was originally designed as a basis for rebates paid to the states. It is now being expanded as the basis for payments of drugs to pharmacies under the Medicare Part D program. It will eventually replace AWP as the basis for retail pharmacy payments.

---

8. (a) mckessonawpsettlement.com/PDFs/AmendedSettlementAgreemt.pdf.
    (b) online.wsj.com/article/SB124467803957704253.html.
    (c) www.firstdatabank.com/download/pdf/FinalJudgment.pdf.
    (d) www.pharmacychoice.com/resources/cdr/060309.cfm.
9. Deficit Reduction Act of 2005 (DRA) Section 6001 that amended Social Security Act Section 1927(k)(1).

AVERAGE SALES PRICE

Average sales price (ASP) is a manufacturer's average price to all purchasers, net of discounts, rebates, chargebacks, and credits for drugs. ASP is determined using manufacturers' sales reports, which include information on total units sold and total revenue for each drug. ASP is commonly used for payment of Medicare Part B drugs and is subject to audit by Medicare. In other words, the average sales price is a reference price based on purchase price rather than drug cost. The ASP price is used for Medicare reimbursements to providers.

WIDELY AVAILABLE MARKET PRICE

Sections 1847A(d)(1) and (2) of the Social Security Act (the Act), as added by the Medicare Prescription Drug, Improvement, and Modernization Act of 2003 (MMA), P.L. No. 108-173, directs the Office of Inspector General (OIG) to undertake pricing studies that compare ASPs to widely available market prices and AMP. Section 1847A(d)(5)(A) of the Act defines the widely available market price (WAMP) to be the price that a prudent physician or supplier would pay for the drug, net of any routinely available price concessions. In determining widely available market prices, OIG is authorized to consider information from sources including (but not limited to) manufacturers, wholesalers, distributors, physicians, and suppliers.

340B PRICING

The 340B Drug Pricing Program resulted from enactment of Public Law 102-585, the Veterans Health Care Act of 1992, which is codified as Section 340B of the Public Health Service Act. Section 340B limits the cost of covered outpatient drugs to certain federal grantees, federally qualified health center look-alikes and qualified disproportionate share hospitals. Significant savings on pharmaceuticals may be seen by those entities that participate in this program.

APPENDIX 10.3
MEDICATION EQUIVALENCE

Generic drugs play an important role in prescription drug plans. Generic drugs are nonbranded medications. They contain components identical to those of their name-brand counterparts. Generics are produced by a variety of manufacturers and can typically save the buyer 20 to 50 percent or more of the cost of branded drugs.

Major pharmaceutical firms spend millions of dollars developing new ("innovator" or "pioneer") drugs. Once created, drugs are patented and become the sole property of the firm. Drugs are typically patented for an average of 20 years, although patents may be extended if the product develops a new and unique "extender," such as an "extra-strength" or "sustained-release" version. At the end of 2005, 14 significant drugs with almost $15 billion in sales lost their patents. In 2006, six branded drugs lost patent protection with over $2.5 billion in sales. In 2007 and 2008, 12 and 13 drug patents, respectively, expired resulting in the loss of billions of sales dollars. Currently, patents for many blockbuster brand-name drugs—drugs with sales of over one billion dollars per years—have begun to expire at a rapid pace, and this will continue for the next few years. As a result, the development of a pipeline of new drugs has become vital in order to sustain the size of many large drug manufacturers. Drugs with expired patents are now available to other drug manufacturers to produce as nonbranded or generic drugs. Pharmacy benefit managers (PBMs) may use generics to help manage the cost of prescription drug plans, although plan sponsors must be diligent in moving preferred tier brand drugs to nonpreferred status once their patents have expired. Within the first six months to a year of a brand-name drug going off patent, it typically loses 80 percent of its revenues to generic competitors.

The most fundamental question that is frequently asked is: "Are generics as good as brand name medications?" The simple answer is yes. The Food and Drug Administration (FDA) approves generics as safe and effective alternatives to the pioneering branded medication. Generics contain the exact same active ingredients as the branded product and must fulfill the same properties for dissolving and disintegrating in the body as the pioneer brand. The FDA approves generics as therapeutically equivalent to the pioneering branded product and publishes all approved generics in its publication, *Approved Drug Products with Therapeutic Equivalence Evaluations*, frequently called the "Orange Book." Generic drugs are frequently made by the same companies that market the pioneer branded product and by public companies that are listed on the major stock exchanges. Claims that generics contain various binders and fillers that are not the same as the pioneering branded product may be true, but such claims are irrelevant. All companies that manufacture medication, both brand and generic, use the same fillers and binders. A generic may have a different size, shape, and color, but it cannot be marketed without FDA approval.

To further emphasize the credibility of generics, the FDA has published a position statement on generic drugs. In a statement released January 28, 1998, the FDA stated: "To date, there are no documented examples of a generic product manufactured to meet its approved specifications that could not be used interchangeably with the corresponding brand-name drug." This statement was issued in response to concern expressed about drugs with so-called narrow therapeutic indices (NTI), that is, small differences between the therapeutic and toxic doses. This statement provides reassurance to plan sponsors that encourage generic drugs over brand drugs.

The FDA uses guidelines on pharmaceutical equivalence, bioequivalence, and therapeutic equivalence to ensure that generic drugs are interchangeable with brand drugs. *Pharmaceutical equivalence* means that the generic drug has the same active ingredient or ingredients as the brand drug, is in the same dosage form (tablet, liquid, etc.), and is identical in strength. *Bioequivalence* means the generic drug is absorbed into the bloodstream at the same rate and extent as the brand drug. *Therapeutic equivalence* is achieved when a generic drug is proven to be safe and effective and is both pharmaceutically equivalent and bioequivalent.

Much discussion has taken place among physicians about generics having a wider range of strength allowed per dosage unit than branded medications. The branded pharmaceutical industry has promoted this distinction in order to discourage generic usage. The FDA has published the allowable strength and measurement tolerance that must be confirmed by generic manufacturers in their FDA submissions. These tolerances are not different from the measurement error allowable among branded products for their published strengths. As a result, concerns about the lack of strength of a generic product are unwarranted.

The American Association of Retired Persons (AARP) says that manufacturer prices for brand-name prescription drugs commonly used by people on Medicare rose 9.7 percent for the year ending in March 2010—the biggest annual jump since the group started tracking prices in 2002—while generic drug prices dropped 9.7 percent, offering an alternative to the consumer with greater affordability. According to the Generic Pharmaceutical Association, generic medications saved an estimated $121 billion in 2008.[10]

10. www.businessweek.com/bwdaily/dnflash/content/feb2008/db2008025_791527.htm.

APPENDIX 10.4
SPECIALTY/BIOTECHNOLOGY MEDICATIONS AND THEIR PLACE IN PRESCRIPTION DRUG PLANS

Biotechnology medications are drugs that are manufactured by reengineering proteins, manipulating genes, and other sophisticated techniques for generating new molecules. These medications may be self-injectable by patients or require injection by a health care professional. They were originally targeted to treat obscure diseases, but are now being developed to treat common chronic diseases.

As of 2010, biologics comprise 30 percent of the current compounds in the pharmaceutical industry development pipeline, and there is potential that this could grow up to 50 percent within ten years. The growth rate of biologics has been increasing quickly.

Cancer treatments dominate the biotechnology pipeline. As of June 2008, 619 biotechnology medications and vaccines were in drug trials. Of the medications in trials, 292 medications were targeted for treatment of cancer, 24 for autoimmune disease, 79 for HIV and related disorders, and 15 for cardiovascular diseases. In 2009, four monoclonal antibodies (mAbs) gained approval, representing the highest annual number in over a decade and equaling the record set in 1998. In addition, there were many approvals for H1N1 influenza vaccines in response to the swine flu pandemic, as well as the landmark of the first approval for a recombinant protein produced in a transgenic animal.[11]

Yet, the industry faces greater challenges today than it has in the past. According to the Biotechnology Industry Organization, the industry today is being challenged by the financial realities of a recession and many emerging biotechnology companies are struggling for survival. Difficult operating decisions have to be made, including postponing the development of new therapies or laying off employees to reduce operating expenses. In October 2008 alone, over 20 companies publicly announced layoffs. Many other companies are making programmatic adjustments, such as shelving important research to conserve financial resources to reduce cash

11. www.nextpharma.com/pr_march2010_1.html.

burn rates. For example, while the 2008 experience indicated that the industry was heating up and more drugs were being developed for chronic care management over acute care, numerous smaller biotechnology companies were acquired by larger corporations that could withstand losses on investment associated with a failing drug in its pipeline. It is becoming increasingly difficult for companies to develop safe, effective, blockbuster drugs to stay afloat as their older drugs lose patent protection and sales.

CHAPTER 11

Dental Plan Design

Ronald L. Huling

In 2010, 45 percent of small firms (3–199 workers) and 87 percent of large firms (200 or more workers) provided dental benefit plans.[1] It is not surprising that dental plans are so popular. Most of the U.S. population visits a dentist at least once each year.

DIFFERENCES BETWEEN MEDICINE AND DENTISTRY DRIVE PLAN DESIGN

Medicine and dentistry have many differences, and sound dental plan design recognizes these. These differences include practice location, the nature of care, cost, and emphasis on prevention.

Location

The typical physician practices in a group, while many dentists practice almost exclusively in individual offices. Partly because of these practice differences, physicians tend to associate with other physicians with greater frequency than dentists associate with other dentists. This isolation, along with the inherent differences in the nature of medical and dental care, tends to produce a greater variety of dental practice patterns than is the case in medicine. In addition, practicing in isolation does not afford the same opportunities for peer review and general quality control.

1. *Employee Health Benefits, 2010 Annual Survey*, The Kaiser Family Foundation and Health Education Trust, p. 43.

Nature of Care, Cost, and Prevention

Perhaps contributing more significantly to the differences in medicine and dentistry are the important differences between the nature of medical and dental care.

First and perhaps foremost, because of the importance of preventive dentistry, the need for dental care is almost universal to ensure sound oral hygiene. Many individuals sometimes require only preventive or no medical care for years. Individuals routinely visit their dentists for preventive dental care, but in medicine the patient typically visits a physician with certain symptoms—often pain or discomfort—and seeks relief.

Dental treatment, because of its emphasis on prevention, is often considered elective. Unless there is pain or trauma, dental care is sometimes postponed. The patient recognizes that life is not at risk and as a result has few reservations about postponing treatment. In fact, postponement may be preferable to some patients—perhaps because of an aversion to visiting the dentist, rooted many years in the past when dental technology was less developed.

Because major dental care is not life-threatening and time-critical, dentists' charges for major courses of treatment are often discussed in advance of the treatment when there is no pain or trauma. As with any number of other consumer decisions, the patient may opt to defer the treatment to a later time or spend the money elsewhere.

A second difference in the nature of care is that, while medical care is rarely cosmetic, dental care often is. A crown, for example, may be necessary to save a tooth, but it also may be used to improve the patient's appearance. Many people place orthodontics into the same category, although evidence exists that failure to obtain needed orthodontic care may result in problems ranging from major gum disease to temporomandibular joint (TMJ) disorders in later life.

A third major difference between the nature of medical and dental care is that dentistry often offers alternative procedures for treating disease and restoring teeth, many of which are equally effective. For example, a molar cavity might be treated by a composite or resin filling, which may cost twice as much as a simple amalgam filling. In these instances, the choice of the appropriate procedure is influenced by a number of factors, including the cost of the alternatives, the condition of the affected tooth and the teeth surrounding it, and the likelihood that a particular approach will be successful.

There are other significant differences in medical care and dentistry that will have an effect on plan design. These include the cost of the typical treatment and the emphasis on prevention.

Dental expenses generally are lower, more predictable, and budgetable. The average dental claim check is only about $155. Medical claims, on average, are much higher.

The last significant difference is the emphasis on prevention. The advantages of preventive dentistry are clearly documented. While certain medical diseases and injuries are self-healing, dental disease, once started, almost always gets progressively worse. Therefore, preventive care may be more productive in dentistry than in medicine. Certainly, the value of preventive dentistry relative to its cost is acknowledged.

PROVIDERS OF DENTAL BENEFITS

Providers of dental benefits generally can be separated into three categories: insurance companies, Blue Cross and Blue Shield organizations, and others, including state dental association plans (e.g., Delta plans), self-insured, self-administered plans, and group practice or HMO-type plans. The Delta plans currently have the largest single market share, insuring over 31 percent of the covered population. An insurance company, MetLife, insures approximately 12 percent of the market, a share slightly larger than the Blue Cross/Blue Shield plans. All others have less than 10 percent of the market.

The types of dental benefit plans resemble today's medical plans. There are three basic design structures: the fee-for-service indemnity or reimbursement approach, the preferred provider (PPO) approach, and the dental health maintenance organization. As with medical plan design, the PPO is the prevailing dental benefit approach, and fee-for-service and reimbursement arrangements are gradually disappearing.

Most self-insured, self-administered plan benefits are provided on either an indemnity or preferred provider basis. Preferred provider benefits are payable directly to the treating dentist, generally according to a contract, which fixes the reimbursement level between the dentist and the plan. In most instances, this payment actually may be lower than what would be charged to a direct-pay or indemnity patient.

Under the indemnity approach, expenses incurred by eligible individuals are submitted to the administrator, typically an insurer, for payment. If the expense is covered, the appropriate payment is calculated according to the provisions of the plan. The indemnity plan payment is generally made directly to the covered employee, unless assigned by the employee to the treating dentist.

The dental benefits of the dental service corporations, most insurance companies, and the Blue Cross/Blue Shield plans are generally provided on a preferred provider basis. The major differences between indemnity and preferred provider benefits relate to the roles of the provider and the covered individual. Under either approach, the plan sponsor normally has substantial latitude in determining who and what is to be covered and at what level.

Under the group practice or HMO-type arrangement, a prescribed range of dental services is provided to eligible participants, often in return for a prepaid, fixed, and uniform payment. Services are provided by dentists practicing in group practice clinics or by those in individual practice but affiliated for purposes of providing plan benefits to eligible participants. Some individuals eligible under these arrangements are covered through collectively bargained self-insurance benefit trusts. In these instances, trust fund payments are used either to reimburse dentists operating in group practice clinics or to pay the prescribed fixed per capita fee. Group practice HMO-type arrangements, which often have cost, quality assurance, and administrative advantages but more limited provider selection, generally offer little latitude in plan design. As a result, the balance of this chapter, since it is largely devoted to the issue of plan design, may have limited application to these types of arrangements.

COVERED DENTAL EXPENSES

Virtually all dental problems fall into 10 professional treatment categories:

1. *Diagnostic.* Examination to determine the existence of oral disease or to evaluate the condition of the mouth. Included in this category would be such procedures as X-rays and routine oral examinations.
2. *Preventive.* Procedures to preserve and maintain dental health. Included in this category are topical fluoride applications, cleaning, space maintainers, and the like.
3. *Restorative.* Procedures for the repair and reconstruction of natural teeth, including the removal of dental decay and installation of fillings.
4. *Endodontics.* Treatment of dental pulp disease and therapy within existing teeth. Root canal therapy is an example of this type of procedure.
5. *Periodontics.* Treatment of the gums and other supporting structures of the teeth, primarily for maintenance or improvement of the gums. Periodontal curettage and root planing are examples of periodontic procedures.

6. *Oral surgery.* Tooth extraction and other surgery of the mouth and jaw.
7. *Prosthodontics.* Construction, replacement, and repair of missing teeth. Examples include onlays, crowns, and bridges, which are fixed prostheses, and dentures and partials, which are removable prostheses.
8. *Orthodontics.* Correction of malocclusion and abnormal tooth position through repositioning of natural teeth.
9. *Pedodontics.* Treatment for children who do not have all their permanent teeth.
10. *Implantology.* Use of implants and related services (e.g., over-dentures, fixed prostheses attached to implants, etc.), to replace one or all missing teeth on an arch.

In addition to the recognition of treatment or services in most of these 10 areas, the typical dental plan also includes provision for palliative treatment (i.e., procedures to minimize pain, including anesthesia), emergency care, and consultation.

These 10 types of procedures are usually categorized into three, four, and sometime five general groupings for purposes of plan design. The first classification often includes both preventive and diagnostic expenses. The second general grouping includes all minor restorative procedures. The third broad grouping, often combined with the second, includes major restorative work (e.g., prosthodontics), endodontic and periodontic services, oral surgery, and implantology. A fourth separate classification covers orthodontic expenses. Whether to cover implantology and to what extent is often a separate, cost-driven, design decision. If covered, implantology services typically fall into the major restorative grouping, although these services are sometimes covered under a separate fifth classification.

Pedodontic care generally falls into the first two groupings. Later in this chapter, plan design is examined in greater detail, with specific differences evaluated in traditional plan design applicable to each of these general groupings.

TYPES OF PLANS

Dental plans covering the vast majority of all employees can be divided broadly into two types: scheduled and nonscheduled. Other approaches discussed below are essentially variations of these two basic plan types. The number of nonscheduled plans far exceeds the number of scheduled and hybrid ones.

Scheduled Plans

Scheduled plans are categorized by a listing of fixed allowances by procedure. For example, the plan might pay $50 for a cleaning and $400 for root canal therapy. In addition, the scheduled plan may include deductibles and coinsurance (i.e., percentage cost-sharing provisions). Where deductibles are included in scheduled plans, amounts are usually small or, in some cases, required on a lifetime basis only.

Coinsurance provisions are extremely rare in scheduled plans, since the benefits of coinsurance can be achieved through the construction of the schedule (i.e., the level of reimbursement for each procedure in the schedule can be set for specific reimbursement objectives). For example, if it is preferable to reimburse a higher percentage of the cost of preventive procedures than of other procedures, the schedule can be constructed to accomplish this goal.

There are three major advantages to scheduled plans:

1. Cost control. Benefit levels are fixed and therefore less susceptible to inflationary increases.
2. Uniform payments. In certain instances, it may be important to provide the same benefit regardless of regional cost differences. Collectively bargained plans may occasionally take this approach to ensure the "equal treatment" of all members.
3. Ease of understanding. It is clear to both the plan participant and the dentist how much is to be paid for each procedure.

In addition, scheduled plans are sometimes favored for employee-relations reasons. As the schedule is updated, improvements can be communicated to employees. If the updating occurs on a regular basis, this will be a periodic reminder to employees of the plan and its merits.

There also are disadvantages to scheduled plans. First, benefit levels, as well as internal relationships, must be examined periodically and changed when necessary to maintain reimbursement objectives. Second, where participants are dispersed geographically, plan reimbursement levels will vary according to the cost of dental care in a particular area unless multiple schedules are utilized. Third, if scheduled benefits are established at levels that are near the maximum of the reasonable and customary range, dentists who normally charge at below prevailing levels may be influenced to adjust their charges.

Services under the typical dental HMO are also provided on a scheduled basis—in a fashion. Since the contract between the participating dentist and the HMO generally specifies the basis on which the provider will be paid by the HMO and also fixes the amount that can be charged to the participant, the schedule furnished to participants typically identifies the amount the participant is required to pay rather than the amount the plan pays.

Nonscheduled Plans

Nonscheduled plans are by far the most common designs today. Sometimes referred to as comprehensive plans, nonscheduled plans are written to cover some percentage of the "reasonable and customary" charges, or the charges most commonly made by dentists in the community. For any single procedure, the usual and customary charge typically is set at between the 75th and 90th percentiles, depending on the administrator. (The trend is toward the lower number.) This means that the usual and customary charge level will cover the full cost of the procedure for 75 to 90 percent of the claims submitted in that geographic area.

Nonscheduled plans generally include a deductible, typically a calendar-year deductible of $50 or $75, and they reimburse at different levels for different classes of procedures. Preventive and diagnostic expenses are typically covered in full or at very high reimbursement levels. Reimbursement levels for other procedures are usually then scaled down from the preventive and diagnostic level, based on the design objectives of the employer.

There are two major advantages to nonscheduled plans:

1. Uniform reimbursement level. While the dollar payment may vary by area and dentist, the percent of the total cost reimbursed by the plan is uniform.
2. Adjusts automatically for change. The nonscheduled plan adjusts automatically, not only for inflation, but also for variations in the relative value of specific procedures.

This approach also has disadvantages. First, because benefit levels adjust automatically for increases in the cost of care, in periods of rapidly escalating prices cost control can be a problem. Second, once a plan is installed on this basis, the opportunities for modest benefit improvements, made primarily for employee-relations purposes, are limited, at least relative to the scheduled approach. Third, except for claims for which predetermination of benefits is appropriate, it rarely is clear in advance what the specific payment for a particular service will be, either to the patient or the dentist.

Preferred provider benefits are usually provided on an unscheduled basis. Reimbursement for services provided by network dentists, however, is based on an agreed-upon discounted charge level, rather than the reasonable and customary charge. Deductible, coinsurance, percentage copayment, and other benefit provisions are generally applied to the discounted charge level, not the reasonable and customary amount.

Other approaches are, for the most part, merely variations of the two basic plans. Included in this list are combination plans, incentive plans, and dental combined with major medical plans.

Combination Plans

This is simply a plan in which certain procedures are reimbursed on a scheduled basis, while others are reimbursed on a nonscheduled basis. In other words, it is a hybrid. While many variations exist, a common design in combination plans is to provide preventive and diagnostic coverage on a nonscheduled basis (i.e., a percentage of usual and customary, normally without a deductible). Procedures other than preventive and diagnostic are provided on a scheduled basis.

The principal advantage of a combination plan is that it provides a balance between (1) the need to emphasize preventive care and (2) cost control. Procedures that traditionally are the most expensive are covered on a scheduled basis, and, except where benefit levels are established by a collective bargaining agreement, the timing of schedule improvements is at the employer's discretion. Preventive and diagnostic expenses, however, adjust automatically, so the incentive for preventive care does not lose its effectiveness as dental care costs increase.

The combination approach shares many of the same disadvantages as the scheduled and unscheduled plans, at least for certain types of expenses. Benefit levels—for other than preventive and diagnostic expenses—must be evaluated periodically. Scheduled payments do not reimburse at uniform levels for geographically dispersed participants. And dentists may be influenced by the schedule allowances to adjust their charges. Also, actual plan payments for preventive and diagnostic expenses are rarely identified in advance. Finally, it can be said that the combination approach is more complex than either the scheduled or unscheduled alternatives.

Incentive Plans

This type, a second variation, promotes sound dental hygiene through increasing reimbursement levels. Incentive coinsurance provisions generally apply only to preventive and maintenance (i.e., minor restorative) procedures, with other procedures covered on either a scheduled or a nonscheduled basis. Incentive plans are designed to encourage individuals to visit the dentist regularly, without the plan sponsor having to absorb the cost of any accumulated neglect. Such plans generally reimburse at one level during the first year, with coinsurance levels typically increasing from year to year only for those who obtained needed treatment in prior years. For example, the initial coinsurance level (i.e., the benefit paid by the plan) for preventive and maintenance expenses might be 60 percent, increasing to 70 percent, 80 percent, and, finally, 90 percent on an annual basis as long as the individual visits the dentist regularly. If, in any one year, there is a failure to obtain the required level of care, the coinsurance percentage reverts back to its original level.

The incentive portion of an incentive plan may or may not be characterized by deductibles. When deductibles are included in these plans, it is not unusual for them to apply on a lifetime basis.

On the one hand, the incentive concept, has two major advantages. In theory, the design of the plan encourages regular dental care and reduces the incidence of more serious dental problems in the future. Also, these plans generally have lower first-year costs than most nonscheduled plans.

On the other hand, there are major disadvantages. First, an incentive plan can be complicated to explain and even more complicated to administer. Second, little evidence exists to suggest that the incentive approach is effective in promoting sound dental hygiene. Finally, this particular plan is vulnerable to misunderstanding. For example, what happens if the participant's dentist postpones the required treatment until the beginning of the next plan year?

There are other incentive approaches that have been introduced in recent years. One approach allows participants to carry over part or all of any unused annual benefit maximums into future periods. The goal is to encourage participants to seek less costly care.

Plans Providing Both Medical and Dental Coverage

The last of the variations is the plan that provides both medical and dental coverage. During the infancy of dental benefits, such plans were quite popular.

These plans are generally characterized by a common deductible amount that applies to the sum of both medical and dental expenses. Coinsurance levels may be identical, and sometimes the maximum applies to the combination of medical and dental expenses. However, recent design of these plans has made a distinction between dental and medical expenses so that each may have its own coinsurance provisions and maximums.

The advantages of this approach are the same as for the nonscheduled plan (i.e., uniform reimbursement levels, automatic adjustment to change, and relative ease of understanding). But this approach fails to recognize the difference between medicine and dentistry unless special provisions are made for dental benefits. It must be written with a medical carrier, whether or not this carrier is competent to handle both medical and dental protection; it makes it extremely difficult to separate and evaluate dental experience; and it shares the same disadvantages as the nonscheduled approach.

ORTHODONTIC EXPENSES

With possibly a few exceptions, orthodontic benefits are never written without other dental coverage. Nonetheless, orthodontic benefits present a number of design peculiarities that suggest this subject should be treated separately.

Orthodontic services, unlike nonorthodontic procedures, are generally rendered only once in an individual's lifetime; orthodontic problems, treated properly, are unlikely to recur. Orthodontic maximums, therefore, are typically expressed on a lifetime basis. Deductibles that are applicable only to orthodontic services are also often expressed on a lifetime basis. However, it is quite common for orthodontic benefits to be provided without deductibles, since a major purpose of the deductible—to eliminate small, nuisance-type claims—is of little consequence.

Because adult orthodontic treatment is generally cosmetic and also because the best time for orthodontic work is during adolescence, many plans limit orthodontic coverage to persons under age 19. However, an increasing number of plans are including adult orthodontics as well, and many participants are taking advantage of this feature.

The coinsurance level for orthodontic expenses is typically 50 percent, but it varies depending on the reimbursement levels under other parts of the plan. It is common for the orthodontic reimbursement level to be the same as that for major restorative procedures.

Reflecting the nature of orthodontic work, and unlike virtually any other benefit, orthodontic benefits are often paid in installments instead of at the conclusion of the course of treatment. Because the program of treatment frequently extends over several years, it would be unreasonable to reimburse for the entire course of treatment at the end of the extended time. It would be equally unreasonable to pay for the entire course of treatment at its beginning.

IMPLANTOLOGY AND ITS SERVICES

Today's typical dental plan often excludes implantology, because it is expensive to cover some of these services. In some instances, implantology services are an effective and cost-advantageous technique for addressing certain dental problems. In others, they are an expensive and often unnecessary option. For these reasons, whether to cover these services and to what extent is a cost-driven plan design decision.

Implants, like orthodontic services, are generally rendered only once in an individual's lifetime. As a result, implant benefits design, at least if the plan will be covering the more expensive services, often includes the following features:

1. The maximum benefit is expressed on a lifetime basis, typically at the same level that applies to orthodontic services.
2. Deductibles, where they apply, are also on a lifetime basis.
3. Coinsurance levels are the same as that for orthodontic services.

Because implants are not usually appropriate until an individual has reached adulthood, benefits are usually not extended to children.

FACTORS AFFECTING THE COST OF THE DENTAL PLAN

A number of factors, including design of the plan, characteristics of the covered group, the employer's approach to plan implementation, and plan administration, affect the cost of the dental plan.

Plan Design

Many issues must be addressed before a particular design that is sound and reflects the needs of the plan sponsor can be established. Included in this list are the type of plan, deductibles, coinsurance, plan maximums, treatment of preexisting conditions, whether covered services should be limited, and orthodontic coverage.

An employer's choice between scheduled and nonscheduled benefits requires a look at the employer's objectives. The advantages and disadvantages of scheduled versus nonscheduled plans, combination plans, and others have been described earlier in this chapter.

Deductibles may or may not be included as an integral part of the design of the plan. Deductibles are usually written on a lifetime or calendar-year basis, with the calendar-year approach by far the more common.

Numerous dental procedures involve very little expense. Therefore, the deductible eliminates frequent payments for small claims that can be readily budgeted. For example, a $50 deductible can eliminate as much as 10 percent of the number of claims. A deductible can effectively control the cost of claim administration.

However, evidence exists that early detection and treatment of dental problems will produce a lower level of claims over the long term. Many insurers feel the best way to promote early detection is to pay virtually all the cost of preventive and diagnostic services. Therefore, these services are often not subject to a deductible.

A few insurance companies are advocates of a lifetime deductible, designed to lessen the impact of accumulated dental neglect. This is particularly effective when the employer is confronted with a choice of (1) not covering preexisting conditions at all, (2) covering these conditions but being forced otherwise to cut back on the design of the plan, or (3) offering a lifetime deductible, the theory being, "If you'll spend X dollars to get your mouth into shape once and for all, we'll take care of a large part of your future dental needs."

Opponents of the lifetime deductible concept claim the following disadvantages:

- A lifetime deductible promotes early overutilization by those anxious to take advantage of the benefits of the plan.
- Once satisfied, lifetime deductibles are of no further value for the presently covered group.
- The lifetime deductible introduces employee turnover as an important cost consideration of the plan.
- If established at a level that will have a significant impact on claim costs and premium rates, a lifetime deductible may result in adverse employee reaction to the plan.

Most dental plans are being designed, either through construction of the schedule or the use of coinsurance, so that the patient pays a portion of the costs for all but preventive and diagnostic services. The intent is to reduce spending on optional dental care and to provide cost-effective dental practice. In addition, many believe that employees that participate financially in the plan make better use of it. Preventive and diagnostic expenses are generally reimbursed at 80 to 100 percent of the usual and customary charges. Full reimbursement is quite common.

The reimbursement level for restorative and replacement procedures is generally lower than that for preventive and diagnostic procedures.

Restorations, and in some cases replacements, may be reimbursed at 70 to 85 percent. In other cases, the reimbursement level for replacements is lower than for restorative treatment.

Orthodontics, implantology (where covered), and occasionally major replacements have the lowest reimbursement levels of all. In most instances, the plans reimburse no more than 50 to 60 percent of the usual and customary charges for these procedures.

Most dental plans include a plan maximum, written on a calendar-year basis, which is applicable to nonorthodontic expenses. Orthodontic and implantology expenses are generally subject to separate lifetime maximums. Also, in some instances, a separate lifetime maximum may apply to nonorthodontic expenses.

Unless established at a fairly low level, a lifetime maximum will have little or no impact on claim liability and serves only to further complicate design of the plan. Calendar-year maximums, though, encourage participants to seek less costly care and may help to spread out the impact of accumulated dental neglect over the early years of the plan. The typical calendar-year maximum is somewhere between $1,000 and $1,500. To put things in perspective, in 2003, only about 33 percent of people visiting a dentist spent from $300 to $999 annually, including insurance company payments, and just 23 percent spent $1,000 or more, including insurance company payments. Most claims are small (34 percent spent $100 or less), and therefore the maximum's impact on plan costs is minor.

Another major consideration is the treatment of preexisting conditions. The major concern is the expense associated with the replacement of teeth extracted prior to the date of coverage. Preexisting conditions are treated in a number of ways:

- They may be excluded.
- They may be treated as any other condition.
- They may be covered on a limited basis (perhaps one-half of the normal reimbursement level) or subject to a lifetime maximum.

If treated as any other condition, the cost of the plan in the early years (nonorthodontic only) will be increased by about 5 to 7 percent.

Another plan design consideration is the range of procedures to be covered. In addition to orthodontics and implantology, other procedures occasionally excluded are surgical periodontics and temporomandibular joint (TMJ) dysfunction therapy. It is difficult to diagnose TMJ disorders, and many consider them a medical and not a dental condition. Claims are large, and the potential for abuse is significant.

Although rare, some plans cover only preventive and maintenance expenses. These plans are becoming more common in flexible benefit plans, where employees often may pick either a preventive plan or one that is more comprehensive.

Orthodontic expenses, as noted, may be excluded. However, where these are covered, the plan design may include a separate deductible to discourage "shoppers." The cost of orthodontic diagnosis and models is about $350 to $400, whether or not treatment is undertaken. The inclusion of a separate orthodontic deductible eliminates reimbursement for a portion of these expenses. Also, orthodontic plan design typically includes both heavy coinsurance and limited maximums to guarantee patient involvement.

An indication of the sensitivity of dental plan costs to some of the plan-design features discussed can be seen in the following illustration. Assume a nonscheduled base model plan with a $50 calendar-year deductible applicable to all expenses other than orthodontics. The reimbursement, or employer coinsurance, levels are as follows:

- Diagnostic and preventive services (Type I): 100 percent
- Basic services, including anesthesia and basic restoration (TypeII): 75 percent
- Major restoration, including oral surgery, endodontics, periodontics, and prosthodontics (Type III): 50 percent
- Orthodontics (Type IV): 50 percent

There also is an annual benefit maximum of $1,500 for Type I, II, and III services and a lifetime maximum of $1,500 for orthodontics. Based on this base model plan, Table 11-1 shows the approximate premium sensitivity to changes in plan design. If two or more of the design changes shown in this table are considered together, an approximation of the resulting value may be obtained by multiplying the relative values of the respective changes.

The change in deductibles has a significant impact on cost—as much as a 12 percent reduction in cost to increase the deductible from $50 to $100. The change in benefit maximums has some impact, but it is minor. Coinsurance has a definite effect, especially changes in restoration, replacement, and orthodontic portions of the plan, all of which represent about 80 to 85 percent of the typical claim costs. Finally, the inclusion of orthodontics in the base plan is another item of fairly high cost.

TABLE 11-1

Model Dental Plan

	Relative Value (%)
Base model plan	100
Design changes	
Deductible	
Remove $50 deductible	112
Lower to $25	106
Raise to $100	88
Benefit maximum (annual)	
Lower from $1,500 to $1,000	97
Raise to $2,000	103
Coinsurance	
Liberalize percent to 100—80—60—60*	111
Tighten percent to 80—70—50—50*	88
Orthodontics	
Exclude	95

*For Types I, II, III, and IV services, respectively.

Characteristics of the Covered Group

A second factor affecting the cost of the dental plan is the characteristics of the covered group. Important considerations include, but are not limited to, the following:

- Age
- Gender
- Location
- Income level of the participants
- Occupation

The increased incidence of high-cost dental procedures at older ages generally makes coverage of older groups more expensive. Average charges usually increase from about age 35 to 40. As one ages, the need for more expensive restorative services increases for those who need dental care.

Gender is another consideration. Women tend to have higher utilization rates than men. For a given age, costs among females are 5 percent higher than the costs among males. One study showed that women average 1.9 visits to dentists per year, compared with 1.7 for men. These differences may be attributable to a heightened sensitivity to personal appearance by women rather than to a greater need.

Charge levels, practice patterns, and the availability of dentists vary considerably by locale. Charge levels within the United States range anywhere from 75 to 135 percent of the national average, except for Alaska, California, and certain metropolitan areas. Differences exist in the frequency of use for certain procedures as well. There is evidence, for example, that more expensive procedures are performed relatively more often in Los Angeles than, say, in Philadelphia.

Another consideration is income. One study shows that dental care expenditures per participant were 5 to 30 percent higher for members of families with higher incomes. Generally, the higher the income, the greater the differenceis.

Essentially four reasons may account for income being a key factor. First, the higher the income level, the greater the likelihood the individual already has an established program of dental hygiene. Second, in many areas, there is greater accessibility to dental care in high-income neighborhoods. Third, a greater tendency exists on the part of higher-income individuals to elect higher-cost procedures. Last, high-income people tend to use more expensive dentists.

Another important consideration is the occupation of the covered group. While difficult to explain, evidence suggests considerable variation between plans covering blue-collar workers and plans covering salaried or mixed groups. One possible explanation is differences in awareness and income levels. One insurer estimates that blue-collar employees are 15 to 25 percent less expensive to insure than white-collar employees.

Sponsor's Approach to Implementation

The last of the factors affecting plan costs is the sponsor's approach to implementation. Dental work, unlike medical care, lends itself to "sandbagging" (i.e., deferral of needed treatment until after the plan's effective date). Everything else being equal, plans announced well in advance of the effective date tend to have poorer first-year experience than plans announced only shortly before the effective date. Advance knowledge of the deferred effective date can easily increase first-year costs from 10 to 20 percent or even more.

Employee contributions are another consideration. Dental plans, if offered on a contributory basis, may be prone to adverse selection. While there is evidence that the adverse selection is not as great as was once anticipated, many insurers continue to discourage contributory plans. Most insurance companies will underwrite dental benefits on a contributory basis, but some require certain adverse selection safeguards. Typical safeguards include the following:

- Combining dental plan participation and contributions with medical plan participation.
- Limiting enrollment to a single offering, thus preventing subsequent sign-ups or dropouts.
- Requiring dental examinations before joining the plan and limiting or excluding treatment for conditions identified in the examination. The Health Insurance Portability and Accountability Act (HIPAA) limitations do not apply as long as the dental benefits are "limited in scope" and are available under a separate policy or rider.
- Requiring participants to remain in the plan for a specified minimum time period before being eligible to drop coverage.

Plan Administration

The last item to be addressed is claims administration. The nature of dentistry and dental plan design suggests that claims administration is very important. While several years may lapse before an insured has occasion to file a medical claim, rarely does a year pass during which a family will not visit the dentist at least once. Therefore, claims administration capability is an extremely important consideration in selecting a plan carrier—and might very well be the most important consideration.

One key element of claims administration is "predetermination of benefits." This common plan feature requires the dentist to prepare a treatment plan that shows the work and cost before any services begin. This treatment plan is generally required only for nonemergency services and only if the cost is expected to exceed some specified level, such as $300. The carrier processes this information to determine exactly how much the dental plan will pay. Also, selected claims are referred to the carrier's dental consultants to assess the appropriateness of the recommended treatment. If there are any questions, the dental consultant discusses the treatment plan with the dentist prior to performing the services.

Predetermination is very important both in promoting better quality care and in reducing costs. These benefits are accomplished by spotting unnecessary expenses, treatments that cannot be expected to last, instances of coverage duplication, and charges higher than usual and customary before extensive and expensive work begins. Predetermination of benefits can be effective in reducing claim costs by as much as 5 percent. Predetermination also advises the covered individual of the exact amount of reimbursement under the plan prior to commencement of treatment.

Also important are alternate treatment provisions. These provisions enable the plan administrator either to approve the least costly, equally effective treatment option or to cover more expensive procedures only at the level of the less expensive alternative. Alternate treatment provisions, adopted by most plan sponsors, can reduce plan costs up to 5 percent.

TECHNOLOGY AND DENTAL PLAN DESIGN

Dental technology is constantly changing. The goal is to provide treatments and techniques that are more efficient, more effective, and/or more comfortable. Many of these technologies may be unproven, but today's investigational technologies are often mainstream practices tomorrow.

In dental plan design, it is important to differentiate between new techniques and new procedures. A new technique is a different way to provide an already-covered service. Laser technology is an example. The use of lasers may cut down on the time and discomfort associated with certain procedures that have historically involved the use of surgical instruments, sutures, etc. There are many other examples of technologies that represent new techniques. New techniques, once officially recognized by the American Dental Association, are generally covered as any other service under the plan, since they are considered another way to deliver already-covered services.

On the other hand, new procedures are not covered so readily. Generally, before such a service becomes covered, it must, first, be recognized by the American Dental Association as an accepted procedure and, second, must have a proven track record of success. There are many factors that go into this determination, including the procedure's effectiveness relative to other options, its acceptance by respected practitioners, how broad its usage, and even its cost. The procedure is then approved for coverage or tabled for further study. If approved, a separate decision establishes whether the procedure and similar ones will be covered routinely or instead as a design option, that is, at the plan sponsor's discretion.

Whether new techniques or procedures, plan administrators closely monitor emerging technology to ensure that plan design appropriately recognizes changes in effective practice.

CHAPTER 12

Long-Term Care Insurance

Jan McFarland

No discussion of employee benefits can be considered complete without a mention of long-term care (LTC) insurance. The benefit's popularity has grown significantly over the past several years, with an 862 percent increase in employer groups installing an LTC insurance plan between 1995 and 2009.[1] The benefit is primarily offered on a voluntary basis, giving employers a low-cost way to provide their employees with access to insurance protection that is generally not available with their other benefits.

DEFINITION OF LONG-TERM CARE

Long-Term Care (LTC) is personal care or supervision needed by persons of all ages for an extended period of time. Although many LTC situations result from the effects of aging, many others are caused by accident or illness. Some conditions that may require LTC are listed in Table 12-1.

WHY LTC IS AN IMPORTANT ISSUE

LTC is an important issue because the need for care is growing and the funding resources for care are limited. Although we may not like to think about a time in our lives when we may need personal assistance in performing some of the basic activities of daily living, like eating or

1. LIMRA Reports, U.S. Group Long-Term Care Insurance Sales and In-Force, 1995–2009.

TABLE 12-1

Conditions That May Require Long-Term Care (LTC)

▪ Head injury	▪ Rheumatoid arthritis
▪ Stroke	▪ Parkinson's disease
▪ Cancer	▪ Alzheimer's disease
▪ Multiple sclerosis	▪ Paralysis
▪ Heart disease	▪ Amyotrophic lateral sclerosis (Lou Gehrig's disease)

dressing, the need for LTC can happen to anyone at any time. In fact, of the 12.1 million Americans currently needing LTC, 41.3 percent are under age 65.[2]

Impact of National Demographics

Of course, aging is an important factor in determining the potential need for LTC. While recent medical advances have contributed to our overall longevity, they have not necessarily improved the quality of life, particularly in terms of the ability to function independently. It is estimated that at least 70 percent of people over the age of 65 will require LTC services at some point in their lives.[3] Looking ahead, we can expect the number of care recipients to skyrocket, as 78.2 million baby boomers begin turning 65 in 2011.

Current and Projected Costs

There is also the matter of expense. The national average for nursing home stays is almost $75,000 annually, with home care costs averaging nearly $40,000 a year.[4] According to one survey, 64 percent of Americans age 45 and older think that the recent economic downturn has hurt their ability to

2. Georgetown University Long-Term Care Financing Project, "Long-Term Care Financing Policy Options for the Future," June 2007.
3. U.S. Department of Health and Human Services, National Clearinghouse for Long-Term Care Information, September 2008, www.longtermcare.gov.
4. John Hancock Cost of Care Survey, conducted by CareScout, 2008.

TABLE 12-2

Geographic Variations in Cost of Care

	Nursing Home Semi-Private (Daily)	Home Health Care (Hourly)
Atlanta, GA	$159	$17.44
Boston, MA	$289	$22
Chicago, IL	$148	$19.65
Denver, CO	$194	$19.69
Houston, TX	$128	$17.28
Los Angeles, CA	$151	$21
Minneapolis, MN	$147	$26.50
Nashville, TN	$161	$17.42
New York, NY	$373	$17.23
Phoenix, AZ	$161	$20.53
Seattle, WA	$221	$24.28
Tampa, FL	$193	$18.72

Source: Based on the John Hancock Cost of Care Survey, conducted by CareScout, 2008.

pay for LTC services should they be unable to take care of themselves for an extended period of time.[5]

The cost of care can vary widely, as illustrated in Table 12-2.

Like everything else, LTC expenses are expected to rise. By some estimates, the projected cost for a three- to five-year care event in 30 years will be $750,000 to 1,250,000 (based on the John Hancock 2008 Cost of Care Survey and projected at the average rate of inflation of 4.1 percent over the 50-year period ending December 31, 2009).

Lack of Traditional Care Resources

The issues surrounding LTC have changed, along with the social fabric of the country. At one time, it was common for LTC services to be provided

5. Life and Health Insurance Foundation for Education, Arlington, VA, 2008.

by family members, with women taking on most of the responsibility for caregiving. This might have been a reasonable option years ago, when grown children tended to settle near their parents and women stayed at home. In today's society, children may live across the country or on the other side of the world. And, many more women are active in the workforce and may not be able to fulfill the traditional caregiver role.

Even if that were not the case, caregiving can place a burden on family members that most people would prefer to avoid. A survey of caregivers revealed that 83 percent were concerned with losing their physical or mental health as a result of their caregiving responsibilities.[6]

Misconceptions about Who Pays for Care

In the absence of unpaid, informal care, individuals look to other resources for funding. Unfortunately, misconceptions abound, with many people thinking they can rely on existing employee benefits or government programs. Let us review some of the most common held misconceptions.

LTC Is Covered by Medical or Disability Benefits

Health insurance is designed to provide coverage for illnesses that are acute, or short term, in nature. It will pay for hospital stays or doctor's care for conditions where recovery is expected, for example, kidney stones or a broken leg. Most health insurance will not pay for a home health aide to help manage a chronic illness at home or for the nursing home care that may be needed after the diagnosis of Alzheimer's disease.

Likewise, long-term disability (LTD) insurance is designed to replace income, not cover LTC costs. In addition, LTD usually ceases at age 65—though the need for LTC does not.

Medicare Pays for LTC

Medicare is a national health insurance program designed to assist people age 65 and older with their medical expenses. It is intended to pay for acute illnesses, where recovery is expected. Medicare does pay some LTC expenses, but certain requirements must be met. Benefits may be paid for the first 100 days in a nursing home, if confinement takes place within 30

6. National Association of Professional Geriatric Care Managers (NAPGMCM), Geriatric Care Manager/Aging Study, January 2008.

days following a hospitalization of at least three days and if skilled care is being received. Unfortunately, most conditions requiring LTC do not call for hospitalization or skilled care, for example, Alzheimer's disease or rheumatoid arthritis, so Medicare may only be of limited usefulness to a minority of LTC recipients.

Medicaid Pays for LTC

The other government program that some individuals view as a personal safety net is Medicaid. Medicaid was created to help low-income families with their medical expenses, but has unintentionally become one of the leading ways to fund the cost of LTC.

Recent legislation, specifically the passage of the Deficit Reduction Act in 2005, has made it more difficult to transfer assets in order to qualify for benefits, forcing individuals to spend down to state-prescribed levels before being considered Medicaid-eligible. Regrettably, this strategy can put other family members at serious financial risk. Moreover, it can limit choices regarding care, since Medicaid primarily pays for nursing home, rather than home care.

LTC INSURANCE AS AN EMPLOYEE BENEFIT

There are a number of reasons why an employer might consider the addition of LTC insurance to its portfolio of benefits. The benefit has advantages for both employers and employees.

Advantages for Employers

The offer of LTC insurance allows employers to enhance their existing benefits package, by giving employees access to insurance protection that their other benefits do not provide. It also helps prevent the productivity that is lost when employees find themselves in the role of caregiver for a loved one. Caregiving imposes a tremendous cost on employers, with disruptions and absenteeism costing U.S. employers up to $33.6 billion per year.[7] It is also worth nothing that if an employer pays all or a portion of the tax-qualified LTC insurance premiums on behalf of an employee, the *total* amount paid is deductible as a business expense [IRC 162 (a)].

7. The Caregiving Project for Older Americans, "Caregiving In America," 2007.

Advantages for Employees

For employees, LTC insurance can help them protect their savings and assets from the high cost of care, should they ever face an LTC event. It can also provide the support they need as caregivers, since many policies extend available provider discounts and other support services to family members.

EMPLOYER DECISIONS

Employers who are considering the introduction of a plan will have to make a number of decisions with regard to the structure and funding of the coverage.

Policy Structure—True Group versus Multilife

There are two basic policy structures: true group insurance and multilife (individual insurance). With a true group plan, the employer is the policyholder and employees are issued certificates of insurance. The employer can choose to include retirees, spouses, adult children, parents/in-laws, and siblings as part of the eligible group. With a multilife approach, individual insureds are the policyholders and are issued individual policies. In most cases, true group is a better match for larger employers, particularly those with widely dispersed populations. True group plans offer the following advantages:

- Availability of guaranteed issue for eligible, actively-at work employees
- No minimum participation requirements
- Fully portable coverage
- Low group rates, in many cases, with a rate guarantee period
- Transfer of reserve capabilities
- Turnkey approach to enrollment and administration
- Employer-dedicated website to support enrollment

A multilife approach may be attractive to smaller employers or those wishing to give their employees greater flexibility in customizing their coverage. Some other advantages of a multilife approach are

- Simplified underwriting for eligible, actively at work employees
- Availability of preferred health and spousal/family member discounts
- Broker-assisted enrollments, with one-on-one consultations
- Availability of list and split billing

LTC PLAN DESIGN

There are two claims-paying approaches offered by the LTC carriers.

Reimbursement versus Disability

Under a reimbursement approach, the insured is reimbursed for the actual costs of the covered services received on any given day up to the maximum daily dollar limit stated in the policy. For charges that are less than the daily maximum, the difference is retained by the policy in a "pool of money" and can be accessed at a later date. This approach differs from the indemnity/disability model, which provides a daily benefit regardless of the actual charges incurred by the insured. As a general rule, the reimbursement model is less costly than the disability model because claims payments are tied to the services received, rather than being automatically issued once benefit triggers have been met.

Coverage Features

Most LTC insurance pays benefits for care received in the following settings:

- Nursing homes
- Assisted living facilities
- Adult day care centers
- The claimant's home

In addition to this basic coverage, there are core benefits that are included in most policies. These may include benefits for informal care by family members, benefits designed to support care in the home, respite care benefits, or international benefits. There are also optional benefits, which add to flexibility, but also increase premiums, such as inflation provisions, return of premium at death, nonforfeiture benefits, or provisions that allow spouses or family members to share available benefits. Some carriers may extend care coordination services to noninsured family members, thereby providing important resources for employee-caregivers. These are described in detail in the carrier's response to the employer's request for proposal. When selecting a LTC insurance plan, employers should try and strike a balance between meeting their populations' needs and keeping coverage affordable, particularly if the coverage is to be offered on a voluntary basis. The primary determinants of the plan's cost are summarized below.

Daily Benefit

The daily benefit is the most that may be paid for covered services received on any one day. Since the costs for LTC services vary geographically as well as by type of service provider, employers may wish to offer participants three to six daily benefit options to choose from at the time of enrollment to ensure that the daily benefit meet the needs of potential applicants. Weekly and monthly benefits may also be available, for additional premium.

Lifetime Maximum Benefit

The lifetime maximum benefit is the most the LTC insurance policy will pay over the lifetime of the policy. Often, the lifetime maximum benefit ("pool of money") is expressed in years, because the total amount is calculated by multiplying the daily benefit by a number of years, usually three or five, although other options may be available.

Waiting Period

The policy's waiting (elimination) period works much like a deductible. It is the number of days a claimant must wait after becoming benefit-eligible before benefits are payable. Sometimes, services must be received for a day to count toward the waiting period, but most often the waiting period is expressed as calendar days, with no LTC services required. The most common waiting periods are 60 or 90 days and the longer the waiting period, the lower the cost. In addition, waiting periods based on the receipt of services are less costly than calendar-day waiting periods because they generally take longer to satisfy.

Inflation Options

LTC insurance is a benefit that an individual may not have to use for many years. Therefore, it is important that coverage keeps pace with inflation.

An employer's choice of inflation options can also influence the cost of coverage. There are three approaches to inflation available in today's LTC insurance market:

1. Future purchase option
2. Automatic benefit increase option
3. Consumer price index option

Future Purchase Option

Under the future purchase option, an inflation increase will be offered with guaranteed issue on a regular, periodic basis from the employer's plan effective date. Insured individuals are free to elect or decline each offer, with premiums for the increase amount based on their age at time of purchase. Rules for continuing offers vary by carrier.

Essentially, this is a "pay as you go" approach to inflation and is the least expensive of the three options, at initial enrollment.

Automatic Benefit Increase Option

With an automatic benefit increase approach, the insured's daily benefit (as well as the lifetime benefit) automatically increases each year at an annual rate, usually 3, 4, or 5 percent compounded, with no corresponding increase in premium. The increases continue to be made regardless of age or whether the insured is eligible for benefits. It is the option most often recommended by consumer agencies and is required to be offered in all states. However, it is significantly more expensive than the other inflation approaches.

Consumer Price Index Option

Under the consumer price index inflation option, inflation increases are based on percentage changes in the All Urban Consumers–All Items–CPI (CPI-U), and automatically increase the insured's daily maximum benefit by the same percentage, with no corresponding increase in premium. This is the most recent approach developed to address inflation and falls between the future purchase and automatic benefit increase options in terms of cost.

Underwriting

The LTC insurance benefit can be offered on a guaranteed issue basis or be underwritten, depending on the size of the employer's population. Larger groups, that is, those with more than 1,000 employees, are the best candidates for guaranteed issue, where simplified or full underwriting is more appropriate for smaller employers or for associations looking to introduce the benefit to their membership. Guaranteed issue adds a small cost to the overall premium structure.

LTC PRICING

LTC insurance is priced on a scale of premiums that varies by issue age and plan design selected. The intent is that the premium rates remain level for the insured's lifetime, although rates are not guaranteed. If actual and expected experience differs from the actuarial pricing assumptions used to price the LTC insurance, the policyholder may be subjected to a rate increase.

Most LTC insurance sold as an employee benefit is issued to people in their 40s and 50s, while the expected claims will not occur until people are in their 70s, or older. Therefore, the pricing actuary must develop an assumed set of claim costs over the insured's lifetime. These claim costs are based upon plan design, sex, issue age, type of underwriting, and other potential factors, such as marital status. Significant additional assumptions include the expected rate of return on invested assets, lapse rates, mortality rates, administrative expenses, taxes, and risk charges. The long time frame over which pricing assumptions must be made presents significant challenges for the actuary. In other words, a relatively small deviation in these pricing assumptions relative to actual experience can result in a large difference in the level of required premium. Thus, it is prudent to conservatively set these pricing assumptions. This process is sometimes referred to as including "provisions for adverse deviations" (PADs). In fact, the pricing actuary is required to certify to state regulators that the premium rate schedule is sufficient to cover anticipated costs under moderately adverse experience.

The "level" premium structure of LTC insurance is different from the premium structure of most other employee benefits, where the premium is expected to change each year. Since premiums are designed to remain level as the insured person ages, while their expected level of claims increases, the premium must be set at a level that is higher than expected claims in the early years of coverage, so that sufficient funds are available to pay claims

FIGURE 12-1

Premium and Claims by Age for Issue Age 40

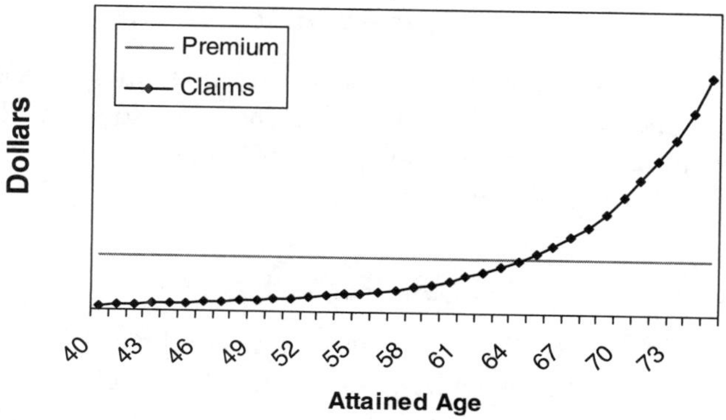

in the later years of coverage. The pattern of premiums and claims by age is illustrated in Figure 12-1 for a person who buys LTC insurance at age 40.

Note that, until around age 66, this person will be paying more in premium than the insurer expects to pay out in claims. Some of this "excess" premium is needed to pay for administration expenses and taxes, but most will be set aside to pay future claims and is referred to as "active life reserves". These active life reserves are set aside and invested by the insurer, so that they will be available in the later policy years when expected claims are higher than expected premium.

OTHER LTC CONTRACT PROVISIONS

Beyond the basic and optional plan design features, employers should also be acquainted with some other key policy provisions.

Guaranteed Renewable Provision

Most LTC insurance today is sold on a "guaranteed renewable," basis, which means that the carrier cannot cancel coverage for any reason (other than nonpayment of premiums), unilaterally change the coverage, or raise rates on a single person for any reason. If a carrier demonstrates a financial need to raise rates, it must be on an entire class of policies and be filed and accepted by each and every state where the policies were sold. As with similar insurance product lines, for the LTC insurance business to be financially viable, the design of these products must allow for pricing that can be adjusted to reflect actual experience.

Portability

LTC insurance coverage is fully portable, meaning employees can take it with them if they retire or otherwise terminate employment. Portability also applies to family members, who may continue their coverage even if the employee elects to terminate coverage.

30-Day Free Look

Upon receipt of the certificate or policy, an insured has a 30-day window of opportunity to decide whether to continue with the plan. If the insured decides not to take the coverage during this period, all premiums paid will be refunded.

Coordination of Benefits

Most group LTC insurance policies contain a coordination of benefits (COB) provision that governs which policy pays first, in the case of multiple policies or coverage. The National Association of Insurance Commissioners (NAIC) Coordination of Benefits Model Regulation permits group LTC policies to coordinate benefit payments with other LTC plans.

LTC INSURANCE FINANCING

There are four basic approaches to LTC insurance financing: voluntary, employer-paid, core plus buy-up, and executive carve-out.

Voluntary Plans

It is not surprising, in the wake of the recent financial crisis, that the popularity of voluntary benefits is on the rise, since they allow employers to enrich their benefits packages at little or no cost. According to *Top Trends in Voluntary Benefits*, a study conducted in 2009 by the International Foundation of Employee Benefit Plans revealed that 84 percent of employer-respondents indicated that they offer voluntary benefits, with an additional 5 percent saying that they were planning to offer them in the future. LTC insurance placed third in the survey, with 51 percent of the 833 participating companies offering the coverage, ahead of long-term disability insurance and dental insurance.

In order to ensure good participation, the employee population should be well paid, with employee salaries averaging over $50,000, and well educated. Even more important is the employer's willingness to support the benefit's introduction, since a robust marketing campaign is necessary to establish the need for coverage and the value of the benefit.

Employer-Paid

Some employers have chosen to pay for the LTC coverage, just as they do for their life and health benefits. All employer-paid LTCI plans offer significant tax advantages for both employers and employees:

- Employers can deduct 100 percent of the premiums paid as a business expense.
- Employers have the flexibility to determine eligible classes, so they can limit the plan's offer to key executives or broaden the eligible class to include the remaining employee population; in either case, they would still enjoy applicable tax advantages.
- Most employees can exclude premiums from gross income and are not taxed on the LTCI benefits they receive.
- Employees living in certain states are also eligible for either tax credits or deductions for premiums they pay, as part of a voluntary offering.

Executive Carve-Out

Some employers choose to reward their management teams by providing incentives outside of traditional compensation programs. Those who opt to pay for the premiums for their executive's LTC insurance enjoy the same tax advantages that apply to health insurance.

Core Plus Buy-Up

Another approach to LTC insurance funding is the core plus buy-up approach whereby the employer pays for a core level of coverage and allows members of the eligible group to buy additional coverage so that they can choose the amount that best fits their needs. Core plus buy-ups generally have strong participation, since employees may be encouraged by their employer's solid support of the plan, and therefore tend to purchase additional coverage beyond the core coverage. Employer-paid premium tax advantages also apply.

LTC ENROLLMENT

LTC enrollments generally take place over four to six weeks and tend to be either broker-driven or carrier-driven, depending on the size of the employer. In both scenarios, the goal is to take the burden of benefit introduction off of the employer. For larger employers, the carrier's role includes

- Developing and executing the marketing campaign
- Setting up the administrative protocols for payroll deduction
- Overseeing customer support at a carrier-run call center
- Coordinating human resource training sessions and employee meetings

The employer's main responsibilities are confined to determining the eligible class and providing ongoing eligibility information, selecting a final plan design, reviewing marketing materials, and providing general plan support. Support can be as simple as allowing the communications material to be co-branded with the company logo and also permitting the carrier access to the employee population, so that it can conduct an effective communications campaign.

LTC insurance presents a different set of communications challenges than most other voluntary benefit offerings. LTC is not an issue that people like to think about and so people often rely on misconceptions about the likelihood of need or the sources for funding. Most applicants are not familiar with the coverage and sometimes confuse it with other, existing benefits, such as long-term disability. In order to provide the prospective applicants with the information they need when considering the benefit's purchase, numerous communications "touches" are needed, using various media, including Web-based communications.

Web enrollments have become increasingly popular, as employees seem to appreciate the convenience of learning about and enrolling in the benefit online. Online enrollments are largely limited to guaranteed issue scenarios, though it is also possible to download medical applications, when underwriting is required.

LTC UPGRADES AND TRANSFERS

Some LTC insurance plans allow the employer to transfer its existing plan to a new plan, either with the same insurer or with a new insurance carrier.

There are a number of reasons why an employer might want to transfer its LTC insurance plan to a new plan, including the following:

- A desire to update their plan design to a newer plan design with additional features
- To get a lower-priced plan for its employees
- Post merger consolidation of LTC insurance plans
- Dissatisfaction with the current insurer's service, or the perceived financial strength of the insurer

If an employer decides to transfer its current LTC insurance plan, it may allow the insured person the option to transfer to the new LTC plan or to stay in his or her current LTC plan. To offset the cost of the higher attained age premiums of the new LTC plan and to recognize that the insured has contributed to a LTC insurance plan, the active life reserves that the insured has accumulated will be transferred to the new plan, if the insured decides to transfer. Transferring the reserves enables the new LTC plan to reduce premiums for the transferee by subtracting a discount from the insured's attained age premiums or allows the LTC plan to use the insured's original issue age under their prior plan when setting premium rates.

The insurer(s) and the employer will need to negotiate the terms of the transfer, such as who is eligible to transfer, what type of underwriting is to be used, and how the new premiums will be calculated. Transfers and upgrades require a considerable amount of administrative effort, including a customized premium quote for the new plan, the tracking of who has elected to transfer, and, for a transfer between insurers, the reconciliation of the final transfer list between insurers. Thus, a transfer provision is often included only in larger employer LTC insurance policies.

LTC CLAIMS ADJUDICATION

Since LTC benefits purchased during the working years may not be needed until well after retirement, it is important that employers verify the carrier's claims paying ability. Employers who are considering the introduction of LTC should ask about the carrier's track record of benefits payment and find out its ratings from the financial ratings agencies, such as A.M. Best or Standard & Poors, which evaluate future claims-paying abilities. It is also advisable to ask about the kind of support a claimant can expect and what the claims-adjudication process involves, once benefit triggers have been met and the waiting period has been satisfied.

Benefit Triggers

Insureds are eligible to receive benefits under the policy when they become either functionally dependent or cognitively impaired and have fulfilled a waiting period requirement. To prove functional dependency, an insured must be unable to perform, without substantial assistance from another person, at least two of the six activities of daily living (ADLs: bathing, dressing, eating, toileting, transferring, and continence) because of a loss of functional capacity that is expected to last for a period of at least 90 days. The 90-day period requirement, a part of what qualifies the plan for tax-favored status, is not a "waiting" period. It indicates only the expectation by a medical professional that an insured will be unable to perform any two ADLs for at least 90 days without substantial assistance from another person (hands-on or stand-by). Its purpose is to ensure that the particular illness or disability is long-term in nature.

Separate Cognitive Impairment Trigger

An insured can qualify for benefit payments without being certified ADL-dependent if he or she is determined to have a severe cognitive impairment that requires substantial supervision to protect the person from threats to health and safety. The insured individual should be expected to demonstrate a loss or deterioration in intellectual capacity that is (a) comparable to (and includes) Alzheimer's disease and similar forms of irreversible dementia, and (b) measured by clinical evidence and standardized tests that reliably measure impairment in the individual's (i) short- or long-term memory, (ii) orientation as to people, place, or time, and (iii) deductive or abstract reasoning.

LTC REGULATION

LTC insurance is one of the most extensively regulated products in the insurance marketplace. The basis of this regulation is the Model Act and Regulations developed by the National Association of Insurance

Commissioners. The goal of the NAIC is to protect the interests of insurance consumers and to develop uniform public policy and regulatory templates that states may adopt. These Model Act and Regulations establish rigorous standards for long-term care insurance products (i.e., uniform definitions, benefit triggers, and policy provisions), disclosure, rate stability, suitability, and carrier and producer/agent marketing and sales practices. These Model provisions have been widely adopted at both the state and federal levels.

State Jurisdiction

The kind of LTC insurance product an employer selects will dictate how state requirements will apply to plan design. For those employers who offer a multilife LTC insurance product, the requirements of the insured individual's state of residence will apply. However, if an employer decides to offer a true group plan, the location where the policy is delivered (usually the employer's headquarters) is considered the situs and dictates which insurance regulations apply. For example, if the employer is sitused in New York, New York State insurance regulations will apply to those insureds issued coverage in New Jersey, as well as those insureds issued coverage in New York.

There are also some states that apply their regulations to all individuals resident in their state, regardless of the situs state of the employer. These are referred to as extraterritorial states, or "ET" states, and can affect an employer's plan design and enrollment planning.

ERISA

An ERISA plan is an employee benefit plan voluntarily established and maintained by an employer, an employee organization, or a combination of the two. There are two types of employee benefit plans: retirement plans and welfare plans. LTC insurance plans are considered a type of welfare plan, as are other forms of health plans.

Sponsoring an ERISA plan does involve a few reporting and disclosure requirements, which are the same for LTC insurance plans and health plans. ERISA requires the employer to file an annual report to the IRS: Form 5500. Form 5500 is designed to provide detailed information on the financial condition and operations of the plan. Schedule A to Form 5500 includes information supplied by the insurance carrier. Electronic filing of Form 5500 has been required for plan years beginning on or after January

1, 2008. In addition, a brief summary of Form 5500—the Summary Annual Report—must be filed with the IRS and distributed annually to participants. (Starting in 2008, no Summary Annual Report was required for defined benefit pension plans.) The plan must also furnish participants with a summary plan description (SPD).

Some employers are initially reluctant to consider the plan governed by ERISA because of these reporting and disclosure requirements. A voluntary plan will not be considered an ERISA plan if the employer avoids certain activities—most importantly, if the employer does not contribute to premiums, does not endorse the program, and limits its activities to collecting premium by payroll deduction and sending the premium to the insurer. There is a downside to minimizing the employer's involvement in this way, however. The employer loses the opportunity to help design the plan design and to take credit for offering it. In addition, the enrollment results will likely suffer without the employer's endorsement. Employers may want to explore with the insurer what assistance can be provided in meeting the reporting and disclosure requirements so they can be as involved as they want with the introduction of the plan.

HIPAA

The Health Insurance Portability and Accountability Act (HIPAA) of 1996 was another key regulatory milestone for LTC insurance as it clarified the federal income tax status of LTC insurance benefits and premiums, defined LTC insurance benefit triggers, and adopted the core consumer protections provisions found in the NAIC LTC Model and Act as federal standards for this product. LTC insurance plans that meet the criteria for a tax-qualified plan as defined by HIPAA allow individuals to deduct their LTC insurance premiums as medical expenses up to specified amounts, and any benefit payments they receive are not considered taxable income. Policies sold prior to January 1, 1997 are grandfathered and are automatically eligible for favorable tax treatment so long as they met applicable state requirements at time of policy issuance. Virtually all LTC insurance plans sold today are tax-qualified plans.

LTC DRA PartnershipPlans

The Deficit Reduction Act of 2005 (DRA) represented the government's attempt to encourage Americans to take more personal responsibility for covering their own LTC costs. One provision in the DRA allows states to establish Qualified State Long Term Care Insurance Partnership Programs (QSLTCIP) that would

- Help protect the stability of state Medicaid programs
- Promote the importance of private LTC insurance coverage
- Offer Medicaid Asset Protection to consumers who buy LTC insurance, enabling them to protect a specific dollar amount of personal assets and still remain eligible to apply for Medicaid LTC coverage, if needed

The DRA Partnership concept was based upon the original Partnership programs as developed by California, Connecticut, Indiana, and New York in the mid-1990s. As of July 2010, 33 states had DRA Partnership Programs in place. To qualify, an individual

- Must be a resident of the state at the time the policy is issued.
- Must select the appropriate amount of inflation protection, based on his or her age at the time of purchase:
    - Applicants who are 60 or younger must select coverage with automatic inflation protection with annual compounding.
    - Applicants who are between ages 61 and 75 must select coverage with some level of automatic inflation protection (either annual compounding or simple).
    - Applicants who are age 76 or older have no inflation requirements.

The implementation of these programs poses unique challenges in a group setting that have yet to be addressed by the Centers for Medicare & Medicaid Services (CMS) or the states. For example, the extent to which there will be reciprocity between the situs state and state of issuance of the certificate is not clear. In reality, the DRA Partnership model was structured on individual insurance framework, not group insurance. As a result, availability of DRA Partnership plans is relatively limited in the group marketplace.

CONSUMER PROTECTION PROVISIONS

The LTC insurance industry must adhere to a number of consumer protection provisions aimed at preventing unintended lapses and unfair claims practices. Some of these provisions, which are included in the NAIC Models, are described below.

Third-Party Billing Notification

This feature provides added protection against an accidental policy lapse by giving applicants the opportunity to designate a person(s) to receive notice of cancellation in case of nonpayment.

Policy Reinstatement Provision

This provision allows the insured a certain time period to request a reinstatement of coverage, in the event that a physical or cognitive impairment resulted in failure to pay premiums when due, resulting in a lapse of coverage.

Contingent Nonforfeiture

The Contingent Nonforfeiture benefit allows an insured to keep reduced paid-up coverage with the full daily benefit amounts and a reduced lifetime maximum, equal to the total amount of premiums paid since the coverage was issued, but not less than 30 times the Nursing Home daily maximum benefit (DMB). The Contingent Nonforfeiture benefit only applies in the event of a substantial premium rate increase, ranging from an increase of 10 percent at issue age 90 or older to an increase of 200 percent for those applicants at issue age 29 or younger.

Independent Third-Party Review

One of the newer requirements is that in the event that a claim is denied because the benefit trigger has not been met, insured individuals have the right to request an independent third-party review. The decision of that third party will be binding and must be upheld by the carrier.

Timely Payment of Claims

This is another new NAIC model requirement, which calls for the carrier to pay an interest penalty to the claimant of 1 percent per month of the claim amount, in the event that claims payments are not processed within 30 days, provided the claim is valid and substantiated. Some states have different time standards and interest amounts.

HEALTH CARE REFORM AND LTC

The health care reform law (the Patient Protection and Affordable Care Act) enacted in 2010 includes a provision for long-term care coverage under the Community Living Assistance Services and Supports (CLASS) Act.

Overview of CLASS Act

This new program allows for the creation of a voluntary government plan that provides some LTC coverage, once certain requirements are met. Participation is completely voluntary, so an employer can choose to opt out of the program without penalty and employees will not be required to join.

Program Timing

Based on current understanding, the CLASS Act is not expected to be operational until 2013 as the plan details and administrative infrastructure still need to be developed by the Department of Health and Human Services.

Program Eligibility

The CLASS program will be available to all actively at work individuals who are at least 18 years of age, on a guaranteed-issue basis, meaning that proof of good health will not be required for participation.

CLASS Premiums

The CLASS program is required to be paid for by enrollee premiums and not with taxpayer dollars. Although premiums have yet to be determined, the Chief Actuary of the Centers for Medicare & Medicaid Services (CMS) has estimated that "an initial average premium level of about $240 per month would be required to adequately fund CLASS program costs for this level of enrollment [2 percent], adverse selection, and premium inadequacy for students and low-income participants."[8] Students and the working poor will be able to access the program for $5 a month subject to an annual CPI increase.

8. Richard S. Foster, Chief Actuary, "Estimated Financial Effects of the 'Patient Protection and Affordable Care Act of 2009,' as Passed by the Senate on December 24, 2009," January 8, 2010, p. 14.

The law permits premiums to be increased yearly to ensure that the CLASS fund is actuarially sound.

CLASS Act Benefits

The CLASS benefit plan has not been formulated as of this writing—it is required to be finalized by October 1, 2012. The law requires that it provide benefits of no less than $50 per day on average, with benefit amounts scaled based on the degree of impairment. If the minimum required benefit plan becomes the plan adopted for the program, this means that some claimants will receive less than $50 per day while others will receive more than $50 per day. To keep things in perspective, the average cost of long-term care in the United States today ranges from $97 per day at home to $202 per day in a nursing home.[9] Benefits will increase annually based on changes in the Consumer Price Index (CPI), and will be paid as long as the individual remains disabled.

Benefit Eligibility and Five-Year Vesting Period

The CLASS program has a vesting period requirement whereby participants would need to pay premiums into the program for five years and must earn wages for at least three of those years before they could be eligible for benefits. Once the vesting period has been satisfied, participants must meet certain benefit triggers, just as they would under private LTC coverage. The benefit trigger can be met in one of two ways.

Functional Limitations

A participant must demonstrate his or her inability to perform at least two or three of the activities of daily living (eating, bathing, dressing, continence, toileting, and transferring) without substantial assistance from another individual (a final determination of whether the minimum requirement will be two or three activities of daily living has yet to be made). It must be certified by a licensed health care practitioner that this functional limitation is expected to last for a continuous period of more than 90 days. Individuals may also qualify if they demonstrate a level of functional limitation similar (as determined under regulations prescribed by the Secretary) to the level of functional limitation described above.

9. John Hancock Cost of Care Study, 2008.

Cognitive Impairment

A participant must demonstrate the need for substantial supervision to protect the individual from threats to health and safety due to substantial cognitive impairment.

The Future of Private LTC Insurance

Once the CLASS Program rolls out, which presumably will be in 2013 after the CLASS benefit plan has been finalized, it will perform the valuable service of raising awareness about the many issues surrounding LTC, including need, cost, and the desirability of planning ahead for the possibility. It will not preclude the need for private LTC insurance, which may be better suited to meet the need of both employers and employees. For employers, the introduction of LTC insurance coverage allows them to enhance their benefits packages at little cost. It also allows them to extend insurance protection to their retiree population and to the eligible family members of actively at work employees. In addition, private LTC insurance offers employers more control over plan design and enrollment timing, with administrative tasks largely undertaken by the insurance carrier. For employees, an LTC insurance benefit may prove to be a better financial or retirement planning tool, since the coverage may be better able to meet the cost of care in their area and offer optional benefits that provide greater flexibility for the management of their care.

CHAPTER 13

Disability Income Benefits

John S. Roberts

Mark A. Andruss

Loss of income because of a long-term disability is among the most devastating financial losses a person can face. This chapter focuses on disability income benefits, both short-term and long-term. It begins with an overview of disability risk and an explanation of how disability income protection evolved in the United States, both in the public sector and in employment-based programs. Plan design issues associated with sick leave, short-term disability, long-term disability, self-insurance options, integration of plans, and integration with public programs are discussed.

DISABILITY RISK

About 24.5 million Americans are out of work or limited in the amount of work they can do at any given time because of a health problem or disability.[1] Most of these are short-term conditions, but millions of workers have severe conditions that can keep them from work. In 2009, 7.8 million workers qualified for disability benefits under Social Security OASDI (Old Age, Survivors, and Disability Insurance).[2] To qualify under Social Security, these were severe disabilities that prevented the person from

1. *Statistical Abstract of the United States: 2011*, 130th edition, Washington, DC: U.S. Census Bureau, 2011, Table 590.
2. Ibid., Table 543.

doing any kind of work for which he or she was suited and that could be "expected to last for at least a year or to result in death."[3]

Estimates of the number of people with disabilities vary depending upon how disability is defined. The most recent U.S. Census Bureau figures show that roughly one in six people age 16 and older in the United States have some type of disability, with disability defined as a reported sensory, physical, mental, self-care, go-outside-home, or employment disability. By this definition, the Census Bureau reported that about 38.4 million of the approximately 242.9 million Americans over age 15 had a disability.[4]

The risks of both short- and long-term disability increase with age. The average incidence of an employment disability lasting three months or longer is 3.5 per 1,000, according to Society of Actuaries estimates.[5] The figure grows to 20 per 1,000 near age 65 and can be as low as 0.5 per 1,000 in younger age groups.[6]

As the baby boomers age, the number of people with a disability will grow. In the period from 2003 to 2009, the number of individuals receiving disability benefits from Social Security increased 32.6 percent.[7] Disability is a low-incidence event in comparison with some other insurable events. However, if one makes the same comparison in terms of impact, disability is a dramatically more serious financial threat. A 40-year-old earning a gross salary of $50,000 per year will forgo almost $2.4 million in pay if he or she is disabled and is not able to return to work before age 65 (see Table 13-1). http://www.census.gov/compendia/statab/2011/tables/11s0588.pdf

EARLY HISTORY

The first disability-type insurance policies were created as the United States made the transition from an agricultural to an industrial economy. These forerunners of disability income insurance—called "establishment

3. Social Security Administration, *Social Security Disability Benefits*, SSA Publication No. 05-10029, May 1996, p. 3.
4. (a) "Annual Estimates of the Population by Sex and Five-Year Age Groups for the United States: April 1, 2000 to July 1, 2008 (NC-EST2008-01)" (released May 14, 2009); and (b) Statistical Abstract of the United States: 2011, 130th edition, Washington, DC: U.S. Census Bureau, 2011, Table 2006, B18002.
5. *Commissioner's Disability Table, Society of Actuaries*, Vol. 39, 1987.
6. U.S. Department of Commerce, Bureau of the Census, *Statistical Abstract of the United States, 2003*, March 2003, p. 362.
7. *Statistical Abstract of the United States: 2011*, 130th edition, Washington, DC: U.S. Census Bureau, 2011, Table 543.

TABLE 13-1

Potential Lost Salary ($) Due to Disability at Various Ages to Age 65

Gross Pay at Disability	Age at disability		
	25	40	50
7,500	906,000	358,000	162,000
18,000	2,174,000	859,000	388,000
50,000	6,040,000	2,386,000	1,079,000

Note: This table assumes a 5 percent salary increase per year if disability had not occurred. For example, if the person became disabled at age 40 with a salary of $18,000, then future earnings lost would be $859,000 to age 65.

funds"—were seen in the industrial regions of the Northeast in the early 1800s. Employers created the funds and paid employees a small cash payment if they became sick or were injured on the job.

Insurance companies followed with other measures to protect against accident or illness. The first disability policies were sold to individuals in the late 1840s, and related travel and accident-type coverages followed in the 1850s.

Few people were covered by these early policies, but their existence signaled that society was beginning to think about disability risk and how to protect against it. The industrial revolution had created new industries, new machinery, and faster production. In turn, this progress created new hazards for employees and business. By 1900, businesses were seeking insurance to protect against accident-related lawsuits. At the same time, government was responding to the new economic and social conditions. In 1911, state governments enacted the first workers' compensation laws, requiring employers to provide employees with insurance protection for job-related injury and sickness.

The workers' compensation laws created more awareness of disability risk and marked a new stage of development for disability insurance. The first group disability insurance came on the market in 1915, modeled after group life insurance.

These early chapters of the nascent disability income insurance market were virtually closed by the Great Depression. By 1932, 14 million Americans were unemployed. Sales of disability and accident-related insurance to both individuals and groups fell, and claims under existing policies climbed.

Looking back, it seems clear that even without the vast economic disruption of the 1930s, the disability income insurance contracts of that day were destined for poor results. These early contracts used a flat-rate structure, applying the same rate to all ages. Some contracts provided for increased benefits the longer the disability continued, greatly reducing the likelihood of return to work. In addition, contracts did not include a number of underwriting safeguards that are common today, such as a maximum age beyond which benefits cannot be received. And because their benefits were often determined as a percentage of a related life insurance contract, over-insurance was common.

THE MODERN ERA OF DISABILITY INCOME BENEFITS

The modern era of disability income benefits took shape in the 1950s and 1960s. Two demand factors are worth noting. First, organized labor became more active in seeking noncash compensation. Second, government addressed the problem of disability. In 1960, an amendment to the Social Security program extended disability income protection to all workers. This initiative had a strict definition of disability and a six-month waiting period, as well as a benefit structure that became increasingly inadequate for higher wage earners, so it hardly met the full need for disability income protection. However, it did propel awareness of the need for protection, encouraging bargaining units and individual workers to seek disability income benefits through the workplace.

In the 1960s, the quality of disability income insurance products caught up with the emerging demand of a modern economy and workforce. Before this time, group long-term disability (LTD) contracts provided a low level of benefits. Insurance carriers did not understand how to manage LTD risk and, in the wake of their 1930s experience, they took a highly conservative approach. In the 1960s, innovative insurers developed the methods for insuring the unique risks of disability. One of the most important changes was insuring the loss of income specifically. By contrast, contracts of the past often triggered payment when a person was disabled, without attention to loss of income. The focus on income protection allowed insurers to manage risk more effectively and offer more appropriate and meaningful benefits.

The recent decades have also been characterized by a new level of awareness about disability issues and the capabilities of people with disabilities. This culminated in 1990 with passage of the Americans with

Disabilities Act (ADA). The law prohibits discrimination on the basis of disability. In relation to employment, the ADA states that employers cannot discriminate against qualified individuals with disabilities. Qualified individuals with disabilities are those who can perform the essential functions of the job they hold or desire, with or without reasonable accommodation. Other ADA sections cover the issues of discrimination in public services, public accommodations and services operated by private entities, and telecommunications.

In addition, public policy has begun to focus more on aiding people with disabilities in returning to work. In 1999, the Work Incentives Improvement Act broadened access to the major federal health insurance programs—Medicare and Medicaid—in supporting a return to work among those who receive Social Security disability benefits (both under OASDI and Supplemental Security Income). Under prior policy, those on Social Security disability risked loss of their access to federal health insurance programs if they attempted to return to work. Advocates for people with disabilities consider the new Work Incentives Law as the most important policy step in supporting return to work since ADA.[8]

TYPES OF DISABILITY INCOME IN THE PUBLIC AND PRIVATE SECTORS

This section describes the various public and private income replacement programs. Four major areas are covered within each program:

- Eligibility
- Benefit levels and approximate replacement ratios
- Duration of benefits
- Definition of disability

Specified limitations and exclusions are also pointed out where appropriate. A description of the public programs is followed by a discussion of private-sector benefit programs, including sick pay, short-term disability (STD), and long-term disability (LTD). Plan design and funding issues also are addressed.

8. "Clinton Signs Law to Help Workers With Disabilities," *The New York Times*, December 18, 1999.

Public Programs

Public-sector disability programs include the following:

- Social Security (OASDI/SSI)
- Workers' compensation
- Veterans' benefits
- State retirement systems (disability rider)
- State-mandated (short-term) plans

These various public-sector programs provide a modest, yet important, foundation of disability income protection to the working population.

The most comprehensive level of coverage is provided by the state workers' compensation programs covered in Chapter 22. However, those apply only to work-related disabilities. Work-related disabilities represent less than 10 percent of total disabilities that last more than 90 days.

Social Security disability income provides protection for both occupational and nonoccupational disabilities, but its strict definition of disability and general benefit levels are not intended to support disability protection needs at all income levels. Similarly, state retirement systems often apply in lieu of participation in the Social Security disability income system, with equivalent replacement ratios and claim approval rates.

The state-mandated (short-term) programs also are modest and, by definition, apply only to short durations. Moreover, they are only available in a handful of states. Veterans' benefits can provide significant income protection, depending on the degree of disability. These benefit levels are normally provided regardless of benefits received from other programs.

Private group disability plans generally integrate with public programs. The income replacement remitted under private plans usually reflects income replacement that was not available from public programs or is an addition to payments received under public programs. The most significant exceptions to this rule are payments under veterans' disability income, which are not normally offsets to benefits under private group disability plans.

Social Security: SSDI and SSI

Chapter 20 discusses eligibility and insured status of individuals participating in Social Security OASDI (Old Age, Survivors, and Disability Income). This section addresses Social Security Disability Income (SSDI) and Supplemental Security Income (SSI). Both are administered by the

Social Security Administration. Employers and employees share the funding of SSDI through regular withholding. SSI is funded through general revenue of the federal government.

SSDI

A worker is generally eligible for Social Security Disability Income (OASDI) if the following five conditions are met:

1. The person is insured. In most circumstances, the standard that will apply here is that the person has worked under Social Security for at least 5 of the last 10 years before becoming disabled.
2. The person is under age 65.
3. The person has been disabled for 12 months, is expected to be disabled for at least 12 months, or has a disability that is expected to result in death.
4. The person has filed an application for disability benefits.
5. The person has completed a five-month waiting period or is exempted from this requirement.

Benefits

The benefit generally equals the worker's primary insurance amount (PIA) as defined by Social Security. Broadly, the PIA is based on a person's taxable earnings averaged over the number of years that he or she has worked before becoming eligible for benefits.

Disability benefits are normally lowered by any workers' compensation benefits. Auxiliary beneficiaries receive a portion of the PIA (see Table 13-2).

Duration

Benefits are payable to age 65.

Definition of Disability

It is vital to keep in mind that the definition of disability under Social Security is narrow. Disability is defined as the inability to engage in any substantial gainful activity by reason of any medically determinable physical or mental impairment that can be expected to result in death or that has lasted or can be expected to last for a continuous period of not less than 12 months.

TABLE 13-2

Benefits as a Percentage of Primary Insurance Amount (PIA)

	Percentage of PIA
Disability benefit	100
Spouse's benefit (husband or wife of retired or disabled worker)	50*
Child's benefit: child of retired or disabled worker	50*
Mother's or father's benefit: caring for child under 16 or disabled	75*
Disabled widow(er)'s benefit: starting age 50–59	71.5

*Subject to a Maximum Family Benefit.

In 2008, processed applications for disability benefits under OASDI totaled 2,781,600; 877,226 workers were awarded benefits (roughly 32 percent)[9] (See Table 13-3). The benefit process, viewed as a whole, is a difficult course of applications, denials, and appeals. An audit by the Office of the Inspector General of OASDI disability claims finalized in 2006

TABLE 13-3

OASDI Disability Benefits Awarded–Number and Average Monthly Benefit, 2008

Age	Number	Average Monthly Benefit ($)
Under 30	70,730	687.69
30–39	98,176	935.02
40–49	204,645	1,057.56
50–54	168,529	1,155.80
55–59	198,350	1,248.70
60 or older	136,796	1,303.80
Total	877,226	1,114.50

Source: Social Security Bulletin, Annual Statistical Supplement, 2009, Table 6.A4.

9. *Social Security Bulletin, Annual Statistical Supplement*, 2009, Tables 2.F5 and 6.A1, p. 269.

showed that the average time to a decision, pro or con, at the initial consideration stage was 131 days from date of application, 279 days for claims decided at the reconsideration level, 811 days for claims decided at the Administrative Law Judge level, 1,053 days at the Appeals Council level, and 1,720 days in the Federal Courts. Growing backlogs, budgetary constraints and increasing retirements of experienced adjudicators have combined to make this a persistent and intractable problem.

SSI

Supplemental Security Income (SSI) is a need-based program that makes cash payments to individuals who fall under designated income thresholds and are disabled. In 2008, more than 7.5 million people with disabilities received SSI payments. The average monthly payment was $477.79.[10]

Workers' Compensation

Workers' compensation provides reasonable income and medical benefits to work-accident victims, or income benefits to their dependents, regardless of fault. Most employees have a solid replacement level of income for a good-to-excellent duration of benefit payments for disabilities that result from work-related injuries and diseases. However, as stated previously, these work-related disabilities represent less than 10 percent of all disabilities of significant length that occur in the employee population.

The following provides a brief description of the benefits under the workers' compensation program. Chapter 22 explains the program in detail. All 50 states have workers' compensation laws. Although there is broad agreement that coverage under these laws should be universal, in fact no state law covers all forms of employment. In 2007, 131.7 million employees were covered by job injury laws.[11] In 13 states, smaller employers are exempt from the law.[12] Generally these are firms with fewer than three to five employees. In some states, employers are exempt from mandatory coverage of some types of employees, for instance certain agricultural workers, household employees, employees of charitable or religious institutions, or employees of some units of state or local governments. Interpretations of the law in different states also can affect uniformity of

10. *Statistical Abstract of the United States: 2011*, 130th edition, Washington DC: U.S. Census Bureau, 2011, Table 561.
11. SSI Annual Statistical Report, Social Security Administration, 2009, p. 66, http://www.ssa.gov/policy/docs/statcomps/supplement/.
12. Business Owners Toolkit, http://www.toolkit.com/small_business_guide/sbg.aspx?nid=P05_4403.

coverage among all workers, but the intent of the laws is to cover all work-related injuries and diseases. These compensation laws are theoretically compulsory or elective. Under an elective law, the employer may reject the act, but if it does so, it loses the three common-law defenses: assumption of risk, negligence of fellow employees, and contributory negligence. As a practical matter, this means that workers' compensation laws are generally "compulsory." Coverage is still elective in Texas, although Texas law provides for mandatory workers' compensation for occupations engaged in transportation as defined in state law. In Wyoming, the law is compulsory for all employees engaged in extra-hazardous occupations and elective for all other occupations. Most states require employers to obtain insurance or prove financial ability to carry their own risk. Self-insurance is permitted in all but a few states, usually after obtaining approval of the state regulatory authority. Employers may set up a reserve fund for self-insurance to pay compensation and other benefits.

Benefits Provided

Because workers' compensation imposes an absolute liability upon the employer for employee disabilities caused by employment, the benefits payable to the injured employee attempt to cover most of the worker's economic loss. Specifically, the following three benefits are provided:

1. *Cash benefits*, which include both impairment benefits and disability benefits. The former are paid for certain specific physical impairments, while the latter are available whenever there is both an impairment and a wage loss. Four classes of disability are used to determine cash benefits: (1) temporary total, (2) permanent total, (3) temporary partial, and (4) permanent partial. Most cases involve temporary total disability: the employee, although totally disabled during the period when benefits are payable, is expected to recover and return to employment. Permanent total disability generally indicates that the employee is regarded as totally and permanently unable to perform gainful employment. In general, most states provide payments extending through the employee's lifetime on permanent total disability. Replacement ratios vary somewhat by various states, but are generally reasonable and are a percentage of "current" predisability income.
2. *Medical benefits*, which are usually provided without dollar or time limits. In the case of most workplace injuries, only medical

benefits are provided, since substantial impairment or wage loss is not involved.

3. *Rehabilitation benefits*, which include both medical rehabilitation and vocational rehabilitation for those cases involving severe disabilities.

Veterans' Benefits (Disability Income)

Members of the military are provided with a noncontributory pension plan. Retirement is provided for after 20 years of service. If a member is disabled before retirement, he or she becomes eligible for veterans' compensation, provided the disability is service-connected. Compensation varies by degree of disability, ranging in 2010 from $123 per month for a 10 percent disability (with no dependents involved) to $3,172 or more for a 100 percent disability (veteran with spouse, two dependent parents, and at least one dependent child).

Additional amounts above those base disability-compensation rates are paid when an individual has a severe disability as defined in law. In addition, those with at least a 30 percent disability can receive additional allowances for dependents. These additional allowances are tied to the level of disability.

State Retirement Systems (Disability Features)

Pension programs, especially public employee retirement systems (PERS), frequently have a disability component to protect the income of disabled members. The PERS programs are often a substitute for the OASDI program of Social Security. State and local governments can opt out of the Social Security system, if their employees are covered by their own retirement system.

Eligibility

The PERS programs are established by each state to provide for the retirement and disability income needs of their employees. The eligibility point for disability benefits varies from immediate to up to five years of service; in some states, 10 years of service are required to qualify for benefits.

Benefits

The benefit levels are frequently based on a service-type formula, such as 2 percent of salary for each year of service times a final average salary (FAS), to a maximum percentage of salary. Other states provide straight formulas, such as 50 percent of FAS or 62.5 percent of average monthly salary (AMS). The number of years required in these averages varies by state, but the most frequent requirements are "latest *x* years," or all years since a certain date, excluding the five years of lowest earnings. In general, replacement ratios are not applied to current incomes prior to disability, and benefit levels generally are in the range of the Social Security disability income programs, with some exceptions.

Duration

Benefits are usually paid to normal retirement (age 65).

Definition of Disability

The definition of disability is usually permanent and total disability. The approval rates on PERS programs (i.e., of the claims submitted, how many are approved for payment by the PERS) are generally not available. However, because the definition of disability is permanent and total, similar to that of the Social Security disability income system, there probably is a sizable declination rate that may be more severe than that of Social Security. The Social Security Administration declines in excess of 50 percent of applications for disability benefits under OASDI.

State-Mandated Plans

California, Hawaii, New Jersey, New York, Rhode Island, and the territory of Puerto Rico have modest programs that provide or require employers to provide disability benefits for all workers. These programs all provide benefits for short-term disabilities (STD).

Public-Sector Benefits Changes on the Horizon

Public-sector benefits may face changes in the coming years as the U.S. government deals with the problem of an aging population and the potential impact on budget deficits. The Social Security Board of Trustees 2009 Annual Report noted that trust fund expenditures will begin to exceed tax revenues in 2016. Beginning in 2016, the report said, trust fund reserves will be drawn down to pay benefits until the funds are exhausted in 2037. Disability Insurance program costs have exceeded tax revenues since 2005, and trust fund exhaustion is projected for 2020. The recent recession and projected slow recovery as well as more rapidly improving mortality rates have negatively impacted the projected solvency period, and the trustees have urged bipartisan legislative action to restore the long-term balance to

Social Security. Other major programs, most notably Medicare and Medicaid, are also expected to feel the financial strain of an older population requiring more benefits.

In 1950, there were 16.5 covered workers for every Social Security beneficiary; in 1994, there were 3.2 workers per beneficiary, according to Social Security Administration figures. By 2040, this figure is projected to fall to about two workers per beneficiary.[13] Potential reforms for coping with this situation include raising the eligibility age and/or changing eligibility criteria for Social Security benefits, raising taxes, or both.

Workers' compensation has undergone significant reform at the state level. Most states have gone through repeated cycles of substantial reforms aimed at lowering costs and stabilizing the market for corporations and insurers. These reforms have included use of managed care practices to contain costs. Some states and businesses have also turned to 24-hour coverage plans, which integrate disability management, workers' compensation, and group health insurance in a single program. This approach is designed to reduce the complexity and cost of managing workplace disabilities and to increase productivity. At the same time, organized labor and other interests have pushed for an expansion of the scope of coverage, and in other ways attempted to protect workers.

While the public-sector programs discussed above provide a critical foundation for disability coverage, they do not cover all disabilities or income protection needs sufficiently. That makes additional disability income protection a fundamental need to be met through private-sector insurance or self-insurance plans.

Private-Sector Benefits

Three major benefits in the private sector address group disability concerns: sick leave, short-term disability (STD), and long-term disability (LTD). An employer can elect to provide these benefits through a self-insured, partially insured, or fully insured plan. The following is an overview of each benefit and related plan design issues.

Sick Leave

Employers will often continue full salary for the time missed when an employee misses work due to illness or accident. These sick leave or

13. *Workers' Compensation: Benefits, Coverage and Costs*, Washington, DC: National Academy of Social Insurance, 2007, p. 8.

medical leave plans generally cover a period from 10 to 30 days. Most often, the plan is self-funded by the employer.

Salaried personnel are more likely to have a sick-leave plan that is combined with a long-term disability plan. A short-term disability plan that follows a brief period of sick pay may also be part of this package. These benefits should be explained to employees in writing as part of the total benefits package.[14]

The design of the sick-leave plans can allow employees to accumulate unused "sick days" over several years. This permits employees to apply their accumulated time to an extended illness or disability. Some employers also increase the number of sick days per year based on time of service. Such a design will have a maximum for accumulated sick-leave days; most often, 180 days is the limit.

Short-Term Disability

Employees generally must be off the job for five or six days because of illness or one day because of a nonjob-related accident to qualify for benefits under a group STD plan. Such a plan, unlike sick pay, is more likely to be insured. The waiting periods before STD benefits begin will vary among workplaces. The goal is to structure a waiting period so that the plan does not encourage staying off the job. The level of income replaced also is a key part of this design goal. Most STD plans replace 50 to 66.6 percent of income for up to 26 weeks. Some plans may base benefits on a percentage of take-home pay or spendable income.

Whether an STD plan is insured or self-insured, payments during this 26-week period are considered wages and are subject to income, Social Security, and unemployment taxes, provided that the premiums are paid by the employer or with pretax dollars by the employees. (FICA, FUTA, and SUTA taxes are only assessed on otherwise taxable benefits that are actually paid within the first six full calendar months following the onset of the disability.)

Long-Term Disability

LTD plans usually provide income replacement after 13 or 26 weeks under a two-part definition of disability. The first part usually applies to the initial two years that LTD benefits can be paid and focuses on the employee's own occupation. It states that employees must be disabled to an extent that

14. Stephen C. Goss, Chief Actuary, Social Security Administration, Testimony for the Senate Finance Committee on February 2, 2005.

they cannot perform the duties of their own occupation. Employers also have the option of plan structures that will extend the "own occupation" definition of disability beyond the initial 24 months.

The second part of the definition usually applies to the time after the initial 24 months of LTD benefits. It states that benefits will continue to be paid if the person is unable to engage in any work or occupation for which he or she is reasonably fitted by education, training, or experience.

The benefits continue until normal retirement age. While that is often age 65, many contracts now extend to age 67 in order to cover younger workers who may have a Social Security retirement age of 67. Some workers may also be eligible for benefits after age 67. The Age Discrimination in Employment Act (ADEA) requires that the benefit period provide cost-equivalent benefits for older workers when compared with younger workers. (This is covered in more detail below in the section on age under "Elements in Plan Design.")

Basic benefits cease if the person is able to return to full-time work without material limitations or dies before normal retirement age. The percentage of income replaced is normally a percentage of gross salary and can vary significantly from one plan to another. While benefit rates ordinarily range from 50 to 80 percent of gross predisability salary, the preponderance of plans offer a 60 percent replacement rate. In addition, some higher-income professionals will supplement these group benefits with an individually purchased disability income protection plan.

In comparison with medical and life insurance, LTD is relatively under-penetrated in the marketplace. The coverage is most commonly found among white-collar employees (see Table 13-4).

TABLE 13-4

Percentage of Employees with Access to Indicated Benefit Programs on the Job

	All Employees	White Collar	Blue Collar	Service
Medical	69	76	76	42
Life	51	58	54	27
LTD	30	41	22	12

Source: U.S. Department of Labor, Bureau of Labor Statistics, National Compensation Survey: Employee Benefits in Private Industry, March 2009.

LTD benefits are subject to the same tax rules as STD benefits (see above). In both STD and LTD, if the employees paid for a disability plan with their own post-tax dollars, benefits are tax-free. This is most likely to be the case with an individual disability plan, which executive and professional employees often access and buy through the workplace. When a portion of the plan was paid by the employer and a portion by the employee with post-tax dollars, the proportion of plan benefits funded by the employer are taxable as income.

Integrated Disability Coverage

Among our largest employers, disability plans are moving toward designs that integrate traditional occupational coverage such as workers' compensation and the coverage more oriented to nonoccupational risk (e.g., STD, LTD, individual disability, and certain voluntary employee benefits). These designs offer a single point of entry to the benefits process for employees, making coverage more seamless and facilitating claim filing. Employers have a more seamless picture of their overall absenteeism and employee risk profile through integrated information reporting. Information that follows trends across the full spectrum of coverage is a valuable tool in assessing effectiveness of the benefits program design and disability management initiatives.

Voluntary Disability Coverage

Since 2000, voluntary disability coverage has increased in popularity, as employers have sought to control benefits costs and at the same time to afford workers in different life stages more options in the benefits in which they participate. Voluntary coverages are defined as those insurance products offered by the employer and fully paid for by employees. While plan designs offered by insurance companies must take the anti-selection risk into account, plans generally equivalent to those available in the employer-paid market are widely available in the voluntary market as well, so far as qualifying or elimination periods, benefit replacement rates, maximum benefit durations, and other core plan features are concerned. Less liberal benefit plans are more common in the worksite benefits arena. Voluntary and worksite disability programs combined became a top-selling product, yielding $1.1 billion sales in 2008.[15]

15. Eastbridge Consulting Group, Inc., *2008 Worksite Marketing Industry Snapshot and Competitor Profiles*, p. 7.

Elements in Plan Design

Some of the elements to consider in designing a group LTD plan are group size, age of individuals, preexisting conditions, gender, and occupation.

Group Size

Many LTD carriers require at least 10 participants in a group plan. Individual underwriting applies to smaller groups. In general, individuals and extremely large groups tend to produce the highest claim incidence. In the case of groups with 5,000 or more participants, higher incidence is attributable to a lower level of employer contact and control, as well as to the types of work typically performed in our economy in enterprises of that size. By contrast, on the individual and small-groups end of the spectrum, small numbers and anti-selection play the larger role in the incidence picture.

Age

Age of a group is the key factor in determining rate. However, it is discriminatory under the Age Discrimination in Employment Act (ADEA) to use age to determine eligibility for the group. Some employers prefer offering disability benefits based on years of service. This is not a discriminatory practice, because all employees have access to the plan once they have been employed for the predetermined amount of time.

Table 13-5 illustrates the relationship between age and disability incidence. On average, younger workers, in addition to experiencing fewer disability events, have higher motivation for both rehabilitation and retraining.

The rule on discrimination issues generally is that all employees within an eligible class must be included in the plan. In voluntary or contributory plans, all employees in the eligible class must be invited to participate in the plan.

Under the ADEA, benefit programs can define benefit periods without discriminating against the older employee. The contract can specify the maximum number of months of income replacement for older employees. The key issue is that this benefit period must provide cost-equivalent benefits when compared with benefits for younger workers. Because the claim incidence and disability duration of younger employees is lower on average than those of older employees, the maximum benefit duration of the younger employees can be longer in years than the maximum benefit duration of employees who are older when first disabled.

The ADEA also specifies that employees age 70 or older must receive a minimum of 12 months of disability benefits.

TABLE 13-5

Group Long-Term Disability Insurance Rate of Disablement in Men and Women per 1,000 Lives Exposed (Calendar Years of Experience 1976–1980)

Six-Month Elimination Period	Male Experience	Female Experience
Under 40	1.02	1.39
40–44	2.02	3.04
45–49	3.56	4.52
50–54	6.33	7.41
55–59	12.20	10.88
60–64	16.63	12.98
All ages	3.78	3.40
Three-Month Elimination Period	**Male Experience**	**Female Experience**
Under 40	1.70	2.83
40–44	3.41	4.84
45–49	5.75	7.67
50–54	8.35	9.50
55–59	15.41	13.30
60–64	21.26	17.63
All ages	4.85	5.24

Source: Transactions of the Society of Actuaries, 1982 Reports on Mortality and Morbidity Experiences, 1985, p. 279.

Preexisting Conditions

Preexisting-condition exclusion clauses are used in LTD contracts to minimize the risk of anti-selection. Here is a typical example of how they may work. If a person insured under a policy with such a clause becomes disabled in his or her first year of coverage, the claim adjudicator is allowed to investigate the issue of whether, during the three months before the claimant's coverage commenced, he or she received medical care, treatment, or took prescribed medication for a condition that caused or is related to the condition for which he or she now claims disability. If it is found that he or she did have a relevant preexisting condition, then his or her claim will be denied. Some policies may provide an exception if it can be shown that he or she went three or more months without such care, treatment, or medication, between the time he or she was treated before becoming insured and the time his or her disability commenced. The general idea is the same as the adage from the property and casualty area—that a person whose barn is already burning should not be able to purchase fire insurance and expect to recover benefits.

Preexisting conditions are normally not used as part of STD plans, because the total insured exposure is relatively low, there is a marketplace expectation that claimants should not be forced to make dramatic financial rearrangements in cases of short-term absence from work, and preexisting claim investigations take time to conclude while benefits are expected to commence rapidly. But these clauses are almost always a standard for LTD plans, given the increased exposure. As a result, an employee could be eligible for benefits under the STD plan and later be denied benefits because his or her condition existed prior to the effective LTD contract date. When STD benefits are offered on a voluntary basis, preexisting condition language may apply to the short-term period as well.

Gender

As Table 13-5 indicates, women have a higher incidence of disability than men at younger ages, but a lower incidence at older ages. The primary, though not the only, reason is that pregnancy is, by law, treated as any other "illness," and it is a condition common among younger females rather than older. This can increase disability incidence in some groups with a high percentage of young female employees.

Occupation

Claim frequency will vary from one occupation to the next. Some of these differences are obvious. Blue-collar workers, for example, face more physical hazards on the job. Other occupational connections with incidence are more complex. An economic downturn in a particular type of business or major changes in the job environment of professional groups will increase disability incidence.

The existence of workers' compensation insurance also does not eliminate the impact of occupational hazards on disability plans. Medical leave or STD is needed in some states before workers' compensation is available. LTD benefits are paid when workers' compensation is not adequate to reach the targeted income replacement rate.

Hourly paid workers and lower-paid workers historically have been declined or heavily rated in LTD plans. This is related to the likelihood of over-insurance. The percentage of hourly paid or lower-paid jobs and the type of work done will often determine whether a group is insurable. Seasonal work, such as agriculture and construction, is generally more tightly underwritten as well. In businesses with high employee turnover, service requirements are often imposed so that temporary employees with less demonstrated commitment to the business do not qualify for coverage, as they would represent a greater than average risk.

Other Plan Design Considerations

Along with fundamental plan features such as the eligibility requirements for coverage, the benefit rate, maximum benefit duration, and elimination or qualifying period (which functions like a "deductible," being the period at the beginning of a disability for which benefits are not available), a few other issues merit mention. Defining the covered earnings can be important, especially for more complicated situations such as those involving business owners or partners in a professional firm, or individuals with a substantial variable component to their compensation in the form of bonuses or commissions. The plan sponsor or insurance carrier usually tries to balance the goal of adequate income protection against the goal of avoiding the moral hazard associated with over-insurance, in the latter case generally by some smoothing formula.

Another major consideration is the net benefit calculation. As mentioned, private group disability insurance is intended to supplement other forms of income protection available, while avoiding over-insurance. So the vast majority of plans involve some form of offset formula, whereby the targeted income replacement rate is achieved by the combination of various types of income obtained by the claimant. A variety of calculation approaches have been developed in order to enable employers to pick from different price points, depending, among other things, on their approach to offsets.

Finally, we should mention briefly the wide variety of benefit riders that have been developed to address specific additional needs or wants. Three of the more common such riders are (1) cost-of-living adjustments, so that benefits over time keep up with inflation; (2) pension supplement benefits, so that the funding of retirement needs can continue even during an extended period of disability; and (3) additional benefits available when the claimant meets a more severe test based on restrictions to activities of daily living, intended to fund the additional financial burdens associated with such severe disabilities. Constraints on employers' willingness to pay higher total compensation costs have set limits on the extent to which these or other features have been adopted, but they are available for those who recognize the need.

Funding

Risk is the primary concern in designing a disability-income benefits plan. LTD is a catastrophic coverage. Employers must take great care in considering whether to fully self-insure this kind of risk. A fully insured or partially insured plan is often the best course. The following are among the considerations for employers:

- *Size of the employee group.* The relatively higher predictability of experience in a large group is important in evaluating the risk of any self-insured or partially self-insured plan. Employers with fewer than 10,000 covered employees are usually urged to insure their LTD plan, while for STD, the cutoff may be 500 covered lives.
- *Structure of the plan.* Employers should look to structure a plan that makes their exposure more predictable, for example, in LTD, self-insuring only the first two years of a claim.
- *Stop-loss insurance.* Stop-loss insurance is a sound option for employers that need special design components. For example, stop-loss insurance can be applied to one or a small number of highly paid employees with very high maximum benefits.

Limiting Exposure

No employer should self-insure any part of its LTD risk without carefully evaluating and limiting its maximum benefit exposure on any given individual. The impact of accounting standards on self-funded plans must also be assessed. In 1993, new accounting standards (Financial Accounting Standard No. 112) required employers to switch from a pay-as-you-go accounting to an accrual method for liabilities associated with self-funded disability benefits, COBRA plans, life insurance, severance pay, salary continuation plans, and workers' compensation.

Other changes also have given employers more incentive to seek out greater claims management expertise. The contractual and legal concept of disability is becoming more complex. New causes of disability, social trends, and the evolution of health care delivery are affecting the success of claims management. LTD insurance carriers and large third-party administrators have the most developed expertise in claims management and are more aware of changes in the medical, social, and economic environment.

Employers face less risk in self-insuring STD, and most employers do self-insure sick leave. However, these also are areas of potential savings for employers that partner with insurance carriers. STD and sickness benefits have become recognized as high-payback targets for disability management programs and can produce cost savings.

The claims management expertise of insurers should be allocated to those disability risks where recovery or rehabilitation has a direct impact on the insurer's profit levels. It is distinctly in the insurer's best interest to fully manage any front-end self-insured portion of these risks. Recoveries within this window create the insurer's desired experience results for the catastrophic insured portion of the claim duration; that is, claim payments in excess of that two-year limit are the liability of the insurer. The insurer's full expertise and resources, including rehabilitation resources, should come to bear as early as feasible and within any self-funded period.

Related plan design issues are also important to weigh in the insure-versus-self-insure evaluation. Insurance carriers with a specialty in disability understand issues of eligibility and nondiscrimination, among other considerations. Often this expertise is not available from other sources or is costly to create within the employer's organization.

Disability Management

Disability management is an important consideration in disability benefits plan design. Disability management encompasses the range of activities that prevent disabilities from occurring or minimize the impact of disabilities on employers and employees. These initiatives can include wellness programs, employee assistance plans, medical clinics focused on minimizing disability, employee safety programs, claims management activities, and return-to-work programs.

The direct and indirect costs of disability were 9.0 percent of payroll in 2010.[16] This includes incidental absence benefits (2 percent), indirect costs for replacement labor and loss of productivity (4 percent), STD and LTD benefits (1 percent), and related indirect costs (2 percent). The disability cost area in which employers see some of the greatest impact and opportunities for better management is that of indirect costs.

16. Denise Fleury and Rich Fuerstenberg, "Managing Disability Absences in the Era of Health Care Reform," Mercer Consulting, 2011, p. 1.

Employers are finding that effective disability management programs reduce total cost. Among the most effective interventions, according to employers, are return-to-work programs, prevention and behavioral health programs, and case management.[17] The best disability management programs begin before a disability occurs. The foundation is a comprehensive, well-integrated disability plan design. In addition, a cost analysis specific to each business is useful to reveal the areas with the most potential savings. The ability of the insurance carrier to help the employer analyze and understand cost impact across the full range of benefits and programs that touch on disability has become increasingly important. The best plan designs integrate information across this spectrum to help improve outcomes. Once a claim does occur, early intervention, rehabilitation, case management resources, and long-term follow-through are critical. Specialized knowledge of the impairment from both a medical and vocational perspective is highly valuable in managing complex claims.

Given the high cost and complexity of disability today, quality disability management efforts have taken on greater importance. Employers with well-coordinated disability management programs can save up to 1 percent or more of payroll.

SUMMARY

A significant likelihood of disability exists for the working population, and the loss of income has a devastating impact. A number of public income sources are provided for the disabled, but these programs do not cover all employees or all types of disabilities. As a result, private-sector insurance coverage is needed on both a short- and a long-term basis to provide adequate and reliable protection. Such private programs usually integrate with the public programs before remitting the additional income support to the covered individual.

Self-insurance of the long-term disability exposure is not a normal solution for employers because of the catastrophic and volatile nature of the coverage. The lowest costs are achieved through appropriate plan design that includes disability management programs.

17. Ibid.

PART THREE

Life Insurance Benefits

Traditionally, most employers have provided some form of group life insurance benefits for their employees. Of course, as is the case with all employee benefits, life insurance plans must be designed to meet both the objectives of an employer and the needs of its employees. As will become clear, even this very popular and relatively inexpensive benefit has fallen prey to the need employers have increasingly faced since the mid-1990s to cut costs in order to remain competitive.

Part Three begins with a discussion in Chapter 14 of some of the most important considerations involved in the design of a life insurance benefit plan and an overview of the most popular method of providing life insurance benefits—group term life insurance. Also briefly included in this chapter are permanent forms of group life insurance and their uses in employee benefit planning. This is followed with a discussion in Chapter 15 of business uses of life insurance in programs to deliver other employee benefits, for example, to executives and retirees, and in supporting business continuation.

CHAPTER 14

Group Life Insurance

William H. Rabel

Jerry S. Rosenbloom

Death benefits are a nearly universal employee benefit in the United States. Almost all employers, except perhaps the smallest of companies, provide death benefits for their employees as an integral part of their employee benefit programs. They also are made available through public-sector programs such as Social Security and workers' compensation. Among the forms of death benefits provided through the employee benefit mechanism are the following:

- Group term life insurance
- Group dependent life insurance
- Group accidental death and dismemberment (AD&D) insurance
- Group travel accident insurance
- Joint and survivor annuity benefits under retirement plans
- Preretirement annuity benefits
- Supplemental/optional life insurance for employees and dependents

---

The authors would like to thank Graham Cox of the Group Life Department of MetLife for his review of this chapter and his very helpful comments and suggestions.

In the past, the following benefits were also offered, but while a few plans may remain in effect, there is no evidence that any are sold as true group today:

- Group paid-up life insurance
- Group permanent life insurance
- Group universal life insurance
- Group survivor income benefit insurance

However, although group permanent and group universal life are no longer sold as true group, they are sold as supplemental or voluntary plans and benefit from the efficiencies of group administration such as payroll deduction.

The emphasis in this chapter is on group term life insurance—the most common means of providing death benefits as an employee benefit. This chapter and Chapter 15 also review some of the permanent forms of group life insurance. While such plans are rarely, if ever, offered in the United States today—primarily because of their tax treatment—they will be covered briefly in this chapter because some remain in effect, and they provide an example of how the group mechanism might be used in the absence of unfavorable tax consequences. Furthermore, as will become evident in the following pages, the features of group life insurance now offered are significantly different from those offered as recently as a decade ago.

Other chapters in the *Handbook* cover the forms of death benefits specific to their topic areas.

Traditionally, group life insurance has covered employees against death during their working years. The protection usually provided is one-year renewable group term life insurance, with an average rate applied to the entire population, with no cash surrender value or paid-up insurance benefits. Normally, in the past coverage was limited to the employee, although some plans allowed dependents to buy a smaller amount of coverage. To an increasing extent, especially when compared with plans in the 20th century, life insurance is also provided and offered on an optional basis to dependents of employees. Amounts now available are relatively large, especially when compared with the $1,000 or $2,000 typically offered in the past. Today, it is not unusual for dependents to have an option to purchase $50,000 and more. Some employee benefit plans may also continue a reduced amount of death benefits on retired employees, although the practice has declined substantially during the past two decades. Survivor income benefit insurance (SIBI) plans are another form of group life that is rarely, if ever, offered today, although some may remain in existence. These plans differ from traditional employer-sponsored death benefit plans in that a benefit is payable only to certain specified surviving dependents of the employee and only in installments. Additionally, survivor benefits to spouses are mandated under certain conditions by the Employee Retirement Income Security Act of 1974 (ERISA). The Retirement Equity Act of 1984 (REA) also provides for a preretirement survivor annuity under pension plans for surviving spouses of vested employees who die in active service and who were not yet eligible for early retirement.

GROUP MECHANISM

While it is beyond the scope of this chapter to fully discuss the intricacies of the group mechanism, it is helpful to develop some basics in order to understand when the mechanism can be used. Five essential features of group insurance should be understood.

First, unlike with individual insurance, in which the risk associated with each life is appraised, group insurance makes use of group selection whereby an entire group can be insured without medical examination or other evidence of individual insurability. For many years, state regulation and prudent practice mandated stringent underwriting rules concerning such things as the minimum number of individuals in a group and the minimum proportion to be insured. However, over the years, these rules have been relaxed somewhat as a result of competitive pressure, reinsurance, and decades of experience with the group underwriting process. Today, even a certain amount of voluntary coverage, such as that offered to dependents, may be issued without any, or at least somewhat limited, individual underwriting of the insured. (Supplemental insurance that involves some individual underwriting is also offered, but is not true group insurance. This topic is covered in Chapter 15.)

A second feature of group insurance is that premiums on a plan, at least for larger groups, are often subject to experience rating. The larger the group, the greater the degree to which its cost of insurance reflects its own loss experience. Experience rating can either be on a prospective or a retrospective basis. Normally, if experience has been favorable, an experience credit (sometimes called a dividend) may be paid at the end of the year to adjust the renewal premium for the next year (prospective basis), Credits may be applied to the current year's original premium (retrospective basis), but today retrospective rating is rare.

A third feature of the group mechanism calls for economies of administration. The plan is administered by an insurance company, an employer, a union, or some other agency positioned to obtain administrative efficiencies through payroll deductions or other centralized functions, or both. In the past, economies of administration and the group underwriting concept were almost always associated with the employer paying at least some of the premium for the employee's coverage. This is no longer true. Today, some plans are written on an employee-pay-all basis. This being the case, employees now have the option of opting out of coverage or choosing the amount of coverage they want, opening the plan up to the possibility of adverse selection caused by the younger, and healthier, employees opting out and leaving the older and potentially less healthy employees in the plan. The pricing of group insurance today must reflect these changing practices.

Group insurance makes use of a fourth feature—a master contract—containing all conditions concerning the coverage. Insured individuals receive a group certificate as proof that they are covered, which shows the coverages provided, and the amounts of the coverage, plan features, and the like. The insured employees receive a summary plan description (SPD) booklet describing the plan in relatively easy-to-read language.

The existence of a master contract indicates a fifth feature—that the plan may last long beyond the lifetime (or participation in the group) of any one individual, although any group life contract can generally be cancelled by the employer or plan sponsor, or by the insurance carrier.

GROUP LIFE INSURANCE

Group life insurance is an extremely important employee benefit plan. At the end of 2008, group life insurance in the United States totaled $8.7 trillion of protection and represented 46 percent of all life insurance policies in force.[1]

Benefits

Group term life insurance benefit amounts should be based on a plan designed to avoid or at least minimize possible adverse selection either by the employees or by the employer. Factors to consider in the selection of a benefit schedule include (1) the employees' needs, (2) the overall cost of the plan, (3) the nondiscrimination requirements of the law, and (4) the employees' ability to pay if the plan is contributory.

The interrelationship of these four factors has resulted in the development of group term life insurance benefit schedules that are related to (1)

1. *Life Insurers Fact Book 2009*, Washington, DC: American Council of Life Insurance, 2009, p. 15.

earnings (typically limited to a maximum amount), (2) occupation or position, or (3) a flat benefit amount for everyone covered. In the past, earnings-based benefit schedules often clustered employees into salary groups for ease of administration. Today, however, the use of computerized benefit administration systems makes it possible for benefits to be a direct multiple of an employee's salary, usually rounded to the nearest hundred dollars. Benefit schedules that are a combination of these types of benefits schedules have also been used in the past, but today the practice is rare.[2]

Financing

Any employee benefit program, including group term life insurance, may be financed on either a noncontributory basis (where the employer pays the total amount for the insurance) or a contributory basis (where the employees share the cost with the employer or, in some plans, may pay the entire cost). Furthermore, as described elsewhere in this book, favorable experience can result in dividends to the employer and, for contributory plans, employees. As a result of revenue rulings beginning in 1971, contributions to the employer's account may not subsidize the employee's account, or vice versa. In other words, each account must stand on its own. Furthermore, favorable experience credits (dividends) must be allocated to the account from which they originate, whether it is the employer's or the employee's account. If discovered, any cross-subsidization in a plan that contravenes the Internal Revenue Code can lead to severe penalties.

A number of advantages are claimed for each approach—the following for noncontributory plans:[3]

- *All employees are insured.* All eligible employees who have completed the probationary period and are actively at work have coverage. Thus, the plan has maximum participation and minimizes adverse selection.
- *Tax advantages.* Under conditions described later in this chapter, employer premium costs are deductible as an ordinary business expense for federal income tax purposes, whereas employee contributions under a contributory plan are not deductible unless they are under an Internal Revenue Code (IRC) Section 125

2. See Davis W. Gregg, "Fundamental Characteristics of Group Insurance," in *Life and Health Insurance Handbook*, 3rd ed., eds. Davis W. Gregg and Vane B. Lucas, Burr Ridge, IL: Richard D. Irwin, 1973, pp. 357–358.
3. Ibid., pp. 358–360.

flexible benefit plan, but then only up to a maximum total of $50,000 of life insurance. Because of this restriction, and the fact that many group life plan benefits exceed $50,000, group life plans are rarely offered in a Section 125 plan. (See Chapter 25.)

- *Simplicity of administration.* Records for individual employees are easier to maintain than under contributory plans, primarily because no payroll-deduction procedures are involved.
- *Economy of installation.* Because all employees are covered, it is not necessary to solicit individual employees to join the plan.
- *Greater control of plan.* The employer may have more control over changes in benefits under noncontributory plans because, in the absence of collective bargaining, unilateral action may be more feasible when employees are not sharing in the cost of the plan.

The following advantages are claimed by contributory plans:[4]

- *Larger benefits.* Possibly more liberal benefits or higher benefit amounts are possible if both employers and employees contribute.
- *Better use of employer's contributions.* Provided enough individuals participate to meet the nondiscrimination requirements, a contributory plan may allow the employer to provide more coverage to the employees with the greatest needs. Employees who elect not to contribute, and hence who are not covered, tend to be young single individuals who may have few life insurance needs and among whom employee turnover also may be high. In such a case, a contributory plan allows employer funds to be used most effectively by sharing the cost of benefits for the employees who have greater needs for life insurance and who are also most likely to be long-service employees.
- *Employees may have more control.* The contributory plan may afford employees a greater voice in the selection of their own benefits, because they are paying part of the cost, and, within certain limits, may be able to design the coverage to meet their own needs.
- *Greater employee interest.* Employees may have a greater interest in plans in which they are making a contribution.

4. Ibid.

Important Group Term Life Insurance Provisions

Some important group term life insurance provisions are beneficiary designation, settlement options, assignment, and conversion privilege.

Beneficiary Designation

Under group term life insurance, an employee may name and change his or her beneficiary as desired.[5] The only restriction is that the insurance must benefit someone other than the employer. If, at the death of the employee, no beneficiary is named, or if a beneficiary is named but does not survive the employee, the proceeds may be payable at the insurer's option to any one or more of the following surviving relatives of the employee: spouse, mother, father, child or children, or the executor or administrator of the estate of the deceased employee. If any beneficiary is a minor or otherwise incapable of giving a valid release, the insurer is able to pay the proceeds under a "facility of payment" clause, subject to certain limits.

Settlement Options

The covered employee or the beneficiary may elect to receive the face amount of the group term life insurance on an installment basis, rather than in a lump sum. The installments are paid according to tables listed in the group master policy. An insurer generally offers optional modes of settlement based on life contingencies. But the basis is seldom mentioned or guaranteed in the contract and is governed by insurance company practices at the time of death.[6] Depending on the state law governing the contract, insurers may pay interest on funds held between the date of death and the date the claim is paid as a lump sum or converted into a life annuiy or installment settlement option.

Assignment

Group term life insurance generally may be assigned if permitted by both the master policy and state law. The right to assign group life insurance is important as a means for an employee to remove the group life insurance proceeds from his or her gross estate for federal estate-tax purposes. A properly executed absolute assignment conveys all incidents of ownership

5. See William G. Williams, "Group Life Insurance," in *Life and Health Insurance Handbook*, 3rd ed., eds. Davis W. Gregg and Vane B. Lucas (Burr Ridge, IL: Richard D. Irwin, 1973), pp. 373–377
6. Ibid., p. 376.

in group term life insurance to another person or to an irrevocable insurance trust. This is an important estate-planning technique for some employees whose estates are potentially subject to federal estate taxation.

Conversion Privilege

An employee may convert group term insurance to an individual permanent life insurance policy if the employee's coverage ceases due to termination of employment, termination of membership in a classification(s) eligible for coverage, or retirement. The employee must apply to the insurer in writing within 30 days of termination and pay the premium for his or her attained age, type of insurance, and class of risk involved (if applicable); however, medical evidence of insurability is not necessary. Under most state laws, employers must notify employees of their conversion rights within 30 days after they take effect.

A more restricted conversion privilege may be provided for an employee if the group master policy is terminated or amended so as to terminate the insurance in force on the employee's particular classification. Generally, in this scenario, the employee may not convert more than $2,000 of coverage. The reason for such a limitation is to avoid the situation where an employer purchases group life insurance and quickly terminates the plan to allow those who are individually uninsurable to obtain, by conversion, large amounts of individual life coverage.

Thirty-One-Day Continuation of Protection

This provision gives a terminated employee an additional 31 days of protection while evaluating the conversion privilege or awaiting coverage under the group life insurance plan of a new employer.

Continuation of Insurance

The employer can elect to continue the employee's group term life insurance in force for a limited period, such as three months (or even longer, if negotiated with the carrier, or as part of a leave of absence (LOA) program), on a basis that precludes adverse selection during temporary interruptions of continuous, active, full-time employment. Upon expiration of the continuation period, premium payments are discontinued, and the employee's insurance is terminated, and then subject to the conversion or portability features of the contract. However, in this event, the insurance, as well as the right to exercise the conversion privilege, is still extended for 31 days after termination of the insurance.

Some states (e.g., Minnesota) have a state-required COBRA-type option for the continuation of group life insurance rather than for medical insurance.

Waiver of Premium Provision

Because employees may become disabled, approximately 93 percent of group life insurance policies generally contain a waiver-of-premium provision. Under a typical waiver-of-premium provision, the life insurance remains in force if (1) the employee is under a specified age, such as 60 or 65, at the date of commencement of total disability; (2) total disability commences while the person is covered; (3) total disability is continuous until the date of death; and (4) proof of total and continuous disability is presented at least once every 12 months.[7]

The waiver-of-premium provision is one of several types of disability benefit provisions used for group life plans. The second, disability income, accounts for less than 1 percent of plans. A third type, the extended death benefit, is found in almost 5 percent of contracts. It pays group life insurance death claims incurred within one year after termination of employment. It requires that the employee be continuously and totally disabled from the date of termination of employment until death occurs.

Accelerated Benefits

Some plans provide for the payment of all or part of the death benefit if a patient can prove that he or she has a terminal illness that is typically expected to result in death within 12 months and can be and is certified by a physician. These so-called accelerated benefits have become increasingly popular where permitted by law, and barriers to the practice have decreased as third-party organizations have emerged to purchase the rights to life insurance benefits covering the terminally ill.

Dependent Coverage

Dependent group life insurance may be offered as part of the basic group term life insurance plan, as optional additional coverage, or as both. The growth of dependent group life insurance has been relatively slow until recent years, partly because of the taxation of amounts greater than $2,000 and partly because only limited amounts were offered on a true group basis. When provided, a typical schedule of benefits might have given the dependent spouse life insurance equal to 50 percent of the employee's coverage but not more than $2,000. Typical benefits for dependent children were often graded from $100 between the child's age of 14 days to six months up to, for example, $1,000 or $1,500 between ages 5 and 19 years. Today, much larger

7. Ibid., pp. 374–375.

amounts of coverage are offered under true group plans that are fully paid for by the employee. The death benefit is normally payable automatically in one lump sum to the insured employee or, in the event of the prior death of the employee, either to the employee's estate or, at the option of the insurer, to one of certain specified classes of order-of-preference beneficiaries.

Post-Retirement Coverage for Employees

Upon retirement, a former employee's group term life insurance would normally be discontinued, and the high cost of conversion at the retiree's advanced age usually makes use of the conversion privilege impractical.[8] Therefore, some employers continue to provide reduced amounts of group term life insurance on retired employees under various types of reduction formulas. One formula reduces the insurance by 50 percent at retirement. Another uses a graded percentage system, decreasing the amount of coverage each year after retirement age until a certain minimum benefit is reached; for example, 10 percent per year until 50 percent of the amount in force immediately prior to retirement is attained. Still other employers provide a flat dollar amount, such as $15,000 or $20,000, at retirement. Taxation of post-retirement benefits is the same as that for active employees. Because continuing group life insurance on retired lives is costly, employers may consider funding coverage for retired employees through some other means, such as group paid-up, or a separate "side fund."

Active Employees After Age 40

Coverage requirements for active employees after age 40 are strongly influenced by the Age Discrimination in Employment Act of 1967 (ADEA), as amended in 1978 and in 1987. The latest amendment eliminated the age-70 ceiling on active employment and any ambiguity was clarified by the Older Workers Benefit Protection Act in 1990. Essentially, employees aged 40 and above are considered a "protected group." Benefits may be "cut back or reduced," but individual plans must be actuarially analyzed to determine cost-justified reductions.

Under a "benefit by benefit" cost comparison, an employer may reduce the amount of coverage for older workers provided that the actuarial cost of providing the coverage is at least the same as that for younger workers. The analysis compares consecutive age bands of five years or less. A reduction in benefits is permissible if the actual cost of providing a lesser

8. Jerry S. Rosenbloom and G. Victor Hallman, *Employee Benefit Planning*, 3rd ed., (Englewood Cliffs, NJ: Prentice Hall 1991), pp. 48–49.

benefit to the workers in the upper age band is the same as the cost of providing a greater benefit to the workers in the lower age band. For example, the level of coverage for workers aged 65 to 69 may be less than that for workers aged 60 to 64 if the costs are equal.

Within that general framework, the guidelines allow cost-justified reductions that permit an employer to (1) reduce an employee's life insurance coverage each year starting at age 65 by 8 to 9 percent of the declining balance of the life insurance benefit or (2) make a one-time reduction in life insurance benefits at age 65 of from 35 to 40 percent and maintain that reduced amount in force until retirement. The 8-to-9 percent annual reduction is justified by mortality statistics showing, for example, that the probability of death increases by that amount each year for the age 60-to-70 group. The one-time 35-to-40 percent reduction is justified by the difference in mortality expected, for example, by employees in the age 65-to-69 bracket, compared with the mortality expected in the age-60-to-64 bracket. An employer also may be able to cost justify greater reductions in group term life insurance benefits on the basis of its own demonstrably higher cost experience in providing group term life insurance to its employees over a representative period of years.

The ADEA also permits use of a "benefit package" approach for making cost comparisons for certain benefits that offers greater flexibility than a benefit-by-benefit analysis as long as the overall result is of no lesser cost to the employer and is no less favorable in terms of the overall benefits provided to employees.

Advantages and Disadvantages of Group Term Life Insurance

In summary, employers and employees are interested in evaluating the relative advantages and limitations of group term life insurance as an employee benefit.[9]

Advantages to the Employer

From the employer's perspective, the following might be considered advantages of including a well-designed group term life insurance program as one of its employee benefits:

- Employee morale and productivity may be enhanced by offering this element of financial security.

9. Ibid., pp. 377–378.

- The coverage is necessary for competitive reasons, since most employers offer this form of protection.
- The life insurance protection is an aid to attaining good public and employer–employee relations.
- When employees are adequately covered, employers no longer have the moral obligation connected to having employees who work long hours at the cost of neglecting their personal protection planning.

Advantages to Employees

Group term life insurance dovetails into an employee's financial security planning in the following ways:

- It adds a layer of low-cost protection to personal savings, individual life insurance, and Social Security benefits.
- It helps reduce anxieties about the consequences of the employee's possible premature death.
- If the plan does not favor key employees, the employer's contributions are not reportable as taxable income to the insured employee for federal income-tax purposes unless the total amount of group insurance from all sources exceeds $50,000. If so, then the employee is only taxed on the value of amounts in excess of $50,000, as determined by a table in the Internal Revenue Code, less any after-tax contributions the employee made to the plan. However, if the plan discriminates in favor of key employees, the actual cost of all coverage (or the amount of its value as determined in the code, whichever is greater) will be taxable to the key employee. In other words, the key employee loses the $50,000 worth of tax-free life insurance, and may end up paying a higher rate on amounts in excess of $50,000. However, even if the plan is discriminatory, "rank-and-file" employees will not suffer adverse tax consequences. A group term life insurance plan may be considered to discriminate in favor of key employees with respect to eligibility unless (1) the plan benefits at least 70 percent of all employees, (2) at least 85 percent of the participants are not key employees, (3) the plan is part of a cafeteria-type plan, or (4) the plan complies with a reasonable classification system found by the Internal Revenue Service (IRS) to be nondiscriminatory. In applying these IRS rules, part-time and seasonal workers as well as those with fewer than three years of service do not have to be

considered. Employees covered by a collective bargaining agreement by which group term life insurance has been bargained for may also be excluded. Special rules apply to groups of fewer than 10 employees. The plan may be considered to discriminate in favor of key employees if benefits available to them are not available to all participants. Coverage levels based on a uniform multiple of salary are not discriminatory.

- If employees are contributing toward the cost, their contributions are automatically withheld from their paychecks, making payment convenient and also reducing the possibility of lapse of insurance.
- The conversion privilege enables terminated employees to convert their group term life insurance to individual permanent policies without having to provide individual evidence of insurability, but at a very high cost.
- Liberal underwriting standards provide coverage for those who might be uninsurable or only able to get insurance at otherwise substandard rates.

Disadvantages

Despite its many advantages, group term life insurance has some disadvantages. First, the employee usually has no assurance or guarantee that the employer will continue the group policy in force from one year to the next. Group life insurance plans are seldom discontinued, but business failures can and do occur, and the conversion privilege upon termination of a group life policy may be of limited value to the employees because of the high cost of conversion on an attained-age basis.

Another limitation exists when employees change employers, because group term life insurance is not often "portable" as term insurance, although that option is becoming more popular. Only about one out of every 100 departing employees uses the conversion privilege. However, most employees changing jobs expect to be insured for the same or a higher amount of group life insurance with their new employers. Group term life insurance provides "protection only," while employee needs, at least partially, may dictate some other form of life insurance for a long-term need or one that has a savings or cash value feature. Also, with salary-related plans, coverage may be lowest when it is most needed (e.g., for a young employee with dependents). The next section looks at some permanent forms of group life insurance.

PERMANENT FORMS OF GROUP LIFE INSURANCE

Given the expense of providing retired employees with group term life insurance, it is not surprising that permanent forms of group life have engendered some degree of interest over the years. After all, even though most retired workers do not have dependent children, many of them have dependents, most often spouses, and some have problems of estate liquidity. Furthermore, a lifetime of work may not be sufficient to provide the legacy hoped for by many retirees, and their financial goals are made particularly elusive by the high level of inflation that has plagued most countries since World War II. Therefore, the thought of obtaining permanent insurance through the relatively low-cost group mechanism has a certain amount of appeal.

Several forms of group permanent life insurance have been developed over the years, almost exclusively in forms that attempt to take advantage of government policies providing favorable tax treatment to group term life insurance. Among those to be briefly examined here are group paid-up insurance and various forms of continuous premium coverage, including level-premium group, supplemental group, and group ordinary life insurance. However, *it is important to note that only a relatively insignificant amount of group permanent remains in effect*, because of (1) potential adverse tax consequences, and (2) the advent of employee-pay-all supplemental policies that have many advantages of the group mechanism, such as payroll deduction.

GROUP PAID-UP LIFE INSURANCE

Group paid-up life insurance was first written in 1941. Although today it is largely superseded by other types of plans, it is nevertheless useful to understand how it works in order to understand the development and current status of tax laws on group insurance, which are a driving force in plan design.

Group paid-up life insurance allows all or part of an employee's scheduled group coverage to be written so that it will be fully paid up when the employee retires. During his or her working life, the employee makes a regular contribution that is used to purchase paid-up increments of whole life insurance. Each purchase increases the total amount of paid-up insurance owned.

For tax reasons, discussed in the next section, employers do not purchase permanent insurance for their employees under this plan. Rather, they supplement the employees' purchases of permanent insurance with decreasing amounts of term insurance. After each contribution, the amount of term insurance decreases by exactly the amount by which the paid-up insurance increases. Thus, the combined amount of both types of insurance remains constant at the amount set by the benefits schedule.

Contributions

Employee contributions are generally designed to be level throughout the employee's working life. Naturally, because of actuarial considerations, the amount purchased with each contribution decreases as the employee gets older. Furthermore, costs are higher for individuals who enter the plan at older ages, because they have fewer years in which to accumulate paid-up coverage. Therefore, in theory, a schedule of contributions should be graded for age of entry into the plan and anticipated length of service, and this was the normal practice when these types of plans were offered.

Plan Provisions

As is normal for group insurance, benefits are determined by a schedule. In general, the provisions found in group term contracts apply to the term portion of the paid-up plan as well. These include conversion and disability (such as waiver-of-premium) benefits.

Coverage is not automatically surrendered if the master contract terminates. Paid-up coverage remains intact as long as employment is not terminated and for life unless it is surrendered. Term coverage is convertible under the same rules as under a group term plan.

Premium Rates and Experience Rating

Group term policy owners (usually an employer) normally receive a dividend or "experience credit" each year if plan experience has been favorable. As a result of revenue rulings beginning in 1971, the term account may not subsidize the permanent account, or vice versa. In other words, each account must stand on its own. Thus, favorable experience credits must be allocated to the account from which they originate, whether it is the term or the paid-up account. Favorable experience may be passed on to the paid-up account in the form of a dividend to insureds or as reduced rates for future purchases.

All normal or customary practices in experience rating are subject to change under the pressure of competition. When competition is intense, insurers may expand their tendency to pool the underwriting experience of different coverages or even different lines (e.g., group term and group permanent, or group life and group health). Pooling may lead to changes in the experience-rating practices.

Uses of Group Paid-Up Insurance

Group paid-up, to the extent that it is offered today, appeals primarily to firms with fewer than 500 employees. Then or now, it is generally underwritten only for those employers that provide stable employment, because strikes and layoffs interrupt employee contributions and therefore interfere with the accumulation of paid-up coverage. Therefore, such events should be most unusual for the industry in which the policy owner operates. Furthermore, the firm may be required to have been in business for a minimum period (e.g., three years).

Turnover should be very low for the employer. To a degree, the turnover problem can be controlled by a long probationary period, but the underwriting rules of some carriers exclude employers that have an annual turnover rate in excess of 5 percent. In addition, some establish minimum-age requirements for participation (e.g., ages 30 to 35).

Advantages of Group Paid-Up Life Insurance

Adherents of group paid-up life insurance claim it provides several advantages to employers or employees, or both. First and foremost, as contrasted with group term, it does provide permanent protection. Related to this is the advantage of cash-value accumulations by the insured that can be made available when employment terminates. Both these features are related to a third, which is that group paid-up provides a scientific way to fund post-retirement coverage over the working life of the employee.

Fourth, group paid-up plans facilitate the conversion by long-service employees of any term coverage remaining at age 65, because it is usually a relatively small proportion of the scheduled amount and because converted coverage is purchased at net rates. For these two reasons, retirees may end up being able to afford even more permanent coverage than they had anticipated.

A fifth advantage to group paid-up is that employers electing to continue all or part of the coverage on retirees find the scheduled amount of term reduced well below the amount needed in the absence of paid-up insurance. This smaller financial burden may be easier for a business to justify.

A sixth advantage, when group paid-up is compared with other forms of permanent group coverage (discussed later), is that the status of these plans is well established with the IRS. They are a known commodity, and no serious modification of existing plans has been required by tax rulings to date. Therefore, it is highly unlikely that they will be subject to unfavorable rulings in the future. Another important tax factor is that the employer-purchased term coverage receives the favorable tax treatment accorded to all group term coverage.[10]

The group paid-up system provides still other advantages. Being contributory, the plan encourages participation only by those who need insurance. At the same time, in contrast to group term plans, employees may be more willing to contribute to the cost of group paid-up because they can see a permanent benefit growing out of their premiums.[11]

It is worth noting that insurers may be willing to offer higher limits on group plans containing permanent coverage than on term alone. The amount at risk for each individual continually diminishes throughout his or her working life. Furthermore, margins in interest earnings on reserves may support a more liberal benefit schedule.

Disadvantages of Group Paid-Up Life Insurance

Among the greatest disadvantages of group paid-up insurance is that the type of employer that can use it is limited, as previously explained. Another drawback is the relatively high cost of administering the plan, when compared with term insurance, because more professional advice is needed in designing, installing, and operating it. Furthermore, changes in benefits, eligibility status, and the like often require more record changes than would be required for term. A third disadvantage is that employer costs are higher in the early years of the plan than they would be for group term. Thus, the employer may delay the plan until it can be afforded. The high cost in the early years is caused by start-up costs. In some cases, the employer may decide not to purchase a term plan to provide temporary protection, with the result that there is no protection at all.

Finally, the principal advantage of group paid-up is also its principal weakness. Employee contributions purchase permanent coverage, and, therefore, afford less current protection for each premium dollar.

---

10. For a thorough discussion of this topic, see William H. Rabel and Charles E. Hughes, "Taxation of Group Life Insurance," *Journal of Accounting, Auditing, and Finance*, Vol. 1, No. 2, p. 177.
11. For a discussion of the advantages of contributory group life plans, see Robert Batten et al., *Group Life and Health Insurance*, Atlanta, GA: Life Office Management Association, 1979, p. 42.

LEVEL-PREMIUM GROUP PERMANENT LIFE INSURANCE

In exploring various approaches to providing post-retirement coverage through the group mechanism, it was only a matter of time before someone suggested taking standard, level-premium, whole-life insurance and writing it on a group basis. The idea was to have the employer pay all or part of the premium and to have the employee pay any amount not paid by the employer. However, before this approach could develop much of a following, the Treasury Department quashed it for all practical purposes in a 1950 tax ruling (Mimeograph 6477). The ruling required employees to include as current taxable income any employer contribution toward the cost of permanent insurance, unless the insurance is nonvested and forfeitable in the case employment is terminated. As a result of this ruling, the use of traditional level-premium group life insurance has been limited principally to supplemental group life plans. A prominent form of supplemental life, group universal (sometimes called GUL) is discussed in Chapter 15.

Group Ordinary Life Insurance

In the mid-1960s, a new type of permanent coverage was introduced; it purported to allow employers to contribute to permanent policies because of some newly introduced standards in the tax law. Over the years, these products have varied widely in design, but are known collectively as "group ordinary" or "Section 79" plans.

In concept, group ordinary allows employees to elect to take all or a part of their term insurance as permanent coverage. In effect, the contract is divided into protection and savings elements. Employer contributions are used to pay only for the term insurance component of the permanent contract, while employee contributions are credited to cash values. The plan can be limited-payment (e.g., life paid up at 65) or ordinary whole-life. Had plans been limited to this simple design, the taxation of group life insurance would be less complex than it is today.

However, inherent in the group ordinary concept is the fact that premium contributions will vary from year to year, as the amount at risk under the policy and the insured group's death rate vary. This variability of premium limited the attractiveness of the product, and companies began to seek ways of smoothing or leveling the premium. Of course, such designs fly in the face of the tax rules providing that payments can be used to purchase term insurance only; premium leveling by its very nature creates a reserve. Furthermore, the IRS suspected that some products were so designed that employers were paying more than their fair share of expenses under the contract. (This practice had been common under group paid-up, and was never brought into question until the IRS began to scrutinize group ordinary.) As a result, during the 1960s and 1970s, a tug of war developed in which the IRS would write regulations and carriers would try to design plans that would comply while still being attractive in the marketplace. The final result is that today all group permanent insurance issued must meet stringent, complex rules that ensure that (1) employer contributions are not used to purchase permanent insurance and (2) employee-owned benefits are self-supporting. A few group ordinary plans remain in force under these circumstances, but the coverage is not widely marketed.

RETIRED-LIVES RESERVE

Another approach used to fund life insurance benefits for retired employees is a retired-lives reserve plan. A retired-lives reserve arrangement can be set up as a separate account through a life insurance company or through a trust arrangement for providing group term life insurance for retired employees. Such an approach provides for the funding of retiree life insurance over the employees' active employment period.

Retired-lives reserve plans were once a popular mechanism for providing life insurance for retired employees, because of very favorable tax implications for the employer. Restrictions imposed by the Deficit Reduction Act of 1984 (DEFRA) have limited the previous favorable tax aspects of retired-lives reserve plans for both employers and employees, and such plans have decreased in importance.

ACCIDENTAL DEATH AND DISMEMBERMENT INSURANCE

In addition to providing group term life insurance, employers typically also provide accidental death and dismemberment insurance (AD&D). The AD&D benefit is usually the same multiple of the amount of group term life insurance provided to the employee under the plan's benefit formula. AD&D insurance is payable only if the employee's death is a result of accident. Percentages of the AD&D coverage amount are payable in the event of certain dismemberments enumerated in the contract or employee booklet.

SUPPLEMENTAL GROUP LIFE INSURANCE

In the past few years, interest has been kindled in an employee-pay-all approach to providing permanent insurance, which has some features of both group and individual insurance. Sometimes called supplemental insurance, sometimes payroll deduction, it may be provided under a master policy, with a certificate being issued to each employee. Group universal life is also in this category. Alternatively, individual policies are sometimes issued when the coverage is written. Premiums are paid through payroll deduction and do not receive favored tax treatment. Depending on competitive factors, number of employees insured, and amounts available, coverage may be purchased with minimal individual underwriting. Since the employee owns the coverage, it goes with him or her if employment is terminated.

Supplemental group life insurance appears to be giving way to "mass-marketed" or "wholesale" life insurance. This approach involves the issue of individual insurance through the endorsement (and sometimes the administrative support) of a third party. It seems likely that much of this coverage would have been sold as supplemental group if the mass-marketed coverage were not available.

GROUP CARVE-OUT PLANS

While supplemental coverage may be purchased above and beyond group term benefits, another approach provides that all or part of a group term benefit may be "carved out" and permanent insurance substituted. Typically, amounts in excess of $50,000 are carved out. While premiums are paid with dollars that are taxable to the employee, the actual cost for the employee typically may be favorable when contrasted with imputed income (based on government Tables 1 rates) for term insurance of an amount equal to the carve out. Thus, an overall advantage is created for the employee. Various forms of permanent coverage can be used, depending on employee objectives, funding levels, and the like.

GROUP UNIVERSAL LIFE (GUL) PLANS

Interest in supplemental protection was substantially increased through the addition of group universal life (GUL) in the mid-1980s. GUL is a permanent form of insurance. Like individual universal life, it has two separate parts: (1) pure term protection and (2) an accumulation fund. The employee contributes periodically to the fund, which is credited with interest at a competitive short-term rate. Each month, the carrier deducts the cost of pure term protection for the amount at risk under the policy and the cost of administering the policy. The insured may elect to increase the face amount of the policy, provided that certain requirements are met. Like other insurance products, reserves accumulate on a tax-deferred basis and are tax-free if paid as a death benefit.

CHAPTER 15

Business Uses of Life Insurance

Susan Conant

Chapter 14 has covered the use of yearly renewable term life insurance on a group basis in a qualified employee benefit plan. Businesses have numerous further uses for life insurance. Generally, these fall into two broad categories: delivering other employee benefits and supporting business continuation.

In delivering other employee benefits, life insurance can be used in the context of supplemental or voluntary benefits offered to the entire employee population, retiree life insurance benefits, and executive benefits. Life insurance used in supplemental, voluntary or executive benefits may be group life insurance, individual life insurance, or something in between: worksite or workplace life insurance.

Life insurance can provide funds to ensure that a partnership or small proprietorship continues upon the death of an owner, partner, or other key person through the use of buy-sell agreements and key person insurance. Figure 15-1 illustrates these business uses of life insurance.

LIFE INSURANCE BENEFITS FOR EMPLOYEES

Frequently, employer-provided employee benefits packages include group life insurance, including forms of universal life insurance and ancillary

FIGURE 15-1

Topics in Business Uses of Life Insurance

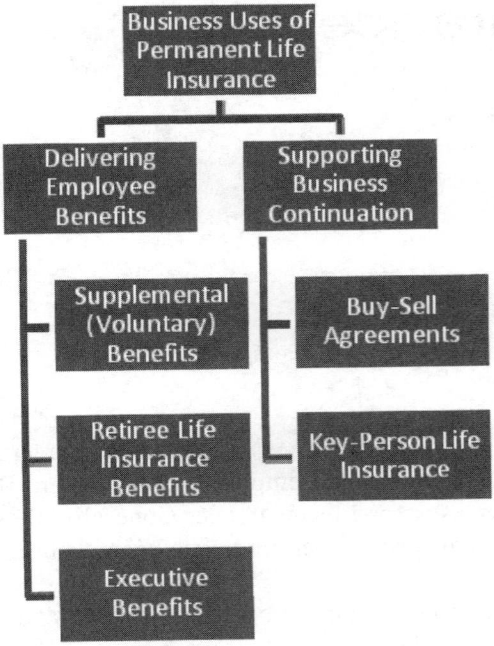

benefits such as dependent life insurance and accelerated death benefits. However, some employers offer permanent life insurance to employee groups on a supplemental or voluntary basis. Appendix 15.1 presents an overview of permanent life insurance plans and features. Permanent life insurance sold on a supplemental basis can be structured as group insurance, individual insurance, or worksite insurance.

In this section, first we discuss supplemental life insurance benefits, offered either on a group basis or on a worksite basis. Next, we discuss life insurance for retirees. Then, we discuss uses of life insurance for supporting executive benefits, through mechanisms including corporate-owned life insurance, bank-owned life insurance, and split-dollar life insurance arrangements. Finally, we consider formal financial evaluations of permanent life insurance, as these may be relevant for decisions concerning large executive life insurance policies.

Supplemental or Voluntary Life Insurance Benefits

Most employer group plans today provide a basic true group term life insurance benefit on a noncontributory basis, typically in an amount equal to salary. Under a true group plan, this term life coverage is not individually underwritten. Often, within the same plan, the employee is able to elect optional additional amounts of term life insurance coverage paid for through payroll deduction. This additional insurance is also true group insurance and is not individually underwritten. The true group plan may also offer dependent group term life insurance either as part of the basic group plan or as optional additional coverage.

When the covered employee changes employers and leaves the group, this additional optional group term life insurance does not necessarily end. When an employee who leaves the group chooses to continue the insurance, it is not converted. Rather, the certificate of insurance is rolled into a trust administered by the life insurance company and the provisions and conditions of the original plan prevail.

A contrasting supplemental life insurance offering through the employer is known as workplace or worksite insurance. These life insurance products are chosen by the employer for the workplace and are offered to employees for purchase through payroll deduction. The employer does not contribute to the premiums. The employee owns the coverage, which continues with the employee upon termination of employment.

Underwriting for worksite life insurance policies mixes features typically associated with group and individual insurance plans. Depending on competitive factors and the amounts offered, coverage may require minimal individual underwriting, guaranteed issue, or simplified underwriting. Typically, under worksite coverage, life insurance must be incidental to the purpose of the group; the employer selects the insurance company and the plans offered, the employee pays the premium through payroll deduction and mass billing, the insurance company issues individual policies, underwriting is approached individually on simplified or guaranteed issue principles, the type of insurance is long-term level premium term or permanent life insurance, and the coverage may be portable. The features of group and worksite insurance are illustrated in Table 15-1.

Accelerated Death Benefits

Many policies permit a purchaser to add a type of accelerated death benefit, often at an extra premium. An accelerated death benefit, also known as

TABLE 15-1

Worksite and Group Life Insurance Features

Worksite Life Insurance Features	Group Features
Insurance must be incidental to the group	✓
Employer selects the coverage	✓
Employee pays the premium	✓
Payroll deduction and mass billing	✓
Individual policies	
Individual underwriting on simplified or guaranteed issue principles	
Coverage does not automatically end with employment	
Long-term level-premium term or permanent life insurance	

a living benefit, provides that a policyowner-insured may elect to receive all or part of the policy's death benefit before death if certain conditions, called insured events, are met.[1] A statement by an attending physician establishes evidence of the required insured event.

The accelerated death benefit is usually paid in a lump sum. After the death of the policyowner-insured, the beneficiary may still be eligible to claim a death benefit. The payment of an accelerated death benefit reduces the later death benefit paid to the beneficiary at the insured's death by the amount of the living benefit paid earlier to the policyowner-insured.

The amount of an accelerated death benefit payment depends on the wording of the benefit provision. Three types of accelerated death benefits are the terminal illness benefit, the dread disease benefit, and the long-term care benefit.

- *Terminal illness benefit.* Under a terminal illness (TI) benefit, the insurance company pays a portion of the policy's death benefit to a policyowner-insured who suffers from a terminal illness and has a physician-certified life expectancy of 12 months or less. Typically, when a policyowner-insured elects to exercise the TI benefit, the insurer assesses an administrative charge to pay for the election.

1. Harriett E. Jones, *Principles of Insurance: Life, Health, and Annuities*, Third Edition, Atlanta: LOMA (Life Office Management Association, Inc.), 2005, 124–126.

- *Dread disease benefit.* Under a dread disease (DD) benefit, also known as a critical illness benefit, the insurer agrees to pay a portion of the policy's face amount to the policyowner if the insured experiences an insured event. Insured events under this provision usually include life-threatening cancer, acquired immune-deficiency syndrome (AIDS), end-stage renal (kidney) disease, myocardial infarction (heart attack), stroke, and coronary bypass surgery. They sometimes include vital organ transplants and Alzheimer's disease.
- *Long-term care benefit.* Under a long-term care (LTC) benefit, the insurer agrees to pay a monthly benefit if the insured requires constant care for a medical condition under terms specified in the contract.

Dependent Life Insurance Benefits

Under typical group term life insurance, employees are able to add optional life insurance coverage for their dependents—the spouse or second insured only, the spouse and children, or the children only.

Group Carve-Out Plans

All or part of a noncontributory group term benefit may be carved out and a variety of permanent insurance substituted. Typically, the carve out applies to coverage amounts in excess of $50,000. Although premiums are paid with dollars that are taxable to the employee, the employee gains an overall advantage through a carve-out arrangement. The actual cost for the employee typically may be favorable when contrasted with imputed income in tax tables for term insurance of an amount equal to the carve out.

LIFE INSURANCE BENEFITS FOR RETIREES

Retirement renders a retiree ineligible to continue participating in employee life insurance benefits. Although the retiree may be eligible for conversion of group benefits to an individual basis, the cost of conversion may be prohibitive for most retiring individuals. To address a need for affordable post-retirement life insurance, some employers provide small amounts of group term life insurance to retired employees. Continuing group life insurance on retired lives is costly for employers, too. Thus, some companies provide life insurance coverage for retirees through group paid-up life insurance, group ordinary life insurance, or a side fund to pay the premiums at retirement.

A retired lives reserve is a side fund set up as either a separate account through a life insurance company or a trust arrangement. A retired lives reserve funds retiree life insurance over the employees' active employment period. Retired lives reserve plans were once a more popular mechanism when they supported very favorable tax implications for the employer. However, the Deficit Reduction Act of 1984 (DEFRA) limited the favorable tax aspects of retired lives reserve plans, and funding of these plans diminished.

LIFE INSURANCE FOR EXECUTIVES

Individual insurance products are sometimes used under excess benefit plans to provide employee benefits for company executives and other selected classes of employees. For various reasons, group universal life insurance has enjoyed popularity for executive excess benefits in recent years, and is discussed at length in Appendix 15.2.

Permanent life insurance coverage for executive employees may be structured so that the employer fully or partially owns the insurance policy, under either corporate-owned life insurance or split-dollar life insurance.

Under corporate-owned life insurance (COLI), the corporation is full owner and sole beneficiary of the insurance policy on the life of an employee. Under COLI, the cash value accumulation and death benefit are intended to provide funding for other employee benefits. Under a split-dollar arrangement, the corporation and the executive split the ownership and beneficial interest in an individual life insurance policy. They also share paying premiums. The split of ownership can generally be handled in one of two ways: Either the employer can own the policy and create the executive's interest by endorsement, or the employee can own the policy and collaterally assign a portion of the proceeds to the employer.[2]

Corporate-Owned Life Insurance

The purchase of COLI is separate and distinct from the employer's executive compensation plan or agreement to provide benefits for the executive. For example, the executive compensation agreement might provide for ERISA-excess benefits; the restoration of other benefits lost because of the tax law, deferred compensation, or other supplemental retirement or death benefits; or both. Regardless, the employer's promise of other benefits generally has no legal link to the COLI policy value.

2. Another arrangement, often called sole-owner split dollar, may be used in some cases. Here, all ownership rights are held by a third-party owner and there is a separate agreement between the owner and the employer.

With COLI, the employer is both owner and beneficiary of permanent life insurance covering the lives of participating executives. Because the employer owns the policy, the arrangement does not provide benefit security for the executive. The insurance amount is usually related to the benefits projected to be payable on the basis of current pay, or sometimes in amounts that anticipate some future pay increases.

Upon death of a covered executive, the employer collects the policy proceeds and may pay a death benefit to the executive's beneficiary. To obtain full benefit of the arrangement, the corporation should keep the policy in force until the covered executive dies. Thus, most COLI programs continue insurance on the lives of retired or otherwise inactive executives. Any benefit payable to a living executive is paid from employer assets, with the employer recovering the funds through policy loans or, later, from insurance proceeds when that executive dies.

COLI and Tax Treatment of an Employer

The employer is subject to the following federal tax treatment of COLI and certain executive benefits:

- COLI premiums paid by the employer are not tax-deductible to the employer. However, payments made by the employer to the executive or beneficiary under a separate benefit plan are generally tax-deductible by the employer.
- The employer generally receives COLI policy death proceeds free of income tax, although death proceeds may be considered in determining whether a company must pay the corporate alternative minimum tax.[3]
- The inside buildup of COLI policy cash values is not currently taxable to the corporation, although such values may be considered in determining whether the employer must pay the corporate alternative minimum tax.[3]
- If the employer surrenders the COLI policy before it matures as a death claim, any excess of the gross cash surrender value (without regard to any outstanding policy loans) over the premiums

3. It may be noted, however, that pursuant to the Tax Reform Act of 1997 the corporate alternative minimum tax (AMT) no longer applies to "small business corporations" for tax years beginning after 1997. "Small business corporations" generally are those whose initial average gross receipts do not exceed $5 million and thereafter do not exceed $7.5 million. Thus, for these smaller corporations, the corporate AMT is not a factor.

paid will be considered a taxable gain. The tax deductibility of interest paid or accrued on loans with respect to COLI is complicated.[4] The general rule is that no income tax deduction is allowed for any interest paid or accrued on any indebtedness with respect to one or more life insurance policies owned by a taxpayer covering the life of any individual, with the following exceptions:

1. Interest paid or accrued on indebtedness with respect to policies on the lives of key persons (officers or 20-percent-or-more owners of the employer) is exempted, but only up to $50,000.[5] Interest within this exception is deductible, but deductibility is subject to an interest rate cap that is based on Moody's Corporate Bond Yield Average-Monthly Average Corporates for each month.
2. In addition, the portion of a taxpayer's total interest expense (from whatever source) that is allocable to unborrowed policy cash values is not tax-deductible.[6] However, an important exception to this rule applies for policies covering one individual who is a 20 percent or more owner, an officer, a director, or an employee of a trade or business entity.
3. Transition rules apply for certain policies purchased before the inception of these rules.[7]

COLI and Tax Treatment of an Employee

For the insured employee and beneficiaries, federal tax treatment of COLI, along with certain separate executive benefits, is as follows:

- The value of the death benefit protection provided under the COLI plan does not create imputed income each year for the insured employee.
- Payments received by the executive under a separate benefit plan are taxable income to him or her.

---

4. See, in general, IRC Section 264.
5. The number of such "key persons" for any taxpayer may not exceed the larger of (1) five individuals, or (2) the lesser of 5 percent of all officers and employees of the taxpayer or 20 individuals.
6. This portion is the same ratio as the taxpayer's average unborrowed policy cash values bears to the sum of (1) the average unborrowed cash values, and (2) the average adjusted income tax bases of the taxpayer's other assets.
7. For example, different rules apply under the general rule and the pro rata rule, noted above, for policies issued prior to June 9, 1997.

- Payments received by the executive's beneficiary under the separate benefit plan are taxable income to the beneficiary as income in respect of a decedent (IRD) and generally are includable in the employee's gross estate for estate tax purposes.
- As an IRD distribution, the death benefit may qualify for the marital deduction if paid to a spouse. In large estates, this rule may serve only to defer estate taxation, because the benefit may remain in the spouse's estate and be taxed on his or her subsequent death.
- An income tax deduction by the beneficiary for any estate tax attributable to the IRD distribution can mitigate, but not eliminate, the combined effect of federal income and estate taxes.
- State income and estate or inheritance taxes vary. In most states, however, tax treatment will be consistent with that of federal tax law.

Other Arrangements Comparable to COLI

COLI is not the only arrangement in which an organization owns life insurance on an individual. Organizations have a variety of business uses for ownership of life insurance on individuals. Forms of ownership in this category include charity-owned life insurance, church-owned life insurance, foundation-owned life insurance, and trust-owned life insurance. One use is to secure a debt, whether the insured's debt is to the employer, to a bank (bank-owned life insurance, BOLI), or to a trust (trust-owned life insurance, TOLI). Another use is to leave the policy proceeds as a charitable donation. For this purpose, life insurance may be owned by a charitable organization or a trust.

Finally, some insureds engage in a viatical settlement in which they sell their rights to their policy's death benefit to investors in an arrangement sometimes called stranger-owned life insurance (STOLI).

Split-Dollar Life Insurance Arrangements

Split-dollar arrangements are funding approaches using permanent life insurance. Many such plans are intended to fund employee benefits. For split-dollar plans as part of a benefit program, the employer usually purchases permanent life insurance on the life of an executive. Premiums may be paid entirely by the employer or they can be split between the employer and executive. Any death benefit is split between the employer and the executive's beneficiary.

The Sarbanes-Oxley Act, in 2002, prohibited publicly traded companies from making loans to their executives. New split-dollar plans have been scarce since 2003. In this environment, new split-dollar arrangements are used mainly for providing retirement benefits to executives of businesses that have tax-exempt status. Even this application of split-dollar plans faces pitfalls in the IRS code.

Many pre-2003 split-dollar plans remain. The two general types of split-dollar life insurance arrangements are endorsement split dollar and collateral assignment split dollar.

- *Endorsement split-dollar.* In endorsement split-dollar, the employer is the owner, beneficiary and normally the premium payor of a permanent policy on the executive's life. The endorsement provides that, in the event of the insured executive's death, the death proceeds are divided (split) between the employer (to recover the premium costs) and the beneficiary named by the executive in the agreement. In effect, the executive receives pure insurance protection for his or her share of the policy death benefit.
- *Collateral assignment split-dollar.* Under collateral assignment split-dollar, the policyowner is either the executive, or an irrevocable trust established by the executive. The employer normally pays the premiums. The executive, as policyowner, executes a collateral assignment of the policy cash values and death benefit to the employer to secure the repayment of the employer's outlays if the executive dies or surrenders the policy. Sometimes, the collateral assignment involves less than the policy's full cash value—such as when, after a certain policy duration, the cash value may be less than the premiums paid. In these situations, the arrangement is called *equity split-dollar.*

IRS regulations issued in 2003 dealing with split-dollar plans provided two approaches for the income taxation of split-dollar plans: the economic benefit approach and the split-dollar loan regime.

- The economic benefit approach generally applies under endorsement split-dollar, when the employer, in the role of premium payor, owns the policy and the insured executive has imputed gross income for the economic value (economic benefit) of the pure insurance protection.

- The split-dollar loan regime generally applies where the insured, a trust, or another third party (not the employer) owns the policy. Here the employer's premium payments are treated as loans to the policyowner, and the loans must carry adequate interest or interest will be imputed to them under the below-market loan rules.

Consideration of Life Insurance Proposals for Executive Benefits

COLI and split-dollar arrangements warrant careful scrutiny and analysis. A financial analysis of these arrangements should take into consideration employer objectives, ERISA compliance, long-term financial returns, tax treatment, time period expected for the program, interest rates, mortality rates, and expenses.

Employer Objectives

An employer contemplating the purchase of executive life insurance must set the objectives of the plan exactly. After the employer has set its objectives, the employer is in a solid position to evaluate an insurance proposal. For example, suppose the employer's primary objective is to prefund supplemental executive retirement benefits. The amount of life insurance required to generate sufficient cash values might far exceed the employer's targeted amount of death benefits. Other funding arrangements—such as a rabbi trust, secular trust, or stock-based supplemental executive retirement plan (SERP)—might be more efficient for this objective.

Insurance proposals typically project financial results that reflect current tax law. Any future changes in tax treatment could adversely impact projected results of financial analyses.

ERISA Compliance

Executive retirement plans generally fall within Title I of the Employee Retirement Income Security Act (ERISA), and must comply with all requirements of Title I unless they are both (1) unfunded and (2) limited to a select group of management or highly compensated employees. However, pure excess benefit plans for benefits lost by reason of IRC Section 415 are generally exempt from Title I requirements.

Implications of Long-Term Financial Projections

COLI and split-dollar arrangements produce maximum financial advantages only in the long term, when policies mature as death claims. Sales proposals for these arrangements often rely on long-term financial projections to illustrate future financial results. Such long-term projections should avoid the following oversimplifications:

- Wrongly assuming that interest rates will remain level for the entire period
- Wrongly assuming that actual deaths in the employee group will follow the pattern of the insurer's mortality table used in the proposal
- Wrongly assuming that the employer will maintain the same tax profile for a period of many years

Interest-Rate Movements

The interest rate typically used in an insurance proposal is a flat-level total rate of return comprising the guaranteed interest rate and excess (nonguaranteed) interest. Interest rates actually fluctuate, and thus projected results under an insurance proposal should be analyzed with several different interest-rate assumptions. Assumed interest rates should take into consideration the insurer's investment performance for prior years, the insurer's history of excess interest rates actually credited, and anticipated turns in the business cycle over a long period.

Mortality Rates

Insurance sales proposals usually project the payout of tax-free life insurance proceeds based on the insurer's expected mortality rates. If an employee group has a lower actual mortality rate than shown in the insurer's mortality table, the employer will collect life insurance proceeds more slowly. If an employee group has a higher actual mortality rate than shown in the insurer's table, the employer will collect life insurance proceeds faster, which would be favorable for COLI projections.

Loss or Deferral of Tax Benefits

Employers cannot know in advance in which year they will receive expected tax benefits from a life insurance arrangement. Competent analysis should assess the implications of losing or deferring tax benefits at various times. Life insurance sales proposals typically assume that the employer will always pay taxes at regular corporate rates. This assumption is untrue in two cases:

1. A corporation may become subject to an alternative minimum tax and then have to include a part of the life insurance proceeds and the inside buildup in determining its corporate income tax.
2. An employer may suffer tax losses and then have to defer tax benefits.

Evaluation of Insurance Providers

After an employer has decided to fund a benefit plan with life insurance, the company's human resources department still has more to consider than simply the rate of return. Important other factors to evaluate are the insurance company's overall stability and quality rating(s), the employer's established relationship with a broker and the quality of service provided by the insurance company and the broker.

Plan Costs for Executive Life Insurance

An executive benefit plan has the same costs as any other employee benefit plan. In general, the cost of a plan ultimately will equal the sum of the benefits actually paid plus the expense of the plan operation. If the plan is funded, this outlay of principal is reduced by any investment income on plan assets. However, if the investment income is less than the company could earn investing the funds elsewhere, funding could create additional costs. If a company can earn a 5 percent after-tax return on retained assets, but plan assets (an insurance policy, a pension fund, and the like) earn only 3 percent, the company should acknowledge an opportunity cost of 2 percent for the choice of investment vehicle.

If an employer buys permanent life insurance for a group of executives and maintains this insurance in force, actual long-run mortality experience will probably not exactly match the estimated mortality rates in the insurer's mortality table. However, if the actual mortality did match estimated mortality, the employer's cost of funding the program would equal the sum of benefits paid and expenses of operation, adjusted for investment considerations.[8] If this formula correctly expresses the long-term cost of an

8. Not surprisingly, the pricing of insurance works the same way from the insurer's viewpoint. The insurer must collect enough money from premiums and investment income to cover its expenses, profit, and the amount of benefits it pays; in other words, the price of insurance is equal to the sum of the claims paid plus expenses and profit, less income received on investments.

executive benefit plan, the benefits paid to the executives or their beneficiaries will be determined by the group's actual mortality experience and the effect of plan provisions on amounts payable.

Executive benefits funded with permanent life insurance have a cost to the employer. When an employer purchases life insurance, the employer assumes an obligation to pay benefits to the executive or his or her estate. The insurance proceeds, over the long term, represent employer assets—partly a return of the premiums and partly the investment return that could have been realized if the employer had otherwise invested the money used to pay premiums.

Example. An employer agrees to pay Executive A the sum of $1,000,000 in exactly one year. In order to have funds on hand to meet this obligation, the employer invests $909,000 in a 12-month certificate of deposit yielding 10 percent annually. At the end of one year, the certificate matures for $1,000,000 and the employer uses this amount to pay Executive A.

This employer incurred a cost of $1,000,000 to provide Executive A with a $1,000,000 benefit even though the employer invested only $909,000 for the certificate and did not have to expend any current income to meet the obligation when it came due. The interest earned during the year that became part of the total payment made to Executive A was the employer's asset. The employer incurred an expense by applying an existing asset, rather than current income, to make the payment.

Financial Analysis of Permanent Life Insurance

A purchase of permanent life insurance can be analyzed with standard approaches to analyzing a proposed investment. Analysis of a proposed purchase of a permanent life insurance policy should take into account the risk levels inherent in alternative investment opportunities and the effective rate of return to be credited to the premium. This rate of return is highly sensitive to the amount of tax leverage generated.

Table 15-2 shows the payments comprising the employer's cash inflows and outflows for a life insurance policy on an employee.

Internal Rate of Return Calculation for Life Insurance

Discounted cash-flow analysis techniques can be used to compute the policyowner's after-tax yield on an insurance product. Here, we describe the

TABLE 15-2

Policyowner's (Employer's) Cash Inflows to and Outflows from a Life Insurance Policy

Cash inflows (Income) to the Policyowner:*	Cash Outflows from the Policyowner:
1. Any annual policy loans.	1. Premiums paid.
2. Interest credits awarded by the insurer.	2. After-tax interest paid on any policy loans.**
3. Any net death benefits received from the insurer. (*Net* death benefits are equal to gross policy death benefits less any policy loans outstanding at date of death.)	3. Any administrative fees.

* Dividends from participating life insurance typically are not considered as cash flow, because they are usually used to purchase additional death benefits, which are included in the total proceeds received at death.
** The deductibility of policy loan interest is severely limited. In general, the deductibility extends only to interest paid or accrued on indebtedness for policies on the lives of key persons—officers, or 20 percent or more owners of the taxpayer—up to $50,000 of indebtedness per key person

internal-rate-of-return calculation.[9] For a life insurance policy, the internal rate of return (IRR) is the percentage rate at which the policy's earnings must be discounted, using present-value techniques, in order to exactly repay the investor's initial investment in the policy. In simpler language, the IRR shows the rate of return that the policyowner can expect to earn on premiums. IRR results can be interpreted using the following basic decision rule:

> For an IRR to be acceptable for the level of risk the investment represents, the estimated IRR must exceed the investor's required rate of return (hurdle rate) for the investment.

For example, if an investor has a required rate of return of 5 percent, the investor will likely accept a new investment that shows an IRR of 6 percent.

The IRR is often used to compare investment alternatives. If an investor can realize a higher rate of return elsewhere, the policies have a cost—the loss of the excess earnings otherwise available. An investor can take

9. Material in this section is adapted from Susan Conant, *Product Design for Life Insurance and Annuities*, Atlanta: LOMA (Life Office Management Association, Inc.), 2001, pp. 113–114. Used with permission. All rights reserved.

into account the relative riskiness of decision alternatives by setting a higher required rate of return for riskier investments and a lower required rate of return for less risky investments. The following example demonstrates the interpretation of IRR results:

Example. Consider Policies A and B in Table 15-3.

Policy A has an estimated IRR of 6 percent. Because the risk associated with the policy's cash flows is low, the investor will proceed with developing the product if the IRR exceeds 5 percent. In other words, the investor's required return for Policy A is 5 percent. Because the estimated IRR of 6 percent exceeds the required return of 5 percent, the investor will proceed with purchasing Policy A.

Policy B is riskier than Policy A. Thus, the investor sets a higher required rate of return of 7 percent for Policy B. Policy B has an estimated IRR of 6 percent. Because this IRR is lower than the hurdle rate set for this policy, the investor will not purchase Policy B.

Finding the internal rate of return requires the following steps:

1. Estimate each year's income and expenses in a manner that reflects their probability of occurrence. For the anticipated income from death benefits, for each year the policy's face amount is multiplied by the appropriate mortality rate—that is, the probability that each insured person will die at the given age.

   Example. Consider a one-year term policy with a death benefit of $100,000 and an insured 35-year-old male for whom the mortality rate is 0.025. The death benefit of $100,000 multiplied by 0.025—the probability of the insured's death—equals $250. Thus, the expected or probable income for that year would be $250. For an insured who is now aged 33, the

TABLE 15-3

Example of IRR Decision Rule

Policy	Estimated IRR		Required IRR	Decision
A	6%	>	5%	Accept
B	6%	<	7%	Reject

insured's age 35 is two years into the future, so the analyst would need to discount the $250 at the appropriate hurdle rate of interest for two years.

2. Find the discounted present value of the net amounts for each future year and use a trial-and-error process to find the highest interest rate for which the current value of the income equals the current value of the outgo.

The following additional considerations affect the financial analysis of life insurance policies: tax implications, termination of the life insurance policy, interest and dividends, and potentially other factors.

Tax Implications

Permanent life insurance can be an effective tax shelter. Investment income under a life insurance policy is said to be tax-deferred because it is taxable only when and if the policy is surrendered. In a surrender transaction, investment earnings—defined as the combination of total increase in cash value (inside buildup) plus any dividends, minus premiums paid—are tax-deferred.

Life insurance death proceeds are income-tax-free, within limits. The tax advantage applies to only part of the death proceeds.

For policies owned by a corporation, both the investment earnings (inside buildup) and the death proceeds will be considered in determining the corporate alternative minimum tax, if applicable. Further tax advantages may accrue if the corporation has taken policy loans. A tax advantage occurs if the after-tax cost of borrowing is less than the interest credited by the insurer. Any tax advantage depends on the corporation's ability to deduct the interest expense.

Example. The following analysis of a $1,000 loan illustrates this effect. If a corporation takes a policy loan at an 8 percent interest rate, the after-tax cost of borrowing—for a 35 percent tax bracket—is 5.2 percent. If the insurer is crediting 7 percent interest to the policy, the difference is 1.8 percent, as shown in Table 15-4.

Termination of a Life Insurance Benefit

Financial analysis of a permanent life insurance program should project the potential after-tax financial results for termination of the program at various future points in time—for example, at the ends of the 5th, 10th,

TABLE 15-4

Example of Policy Loan Tax Advantage

Stated Interest Cost of Borrowing $1,000	7% Guaranteed Interest Plus Excess Interest (Crediting Rate)	5.2% After-Tax Interest Cost of Corporate Borrowing	1.8% Tax Saving
–$80	+$70	$52	+ $18

15th, and 20th years. A permanent life insurance benefit program terminated after only a few years will often produce only minimal returns and possibly even losses, for several reasons, including surrender charges, taxation issues, unrealistic interest assumptions, and other subtleties of analysis:

- Most types of permanent policies impose a surrender charge for a specified number of years—often seven or eight years—after policy issue.
- If the policies are surrendered, any investment gain will be taxable as income.
- Because many permanent life insurance policies are front-loaded to recover acquisition expenses, early year cash values will not reflect significant investment gains.
- Long-term financial projections incorporate assumptions for the collection of tax-free life insurance death proceeds. For as long as the projected rate of deaths exceeds the group's actual rate of deaths, however, the financial projections for life insurance proceeds will not be realized.

Assumed Interest and Dividends

Financial projections for insurance proposals incorporate assumptions about future nonguaranteed payments from the insurer. Proposals should be analyzed under several different interest-rate assumptions. In selecting an array of interest-rate scenarios, the analyst should select an array of worst-case, moderate, and best-case scenarios. The best-case projections might be based on the insurance carrier's historical performance.

Other Factors

An analysis of an insurance proposal should

- Show all costs and cost summaries on an after-tax basis for both the employer and the executive.
- Account for all costs to the executive including direct contributions, taxes, or the time value of any money he or she has advanced.
- Project financial results over the life expectancies of insured individuals.
- Use nonstandard premium rates for executives who are not insurable at standard rates.
- Project alternative financial results that would occur if the employer has tax losses or becomes subject to the alternative minimum tax.
- Assign a risk factor to the insurer's quality rating for claims paying ability.
- Assign risk factors to alternative investment opportunities available within the policy.
- Identify alternative ways of achieving the same financial objectives.

INSURANCE FOR BUSINESS CONTINUATION ARRANGEMENTS

A business continuation insurance plan is an insurance plan designed to enable a business owner (or owners) to provide for the continued operation of the business if the owner or a key person dies. A key person is any person or employee whose continued participation in the business is necessary to the success of the business and whose death would cause the business a significant financial loss.

A large corporation typically has the financial resources to ensure that its business continues beyond the death of any individual, and thus does not have a need to ensure continuation of the business. However, a closely held business—that is, a sole proprietorship, a partnership, or a corporation that is owned by only a few individuals—may need to establish a business continuation insurance plan to ensure that the business will continue in the event of the death of its owner or key employee.

Business continuation insurance plans include those that closely held businesses can use to fund the purchase of a deceased owner's or partner's share in the business and business continuation insurance plans that protect a business against the financial consequences of the death of a key person.

Buy-Sell Agreements

Ideally, the owners of any closely held business should arrange for the continuation of the business after the death of an owner, a partner, or a shareholder. As noted earlier, an individual's estate includes any ownership interest he or she had in a business. Thus, if one of the owners of a closely held business dies, the deceased owner's share of the business becomes part of that owner's estate. For example, when the owner of a sole proprietorship dies, all of his or her assets—including the assets of the business—pass to the owner's estate. All of his or her liabilities—including the liabilities of the business—must be paid by the estate. The executor or administrator of the deceased's estate may be forced to liquidate the business to provide funds to pay these liabilities. Liquidation places the surviving heirs in the position of having to take whatever price they can get for these assets at the time of the sale. The heirs often receive far less than if they had been able to wait for more acceptable offers.

A buy-sell agreement prepared in advance can address the potential problems associated with the untimely death of a business owner. In a buy-sell agreement, one party agrees to purchase the financial interest that a second party has in a business following the second party's death and, in reciprocal fashion, the second party agrees to direct his or her estate to sell the interest in the business to the purchasing party. Parties to a buy-sell agreement often purchase life insurance to fund it.

Although a partnership usually dissolves upon the death of a partner, the surviving partner(s) may create a new business. Partners often enter into a buy-sell agreement that expresses the arrangements for surviving partners to purchase a deceased partner's interest in the partnership. The partners may purchase insurance on the lives of the other partners to fund the buy-sell agreement, or the partnership can purchase insurance on each of the partners' lives. Sometimes, a split-dollar arrangement is used in these cases.

Key Person Insurance

Another form of business continuation insurance is key person life insurance. Key person life insurance—or key employee life insurance—is insurance that a business purchases on the life of a person whose continued participation in the business is necessary to its success and whose death would cause financial loss to the business. A key person could be an owner, a partner, or an employee of the business. When a business purchases key person life insurance, the business owns, pays the premiums on, and is the beneficiary of the insurance policy. If the key person dies, the policy proceeds are paid to the business.

For many businesses, the loss of a key person's expertise and services may seriously affect the firm's earnings. For example, a top salesperson or a person with important business contacts may be responsible for a large portion of the firm's income. The business must also consider the cost of training or finding a replacement for the key person. A business can provide itself with an extra layer of financial security by purchasing an insurance policy on the life of the key person. The policy proceeds can supplement the firm's earnings while it searches for and trains a replacement for the deceased employee.

A company's credit position can become impaired during the adjustment period following the death of a key person. However, the existence of key person insurance typically will forestall any damaging actions on the part of banks, creditors, and suppliers at the difficult time of a key person's death.

APPENDIX 15.1

PERMANENT LIFE INSURANCE PLANS AND FEATURES

Permanent life insurance policies have an owner who exercises all incidents of ownership in the policy. A policyowner has the rights to name a beneficiary, temporarily or permanently assign the policy to another party, take a loan from the cash value of the policy, surrender the policy for cash, exercise other nonforfeiture rights in the policy, select the allocation of premiums to any investment choices, and exercise any dividends connected with the policy. Permanent life insurance policies can pay dividends, if any are declared by the insurance company. Policies eligible for dividends are classified as participating policies, while those not eligible for dividends are nonparticipating.

Individual insurance is underwritten on the basis of individual characteristics and sold to individuals. Group insurance is designed for groups and underwritten on the basis of group characteristics. Some insurance is designed to be sold to individuals at the workplace, and is underwritten on a basis that combines principles of group and individual insurance.

Insurance companies provide a broad array of term and permanent life insurance plans. Term life insurance plans were covered in Chapter 14. Many of the available plans of permanent insurance are defined here. Any plan of permanent life insurance may have uses in business markets.

Whole-life insurance is a plan of cash-value life insurance that provides lifetime insurance coverage at a level premium rate that does not increase as the insured ages, along with a cash-value component that increases over the term of the policy.

Modified whole-life insurance is a type of cash-value life insurance under which the amount of insurance decreases by specific percentages or amounts either when the insured reaches certain stated ages or at the end of stated time periods.

Joint whole-life insurance, also called first-to-die life insurance, is a plan of cash-value life insurance that has the same features and benefits as individual whole-life insurance, except that it insures two lives under the same policy.

Last-survivor life insurance, also called *second-to-die life insurance*, is a type of joint life insurance that pays the policy benefit only after both people insured by the policy have died.

Family life insurance provides cash-value life insurance on a primary insured and also provides term life insurance on the insured's spouse and any children. Insurance companies offer a number of variations on dependent coverage, including the following:

- A spouse and children's benefit is a supplemental benefit offered in increments that usually provide $5,000 of term insurance coverage on the spouse and $1,000 of term insurance coverage on each child. Most insurance plans set a maximum number of increments, called coverage units. The term insurance coverage on each child expires when that child reaches a stated age, typically 21 or 25.
- A children's insurance benefit provides term life insurance coverage on children of an unmarried person.
- A spouse or second-insured benefit, also called an optional insured rider or an additional insured rider, provides term insurance coverage on the life of a second person insured, known as the second insured. The second insured may be the spouse of the insured, another relative, or an unrelated person, such as a business partner of the insured.

Indeterminate-premium life insurance, also known as *nonguaranteed premium life insurance* or a *variable-premium life insurance*, is a type of cash-value life insurance that specifies two premium rates—both a maximum guaranteed premium rate and a lower premium rate. The insurance company charges the lower rate when the policy is issued and guarantees that rate for at least a stated period of time. After the expiration of the stated period, the company periodically sets a new premium rate, which cannot exceed the maximum guaranteed rate.

Interest-sensitive life insurance, also known as *current-assumption life insurance*, is a type of indeterminate premium life insurance that provides that the policy's cash value can be greater than the amount guaranteed in the policy if the company's experience warrants such an increase.

Universal life insurance is a form of cash-value life insurance characterized by flexible premiums, a flexible face amount and death benefit amount, and various specific charges to the policyowner.

Variable life insurance is a form of cash-value life insurance in which premiums are fixed, but the face amount and other values may vary, reflecting the performance of the investment subaccounts selected by the policyowner. Variable life insurance is a type of security, and is subject to securities regulations.

Variable universal life insurance, also known as *universal life II* or *flexible-premium variable life insurance*, combines the premium and death benefit flexibility of universal life insurance with the investment flexibility and risk of variable life insurance. Variable universal life insurance is a type of security, and is subject to securities regulations.

APPENDIX 15.2

UNIVERSAL LIFE INSURANCE PROGRAMS

Interest in supplemental protection was substantially increased through the introduction of universal life (UL). Individual universal life is permanent life insurance and represents a major product line for many life insurers.

GENERAL CHARACTERISTICS OF UL PLANS

UL has the following characteristics:

- UL consists of a life insurance element and a savings element.
- Each premium is applied to pay for the life insurance in the form of a mortality and expense charge; the remainder of each premium is added to the policy's cash value accumulation. For example (see Table A15.2-1), a policyholder might pay a premium of $120 per month. Suppose that $55 exactly covers the mortality and expense charge for the life insurance. Then, the remaining $65 of premium would be added to the policy's cash value.
- For UL policies, the addition to cash value is the UL premium minus the mortality and expense charges. The UL policy's cash value is credited with interest or other earnings to reflect the experience of an investment account operated by the insurer. The specifics of the investment earnings depend upon whether the universal life plan is fixed or variable.
- In fixed UL plans, these cash value accumulations are credited with interest at the current rate declared by the company. This

TABLE A15.2-1

Example of UL Premium Application

UL Premium	Minus	Mortality and Expense Charge	Equals	Addition to Cash Value
$120	–	$55	=	$65

interest accumulates tax-free and, if ultimately paid out as a death benefit, can totally escape income taxation.

- The current interest rate credited to UL cash values under fixed guaranteed accounts changes periodically, to reflect investment experience. The permanent guaranteed minimum interest rate also applies.
- Variable universal life (VUL) differs from fixed UL mainly in one important aspect. In variable universal plans, the savings element offers policyholders a choice of several nonguaranteed investment allocations, such as money market funds, growth funds, bond funds, international funds, and index funds. An insurer may offer 20 or more nonguaranteed investment options. Most of the optional investment accounts under a variable contract offer no investment guarantees and, with these so-called variable subaccounts, the policyholder bears the full investment risk. Thus, a policyholder can experience losses in cash value due to poor investment performance. For this reason, VUL products are registered as securities and the applicable set of policy charges differs from the charges for fixed UL.
- Most VUL products also offer one fixed-rate, guaranteed account that gives policyholders a minimum interest-rate guarantee. This guaranteed account is the equivalent of the sole investment arrangement available under a fixed UL contract rather than a variable UL contract.
- Some UL plans, mostly those underwritten on an individual basis, permit a choice between two death benefit options, the level death benefit and the increasing death benefit.
    - A level death benefit is structured by combining the policy's cash value plus whatever amount of life insurance is required to provide the selected level of benefit. Over time, the policy's cash value is expected to increase. If the cash value does increase, then the amount of life insurance would decrease. For example, suppose that at one point in time an insured has a policy cash value of $200,000. To achieve a total death benefit amount of $600,000, this insured must also have life insurance in the amount of $400,000. After the same policy's cash value rises to $225,000, this insured can achieve the same death benefit of $600,000 by adding a life insurance amount that is decreased to only $375,000, as shown in Table A15.2-2.

TABLE A15.2-2

Example of Level Death Benefit

Year	Level Death Benefit	Equals	Policy Cash Value	Plus	Life Insurance Face Amount
1	$600,000	=	$200,000	+	$400,000
2	$600,000	=	$225,000	+	$375,000

  - An increasing death benefit structure combines a level amount of life insurance plus the policy's cash value. In this structure, the insured policyowner purchases a set amount of life insurance, say $250,000, and then begins to accumulate a policy cash value to supplement the death benefit amount.

- UL policyowners can withdraw or borrow against cash values at any time. Loans may be subject to transaction fees. Withdrawals may be subject to surrender charges and transaction fees, usually about $10 or $20. The interest rate charged for loans exceeds the interest rate being credited to cash values—possibly by 1.5 or 2.0 percent or in some cases even less. Insureds may later make supplemental contributions to replace any amounts withdrawn.
- UL policyowners can use cash values to purchase paid-up life insurance.
- If UL policyowners cease paying premiums and leave the policy in force, mortality charges and administrative expenses (including premium taxes), when due, are automatically withdrawn from the cash values. When no more cash values remain to cover premiums due, the policy automatically terminates.

GROUP UNIVERSAL LIFE PLANS

Many employers install group universal life benefits either in addition to or as a replacement for conventional group life insurance. A group UL plan can supplement or replace an existing group life insurance plan. In addition, a UL plan may have the following applications:

- Funding ERISA-excess and top-hat plans.
- Replacing coverage lost under discriminatory post-retirement life insurance plans.

Most statements about individual UL are true for group UL.

Several of the differences tend to revolve around the employer's need for streamlined administration and the insurer's need to apply group underwriting practices to employee groups. Other differences arise because insurers administer and sell group plans differently from individual coverage.

Group UL provides many of the same opportunities as individual UL, but with a key difference: group UL coverage is similar to the coverage available under an employee benefit plan. Group UL differs from individual UL in the following respects:

- *Separable policy elements.* Under group UL, the purchase of a life insurance policy can be separated from the savings or cash-value element. Thus, employees can buy term insurance alone or in whatever combination of term insurance and savings that best meets both their death benefit and capital-accumulation objectives.
- *Restricted coverage options.* Employees are offered a restricted selection of amounts of term insurance—either a flat amount or a multiple of pay. Some group UL plans provide for coverage to increase automatically in relation to pay. Some group UL plans offer waiver-of-premium coverage, payable in the event of an employee's disability, with the life insurance. Although some group UL plans limit coverage to employee life insurance, other plans include accidental death and dismemberment insurance for the employees and dependent coverage for spouses and children. Typically, children are covered only for term insurance, but spouses may be able to accumulate cash values.
- *Payroll deduction for premium payment and contributions to the cash value.* Employee payments for the plan's mortality and expense charges (term insurance premiums) are automatically withheld from after-tax pay. Pretax premium payments are not permitted. Employees who have elected a savings element authorize an additional amount, above the mortality and expense charges, to be deducted from pay. In theory, these savings contributions could be variable.
- *Guaranteed future group life premium rates.* Generally, the life insurance premium rates are guaranteed for a specified period (e.g., one year, three years, or five years). Higher rates would presumably apply for extended premium rate guarantees.

- *Benefit portability.* Insured employees may be able to continue their coverage after they retire or otherwise terminate employment. Insurers permit such "nonactive" insureds to continue making premium payments directly to the insurance company up to the oldest age in the applicable mortality table (e.g., to age 100).
- *Lower administrative charges.* The insurance carrier's charges for any administrative services typically would be lower for group than for individual UL coverage.
- *Guaranteed issue coverage.* Subject to a maximum limit, group coverage amounts are guaranteed for issue without evidence of insurability. The coverage limits depend upon (1) plan provisions, (2) the size of the participating group, and (3) the insurer's underwriting standards. Insurance of additional individual UL coverage may be subject to individual underwriting.
- *Group underwriting practices.* Group UL is generally underwritten on a group basis, whereas individual UL policies are subject to individual underwriting. The following group underwriting requirements limit adverse selection for group UL:
    - Actively-at-work requirements generally apply to group coverages.
    - A pay-related formula (e.g., one, two, five or more times pay) or some other fixed rule may be applied to determine amounts of group coverage available.
    - Health statements or other evidence of insurability may be required in some situations—for example, if group participation falls below some stated level or for older ages.

Group UL Plan Design

Each group UL plan design typically is highly flexible and involves many of the design and financial issues applicable to other employee benefit plans, such as

- Selecting eligibility requirements.
- Establishing insurance schedules.
- Fixing contribution schedules, obtaining competitive bids and possibly negotiating contract provisions.

Moreover, the plan design must be negotiated with the insurer and must be included in a competitive bidding process. Table 15-1 in the main text of the chapter presents a list of the key issues involved in designing a group UL plan.

Advantages for Employers

- Nonsubsidized group UL plans can replace an existing subsidized flat-rate life insurance plan.
- With voluntary plans, group UL plans are paid for entirely by participating employees.
- The insurance carrier offers support for benefit administration, including enrollments, employee communication, payroll deductions, claims, itemized electronic billing, and electronic bill pay.
- A group UL plan is a low-cost benefit improvement, much like a 401(k) plan without necessarily any employer-matching contribution.
- A group UL plan may relieve pressure on the employer to provide post-retirement life insurance coverage.
- Group UL plans offer important benefits for key employees and highly compensated employees.
- If a former employee continues group UL plan coverage after termination of employment, the employer will not face conversion charges.

Limitations for Employers

- Employees sometimes elect to decrease their 401(k) participation in favor of group UL plan participation. If 401(k) participation were to drop, then the employer's 401(k) plan could fail the actual deferral percentage (ADP) test for nondiscriminatory participation by higher-paid employees.
- Although employers do not administer group UL plans, they may face employee dissatisfaction if servicing problems arise.
- Group UL plans may pose challenges in communicating benefits to employees.

- If a group UL plan attracts only low voluntary participation, employers take on new administrative burdens but gain no offsetting advantages.
- To remain outside of the scope of IRC Section 79, a group UL plan cannot be
    - Included directly in a flexible benefit program.
    - Funded with before-tax employee contributions.
- The employer should learn whether the subsequent mortality experience of former employees will be charged back to the employer group and reflected in future premium levels.
- Laws, regulations, and rulings could change and, for example, bring group UL plans under the scope of Section 79.

Advantages for Employees

- Group UL plan premiums are somewhat flexible in amount and timing, and they can be made through payroll deductions.
- Participation in the plan is voluntary.
- Group UL plans offer important savings opportunities to employees at all pay levels.
- Investment income from group UL plans is tax-deferred or tax-free.
- With group UL plans, employees can consolidate all coverages for themselves and their dependents under one contract.
- Under group UL plans, guaranteed issue amounts are high enough to cover most employee needs.
- Group UL plan cash values offer a source of funds for emergencies. By contrast, withdrawals from qualified defined-contribution plans are typically limited and are usually subject to excise taxes.
- Interest guarantees for fixed group UL plans shield the employees from any risk of investment loss.
- A group UL plan may be more attractive to employees than an employer-sponsored 401(k) plan.
- Employees receive periodic reports on the status of their group UL insurance.

- Upon termination of employment for any reason, the life insurance coverage is portable.
- Group UL insurance allows retirees to continue meaningful amounts of life insurance coverage after retirement.
- Upon retirement, an employee may be able to reduce the face amount of life insurance to a more affordable level for him or her.
- Group UL plans can help to avoid the tax implications of Section 79.

Limitations for Employees

- Surrender charges may apply for early withdrawals or surrenders, and participants might face adverse financial results if coverage is surrendered early.
- The employee usually must fully fund the group UL plan coverage; employers often do not fund it.
- Laws, regulations, and rulings could change and bring group UL plans under the scope of Section 79 or make taxable the investment earnings on cash values.

PART FOUR

Work/Life Benefits

Part Four consists of four chapters dealing with work/life programs and several service-type plans. Chapter 16 reviews traditional time-off benefits and family leave programs that are the basis of all work/life programs. Chapter 17 focuses on two major forces behind most work/life programs: child care and elder care needs. This chapter explores the various approaches that have been developed as employee benefits to help meet the financial needs of employees for these special concerns.

Educational assistance programs, the nature and uses of legal service plans provided through the employer, qualified transportation fringe benefits, and the recent addition of voluntary benefits are covered in Chapter 18. Part Four concludes with Chapter 19, which discusses financial planning as an employee benefit.

CHAPTER 16

Time-Off Benefits and Family and Medical Leave Programs

Serafina Maniaci

Today's technological revolution is enabling companies to reengineer work processes and transform many job duties. Business literature is replete with stories describing the latest innovations in production, distribution, and marketing. Many of these technological advancements are creating unprecedented flexibility in work schedules and allowing work to be done at irregular times and off-site, in many cases from the employee's home. Many work/life programs strive to help employees balance work and home responsibilities by providing flexible working arrangements. Some components of work/life programs are discussed in Chapter 17 of the *Handbook*. This chapter discusses traditional time-off benefits. These are the benefits that employees for years and across a broad spectrum of industries have depended on and continue to depend on to balance basic work and personal commitments. Companies have relied on these types of traditional time-off benefits to manage employee burnout and unscheduled absences and also to reward longer-service employees. The U.S. Chamber of Commerce in its 2007 *Employee Benefits Study* reported that of the 42.7 percent of payroll spent on benefits, 9.8 percent was for time not worked. The Chamber defines time not worked as (1) payments for holidays, (2) paid breaks, etc., (3) sick leave pay, (4) payments for vacations, (5) paid time off, (6) family and medical leave pay, and (7) other payments.

Not included in the Chamber of Commerce category of "payment for time not worked" are payments for short-term disability, sickness or accident insurance, or severance.

This chapter's focus is on

1. Paid leave time
   - *a.* Nonproduction time
   - *b.* Holidays
   - *c.* Sick days
   - *d.* Personal days
   - *e.* Vacation days
2. Paid time-off (PTO) plans
3. Miscellaneous paid leave time
   - *a.* Bereavement leave
   - *b.* Jury duty pay and leave required by law
   - *c.* Military pay and leave required by law
4. Extended leaves of absence
   - *a.* Family and Medical Leave Act (FLMA)
   - *b.* Military leave under FLMA
   - *c.* Sabbatical leave

PAID LEAVE TIME

Paid leave time are nonproduction time, holidays, sick days, personal days, and vacation days.

Nonproduction Time

The payment of nonproduction time such as rest periods and clothes-change time is considered an intrinsic part of labor costs. The federal Fair Labor Standards Act (FLSA) mandates such payments.[1] Specifically FLSA requires payments for

- Break periods shorter than 20 minutes (rest periods and lunch periods are not required under FLSA)

1. The Fair Labor Standards Act (FLSA) was passed in 1938, and its regulations remained largely unchanged until August 2004 when new regulations redefined the "white collar" exemption tests. The statute's basic requirements are payment of the minimum wages, overtime pay for time worked over 40 hours in a work week, restrictions on the employment of children, and record keeping. The Act covers employees who are engaged in the production of goods for interstate and foreign commerce, including those whose work is closely related to or essential to such production.

- Preparation and cleanup before and after shifts
- Travel between job sites
- Downtime or call-in time, where the employee must be readily available for work

There also are state labor laws that regulate whether paid or unpaid rest periods must be provided. State laws also require meal breaks to be provided, but in general they do not require that the meal breaks be paid. Employees who are likely to be paid for meals are blue-collar workers in large private establishments and workers who cannot leave their worksite or are on constant call, such as coal miners, police officers, and firefighters.

Holidays

Although payments for holidays are not mandated by law, they are perceived by employers as an unavoidable component of labor costs, especially for full-time permanent employees. After completing a probationary or introductory period, most employees are eligible to receive paid time off for holidays. Part-time employees and seasonal workers may receive full or prorated pay for holidays. If employers pay for holidays, the six holidays that virtually every company provides paid time for are

1. New Year's Day
2. Memorial Day
3. Independence Day
4. Labor Day
5. Thanksgiving Day
6. Christmas Day

Many employers also pay employees for the day after Thanksgiving. Other paid holidays are provided by some employers. The next most popular days are President's Day and Christmas Eve Day. Also, Martin Luther King, Jr. Day is not universally provided, but the day has gained popularity as an observed paid holiday. Another customary holiday in the public sector is Election Day. In the private sector, Election Day is not a paid holiday unless negotiated in a collective bargaining agreement. However, most states have laws that protect employees' right to time off to vote. Companies also may provide one or two floating holidays (the time may be prorated during the first year of employment) for employees to use at their discretion for personal holidays, such as Good Friday and Martin Luther King, Jr. Day.

A general requirement of holiday pay, particularly for FLSA nonexempt (hourly paid) employees, is that the employee must work the day before and after a holiday. (See Appendix 16.1 for information on the FLSA designation of exempt and nonexempt workers.)

Employees who take an unscheduled day off either before or after a holiday are often denied payment for the holiday if they are unable to provide medical documentation for the absence. Also, nonexempt employees who are required to work on a company-designated holiday are likely to receive a pay differential for that day or compensatory time. Compensatory time is an option only if the nonexempt employee has worked less than 40 hours in the workweek; otherwise, according to FLSA rules, the employee must receive overtime pay. According to the Bureau of Labor Statistics (BLS), the average number of paid holidays provided each year to full-time employees by prite industry is eight; union employees average nine days.[2]

Sick Days

Eligibility for sick days is determined by length of service and, in some cases, employment category. A common variable used for employee differentiation regarding sick time is the FLSA-exempt or nonexempt status. For example, a nonexempt employee may accrue one sick day or a stated number of hours of sick time per one completed month of service, while an exempt (salaried) employee may accrue one-and-one-half days during the same period. In general, the total number of sick days is available immediately for use upon the completion of the accrual period. Some plans may allow employees to use a limited number of sick days to care for immediate family members.

To promote the conservation of sick days, companies may permit employees to accumulate sick days from one year to another up to a maximum amount. A sick-leave program often allows employees to transfer unused, carried-over sick days at a one-to-one or two-to-one exchange rate to a short-term disability (STD) bank for an employee to use in the event of an extended illness or when applicable, during the waiting period before long-term disability benefits begin. BLS data show that 72 percent of

2. "National Compensation Survey: Employee Benefits in the United States, March 2009," *U.S. Department of Labor, U.S. Bureau of Labor Statistics*, September 2009. Table 31, pp. 285–286.

workers at medium and large private establishments (100 or more employees) have access to paid sick leave.[3]

Personal Days

Paid time for personal days grants employees a few extra days off a year without requiring employees to identify the reason for the absence. The availability of personal days is believed to reduce unscheduled absences. With less restrictive advance-notice requirements than those for vacation days, personal days are likely to reduce the incidence of employees calling in sick to attend to a personal matter. For part-time employees and employees in their first year of service, personal leave days are typically prorated. Paid time-off plans, which are discussed later in this chapter, extend this concept of employee discretion in using an allotted number of days as the employee wishes, rather than necessitating that specific types of leave time be used for specific purposes.

Vacation Days

Paid vacation time also is not mandated by law, although there are state labor laws that protect vacation time once it has been accrued. A typical vacation policy grants two weeks of vacation after one year of employment, with days being prorated during the first year of employment. Some companies may have varying accumulation rates, with lower rates for nonexempt employees or nonexecutive staff. The amount of vacation time generally increases with length of service, often capping at four or five weeks after 15 or 20 years of service. BLS data show that full-time participants in private industry receive 10 days after 1 year of service, 14 days after 5 years of service, 17 days after 10 years, and 19 days after 20 years.[4]

A number of employers supplement vacation plans by offering in their flexibile benefit programs the option to buy additional vacation days. Under Internal Revenue Code (IRC) Section 125,[5] employers may allow on a tax-favored basis the option of purchasing (or selling) vacation days. These plans appeal not only to current employees, but also to prospective

3. Ibid., Table 30, pp. 281–282.
4. Ibid., Table 34, pp. 297–298.
5. Recent Section 125 rules consolidated vacation days, sick leave, and personal days into a single category of "paid time off." The ordering rules and restrictions regarding carryovers and forfeitures discussed here continue to apply.

employees who may be reluctant to switch jobs if it means a reduction of one or two weeks of vacation time. In a typical flex vacation plan, an employee can purchase up to five additional vacation days with the cost usually being based on the employee's base salary.[6] When vacation days are purchased under a Section 125 arrangement, the IRC places restrictive conditions on the operation of the plan. The employee must use all of his or her nonelective (core) days before accessing the vacation days purchased, and the law prohibits carryovers of these elective days to a succeeding tax year. However, companies are permitted to reimburse employees for unused days as long as they do it by the end of the employer's tax year or the plan year, whichever is earlier. Some companies that offer the option to buy vacation time also offer their employees the option of selling back the vacation time to the employer. In these plans, the number of days that an employee is eligible to sell, regardless of whether he or she sells them, is subject to Section 125 forfeiture rules. If a week of vacation that could have been sold is not used in the plan year, the week must be cashed out by the end of the plan year—or employer tax year, if earlier—in which the election is made; otherwise, it will be forfeited. Offering the option to buy and sell vacation time in a flexible benefit program enables employees to buy vacation days with flex credits or sell vacation days back for flex credits or cash. Offering a similar program outside of Section 125 on an after-tax basis allows plan participants to avoid the forfeiture penalties required by Section 125.

PAID TIME-OFF PLANS

Paid time-off (PTO) plans have gained in popularity for two reasons. First, these plans are appealing given the diversity in the workforce because they allow employees to use their block of time as they choose. Second, such plans typically reduce administrative record keeping because time need not be tracked for separate purposes. Under a PTO plan, employers bundle most of their paid time-off benefits into one package. A PTO plan consolidates the benefits of floating and personal days, vacation, sick days, and, in some cases, salary continuation programs and holidays into one single plan that provides benefits for scheduled and unscheduled short-term absences. The absences require no specific designation from the employee. The objective of a PTO is to give employees

6. Depending on employer objectives, the price for buying vacation days can be discounted from the base salary price, and for selling vacation days it can be set higher than the base salary price. Also employers can establish a salary cap and exclude highly paid employees from participating in a flex vacation plan.

more control over their work schedule by eliminating the restrictions found in traditional paid time-off policies. Under a PTO plan, in nonemergency cases, employees have the freedom to take a day off to attend to personal matters without worrying about whether their managers will approve the leave. For example, an employee can schedule a day off for the delivery of an appliance without having to designate the day as a vacation day, a personal day, or a floating day. PTO advocates believe that this kind of freedom dissuades employees from calling in sick on the day of the delivery. By reducing unscheduled absences, a PTO plan can curtail work disruptions and reduce labor costs. Unplanned and unscheduled absences are estimated to cost employers 8.7% of payroll according to an online survey of 276 organizations representing all major industry segments, sizes, and regions throughout the U.S.[7]

Other savings may be derived from the implementation of a PTO plan. Employers often reduce the total amount of paid time that they provide,[8] although in some cases the reduction affects only new hires. The combined amount of time off under these converted PTO plans is less than the sum of what was available under the separate policies. The justification for the reduction is that by combining the various categories of time off—especially sick time with vacation time—many employees have access to more paid time under the new PTO plan. Also, under some PTO plans, those employees who have not used all the time available at the end of the plan years may be allowed to carry over or cash-out unused time.

MISCELLANEOUS PAID LEAVE TIME

Miscellaneous paid leave time are bereavement leave, jury duty leave, and military leave.

Bereavement Leave

Bereavement leave is specifically designated for use when a member of the employee's immediate family dies. Employers today are granting bereavement leave in other situations. Companies recognizing the diversity of today's family arrangements have expanded the definition of a family and

7. *Survey on the Total Impact of Employee Absences*. Mercer (2010) on behalf of Kronos Incorporated. http://wwmercer.com/summary.htm/idContent=1383785 (July 2010).
8. An employer implementing a PTO plan should consider state laws governing accrued vacation time.

are granting the leave not just for mothers, fathers, spouses and children, but also for stepparents, domestic partners, in-laws, and ex-spouses.

Jury Duty Pay and Leave Required by Law

Jury duty pay is provided by many employers, with some paying up to a designated number of days and others paying for the entire leave regardless of the number of days the employee serves on a jury. Some companies that do provide some paid jury duty benefits reduce the employee's pay by any fees the employee receives for jury duty service. BLS has no data available on the average number of days employers pay for such a leave, but BLS data do show that 78 percent of full-time employees in private industry receive paid jury duty leave.[9]

As for legislation regulating jury duty leave, the Federal Jury System Improvement Act of 1978 makes it unlawful for an employer to discharge, intimidate, and coerce employees because of their service on jury duty. However, the law does not require employers to pay salaries during jury duty. The law only requires that jury duty be considered an excused leave of absence with no loss of seniority and with benefits continuing to accrue. There are also state laws that govern jury duty leave, but only a few states stipulate that the time off must be with pay.

Military Pay and Leave Required by Law

Military leave is paid time off granted to employees who are members of the National Guard or a reserve component of the United States Armed Forces. Typically, the leave grants time off with pay for annual military duty provided it is obligatory to maintain military status. Any period of time spent on military duty in excess of the maximum time allowed by the leave may be taken as vacation or personal days.

This type of leave obviously is not meant to address nonpeacetime situations. In the event of war, the time off needed by employees who are called to or volunteer for active military duty cannot be accommodated by paid military leave policies. Employees can look to federal law in such situations. Under the provisions of the Uniformed Services Employment and Reemployment Rights Act (USERRA), veterans, reservists, and

---

9. "National Compensation Survey: Employee Benefits in the United Stated, March 2009," U.S. *Department of Labor, U.S. Bureau of Labor Statistics*, September 2009. Table 30, pp. 281–282.

National Guard members participating on active duty or required training must be allowed up to five years of excused absences for military service. This is required as long as, when possible, advance notice is provided to the employer and the employee returns to work in a "timely manner" after completion of his or her tour of duty. The USERRA defines what is considered a timely manner. The applicable time limits are as follows:[10]

- *Less than 31 days of service.* By the beginning of the first regularly scheduled work period after the end of the calendar day of duty plus time required to return home safely and an eight-hour rest period. If this is impossible or unreasonable, then as soon as possible.
- *31 to 180 days of service.* Application for reemployment must be submitted no later than 14 days after completion of a person's service. If this is impossible or unreasonable through no fault of the person, then as soon as possible.
- *181 days or more of service.* Application for reemployment must be submitted no later than 90 days after completion of a person's military service.
- *Service-connected injury or illness.* Reporting or application deadlines are extended for up to two years for persons who are hospitalized or convalescing.

In addition to granting reemployment rights after a military leave, USERRA also provides other rights, which include continuation of medical benefits up to 24 months and the accrual of retirement benefits during a military leave. Lastly, USERRA requires that an individual on a USERRA leave must be provided with those pay and benefits levels available under the company's most generous leave-of-absence policies.

EXTENDED LEAVES OF ABSENCES

Extended leaves of absences are eligible leaves covered under FMLA, military leave covered under FMLA, and sabbatical leave.

10. "Uniformed Services Employment and Reemployment Rights Act, Employment Law Guide," *Department of Labor*; http//:www.dol.gov/compliance/guide/userra.hrm#BasicPro (July 2010).

Family and Medical Leave Act

Signed into law in 1993, the Family and Medical Leave Act (FMLA)[11] allows 12 weeks of unpaid leave within a 12-month period, with job protection and continued health care benefits on the same terms as if the employee had continued to work. Eligible employees are entitled to FMLA for the following reasons:

1. The employee's serious health condition (see Appendix 16.2)
2. The birth and care of the employee's child
3. Placement with the employee of a child for adoption or foster care
4. Care of the employee's spouse, child, or parent with a serious health condition

FMLA leave for the birth and care, or placement and care, of a child must be completed within a one-year period, beginning on the date of the birth or placement of the child. The Act also provides that the leave can be taken intermittently or on a reduced work schedule. Most employers have integrated FMLA into their existing paid and unpaid time-off programs. Provided employees are immediately notified of the designation,[12] companies are permitted to designate any leave request because of a reason that qualifies for FMLA event as an FMLA leave. The effect of the designation is to draw down time from the FMLA's 12-week bank. In such cases, the employee does not have the choice of selecting FMLA's unpaid leave and not accessing paid leave, such as vacation or sick days if the leave is because of the employee's medical condition. For those employees who already had access to generous paid time-off benefits and liberal unpaid leave programs before the passage of the FMLA, the benefits of FMLA are statutory protection of employment and insurance, but not an extra 12 weeks of unpaid leave. However, FMLA does compel recalcitrant employers to acknowledge and accommodate the needs of employees when attributable to FMLA-covered events. An example is paternity leave. Before the passage

11. FMLA applies to employers that have had 50 or more employees for at least 20 weeks in the current or preceding calendar year. Only employees who have worked for at least 12 months and for at least 1,250 hours during the preceding 12-month period are entitled to take a leave.
12. FMLA imposes notification requirements also on employees. Employees must give their employers at least 30 days prior written notice of the proposed leave. Where advance notice is not possible, such as in the event of a medical emergency, notice should be given as soon as practicable.

of FMLA, in companies where such a leave was unheard of, a father who wanted to take time off to care for his newborn child could do so only if he had vacation available and the duration of the leave could not exceed the vacation time available. FMLA mandates that he be granted up to 12 weeks of leave with no threat of retaliation. Successful lawsuits brought against employers attempting to deny or circumvent the law are ensuring the accessibility of FMLA benefits across all sectors of the labor market.

Military Leave under FMLA

In the late 2000s, FMLA coverage was extended to military family members with the creation of two new benefit entitlements: qualifying exigency leave and military caregiver leave.

The qualifying exigency leave requires an employer to grant an eligible employee up to a total of 12 weeks of unpaid leave for qualifying exigencies arising out of the fact that the employee's spouse, son, daughter, or parent is on active duty or called to active duty status as a member of the National Guard or Reserves or, subject to certain conditions, as a member of the Regular Armed Forces.

The military caregiver leave requires an employer to grant an eligible employee up to a total of *26* weeks of unpaid leave to care for a spouse, son, daughter, parent or "next of kin" who is: 1) a current member of the Armed Forces, including a member of the National Guard or Reserves, with a serious injury or illness incurred in the line of duty while on active duty; or 2) a veteran with a serious injury or illness that arises within 5 years of military service. The definition of serious injury or illness with respect to this type of leave is very broad allowing a leave for a preexisting injury or illness aggravated by active duty in the military.[13]

Sabbatical Leave

In the past, sabbatical leave has been available only to employees of a select group of organizations such as educational and religious institutions. But sabbatical leave plans have been surfacing in more traditional corporate settings. A sabbatical program allows an employee to take an extended

13. The definition reflects changes made by the National Defense Authorization Act of 2010 to the National Defense Authorization Act of 2008 which amended FMLA to provide additional leave rights to families of service-members. http//: www.dol.gov/whd/regs/compliance/whdfs28.htm. (July 2010).

unpaid leave (or paid leave, in a few cases) with a guarantee of a job upon returning to work, with no risk of being demoted. The program may restrict the types of projects or endeavors for which a leave will be granted, perhaps allowing a leave for community service or job-related education, but not for an extended vacation; and the program is likely to limit eligibility to employees with more than five years of service. The actual leave time allotted can vary from several weeks or months to a year. Sabbatical leaves are being considered for and, in some cases, incorporated in work/life programs with the view that they enhance employee morale and foster employee loyalty, creativity, and productivity.

SUMMARY

Paid time-off benefits have a tremendous effect on recruitment efforts, employee relations, productivity, and, ultimately, profitability. Companies face many challenges in maintaining paid time-off benefits that meet both the needs of their workforce and their business strategies. In administering these benefits, companies must contend with a myriad of federal and state laws that can precipitate employee litigation if human resource managers and line supervisors overtly or inadvertently fail to adhere to the relevant legislation. Also, a company's time-off policies contribute to the attitudes and perceptions employees hold about the company itself. Paid time off from work is just as important to employees as medical and retirement benefits. Therefore, as companies look to establish the latest innovative work/life initiatives, they should begin by examining their traditional paid time-off benefits.

APPENDIX 16.1

FLSA-EXEMPT AND NONEXEMPT WORKERS

In the broadest terms, the Fair Labor Standards Act (FLSA) exempts from its basic rules employees who require minimal supervision and exercise much discretion in performing their duties. According to the Department of Labor (DOL), the exact terms and conditions of an exemption must be made in light of the employee's actual duties and not just the designation of the position as a nonexempt position. The ultimate burden of supporting the actual application of an exemption rests on the employer. The Act also exempts specific categories and businesses. Examples of exemptions include the following:[14]

1. Executive, administrative, professional and outside sales employees (as defined in Department of Labor regulations) who are paid on a salary basis are exempt from both the minimum-wage and overtime-pay provisions of the FLSA.
2. Employees employed by certain seasonal and recreational establishments are exempt from both the minimum-wage and overtime-pay provisions of the FLSA.
3. Commissioned sales employees of retail or service establishments are exempt from overtime if more than half of the employee's earnings come from commissions and the employee averages at least one and one-half times the minimum wage for each hour worked.
4. Certain computer professionals under Section 13(a)(17) of the FLSA who are paid at least $27.63 per hour are exempt from the overtime provisions of the FLSA.
5. Farm workers employed on small farms are exempt from both the minimum-wage and overtime-pay provisions of the FLSA. Other exemptions and regulations apply to farmworkers.
6. Salespeople, partsmen, and mechanics employed by automobile dealerships are exempt from the overtime-pay provisions of the FLSA.

14. http://www.dol.gov/elaws/esa/flsa/screen75.asp# (July 2010).

APPENDIX 16.2

GUIDELINES FOR THE TERM "SERIOUS HEALTH CONDITION" UNDER THE FAMILY AND MEDICAL LEAVE ACT

Serious health condition means an illness, injury, impairment, or physical or mental condition that involves either:

- Inpatient care (*i.e.*, an overnight stay) in a hospital, hospice, or residential medical-care facility, including any period of incapacity (*i.e.*, inability to work, attend school, or perform other regular daily activities) or subsequent treatment in connection with such inpatient care; or
- Continuing treatment by a health care provider, which includes:
  1. A period of incapacity lasting more than three consecutive, full calendar days, and any subsequent treatment or period of incapacity relating to the same condition that **also** includes:
     - Treatment two or more times by or under the supervision of a health care provider (*i.e.*, in-person visits, the first within 7 days and both within 30 days of the first day of incapacity); or
     - One treatment by a health care provider (*i.e.*, an in-person visit within 7 days of the first day of incapacity) with a continuing regimen of treatment (*e.g.*, prescription medication, physical therapy); or
  2. Any period of incapacity related to pregnancy or for prenatal care. A visit to the health care provider is not necessary for each absence; or
  3. Any period of incapacity or treatment for a chronic serious health condition which continues over an extended period of time, requires periodic visits (at least twice a year) to a health care provider, and may involve occasional episodes of

---

This appendix is taken from http://www.dol.gov/whd/regs/compliance/whdfs28.htm (July 2010).

incapacity. A visit to a health care provider is not necessary for each absence; or

4. A period of incapacity that is permanent or long-term due to a condition for which treatment may not be effective. Only supervision by a health care provider is required, rather than active treatment; or
5. Any absences to receive multiple treatments for restorative surgery or for a condition that would likely result in a period of incapacity of more than three days if not treated.

The definition of *health care provider* encompasses:[15]

- Doctors of medicine or osteopathy authorized to practice medicine or surgery by the state in which the doctor practices; or
- Podiatrists, dentists, clinical psychologists, optometrists and chiropractors (limited to manual manipulation of the spine to correct a subluxation as demonstrated by X-ray to exist) authorized to practice, and performing within the scope of their practice, under state law; or
- Nurse practitioners, nurse-midwives, clinical social workers and physician assistants authorized to practice, and performing within the scope of their practice, as defined under state law; or
- Christian Science practitioners listed with the First Church of Christ, Scientist in Boston, Massachusetts; or
- Any health care provider recognized by the employer or the employer's group plan benefits manager.

15. http://www.dol.gov/dol/allcfr/title_29/Part_825/29CFR825.125.htm (July 2010).

CHAPTER 17

Dependent Care Programs

Ann Costello

Today, an increasing number of employees face conflicts between work and family stemming from dependent care responsibilities. As a result, many employers have introduced dependent care as an employee benefit. Dependent care benefits, originally thought of as child-care assistance, actually encompass employer support for the care of other dependents, including elderly parents, elderly, ill, or disabled spouses, and dependent adult children. An employer that offers dependent care benefits usually considers them an important element of its human resources policy directed at maintaining or improving its competitive position.

In the last 20 years, the benefit portion of employee compensation began to change in a number of ways in response to social and demographic changes in the American family. The family stereotype composed of working father, housewife, and two or three children was rapidly being replaced by different family units. The overwhelming majority (60 percent) of two-parent families have both parents in the workforce and the majority of single parents also are employed.

At the same time, life expectancy had increased: a 65-year-old male could expect to live until age 82.2 and a female to age 84.3. The U.S. Census Bureau estimated that there were 36.8 million persons age 65 and over in 2008, and that number will double to 72.1 million by the year 2030. This will be approximately 20 percent of the population. A 2009 survey by the National Alliance for Caregiving and the AARP found that more than 70 percent of elder caregiving was done by employed individuals.[1]

Many caring for elders also have child-care responsibility and have been referred to as the sandwich generation. Thus, family responsibilities are not only extended to children but also to the older generation. With far more of the adult population participating in the labor force, the need for some accommodation on the part of employers for employees' dependent care needs came forcefully to both the public's and employers' attention.

EMPLOYEE PROBLEM

For the past 25 years, the more troubling aspects of working parents and child care have received increasing attention. First, child care represents a considerable expense for employed parents; second, the desired quality of child care may be difficult to obtain and too costly to be a realistic alternative; and third, employers of working parents have had to face the issue of either providing or subsidizing child care.

Infant care averaged $4,560 to $15,895 per year in 2008 and care for a four-year-old in a child-care center ranged from an average of $3,380 to $10,787.[2] In every region, this was higher than what the family spent on average for food. The yearly cost of care for an infant exceeded the annual tuition at a four-year public college in 39 states and the District of Columbia.[3]

Elder care, depending upon the degree of skill needed for the caregiver or for special treatments, can be inexpensive for occasional at-home services or very expensive for a special daycare center with a nursing staff. The national average cost of a home health care aide for 2009 was $21 per hour and $67 per day for adult day services.[4] Both child care and elder care can best be seen as part of the human resource challenge in an ever-increasing competitive environment facing employers in the United States. Employers are challenged to provide the type of employee benefits that make the greatest contribution to overall productivity and employee morale and to do so in a cost-effective manner. Well-designed dependent child-care and elder care benefits offer an important means to meet this challenge and

1. National Alliance for Caregiving, www.caregiving.org/data/caregivingusallagesexecsumpdf.
2. NACCRRA, *Parents and the High Price of Child Care*, 2009 Update, www.NACCRRA.org/docs/publications/supporting-docs/parents-and-the-high-price-of-child-care-2009-update/executive-summary.pdf.
3. Ibid.
4. Metlife Mature Market Institute, The 2009 MetLife Market Survey of Nursing Home, Assisted Living, Adult Day Services, and Home Care Costs, www.maturemarketinstitute.com

to attract and retain employees, which will be of major importance due to the projected shortage of future workers.

CHALLENGE FOR EMPLOYER

Employers that recognized they had human resource management problems—such as recruiting and retention of certain categories of workers, high turnover rates, high rates of absenteeism, and requests for time off the job—turned to employer-supported child care as a problem-solving technique. Several factors have stimulated the growth of the dependent care benefit, including the following:

- Information given to employees by labor organizations
- Media attention to child care as a significant issue
- A gradual understanding that dependents other than children require similar care and that employers could increase management efficiency by assisting their employees in solving these problems
- The granting of tax-preferred status to employee benefit dependent care and the use of flexible spending accounts

In 2009, the National Compensation Survey of Private Industry showed that 10 percent of all civilian employees were eligible for employee assistance for child care. This involved a workplace program that provided full or partial cost of care. Registered nurses (21 percent) and management, professional, technical, and related employees (17 percent) had the most access. Thirty-six percent had access to dependent care reimbursement accounts and 62 percent of employees of large employers have access to these accounts. Elder care statistics are not available in these studies, but the 2010 survey conducted by the Society for Human Resource Management indicated that only 3 percent of responding HR departments subsidized elder care cost. The most common benefit offered (11 percent) was a referral service. Geriatric counseling, access to backup elder care services, elder care assisted-living assessments, elder care home assessments, and on-site elder care were less commonly offered.

TYPES OF EMPLOYEE DEPENDENT CARE BENEFITS

The mass media often present child care and elder care as synonymous. While there are similarities, human resource and benefit consultants should be aware of the differences. Families often seek elder care assistance in a time of emotional crisis. The needed types of care can change quickly, and the strain of dealing with physical and mental deterioration of the dependent is extremely stressful on the caregiver. They often do not know where to seek help or who to ask. They may feel uncomfortable talking about family matters at work. Also, there may be conflicts within their own family as to who will be responsible and what each will do or how to deal with financial and personal decision making. Many times, there may be need for care in a geographic location different from the employee's.

In contrast, the types of child care that are needed are more predictable (except for a child with special needs). The major stress factor is trying to do the two full-time jobs of parent and employee at once. Table 17-1 shows a comparison of two forms of dependent care—child care and elder care—as an employee benefit. A discussion of the different programs follows. Categorizing the programs by costs is made difficult by the different degrees of possible actions. In designing the program, the cost should be viewed in relation to the productivity issues it is attempting to address.

The different types of benefits can be classified according to the function or purpose of the program and according to ease of administration. The purposes of dependent care programs include

- Resource and referral assistance
- Emergency or short-term services
- Direct or contractual provision of services
- Financial approaches

Employers should consider the ease of administration, the cost/benefits, and the risk of implementation of the particular form of the benefit. They should examine questions of employee equity that may arise, so employees do not feel that only limited numbers of their coworkers will benefit from dependent care. The five categories of employer-provided dependent care assistance serve different purposes, take different forms, and vary in relation to the nature of the dependent because children and the elderly differ in caregiving and service needs.

Resource and Referral Services

Employers may choose to limit their dependent care assistance programs to the provision of resource of information pertinent to their employees'

TABLE 17-1

Dependent Care as an Employee Benefit

	Child Care	Elder Care
Eligibility of dependent	Child under 13—worker claims as tax exemption	Mentally or physically incapacitated dependent or spouse of the taxpayer—lives in employee's home at least half of the tax year
Annual limit	Lesser of $5,000 total ($2,500 if married and file a separate tax return), or earned income of either spouse	Lesser of $5,000 total ($2,500 if married and file a separate tax return), or earned income of either spouse
Tax code	IRC Section 129 subject to definition and requirements of Section 21	IRC Section 129 subject to definition and requirements of Section 21
Care	Very routine—generally same type for almost all children of same age	Individualized with rapid change in needs—must be closely monitored
Decision-making on care and type	Parent-employee for child	Employee in conjunction with dependents or spouse—level of resistance or resentment possible
Benefit options	Straight benefit, flexible spending account (FSA), flexible benefits, vouchers, resource and referral, employee assistance program (EAP), family daycare, and worksite daycare	Straight benefit, FSA, flexible benefit, vouchers, resource and referral, EAP, family daycare, adult daycare, wellness, flextime, telecommuting

needs or to combine this with an actual referral service. The use of employer resource and referral services for child-care services has been well established, and, while employer experience in using these services for employee elder care is more limited, the results appear to be positive. The great contrast in the nature of the two different kinds of information and referral services means that very different types of community resources are involved in service provision.

For child care, the employer's objective in establishing an information service is to provide employees in need of child-care services with a listing of available providers. These providers control the quality of care. Employers can exercise quality control only insofar as they limit information and referrals to state-licensed, registered, or certified providers. Employers generally have to make a financial contribution to support the information system.

Frequently, employers may contract with a nonprofit agency, such as the United Way, to provide the information service and to make referrals if that service is included. The nonprofit agency then has the responsibility to compile the listing of providers and, frequently, to attempt to ensure quality control through an on-site inspection process. The quality of service, however, is not guaranteed. The addition of referral services usually entails additional costs for the employer. This needs to be weighed against the possible work time lost by requiring the employee to find a service provider, particularly on short notice.

Resource and referral services are the most common form of employer-supported elder care. The service is similar to that for child care. However, the range of community resources and the types of service provided may be much greater. Some of the types of services are adult daycare, home health care, nursing homes, elder law assistance, home-delivered meals, respite care, senior centers, companion visits, emergency response, continuing-care communities, and special transportation. Employee questions may deal with many different problems, such as home safety, finance, choice of a proper facility, end-of-life issues, talking to elder and doctors, moving and lifting elder, characteristics of different health problems, dealing with emotional and behavioral factors, choice of a rehabilitation facility, choosing a home health care aide, and caring for the caregiver.

Today, a tremendous amount of information from very reliable and highly qualified groups is available on the Internet. Employers could simply provide employees with a listing of computer sites such as www.AgingCare.com and www.AARP.org. However, most go beyond this by also providing listings of community services. Community services funded through the Older Americans Act are provided without charge, as they are an entitlement based on age. Other community-based services charge fees, usually based on a sliding scale to match the income of the elderly person.

Some employers provide a certain number of hours for individual in-person help from professional care managers. This may involve case management, and geriatric evaluation that goes from simple questions to complex situations. There may be visits to a nursing home or hospital and discussions with different health care professionals. The purpose of this is to assist the employee with information and sources that would help them decide what kind of care is best for their dependent. This may be a very stressful and difficult time.

The elderly dependent, unless mentally incapacitated, likely will want to be involved in the choice of service. Care arrangements may change more frequently in instances where the elderly dependent insists upon service changes or criticizes the care provider or has a determination of lack of mental or physical capabilities. This may add to the emotional stress of the employee.

As a result of these problems, resource and referral service may be linked to the employer's employee assistance program (EAP). The employer may structure the information service so that it is linked to a counseling service. This may facilitate the employee's ability to express the tension and frustration that are often found in a dependent care situation for an elderly parent or disabled spouse or child. Some employers have made use of employee support groups for those employees who serve as care providers for elderly parents or other relatives. A hotline service may be included for either child care or elder care to provide immediate information in the case of a crisis, such as a sudden illness or the disruption of existing dependent care services. One major employer provides access to an online course that helps the employee become a better caregiver and to find ways to deal with their own stressful life professionally and personally.

Emergency or Short-Term Services

Even if parents have made satisfactory arrangements with a child-care center to care for their child or children, a sudden illness can leave working parents with the need to make alternative arrangements on short notice. In many cases, the demands of a job make it extremely difficult for a parent to stay at home to care for a sick child. Also, even when children are well, emergencies may happen, and employees may need backup services. Some employers have contracted with local daycare centers or hospitals that provide sick child care, while others have developed lists of nannies and home health care professionals to deliver the care, and some have subsidized the emergency care.

Contractual or Direct Provision of Services

Employers may directly provide, or provide through a contractual arrangement, an array of services ranging from resource and referral or employee-counseling programs to the provision of emergency care and even on-site daycare services. Only a limited number of employers offer on-site elder care services; there is a possibility that future demographic changes may provide for some employers with exceptional need to provide this services.

Family Daycare Home Support

In some communities, daycare services for children are available in family homes as well as in daycare centers, and some employers have made arrangements to make use of these facilities as an alternative to on-site care. Family daycare homes offer care by an individual for up to six children in a home. This form of care is often cited as being preferred for children from one to three years old, and many homes accept infants and toddlers. The family daycare home is often more convenient and less expensive than daycare centers and provides a homelike atmosphere.

This benefit is noted as being the best for companies that have employees living in a broad geographical area who must commute distances to work. The individual employees have a broader choice in the selection of provider and can leave their children close to home. However, while these advantages make this an attractive option, the quality of care may vary greatly. The employer does not have management or financial control over the homes and is, therefore, not legally liable. The employer may or may not use some form of financial assistance to help employees with the cost of using the homes. (Vouchers, discounts, flexible benefit plans, and reimbursement accounts also can be used, subject to Internal Revenue Code (IRC or Code) requirements.)

Daycare Centers

Child-care centers provide institutional care for more than six children, from infants through school age (but normally over the age of three), and as many as several hundred children may be cared for at one center. Centers usually are licensed and follow extensive safety, health, and sanitation requirements imposed on centers by local and state laws. If there are any educational services, such as preschool or kindergarten, the programs must meet the appropriate educational standards of the community and state.

Employers may offer child care in one of the several ways. Centers may be

- Owned and managed by the employer.
- Owned by the employer and operated by an outside group.
- Contracted out to a nonprofit agency.
- Contracted with a profit-making service.

An employer may act alone or join a consortium of other firms. The consortium concept has been used by some employers in locating care in downtown urban areas, but difficulty in meeting varying employer objectives has limited its use. Employer-supported daycare centers may be at the worksite (on-site) or located elsewhere (off-site), and the financial arrangements of the employers may vary. Some firms have supplied the startup costs and expect the program to be self-sustaining; others have supplied full financial support and subsidized yearly center losses. Major employer concerns are cost, usage, and quality. These programs have high startup costs, and attendance may fluctuate. In exchange for financial support, employers may want preferential treatment for their employees, reduced rates, or reserved spaces.

The positive aspect of this option is that the center may be more flexible in providing the types of service required by the company's employees. The center may be open for different shifts of workers and be easily accessible during breaks and lunch, parents may be able to visit their children, and the available resources may permit children to have broader experiences than available with a babysitter or daycare home. The employer has the greatest amount of control with this arrangement, and the center may enable the employer to recruit new employees from a broader range of the community population and foster a positive image for the firm in the community.

However, there are negative considerations for the firm. The employer must be concerned with pricing. The benefit may be provided free to the employee, or, more commonly, the employee will pay part of the cost. The existence of other child-care services in the community that offer lower prices and more desirable locations may offer competition for the center. If the center is in an urban location, employees may not want to transport their children long distances daily or on public transportation. Also, the employer may incur extensive administrative and legal problems imposed by providing a center. Some companies set up a 501(c) (3) nonprofit corporation to avoid financial loss, but a firm's reputation can be severely damaged by claims of injury to children.

Financial Approaches

Dependent care assistance plans may be financed totally by the employer and treated as a separate benefit following IRC Section 129 and Section 21 guidelines. However, if employee contribution is involved, Section 125 of the Code allows this to be done on a pretax basis subject to the dependent care assistance plan (DCAP) requirements. Flexible spending accounts and flexible benefit (Section 125) plans provide attractive options for dependent care.

Flexible Spending Accounts

Flexible Spending Accounts (FSA), commonly referred to as reimbursement accounts, can be used to provide employees with dependent care benefits. Such an account may be established at a very low or negligible cost to the employer, and employees can pay for dependent care expenses with pretax dollars by using a salary reduction program. Employers may contribute to the account, but most do not. The total amount of the dependent care account is restricted by the requirement of Section 129 of the Code—the total maximum amount that may be in the account is $5,000 for a single person or married couple filing jointly, or $2,500 for a married person filing separately. This also is subject to the earned-income limitation. The employer pays no Social Security taxes or unemployment taxes on the amount of the employee's salary reduction.

As discussed below, eligible employment-related expenses provided for qualifying individuals by approved caretakers are governed by IRC Sections 129 and 21. While the plan may be funded by employee and employer contributions, if any form of salary reduction is used, the plan is subject to the Section 125 flexible benefit plan regulations. The amount of funds to be committed to the account must be decided in advance by the employee and must cover the whole period of the plan. Thus, an individual may not choose to participate for only three months, rather than 12 months, in order to protect the tax exclusion. The financial advantage of using an FSA for elder care or child-care expenses is shown in Table 17-2.

The plan requires that the employee forfeit any money left in an account at the end of the year—"Use it or lose it"—and the employer must use the remaining funds for the exclusive benefit of the employees. It is essential that the employee do the comparison between the benefit of a salary reduction versus the tax credit of Section 21 discussed later. A Section 125 plan document is required for all salary-reduction plans, and strict adherence to the nondiscrimination rules and to reporting requirements is required.

The reimbursement account satisfies the equity issue so often raised about dependent care. Those not needing the benefit are not deprived of employer funds that could be used for some more desired benefit. Also, because the employer does not pay Social Security or unemployment taxes on the amount of the employee's salary reduction, these savings are often used to offset the administrative costs of setting up an individual account and reimbursing the employee for eligible expenses. Thus, in effect, the employee is paying for the cost of the benefit by trading Social Security and unemployment earnings credits for it, and the cost is borne only by those participating in the plan.

TABLE 17-2

Usage of Flexible Spending Account (FSA) Tax Savings on Elder care or Child-Care Expenses (in $), with $5,000 Eligible Expenses

	With Dependent care Assistance Plan	Without Dependent care Assistance Plan
Taxable income	$50,000	$50,000
Contributions to FSA (elder or child)	5,000	0
Net taxable income	45,000	50,000
Taxes		
Federal	6156	7,354
State*†	1,800	2000
Social Security	3,443	3,825
Total	11,399	13,179
Disposable income	33,601	36,821
Elder- or child-care expense	0	5,000
Spendable income after dependent care expenses	33,601	31,821
Increase in spendable income with FSA	1,780	

*Assume 4% rate.
†Assume state is following federal laws for withholding head-of-household tax status (2010 rates).

DCAP as Part of a Flexible Benefit Plan

While a dependent care assistance plan may be offered as a separate benefit, it also may be one of a choice of benefits under a Section 125 flexible benefit or "cafeteria" plan. A cafeteria plan is a written plan under which participants may choose among two or more qualified benefits and cash. Whether or not the flexible benefit plan offers the DCAP choice to employees, it must meet numerous requirements under Section 125 of the IRC; these are covered in detail in Chapter 25 of the *Handbook*.

The flexible benefit plan must follow the dependent care assistance plan rules of Section 129 for the DCAP to be a qualified benefit. The plan may allow for care of children, handicapped dependents, and elderly parents. Reimbursement accounts using salary reduction are governed by Section 125. Requirements for dependent care administration exist for salary-reduction plans as well as the flexible benefit program, both being governed by Section 129.

Other Financial Approaches

Instead of or in addition to the methods just described, there are methods of more direct financial assistance for employees' dependent care expenses. These are employer-negotiated discounts at local daycare centers, subsidies, and child-care or elder care vouchers.

Employer Discounts and Subsidies

Certain national child-care provider chains offer employers a discount on employee child-care services if the employer meets the provider's requirements for use. The Department of Labor found that a number of employers match the discount with an equivalent subsidy. The employer subsidy can be either a flat amount or a percentage of child-care/elder care expenses and can be available for all employees or for only those employees in the lower-income brackets.

Vouchers

Vouchers for elder care services are relatively new and are used more widely for dependent child-care payments. Most voucher programs operate as Section 125 flexible spending accounts for dependent care, but the plans can be attractive to firms that choose not to adopt flexible benefit plans. The programs are limited to licensed care and are more common in the retail field.

Employers usually contract with a voucher vendor to administer the voucher program. Employees enroll in the program during an enrollment period and select a specific amount of pretax dollars to be deducted from each paycheck to cover all or part of the dependent care expenses. The employer advances monthly payments to the voucher vendor, who issues four vouchers per month to individual program participants. The voucher represents a fixed amount of available funds. The employee receives the voucher from the vendor and either endorses it over to the dependent care service provider or pays the provider directly and then turns the voucher in for reimbursement. To be reimbursed, the employee must submit identification information on the provider, as required by the IRC.

To implement a dependent care voucher program, an employer enters an agreement with the vendor firm and pays both a startup fee (based on the employer's total number of employees) and a small monthly administrative fee. The fees paid to the vendor are structured so that the employer incurs little or no cost, because of the savings on Social Security and unemployment taxes.

Vendor Plan

An employer may join other employers and buy "slots" or spaces from a local daycare provider. Their employees have priority for these openings; this is especially common for emergency daycare.

TAX POLICY

As already mentioned, the tax treatment of dependent care costs is governed by IRC Sections 21 and 129. Section 21 was passed by Congress in 1976 in response to rising dependent care costs and provides a tax credit on the individual's federal income tax liability. Also, important definitions such as "dependent" and "employment-related expenses," required for Section 129 plans are stated in this part of the Code. The tax-preferred treatment of employer-provided DCAPs was added in 1981 by Section 129 and amended several times in the 1980s. Under the provision, payments made in accordance with the tax law are deductible for the employer and excluded from the employee's gross income. The maximum exclusion for a tax year is the lesser of $5,000 or the earned income of the worker or spouse. Eligible expenses and the method for determining the earned income of a spouse who is disabled or is a student are set forth in Section 21 of the code. The employee must provide over one-half of the financial support of the dependent.

A dependent care program organized to meet Section 129 requirements can assist employees in securing services required for the supervision and care of children and of elderly or disabled dependents of the employee so long as the employee is employed full time. The term dependent care assistance must meet the code definition.[5] The code requires that dependent care assistance be in connection with "employment-related expenses" incurred to enable the employee to be gainfully employed.[6] The expenses must be

5. IRC Section 129 (e) (1) and as defined under Section 21 (b) (2).
6. 23 IRC Section 21 (b) (2).

incurred for household services and the care for a "qualifying individual,"[7] defined as (1) a dependent of the taxpayer under the age of 13; (2) a dependent who is physically or mentally incapable of caring for himself or herself and lives at the taxpayer's principal place of abode more than one half of the taxable year; or (3) the spouse of the employee if the spouse is physically or mentally incapable of caring for himself or herself and lives at the taxpayer's principal place of abode more than one-half of the taxable year.[8] For services provided outside the home, dependents in the last two categories must also live at the taxpayer's residence each day for eight hours.

If the dependent care services are provided by a dependent care center, to meet the Code requirements, the center must comply with all applicable laws and regulations of a state or local government and receive a fee for the provisions of care for more than six individuals.[9] In addition, the DCAP must pass a special nondiscrimination test. The average employer-provided benefit for those not defined by the Code as highly compensated must be at least 55 percent of the employer-provided benefits given to those who are so defined.[10] Employees who are covered by collective bargaining agreements, who are under 21 years old, or who have less than one year of service may be excluded from the calculation. For plans that involve the use of salary reduction, employees with compensation below $25,000 may also be disregarded. The reasoning for this provision is that the existence of the tax credit for dependent care would benefit this group of employees more than would a salary reduction.

In order to meet the requirements for the federal income tax exclusion, a DCAP must meet the following eligibility requirements:

- The plan must be in writing.
- The employee's rights under the plan must be enforceable.
- Employees must be given reasonable notification of the benefits available under the plan.[11]
- The plan must be maintained for the exclusive benefit of employees.

7. 24 IRC Section 21 (b) (1).
8. IRC Section 21 (b) (1) (A, B, C).
9. IRC Section 21 (b) (2) (c) (d).
10. IRC Sections 129 (d) (2) and (8).
11. The notification must include a description of the dependent care credit (IRC Section 21) and the circumstances under which the credit is more advantageous than the exclusion. Also, on or before January 31, the employee must be given a written statement showing the employer's expenses or amount paid for the dependent care during the previous year. This may be done on Form W-2.

Employees must be informed that they have to make a choice between use of the DCAP and use of the dependent care tax credit (DCC) in a given tax year, and employees are responsible for determining whether the tax credit offers them more tax savings than the use of the DCAP. Employers can assist employees in understanding which option provides the employee with the greater tax savings.

The dependent care credit under Section 21 and the exclusion for employer-provided dependent care assistance benefits under Section 129 both require the taxpayer to report on his or her tax return the correct name, address, and taxpayer identification number of the dependent care provider.[12] If the caregiver refuses to provide the correct information, he or she may be penalized. If the taxpayer cannot report the required information, he or she must be able to prove to the Internal Revenue Service (IRS) that the taxpayer exercised due diligence in attempting to provide the information on the service provider; otherwise, the taxpayer may forfeit the Section 21 or Section 129 exclusion.[13] The reporting requirement often restricts the use of either benefit, because some care providers do not report the income to the IRS and may not be providing "legal" services. Thus, they are unwilling to provide the required information, and the taxpayer must choose between the needed services or the benefit.

EMPLOYER OBJECTIVES

In the context of its overall benefit philosophy, an employer may decide to offer dependent care benefits when it finds it advantageous to meet its objectives. These objectives fall into three major categories:

- Employee needs
- Employer productivity goals
- Improved external relations

Employee Needs

If the absence of available dependent care alternatives or the high costs of available care are creating hardships for employees, the employer may find

12. Taxpayers report this information on Form 2441, the form on which the credit for child and dependent care expenses is computed. If the dependent care provider is exempt from federal income taxation under Section 501 (c) (3) of the Code, the taxpayer is only required to report the correct name and address of the exempt organization.
13. IRC Section 21 (e) (9).

it advantageous to offer dependent care benefits in recognition of employee needs. Personal considerations often dictate whether an individual accepts one particular employer's job offer or another's. Willingness to relocate is not as common as it was in the past, and family considerations are much more important. Individuals examine what the employer is willing to provide in total compensation, of which benefits are a major component. Employees see the employer's commitment to a benefit, such as dependent care, as recognition that employees are more than just workers, and assistance in finding high-quality dependent care or in reducing its cost bond the employee to the company. The design of the actual benefit affects the level of freedom from concern, but almost any form of assistance provides some form of relief. An employee with dependent care concerns may see the need for and importance of such a benefit as greater than such benefits as a pension. The dependent care problem exists now; the other benefits are something for the future.

Employee Productivity

An employer considering the addition of a benefit wants to know how the additional benefit will promote its goals. If the addition of dependent care benefits will contribute to productivity by reducing absenteeism and employee turnover and the attendant costs of hiring and training new employees, then the employer may decide that potential improvements in productivity outweigh the additional costs of the benefit. The 2008 National Study of Employers by the Families and Work Institute, involving 1,100 employers, found that the largest obstacle to implementing child-care or elder care assistance, caregiving leaves, or work flexibility was the cost of the benefit (30 percent of respondents), followed by potential loss of productivity (11 percent). Employers in the report that cited less difficulty in hiring self-starters, honest reliable workers, and managers were more likely to provide child- and elder care assistance.[14]

A major study on Caregiving in the United States by the National Alliance for Caregiving and AARP (2004) found that approximately 44 million Americans provide care for a family member or friend over 18. The majority of care was provided by employed workers. A MetLife study quantified the costs of full-time employee intense caregivers as $17 billion and the total estimated costs to employers for all full-time employee

14. Ellen Galinsky, James T. Bond, and Kelly Sakai, *2008 National Study of Employers*, Families and Work Institute, p. 7.

caregivers as $33.6 billion.[15] They estimated the cost of replacing employees, workday interruptions, absenteeism, partial absenteeism, supervisor time, elder care crisis, unpaid leave, and change of full-time to part-time work. All of these are major productivity issues and show the tremendous dollar cost as well as personal costs.

Consulting Practice at Bright Horizons and Professor Ladge surveyed 4,000 working adults on dependent care. The sample was composed of one half who used employer-supported worksite child care, adult care, or backup care for children and one half with children under 13 who did not have the employee benefit. The results of the study were those with the benefit were healthier, had less stress, reported fewer mental and physical health issues, were less likely to seek employment elsewhere, and had less loss of productivity than those without.[16] Children's Healthcare of Atlanta found that expanding dependent care benefits provided measurable increases in employee retention and return to work rates.[17] A Metlife study of one large company suggests that caregivers for elders have higher health care costs. Therefore, to increase productivity, wellness benefits should be linked to elder care programs.[18]

Improvements in External Relations

Besides productivity gains, an employer may gain additional advantages external to the organization. The installation of new benefits is often announced in the local press and industry publications. The image of a "caring" employer is reinforced; a message is transmitted that the company is progressive and a leader in human resource management.[19] Other firms may use the plan as a prototype for their benefit packages, and the company's name is often repeated as a trendsetter. Positive public relations may be furthered by actual involvement of the company in increasing the

15. MetLife Mature Market Institute, *Caregiving Cost Study: Productivity Losses to U.S. Business*, 2006.
16. Bright Horizons, The Consulting Practice at Bright Horizons, *Enhanced Employee Health, Well-Being, and Engagement through Dependent Care Supports*, 2010.
17. "Dependent care Plan Boosts Retention & Return-to-Work Rates," *Managing Benefit Plans*, No. 07-06, June 2007, www.IOMA.com/HR.
18. Metlife Mature Market Institute, The Metlife Study of Working Caregivers and Employer Health care costs: New Insights and Innovations for Reducing Health care costs for Employees, 2010. www.maturemarketinstitute.com
19. An example of this is being named as one of the "100 Best Companies for Working Mothers" by *Working Mother*: the magazine is inundated by companies trying to be so named. Also, it is very common for the media to report the findings.

quantity and quality of dependent care in the community; this depends, however, on the actual design of the benefit.

ISSUES

While dependent care may offer many advantages to a company, there are major issues that affect its acceptance and are probably causing many firms to hesitate.

Equity

In a conventional employee benefit plan option, such as health care coverage, an employee may or may not use the benefit during a given year; but all employees are eligible to use it at any time, and over time all employees may have occasion to rely on it. However, dependent care may be used only by those who have "qualifying individuals" as dependents.

While employees who do use it will change over time, resentment could arise among employees who have no need for such a benefit—compensation funds are being spent for something that does not help them at all. Equity is a fundamental issue in employee benefits, as can be seen from the nondiscrimination rules applicable to many benefits that exist to protect against a disproportionate amount of funds for a benefit being spent on top management, owners, and stockholders. The equity issue in dependent care benefits could lead to individual personnel issues, and the actual composition of the employee group is important in determining the size of the potential problem.

Upper Management

Decision-making about dependent care benefits is done by upper management. Some have argued that the increasing number of baby boomers who are senior managers faced with elder care problems will put a new emphasis on elder care as a benefit. The 2008 National Study of Employers by the Families and Work Institute found that firms most likely to provide child and elder care assistance had more women and minority members in executive positions or who reported to executives.

Firm's Reputation

While there are positive outcomes for the reputation of a company offering dependent care, a risk manager would advise caution when considering the benefit from an external relations perspective. Firms do not want to be involved with a program that may be substandard, as the expected gain from such a plan would be more than offset by the problems presented. Personnel complaints and, ultimately, liability suits could severely damage the company's reputation. A firm must be very careful about the qualifications of any daycare provider with which it associates and may decide to deal only with state-licensed or registered providers.

Attempts to limit liability by having a nonprofit foundation or a professional daycare chain control and manage the on-site or off-site facility have been utilized. In plans that simply make referrals, the choices given have often been limited to licensed care; here the purpose is to inform, not to be the provider. Flexible benefit plans and reimbursement accounts merely provide financial aid; choosing the provider, within the requirements of the IRC, is left to the employee, and the employer would not be liable for the actions of the dependent care provider.

Usage

In the past, researchers have explored nonusage by some caregivers of workplace dependent care plans, specifically elder care. While the results are not conclusive, they do raise interesting points. The discussion often involves financial issues and the use or possible use of Medicaid. Also, employees may be afraid of potential problems for career advancement. Workplace dependent care programs must stress confidentiality and provide extensive communication processes to achieve the employer's objectives.

DESIGN OF BENEFITS

In designing the benefits package, feasibility studies are considered as well as employer's objectives, employees' needs, and the local market.

The Feasibility Study

In the process of designing or redesigning a benefit package, feasibility studies are often conducted to explore the possibilities of a particular benefit. Employers considering adopting or modifying dependent care benefit policies need to research the specific needs and opportunities of their labor force. The analysis may be undertaken by management, but outside consultants are often used for their specific expertise. Expert assistance may be needed not only in the employee benefit field but also in the child-care and elder care fields, and may require the use of more than one consultant.

Set Objectives

The employer's overall employee benefit philosophy is the first consideration, and then the employer's objectives in adding dependent care can be established. With the objectives clearly defined and the need of the employees and their dependent care problems identified, those responsible for designing the new benefit may proceed. The personnel problems that appear to diminish productivity should be reinforced by the benefit design.

The feasibility study should identify and further examine those relevant employee characteristics that suggest dependent care would meet the company's objectives, keeping in mind that, while the benefit may not be useful for all employees, the productivity impact of dependent care problems on the entire organization may make alleviating those problems a priority.

Assess Employee Needs

Economic projections about future requirements for employees will help management to understand not only the immediate situation but also long-term implications. Data from personnel records are an important source of information. Examination of the demographics of the employee group will show how many present employees are members of two-income families or are single parents; these data will assist in making projections on future child-care requirements. Comparative data about tardiness, absenteeism, and turnover can be collected for groups of employees with and without children.

From this, the company can cost out the possible personnel problems as well as advantages associated with child-care programs. Since the collected data are very limited, other techniques may be implemented. For example, a company could use informal means and target groups for the feasibility study. Information as to whether child care has been mentioned as a problem by employers may be gathered from individuals by the personnel department and supervisors. Focus groups involve discussions among a small number of specifically selected individuals led by an expert whose purpose is to elicit individual viewpoints concerning dependent care needs and propose alternative responses to the identified needs. The leader tries to keep the discussion focused on plan-design options that would be acceptable to the company.

Analysis of personnel records will not disclose the need for elder care, so the use of employee surveys is the most recommended tool. There may be a wide variation between the need and the types of care involved from one employee group to another. Also, the type of care needed may change drastically with the normal process of aging. The survey may provide important information totally unknown to management, and the data will demonstrate which elder care benefit options are viable.

Evaluate Local Market

Management or its consultant, or both, should have the most current cost and tax implications of the different options available. To assist in choosing those possible for the firm, information must be collected on dependent care in the local community. The employer must try to establish the existing availability of daycare homes and dependent care facilities. The ages of children and appropriate facilities for each age group are important considerations; children may be infants, toddlers, preschoolers, school age, or those with special needs. Care for infants is the most expensive and is often in the shortest supply. Special children may be handicapped or temporarily sick; care of this type may not be available at all. Data are gathered about licensed or registered caretakers' costs, hours of operation, and services provided. If any other local businesses offer dependent care assistance, their programs should be examined.

As with child care, the availability of elder care services is an important factor in the employer's decision-making process, and a similar study should be done for elder care by an employer considering that benefit. The employer-supported benefit plan should not duplicate but complement any programs the community provides and to which the dependent may be entitled.

Select Option

At this point in the feasibility study, company executives should be equipped to decide which design options are viable. Besides the obvious factor of cost, the firm must decide what level of involvement should exist in actually providing the dependent care. A firm's inability to spend additional dollars on a new benefit will place constraints on acceptable alternatives. A constantly updated resource and referral program may be invaluable for elder care; a flexible benefit plan that includes dependent care but also allows the employer more financial control may be attractive for child care.

After analyzing the possible acceptable options, the firm does a formal needs assessment, and management should be seriously committed before doing this, as employees' expectations may be raised, and negative feelings toward the employer could result if the process is not handled properly.

Besides the normal demographics, the first section should also cover the types and operating features of dependent care currently available. This assessment data will assist the firm in deciding which of the acceptable options would most satisfy employees' needs now and in the future. On completion of the feasibility study, the employer should have identified the dependent care needs and associated problems that inclusion of dependent care as an employee benefit may alleviate, thus meeting the employer's objectives.

CONCLUSION

Employers concerned with their responsibility to design benefits that both meet employee needs and contribute to productivity will continue to search for ways to integrate dependent care into their existing benefit plans. Employers have gained an increased understanding that parents in the labor force who have young children currently comprise, and in the foreseeable future will continue to comprise, a substantial portion of the labor force.

An even greater number of employees have and will have elder care needs. The high cost of good-quality elder care and child care and problems with their continuing availability can contribute to the economic insecurity of those employees, particularly single parents and those with low incomes. Current evidence indicates that concerns over dependent care affect employee performance detrimentally. Responsible employers will seek to improve their ability to analyze the dependent care needs of their employees and to design benefits that meet employee needs as well as employer objectives and that are administratively feasible.

CHAPTER 18

Selected Additional Benefits: Educational Assistance Programs, Group Legal Services Plans, Qualified Transportation Fringe Benefits, and Voluntary Benefits

Craig J. Davidson

EDUCATIONAL ASSISTANCE PROGRAMS (SECTION 127 PLANS)

The relationship between education and work is well known. Education has a positive effect on incomes, job potential, and workplace performance. The importance of education in today's workplace is particularly acute given the shortage of qualified workers. Employee benefits that offer workers educational assistance are a win–win proposition. Employers gain through a more highly educated and skilled workforce, increased employee morale, possible tax deductions, and a strategic hiring and retention advantage over employers who do not offer educational assistance benefits. Similarly, employees gain from employer-sponsored educational assistance through increased knowledge and skills that can lead to higher pay and better career opportunities.

JOB-RELATED VERSUS NONJOB-RELATED EDUCATIONAL ASSISTANCE

Employer-sponsored educational assistance represents a variety of arrangements. Those arrangements, and the accompanying tax issues, can be separated into two categories—job-related and nonjob-related. The most common form of job-related educational assistance is an educational reimbursement program (ERP). Employers that offer ERPs can reimburse an employee for job-related educational expenses as a working condition fringe and exclude the expense from the employee's gross income.[1] Educational assistance is job-related if it helps to maintain or improve skills required for a job, trade, or business, or meets the requirements imposed by an employer (or by law) as a condition to retaining an employee's job, status, or salary. Deductible education expenses include

- Tuition, books, laboratory fees, and supplies[2]
- Travel and transportation costs[3]
- Graduate or undergraduate level courses[4]
- Courses qualifying employee for new trade or business[5]
- Reasonable expenses incurred while typing a paper or conducting research in connection with the eduation
- Expenses for tutorial instruction or correspondence courses
- Certain transportation expenses

Deductibility of local transportation costs incurred for transportation to and from school depends on (1) where the transportation is to and from, and (2) whether or not the employee is attending school on a "temporary basis." Temporary basis means irregular or short-term attendance. Transportation from work to school is generally deductible when the employee goes directly from work to school. Transportation from school to home is deductible if the employee is attending school on a strictly temporary basis. Transportation from home to school and back home is deductible if the employee is attending school on a temporary basis. Deductible transportation expenses include

- Bus, subway or cabfare
- Cost of an employee using the employee's own car[6]

Exclusions or deductions are not permitted for (1) education required for the employee to meet the minimum educational requirements for qualification in his or her employment or other trade or business, or

1. See IRC Sec. 132(d); Treas. Reg. Sec. 1.162-5(a)(1).
2. Treas. Reg. Sec. 1.162-6
3. Treas. Reg. Sec. 1.162-5(d)
4. Treas. Reg. Sec. 1.162-5(a)
5. Treas. Reg. Sec. 1.162-5(b)(3)
6. BNA Compensation and Benefits Guide, *Welfare and Fringe Benefits*, 2004, pp. 4–5.

(2) expenditures made by an individual for education that is part of a program of study that will qualify him or her in a new trade or business.[7] Employers are not limited on the amount of excludable assistance if the education is job-related. An example could include software training for an employee who needs to use that software on the job.

The remainder of this chapter will deal with programs that can offer both nonjob-related educational assistance and job-related educational reimbursement. These arrangements, known as educational assistance programs, are sanctioned under Section 127 of the Internal Revenue Code (IRC).

OVERVIEW AND HISTORY OF EDUCATIONAL ASSISTANCE PROGRAMS

Congress created educational assistance programs with passage of the Revenue Act of 1978. Under these programs, employees can exclude up to $5,250 of employer-provided educational assistance from gross income.[8] Amounts of educational assistance provided above the $5,250 limit for educational assistance programs may be excludable under other sections of the IRC if the conditions of those sections are met. Actual amounts excludable from an employee's gross income are reported on the employee's W-2. Where an employee works for more than one employer, the $5,250 limitation applies to the aggregate amount of educational assistance benefits received from all employers.[9]

Congress designed Section 127 with sunset provisions that have allowed these programs to expire and lose their tax-qualified benefits over the years. The Economic Growth and Tax Relief Reconciliation Act of 2001 (EGTRRA), Section 411 made the exclusion permanent and extended deductibility to include graduate education, effective January 1, 2002. Employers can now exclude from employees' gross incomes the cost of undergraduate and graduate courses.[10]

DEFINITION AND ADMINISTRATION OF AN EDUCATIONAL ASSISTANCE PROGRAM

Educational assistance programs are qualified plans under the IRC and must meet strict requirements set forth in the Code. Unlike the process for

7. Treas. Reg. Sec. 1.162-5.
8. See IRC Sec. 127(a).
9. See H.R. Rep. 1049, 98th Congress, 2nd Session,
10. See the Economic Growth and Tax Relief and Reconciliation Act of 2001, Sec. 411.

qualified retirement plans, employers who sponsor educational assistance programs do not have to request a determination letter from the Internal Revenue Service (IRS) for the plan to be qualified.[11]

An educational assistance program is an arrangement under which an employer provides education to an employee or pays the employee's educational expenses. The term educational expense means the payment, by an employer, of expenses incurred by or on behalf of an employee for education of the employee (including, but not limited to, tuition, fees, and similar payments, books, supplies, and equipment), and the provision, by an employer, of courses of instruction for such an employee (including books, supplies, and equipment), but does not include payment for, or the provision of, tools or supplies that may be retained by the employee after completion of a course of instruction, or meals, lodging, or transportation. The term "educational assistance" also does not include any payment for, or the provision of any benefits with respect to, any course or other education involving sports, games, or hobbies.[12]

Separate Written Plan

Section 127 requires that these plans be written exclusively for educational assistance benefits and solely for the exclusive benefit of employees.[13] Plans must be administered in a nondiscriminatory manner. Employers can, and typically do, offer educational assistance programs as part of a more comprehensive employee benefit arrangement. These arrangements may include cafeteria plans.[14] The written plan must set forth the details of the program, and the employer must provide reasonable notice to eligible employees of the plan's terms and conditions.[15]

Exclusive Benefit of Employees

Educational assistance programs must be established exclusively for employees. Spouses and other dependents are ineligible to participate in the plan, unless they are also employees. The term "employee" includes certain self-employed individuals; retired, disabled, or laid-off employees;

11. Treas. Reg. Sec. 1.127-2(a).
12. IRC Sec. 127(c)(1).
13. IRC Sec. 127(b)(1).
14. IRC Sec. 127(b)(4) and Treas. Reg. Sec. 1.127-2(b).
15. IRC Sec. 127(b)(6).

and employees on leave.[16] For purposes of an educational assistance program, any individual who owns an entire interest in an unincorporated business is considered both the employer and the employee. A partnership includes the employer and each of the equity partners, if any. The partners are considered employees of the partnership.[17]

Nondiscrimination Rules

Employers that offer educational assistance plans to their employees must comply with nondiscrimination rules or risk plan disqualification and the loss of Section 127 tax benefits. An explanation of the nondiscrimination rules for educational assistance plans is as follows:

1. Highly compensated employees (HCEs): An employer's educational assistance plan cannot discriminate in favor of HCEs with respect to eligibility for benefits under the plan. An HCE includes owners, officers, or self-employed individuals, or their spouses or dependents who are employees.[18]
2. Five-percent owners: The plan cannot provide more than 5 percent of the benefits paid under the program during the year to shareholders or owners (or their spouses or dependents) who on any day of the year owned more than 5 percent of the stock, capital, or profits of the employer.[19]

The IRS will not treat a plan as discriminatory merely because different types of educational assistance available under the plan are used to a greater degree by employees for whom discrimination is prohibited. Similarly, a plan may base benefits on the successful completion of a course, attainment of a particular grade, or satisfaction of a reasonable condition (such as remaining with an employer for a period of time after completion of a course).[20] Finally, employees participating in a collective bargaining agreement unit are excluded from nondiscrimination testing if the educational assistance benefits were established through good-faith bargaining.[21]

16. IRC Sec. 127(c)(2) and Treas. Reg. Sec. 1.127-2(h)(1).
17. Treas. Reg. Sec. 1.127-2(h)(2).
18. IRC Sec. 127(b)(2) and Treas. Reg. Sec. 1.127-2(e).
19. IRC Sec. 127(b)(3). The term "shareholder" includes an individual who is a shareholder as determined by the attribution rules under IRC Sec. 1563(d) and IRC Sec. 1563(e) without regard to IRC Sec. 1563(e)(3)(C).
20. IRC Sec. 127(c)(5) and Treas. Reg. Sec. 1.127-2(e)(2).
21. IRC Sec. 127(b)(2) and Treas. Reg. Sec. 1.127-2(e)(1).

Reporting and Record-Keeping Requirements

Section 127 plans are required to comply with certain reporting and record-keeping requirements under the Employee Retirement Income Security Act of 1974 and the IRC. An employer's reporting requirements include filing information annually with the IRS, on behalf of the plan, that includes the following:

- Number of employees
- Number of employees eligible to participate in the plan
- Number of employees actually participating in the plan
- Plan's total cost for the year
- Name, address, and taxpayer identification number of the employer and the type of business in which the employer is engaged
- Number of highly compensated employees

The vehicle for providing this information to the IRS is Form 5500. In Notice 2002-24, the IRS suspended until further notice the reporting requirement for Section 6039D for educational assistance programs. The Notice, which went into effect April 5, 2002, also suspends the requirement to file Schedule F from the Form 5500 series.[22] Educational assistance program sponsors must also retain records of financial transactions on behalf of the plan.[23]

Coverdell Education Savings Accounts

Coverdell education savings accounts (ESAs), fomerly called Education IRAs, were created by Congress in EGTRAA.[24] The plans went into effect in 2002. These ESAs are sanctioned under IRC Section 530 and allow employers to make contributions to individual educational savings accounts. Coverdell ESAs—certain trusts or custodial accounts—must be exclusively for paying qualified higher-education expenses of a designated beneficiary, and on a tax-exempt basis. Contributions to the ESAs must be made in cash. Annual contributions cannot exceed $2,000 per beneficiary (except for certain tax-free rollovers) and may not be made after the designated beneficiary reaches age 18.

Contribution limits are phased out ratably for contributors with modified adjusted gross incomes (AGI) between $95,000 and $110,000. The

22. See IRS Notice 2002-24.
23. IRC Sec. 6039D.
24. See EGTRRA, Sec. 411.

phase-out range for married individuals filing a joint return is $190,000 to $220,000 of modified AGI. Individuals with modified AGI above the phase-out range are not permitted to make contributions to an education IRA.[25]

SUMMARY

Support for educational programs can play a vital role in an employer's overall mix of employee benefits. Reimbursement for job-related educational expenses is the most common approach. Increasingly though, employers recognize the need for formal employee assistance programs under IRC Section 127 that help employees expand their knowledge and skills beyond their current job responsibilities.

That strategy squares nicely with a new, unwritten contract that has emerged among forward-thinking organizations and their employees during this early part of the 21st century. That contract places less emphasis on job security and more emphasis on investment in worker education and skill training to attract and retain qualified employees. Educational assistance programs represent a powerful tool for organizations that adopt this philosophy.

25. Ibid.

GROUP LEGAL SERVICES PLANS

Contemporary employee benefit systems are a reflection of societal needs, economic constraints, laws, and demographic trends. Group legal services plans are one such reflection of our current times. One study by the American Bar Foundation estimated that 37 percent of all employees face a legal problem every year that a lawyer can help with, but fewer than one in 10 seek legal help.[26] While a relative minority of individuals seek professional legal help with their legal problems, the need for such assistance is certain and growing. Population demographics also play a role in the advent of group legal services plans. According to one researcher, "a high correlation exists between age and the use of lawyers because most people wait until they are older to consider estate planning issues"—a highly utilized service in group legal assistance plans.[27] According to one study, 24 percent of surveyed U.S. private employers (581 respondents) offered group legal service plans as a benefit to their employees in 2007.[28]

LEGISLATIVE BASIS FOR GROUP LEGAL SERVICES PLANS

Congress provided the early incentive behind group legal services plans with the passage of key laws in the 1970s and subsequent provisions in the IRC. For example, the Labor Management Relations Act (LMRA) gave organized labor the right to collectively bargain for legal plans. In 1974, President Gerald Ford signed into law the Employee Retirement Income Security Act (ERISA), which preempted state insurance regulations. ERISA effectively provided a federal framework for group legal services plans.

The Tax Reform Act of 1976 added a new section to the tax code—Section 120. Under Section 120, employees, spouses, and dependents could exclude the following from gross income:

- Amounts contributed by an employer under a qualified group legal services plan, or
- The value of legal services received under a qualified group legal services plan.

---

26. See Sandra H. Dement, "Advice for Employers: How to Select a Prepaid Legal Benefit," *Employee Benefits Journal*, June 1999, p. 22, citing American Bar Foundation study.
27. Ibid., p. 22.
28. See Hewitt Associates, LLC, 2007.

IRC Section 120 also permitted the creation of tax-exempt trusts to fund qualified group legal services plans.

Congress capped the amount that could be contributed to a group legal services plan at $70 per person.[29] This exclusion cap applied to the plan's "premium value" for insured and self-insured plans. The exclusion did not apply to the value of legal services provided under the plan. Under an insured plan, the premium value was equal to the premium paid by an employer for the plan. For self-insured plans, the premium value was the total amount paid by the employer under the plan during the year divided by the total number of individuals entitled, in their own right, to benefits under the plan.[30]

Qualification under Section 120 required the plan to

- Be in writing and for the exclusive benefit of employees, their spouses, and dependents.
- Provide only personal legal services.
- Not discriminate in favor of highly compensated employees with respect to contributions or benefits and eligibility.
- Provide that no more than 25 percent of amounts contributed be provided to shareholders or owners (or their spouses or dependents) owning more than 5 percent of the stock, capital, or profits.
- Notify the IRS of application for qualified status.
- Be financed through payments to insurance companies, or persons or organizations providing legal services or indemnification against the cost of such services; trusts or organizations described in IRC Section 501(c) (20); other 501(c) organizations permitted to receive employer contributions for qualified group legal services plans; providers of legal services; or a combination of the above.[31]

Passage of the Revenue Act of 1978 established cafeteria plans under IRC Section 125. This section of the Code permitted employers to set up plans that gave employee participants a choice between taxable cash and nontaxable employee benefits. This tax provision proved to be popular and many employers established cafeteria plans as a result. The tax advantages under Section 120 made group legal services benefits ideal for

29. IRC Sec. 120(a).
30. See *Benefits Coordinator*, New York: Research Institute of America, 1992, pp. 20, 102A, citing Congressional Record, October 11, 1988, p. S 15458.
31. See IRC Sec. 120(b), IRC Sec 120(c), Prop. Treas. Reg. Sec. 1-120-2, and Treas. Reg. 1.120-3.

cafeteria plans. As a result, group legal services plans grew in popularity during the 1980s.

In 1992, Congress voted to sunset Section 120, effectively removing any tax advantage for employers to set up or maintain group legal services plans. Employers may still establish group legal services plans. Most common today, those services are offered as voluntary, employee-pay-all benefits. Despite the loss of tax advantages, employees still benefit through group purchasing of legal services and the advantages of group administration.

DEFINITION OF A GROUP LEGAL SERVICES PLAN

The term "group legal services" describes a variety of plan arrangements that offer legal services as the core benefit. In general, plans take on one of two basic forms—access plans and comprehensive plans:

- Access plans are the more basic of the two forms. These arrangements provide participants with easy access, usually over the telephone, to legal advice and consultation for simple legal issues.
- Comprehensive plans typically offer the same benefits as access plans, but are usually established based on a traditional group benefits design. These plans can offer services for more complex legal problems such as financial guidance, consumer protection, property protection, family matters, and standard wills. Comprehensive plans typically also cover in-office consultation, research, negotiation, and trial presentation.

Legal services plans are also referred to as "prepaid" plans. A "prepaid" legal services plan is an individual or group arrangement that is funded in advance of services being rendered through employer or employee contributions to a trust, through a group of legal service providers, or through insurance premiums.[32] These programs can be designed as either access plans or comprehensive plans. According to one study, the average hourly billing rate for attorneys across all fields was $325 in

32. Some researchers maintain that a plan funded with insurance premiums is not a prepaid plan. Research suggests that an insured plan is merely a prepaid plan where the insurance company holds the risk of loss.

2009.[33] Annual coverage in a prepaid legal plan could be secured for less than the cost of one hour with an attorney.[34]

GROUP LEGAL SERVICES PLANS AS AN EMPLOYEE BENEFIT

Many employers today offer these plans as a response to the tight labor market facing the U.S. workforce long term. The maxim that employee benefits are offered to attract and retain qualified employees holds true with group legal service benefits. According to a recent study, 70 percent of full-time U.S. workers had experienced some kind of "legal life event" in the past year. Of these, 20 percent said they were less productive at work, and one-third took time off of work—an average of 13 days—to deal with legal needs.[35]

DESIGN, FUNDING, AND ADMINISTRATION

The decision to add group legal services as an employee benefit launches a series of questions and processes. What type of plan best suits my organization and its employees? How should the plan be funded? What administrative burden does my organization assume in adopting a group legal services benefit plan? These are all valid questions.

Type of Plan

Selection of a plan design should start with an examination of the characteristics of the workforce. Is the employee population older or younger? A low-cost telephone access plan may be ideal for an older workforce. Where are employees located? Try to match your organization's choice of a legal provider network with the geographic distribution of employees. Telephone access plans may be ideally suited for rural workforces, while urban workforces may be better matched with legal provider office locations. What is the compensation level of employees? A population with more highly compensated employees may require a plan that offers financial counseling as a

33. Ronald L. Burdge, *United States Consumer Law Attorney Fee Survey 2008–2009*, 2nd ed., Dayton, OH: Burdge Law Office, 2010, p. 8.
34. 2001 Survey of Law Firm Economics Executive Summary, Altman Weil, Inc.
35. The Amerisc Corporation, Employee Benefits Report, November 2009, p. 1, citing 2007 study by Russell/ARAG.

benefit.[36] Finally, and perhaps most importantly, these plans are designed so an employer or family member cannot use the program to sue the employer.

ADMINISTRATION

An organization's funding method will determine, in large part, the type of administrative procedures required to be compliant with federal and state laws. Employee-pay-all plans, for example, may be exempt from ERISA and therefore do not have to comply with the reporting and disclosure requirements found in Title I of the Act. To receive this exemption, the plan must comply with each of the following four conditions set by the Department of Labor:

1. No contributions are made by the employer or employee organization.
2. Participation in the program is completely voluntary for employees or members.
3. The sole functions of the employer or employee organization with respect to the program are, without endorsing the program, to permit the insurer to publicize the program to employees or members, to collect premiums through payroll deductions or dues checkoffs, and remit them to the insurer.
4. The employer or employee organization receives no consideration in the form of cash or otherwise in connection with the program, other than reasonable compensation, excluding any profit, for administrative services actually rendered in connection with payroll deductions or dues checkoffs.[37]

Plans that do not meet these criteria are subject to ERISA and required to comply with the reporting and disclosure requirements identified in Table 18-1.[38]

Record-Keeping

Administrators of group legal services plans (if the program is subject to ERISA) are also required to keep records that support and verify information

36. See Sandra H. Dement, "Advice for Employers: How to Select a Prepaid Legal Benefit," *Employee Benefits Journal*, June 1999, p. 23.
37. See DOL Regs. 2510.3-1(j).
38. See ERISA Sec. 101.

TABLE 18-1

Reporting and Disclosure Requirements for Organizations (100 or more participants)

Item	File With	Disclose to Participants	When Due
Form 5500 (Annual Report) and Schedules	ERISA Filing Acceptance Systems (EFAST)	On written request; available for viewing	Last day of 7th month after the end of the plan year (unless extension is obtained)
Summary Annual Report	None	Yes, if plan is insured or otherwise funded	9 months after the end of the plan year (unless extension is obtained)
Summary Plan Description	Department of Labor (DOL) on written request	Yes	120 days after the plan becomes effective; for new participants, 90 days after becoming a participant
Summary of Material Modification	Department of Labor (DOL) on written request	Yes	210 days after the end of the plan year in which the change occurs

For a complete list of the Reporting and Disclosure Requirements, see: Reporting and Disclosure Guide for Employee Benefit Plans, Employee Benefits Security Administration, U.S. Department of Labor, Revised October 2008.

required in Form 5500 or disclosed under ERISA in summary plan descriptions or summary annual reports. Records must be retained for six years after the Form 5500 filing date.

Enrollment

Enrollment in a group legal services plan can be voluntary or automatic. Voluntary enrollment plans require employees to make an election to participate in the plan and pay the enrollment fee or premium. Fees or premiums are generally paid through payroll deduction. Voluntary enrollment periods are generally held once a year. An automatic enrollment plan requires that all employees participate in the plan as a condition of employment. These automatic enrollment plans will be subject to ERISA.

SELECTING AN ATTORNEY PANEL

Providers in group legal services plans fall into one of two broad categories: open and closed panels. Employers must decide how much choice plan participants will have in selecting an attorney. If freedom of choice is important, the plan can be designed using an open panel of attorneys. Participants can use any licensed attorney on a fee-for-service basis. Under this design, plan participants utilize the services of an attorney of their choice and are billed directly by the attorney. When services are complete, the participant submits a claim form and the attorney's billing statement for reimbursement according to plan limits.[39]

The closed panel approach allows a plan to contract with a group of attorneys to form a network. Using a network of attorneys affords the plan an opportunity to negotiate rates and services with a single entity. Generally, the plan design will provide financial incentives for participants to use attorneys in the network, or may restrict participants to using in-network attorneys.

Administrators of plans that use a network of providers have a responsibility to perform due diligence on the qualifications of the attorneys in the network. This due diligence can be performed by establishing and enforcing written guidelines of performance. The following is a sample list of reliable indicators of an attorney's level of expertise that can be incorporated into a plan's guidelines for attorney participation:

- Licensed to practice in a particular state.
- Member in good standing with the state bar association.
- Maintains an office for regularly engaging in the practice of law.
- Agrees to the methods and rates of payments for covered services.
- Agrees to provide services to plan members.
- Committed to client service.
- Adequate number of years in practice and breadth of practice (knowledgeable in areas frequently generating questions from plan members).

39. See Jim Brennan, "Group Legal Insurance: An Effective Recruiting and Retaining Tool," *Compensation & Benefits Review*, May/June 1999, p. 88.

- Adequate level of support (associate attorneys, staff, etc.) and technology (phone lines, computer equipment, etc.).
- Accessibility during regular business hours and for emergencies.
- Good telephone demeanor.
- Acceptable levels of professional liability coverage ($100,000 is standard).
- Speaks foreign languages.
- Percentage of time spent offering advice and counsel.
- Reasons the attorney wishes to provide services to plan members.
- No record of fraud or felony convictions.
- Disclosure of any complaints or disciplinary actions filed and the outcomes.
- Community involvement.[40]

SUMMARY

Providing legal services through a group benefit plan offers an employer an opportunity to meet a need among its workforce and to offer an attractive recruitment tool if communicated properly. Employers today struggle to compete for skilled employees who will bring maximum productivity to the workplace. Group legal services plans offer those employees important peace of mind for when inevitable legal issues arise.

40. Ibid, p. 89.

QUALIFIED TRANSPORTATION FRINGE BENEFITS

Qualified transportation fringe benefits are benefits that organizations can offer their employees tax-free under the provisions of Section 132(f) of the IRC.[41] Such benefits have become popular with organizations and their employees because the cost of transportation to work and parking at work has become increasingly costly. Specifically, qualified transportation fringe benefits include:

- Transportation in a commuter highway vehicle if such transportation is in connection with travel between the employee's residence and place of employment
- Transit passes
- Qualified parking[42]

COMMUTER VEHICLE TRANSPORTATION

In general, transportation benefits are employer-sponsored programs that assist employees with their trip to work and back home again. The benefit is designed to encourage energy-efficient forms of transportation instead of single-occupant use of an automobile. Examples include public transportation, commuter vehicles (vanpooling), and van pools. Commuter vehicles must seat at least six adults, not including the driver to receive tax qualification. Additionally, at least 80 percent of the vehicle's mileage must be reasonably expected to be used:

- Transporting employees between their residence and place of employment, and
- On trips during which the number of employees transported for commuting purposes averages at least half of the adult seating capacity of the vehicle.[43]

Qualified transportation fringe benefits are subject to dollar limits. The aggregate benefit of commuter vehicle use cannot exceed $110 dollars per month. The maximum monthly benefit is indexed for inflation.[44] The benefit provided must be in addition to, and not in lieu of, any compensation

41. IRC Sec. 132(f).
42. Ibid.
43. See IRS Revenue Procedure 2003-85.
44. IRC Sec. 132(f)(2)(A).

otherwise payable to employees.[45] If the value of all qualified transportation benefits exceeds the appropriate dollar limit, only the excess is includible in employee income.

QUALIFIED PARKING

Employees can exclude up to $200 per month in qualified parking expenses. Qualified parking must be situated on or near

- The employer's business premises
- The location from which employees commute to work in a commuter highway vehicle or carpool, or
- The location where employees board public transportation, that is, buses or subways

In general, the value of qualified parking to an employee must be based on the cost (including taxes and other fees) that an individual would pay in a retail transaction to park at the same site.[46]

THE BENEFIT COORDINATION RULE

Code rules for "Qualified Transportation Fringes" contain a "benefit coordination rule." This says that any transportation fringe benefit violating the qualification requirements under the Code (including, in particular, the monthly dollar caps under Section 132(f)(2)) cannot qualify for the working condition or de minimis fringe benefit exclusions. The IRS takes the position that this benefit coordination rule is designed to ensure that any common law employees who receive transportation benefits exceeding the Section 132(f)(2) dollar caps are taxed on the excess value. The benefit coordination rules do not apply to partners, independent contractors or 2 percent shareholders in S corporations.[47]

REPORTING AND DISCLOSURE REQUIREMENTS

Qualified transportation fringe benefits are not wages for purposes of the Federal Insurance Contributions Act (FICA), the Federal Unemployment Tax Act (FUTA), and federal income tax withholding if the requirements

45. See IRS Revenue Procedure 2003-85.
46. Ibid.
47. IRC Sec. 132(f)(7).

of Section 132(f) are satisfied. Benefits exceeding the applicable monthly limit (or reimbursements exceeding the monthly limits) or for which the statutory requirements are not satisfied are wages for purposes of FICA, FUTA, and federal income tax withholding. These amounts are reported on the employee's Form W-2, unless the employer reasonably believed the employee would be able to exclude that amount at the time the benefit was provided.[48]

SUMMARY

Employers and employees will likely continue to embrace Section 132(f) benefits and Congress will likely continue to make tax-favored provision for these benefits as the costs of transportation in urban areas grows. Because of the tax-preferred nature of these benefits, employers and employees win by offsetting the true cost of transportation and related costs for going to and from work.

48. The Thompson Publishing Group, *Employer's Guide to Fringe Benefit Rules,* Tab 600: *Qualified Transportation Fringes,* Par. 606, February 2009, p. 11.

VOLUNTARY BENEFITS

Voluntary benefits came into being in the 1990s as a way for employers to shift some of their benefits costs to employees by eliminating coverage of noncore benefits from their plans and giving employees a choice of which of these ancillary benefits they most wanted and would be willing to purchase through the employer. For example, if dental and vision benefits were once part of the employer's group health care plan, they were spun off into the voluntary benefit category. Voluntary plans offer employees the convenience of not having to shop around for the various benefits and the advantage of getting them at a reduced rate through the employer's group discount. Some benefits may be paid for with pretax dollars.[49] Employer responsibilities generally involve surveying employees to determine interest in the benefits, reviewing vendors and signing contracts, setting up payroll deduction or other payment forms, and communicating with employees.[50] Since their inception, their popularity has grown and ebbed with upturns and downturns in the national economy.

ADVANTAGES OF VOLUNTARY BENEFITS

Voluntary benefits are advantageous for employers because they can be viewed as offering more benefits without significant added cost to their bottom lines. For instance, they may wish to offer voluntary benefits such as dental, vision, critical care, and the like that are not otherwise available through the employer plan. They also may use voluntary benefits to supplement or replace employer-sponsored benefits that have been reduced or eliminated.[51] The benefits can act as an employee recruitment or retention tool with employers paying only for administrative costs. In addition, some companies are making available voluntary and work-life benefits (such as flex time) to employees that meet performance targets.[52]

Employees like the convenience of obtaining benefits through the workplace, and employers should consider allowing insurers offering voluntary benefits to meet with employees during paid work time.

49. BNA, Compensation and Benefits Guide, Welfare and Fringe Benefits, Voluntary Benefits, 2010.
50. Ibid.
51. CCH, Inc., *Employee Benefits Answer Book*, 2010, Par. 158,265.
52. BNA Compensation and Benefits Guide, 2010.

Approximately half of employers allow such meetings.[53] Employees also appreciate the fact that in many cases, these benefits are portable so they can take them with them to a new job.[54]

TYPES OF VOLUNTARY BENEFITS

Group term life insurance was the first voluntary benefits product and still remains the one most frequently offered by employers. It is also among the voluntary benefits most often purchased by employees. Other commonly offered voluntary benefits include

- Dependent life insurance
- Supplemental life insurance
- Long-term and/or short-term disability income insurance
- Dental insurance
- Long-term care coverage
- Adoption assistance
- Accidental death and dismemberment (AD&D) insurance
- Automobile insurance
- Homeowners insurance
- Benefits under a legal services plan
- Vision benefits coverage[55]

In recent years, voluntary benefits have grown to include a new list of benefits, such as

- Critical care insurance
- Cancer insurance
- Group homeowners insurance
- Hospital indemnity insurance
- Travel accident insurance
- Student medical insurance

Cancer policies, for example, are designed to cover health care costs associated with certain cancers. While cancer treatment and related costs are normally a covered expense under major medical group plans, some plans

53. CCH, Inc., *Employee Benefits Answer Book*, 2010.
54. Ibid.
55. CCH, Inc., *CCH, EXP-Benefits*, 2010.

would "laser" individuals with past or current cancer diagnoses, giving rise to a need for group health policies specifically designed to cover a plan participant who contracts cancer. It should be noted that the "lasering" of cancer as a medical condition in group medical health care policies is now prohibited under the Patient Protection and Accountability Act of 2010.

Group property and casualty insurance is another voluntary benefit that has grown popular with employees. This consists primarily of group home and automobile insurance policies, which are offered by many property and casualty insurance carriers as a voluntary benefit. One of the key benefits for plan participants is the advantageous pricing that can be had because the policies are underwritten as group policies. Another benefit of these plans is that the purchase is made through salary reduction like other employee benefits.

Travel insurance is another of the newer voluntary benefits. Travel can be expensive, and it is possible to lose any prepaid trip expenses if it is necessary to cancel or interrupt a trip. Travel interruption insurance applies when an employee or a family member travels and either gets sick, is injured or dies; the tour operator, airline or cruise line declares bankruptcy; or the reservation needs to be cancelled for any reason. The policy can even include a job-loss protection feature, so that if the employee becomes unemployed, it is easy to recover the trip costs. Travel insurance usually includes medical expense and medical evaluation coverage and provides 24-hour access to multilingual emergency assistance services.

LEGAL COMPLIANCE

Most voluntary benefits are treated by the tax code as taxable benefits. As such, voluntary benefits cannot be provided on a pretax basis through a Section 125 flexible spending plan. Voluntary benefits may be available, however, for employees to purchase through a cafeteria plan with after-tax dollars or credits.[56]

ERISA versus NonERISA Governance

Most voluntary benefits are not treated as plans subject to the Employee Retirement Income Security Act. They may be covered by ERISA, however, if they do not meet requirements established by regulations.[57] That being said, some employers choose to treat group benefits as ERISA-covered plans to ensure compliance with ERISA and the administrative structure and legal

56. IRC Sec. 125(f).
57. DOL Reg. Sec. 2510.3-1(j).

protection that ERISA provides.[58] The question of ERISA governance over voluntary benefits is addressed in DOL regulations. A plan is governed by ERISA if it is established or maintained by an employer, an employee organization, or both. The DOL has issued a regulation for determining when a group or group-type insurance arrangement may be excluded from ERISA.[59] Group or group-type programs that an insurer offers to employees or members of an employee organization will be excluded from ERISA coverage if the following four requirements are met:

1. The employer or employee organization does not make any contributions.
2. Participation in the program is completely voluntary for employees or members.
3. The employer's or employee organization's sole functions with respect to the program are, without endorsing the program, to (a) permit the insurer to publicize the program to employees or members, (b) collect premiums through payroll deductions or dues checkoffs, and (c) remit the premiums to the insurer.
4. The employer or employee organization receives no consideration (cash or otherwise) in connection with the program other than reasonable compensation, excluding any profit, for administrative services actually rendered in connection with payroll deductions or dues checkoffs.[60]

Prohibition of Employer Contributions

As noted above, employers are prohibited from making contributions for voluntary benefits on behalf of plan participants to avoid triggering ERISA compliance. In one case, an employer was held to have established an ERISA plan when it subsidized the cost of health insurance policies for several of its employees. The fact that the employees were permitted to choose the insurers they wanted did not make the arrangement too loose to constitute a plan.[61]

In another case, voluntary benefits were considered a group medical plan under which the employer paid the premium cost for its employees, but the employees were required to pay the entire premium cost for dependent coverage. In this example, an employee lost spousal coverage

58. DOL Opinion Letter 94-25A.
59. DOL Reg. Sec. 2510.3-1(j).
60. CCH, Inc., *Employee Benefits Answer Book*, 2010, Q. 2:5.
61. Madonia v. Blue Cross and Blue Shield of Va., 11 F.3d (4th Cir. 1993).

because of nonpayment of premiums for dependent coverage. The employee and his wife sued the insurance company under state law. Holding that state law was preempted by ERISA, the Circuit Court of Appeals refused to sever the dependent coverage from the employee coverage under the plan. As a result, the plan was found to be governed by ERISA because the employer did make contributions to the overall plan.[62]

In still another case, the employer paid all employee premiums for the insurance, except the premium for one employee who had reimbursed the employer for the premiums paid on his behalf. The employee, who wanted to sue the insurer under state law, claimed that since he paid his own premiums, there was no plan subject to ERISA, and hence his lawsuit was not preempted. However, the Circuit Court of Appeals in this case held that if an employer contributes to any employee's payment of premiums, ERISA must apply to the entirety of the insurance program, regardless of whether one employee pays his own premiums in full. According to the court, the ERISA policy of uniform regulation dictates a finding that a single plan may not be variously governed by ERISA and state law depending on the particular employee in question.[63]

Prohibition of Employer Endorsement of Voluntary Benefits

Employers offering voluntary benefits are also prohibited from endorsing the benefit program or the insurance carrier offering the benefits. This rule is particularly important if an employer wishes to avoid having an ERISA plan. Employer actions such as negotiating fees, processing claims, producing summary plan descriptions (SPDs), or selecting among options to be offered to its employees could constitute sufficient employer involvement to fall outside the exemption and cause an ERISA plan to exist.[64]

The federal courts have also considered how limited the employer's involvement in an employee-pay-all group insurance plan must be to fall within the preceding regulatory exemption. In one case, an employer provided accidental death and dismemberment insurance to its employees on an employee-pay-all basis, and participation by employees was voluntary. The employer collected and remitted premiums to the insurance company, hired an employee benefits administrator to forward employee claims to the insurance company, presented the plan as a supplement to the rest of its

62. Smith v. Jefferson Pilot Life Ins. Co., 14 F.3d 562 (11th Cir. 1994).
63. Helfman v. GE Group Life Assurance Co., 2009 U.S. Dist. LEXIS 112889 (E.D. Mich. Dec/ 4. 2009).
64. CCH, *Employee Benefits Answer Book*, 2010, Q. 2-11.

benefit program, and distributed to employees a descriptive benefit booklet with the employer's own name and logo on it. The booklet encouraged employees to give participation in the plan careful consideration because it could be a valuable supplement to their existing coverage.[65] The appellate court in this case concluded that the employer endorsed the plan and that its involvement in the plan was not limited to the activities specified in the regulation. It also found that, apart from DOL regulations, the employer clearly intended to establish an ERISA plan and had indeed "established" an ERISA plan, because there was a meaningful degree of employer participation in the creation and administration of the plan.[66]

SUMMARY

Voluntary benefits are closely tied to the national economy in that participation rates in these benefits tend to drop when the economy goes into recession and pick up again as economic recovery occurs. Having recently gone through an especially deep recession, it is understandable that voluntary benefits may have lost some of their sheen because of loss of headcount among employers and belt-tightening among employees.

Voluntary benefits have a bright future for employers and those who sell these benefits, considering the merit of a recent study that found that 34 percent of small employers do not offer voluntary benefits to their employees.[67] This is an important finding, since small business is the primary employer of American workers and the main generator of new jobs as the economy moves into recovery in any economic cycle. Thus, insurers, employers, and employees will likely continue to look to voluntary benefits as a vehicle to meet employer and employee needs in a cost-conscious employee benefits environment.

---

65. Ibid.
66. Hansen v. Continental Insurance. Co., 940 F.2d 971 (5th Cir. 1991). Similarly, the Eleventh Circuit concluded that an employer's involvement with an employee-pay-all disability plan was governed by ERISA. The employer's employee handbook referenced the plan as an available benefit, the employer selected the plan and established a fund to pay benefits, and the employer involved itself in the benefit payment process by supplying claim forms. [Moorman v. Unum Provident Corp., 464 F.3d 1260 (11th Cir. 2006)]. On the other hand, an employer that made a group insurance program available to its employees was held not to have established an ERISA plan where the employer performed only ministerial functions under the plan. The employer did not become involved in plan design or operation and did not endorse the program or include it as part of its employee benefits package. [Johnson v. Watts Regulator Co., 63 F.3d 1129 (1st Cir. 1995)].
67. Small Business, Big Benefits: How Smaller Employers Can Use Voluntary Benefits to Create a Competitive Advantage, Colonial Life Insurance Company Whitepaper, April 2010, p. 8.

CHAPTER 19

Financial Planning as an Employee Benefit

Robert T. LeClair

Today's business environment places extraordinary demands on individuals, couples, and families. Two-career couples, downsized corporations, home computers, smart phones, laptops, telecommuting, globalization, and other factors have contributed to a hectic, fast-paced, and sometimes frantic modern lifestyle.

Few people today have the luxury of adequate personal time to plan and to manage their own affairs, including their financial situations. They are rightly concerned that, despite all their hard work, they may not achieve the financial security and peace of mind they desire.[1] The economic crisis of 2008–2009, often labeled the "Great Recession," has only added to the anxiety and stress felt by many.

Similarly, corporations, faced with challenging labor markets, intense competition, and demanding shareholders, are anxious to attract and retain capable employees. In addition to paying higher salaries, firms have greatly expanded the menu of benefits available to their employees. Included in this menu, especially for officers and other highly compensated individuals, is the availability of personal financial planning services. Hopefully, freed to a degree from at least this one burden of modern life, employees may feel more relaxed and secure personally, and be able to contribute even more effectively in their work.

1. For a discussion of these concerns see, Juliet B. Schor, *The Overworked American: The Unexpected Decline of Leisure*, New York: Basic Books, 1992.

To make an informed decision on whether to offer these services as an employee benefit, an employer must understand the elements of financial planning. The first part of this chapter provides background information on the need for financial planning and the role of the financial planner and then outlines the financial planning process. The chapter concludes with an examination of financial planning as an employee benefit, discusses the providers of the needed services, and looks at the cost factors involved in providing them.

FINANCIAL PLANNING

Personal financial planning is concerned with acquiring and employing funds in a manner consistent with established financial objectives. Because money is a limited resource that can be spent in an endless variety of ways with widely different results, financial planning plays a critical role in the satisfactory achievement of objectives.

Individuals or families may experience problems in managing debt, current income and expenditures, protection, savings, investments, conflicting objectives, and haphazard or impulsive financial decisions. Perhaps most important, the individual or family may fail to meet needs and objectives in an economical and satisfactory way. Therefore, advice or consultation on the management of financial matters becomes a valuable service.

At one time it was common to think that only the wealthy needed to be concerned with personal financial planning. This is no longer the case. Increased income levels and benefits, taxation, inheritances, sophisticated financial markets and instruments, increasing longevity, and a generally higher standard of living have all added to the complexity of managing personal finances. The growth and change of our economy and social structure have contributed to the widespread acceptance of the need for planning.

The need for and applicability of financial planning is much broader in our society today than most individuals realize. Many people look only at their bank accounts or investment portfolios in determining the extent of their wealth. They fail to consider other assets, including their equity in a home, personal property (such as automobiles, furniture, and paintings), the cash value of life insurance, pension benefits, divorce settlements, profit-sharing programs, Social Security benefits, and other hidden assets as part of their financial position. Finally, individuals or couples concentrating on the demands of careers simply do not have time to explore all the possibilities for putting money to work, and may fail to consider the consequences that can occur if financial planning is neglected.

The Role of the Financial Planner

The management of financial affairs has been changing through the years. There was a time when setting a budget for household expenditures was considered to be adequate financial planning. If adhering to that budget was difficult, or if carrying out the plan seemed impossible, an individual might have sought the advice of a counselor. Such an adviser would have reviewed the client's income and expenditures and devised a spending plan that made efficient use of the available income.

As income levels increased, larger amounts of disposable income became available beyond basic needs. Individuals and families sought ways of making money work harder for them. Various investments may have looked interesting, but the complexities of the securities markets appeared to be overwhelming. At this point, the counselor also was asked to take on the role of an investment adviser. However, investment opportunities were much broader than just securities. The adviser was also expected to be knowledgeable concerning real estate, tax-advantaged investments, and even such "hard" assets as gold or diamonds.

Added to this were the client's needs for an accountant to prepare tax returns, a lawyer to draft wills and other documents, and an insurance agent to assist in the protection, preservation, and distribution of an estate. Today, the adviser has become someone who counsels clients in all of these areas and who serves as an intermediary in all these functions. From the growing needs of consumers has emerged a new professional, the financial planner.

The role of the financial planner is to provide total financial management for individuals or families to enable them to realize the maximum enjoyment of their finances in an efficient and economic manner. The best way to accomplish the financial objectives of a client is to develop specific plans to direct and control financial activity and progress. The financial planner must (1) assess the client's current financial position, (2) assist in establishing his or her objectives, (3) consider all constraints and variables that bear on those objectives, and (4) develop realistic projections and plans based on these factors. Financial planning is a process, an ongoing series of interrelated activities.

The Financial Planning Process

It is most important to understand the concept of financial planning not as a product or service, but as a process. Many persons who claim to provide planning services are really selling products and nothing more. For them, a "good plan" is simply one that requires extensive use of their products, whatever they may be. Similarly, a view of financial planning as a service provided at one point in time is also inadequate. This concept does not provide for the continuing and changing needs of an individual or family for information, analysis, and review of its program.

Financial planning should be thought of as a series of interrelated activities that a person participates in on a continuing basis. It is not something that is completed, even successfully, and then put away or forgotten. This is similar to the modern view of education that embraces learning not only through formal schooling but also throughout one's lifetime. In the same way, financial planning must be done regularly and continuously to take account of changes in an individual's circumstances, the availability of new products, and varying financial market conditions.

New tax legislation, fluctuating market interest rates, and the introduction of new or modified investment vehicles are examples of changes that can alter the way people and businesses handle money as well as the rates of return earned on liquid funds. As new products appear and market conditions change, even the most comprehensive and best-prepared financial plan may become obsolete. Changes in an individual's personal situation also may require adjustments in the overall plan. Births, deaths, marriages, divorces, or a new business venture can have a great impact on financial as well as personal planning.

The following activities in the process of financial planning must be carried out regularly and, when necessary, should involve qualified, professional advisers:

1. Gathering background information.
2. Establishing objectives.
3. Developing financial plans.
4. Executing and controlling plans.
5. Measuring performance.

The flowchart shown in Figure 19-1 provides a summary of the individual activities involved in the process and shows the relationships among them.

Background Analysis

Financial planning requires comprehensive data on everyone participating in the program. Such information includes a record of income and expenditures, as well as the current financial position of the individual or family. Prior to determining objectives, the financial planner needs

FIGURE 19-1

The Financial Planning Process

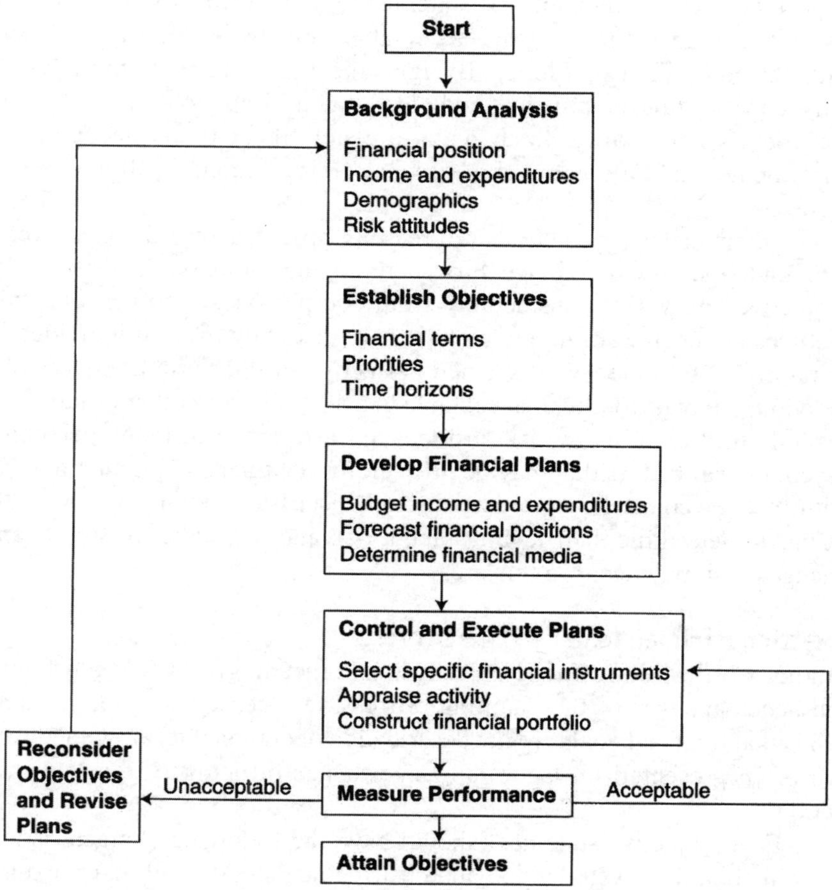

Source: The American College, *Introduction to Financial Counselling*, Bryn Mawr, PA: The American College, 1982, p. 133.

information regarding the sex, health, age, lifestyle, tastes, and preferences of individual family members. Much of this information is subjective, and attitudes may shift considerably over the years. Such changes make it important that the financial planner maintain frequent contact with the client to be aware of important changes in these personal and family characteristics.

Another important area of background analysis is the client's attitude toward the degree of risk in the overall financial plan. Feelings about investment risk, personal financial security, and independence are just as important as the client's income statement or net worth. An awareness of risk attitudes permits realistic, acceptable objectives to be established with the individual or family. By ignoring these feelings, the adviser runs the risk of developing a "good plan" that is simply out of touch with the client's personality. Such plans are not likely to be accepted or implemented, and a great deal of time, effort, and money will have been wasted.

Unfortunately, for a number of reasons, attitudes toward risk are very difficult to measure or to judge. First, defining the nature of "risk" is highly subjective and varies considerably from one person to another. Second, attitudes about risk are likely to change dramatically over an individual's or family's life cycle. What seemed perfectly reasonable to a 25-year-old individual may be totally unacceptable to a 40-year-old mother or father of several children. Finally, risk attitudes are a function of many personal, psychological factors that may be difficult for the financial planner to deal with. Yet, the counselor should try through discussions and interviews with clients to determine their feelings about risk and to be alert to significant changes that may occur in this area.

Setting Financial Objectives

Stating worthwhile financial objectives in a meaningful way is a difficult but necessary part of the planning process. One reason why many plans fail is that financial goals are not described in operational terms. Objectives are often presented in vague language that is difficult to translate into action.

Each objective statement should have the following characteristics. First, it should be well defined and clearly understood by all participants, including members of the financial planning team. Unless individuals really know and understand what they are trying to accomplish, it is not likely they will succeed. Writing down objectives is one way of working toward a set of clear and useful statements. Such comments as, "I want a safe and secure retirement income," do not provide much guidance for financial planners. They merely express an emotion that may be very real to the speaker but one that is hard to translate into effective terms and plans.

Second, good financial objectives are generally stated in quantitative terms. Only by attaching numbers to our plans can we know when the objective has been accomplished. For example, the objective could be stated as "I want to have an inflation-adjusted monthly income of $10,000 in retirement." This is a particularly important factor for long-term objectives, such as those concerning educational funding or retirement. It is desirable to measure progress toward these goals at regular intervals along the way.

The goal of having a particular sum for retirement in 20 years can be reviewed annually to see if the necessary progress has been made. If earnings have been lower than anticipated, larger contributions may have to be made in succeeding years. If a higher rate of return has been realized, future contributions can be reduced. Such fine tuning is impossible unless numbers are associated with plan objectives. Adding numbers to objectives also helps to make them more understandable to all members of the planning team as well as to participants in the plan.

Finally, each goal or objective should have a time dimension attached to it: When will a particular goal be accomplished? How much progress has been made since the last review? How much time remains until the goal is to be accomplished? These questions and similar ones can be answered only if a schedule has been established with objectives listed at particular points in time.

Some aspects of the plan, such as retirement objectives, will have very long timelines associated with them. Others, such as an adjustment to savings, may be accomplished in a few months or a year. Whether long-term or short-term in nature, the timing feature of objective statements is very important. Even long-term goals can be broken down into subperiods that can coincide with an annual review of the plan.

After the objectives have been stated, they must be put in priority order. This ranking process is necessary since different objectives normally compete for limited resources. It is unlikely that a planner will be able to satisfy all the client's objectives at the same time. Some goals are more important, more urgent, than others. Critical short-term needs may have to be satisfied ahead of longer-range plans.

Once certain goals have been reached, funds may be channeled to other areas. An example would be the funding of children's education. After this goal has been met, resources previously spent on education costs may be allocated to building a retirement fund or some other long-range objective. Unless these and other goals have been assigned specific priorities, it is impossible to organize and carry out an effective plan. Conversely, a set of well-integrated financial objectives can make the actual planning process a relatively easy task.

Individuals and families should have workable objectives in each of the following areas:

1. *Standard of living.* Maintaining a particular "lifestyle" normally takes the majority of an individual's financial resources. Setting an objective in this area calls for an analysis of required expenditures, such as food and shelter, as well as discretionary spending on such items as travel, vacations, and entertainment. If almost all income is being spent in this area, it is virtually impossible to accomplish any other objectives.

   One widely used rule of thumb states that no more than 80 percent of income should be spent on maintaining a given standard of living. The remaining 20 percent of disposable income should be allocated among the other financial objectives. Obviously, this guideline varies from one person or family to another. But, unless a significant portion of income can be channeled toward the remaining objectives, those goals are not likely to be reached.
2. *Savings.* Almost everyone recognizes the need for funds that can be used to meet an emergency or other special needs. However, determining the ideal level of savings can be a complex problem. It is influenced by the nature of income received, individual risk attitudes, stability of employment, and other factors, such as the type of health and dental insurance coverage.

   It is commonly recommended that savings balances be equal to at least three months' disposable income. These funds should be maintained in a safe and highly liquid form where rate of return is a secondary consideration. Today, the typical bank money market account or money market mutual fund offers an excellent vehicle for maintaining savings balances. These funds offer a high degree of safety, ready access through the use of checks, telephone, or online redemption of shares, and an acceptable rate of return for this type of highly liquid asset.
3. *Protection.* This objective has traditionally incorporated property, liability, disability, life, and medical insurance coverage. In recent years, reflecting our aging population and longer lifespans, long-term care insurance has been added to the menu. Overall, an insurance program should be designed to provide protection against insurable risks and related losses.

Objectives in this area should also take account of coverages provided through public programs, such as Social Security and Medicare, as well as group insurance plans offered as a related employee benefit. Such plans, subject to a wide range of political influences, are constantly changing and require planners to update their work on a regular basis. For example, in the medical area, Congress passed the Medicare Prescription Drug, Improvement, and Modernization Act of 2003, which permitted eligible individuals to establish health savings accounts (HSAs) for tax years beginning after 2003.[2] More recently, in March 2010, the Patient Protection and Affordable Care Act (H.R. 3590) became law. It extends health insurance coverage to many millions of previously uninsured persons.

4. *Accumulation (investment).* This is possibly the most complex objective in a number of ways. It relates to the buildup of capital for significant financial needs. These needs can be as diverse as a child's college education, a daughter's wedding, or the purchase of a vacation home. The sheer number and variety of such goals makes it difficult to define this objective and to set priorities.

   Adding to the difficult nature of planning in this area is the generally long time horizon, which may encompass 20 years or more. Finally, the wide variety of possible investment vehicles that can be used in the planning process adds to the overall complexity. Regardless of the reason for building capital, the critical ingredients in this objective are the ability to quantify the needed amount and to state a target date for its accumulation.

5. *Financial independence.* This objective may be thought of as a particularly important subset of the accumulation objective. It concerns the buildup of assets over a relatively long time in most cases. Such independence may be desired at a particular age and may or may not actually correspond with retirement from employment. Many persons may wish to have complete financial security and independence while continuing to work in a favored occupation or profession.

2. For a more complete description and analysis of HSAs see Stephan R. Leimberg and John J. McFadden, "Health Savings Accounts – An Important New Tool for Estate Planners," *Estate Planning*, Vol. 31, No. 4, 2004, pp. 194–199.

Since the planning horizon is such a lengthy one, this objective should be broken down into subgoals that can be evaluated, analyzed, and reworked over the years. More than most others, this area is affected by changes in government programs, such as Social Security, and in benefits paid by employers. For example, the recent removal of the Social Security earnings test will increase the retirement income of many working "retirees."

6. *Estate planning.* Objectives in this area are typically concerned with the preservation and distribution of wealth after the estate owner's death. However, accomplishing such goals may call for a number of actions to be taken well before that time. Writing a will is probably the most fundamental estate-planning objective, and yet thousands of persons die each year without having done so. These people die "intestate," and the distribution of their assets is determined by state laws and the courts.

   For larger estates, avoidance or minimization of estate taxes is an important consideration. These objectives can be accomplished, but they call for careful planning and implementation prior to the owner's death. The use of various trust instruments, distribution of assets through gifts, and proper titling of property all can result in a smaller taxable estate. Carrying out such a program, however, takes time and should be considered as various assets are being acquired. This also is an area where professional guidance generally is necessary. If the financial planner is not an attorney, one should be consulted in drafting a will or in preparing a trust document.

Developing Financial Plans

Once a realistic, well-defined set of objectives has been established, the financial planner can begin to develop actual plans. This planning stage includes the budgeting of income and expenditures for the near term, along with a forecast of future activity. A projection of the client's financial position for the next several years should also be made.

These plans should identify the financial instruments to be included in programs to meet specific objectives. For example, specific savings media should be recommended for those who need more in the way of emergency funds. Should a family increase its regular savings accounts, purchase money market certificates, or buy shares in a money market fund?

If an investment program is called for in the plan, recommendations should be made on the appropriate types of investments, such as securities, real estate, or tax shelters.

Executing and Controlling Plans

The next stage of the model calls for the financial planner to assist in setting the plan in motion. This may involve the purchase or sale of various assets, changes in life insurance protection, additional liability coverage, and other changes. All these activities should be monitored closely and appraised to see that they are effective in accomplishing the stated objectives. The outcome of some actions will be quickly apparent, while others may take a long time to produce results that can be evaluated.

Measuring Performance

The financial planner is responsible for gathering data on the plan's operations that are used to evaluate his or her performance and the actions of other professionals who may be involved. Such persons may include a banker, an attorney, a life insurance consultant, and an accountant.

This important step determines progress made toward the attainment of objectives. If performance to date is acceptable, no particular corrective action need be taken until the next scheduled review. However, if it is discovered that progress to date is unacceptable, several actions may need to be taken. These would include a review of the plans to see if they are still valid and an analysis of the market environment to take note of unanticipated changes.

It also may be necessary to review and alter the original objectives if they are no longer realistic and desirable. When this occurs, the entire plan may have to be recycled through each of the stages described previously. This model of financial planning is a dynamic one that is repeated continually as personal, financial, and environmental factors change.

FINANCIAL PLANNING AS AN EMPLOYEE BENEFIT

The array of programs, plans, and services that have been added to an employee's benefit package has expanded greatly over the past several years. Most benefits, by design, are selected or offered as part of a package for all employees; some are offered only to specific employees or groups of employees.

Financial planning is one benefit that has been limited primarily to key executives or other highly compensated employees. This came about partly from the belief that aspects of the program dealing with estate planning apply only to those individuals who will accumulate sufficient wealth to be subject to significant estate taxes.[3] Also, because programs recommended by financial planners may include forms of tax shelters that contain considerable risk, employees other than top executives might not have sufficient assets or income to justify the amount of risk involved. Finally, from the point of view of the employer, the full financial planning process is generally expensive, and this fact limits extending the benefit to large numbers of lower-income employees.

Despite these logical reasons for limiting the financial planning benefit to employees in top management, financial planning is gradually growing in importance as a benefit for those employees in the middle-management category. The increasing cost and complexity of pension, health, and other noncash benefits, increases in the use of flexible benefit plans, the need for counsel regarding the expanding investment options in defined contribution plans, and the growing importance of retirement planning are all reasons why financial planning as an employee benefit is receiving increasing interest.

Services Provided

Because of the relatively high cost, many firms have opted for a partial financial planning service rather than the full process. These separate services include the following:

1. Estate planning—disposition at death, insurance arrangements, minimization of taxes, and estate liquidity
2. Tax preparation—federal, state, and local returns; estate and gift tax returns

3. The Economic Growth and Tax Relief Reconciliation Act of 2001 (EGTRRA) made major changes in the law relating to federal estate taxes. The schedule of excluded amounts was regularly increased as follows: 2004 and 2005—$1,500,000; 2006, 2007, and 2008—$2,000,000; 2009—$3,500,000. EGTRRA repealed the federal estate tax altogether for one year, 2010, but then restored the tax for years 2011 and beyond with an excluded amount of only $1,000,000 and a top tax rate of 55%. However, on December 17, 2010, *The Tax Relief, Unemployment Insurance Reauthorization, and Job Creation Act of 2010* was signed into law by President Obama. This Act increased the estate tax exemption to $5 million, set the top estate tax rate at 35%, and made fundamental changes to numerous other areas of estate and gift tax law.

3. Investment management—short and long-term investment programs, tax shelters
4. Compensation planning—analysis of options available, explanation of benefits
5. Preparation of wills

Some of these services may be provided by employees of the firm, while others are contracted for and performed by outside specialists knowledgeable in a particular area. As the number of individual services available expands, the need for full financial planning becomes more apparent. Many companies are now providing financial planning benefits to their top executives, and some have expanded it to middle managers as well.

Advantages

The major advantages of financial planning as an employee benefit are as follows:

1. Because of such factors as downsizing, outsourcing, or corporate reengineering, many executives do not have sufficient time to devote to their own financial affairs. Financial planning as a benefit relieves them of having to spend time on financial planning and permits them to concentrate on business matters.
2. By reducing the likelihood that a poor decision will be made on his or her own finances, the executive has greater personal peace of mind.
3. The employer is probably better able to screen and select financial planners. Thus, the executive is less likely to receive poor advice from unqualified planners.
4. Salaries offered may appear more attractive and competitive when such compensation is being used more efficiently to reach each executive's goals.

Disadvantages

Although financial planning as an employee benefit would appear to be attractive to both employer and employee, there are several reasons for not providing such services:

1. Financial planning may be construed as meddling in an employee's personal affairs. A related concern on the part of

employees is the rising tide of so-called "identity theft," where an individual's personal and financial information is used for various illegal activities. Collecting and storing large amounts of detailed, individual information in centralized computer files may only add to these concerns.

2. There is a risk that the company could be held accountable for inaccurate or poor advice, since it has endorsed the services or employed the counselor.
3. Although the planning service is considered helpful to highly compensated employees, many companies are reluctant to provide benefits that are restricted to select groups of employees.
4. The cost of providing these services can be substantial.

Who Provides Financial Planning?

Financial planning services are provided by numerous individuals and firms, including banks, insurance companies and agents, investment brokers, benefit consultants, lawyers, accountants, and others. The major firms specializing in financial planning services generally have staffs of professionals who are experts in investments, insurance, tax shelters, and so on, and who work as a team to provide the financial planning service. Smaller organizations may concentrate on one area and hire consultants to complete the planning team.

The selection of a financial planning firm requires care. It is important that the objectives of the employer be satisfied, and, from the employees' standpoint, that their individual confidences be protected and the advice be in their best interests. Some employers have attempted to provide financial planning services through in-house personnel. This is most effective when the benefit is limited to a single service, such as tax advice. However, problems occur because many executives are hesitant to discuss details of their personal financial affairs with fellow employees.

The selection decision is sometimes simply one of identifying the best financial planning firm available. Generally, a firm that operates on a fee-only basis is the preferred type. However, the objectives of the employer may warrant consideration of product-oriented financial planners. For example, if the objective of the benefit is limited to advice on life insurance planning, a competent life insurance agent may be able to satisfy the need. Further, banks, brokerage firms, and life insurance companies have formed financial planning divisions that provide support services for their personnel. Therefore, although an adviser may be product-oriented, he or she has substantial breadth of assistance available to analyze and design broad-based financial plans. In these cases, a fee may be charged even though commissions exist.

Individual professionals call themselves financial counselors, financial planners, or financial advisers. Many of these persons still depend solely on commissions for their income. However, since it is difficult for any single individual to give professional advice in all areas included in a comprehensive plan, the trend is to join together to form firms that are rich in experience and professionally qualified in all aspects of financial planning and that are compensated through fees or a combination of commissions and fees. There exist today many quality individuals and firms that provide financial counseling. The most important ingredient, therefore, is to seek the individual or firm that understands financial planning as a process, one that can have important beneficial results for employers and employees alike.

Fiduciary Responsibility

As financial planners take on a wider range of responsibilities for their clients, a special fiduciary relationship develops between them. This arrangement arises whenever one person places confidence and trust in the integrity and fidelity of another. A fiduciary relationship is characterized by faith and reliance on the part of the client and by a condition of superior knowledge of financial matters and influence on the part of the financial planner.

The existence of a fiduciary responsibility does not depend upon the establishment of any particular legal relationship. Nonlegal relationships can be fiduciary in nature, especially where one person entrusts his or her business affairs to another.

When a fiduciary relationship exists, the fiduciary (adviser) has a duty to act in good faith and in the interests of the other person. A fiduciary is not permitted to use the relationship to benefit his or her own personal interest. Transactions between the client and counselor are subject to close scrutiny by the courts. Especially sensitive are transactions in which the fiduciary profits at the expense of the client. Fiduciaries must subordinate their individual interests to their duty of care, trust, and loyalty to the client.

The Investment Advisers Act of 1940 is particularly important in defining the nature of a fiduciary relationship. One objective of the act is to expose and eliminate all conflicts of interest that could influence an adviser to be other than disinterested. Congress thus empowered the courts to require full and fair disclosure of all material facts surrounding the fiduciary relationship. The adviser must disclose in a meaningful way all material facts that give rise to potential or actual conflicts of interest. For example, an adviser who receives commissions on products, such as securities or life insurance, sold to clients should disclose the amount of sales compensation received on recommended transactions.[4]

Cost

The cost of financial planning varies, based on the range of services to be provided and the type of individuals employed to provide them. A financial counselor or counseling firm may operate on a fee-only basis, a commission-only basis, or some combination of commissions and fees. The existence of commissions, which may eliminate or greatly reduce costs to the employer, can be a strong incentive for companies to seek product-oriented purveyors of financial planning services. It should be understood, however, that insurance or investment advice given to employees could be heavily weighted in favor of products available from the counseling firm. For this reason, employers usually prefer financial counseling on a fee-only basis, since the belief is that this provides the most objective analyses and unbiased recommendations.

Because the financial planning process is often extremely detailed and complicated, costs of $3,000 to $10,000 or even higher per executive are common for a complete counseling program. Another approach used by some counseling firms involves seminars where the counseling process and available services are explained to groups of eligible employees. Some firms charge a separate fee of $1,000 to $3,500 for the initial data-gathering or fact-finding visit with the employee. In addition, if legal documents or certified financial statements are required, there may be additional legal and accounting fees. Finally, after the initial year of the program, the annual fees for maintaining and updating the program are based on required time and effort, generally averaging $1,000 to $2,000 per employee.

The relatively high cost of financial planning as an employee benefit has undoubtedly contributed to its limited availability to only highly compensated executives and perhaps to its limited adoption overall. The cost of

4. Robert W. Cooper and Dale S. Johnson, "The Impact of the Investment Advisers Act of 1940 on CLUs and Other Financial Services Professionals," *CLU Journal*, April 1982, p. 35.

financial planning to the firm can be reduced by offering the benefit to employees on a contributory basis.

The fees paid for financial planning are generally deductible by the corporation for tax purposes if the total compensation to the employee, including the counseling fee, is not considered unreasonable compensation by the Internal Revenue Service (IRS).[5] When this benefit is offered to highly compensated executives, the fee would generally be small, compared with the executive's total compensation, and it is unlikely that total compensation would be considered unreasonable.

The amount the employer pays to the planning firm for services performed for an employee is considered taxable income to the employee and is subject to withholding tax.[6] However, an offsetting tax benefit may be available to the employee because deductions are allowed for services related to tax matters or allocable to investment advice.[7] Therefore, it could be possible for the employee to contribute the cost associated with those services allowed as deductions. The financial planning firm should indicate clearly the charge for these services as a separate item on its billing.

In addition to the tax aspects, when supplemental legal or accounting fees are necessary, these expenses should be borne by the employee. Overall, contributions by employees could reduce the cost to the employer and make it possible for the firm to offer financial planning as an employee benefit.

CONCLUSION

Financial planning has become an increasingly important employee benefit as more employers offer such services and as more employees qualify for eligibility. Other factors contributing to this growth are the maturity of the financial planning industry itself, and an increased need for financial counseling by employees who need to make investment decisions because of their pension plans being changed from the defined benefit to the defined contribution variety. While the costs associated with offering financial planning services as a benefit are not insignificant, clear advantages exist for both the employer and the employee. There also are areas of concern, however, and employers should carefully analyze the nature of their employees and the qualifications of those offering to provide financial planning services for them.

5. IRC Sec. 106.
6. IRC Sec. 61.
7. Fees paid for investment counsel are deductible only to the extent that *all second-tier* miscellaneous itemized deductions cumulatively exceed 2 percent of adjusted gross income.

PART FIVE

Social Insurance Programs

Part Five covers the fundamentals of several social insurance programs that provide a basic layer of protection against various exposures. Chapter 20 discusses Social Security, with a focus on survivorship and disability benefits, as well as Medicare. Chapter 21 focuses on Medicare Part D prescription drug coverage, with particular emphasis on how the rules apply to group health plans. Chapter 22 explores workers' compensation programs, and Chapter 23 examines unemployment compensation systems. It is essential to understand these social insurance programs, because their coordination with private benefit programs is vital to sound employee benefit planning.

CHAPTER 20

Social Security and Medicare: Focus on Disability, Survivorship, and Medicare Provisions

Robert J. Myers

Economic security for retired workers, disabled workers, and survivors of deceased workers in the United States is, in the vast majority of cases, provided through the multiple means of Social Security, private pensions, and individual savings. This is sometimes referred to as a three-legged stool or the three pillars of economic-security protection. It also can be seen as a layered arrangement, with Social Security providing the floor of protection, private-sector activities building on top of it, and public assistance programs, such as Supplemental Security Income (SSI), providing a net of protection for those whose total income does not attain certain levels or meet minimum subsistence needs.

Although some people may view the Social Security program as one that should provide complete protection, over the years it has generally been agreed that it should only be the foundation of protection.

The term "Social Security" is used here with the meaning generally accepted in the United States, namely, the cash benefits provisions of the Old-Age, Survivors, and Disability Insurance (OASDI) program. International usage of the term "social security" is much broader than this and includes all other types of governmental programs protecting individuals against the economic risks of a modern industrial system, such as

This chapter is adapted and updated from *Retirement Plans*, 10th ed. by Allen, Melone, Rosenbloom and Mahoney, Copyright 2008. Reprinted with permission from McGraw-Hill Irwin.

unemployment, short-term sickness, work-connected accidents and diseases, and medical care costs. This chapter focuses on the Disability, Survivorship and Medicare parts of Social Security.

DISABILITY BENEFITS

Listed below are the historical development of disability provisions, the eligibility conditions, the beneficiary categories, the benefit computation procedures, the eligibility test, other restrictions, and freeze provision on disability benefits.

Historical Development of Disability Provisions

It was not until the 1956 act that monthly disability benefits were added to the OASDI program, although the "disability freeze" provision (in essence, a waiver-of-premium provision), described later, was added in the 1952 act.[1] It may well be said that long-term disability is merely premature old-age retirement.

The monthly disability benefits were initially available only at age 50 and over—that is, deferred to that age for those disabled earlier—with no auxiliary benefits for the spouse and dependent children. These limitations were quickly removed by the 1958 and 1960 acts.

Eligibility Conditions for Disability Benefits

To be eligible for disability benefits, individuals must be both fully insured and disability insured.[2] Disability-insured status requires 20 quarters of coverage (QCs) earned in the 40-quarter period ending with the quarter of disability, except that persons disabled before age 31 also can qualify if they have QCs in half of the quarters after age 21.[3] The definition of disability is relatively strict. The disability must be so severe that the individual is unable to engage in any substantial gainful activity, and the impairment must be a medically determinable physical or mental condition that is expected to continue for at least 12 months or to result in prior death.

1. Actually, it was so written in the 1952 legislation as to be inoperative, but then was reenacted in 1954 to be on a permanent, ongoing basis.
2. Blind persons need be only fully insured.
3. For those disabled before age 24, the requirement is six QCs in the last 12 quarters.

Benefits are first payable after completion of six full calendar months of disability. For persons with alcoholism or drug abuse, disability benefits are not payable unless they have another severe disabling condition that, by itself, would be qualifying.

Beneficiary Categories for Disability Benefits

In addition to the disabled worker, dependents in the same categories that apply to old-age retirement benefits can receive monthly benefits.

Benefit Computation Procedures for Disability Benefits

In all cases, the benefits are based on the primary insurance amount (PIA), which is calculated by applying a formula that varies according to the year of eligibility for benefits to the worker's average earnings over a certain number of years. The PIA is computed in the same manner as for retirement benefits, except that fewer dropout years than five are allowed in the computation of the average indexed monthly earnings (AIME) for persons disabled before age 47.[4] The disabled worker receives a benefit equal to 100 percent of the PIA, and the auxiliary beneficiaries each receive 50 percent of the PIA, subject to the Maximum Family Benefit.

An overall maximum on total family benefits is applicable, which is lower than that for survivor and retirement benefits—namely, no more than the smaller of 150 percent of the PIA, or 85 percent of AIME (but not less than the PIA).

Eligibility Test for Disability Benefits and Other Restrictions on Benefits

The earnings or retirement test applies to the auxiliary beneficiaries of disabled workers, but not to the disabled worker beneficiary. However, the earnings of one beneficiary (e.g., the spouse of the disabled worker) do not affect the benefits of the other beneficiaries in the family (e.g., the disabled worker or the children). The test does not apply to disabled worker beneficiaries, because any earnings are considered in connection with whether recovery has occurred, except those during trial work periods (which earnings may possibly lead to removal from the benefit roll later).

4. Specifically four such quarters for ages 42–46, grading down to none for ages 26 and under.

OASDI disability benefits are coordinated with disability benefits payable under other governmental programs (including programs of state and local governments), except for needs-tested ones, benefits payable by the Department of Veterans Affairs, and government employee plans coordinated with OASDI. The most important of such coordinations is with workers' compensation (WC) programs, whose benefits are taken into account in determining the amount of the OASDI disability benefit (except in a few states that provide for their WC benefits to be reduced when OASDI disability benefits are payable—possible only for states that did this before February 19, 1981). The total of the OASDI disability benefit (including any auxiliary benefits payable) and the other disability benefit recognized cannot exceed 80 percent of "average current earnings" (generally based on the highest year of earnings in covered employment in the last six years, but indexed for changes in wage levels following the worker's disablement).

Disability Freeze

In the event that a disability beneficiary recovers, the so-called disability freeze provision applies. Under this, the period of disability is "blanked out" in the computation of insured status and benefit amounts for subsequent retirement, disability, and survivor benefits.

SURVIVOR BENEFITS

Listed below are the historical development of survivor provisions, eligibility conditions, beneficiary categories benefit computation procedures, the eligibility test, other restrictions, and financing provisions of OASDI programs for survivors.

Historical Development of Survivor Provisions

When what is now the OASDI program was developed in 1934–35, it was confined entirely to retirement benefits (plus lump-sum refund payments to represent the difference, if any, between employee taxes paid, plus an allowance for interest, and retirement benefits received). It was not until the 1939 act that monthly survivor benefits were added with respect to deaths of both active workers and retirees, in lieu of the refund benefit.

The term "widow" is used here to include also widowers. Until 1983, the latter did not receive OASDI benefits on the same basis as widows, either being required to prove dependence on the deceased female worker or not being eligible at all. Now, because of legislative changes and court decisions, complete equality of treatment by sex prevails for OASDI survivor benefits.

The minimum eligibility age for aged widows was initially established at age 65 and coincided with the then normal retirement age (NRA) for insured workers. This age was selected in a purely empirical manner.

Beginning in the 1950s, pressure developed to provide early retirement benefits, first for widows and spouses and then for insured workers themselves. The minimum early-retirement age was set at 62—a pragmatic political compromise, rather than a completely logical choice—and was later lowered to age 60 for widows. The three-year differential, however, did represent about the average difference in age between men and their wives (but, of course, as with any average, in many cases the actual difference may be larger or smaller). The benefit amounts were not reduced for widows when they claimed before age 65 under the original amendatory legislation, but this is no longer the case.

Eligibility Conditions for Survivor Benefits

To be eligible for OASDI survivor benefits, individuals must have either fully insured status or currently insured status. The latter requires only six QCs earned in the 13-quarter period ending with the quarter of death.

Survivor Beneficiary Categories

Two general categories of survivors of insured workers can receive monthly benefits. Aged survivors are widows aged 60 and over (or at ages 50–59 if disabled) and dependent parents aged 62 and over. Young survivors are children under age 18 (or at any age if disabled before age 22), children aged 18 who are full-time students in elementary or high school (i.e., defined just the same as in the case of retirement and disability beneficiaries), and the widowed parent of such children who are under age 16 or disabled before age 22. In addition, a death benefit of $255 is payable to widows or, in the absence of a widow, to children eligible for immediate monthly benefits.

A disabled widow receives a benefit at the rate of 71.5 percent of the deceased worker's PIA if claim is first made at ages 50–59. The benefit rate for other widows grades up from 71.5 percent of the PIA if claimed at age 60 to 100 percent if claimed at the normal retirement age which is age 65 for those attaining age 60 before 2000, grading up to 67 for those attaining age 60 in 2022 and after. Any delayed retirement credits (DRCs) that the deceased worker had earned are also applicable to the widow's benefit. Widows, regardless of age, caring for an eligible child (under age 16 or disabled before age 22) have a benefit of 75 percent of the PIA. Divorced spouses, when the marriage lasted at least 10 years, are eligible for benefits under the same conditions as undivorced spouses.

The benefit rate for eligible children is 75 percent of the PIA. The benefit rate for dependent parents is 82.5 percent of the PIA, unless two parents are eligible, in which case it is 75 percent for each one.

The same overall maximum on total family benefits is applicable as is the case for retirement benefits. If a person is eligible for more than one type of benefit (e.g., both as a worker and as a surviving spouse), in essence, only the largest benefit is payable.

Benefit Computation Procedures for Survivor Benefits

In all cases, the monthly survivor benefits are based on the PIA, and then are adjusted to reflect the Maximum Family Benefit, both of which are computed in essentially the same manner as for retirement benefits.[5]

Eligibility Test for Survivor Benefits and Other Restrictions

Marriage (or remarriage) of a survivor beneficiary generally terminates benefit rights. The only exceptions are remarriage of widows after age 60 (or after age 50 for disabled widows) and marriage to another OASDI beneficiary (other than one who is under age 18).

From the inception of the OASDI program, there has been some form of restriction on the payment of benefits to persons who have substantial earnings from employment—the earnings or retirement test. The same test applies to survivor beneficiaries as to retirement benefits for retirees who

5. For individuals who die before age 62, the computation is made as though the individual had attained age 62 in the year of death. In addition, for deferred widow's benefits, an alternative computation based on indexing the deceased's earnings record up to the earlier of age 60 of the worker or age 60 of the widow is used if this produces a more favorable result.

are under the NRA. However, the earnings of one beneficiary (e.g., the widowed mother) do not affect the benefits of the other beneficiaries in the family (e.g., the orphaned children).

If a widow receives a pension from service under a government employee pension plan under which the members were not covered under OASDI on the last day of her employment, the OASDI widow's benefit is reduced by two-thirds of the amount of such pension. This provision, however, is not applicable to women (or to men who were dependent on their wives) who became eligible for such a pension before December 1982 or to individuals who became first so eligible from December 1982 through June 1983 and who were dependent on their spouses.

Financing Provisions of OASDI Program

From its inception until the 1983 act, the OASDI program was financed entirely by payroll taxes (and interest earnings on the assets of the OASDI trust funds), with only minor exceptions, such as the special benefits at a subminimum level for certain persons without insured status who attained age 72 before 1972. Thus, on a permanent ongoing basis, no payments from general revenues were available to the OASDI system; the contributions for covered federal civilian employees and members of the armed forces are properly considered as "employer" taxes.

The 1983 act introduced two instances of general-revenues financing of the OASDI program. As a one-time matter, the tax rate in 1984 was increased to what had been previously scheduled for 1985 (i.e., for both the employer and employee, from 5.4 percent to 5.7 percent), but the increase for employees was, in essence, rescinded, and the General Fund of the Treasury made up the difference to the OASDI Trust Funds. On an ongoing basis, the General Fund passes on to the trust funds the proceeds of the income taxation of 50 percent of OASDI benefits for upper-middle income and high-income persons (first effective for 1984), and, in fact, does so somewhat in advance of actual receipt of such moneys.[6]

The payroll taxes for the retirement and survivors benefits go into the OASI Trust Fund, while those for the disability benefits go into the DI Trust Fund, and all benefit payments and administrative expenses for these provisions are paid therefrom. The balances in the trust funds are invested

6. The income taxes on the next 35 percent of benefits (first effective in 1994) anomalously go to the Hospital Insurance Trust Fund.

in federal government obligations of various types, with interest rates at the current market values for long-term securities. The federal government does not guarantee the payments of benefits. If the trust fund were to be depleted, it could not obtain grants, or even loans, from the General Fund of the Treasury. However, a temporary provision (effective only in 1982) permitted the OASI Trust Fund to borrow, repayable with interest, from the DI and HI Trust Funds. A total of $17.5 billion was borrowed ($12.4 billion from HI). The last of such loans was repaid in 1986. Payroll taxes are levied on earnings up to only a certain annual limit, which is termed the earnings base. This base is applicable to the earnings of an individual from each employer in the year, but the person can obtain a refund (on the income tax form) for all employee taxes paid in excess of those on the earnings base. The self-employed pay OASDI taxes on their self-employment income on no more than the excess of the earnings base over any wages they may have had.

Since 1975, the earnings base for OASDI has been determined by the automatic-adjustment procedure, on the basis of increases in the nation-wide average wage. However, for 1979–1981, ad hoc increases of a higher amount were legislated; the 1981 base was established at $29,700. The 1982 and subsequent bases were determined under the automatic adjustment provision. The base for 2011 is $106,800.

The payroll tax rate is a combined one for OASI, DI, and HI, but it is allocated among the three trust funds. The employer and employee rates are equal. However, under the Patient Protection and Affordable Care Act (PPACA) there is an additional tax on high-income individuals. The specific details of this tax are discussed in the Medicare section of this chapter. The self-employed pay the combined employer-employee rate. Also, until 1991, the earnings base was the same for OASDI and HI, but, in 1991, the base for HI was raised to $125,000; it was $130,200 in 1992, and it was eliminated for 1994 and after.

MEDICARE PROGRAM

Health (or medical care) benefits for active and retired workers and their dependents in the United States are, in the vast majority of cases, provided through the multiple means of the Medicare portion of Social Security (for persons aged 65 and over and for long-term disabled persons), private employer-sponsored plans, and individual savings. As mentioned earlier, this is sometimes referred to as a "three-legged stool" or the three pillars of economic security protection. Another view of the situation for persons aged 65 and over and for long-term disabled persons is of Medicare providing the floor of protection for certain categories, or, in other cases, providing the basic protection. Supplementing this, private insurance is present, with public assistance programs such as Medicaid, providing a safety net of protection for those whose income is not sufficient to purchase the needed medical care not provided through some form of prepaid insurance.

Private health benefit plans supplement Medicare to some extent. In other instances—essentially for active workers and their families—health benefit protection is provided by the private sector. The net result, however, is a broad network of health benefit protection.

Historical Development of Provisions

Beginning in the early 1950s, efforts were made to provide medical care benefits (primarily for hospitalization) for beneficiaries under the OASDI program. In 1965, such efforts succeeded, and the resulting program is called Medicare.

Initially, Medicare applied only to persons aged 65 and over. In 1972, disabled Social Security beneficiaries who had been on the benefit rolls for at least two years were made eligible, as were virtually all persons in the country who have end-stage renal disease (i.e., chronic kidney disease). Since 1972, relatively few changes in coverage or benefit provisions have been made, other than the enactment of prescription-drug benefits in 2003 (described later) and other improvements in benefits under PPACA enacted in 2010. The law also contains many provisions that attempt to reduce Medicare spending as well as reducing overall health care costs.

Medicare now is really four separate programs. Medicare Part A, Hospital Insurance,[7] is financed primarily from payroll taxes on workers covered under OASDI, including those under the Railroad Retirement system. Beginning in 1983, all civilian employees of the federal government were covered under Part A, even though, in general, not covered by OASDI. Also, beginning in April 1986, all newly hired state and local government employees are compulsorily covered (and, at the election of the governmental entity, all employees in service on March 31, 1986, who were not covered under OASDI can be covered under Part A). Medicare

7. Medicare Hospital Insurance is sometimes referred to as HI.

Part B, Medical Insurance,[8] is on an individual voluntary basis and is financed partially by enrollee premiums, with the remainder, currently about 75 percent, coming from general revenues. Medicare Part C, also called Medicare Advantage (MA),[9] offers private plan alternatives to Medicare. Medicare Part D, a voluntary program providing prescription-drug benefits, is financed by a mixture of payments by the insured person and general revenues.

Under PPACA, beginning in 2013, there will be additional Medicare taxes of 0.9 percent on wages and a 3.8 percent tax on unearned income on individuals with adjusted gross income (AGI) over $200,000 for an individual income tax filer or $250,000 for joint income tax return filers. Income from interest, dividends, annuities, royalties, rents, and capital gains (net gain from the sale of a property) are subject to the tax. The unearned income tax does not apply to qualified retirement plan distributions or to income in a business that is not a passive activity.

As an alternative to "traditional" Medicare, persons eligible under both Parts A and B (except those previously diagnosed with end-stage renal disease) can elect to participate in a Medicare Advantage plan. There are several types of such plans, but generally they must provide at least the same benefits as Medicare Parts A and B (usually, they provide more). They often include prescription drug benefits as well. These plans receive per capita payments from Medicare (the participant continues paying the premiums to Medicare), which hopefully are equitable reimbursement. In theory, these plans are supposed to provide better health care at a lower cost through managed care principles, but some critics believe that they do not always provide adequate care, especially because they usually do not allow free choice of physicians to provide the services (and generally little or no choice at all).

Several additional provisions of PPACA affect MA plans. In 2011, it freezes payments to 100 percent of Medicare fee-for-service costs. Beginning in 2012, the law phases in a reduction in payments, and provides bonuses for quality achievements and deductions for what are deemed improper actions.

In 2014, PPACA establishes a minimum Medical Loss Ratio (MLR) for MA plans of 85 percent, with penalties for plans with a lower MLR.

8. Previously known as Supplementary Medical Insurance or SMI.

9. Formerly known as *Medicare + Choice.*

Persons Protected by Part A Hospital Insurance

All individuals aged 65 and over who are eligible for monthly benefits under OASDI or the Railroad Retirement program are also eligible for Medicare Part A Hospital Insurance (HI) benefits (as are federal employees and state and local employees who have sufficient earnings credit from their special HI coverage). Persons are "eligible" for OASDI benefits if they could receive them when the person under whose earnings record they are eligible is deceased or receiving disability or retirement benefits, or could be receiving retirement benefits except for having substantial earnings. Thus, the HI eligibles include not only insured workers, but also spouses, disabled children (in the rare cases where they are at least age 65), and survivors, such as widowed spouses and dependent parents. As a specific illustration, HI protection is available for an insured worker and spouse, both at least age 65, even though the worker has such high earnings that OASDI cash benefits are not currently payable because of election to defer receipt of benefits.

In addition, Part A eligibility is available for disabled beneficiaries who have been on the benefit roll for at least two years (beyond a five-month waiting period). Such disabled eligibles include not only insured workers but also disabled child beneficiaries aged 18 and over who were disabled before age 22, and disabled widowed spouses aged 50 to 64.

Further, persons under age 65 with end-stage renal disease (ESRD) who require dialysis or renal transplant are eligible for Part A benefits if they meet one of a number of requirements. Such requirements for ESRD benefits include being fully or currently insured, being a spouse or a dependent child of an insured worker or of a monthly beneficiary, or being a monthly beneficiary.

Individuals aged 65 and over who are not eligible for HI as a result of their own or some other person's earnings can elect coverage, and then must make premium payments, whereas OASDI eligibles do not. The standard monthly premium rate is $450 for 2011 (but only $248 if they have at least 30 to 39 quarters of coverage).

Benefits Provided Under Part A Hospital Insurance

The principal benefit provided by the Part A program is for hospital services. The full cost for all such services, other than luxury items, is paid by Part A during a so-called spell of illness, after an initial deductible has been paid and with daily coinsurance for all hospital days after the 60th, but with an upper limit on the number of days covered. A spell of illness is a period beginning with the first day of hospitalization and ending when the individual has been out of both hospitals and skilled nursing facilities for 60 consecutive days. The initial deductible is $1,132 for 2011. The daily coinsurance is $283 in 2011 for the 61st to 90th days of hospitalization. A nonrenewable lifetime reserve of 60 days is available after the regular 90 days have been used; these lifetime reserve days are subject to daily coinsurance of $566 for 2011. The deductible and coinsurance amounts are adjusted automatically each year after 2011 to reflect past changes in hospital costs.

Benefits are also available for care provided in skilled nursing facilities, following at least three days of hospitalization. Such care is provided only when it is for convalescent or recuperative care and not for custodial care. The first 20 days of such care in a spell of illness are provided without cost to the individual. The next 80 days, however, are subject to a daily coinsurance payment of $141.50 in 2011 which will be adjusted automatically in the future in the same manner as the hospital cost-sharing amounts. No benefits are available after 100 days of care in a skilled nursing facility for a particular spell of illness.

In addition, an unlimited number of home health service benefits are provided by Part A and/or Part B without any payment being required from the beneficiary. Also, hospice care for terminally ill persons is covered if all Medicare benefits, other than physician services, are waived; certain cost restrictions and coinsurance requirements apply with respect to prescription drugs.

Part A benefit protection is provided only within the United States, with the exception of certain emergency services available when in or near Canada. Not covered by Part A are those cases where services are performed in a Department of Veterans Affairs hospital or where the person is eligible for medical services under a workers' compensation program. Furthermore, Medicare is the secondary payor in cases when (1) medical care is payable under any liability policy, especially automobile ones; (2) during the first 30 months of treatment for ESRD cases when private group health insurance provides coverage; (3) for persons aged 65 and over (employees and spouses) who are under employer-sponsored group health insurance plans (which is required for all plans of employers with at least 20 employees) unless the employee opts out of it; and (4) for disability beneficiaries under the plan of an employer with at least 100 employees when the beneficiary is either an "active individual" or a family member of an employee.

Financing of Part A Hospital Insurance

With the exception of the small group of persons who voluntarily elect coverage, the Part A program is financed by payroll taxes on workers in employment covered by OASDI. This payroll tax rate is combined with that for OASDI. The HI tax rate is the same for employers and employees; self-employed persons pay the combined employer-employee tax rate, but have an offset to allow for the effect of business expenses on income taxes (as described earlier in connection with OASDI taxes). This HI tax rate for employees was 1.45 percent in 1990 (and in all future years). The maximum taxable earnings base for HI was the same as that for OASDI for all years before 1991, but thereafter was a higher amount, and, beginning in 1994, no limit is applicable. As already mentioned, under PPACA, effective in 2013, there will be an additional tax on wages and unearned income for individual tax filers with an AGI over $200,000 and for joint filers with an AGI over $250,000. Also, since 1994, part of the income taxes on OASDI benefits has been diverted to finance HI.

The HI Trust Fund receives the income of the program from the various sources and makes the required disbursements for benefits and administrative expenses. The assets are invested and earn interest in the same manner as the OASDI Trust Funds.

Although the federal government is responsible for the administration of the HI program, the actual dealing with the various medical facilities is through fiscal intermediaries, such as Blue Cross and insurance companies, which are reimbursed for their expenses on a cost basis. Reimbursement for inpatient hospital services is based on uniform sums for each type of case for about 490 diagnosis-related groups.

Persons Protected by Part B Medical Insurance

Individuals aged 65 or over can elect Part B Medical Insurance coverage on an individual basis regardless of whether or not they have OASDI insured status. In addition, disabled OASDI and Railroad Retirement beneficiaries eligible for HI and persons with ESRD eligibility under HI can elect Part B coverage. In general, coverage election must be made at about the time of initial eligibility; that is, attainment of age 65 or at the end of the disability-benefit waiting period. Subsequent election during general enrollment periods is possible, but with higher premium rates being applicable. Similarly, individuals can terminate coverage and cease premium payment of their own volition.

Benefits Provided under Part B Medical Insurance

The principal Part B benefit is partial reimbursement for the cost of physician services, although other medical services, such as diagnostic tests, ambulance services, prosthetic devices, physical therapy, medical equipment, home health services, and drugs not self-administrable, are covered. Not covered are out-of-hospital drugs, most dental services, most chiropractic services, routine physical and eye examinations, eyeglasses and hearing aids, and services outside of the United States, except those in connection with HI services that are covered in Canada. Just as for Part A, there are limits on Part B coverage in workers' compensation cases, medical care under liability policies, private group health insurance applicable to ESRD, and employer-sponsored group health insurance for employees and their spouses.

Part B pays 80 percent of "recognized" charges, under a complicated determination basis that usually produces a lower charge than the reasonable and prevailing one, after the individual has paid a calendar-year deductible of $162 for 2011. Special limits apply on out-of-hospital mental health care costs and on the services of independent physical and occupational therapists. The cost-sharing payments ($162 deductible and 20 percent coinsurance) are waived for certain services (e.g., home health services, pneumococcal vaccine and influenza shots, and certain clinical diagnostic laboratory tests). Since 1993, physicians cannot charge Medicare patients more than 115 percent of Medicare "recognized" charges.

Financing of Part B Medical Insurance

The standard monthly premium rate is $110.50 for most beneficiaries in 2011. The premium is higher for those who fail to enroll as early as they possibly can, with an increase of 10 percent for each full 12 months of delay. The premium is deducted from the OASDI or Railroad Retirement benefits of persons currently receiving them, or is paid by direct submittal in other cases.

The remainder of the cost of the program is met by general revenues. In the aggregate, persons aged 65 and over pay only about 25 percent of the cost, while for disabled persons such proportion is only about 20 percent. As a result, enrollment in Part B is very attractive, and about 95 percent of those eligible to do so actually enroll. The enrollee premium rate is changed every year effective for January. According to "permanent" law, the rate of increase in the premium rate is determined by the percentage rise in the level of OASDI cash benefits in the previous year under the automatic adjustment provisions, and in part by the percentage rises in the per capita cost of the program.

The Supplementary Medical Insurance (SMI) Trust Fund receives the enrollee Part B premiums, prescription drug plan premiums and payments from general revenues. General revenues account for about 75 percent of the SMI Trust Fund revenue. From this fund are paid the benefits for both Medicare Parts B and D, as well as the accompanying administrative expenses. Although the program is under the general supervision of the federal government, most of the administration is accomplished through "carriers," such as Blue Shield or insurance companies, on an actual cost basis for their administrative expenses.

Prescription-Drug Benefits Insurance

Medicare Part D[10] was enacted under the Medicare Prescription Drug Improvement and Modernization Act of 2003. Comprehensive drug benefits became available to beneficiaries in January 2006. Medicare Part D is a voluntary prescription drug program for Medicare beneficiaries and disabled individuals who qualify for benefits.

MEDICAID

Over the years, the cost of medical care for recipients of public assistance and for other low-income persons has been met in a variety of ways. Some years ago, these provisions were rather haphazard, and the medical care costs were met by inclusion with the public assistance payments. In 1960,

10. Chapter 21 covers Medicare Part D in depth.

separate public assistance program legislation in this area was enacted—namely, Medical Assistance for the Aged (MAA), which applied to persons aged 65 and over, both those receiving Old-Age Assistance and other persons not having sufficient resources to meet large medical expenses. Then in 1965, the MAA program and the federal matching for medical vendor payments for other public assistance categories than MAA were combined into the Medicaid program. This new program covered not only public assistance recipients but also persons of similar demographic characteristics who were medically indigent.

The Medicaid program is operated by the states, with significant federal financing available. Some states cover only public assistance recipients.

Medicaid programs are required to furnish certain services in order to receive federal financial participation. These services include those for physicians, hospitals (both inpatient and outpatient), laboratory and X-ray tests, home health visits, and nursing home care. Most other medical services, such as drugs, dental care, and eyeglasses, can be included at the option of the state, and then federal matching will be made available. Also, as a result of legislation enacted in 1988, states must pay the Part B premiums and the Part A and Part B cost-sharing payments for persons who are eligible for Medicare and who have incomes below the poverty level and have resources of no more than twice the standard under the Supplemental Security Income program. Thus, the states have the advantage of the relatively large general-revenues financing in the Medicaid program.

The federal government pays a proportion of the total cost of the Medicaid expenditures for medical care that varies inversely with the average per capita income of the state. This proportion is 55 percent for a state with the same average per capita income as the nation as a whole. States with above-average income have a lower matching proportion, but never less than 50 percent. Conversely, states with below-average income have a higher federal matching percentage, which can be as much as 83 percent. The federal government also pays part of the administrative costs of the Medicaid programs; generally, this is 50 percent, although for certain types of expenses that are expected to control costs the federal percentage is higher.

PPACA provides expanded coverage under Medicaid. More lower-income individuals would be eligible for Medicaid. Households with income up to 133 percent of the federal poverty level for a family of four would be eligible.

CHAPTER 21

Medicare Part D Prescription Drug Benefits

Craig S. Stern

This chapter focuses on Medicare Part D prescription drug coverage, with particular emphasis on how the rules apply to group health plans.

The Medicare Prescription Drug, Improvement, and Modernization Act of 2003 (MMA) was signed into law on December 8, 2003. It created a new Medicare Part D, which established a voluntary outpatient prescription drug benefit for seniors and qualified disabled persons.

The eligible population is enormous. It is estimated that the Medicare and Medicaid populations consist of 43 million eligible Medicare beneficiaries, of whom approximately 14 million may qualify for low-income subsidy assistance, and about 6 million beneficiaries who will move automatically from Medicaid to Medicare. Certain beneficiaries will have the greatest benefit from Part D. They are patients with no current drug insurance, patients who qualify for low-income subsidy assistance, patients in Medicare Advantage plans with no drug coverage, and patients who spend more than $800 per year on prescription drugs. (See Appendix 21.1 for Part D cost projections.)

A portion of the Medicare administration has been completely delegated to the private sector. Part D plans include prescription drug plans (PDPs)—private, stand-alone plans that offer drug-only coverage—and Medicare Advantage prescription drug plans (MA-PD plans)—plans that offer both prescription drug and health coverage. These plans exist in every state except Alaska and Vermont.

PDPs and MA-PDs are established in geographical regions of the United States by the Centers for Medicare & Medicaid Services (CMS), which has established 34 PDP and 26 MA-PD regions across the country.[1]

Residents of Puerto Rico and other territories are not eligible for Part D subsidies. The territories may submit a plan to receive additional Medicaid funds to provide covered Part D drugs to low-income Part D-eligible individuals.

Part D defines prescription drug plans for both a PDP and an MA-PD. The definition includes the following requirements:

- It must offer a basic drug benefit called the "standard benefit."
- It may offer supplemental benefits called "enhanced benefits."
- It can be flexible in benefit design.
- It must follow marketing guidelines.

In addition, Medicare Part D, the voluntary prescription drug benefit, must also integrate with the following three components of traditional Medicare and must not duplicate coverage:

- Part A covers inpatient care (e.g., hospital, skilled nursing facility care, home health care, and hospice)
- Part B covers outpatient care (e.g., medical visits, durable medical equipment (DME), and a few prescription drugs)
- Part C covers managed care (enacted as Medicare + Choice in 1997 and now known as Medicare Advantage)

ENROLLMENT

Each individual entitled to Medicare Part A or enrolled in Part B qualifies for Part D coverage. Individuals enrolled in traditional Medicare will receive their benefits through a stand-alone PDP. Individuals enrolled in a Medicare Advantage plan will have coverage through an MA-PD plan. (See Appendix 21.2 for a list of communications materials used to educate beneficiaries about Part D.)

Most eligible Part D beneficiaries were able to choose a Part D plan starting on November 15, 2005. Two special groups were identified for consideration:

- Dual eligibles (individuals eligible for both Medicare and Medicaid). These individuals were automatically enrolled in a

1. www.hapnetwork.org/assets/pdfs/2011-fact-sheet.pdf.

Part D plan. A dual eligible is a Medicare beneficiary who is currently receiving state Medicaid benefits. Medicaid drug coverage for Medicare eligibles was terminated on December 31, 2005. In order to continue drug coverage, dual eligibles were automatically assigned to qualifying plans starting in October 2005. These individuals can switch out of their automatically assigned plans every 30 days.

- Limited-income beneficiaries. These individuals were eligible for a low-income cost-sharing subsidy (LICS).

The Medicare Part D subsidy starts on the date when the dual-eligible senior becomes eligible. If a delay occurs in starting the senior on the program, the senior is eligible for retroactive coverage for prescription medications back to the eligibility date. Effective in 2011, the annual coordinated election period (also known as the annual open enrollment period (AEP)) will be from October 15 to December 7 for the 2012 plan year. (Note that the first-year open enrollment period was November 15, 2005, through May 15, 2006.) Beneficiaries have an option of at least two Part D plans per region.

Retirees must follow their employers' plan coverage rules to remain eligible for their retiree coverage. However, if retirees decide to leave their employer coverage midyear, they may enroll in a Medicare Part D plan only during the Medicare open enrollment period. For example, if a retiree left the employer's Part D plan in July, he or she would have to wait until the November open enrollment period for coverage for the following year. Exceptions are allowed for the following special circumstances:

- Beneficiaries who permanently move out of the plan service area
- Individuals entering, residing in, or leaving a long-term care facility
- Involuntary loss, reduction, or nonnotification of creditable coverage
- Other exceptional circumstances

Some Medicare patients may be subject to a late enrollment penalty if they do not sign up for Part D when they are first eligible. This late penalty fee is a carryover from Medicare Part B. Two categories of patients are at risk. The first group includes patients who were eligible for Medicare before January 2006 and had to sign up by May 15, 2006, to avoid a higher premium. The second group includes patients who became eligible for Medicare after January 2006 and had to sign up for Part D within 63 days after the end of their initial enrollment period to avoid a higher premium.

The higher premium will be based on an increase of at least 1 percent of the base beneficiary premium (i.e., $31.94 for 2010) per month for every month that they waited to enroll. This premium may change each year. For example, if John Doe is without creditable coverage for 18 months, his penalty is 18 percent (1 percent × 18 months) multiplied by $31.94 (base beneficiary premium) = $5.75. This amount would then be added to the monthly premium, for example $20.00. In this example, John Doe would pay a higher premium of $20.00 + $5.75 = $25.75.

The fees will be reflected in higher monthly premiums for the beneficiary's lifetime. However, if a Medicare beneficiary has a creditable coverage equivalent to or better than Part D (e.g., employer or retirement plan), this penalty does not apply.[2]

CREDITABLE COVERAGE

Some patients will not have to pay a late enrollment penalty if they are currently receiving retiree coverage that is at least as good as Medicare Part D. This current coverage is "creditable." The retiree benefits coordinator for their employer is the contact person for determining whether their coverage is creditable.

Creditable coverage notices must be sent annually and at other times specified by Medicare. These notices are commonly sent when an active worker first becomes eligible for Medicare or when the employer group coverage changes. Most employers send creditable coverage notices with annual open enrollment materials sent to all active workers and retirees. Consolidated Omnibus Budget Reconciliation Act (COBRA) notices have no applicability to the Part D program.

CMS has issued guidance on the content, model language, and timing of creditable coverage notices that must be provided to Part D-eligible Medicare beneficiaries.

LOW-INCOME-SUBSIDY BENEFICIARIES

Potential low-income individuals can apply for eligibility determination through mailings to potential eligibles, applications in pharmacies, Internet applications, walk-ins to state Medicaid offices, or walk-ins to Social Security

2. questions.medicare.gov/app/answers/detail/a_id/2255.

Administration (SSA) field offices. After eligibility has been determined, the applicant is notified of the determination.

These individuals had a two-step enrollment process. First, they were prescreened for income and assets through an application process administered by the SSA. After approval from the SSA, the beneficiary had to choose a Part D plan after November 15, 2005. If the low-income-subsidy (LICS) beneficiary did not choose a Part D plan by May 15, 2006, he or she was automatically enrolled into a qualifying Part D plan. (Note that dual eligibles did not have to fill out SSA applications.)

INCENTIVES FOR EMPLOYER TO PARTICIPATE

Generally, companies have not provided prescription drug benefits to retirees because of the high cost of drugs and the costs of health care overall. According to Leslie Norwalk, CMS deputy administrator, "If you look at large employers back in 1988, about 66 percent offered drug benefits to retirees. By 2002, that percentage had dropped to 37 percent, and we feel it has continued to fall since."

Ms. Norwalk explains the CMS position as follows:

> In this era of corporate austerity companies that think about where they can cut costs to be competitive are choosing to cut retiree benefits, depending on their union contracts. But under Part D, there is a major financial incentive to reconsider. We're saying to them, "Stay in the game, and we'll write you a check that could be worth hundreds of thousands of dollars." Clearly, a major reason why an employer or union may want to do this is because it won't have to pay the entire premium. In other words, for those that don't offer drug benefits, now may be the time to rethink.

As a result of the above concerns, CMS provided several options to incentivize employers to participate in Part D:

1. The first option is the drug subsidy.[3] The Retiree Drug Subsidy (RDS) was enacted in December 2003 as part of the Medicare Prescription Drug Improvement and Modernization Act to subsidize employers that sponsor high-value prescription drug coverage to retirees. The plan sponsor offers its benefit plan as a substitute for Part D. Under this option, the plan sponsor receives a check from the government that represents 28 percent of annual prescription drug spending (ingredient cost plus dispensing fee) otherwise covered by Medicare Part D and

3. RDS Fact Sheet, 2010.

attributable to such drug costs between the applicable cost threshold and cost limit. (For example, for 2010 and 2011, drug spending between $310 and $6,300 with each figure to be adjusted annually after that time). In order to be eligible for the subsidy, the company must pass an actuarial equivalence test. This actuarial attestation means that deductibles, coinsurance, and cost sharing are as good as those found in the Medicare plan. Another option was included in the retiree subsidy through the Employer Group Waiver Plan (discussed later). Rebates received are subtracted from the amount eligible for subsidy.[4]

This option has seemed to be the easiest and potentially the most lucrative for a company. The amount of subsidy available is adjusted annually by law and has increased every year. In 2011, up to $1,677.20 is available per retiree.[5]

The Patient Protection and Affordable Care Act of 2010 (PPACA) retains the retiree drug subsidy but changes its tax treatment. PPACA eliminates the employer tax deduction for the subsidy as of 2013. In effect, this increases the employer's cost of using the RDS.

2. The second option is Part D: PDP or MA-PD. The employer can contract with CMS to become an official Prescription Drug Plan (PDP) under Medicare and offer the Part D benefit to retirees themselves. Alternatively, the employer can hire or outsource to an outside PDP or Medicare Advantage plan to serve as its employer-specific plan. Many health insurers (e.g., Aetna, Blue Cross/Blue Shield, Cigna, Highmark Blue Shield, Humana, and PacifiCare/United Health), pharmacy benefit managers (PBMs) (e.g., CVS/Caremark, Medco, Express Scripts, Ovation/ Walgreens, and Universal American Financial Corp./CVS), and coalitions like the Community Care Rx are offering outsourcing services for companies. Other coalitions include the National Community Pharmacist Association, Computer Sciences Corp., and Member Health.

The concern with this option is how much the company will actually pay for the services of the health plans and PBMs. Furthermore, it is expected that there will be a provider shakeout

4. RDS User Guide, 2010.
5. rds.cms.hhs.gov/downloads/rdsuserguide.pdf.

over time, such that some vendors may exit the market. Until the market stabilizes, this option is considered more risky.

3. The third option is coordination of benefits (COB) in a wraparound plan: the employer can offer a separate benefit plan that "wraps around" Medicare Part D. Under this option, the employer fills in retiree drug-benefit voids that are not covered under Part D. Historically, a company or union can offer a supplemental plan in which Medicare typically pays 80 percent of the cost of a service and the company pays a portion—or all—of the remainder. Under Part D, the company can pay the cost of the deductible in a supplemental plan, or a percentage of the coverage gap (or "donut hole")[6], or, for example, 25 percent of total out-of-pocket costs.

   Companies believe that most pharmacies are not prepared to manage retiree patients with two benefits, nor do they have the technology to administer more than one benefit.[7]

EMPLOYER GROUP WAIVER PLAN

The Employer Group Waiver Plan (EGWP) is a retirement subsidization initiated by CMS that was conceived to be superior to the Retirement Group Subsidy. There are two options for EGWP:

1. Direct contract EGWP is an option where employers and unions contract directly with CMS to provide plan benefits and receive payments directly from the government.
2. The "800" series EGWP is an option in which employers and unions contract with CMS using a third-party Part D sponsor who holds and maintains the contract between the employer, union and CMS and performs the administrative and financial functions of the plan removing this burden from the employer and union. Other benefits are as follows:
   - The employer and union group have no direct covenant with CMS.
   - The low premium of the employer and union group results in a greater "cost savings" (up to 25 percent).

6. PPACA gradually phases down the coverage gap from 2010 through 2020.
7. rds.cms.hhs.gov/reference_materials/rdsfactsheet.pdf.

- There are no compliance or regulatory burdens.
- Compared with the CMS Retiree Drug Subsidy program, this program has less administrative burden.
- Plans can be designed to the individual group's needs.
- The third-party Part D sponsor bears the total risk.
- Their relationships with CMS make the third party Part-D sponsors familiar with the regulatory requirements of CMS.

CMS has fostered several benefits to encourage employers to adopt the EGWP rather than the RDS. In summary, these benefits are as follows:

- Cost savings—According to CMS drug costs, savings are approximately 15–20 percent in RDS compared to 19–35 percent under EGWP.
- Risk avoidance—The risk can be shifted to the Part D plan sponsor by the employer and union group.
- Minimal disruption to the membership—the current pharmacy plan design can usually be maintained.
- Tax savings—Tax obligations are treated equally with taxable entities (not missing out on tax advantages).
- Direct monthly subsidy—There is a direct monthly subsidy received from CMS on the basis of the number of enrollees.
- The Governmental Accounting Standards Board (GASB) Statements 43/45 liability is reduced.[8]
- Administrative functions are handled by a third-party sponsor.
- The Part D benefit provides catastrophic coverage (once the beneficiary reaches $4,350 in out-of-pocket expenses, he or she pays no more than 5 percent coinsurance).

8. The Governmental Accounting Standards Board (GASB) is an independent organization that establishes standards of accounting and financial reporting for U.S. state and local governments. GASB issued Statement No. 43, entitled *Financial Reporting for Postemployment Benefit Plans Other Than Pension Plans*, in April 2004; and Statement No. 45, entitled *Accounting and Financial Reporting by Employers for Postemployment Benefits Other Than Pensions*, in June 2004. The purpose of GASB Statements 43 and 45 is to require the accrual of liabilities and expense in plans providing other postemployment benefits, including retiree medical and pharmacy, over the working careers of plan members rather than on a pay-as-you-go basis, which was the practice for most government-sponsored plans.

On January 12, 2009, three years after its original notice of intent to do so, the CMS issued a final rule stating that the "pass through" model will be the only acceptable methodology for calculating beneficiary cost sharing and gross covered drug costs through the benefit, as well as reporting drug costs on explanations of benefits (EOBs) and prescription drug event (PDE) records. (See Appendix 21.3 for more information on PDEs.) The rule requires Medicare Part D plan sponsors to use the amount ultimately received by the pharmacy as the model for determining cost sharing for beneficiaries and for reporting a plan's drug costs to the CMS. Although the new rule allows plans to continue using the lock-in model, they must also report to CMS the actual price paid to the pharmacy as the negotiated price. The difference in the price paid by the plan to the PBM and the price paid by the PBM to the pharmacy must be reported as an administrative cost. The final rule is effective for the contract year beginning in 2010.[9]

STANDARD BENEFIT DESIGN

The standard benefit design entails a monthly premium of approximately $37 that varies by PDP and MA-PD region. The annual deductible is $310 in 2010 and 2011, and is indexed annually, as can be recognized in the benefit parameters comparison shown in Table 21-1. The primary coverage after the deductible requires the beneficiary to be responsible for approximately 25 percent of drug costs until he or she reaches $2,830 in 2010 or $2,840 in 2011 in drug spending (not including monthly premium).

TRUE OUT-OF-POCKET COST

The true out-of-pocket (TrOOP) cost is the beneficiary cost sharing for Medicare Part D benefits before catastrophic coverage begins. Because several different payments contribute to TrOOP, CMS awarded a contract to NDC Health to provide coordination-of-benefits systems. NDC Health is responsible for systems that will monitor TrOOP on a pharmacy level so that beneficiaries can question their pharmacists about how close they are to catastrophic coverage. To ensure accuracy of this information, NDC Health is required to route claims for benefits paid by entities other than Medicare to the prescription drug plans. This requirement ensures that

9. edocket.access.gpo.gov/2009/pdf/E9-148.pdf.

TABLE 21-1

Medicare Part D Standard Benefit Design Parameters

		2007	2008	2009	2010	2011
After the deductible is met, the beneficiary pays 25% of covered costs up to total prescription costs meeting the initial coverage limit	Deductible	$265	$275	$295	$310	$310
Coverage gap (donut hole) begins at this point	Initial coverage limit	$2,400	$2,510	$2,700	$2,830	$2,840
Including the coverage gap, catastrophic coverage starts after this point	Total covered Part D drug out-of-pocket spending	$5,451.25	$5,726.25	$6,153.75	$6,440.00 plus a $250 brand rebate	$6,447.50 plus a 50% brand discount
True out-of-pocket costs including the donut hole (deductible + initial coverage + coverage gap = true out-of-pocket (TrOOP) cost)	True out-of-pocket threshold	$265.00 $533.75 $3,051.25 $3,850.00	$275.00 $558.75 $3,216.25 $4,050.00	$295.00 $601.25 $3,453.75 $4,350.00	$310.00 $630.00 $3,610.00 $4,550.00	$310.00 $632.50 $3,607.50 $4,550.00
	Catastrophic Coverage Benefit					
	Generic/ preferred multisource drug	$2.15	$2.25	$2.40	$2.50	$2.50*
	Other drugs	$5.35	$5.60	$6.00	$6.30	$6.30*

* The Catastrophic Coverage is either the greater of 5%, or the values in the table above. In 2010, beneficiaries would be charged $2.50 for generic or preferred multisource drugs with a retail price under $50 and 5% for those with a retail price greater than $50. For brand drugs, beneficiaries would pay $6.30 for drugs with a retail price under $130 and 5% for drugs with a retail price over $130 (www.q1medicare.com/PartD-The-2011-Medicare-Part-D-Outlook.php).

what seniors pay at pharmacies takes into account the appropriate level of their Medicare coverage.

A beneficiary's actual out-of-pocket costs are calculated according to the following formula, using 2010 amounts

$310	Deductible
$630	25 percent of drug costs in the initial coverage ($310–$2,830)
$3,610	100 percent of drug costs in the donut hole ($2,830–$6,440)
$4,550	TrOOP costs

The following is an example:

Actual Drug Cost	**Medicare Pays**	**Beneficiary Pays**	**Total Paid**
$0–$310	$0	310 (deductible)	$310
$310.01–$2,830	$1,890 (75%)	$630 (25%)	$940 ($310 + $630)
$2,830.01–$6,440	$0 (coverage gap)	$3,610	$4,450 ($940 + $3,610)
$6,440.01+	About 95%	About 5%	Varies

Beyond drug spending by the beneficiary, other payments can count toward TrOOP. These include payments from

- Another individual (such as a family member or friend)
- A state pharmaceutical assistance program (SPAP)
- A charity
- A personal health savings vehicle such as a flexible spending account, health savings account, or medical savings account

The following beneficiary costs are *not* included in the TrOOP

- Monthly premiums (2010 CMS national average is estimated to be $88 per month)
- Most third-party payment arrangements
- Payments for
  - Drugs purchased outside of the United States
  - OTC drugs
  - Drugs not on the plan's formulary
  - Drugs not covered by law

In addition, the following sources of insurance payments are not applied to the TrOOP

- Employer/retiree group health plans
- TRICARE
- Black lung
- Veterans Administration (VA)
- Workers' Compensation
- Automobile/no-fault/liability insurance
- Supplemental benefit portions of PDP or MA-PD

CATASTROPHIC COVERAGE

After spending $2,830 (not including monthly premiums) in 2010, the beneficiary was responsible for 100 percent of drug costs until he or she reached $4,550 in true out-of-pocket costs. This responsibility corresponds to more than $5,000 of total prescription drug spending (more if a person had a wraparound plan).

After $6,440 of total prescription drug spending, the beneficiary received catastrophic coverage. With this coverage, the beneficiary was responsible for about 5 percent of drug costs after having spent $4,550 in out-of-pocket costs.

LOW-INCOME BENEFIT DESIGN

For beneficiaries eligible for low-income assistance, there is a different benefit design. This design changes on an annual basis and is summarized in Table 21-2 for 2010.

MEDIGAP INSURANCE

Medigap provides a unique problem. Enrollees with Medigap H, I, or J insurance must receive a creditable coverage notice. They also must be notified of their options. These options include that their Medigap insurance will not be sold, issued, or renewed after 2005; however, a policy may be renewed if it is modified to exclude drug coverage or if the person does not enroll in a Medicare prescription drug plan. There are also two new Medigap plans: K and L.

TABLE 21-2

2010 Low-Income Subsidy Groups and Costs*

Standard Benefit	Group 1 Dual Eligibles	Group 2 MSP (QMB, SLMB,QI) SSI with Medicare but without Medicaid	Group 3 Income < 135% FPL Resources Below $8,100/ $12,910	Group 4 Income <150% FPL Resources Below $12,510/ $25,010
Premium $31.94 per month	$0 up to "benchmark"	$0 up to "benchmark"	$0 up to "benchmark"	Sliding scale ($0–$28.00) based on income
Deductible $310 per year	$0	$0	$0	$63
Cost sharing† up to $4550 out-of-pocket	Copays: $0 if institutionalized $1.10/$3.30, <100% FPL $2.50/$6.30, >100% FPL	Copay: $2.50/$6.30	Copay: $2.50/$6.30	15% coinsurance
Catastrophic coverage 5% or $2.50/$6.30 copay	$0	$0	$0	Copay: $2.50/$6.30

*www.medicareadvocacy.org/Print/FAQ_PartD.htm.
†Individuals in these four groups do not have the "Donut Hole" gap in coverage.

Medigap Plan K includes coverage of 50 percent of the cost-sharing applicable under Medicare Parts A and B, except for the Part B deductible. Plan K can cover 100 percent of inpatient hospital coinsurance and 365 lifetime days of inpatient hospital services. Also, Plan K can provide for 100 percent of any cost sharing for preventive benefits. The annual out-of-pocket limit for this insurance was $4,000 in 2006 and is indexed thereafter.

Medigap Plan L includes coverage of 75 percent of cost sharing applicable under Medicare Parts A and B except for the Part B deductible. Similar to Plan K, Plan L can cover 100 percent of inpatient hospital coinsurance and 365 lifetime days of inpatient hospital services. Also, Plan L can provide for 100 percent of any cost sharing for preventive benefits as in Plan K. The 2010 annual out-of-pocket limit for Medigap plans K and L were $4,620 and $2,310, respectively.[10]

PHARMACY NETWORK CONTRACTING

Part D pharmacy network contracts require specific expectations for the plan sponsors. Sponsors expect these plans to meet the following criteria:

- Work plans must be included in the application.
- Performance and service criteria must be included in pharmacy contracts.
- Contracts must contain any-willing-providers provisions.
- Contracts must have convenient access requirements for patients who routinely receive benefits through the network.

Consistent with any-willing-provider requirements, plans must ensure adequate access to out-of-network pharmacies when the patient cannot reasonably be expected to obtain that drug at a network pharmacy. However, the patient must not access an out-of-network pharmacy on a routine basis.

Level-playing-field requirement

There is a so-called level-playing-field requirement that no mandatory mail order is allowed. In addition, PDP sponsors may not include only mail order pharmacies in their networks. This requirement is not completely exclusive. For example, if retail pharmacies refuse the 90-day option, then a PDP can still offer a 90-day mail option. Adequate retail emergency access for enrollees is also necessary. However, the patient is responsible for any higher cost-sharing that applies at a retail pharmacy; for example, the patient may pay the normal copay plus the difference between the mail and retail 90-day rates. The implications of this requirement are as follows:

- If a Part D plan offers a 90-day supply by mail, then it must offer a 90-day supply option at retail.
- The plan is not required to offer a 90-day supply option at retail if it does not have a 90-day mail option.

10. www.cms.gov/Medigap/04_KandL.asp.

Preferred Pharmacies

Plans can offer benefits with preferred pharmacies. These discounts apply to standard benefits but not to dual-eligible or low-income beneficiaries. Plans with preferred pharmacies can provide lower reimbursement to participating pharmacies and, in turn, provide more advantageous copays and coinsurances to beneficiaries. However, plans must maintain actuarial equivalence of 25 percent patient responsibility, meaning that the preferred pharmacy benefits still must conform to the standard benefit package.

Pharmacy Reimbursements

Congress did not set a minimum or maximum requirement for pharmacy reimbursement rates. The plan—that is, the market—determines reimbursement based on its network contracting. Dispensing fees do have some limitations. They are limited only to those costs associated with the transfer and possession of a drug. These costs include checking for coverage information, performing quality assurance (QA) activities as mandated by the state, filling the container and providing to the customer, delivery at the point of sale, and overhead. Also, dispensing fees do not include any activities beyond the point of sale (e.g., pharmacy follow-up telephone calls or medication therapy management).

In accordance with the passage of the Medicare Improvements for Patients and Providers Act (MIPPA) in 2009, MA-PD and PDP plan sponsors are required to pay "clean" claims from pharmacies, excluding mail order and long-term care (LTC), within 14 days after transmission if submitted electronically. If submitted otherwise, the deadline is within 30 days. These are the so-called "rapid payment" criteria promoted by retail pharmacies in response to delayed payments from PBMs. (See Appendix 21.4 for other Part D changes due to MIPPA.)

FORMULARIES AND PART D

Formularies are encouraged for PDP and MA-PD plans. While each plan may develop its own formulary, there are several rules governing the design of these formularies. CMS contracted with the United States Pharmacopoeia (USP) to develop formulary guidelines. USP identified 146 therapeutic categories that must be included in all Part D formularies. In addition, if a generic is available, it must be included in the formulary. Also, if preferred drugs are defined, the rebates collected must go to the payer to decrease the cost of the program. (See Appendix 21.5 for details of drug coverage in Part D formularies.)

Part D formularies must also comply with the following requirements:

- They must include at least two drugs in each therapeutic category and class of covered Part D drugs.
- They may, and likely will, include prior authorizations, step therapy, generic drug requirements, and preferred brand drugs.
- They must include all or substantially all drugs in the following classes: antidepressants, antipsychotics, anticonvulsants, anticancer, immunosuppressant, and HIV/AIDS medications.

Tiered Formularies

Part D allows for preferred drug levels defined by formulary tiers. The first tier (Tier 1) is the lowest level of cost sharing for the beneficiary. Subsequent tiers have higher cost sharing in ascending order. CMS reviews all plan formulary submissions to identify drug categories that may discourage enrollment of certain beneficiaries with Medicare by placing drugs in non-preferred tiers. These plans must have exception procedures for these tiered formularies. The overall appeals process has five levels:

1. Redetermination by the plan sponsor
2. Reconsideration by an independent review entity
3. Review by an administrative law judge
4. Review by the Medicare Appeals Council
5. Review by a Federal District Court

ELECTRONIC PRESCRIBING

CMS defines electronic prescribing, or e-prescribing, as a prescriber's ability to electronically send an accurate, error-free and understandable prescription directly to a pharmacy from the point of care. According to the final e-prescribing rule published in the *Federal Register* on April 7, 2008, three electronic tools may be utilized in the method:

1. Formulary and benefit transactions: give prescribers information about which drugs are covered by a Medicare beneficiary's prescription drug benefit plan.
2. Medication history transactions: provide prescribers with information about medications a beneficiary is already taking,

including those prescribed by other providers, to help reduce the number of adverse drug events.

3. Fill status notifications: allow prescribers to receive an electronic notice from the pharmacy telling them that a patient's prescription has been picked up, not picked up, or been partially filled, to help monitor medication adherence in patients with chronic conditions.

Effective in 2010, incentive payments (2 percent in 2009 and 2010; 1 percent in 2011 and 2012; and 0.5 percent in 2013) will be provided for practitioners using qualified e-prescribing systems utilizing the above tools. In 2011, practitioners will be required to use these qualified e-prescribing systems or face payment reduction. General payments to practitioners who fail to e-prescribe by 2011 will be reduced by 1 percent in 2012, 1.5 percent in 2013, and 2 percent thereafter.[11]

MEDICATION THERAPY MANAGEMENT

The MMA states that a Part D plan must have an established medication therapy management (MTM) program with the following components:

- It is designed to ensure that covered Part D drugs that are prescribed to targeted beneficiaries are appropriately used to optimize therapeutic outcomes through improved medication use.
- It is designed to reduce the risk of adverse events, including adverse drug interactions, for targeted beneficiaries.
- It may be furnished by a pharmacist or other qualified provider and may distinguish between services in ambulatory and institutional settings.

MTM services target beneficiaries based on all of the following criteria: multiple chronic diseases, multiple covered Part D medications, and likelihood of incurring annual costs exceeding $4,000 for covered part D drugs. The following services may be included under MTM:

- Patient health status assessments
- Medication "brown bag" reviews
- Formulating, monitoring, and adjusting prescription drug treatment plans

11. 73 Fed. Reg. 18918-18942 (Apr. 7, 2008).

- Patient education and training
- Collaborative drug therapy management
- Special packaging
- Refill reminders

Other services may also be included. In order to initiate any of the above services for a patient, pharmacies will receive e-mail messages from their plans to provide MTM for specific eligible patients.

The CMS introduced changes effective January 1, 2010 for MTM that include more lenient eligibility requirements than first required: an annual, interactive person-to-person comprehensive consultation and medication review and quarterly, targeted medication reviews to assess drug use and monitor any problems. Specifically, these new requirements are as follows:

- Enroll targeted beneficiaries using an opt-out method of enrollment only.
- Target beneficiaries for enrollment at least quarterly during each year.
- Target beneficiaries who
  - Have multiple chronic diseases (sponsors cannot require more than three chronic diseases as the minimum number of multiple chronic diseases, and sponsors must target at least four of seven named core chronic conditions).
  - Are taking multiple Part D drugs (sponsors cannot require more than eight Part D drugs as the minimum number of multiple covered Part D drugs).
  - Are likely to incur annual costs for covered Part D drugs that exceed a predetermined level as specified by the Secretary (the existing cost threshold, $4,000, will be lowered to $3,000, and sponsors' targeting criteria should be adjusted accordingly).
- Offer a minimum level of MTM services, including
  - Interventions for both beneficiaries and prescribers
  - An annual comprehensive medication review for the beneficiary, which includes a review of medications, interactive, person-to-person consultation, and an individualized, written summary of interactive consultation
  - Quarterly targeted medication reviews
- Measure and report details on the number of comprehensive medication reviews, number of targeted medication reviews,

number of prescriber interventions, and the change in therapy directly resulting from the interventions.

All Part D sponsors must establish an MTM program meeting these requirements. The MTM requirement does not apply to MA Private Fee for Service (MA-PFFS) organizations. However, considering that MA-PFFS organizations have an equal responsibility to provide a quality Part D product, CMS encourages MA-PFFS organizations to establish an MTM program to improve quality for Medicare beneficiaries.[12]

Medicare Part D allows pharmacists to bill for MTM services. These services are to be paid through the medical benefit using current procedural terminology (CPT) codes. There are three separate CPT codes for these services, which are different for physicians and pharmacist providers. These codes are applicable to the MTM services for some Medicare Part D beneficiaries, but they also have been designed to be applicable to any payer type or practice setting.

IMPACT OF SKILLED NURSING FACILITIES, NURSING FACILITIES, AND LONG-TERM CARE

According to the 2010 Kaiser Family Foundation Fact Sheet, 5 percent of the Medicare beneficiaries' population will reside in long-term care facilities for some period of time. There are approximately 16,000 Medicare/Medicaid-certified skilled nursing facilities (SNFs) or nursing facilities (NFs), with even more assisted living facilities.

Nearly 70 percent of NF residents are dually eligible for Medicare and Medicaid benefits. Medicaid continues to have responsibility for daily care needs of the residents. Part D covers their prescription costs. Residents of assisted living facilities are often wealthier at first, but then spend down to Medicaid eligibility. Some state Medicaid programs cover care in assisted living facilities through waiver programs. Some residents are eligible for low-income subsidies, but Medicare Part D can present a challenge due to assets testing.

LTC Pharmacy

LTC pharmacies are specialty pharmacies that provide medication dispensing and consulting services to residents of LTC facilities. CMS recognizes

12. www.cms.gov/PrescriptionDrugCovContra/Downloads/2010CallLetter.pdf

some of these facilities, but not all, for additional pharmacy services and dispensing fees under Part D. The following is a list of facilities providing LTC pharmacy services:

- Medicare- and Medicaid-certified SNF/NF skilled nursing facilities (recognized by CMS for Part D)
- Immediate-care facilities for the mentally handicapped (recognized by CMS for Part D)
- Assisted living facilities
- Board and care homes
- Prisons, jails, and hospice settings

These facilities require compliance issues that are specific for LTC pharmacies, as opposed to retail network pharmacies. These compliance issues include enrollment issues, formularies and drug coverage, coordination of benefits and service location, and exceptions and appeals.

Approximately 60 percent of the market is serviced by three publicly traded companies: Omnicare, Inc., PharMerica, and Kindred Pharmacy Services. The remainder of the market is serviced by independent LTC pharmacies.

Before Medicare Part D went into effect, LTC pharmacies received the most reimbursement from individual state Medicaid programs for NFs. The LTC pharmacies managed and developed formularies. There was little or no managed care intervention. Assisted-living residents primarily paid out-of-pocket for medications.

Under Medicare Part D, LTC pharmacies must enter into network agreements with PDPs. The PDPs manage formularies. Medicaid involvement is limited to payment for Part D-excluded drugs and for coverage gaps during transition. There is still coverage under Medicare Part A. This coverage applies to beneficiaries with skilled nursing facility needs who are admitted to NFs after a three-day hospital stay. Approximately 10 to 15 percent of beneficiaries are covered by the Medicare Part A SNF benefit. The Part A benefit was unchanged in 2008, such that the pharmacy bills the SNF for drugs and the facility bills Medicare directly.

In order to comply with Part D, plans must comply with the following access requirements:

- Offer standard contracting terms and conditions to all LTC pharmacies (classified by CMS) in service areas.
- Contract with any willing LTC pharmacy.
- Ensure convenient access to LTC pharmacies.

Certain requirements are unique to LTC pharmacies. The requirements are as follows:

- A special enrollment period for admission or discharge in NFs
- No copay for dual eligibles in NFs
- Special appeals and exceptions processes
- Formulary transition requirements for movement of patients from NF to PDP formularies

Ultimately, the NF is responsible for all aspects of care for residents, including drugs. If Part D does not cover drug therapy, then the facility, not the LTC pharmacy, is responsible.

Services Required of an LTC Pharmacy

A Part D plan may require that an LTC pharmacy offer the following services:

- Drug packaging (including specialty packaging such as bubble packs), labeling, and delivery systems for LTC medication use
- Pharmacy operations and prescription ordering
- Drug delivery service on a routine, timely basis (including emergencies around the clock)
- Access to urgent medications on an emergency basis
- Pharmacist on-call services (around the clock)
- Emergency boxes and log systems
- Standard ordering systems and medication inventories
- Drug disposition systems for controlled and noncontrolled drugs
- Ability to provide intravenous medications
- Compounding or alternative forms of drug composition
- Miscellaneous reports, forms, and prescription ordering supplies (e.g., medication administration records, MARs)

It is important to note that these requirements reflect the services commonly provided in LTC. These services must comply with standards based upon best practices developed by the LTC industry and standards of compliance with federal and state nursing home, pharmacy, and other pertinent regulators. However, pharmacies may negotiate with PDPs for additional reimbursement for services.

The above services apply to the LTC setting only and not to assisted-living facilities not licensed as NFs. Also, these services do not apply to other state-licensed NFs that are not required to meet federal Medicare or Medicaid conditions of participation.

Additional dispensing fees are allowed and account for additional packaging and delivery services associated with providing medications to residents of NFs. Medicare Part D excludes payment for consultant pharmacies' monthly drug utilization regimen review (DUR). DUR remains the responsibility of the NF under Medicaid as part of the contract with the LTC pharmacy.

Coverage of Infusion/Inhalation Therapy in NFS—A Special Case

Infusion and inhalation therapy are special billing cases under Part D in Nursing Facilities. First, the LTC facility must be used as the location code for inhalation. Second, CMS has indicated that infused medications that are not administered by a physician are covered by Part D, and not Part B, in a nursing facility. The physician should include information on the prescription that administration is to be in an NF. The LTC pharmacy will then dispense the medication and will be paid a dispensing fee, but will not be paid for additional services. In addition, the payment for infusion therapy will not include services unless the provider uses Medicaid Federal Financial Participation. In such cases, there is no payment for dispensing, but there is payment for services and supplies.

Enrollment Issues for LTC

Enrollment provides particular challenges in LTC owing to the uniqueness of the population. First, enrollment information is often incomplete and contains key errors in notification among Medicare, Medicaid, LTC pharmacies, and the NFs. Second, claims processing is not the same as in ambulatory care because of the daily administration of medications. Since January 1, 2010, LTC pharmacies are required to have not less than 30 days, nor more than 90 days, to submit claims to the MA-PD or PDP plan sponsor for reimbursement. Third, many dual eligibles are not listed as Medicaid-eligible.

Formulary Issues in LTC

The application of managed care and PDPs to LTC provides several challenges that are unique to LTC. First, it is necessary to determine how the formulary transition process is managed. For example, patients are permitted

31-day supplies under Medicaid, but PDP plans may not allow for different day supply limits. Second, utilization management tools are mandated under LTC standards, which may differ from PDP tools, leading to application and billing problems. Third, the exception and appeals processes are different in LTC from ambulatory plans. For example, the "expedited" process in LTC requires a more immediate response than is common in ambulatory care. Finally, it is necessary to determine how excluded drugs are to be managed. In addition, coordination of benefits is a major issue for NFs because of the difference in policies for payment for infusion and inhalation medications as opposed to the usual oral medications used in ambulatory care. The difference in payment policies is due to the lack of coordination of Medicare/Medicaid and PDP call centers for payment and coverage policies for residents in NFs. In addition, the location codes for services may not indicate NFs as permanent residences, which creates billing confusions. In response to these COB issues, CMS has issued policy guidance, but not specific guidance for telecommunication standards. The standards have been referred to the National Council for Prescription Drug Programs (NCPDP), which is the standards organization for electronic pharmacy transactions, to develop proposals for handling claims.

The difference between LTC and PDP formularies leads to uncertainties in coverage and payment. For example, there is a conflict between the LTC pharmacy negotiation with manufacturers for purchase pricing and rebates versus the agreements of the same manufacturers with PDPs. However, CMS specifically identifies rebates to LTC pharmacies as contrary to the spirit of the Medicare law. As a result, rebates must be included in the price concessions and bids between LTC pharmacies and PDPs. Of particular concern are utilization management requirements for psychotherapeutic medications and the impact of copay tiers on specialty pharmaceuticals that commonly exceed limits of $500 in monthly costs.

QUALITY MEASURES

Medicare Part D contains a quality mandate. There are 131 references to quality in the MMA. These include standards for DME suppliers, Clinical Laboratory Improvement Amendments (CLIA)—certified laboratories, hospitals, and LTC facilities. MMA extends the oversight of Quality Improvement Organizations to Medicare Parts C and D. Finally, MMA includes funding for demonstration projects. Specific language for PDPs is contained within Part D—PDPs must have "quality assurance measures and systems to reduce medication errors and adverse drug interactions and improve medication use." Furthermore, 30 days prior to the open enrollment period, the secretary of Health and Human Services (HHS) must publish the following information: plan premiums and beneficiary cost shares, comparative plan quality and performance, and results of member satisfaction surveys. (See Appendix 21.6 for a listing of quality measures required in the Part D reporting.)

There is a mandate requiring sponsors to establish quality assurance systems and measures that reduce medication errors and adverse drug reactions. The sponsor must require providers to take responsibility for minimizing these problems.

Part D requires that medication measures be developed that demonstrate the quality of drug use for areas determined by CMS. The measures must be based on clinically supported research and evaluated by a technical expert panel. The measures must consider the technical and data limitations of PDPs. CMS draft guidance for developing these measures was produced in spring 2006.

Consistent with the Institute of Medicine (IOM) domains, the ideal measures in pharmacy programs are directed to improving the use of appropriate therapies for the targeted disease states in accordance with accepted treatment guidelines and regimens; reducing the potential for adverse events that may result from drug therapy; quantifying differences in quality and cost across plan sponsors; and avoiding waste, fraud, and abuse. All these procedures must be measured and reported within the context of what is feasible for use in PDPs and MA-PDs, providing challenges for measurement of these quality criteria. Most notably, the data is limited to claims data from multiple data systems and sources (e.g., claims processing vendors, PBMs, PDPs, and MA-PDs) that use complex and nonstandard data sets for pharmacy and medical claims.

There are reference sets for compliance with the quality measures. The Academy of Managed Care Pharmacy (AMCP) published its Pharmacy's Framework for Quality in 21st Century. This framework is a tool to assist PDPs, MA-PDs, and pharmacies to diagnose and assess their quality gaps. In addition, Joint Commission, Utilization Review Accreditation Committee (URAC), National Committee for Quality Assurance (NCQA), and Health care Effectiveness Data and Information Set (HEDIS) quality measures are available to assess quality gaps.

AUDIT ISSUES

On November 13, 2006, CMS provided the Final MA-PD and PDP Part D Audit Guides for Part D Program Audits. This document has been used to give guidance for the compliance audits mandated in Part D regulations in 42 C.F.R. Section 423 and other CMS standards. Specific reference is made to CMS audit guides for Medicare Advantage Prescription Drug Plan Sponsors Part D Audit Guides, and Prescription Drug Plan Sponsors Part D Audit Guide.[13]

CMS conducts regularly scheduled desk and on-site program audits to assess its compliance with the Part D regulations: 42 C.F.R. Sections 422 and 423, and other standards. These audits are based on 42 C.F.R. Sections 422 and 423, Prescription Drug Benefit Manual, Chapter 9—Part D Program to Control Fraud, Waste and Abuse.[14]

COORDINATION-OF-BENEFITS ISSUES

MMA requires coordination among CMS, State agencies, insurers, and employers to ensure that the benefits provided to Part D beneficiaries are maximized. States have special coordination concerns because of their dual status as employers and insurers. The critical question in COB is "Who pays first?" Table 21-3 summarizes the answers to this question.

Some categories of drugs are made to providers for Medicare Parts A and B, and, therefore, not Part D. Medicare Parts A and B cover bundled payments to acute care hospitals and SNFs that generally cover all treatment provided during the stay. (Exceptions for inpatient hospital stays are clotting factors, while exceptions for SNF stays are high-cost chemotherapy.) Medicare Parts A and B also cover payments to physicians for drugs and biologicals that are administered by infusion or injection, but they do not cover self-injectables and most outpatient prescriptions. (See Appendix 21.7 for a list of medications specifically covered under Medicare Part B.)

Medications Covered Under Medicare Part D

CMS provides the following definitions for medications covered under Part D:

- A Part D-covered drug is available only by prescription, approved by the Food and Drug Administration (FDA) (or is a drug described under Section 1927(k)(2)(A)(ii) or (iii) of the Act), used and sold in the United States, and used for a

13. www.cms.hhs.gov/Prescription Contracting_ReportingOversight.
14. Ibid.

TABLE 21-3

COB Primary Payers

Part D plus...	Pays First
State Pharmaceutical Assistance Programs (SPAPs)	Part D
Retiree covered under former employer's group health plan (GHP)	Part D
Also covered under the GHP of retired spouse	Part D
Retiree GHP + SPAP	(1) Part D, (2) GHP, (3) SPAP
Medicaid	Either Part D or Medicaid
Retiree GHP + Medicaid	Part D, then GHP
GHP, then Medicaid	
Currently working with coverage through GHP	GHP, then Part D
Covered under GHP of actively working spouse	GHP, then Part D
Covered under Workers' Compensation (WC)	WC, then Part D for injury-related treatment
No-fault or liability coverage (NF/LC)	NF/LC, then Part D for injury/illness-related treatment

medically accepted indication (as defined in Section 1927(k)(6) of the Act).

- A covered Part D drug includes prescription drugs, biological products, insulin as described in specified paragraphs of Section 1927(k) of the Act, and vaccines licensed under Section 351 of the Public Health Service Act.
- The definition also includes "medical supplies associated with the injection of insulin (as defined in regulations of the Secretary). We define those medical supplies to include syringes, needles, alcohol swabs, and gauze."
- The definition of supplies associated with the delivery of insulin to the body was expanded to include injection and inhalation, effective June 9, 2008.
- Effective January 1, 2008, fees for vaccine administration were included in Part D.

Drug benefits will now be available or coordinated with Part D for populations that previously did not have pharmacy benefits. These groups include benefits provided to state employees, retirees, and dependants, many of whom may be Medicare beneficiaries; Medicaid coverage provided to low-income beneficiaries, many of whom may be Medicare dual-eligibles who will now receive most drug coverage from Medicare Part D; and supplemental drug coverage offered to seniors through the State Pharmaceutical Assistance Programs (SPAPs). Coordination with SPAPs is a high priority for CMS

Medications Excluded from Medicare Part D

The following medications and categories of medications are not covered under Medicare Part D

- Medications available under Parts A or B (even though a deductible may apply)
- Drugs or classes of drugs, or their medical uses, that may be excluded from coverage or otherwise restricted under Medicaid under Section 1927(d)(2) of the Act, with the exception of smoking cessation agents. The drugs or classes of drugs that may currently be otherwise restricted under Medicaid include
  - Agents when used for anorexia, weight loss, or weight gain
  - Agents when used to promote fertility
  - Agents when used for cosmetic purposes or hair growth
  - Agents when used for the symptomatic relief of cough and colds
- Prescription vitamins and mineral products, except prenatal vitamins and fluoride preparations
- Nonprescription drugs
- Outpatient drugs for which the manufacturer seeks to require that associated tests or monitoring services be purchased exclusively from the manufacturer or its designee as a condition of sale
- Barbiturates[15]
- Benzodiazepines[15]
- Exclusions added, effective June 9, 2008

15. Effective in 2013, plans must cover benzodiazepines, as well as barbiturates if used to treat epilepsy, cancer, or a chronic mental health disorder.

- Drugs used to treat erectile dysfunction (ED)
- Drugs used to treat morbid obesity

Drug plan sponsors can generally include the Part D—excluded medications as part of supplemental benefits, provided they otherwise meet the definition of a Part D drug. For example, because nonprescription over-the-counter (OTC) drugs do not otherwise meet the definition of a Part D drug, they may not be included as part of supplemental benefits; however, OTC medications may be covered under the following condition:

- Under certain conditions as part of a utilization management program (including a step-therapy program), nonprescription drugs can be provided at no cost to enrollees.
- The cost of these drugs to the plan would be treated as administrative costs under such programs.

FDA Nonmatch List

CMS has published a list of "Nonmatched" National Drug Codes (NDCs) that are not eligible for reimbursement under Part D plans after January 1, 2010.[16] CMS will use this updated list to establish new edits that will reject prescription drug event (PDE) submissions from Part D sponsors for NDCs identified on the list. The nonmatched NDC list was developed as part of an ongoing joint initiative between CMS and FDA to increase transparency and clarity with respect to the regulatory status of marketed prescription drug products.

CMS has also provided clarifications to the use of the drug list:[17]

- This list cannot be used to determine a drug's status as approved or unapproved.
- This list may not identify all NDCs not properly registered and listed with the FDA.
- Not all NDCs on the nonmatched NDC list are otherwise Part D drugs (e.g. some NDCs are for excluded drugs) and, therefore, proper listing of such products with the FDA will not necessarily result in coverage under Part D.
- Edits apply only to PDEs with dates of service on or after January 1, 2010.

16. A list of the affected NDCs can be found on the CMS website at www.cms.hhs.gov/PrescriptionDrugCovContra/03_RxContracting_FormularyGuidance.asp.
17. www.nhia.org/Members/documents/20091021CMSMemotoPlansonNDCs.pdf.

- CMS planned to update the list at least twice during the 2010 plan year by deleting NDCs that have been registered and listed with the FDA since the fall 2009 posting of the list and removing associated PDE edits. Removal of edits will apply both retrospectively and prospectively for all dates of service.
- Additional NDCs were not to be added to the CY 2010 Nonmatched NDC list during the 2010 plan year. CMS expects Part D sponsors to rely on the FDA NDC Directory to determine when NDCs get listed and not wait for CMS to update the nonmatched NDC list. While this may result in a time lag between the CMS edit updates and the FDA NDC Directory listings, which could require resubmission of previously rejected PDEs, Part D sponsors should *not* wait to remove associated point-of-sale edits once NDCs are listed with the FDA.
- At this time, CMS is not considering making any changes to the Formulary Reference File or accepting negative formulary change requests in relation to the nonmatched NDC list.
- Questions or concerns about FDA's NDC Directory, FDA's drug listing procedures, or possible inaccuracies in the nonmatched NDC list, should be addressed to the FDA's Drug Registration and Listing Team.[18]
- Questions or concerns about PDE reject edits for NDCs listed on the nonmatched NDC list should be addressed to the CMS.[19]

CMS Contractor for Oversight of COB

In 1999, CMS named Group Health, Inc. (GHI) as the COB contractor. The COB contractor consolidates activities to support the collection, management, and reporting of all health insurance coverage of Medicare beneficiaries to implement an improved plan for coordinating Medicare benefits with other insurance coverage. The COB contractor will use a variety of methods and programs to identify situations in which Medicare beneficiaries have other health insurance that is primary to Medicare. In such situations, the other health plan has the legal obligation to meet the beneficiary's health care expenses first before Medicare.

18. Telephone (301) 210-2897 or e-mail nonlisted@fda.hhs.gov.
19. E-mail PartD_NDC@cms.hhs.gov.

As part of its contract, the COB contractor coordinates the following activities:

- Various questionnaires sent to beneficiaries, employers, providers, and insurers about group health plan coverage
- Voluntary data sharing agreements (VDSAs) among CMS and employers and insurers to exchange enrollment information on Medicare beneficiaries
- Coordination of benefits agreements (COBAs) between CMS and supplemental health insurers to coordinate the payment of claims after Medicare has made its payment
- Sharing of drug enrollment data by
    - Facilitating the calculation of TrOOP by the Part D Plans
    - Facilitating billing in the appropriate order at the pharmacy point of sale
    - Ensuring that SPAPs have the information they need to develop their benefit structures
    - Ensuring that Medicaid agencies know which of their beneficiaries are dual-eligibles
    - Simplifying the exchange of enrollment files for employers claiming the employer subsidy

Voluntary Data Sharing Agreements

VDSAs were originally developed to enable CMS, insurers, and employers to coordinate benefits and reduce mistaken payments and administrative expenses. They also allow an exchange of employer group health program (GHP) coverage information for Medicare entitlement information. Concurrently, they allow GHPs to meet Medicare secondary payer reporting requirements and provide them with Medicare entitlement information so they can determine when Medicare should be the primary payer. VDSAs also collect drug coverage information that is supplemental to Medicare for TrOOP facilitation, in exchange for Part D entitlement information. Finally, they allow employers to use VDSAs to submit drug coverage enrollment files to claim the employer subsidy.

State Pharmaceutical Assistance Programs must also share data. They use a process similar to the VDSA program so that SPAPs can receive Medicare Part D entitlement information. To comply with Part D, the SPAP must submit a monthly electronic file of all its enrollees to the COB contractor. The COB contractor then responds with a file detailing the Medicare

Part D entitlement of those enrollees. This information includes Part D entitlement dates, the enrollee's Part D Plan, the monthly Part D Plan premium amount, and effective dates and the level of the low-income subsidy.

Coordination of Benefits Agreements

CMS consolidated the claims crossover trading partner agreements with Medicare contractors into the COBA process at the COB contractor. These agreements are negotiated and maintained between CMS and supplemental health insurers (and Medicaid State Agencies, and their fiscal agents) for the exchange of entitlement and paid claims data. The overall goal of this process is to (1) coordinate correct claim payments by Medicare and supplemental health insurers; and (2) report other drug coverage that is supplemental to Part D to facilitate the tracking of TrOOP and to facilitate billing at the pharmacy.

FWA PROGRAMS AND THE PERM INITIATIVE

Medicare Part D claims are subject to the CMS-established FWA program to detect and act on potential fraud and abuse cases. In addition, under the Payment Error Rate Measurement (PERM) initiative, Medicare Part D claims are reviewed by a panel of outside contractors to see whether they were processed correctly and whether the service was medically necessary, coded correctly, and properly paid or denied.

CONCLUSION

The Medicare Part D drug benefit is unique in government programs in that it delegates the responsibility for management of the benefit to the health care private sector. As a result, it can be expected that changes and clarifications will be common to this benefit as the Part D experiment faces different challenges in the public-private relationship. Further, changes in drug therapies and in the testing procedures required of new drug therapies, particularly in new biotechnology medications and genomic testing, will certainly lead to new approaches to cost control and utilization management. In the face of new therapies, current cost control techniques will be stressed and inadequate. Part D benefits will probably act as the testing site for new techniques and methods. It is very possible that private group health drug benefits will follow Part D into the new frontier of medication therapy benefit design and management.

APPENDIX 21.1
PART D COST PROJECTIONS

In order to budget for Part D, it is necessary to understand the history of cost projections and their accuracy.

- The Part D cost projections for 2009 were as follows. The 2009 Part D standard plan benefit parameters were based on an increase of 7.5 percent over 2008 parameter values. For example, the initial deductible and donut-hole limits were projected to increase about 7.5 percent. This should be compared with a 4.6 percent increase in 2008 versus 2007 Part D plan parameters. Specifically, the annual deductible in 2009 increased from $270 to $290. The initial coverage limit increased from $2,500 to $2,700. The annual out-of-pocket threshold increased from $4,025 to $4,325. The RDS increased from $275 and $5,600 to $295 and $6,000.[20]
- The Part D cost projections for 2008 were as follows. In January 2008, the Congressional Budget Office (CBO) projected that Part D would cost $45 billion in 2008, down from its 2007 projection of $49 billion. According to the CBO estimate, the cost of PDPs was only approximately 2 percent higher than for 2007. However, because Part D will recover savings from previous years, the costs for 2008 would be less than that for 2007.
- The Part D cost projections for 2007 were as follows. Premiums for Medicare drug plans increased 13 percent over 2006, when the drug plans went into effect. According to House Oversight and Government Reform investigators, prices for 10 of the most prescribed brand-name medications increased an average of 6.8 percent for the first quarter of 2007, while wholesale prices for the same drugs rose just 3 percent. The investigators cite atorvastatin (Lipitor™) as an example. The cost of one month's supply climbed 9.6 percent to $84.27 in mid-April 2007, from $76.91 in mid-December 2006. Over the same period list prices

20. www.medicareaide.com/2009.html.

climbed 5 percent. Rebates were predicted to be a cost offset by Medicare actuaries, who expected insurers in 2007 to secure manufacturers' rebates of 6 percent, and then pass those savings on to seniors and the government. However, drug manufacturer rebates to insurance companies were expected to total 4.6 percent of total drug costs in 2007, which was down from 5.2 percent in 2006.

- In 2010, the annual deductible increased to $310 and the initial coverage limit increased to $2,830. In addition, the annual out-of-pocket increased to $4,550 and the RDS increased to $310 and $6,300 for the cost threshold and cost limit amounts respectively.
- In 2011, the annual deductible will remain at $310 and the initial coverage limit will increase to $2,840. The annual out-of-pocket cost will remain at $4,550. In addition, the amounts for RDS will remain unchanged, with the cost threshold and cost limit amounts at $310 and $6,300 respectively. The annual percentage increase in average per capita Part D spending, which is used to update the deductible, initial coverage limit, and out-of-pocket threshold for the defined standard benefit for 2011, is 4.63 percent.[21]

21. www.rds.cms.hhs.gov/reference_materials/threshold_limit.htm. www.q1medicare.com/PartD-The-2011-Medicare-Part-D-Outlook.php.

APPENDIX 21.2
BENEFICIARY COMMUNICATIONS

CMS provides the following communications to educate beneficiaries about Part D

- *Medicare & You*—a pamphlet that contains health plan benefit and cost information
- *www.medicare.gov*—a price comparison Web site that allows beneficiaries to compare prices, fees, and other drug plan features
- 1-800-MEDICARE—a call center that provides program information

In addition to CMS communications, pharmacists are a major source of information for patients. For example, they were a primary avenue used by seniors to sign up for the Medicare discount card program. A study from the Kaiser Family Foundation found that one-third of senior beneficiaries will likely turn to their pharmacists for advice about the Medicare drug program. As a result, additional services are available for pharmacists and other health care professionals from the following Web sites

- www.medicareresourcecenter.com
- www.ncpanet.org

APPENDIX 21.3

PRESCRIPTION DRUG EVENTS

Medicare Part D prescription drug events (PDEs) are data from prescription claims that are reported to CMS by prescription drug plans (PDPs) and Medicare Advantage Plans (MA-PDs). The PDE data is used by CMS for reporting to Congress and the public on the overall statistics associated with the Medicare prescription drug benefit, reconciliation of payments by plan sponsors, evaluations of the program, making legislative proposals, and conducting demonstration projects. With the passage of the Medicare Improvements for Patients and Providers Act (MIPPA) in 2008, these regulations were clarified in stating that PDEs may be used for research purposes, to improve public health and for congressional oversight.

The PDE dataflow as described in the 2008 PDE Regional Training Participant Guide is as follows

1. Pharmacy Provider
2. True out-of-pocket (TrOOP) Cost Facilitator
3. Plan
4. PDE Record
5. Prescription Drug Front-End System (PDFS)
    - PDFS Response Report
6. Drug Data Processing System (DDPS)
    - DDPS Return File
    - DDPS Transaction Summary Error Report
7. Integrated Data Repository (IDR)
    - Cumulative Beneficiary Summary Report
    - P2P Reports
8. Payment Reconciliation System (PRS)

Because plans are paid by CMS prospectively, this dataflow ensures that plans report all eligible beneficiaries and data for payment reconciliation. Errors in submissions will result in underpayments to the plans or CMS claw backs of payments from the plans.

APPENDIX 21.4
MIPPA PART D CHANGES

With the emergence of the Medicare Improvements for Patients and Providers Act of 2008, many changes are occurring in the Part D benefit in order to offset potential cuts in physician fees. These changes involve a reduction in federal spending on Medicare Advantage and prescription drug programs equivalent to $12.5 billion over five years, due, in part, to the following:

1. Indirect Medical Education (IME) costs were phased out of Medicare Advantage plan payments in 2010.
2. Effective January 1, 2011, drug manufacturers began providing a 50 percent discount on brand-name drugs, and the government began providing a 7 percent discount on generic drugs for those who fall into the coverage gap. In 2010, Part D enrollees with spending in the coverage gap received a $250 rebate. The new add-on aims to close the "donut hole" by reducing the percentage of cost sharing for beneficiaries in the gap.
3. Effective January 1, 2010, drugs provided to beneficiaries by AIDS Drug Assistance Programs or the Indian Health Service were allowed to count toward the annual (TrOOP).[22]
4. Now, in 2011, a majority of private fee-for-service (PFFS) plans will have met the requirement to have a network.
5. The PPO Stabilization Fund, established by MMA in the amount of $10 billion, will be phased out in 2013.

These funding avenues were originally established to encourage PPOs and other managed care organizations to participate in Part D. Now that participation is assured, the need for this encouragement is diminished.

22. www.hapnetwork.org/assets/pdfs/2011-fact-sheet.pdf.

APPENDIX 21.5

DETAILS OF DRUG COVERAGE IN PART D FORMULARIES

CMS originally developed criteria for approval of Part D formularies including a mandate for one drug from each therapeutic category, as defined by USP, to be required in any Part D formulary. These so-called formulary key drug types (FKDTs), expanded the Part D formularies and caused controversy over inclusion of drugs regardless of information on effectiveness and safety. In the 2008 CMS Call Letter, the mandate criteria are removed. Essentially, CMS modified its prior mandate and removed the FKDT criteria. The new formulary guidelines indicate that FKDTs must be considered as part of the "outlier" test for formulary review.

If the pharmacy dispenses a brand drug, they must inform the Part D patient of any differential between the price of the brand drug and the price of the lowest-priced generic version of that drug available at that pharmacy. This disclosure is mandatory, and plans will ensure compliance with this provision at the retail level.

Part D does not cover all medications. The general rule for coverage is that Medicare Part A or Part B pays first, and Part D kicks in only for medications that the other Medicare plans do not cover. Certain classes of so-called "formulary protected," drugs are required to have coverage by PDP sponsors unless there are exceptions based on scientific evidence and medical standards of practice. They include classes of drugs that if restricted would have a major or life-threatening clinical effect, or impede an individual's gaining access to multiple drugs in the same class due to unique chemical actions.

DESI DRUGS

Drug efficacy study implementation (DESI) drugs are excluded from Part D formularies. These are drugs that were approved solely on the basis of their safety prior to 1962. Thereafter, Congress required drugs to be shown to be effective as well as safe, and the FDA initiated DESI to evaluate the effectiveness of those drugs that previously had been approved on safety grounds alone. These drugs, and those identical, related, and similar to them, may continue to be marketed until the administrative proceedings evaluating their effectiveness have been concluded, at which point continued marketing is only permitted if an NDA is approved for such drugs. The vast majority of the DESI proceedings have been concluded, but a few are still pending.[23]

VACCINES—A SPECIAL CASE

The Tax Relief and Health Care Act of 2006 (TRHCA) modified the definition of a Part D drug to include "… vaccines administered on or after January 1, 2008." CMS released detailed operational guidance related to administration fees for Part D vaccines in 2008. In this guidance, CMS has interpreted this requirement to mean that the Part D vaccine administration costs are a component of the negotiated price for a Part D–covered vaccine, including the vaccine ingredient cost, a dispensing fee (if applicable), and a vaccine administration fee. Further, CMS has stated that Part D vaccines, including the associated administration costs, should be billed on one claim for both in- and out-of-network situations. As a result, if an in-network pharmacy dispenses and administers the vaccine in accordance with state law, the pharmacy would process a single claim to the Part D sponsor and collect from the enrollee any applicable cost sharing on the vaccine and its administration. Alternatively, if a vaccine were administered out of network in a physician's office, the physician would bill the beneficiary for the entire charge. The beneficiary would, in turn, submit a paper claim to the Part D sponsor for reimbursement for the total charge: both the vaccine ingredient cost and the administration fee.

If a Part D vaccine had specific storage conditions that would limit physicians' offices from maintaining an inventory for their patients, and the physician has a pharmacy dispense and deliver the vaccine for administration, the pharmacy would submit the vaccine ingredient cost and dispensing fee to the Part D sponsor for reimbursement, and the physician would charge the beneficiary for the administration. CMS has said that pharmacy delivery services would be covered through contracted reimbursements with Part D plans.

23. www.fda.gov/cder/compliance/CPG_QandA.htm.

DRUG CATEGORIES NOT COVERED UNDER MEDICARE PART D

The specific categories of medications that are not covered under Part D are as follows:

- Part A—covered drugs
- Part B—covered drugs
- DME supply drugs
- Immunosuppressant drugs received for a Medicare-covered organ transplant
- Hemophilia clotting factors
- Some oral antiemetic drugs
- Pneumococcal, hepatitis B, and influenza vaccines
- Antigens (e.g., allergy shots)
- Erythropoietin for treatment of anemia in patients in end-stage renal disease (ESRD) who are on dialysis
- Parenteral nutrition
- Intravenous immunoglobulin (IVIG)
- Benzodiazepines[24] (e.g., Valium™, Ativan™, and Xanax™)
- OTC medications (e.g., medications for constipation, heartburn, pain)
- Cough and cold medications
- Prescription vitamins and mineral products (except prenatal vitamins and fluoride preparations)
- Medications for anorexia, weight loss, or weight gain
- Barbiturates[24] (e.g., phenobarbital)
- Fertility-promotion medications
- Medications promoting hair growth
- Outpatient drugs for which the manufacturer seeks to require that associated tests or monitoring services be purchased exclusively from the manufacturer or its designee as a condition of sale

24. Effective in 2013, plans must cover benzodiazepines, as well as barbiturates if used to treat epilepsy, cancer, or a chronic mental health disorder.

APPENDIX 21.6
QUALITY MEASURES IN PART D

The following is a listing of measures as seen in the 2009 Medicare Part D Reporting Requirements.[25]

- Retail, home infusion, and long-term care pharmacy access
- Enrollment and disenrollment
- Claim reversals
- Access to extended day supplies at retail pharmacies
- Vaccines
- Medication therapy management programs
- Generic drug utilization
- Grievances
- Pharmacy and therapeutics (P&T) committees/Part D activities
- Transitions, prior authorization, step edit, exceptions, appeals, and overpayment
- Pharmaceutical manufacturer and long-term care rebates
- Discounts and price concessions
- Licensure and solvency
- Business transactions and financial requirements
- Drug benefit analyses

25. www.cms.gov/PrescriptionDrugCovContra/Downloads/PartDReportingRequirements_2009.pdf.

APPENDIX 21.7

DRUG CATEGORIES COVERED UNDER MEDICARE PART B

The following is a list of medications and medication categories covered under Part B. These medications are billed separately from professional services.

- DME supply drugs
- Immunosuppressive medications
- Hemophilia clotting factors
- Anticancer drugs—oral
- Antiemetic drugs—oral
- Pneumococcal vaccine
- Antigens
- Erythropoietin (EPO)
- Hepatitis B vaccine
- High risk: end-stage renal disease (ESRD), Rx factor VIII/IX, institutions for mentally handicapped, household mate of hepatitis B virus (HBV) carrier, homosexual men, illicit injectable drug abusers
- Intermediate risk: staff of institutions for mentally handicapped, workers in health care institutions with frequent blood or blood-derived body-fluid contact
- Parenteral nutrition
- Intravenous immunoglobulin (IVIG) in home
- Influenza vaccine

The following is a list of medications and medication categories covered under Part B that are prescribed as a consequence of Part B—covered professional services. These medications are billed separately from the professional services billing.

- Drugs furnished "incident" to a professional service
- Separately billable ESRD
- Hospital outpatient department separately billable

- Drugs covered as supplies or "integral to a procedure"
- Blood

In addition, certain drugs are furnished as part of a service in provider settings. These drugs are included in the Part B billing.

- Drugs packaged under a hospital outpatient prospective payment system
- ESRD facilities included in Medicare's ESRD composite rate
- Osteoporosis drugs provided by home health agencies
- Critical access hospitals (CAHs) outpatient departments
- Rural health clinics (RHCs)
- Federally qualified health centers (FQHCs)
- Community mental health centers
- Ambulances
- Separately billable drugs provided by comprehensive outpatient rehabilitation facilities (CORFs)

CHAPTER 22

Workers' Compensation

John F. Burton, Jr.

Workers' compensation programs provide cash benefits, medical care, and rehabilitation services to workers who experience work-related injuries.[1] Each state has a workers' compensation statute and there are several federal programs. There are some common features of these programs, including the use of several legal tests to determine which injuries are work-related and therefore entitle workers to benefits. There are also differences among the jurisdictions, including the weekly amounts and durations of cash benefits. This chapter summarizes the salient similarities and differences, with particular emphasis on the insurance arrangements used to provide the benefits.

HISTORY

Workers' compensation is the oldest social insurance program in the United States, and many of the current features of the program can only be understood if the context in which the program emerged in the early decades of the 20th century is understood.[2] At that time, a negligence suit (a form of tort or civil remedy) was the only remedy an employee injured at work had against the employer.

1. Unless otherwise indicated, "injuries" includes injuries and diseases.
2. Burton and Mitchell (2003) provide a brief history of workers' compensation, as well as other social insurance and employee benefit programs.

If the employee won the suit, the recovery could be substantial, since the damages could include replacement of lost wages, reimbursement of all medical expenses, and payments for nonpecuniary consequences, such as pain and suffering. An injured worker faced substantial obstacles to wining the suit, however, not only because of the necessity to prove that the employer was negligent, but because the courts had established several legal doctrines that a negligent employer could use to avoid liability. An example was contributory negligence, which precluded the employee from any recovery if he or she were negligent, even if the employer was primarily the negligent party. The conventional view is that few employees were successful in these suits, although occasionally employers were found liable and paid large awards, a combination that neither party liked. The approach was also criticized because recovery depended on the worker bringing a lawsuit, and the litigation was costly and time-consuming.

Workers' compensation was designed to overcome some of the deficiencies of the negligence suit approach. All of the workers' compensation statutes incorporate the "workers' compensation principle," which has two elements. Workers' compensation is a no-fault system, which means that in order to receive benefits, a worker does not need to demonstrate that the employer is negligent and the employer cannot use the special defenses, such as contributory negligence. The employee only has to prove the injury is "work related" (although there are legal tests that are obstacles to meeting the work-related requirement in some cases, as discussed below).

The other side of the workers' compensation principle is that the statutory benefits provided by the program are the employer's only liability to the employee for the workplace injury. The exclusive remedy aspect of workers' compensation means that employees cannot bring tort suits against their employers (subject to some limited exceptions discussed later). Workers' compensation laws also prescribe cash benefits by formulas, which are intended to reduce the litigation, delays, and uncertainty associated with tort suits (although in practice, many jurisdictions still have considerable litigation in their programs).

The legal context of the early 20th century also affected the design of the workers' compensation program in a feature that persists. At that time, the U.S. Supreme Court interpreted the commerce clause of the Constitution in a narrow fashion, which limited the ability of Congress to regulate matters that were not directly in interstate commerce. The federal government was able to enact a workers' compensation program for its own employees and for workers who were clearly engaged in interstate commerce, such as railroad workers. However, most workers in the private sector as well as state and local government employees could not be regulated by the federal government, and therefore, of necessity, most initial workers' compensation laws were enacted by the states.

The Wisconsin Workers' Compensation Law of 1911 is the oldest state workers' compensation law in continuous existence. By 1920, most states had enacted workers' compensation laws. Although the Supreme Court changed its interpretation of the commerce clause in the 1930s so that a federal workers' compensation statute covering all private-sector workers would be constitutional, the pattern of states controlling workers' compensation established almost 100 years ago persists today. The most serious challenge to state dominance of workers' compensation occurred in the 1970s, when the National Commission on State Workmen's Compensation Laws proposed federal standards for state programs if they did not significantly improve their laws.[3] Although legislation to implement the National Commission's proposal was introduced in Congress in the 1970s, the effort failed and similar efforts seem unlikely in the near term.

COVERAGE OF EMPLOYEES AND EMPLOYERS

Most employees and employers are covered by workers' compensation.[4] Recent estimates indicate that nationally about 97 percent of all wage and salary workers are covered, not counting self-employed persons. Some states cover virtually all employees, while only about 75 percent of the workers are covered in Texas, the only state in which workers' compensation coverage is elective for employers. The other gaps in coverage occur because some states exempt (1) employers with a limited number of employees (e.g., three or less); (2) certain industries, such as state and local government, and agriculture; and (3) certain occupations, such as household workers.

In addition, the laws are designed to cover employees, which means that workers who are independent contractors normally are not covered. Moreover, certain employees—those who are casual workers or workers

3. Burton (2004) discusses the legacy of The National Commission on State Workmen's Compensation Laws. The program was generally known as "workmen's compensation" until the 1970s, when most jurisdictions adopted "workers' compensation" as a more appropriate term.
4. U.S. Chamber of Commerce (2010) includes tables summarizing state coverage provisions. Sengupta, Reno, and Burton (2010) provide data on national and state coverage of workers.

not engaged in the normal trade or business of the employer—may not be protected by the act even when their employers are within the scope of the act.

COVERAGE OF INJURIES AND DISEASES

Even workers who are covered by workers' compensation statutes must meet certain legal tests in order to receive benefits.[5] There is a four-step test found in most state workers' compensation laws:

1. There must be a personal injury, which in some jurisdictions is interpreted to exclude mental illness.
2. It must have resulted from an accident, which is interpreted in some states to exclude injuries that develop over a long period of time, as opposed to those injuries resulting from a traumatic incident.
3. It must have arisen out of employment, which means that the source of the injury must be related to the job.
4. It must have occurred during the course of employment, which normally requires that the injury occur on the employer's premises and during working hours.

Most work-related injuries can meet these four tests, although there are thousands of cases testing the exact meaning of each of these four steps.

The coverage of diseases is a problem in workers' compensation.[6] Many diseases, such as coal workers' pneumoconiosis (black lung disease), could not meet the accident test because they developed over a prolonged period. In addition, the statutes used to contain limited lists of diseases that were compensable. The restricted lists of diseases have now been abandoned in all jurisdictions. Now, typically, there is a list of specified occupational diseases followed by a general category permitting the compensation of other occupational diseases. Nonetheless, there are restrictions in language pertaining to work-related diseases still found in many laws, such as statutes of limitations that require the claim to be filed within a limited period after the last exposure to the substance causing the disease, even if the disease did not manifest itself for a prolonged period. Also, some state

5. The legal tests are examined in Larson and Larson (2010) and Willborn, Schwab, Burton, and Lester (2007, pp. 894–937).
6. Barth and Hunt (1980) is the best examination of the handling of diseases by workers' compensation programs.

courts have interpreted the general category of occupational diseases to only cover those diseases that are peculiar to or characteristic of the occupation of the employee seeking coverage.

Many states have amended their laws in recent decades to exclude certain types of injuries and diseases from workers' compensation coverage. These developments are discussed in the final section of this chapter.

MEDICAL CARE AND REHABILITATION SERVICES

Most state workers' compensation laws require the employer to provide full medical benefits to the worker with a work-related injury.[7] This portion of the workers' compensation program has become increasingly expensive in recent decades, with medical benefits now accounting for half of all benefit payments, up from one-third in the early 1980s. Unlike most health care plans (with minor exceptions), employees pay no portion of the premium for workers' compensation insurance, and there are no deductibles or co-insurance provisions that require employees to share the expense of medical care.

Fee schedules have been issued by many state workers' compensation agencies that limit medical charges, which have made some medical care providers reluctant or unwilling to provide services to injured workers. Other providers appear to react to fee schedules by increasing the quantity of health care services provided. There is disagreement about whether the fee schedules are effective in reducing expenditures on medical care.

Another approach to reducing workers' compensation health care expenditures used in a number of states is to allow the insurance carrier or employer (rather than the employee) to choose the treating physician. Again, there is disagreement about the effect of such limits on employee choice on the quality and cost of health care.[8] In recent years, there has also been a rapid increase in the use of managed health care in the workers' compensation programs in a number of states, including such techniques as health maintenance organizations (HMOs), preferred provider organizations (PPOs), and utilization review. There is limited evidence about the effect of these cost-containment efforts on medical costs and quality in the workers' compensation system.

7. Burton (2009) examines the medical care component of workers' compensation in more detail. Current data on medical benefits are provided by Sengupta, Reno, and Burton (2010).
8. Neumark, Barth, and Victor (2007) examined the impact of variants of provider choice in several states.

Medical rehabilitation, such as physical therapy, is likely to be provided by the workers' compensation laws. However, many states do not require employers to provide vocational rehabilitation services that may be necessary to equip the injured worker to handle a new job.

CASH BENEFITS

Cash benefits vary substantially among the states, with wide variations in maximum weekly benefits and maximum durations of benefits.[9] Each state also provides a variety of types of cash benefits. A general characteristic of the cash benefits is that they are not subject to state or federal income taxes.

Temporary Total Disability Benefits

These benefits are paid to an employee who is completely unable to work but whose injury is of a temporary nature. The weekly benefit in most jurisdictions is two-thirds of the worker's preinjury wage, subject to maximum and minimum amounts as prescribed by state law. There is also a waiting period during which the worker receives no benefits from the workers' compensation program.[10] However, if the worker is still disabled beyond a specified date, known as the retroactive date, then the benefits for the waiting period are paid on a retroactive basis.

Temporary Partial Disability Benefits

These benefits are paid to an employee who is still recovering from a workplace injury or disease and who is able to return to work but has limitations on the amount or intensity of work that can be provided during the healing period.[11] The weekly benefit in most jurisdictions is two-thirds of the difference between the worker's preinjury wage and the worker's current earnings, subject to a maximum amount as prescribed by state law.

9. U.S. Chamber of Commerce (2010) provides information on the statutory provisions for cash benefits. Sengupta, Reno, and Burton (2010) provide data on benefit payments. Burton (2009) reviews the studies of workers' compensation cash benefits.
10. A worker with a work-related injury will receive workers' compensation medical benefits from the date of injury. Some employers also have disability benefit plans that provide cash benefits or continuation of salary from the date of injury, although many such plans exclude work-related injuries.
11. Burton (2008b) summarizes temporary partial disability benefits.

Permanent Partial Disability Benefits

Permanent partial disability (PPD) benefits are the most complicated, controversial, and expensive type of workers' compensation benefit.[12] They are paid to a worker who has a permanent consequence of his or her work-related injury or disease that is not totally disabling. An example would be someone who has lost a hand in an accident.

There are two general approaches to permanent partial disability benefits. Scheduled PPD benefits are paid for those injuries that are included in a list found in the workers' compensation statute. In New York, for example, 100 percent loss of an arm entitles the worker to 312 weeks of benefits. The schedules are also applied to partial loss of the arm, so that a 50 percent loss of an arm in New York is worth 156 weeks of benefit. The schedules in most jurisdictions provide benefits whether the injury results in amputation or a loss of use of the body part. Normally, the schedule is limited to the body extremities such as arms, legs, hands, and feet, plus eyes and ears.

Nonscheduled PPD benefits are paid for those permanent injuries that are not on the schedule, such as back injuries. The basis for these benefits depends on the jurisdiction. In states such as New Jersey that use the "impairment approach," the back injury is rated in terms of the seriousness of the medical consequences. (In New Jersey, 25 percent of loss of the whole person in a medical sense translates into 25 percent of 600 weeks, or 150 weeks of benefits.) In states such as Iowa that use the "loss of earning capacity approach," the back injury is rated considering the medical consequences as well as factors, such as age, education, and job experience, that affect the worker's earning capacity. (In Iowa, 25 percent of loss of earning capacity translates into 25 percent of 500 weeks or 125 weeks of benefits.)

These benefit durations for scheduled PPD benefits and for nonscheduled permanent partial benefits in those jurisdictions relying on the impairment approach or on the loss of earning capacity approach are fixed in the sense that the worker receives that duration of benefits whether or not he or she has actual wage loss for that period. During the period these types of the permanent partial benefits are being paid, the weekly benefit is normally calculated as $66\frac{2}{3}$ percent of preinjury wages, subject to maximum and minimum weekly benefit amounts.[13]

12. Burton (2005) examines permanent partial disability benefits in more detail.
13. Iowa is one of several states in which cash benefits are based on the spendable earnings approach. In Iowa, permanent partial disability benefits are 80 percent of the worker's spendable earnings, which are gross wages minus federal and state income taxes and the employee's share of the payroll tax for the Social Security program.

The nonscheduled permanent partial disability benefits in New York rely on a fundamentally different approach, usually referred to as the "wage-loss approach." The worker receives benefits only if, in addition to having an injury with permanent consequences, he or she also has actual wage loss due to the work injury. The weekly nonscheduled permanent partial disability benefit in New York is $66\frac{2}{3}$ percent of the difference between the worker's earnings prior to the injury minus his or her earnings after the healing period is over, subject to a maximum weekly amount. In New York, these nonscheduled permanent partial disability benefits can continue for as long as the worker has earnings losses due to the work-related injury, subject to duration limits that vary from 225 to 525 weeks, depending on the severity of the injury.

Permanent Total Disability Benefits

Permanent total disability benefits are paid to someone who is completely unable to work for an indefinite period. Permanent total status is assigned if the worker has specified types of injuries, such as the loss of two arms, or more generally if the facts in the case warrant an evaluation as a permanent total disability. This is a relatively uncommon type of case in workers' compensation. The weekly benefit for a permanent total disability is normally two-thirds of the preinjury wage, subject to maximum and minimum amounts as prescribed by state law. In most states, the permanent total disability benefits are paid for the duration of total disability or for life. In a number of states, however, there are arbitrary limits on total dollar amounts or duration of these benefits.

Death Benefits

Death benefits are paid to the survivors of a worker who was killed on the job. In many jurisdictions, the weekly benefit depends on the number of survivors. For example, a widow or widower might receive a benefit that is 50 percent of the deceased worker's wage, while a widow or widower with a child might receive a weekly benefit that is $66\frac{2}{3}$ percent of the deceased worker's wage. These benefits are subject to minimum and maximum weekly amounts. Most states provide the benefits for the duration of the survivor's lifetime if the survivor is a widow or widower and for children's benefits at least until age 21, but there are a number of states that have limits on the dollar amounts or on the durations of survivors' benefits.

FINANCING OF BENEFITS

Workers' compensation benefits are prescribed by state laws, but these laws assign the responsibility for the provision of the benefits to the employer.

Insurance Arrangements

The employer in turn provides the benefits by one of three mechanisms, as shown in Table 22-1:[14]

1. By purchasing insurance from a private insurance carrier.
2. By purchasing insurance from a state workers' compensation fund.
3. By qualifying as a self-insurer and paying its own employees directly.

Twenty-one states, including California and New York, have all three options available (this is known as the three-way system or competitive state fund approach). Four states, including Ohio and Washington, prohibit private carriers and operate state funds (known as exclusive or monopolistic state funds); two of these states also allow self-insurance. The other 26 jurisdictions, including the District of Columbia and Wisconsin, permit employers to purchase insurance from private carriers or to self-insure. Federal government employees are covered by a government fund. Nationally, about 50 percent of all benefits are paid by private insurance carriers, about 25 percent by state and federal funds, and about 25 percent by self-insuring employers.

WORKPLACE SAFETY AND HEALTH

Most employers purchase workers' insurance from private carriers or state funds, as discussed in the previous section. The process used to determine the employers' costs of workers' compensation insurance is described in Appendix 22.1. An essential feature of the process is that the workers' compensation program in each state relies on two levels of experience rating, which in theory promote workplace safety. Industry-level experience rating establishes a pure premium (or manual) rate for each industry that is largely based on prior benefit payments by the industry. Firm-level experience rating determines the workers' compensation

14. Sengupta, Reno, and Burton (2010, pp. 16 and 20–21) provide information on workers' compensation insurance arrangements.

TABLE 22-1

Workers' Compensation Insurance Arrangements in Effect as of January 1, 2010

States with Exclusive State Funds (4)	
North Dakota (No self-insurance)	
Ohio	
Washington	
Wyoming (No self-insurance)	
States with Private Carriers and Competitive State Funds (21)	
Arizona	Montana
California	New Mexico
Colorado	New York
Hawaii	Oklahoma
Idaho	Oregon
Kentucky	Pennsylvania
Louisiana	Rhode Island
Maine	South Carolina
Maryland	Texas
Minnesota	Utah
Missouri	
Jurisdictions with Only Private Carriers (26)	
Alabama	Michigan
Alaska	Mississippi
Arkansas	Nebraska
Connecticut	Nevada
Delaware	New Hampshire
District of Columbia	New Jersey
Florida	North Carolina
Georgia	South Dakota
Illinois	Tennessee
Indiana	Vermont
Iowa	Virginia
Kansas	West Virginia
Massachusetts	Wisconsin

Self-insurance by qualifying employers is permitted unless otherwise indicated.

The South Carolina fund is the required insurer for state employees and is available to cities and countries to insure their employees, but the fund does not insure private employers.

West Virginia only began allowing private carriers as of January 1, 2009.

Source: Sengupta, Reno, and Burton (2010, Table 8).

premium for each firm above a minimum size by comparing its prior benefit payments to those of other firms in the industry. The actual effects of the workers' compensation program in general, and firm-level experience rating in particular, have been debated by scholars representing various economic approaches.[15]

The essence of the "pure" neoclassical economics approach is that the introduction of workers' compensation will lead to reduced incentives for workers to avoid injuries, assuming that they did not purchase private disability insurance plans prior to the introduction of workers' compensation, since the adverse economic effects of the injuries are reduced by workers' compensation benefits. The disincentive to avoid injuries is an example of the "moral hazard" problem. This economic approach also argues that the introduction of workers' compensation will also lead to reduced incentives for employers to prevent accidents unless perfect experience rating is used to finance the program.

In contrast, the "old" institutional economics (OIE) approach argues that the introduction of workers' compensation with experience rating should improve safety because the limitations of knowledge and mobility and the unequal bargaining power for employees mean that the risk premiums generated in the labor market are inadequate to provide employers the safety incentives postulated by the pure neoclassical economics approach. The modified neoclassical economics approach would also accept the idea that experience rating should help improve safety by providing stronger incentives to employers to avoid accidents. Where the OIE theorists would probably disassociate themselves from the modified neoclassical economics theorists would be the latter contingent's emphasis on the moral hazard problem aspect of workers' compensation, which could result in more injuries.

A number of recent studies of the workers' compensation program provide evidence that should be helpful in evaluating the virtues of the pure neoclassical economics, the modified neoclassical economics, and the OIE approaches. However, the evidence is inconclusive. A survey of the literature by Boden (1995, p. 285) concluded that "research on the safety impacts has not provided a clear answer to whether workers' compensation improves workplace safety." In contrast, Thomason (2005, p. 26) asserted that most (11 of 14) studies he surveyed found that experience rating improves safety and health and that the studies failing to detect the relationship were methodologically weaker than the other studies.

15. This section is largely based on Burton and Chelius (1997) and Burton (2009).

Thomason concluded (2005, p. 26): "Taken as a whole, the evidence is quite compelling: experience rating works." Tompa, Trevithick, and McLeod (2007, p. 91) also surveyed the literature and found moderate evidence that the introduction of experience rating reduces the frequency of injuries (although the severity may increase) and moderate evidence that the degree of experience rating reduces the frequency and severity of injuries.

Some estimates of the magnitude of the safety effect from industry-level and firm-level experience ratings are substantial: Durbin and Butler (1998, pp. 78–79) suggest that a 10 percent increase in workers' compensation costs countrywide between 1947 and 1990 was associated with a 12.9 percent decline in workplace fatalities. This evidence on experience rating is consistent with the positive impact on safety postulated by the OIE approach and the modified neoclassical economists, and inconsistent with the pure neoclassical view that the use of experience rating should be irrelevant or may even lead to reduced incentives for employers to improve workplace safety.[16]

There is also evidence that the presence of workers' compensation benefits leads to changes in worker behavior. Thomason (2005) and Burton (2009) summarize a number of studies that found the reported frequency and severity of workers' compensation claims increase in response to higher benefits, which may suggest that a moral hazard problem exists. Caution is needed in interpreting these studies, however, since the increased frequency or severity reported in the claims can result from a "true injury effect" (workers take more risks as a result of higher benefits and as a result actually experience more injuries) or from the "reporting effect" (workers report claims that would not have been reported as a result of the higher benefits, and/or extend their period of reported disability because of the higher benefits). Most studies of the relationship between workers' compensation benefits and the frequency and severity of claims have not distinguished between the true injury and reporting effects. Durbin and Butler (1998, p. 67) conclude that the latter effect dominates, which implies that the concerns of modified neoclassical economists that the use of workers' compensation benefits to provide ex post compensation for injured workers will lead to more injuries is exaggerated. As a result, Burton (2009, p. 252) asserted that "even though the gross effects of higher workers' compensation

16. Thomason (2005, p. 27) cautions that experience rating may, in addition to encouraging employers to improve workplace safety and health, also lead to increased claims management by employers, including the denial of legitimate compensation claims. While Thomason discusses several studies suggesting that such employer activity occurs, the evidence indicates that overall experience rating is associated with accident prevention activities by employers.

benefits is to increase the frequency and duration of workers' compensation claims, once the contribution of the reporting effect is subtracted, the net effect of higher benefits appears to be an improvement in workplace safety since the favorable effects of experience rating on employer safety efforts dominate the deleterious true injury effect for workers."

ADMINISTRATION OF WORKERS' COMPENSATION

There are wide variations among the states in how the workers' compensation programs are administered. There are several dimensions of the differences among states.

The Initial Responsibility for Payment

Most states use what is known as the direct payment system, in which employers are obligated to begin payment as soon as the worker is injured and the employer accepts liability. Other states use the agreement system, where the employers have no obligation to begin payments until an agreement is reached with the employee concerning the amount due. The agreement system is likely to involve delays in many cases.

The Functions of the Administrative Agency

Most states have a workers' compensation agency that is responsible for administering the program. One function of the agency is adjudication of disputes between workers and employers or insurance carriers. In most agencies, the initial level of decision is made by an administrative law judge (ALJ) or an official with similar duties, such as a hearing examiner. The decisions of the ALJ can normally be appealed to an appeals board (or commission) within the workers' compensation agency. Then, appeals from the workers' compensation board typically enter the state court system at the appellate court level.

The state workers' compensation agencies vary considerably in their administrative styles. At one extreme are agencies, such as those in Illinois and New Jersey, that are passive. They essentially wait for problems to arise and then perform the adjudication function. The other extreme is Wisconsin, where the agency can be characterized as active because it performs three functions in addition to adjudication. The Wisconsin agency engages in extensive record keeping, in monitoring of the performance of carriers and employers, and in providing evaluations (e.g., of the extent of permanent disability) that help the parties reach decisions without resorting to litigation.

Closing of Cases

In many states, cases are closed by private agreements of the parties (subject to approval of the workers' compensation agency in some states). These are generally known as compromise-and-release agreements, because a compromise is reached on the amount of benefits paid and the employer is released from any further obligations. Normally, the benefits are paid in a lump sum. These compromise-and-release agreements are often criticized, because they mean that workers who subsequently have additional need for medical care or income benefits cannot obtain them from the employer.[17] Torrey (2007) discusses some concerns about the increasing use of compromise settlements in several jurisdictions.

Litigation

States vary widely in the extent of litigation (defined here as the use of an attorney by the worker to help receive benefits). The worker's attorney's fee is almost always deducted from the cash benefit. Wisconsin is an extreme example of a state where lawyers are involved in only a minority of cases. At the other extreme, states such as California and Illinois have lawyers involved in the majority of cases, especially those that involve anything other than a relatively short period of temporary total benefits.

RECENT DEVELOPMENTS AND CONTINUING CHALLENGES

The workers' compensation program has experienced significant changes in recent decades, many of which were stimulated by developments between 1985 and 1991.[18] There was a rapid escalation in the employers'

17. Thomason and Burton (1993) summarize the studies of the determinants and consequences of compromise and release agreements. They also report (1993, pp. S27–S28) that in New York, "retention of legal counsel increases the probability of settlement and decreases settlement size, indicating that claimant attorneys are acting contrary to their clients' interests in the settlement of nonscheduled permanent partial disability claims."
18. The discussion of developments in the 1980s and 1990s is largely based on Thomason, Schmidle, and Burton (2001, Chapter 2). The information on costs and benefits as a percent of payroll is from Burton (2010, Figure 1).

costs of workers' compensation, largely due to the increases in benefit payments discussed below. The costs increased from $25.1 billion in 1984 to $55.2 billion in 1991, or an average of 11.9 percent a year, which far outpaced payroll growth. As a result, workers' compensation costs as a percent of payroll increased rapidly, rising from 1.49 percent in 1984 to 2.16 percent in 1991.

Workers' compensation benefits also increased during the period, from $18.0 billion in 1984 to $40.8 billion in 1991, for an average annual increase of 12.4 percent. Benefits increased from 1.09 percent of payroll in 1984 to 1.35 percent in 1991. Medical benefits increased by 14.6 percent per year between 1995 and 1991, more rapidly than both the annual increase of 11.0 percent in cash benefits and the high inflation rate for general heath-care costs. The sources of the relatively high inflation in medical costs in the workers' compensation program included the rapid spread of managed care through the health care system used for nonoccupational medical conditions.

Throughout the late 1980s and early 1990s, many employers became concerned about the increasing costs of workers' compensation. In addition to cost increases resulting from higher statutory cash benefits and escalating medical benefits, employers were also concerned about what they perceived to be widespread fraud and rampant litigation, especially involving conditions, such as workplace stress, that employers felt were outside the proper domain of the program.

The workers' compensation insurance industry was particularly agitated during this period. Several factors contributed to the industry's problems. Benefit payments accelerated during this period. Nonetheless, carriers were unable to gain approval from regulators for the significant premium increases the industry believed were actuarially justified. Even though investment income was relatively high from 1984 to 1991 (always exceeding 12 percent of premium), underwriting losses were so substantial that the overall operating ratio was 103.8 or higher in every year between 1984 and 1991 (Burton 2008a).[19] In other words, the workers' compensation insurance industry lost money in every year during this period, even after taking into account the returns on investments.

19. The combined ratio after dividends is the sum of losses, loss adjustment expenses, underwriting expenses, and dividends. The overall operating ratio is the combined ratio after dividends minus net investment gain/loss and other income. The ratios are expressed as a percent of net premiums. Thus, an overall operating ratio of 103.8 means carriers were losing $3.80 for every $100 of net premiums, while an overall operating ratio of 80 means carriers were earning $20 of profit for every $100 of net premiums.

The major legacy of the period from 1985 to 1991 was the planting of the seeds for reform that bloomed in the 1990s and that have had lasting effects on the program. Over half of the state legislatures passed major amendments to workers' compensation laws between 1989 and 1996, generally with the purpose of reducing the cost of the program. Spieler and Burton (1998) identified five significant developments related to these efforts to reduce costs.

First, the statutory level of cash benefits was reduced in a number of jurisdictions, particularly with regard to benefits paid for permanent disabilities. Second, eligibility for workers' compensation benefits was narrowed due to changes in compensability rules. These included requiring workers to provide objective medical evidence to support their claims, the tightening of procedural rules (such as placing the burden of proof on workers to establish their claims), and the restriction on eligibility when the extent of a worker's disability was due in part to a prior injury.

Third, the health care delivery system in workers' compensation was transformed in many states, most notably by the introduction of managed care, by limitations on the worker's choice of the treating physician, and by the promulgation of fee schedules. The fourth development was the increasing use of disability management by employers and carriers, largely due to unilateral action by these parties, but also in part as a result of inducements provided by state legislation.

Finally, in a development discussed later in more detail, the exclusive remedy doctrine, which precludes workers from bringing tort suits against their employers as a result of workplace injuries, was challenged in several court decisions. In addition to these five factors related to workers' compensation reform efforts, another factor that helps explain the decline in employee benefits and employer costs in the 1990s was the significant drop in the work-related injury rate in the decade (from 8.8 cases per 100 workers per year in the private sector in 1990 to 6.1 cases per 100 workers in 2000).

As a result of these various factors, workers compensation benefits increased modestly or even declined in the 1990s, depending on the measure used.[20] Benefits paid to workers increased from \$42.2 billion in 1991 to \$47.7 billion in 2000, which represented less than a 1.5 percent annual rate of increase. Benefits as a percent of payroll peaked at 1.65 percent of payroll in 1991–1992, and then declined to 1.06 of payroll in 2000. The multi-year decline in benefits relative to payroll is unprecedented in

20. The data on benefits and costs in the next three paragraphs are from Sengupta, Reno, and Burton (2010). The underwriting results are from Burton (2008a).

duration and magnitude since at least 1948, when the annual data for successive years were first published.

Largely as a result of these benefit developments, the employers' costs of workers' compensation only increased from $55.2 billion in 1991 to $60.1 billion in 2000, which is less than 1.0 percent a year. Costs as a percent of payroll peaked at 2.18 percent of payroll in 1990 and then slid to 1.34 percent of payroll in 2000. As benefits and costs relative to payroll declined in the 1990s, the profitability of private carriers quickly improved. The overall operating ratio (which includes net investment income) fell from a peak of 108.7 in 1991 to a low of 81.8 in 1995, and was below 100 from 1993 to 2000. The four years from 1994 to 1997, when the operating ratio was below 90 in every year, represents the most profitable stretch of years in at least 20 years for workers' compensation insurance.

In the 21st century, benefits increased from $47.7 billion in 2000 (1.06 percent of payroll) to $56.1 billion in 2004 (1.13 percent of payroll) and then grew slightly to $57.6 billion in 2008, which was slower than the growth of payroll (0.97 percent of payroll). The employers' costs of workers' compensation increased from $60.1 billion in 2000 (1.34 percent of payroll) to $84.2 billion in 2004 (1.70 percent of payroll) and then declined to $78.9 billion in 2008 (1.33 percent of payroll). During the current decade, both benefits and costs as a percent of payroll remain well below their peaks of the 1990s. The workers' compensation insurance industry was unprofitable in 2001 and 2002, but achieved marginal profitability in 2003 (with an overall operating ratio of 98.1) and substantial profitability in 2004 to 2007 (with the operating ratio below 90 in 2006 and 2007).

Changing Insurance Arrangements

Insurance arrangements have been affected by changes in state insurance funds, by the deregulation of private insurance markets, and by changes in the residual market. These changes are discussed here.

Changes in State Insurance Funds

Workers' compensation has relied on a mixture of state funds, private carriers, and self-insurance from its origins in most states between 1910 and 1920.[21] From the beginning, there were arguments concerning the merits of the various insurance arrangements. State funds were lauded because of lower overhead (notably the absence of a broker's fee) and because

21. The discussion of changes in insurance arrangements in this subsection is largely based on Thomason, Schmidle, and Burton (2001, pp. 32–47).

proponents thought that profits were inappropriate in a mandatory social insurance program. Private carriers were praised because they promoted efficiency and were considered more compatible with our capitalistic society. The arguments that prevailed varied from state to state: some jurisdictions created exclusive state funds; some authorized only private carriers to provide insurance; and some permitted private carriers to compete with state funds.

The initial choices of insurance arrangements by the states prevailed for an extended period. As of 1960, there were seven exclusive state funds, the youngest of which was the North Dakota fund established in 1919. There were also 11 competitive state funds as of 1960; the youngest was the Oklahoma fund established in 1933. Oregon converted its exclusive state fund into a competitive state fund in 1966; this represented the only change in state funds between the early 1930s and the early 1980s.

One of the significant developments in the workers' compensation insurance market in the mid-1980s through the 1990s was the emergence of several new competitive state funds. The "pioneer" of the modern movement was Minnesota, which established a competitive state fund in 1984. Then, in the 1990s, seven new competitive state funds began operation. However, in contrarian moves, the long-existing Michigan competitive state fund was privatized in 1994 and a 2009 law will convert the Arizona competitive state fund into a mutual insurance company by 2013. In addition, the Nevada exclusive state fund was privatized in 1999 and the West Virginia exclusive state fund was privatized in 2009.

The state legislators' motives for establishing the state funds were (1)to reduce the costs of workers' compensation and/or (2) to provide an alternative source of insurance for employers who could not purchase policies in the voluntary market or who did not like the surcharges or other conditions imposed on policies purchased in the residual or assigned-risk markets. And, likewise, part of the rationale for privatizing the Nevada and West Virginia state funds was to reduce the costs of workers' compensation insurance.

The cost-savings motives for these changes in insurance arrangements do not appear to be evidence-based. Thomason, Schmidle, and Burton (2001) found there were no differences in insurance costs between states with exclusive state funds and states with private carriers, after controlling for other factors that influence interstate differences in costs, such as injury rates and benefit levels. Among states with private carriers, they found that states with competitive state funds have insurance costs that are nearly 18 percent higher than the costs in states that only have private carriers.

Deregulation of Private Insurance Markets

Another significant development in workers' compensation insurance arrangements in recent decades has been the deregulation of the markets in which private carriers operate. In contrast to the deregulation that generally occurred in property and casualty insurance in the 1970s, rate setting in workers' compensation insurance continued to be highly regulated until the 1980s. The deregulation of workers' compensation insurance was resisted on several grounds: the distinctive characteristic of workers' compensation as a mandated social insurance program (and the resultant concerns with both rates for employers and solvency for carriers); the existence of competitive measures other than price competition for workers' compensation insurance (primarily through dividends); and the need for a comprehensive data base (with uniform rate classes and information on the experience of a large number of insurers). These arguments helped delay even partial deregulation of workers' compensation insurance in most states until the 1980s and 1990s and still operate to preserve "pure" administered pricing in a few states and vestiges of regulation in most states.

The multiple steps that are involved in moving from a manual rate applicable to an employer to the premium paid by that employer are discussed in Appendix 22.1 in connection with Table A22.1-1. The essence of administered pricing is that all carriers were required to start with the same manual rates, and the various modifications to those rates involved either (1) formulas or constants to which all carriers had to adhere and which modified the manual rates at the beginning of the policy period, or (2) dividends that were paid only after the policy period ended. In short, there was virtually no chance for carriers to compete in terms of price at the beginning of the policy period.

Administered pricing is no longer the dominant approach to workers' compensation insurance pricing in the United States. A fundamental result of the deregulation of the workers' compensation insurance market that has taken place in the last 30 years is that private carriers can now compete for business by varying the insurance rates at the beginning of the policy period. Most jurisdictions now allow deviations and scheduled rating,[22]

22. If a state allows deviations, individual carriers may deviate from the published manual rates and charge lower (or higher) rates than those promulgated by the rating organization. The discounts offered by a carrier are uniform for all policyholders in an insurance classification (although the discounts may differ among classes). Under schedule rating plans, insurers can change (usually decrease) the workers' compensation insurance rates an individual employer would otherwise pay.

and a number of jurisdictions have moved to more comprehensive forms of deregulation, which generally fall under the rubric "open competition" or "competitive rating." These reforms involve various combinations of three different changes to the regulatory environment. First, some states have dropped the requirement that insurers become members of the rating organization or adhere to bureau rates. Second, other jurisdictions no longer require insurers to obtain regulatory approval prior to using rates. Third, some states prohibit the rating organization from filing fully developed rates that include loading factors for administrative expenses and profits; instead, these organizations file loss costs or pure premiums. Each carrier has to decide what loading factor should be used in conjunction with pure premiums to produce the equivalent of manual rates.

The initial phase of deregulation began in the early 1980s, and nine states adopted competitive rating between 1981 and 1985. Several factors help explain the onset of deregulation. First, the overall political climate became more hostile to the notion that "big government" could do a better job than competitive forces in determining prices and allocating resources, and one consequence was a general move towards deregulation involving industries such as airlines and trucking, as well as the insurance industry. Another factor was a perception among some legislators, unions, and employers that profits in the workers' compensation insurance line were excessive. The hope was that deregulation would help reduce costs by squeezing out excess profits. Not surprisingly, most workers' compensation insurers resisted deregulation during this period.

After the initial spurt of deregulation in the early 1980s, there was a slowdown in the introduction of deregulation in the balance of the 1980s, with only seven additional states enacting open competition statutes. However, one consequence of the unprofitability of workers' compensation insurance in the late 1980s and early 1990s was a change in attitude towards deregulation by many in the insurance industry.

Deregulation was now seen as a way to escape from the "onerous" decisions of insurance regulators and to establish rates that would allow carrier profitability. Deregulation reemerged with vigor during the 1990s: open competition statutes became effective in 18 states between 1991 and 1995 and in an additional three states by the end of the decade. Deregulation in some of these states—especially those that adopted open competition in the early 1990s when the industry was still experiencing losses—reflected support from the insurance industry, while deregulation in other states, most notably California in 1995, where rate filings had generally been approved by the insurance commissioner, was generally resisted by the industry.

The effect of deregulation on the costs of workers' compensation insurance depends on several factors, such as the stringency of rate regulation in a state prior to deregulation and the particular form of deregulation. Thomason, Schmidle, and Burton (2001) found that comprehensive deregulation—the use of loss costs (instead of manual rates) that were not subject to prior approval by the state before carriers could establish the rates they would charge—reduced the costs of workers' compensation insurance by about 11 percent below the rates that would have been charged if states had continued to rely on administered pricing. They also found that partial deregulation—for example states that continued to rely on manual rates but allowed carriers to deviate from those rates—resulted in higher workers' compensation rates than would have been paid by employers under administered pricing.

Another consequence of deregulation is that, because deviations and schedule rating allow carriers to compete at the beginning of the policy period, dividends to policyholders paid after the policy period have declined in importance. In the early 1980s, dividends ranged from 8.0 to 10.6 percent of premiums, while between 2002 and 2007, dividends varied between 1.3 to 2.8 percent of premiums (Burton 2008a).

Changes in the Residual Market

Another noteworthy development in workers' compensation insurance in recent decades was the rise and fall of the share of premiums accounted for by the residual market. The traditional reasons why an employer was unable to obtain workers' compensation insurance policies in the voluntary market were that the applicant was engaged in some activity that was unusually hazardous relative to the experience of other firms in the appropriate insurance classification, or had a poor loss record, or was so small that the premium did not adequately compensate the insurer for its expenses (Williams, 1969, p. 48). Prior to the mid-1980s, the residual market share generally accounted for five percent or less of all premiums nationally.[23]

23. Thomason, Schmidle, and Burton (2001, pp. 43–46) provide more details on the pre-1985 experience in the residual market, and note that in 1978–1979 the assigned risk market accounted for 12.7 percent of all premiums nationally as the cost of workers' compensation increased after 1975. However, the share dropped back to 5.5 percent in 1984, reflecting the generally profitable conditions in the workers' compensation insurance market and the declining costs of workers' compensation insurance.

The fiscal stress that the workers' compensation insurance market was under from the mid-1980s to the early 1990s is clearly evident in the explosion of the residual market share from 5.5 percent of all premiums in 1984 to a peak of 28.5 percent in 1992. In addition to the traditional reasons for the applicants being forced to purchase in the residual market, which were basically due to the unattractiveness of individual risks, the dominant factor contributing to the residual market growth in the 1985–1992 period was the general inadequacy of workers' compensation insurance rates because of the reluctance of insurance regulators in many states to approve rate filings with substantial rate increases for the voluntary market. Carriers in such jurisdictions became unwilling to write policies in the voluntary market because they could not make an adequate (or, in many cases, any) profit.

The share of workers' compensation insurance provided through the residual market was 80 percent or more in several states (Louisiana, Rhode Island, and Maine) in one or more years between 1989 and 1991. A vicious cycle ensued in some states:

- Rates were held down in the voluntary market by regulators.
- Carriers were unwilling to write policies in the voluntary market, which forced some employers into the residual market.
- In addition, regulators sometimes responded to political pressures and held insurance rates in the residual market well below the levels that were warranted, which induced some employers who were able to purchase policies in the voluntary market to obtain policies in the residual market because the rates were so low; the residual markets ran substantial deficits because of inadequate rates.
- The carriers in the voluntary market were assessed substantial sums to cover the assigned risk markets deficits.
- When the carriers tried to pass on these assessments to policyholders still in the voluntary market, many employers shifted to the residual market in order to obtain coverage at the suppressed rates, which only increased the size of the residual market and increased assessments in the voluntary market.

The national share of total premiums accounted for by the residual market rapidly declined after 1994 (to less than 5 percent by 1998) due to the three major factors already discussed. First, the overall profitability of the workers' compensation insurance line quickly improved after 1992, which made carriers more willing to provide policies in the voluntary market. Second, several jurisdictions established competitive state funds or other special public or quasi-public funds to provide insurance to employers who could not find policies in the voluntary market. The third factor was a series of changes in assigned risk policies that made these policies more expensive and reduced the subsidy from the voluntary market to the residual market, including the introduction of special experience-rating plans in the residual market that tied premiums more closely to each firm's own benefit payments.

The assessments on insurance policies in the voluntary market to underwrite losses in the residual market had two significant consequences for workers' compensation insurance.[24] Employers received an incentive to self-insure since such employers were usually not assessed to cover losses in the residual market. Benefits paid by self-insuring employers increased from 19.0 percent of all benefits in 1990 to 26.7 percent in 1995. Subsequently, as assessments for the residual market declined, the share of benefits provided by self-insuring employers declined (to 22.0 percent of all benefits in 2000).

The second effect of basing assessments for the residual market on insurance premiums was the rapid growth of policies with large deductibles. Under deductible policies written by private carriers or state funds, the insurer pays all of the workers' compensation benefits, but the employer is responsible for reimbursing the insurer for the benefits up to the specified deductible amount (such as the first $100,000 per injury). The amount reimbursed by the employer is not considered insurance for purposes of assessments for the residual market or other special funds in most states. The amount of benefits paid by employers under deductible provisions increased rapidly from $1.3 billion in 1992 to $8.0 billion in 2003, which represented 14.7 percent of the $54.7 billion total benefit payments in 2003. After 2003, the relative importance of large deductibles has slightly declined, with the $8.1 billion of deductibles in 2008 representing 14.1 percent of the $57.6 billion of total benefit payments. One consequence of the expanded use of deductibles should be added encouragement to workplace safety, since employers are essentially perfectly experience rated for the benefit payments up to the deductible.[25]

24. The data in the next two paragraphs are from Sengupta, Reno, and Burton (2010).

25. However, some states permit employers to purchase insurance for their benefit payments up to the deductible, which reduces the degree of experience rating for these benefits.

The Exclusive Remedy Principle

Since their origins in the United States, workers' compensation programs have incorporated the workers' compensation principle, which has two elements: workers benefit from a no-fault system and employers benefit from limited liability, which means that workers' compensation is the exclusive remedy of employees against their employers for workplace injuries and diseases.[26] There have always been some exceptions to the exclusive remedy doctrine, however, and in recent decades there have been several developments that represent significant challenges to the doctrine.[27]

One traditional exception is that the employer is not protected from a tort suit when there is an intentional injury of the employee by the employer. There are at least five legal approaches that states can take when the employer engages in activity that at least arguably represents an intentional injury to the employee:

1. First, some states do not recognize the intentional injury exception under any circumstances.
2. Second, some states require a conscious and deliberate intent to inflict an injury. Larson and Larson (2010, Section 103.03) indicate that this exception to the exclusive remedy doctrine requires "deliberate infliction of harm comparable to an intentional left jab to the chin."
3. Third, some states allow an exception when the employer's conduct is "substantially certain" to cause injury or death.
4. Fourth, the New Mexico Supreme Court created an exception to the exclusive remedy doctrine when the employer's conduct is willful.
5. Fifth, no state (except perhaps New Mexico) upholds the intentional injury exceptions merely because the employer conduct is negligent, wanton, reckless, or even grossly negligent.

26. The exclusive remedy provision means that the only recovery by the injured worker against his or her employer is workers' compensation benefits, unless the worker can take advantage of one of the exceptions to the exclusivity, such as the intentional injury exception discussed in this section. The injured worker may, however, be able to bring a tort suit against a third party who was at least partially responsible for the worker's injury. Examples of third parties that may be sued are manufacturers of defective machinery that was sold to the employer and producers of asbestos sold to firms whose workers contracted diseases because they were exposed to the substances. The suits against third parties and related issues are discussed in Willborn, Schwab, Burton, and Lester (2007, pp. 889–894).

27. This subsection is largely based on Willborn, Schwab, Burton, and Lester (2007, pp. 868–889), Burton (2002), and Aurbach (2003).

The third and fourth exceptions require explication. The exception when the employer's conduct is "substantially certain" to cause injury or death has been established by the courts in several states. In most of these states, including Michigan, Ohio, and West Virginia, the exception was eliminated or narrowed by subsequent legislation. However, a series of recent New Jersey Supreme Court decisions, beginning with *Laidlow* v. *Hariton Machinery Co.,* 170 N.J. 602, 790 A.2d 884 (2002), endorsed the substantially certain test as one element of the intentional injury exception, and efforts by employers and carriers to eliminate the exception by statutory enactment have been unsuccessful. The New Mexico decision, *Delgado* v. *Phelps Dodge Chino, Inc.,* 131 N.M. 272, 34 P. 3d 1148 (2001), includes as part of the definition of "willful conduct" that the employer's act is "reasonably expected to result in the injury suffered by the employee," and to date that decision has not been overturned by the legislature. Whether the New Jersey–New Mexico axis of exception will spread to other jurisdictions is of concern to employers and insurers.

Another area in which the exclusive remedy provision is being challenged involves situations when an employee alleges sexual harassment at the workplace. The New Mexico Supreme Court held in *Coates* v. *Wal-Mart Stores, Inc.,* 976 P.2d 999 (1999) that a tort suit alleging negligent supervision and intentional infliction of emotional distress was not precluded by the exclusive remedy doctrine. However, courts interpreting the workers' compensation statutes in Delaware and Illinois have precluded tort claims for negligent or intentional infliction of emotional distress resulting from sexual conduct by fellow employees. Where tort suits for sexual harassment are precluded by the workers' compensation exclusivity principle, recovery against the employer may be possible under a state fair employment statute or Title VII of the Civil Rights Act of 1964, which was amended in 1991 to permit compensatory or punitive damages for sexual harassment.

A decision by the Supreme Court of Oregon, *Smothers* v. *Gresham Transfer, Inc.,* 23 P.3d 333 (2001), provides another challenge to the exclusive remedy doctrine. The Oregon legislature passed legislation in 1993 denying workers' compensation benefits unless the worker could prove that work exposure was the major contributing cause of an occupational disease. In 1995, the Oregon legislature amended the workers' compensation statute to provide that workers' compensation was the exclusive remedy for work-related injuries and diseases, even if the condition was not compensable under workers' compensation because the work exposure was not the major contributing cause. In Smothers, the court said that the Oregon constitution did not allow the legislature to eliminate both the workers' compensation remedy and a tort remedy when the employment is not the major contributing cause of the condition. While this case established a clear limitation on the exclusive remedy provision in Oregon, similar constitutional challenges in other states have not been successful. Nonetheless, other challenges to statutes that remove any remedy for workplace injuries and disease may be successful under state statutes and constitutions, and arguably also under the U.S. Constitution.

The Viability of Workers' Compensation

The workers' compensation system in the United States is experiencing stress along several dimensions. One is the conflict between affordability of the program for employers and adequacy of benefits for workers. Although economists argue that most of the costs of workers' compensation are paid for by workers in the form of lower wages,[28] employers nonetheless act as if they bear all of the costs and generally seek to reduce costs. The quest for affordability is encouraged in part to the decentralized nature of the programs, in which states compete for employers in part by offering low workers' compensation costs. The increased competition in the U.S. economy in recent decades as a result of deregulation of many domestic industries and of globalization has added to the pressures for states to reduce costs.

The pressures on states to reduce costs can have salutary effects to the extent that the result is increased efficiency in the delivery system for workers' compensation benefits, which, for example, might result from reduced litigation. However, the cost savings achieved by states in recent years often resulted from limiting eligibility for benefits or from maintaining or further curtailing benefits that were already inadequate. An example of the effects of restricting eligibility on workers is provided by Oregon, where Thomason and Burton (2001) estimate that a series of legislative provisions resulted in benefits (and costs) being about 25 percent below the amounts they would have been in the absence of the more restrictive eligibility standards. Guo and Burton (2010) examined the determinants of workers' compensation cash benefits in 45 states plus the District of Columbia and found that 21 percent of the drop in benefits during the 1990s could be explained by declines in the injury rates but that over 30 percent of the decline in benefits was due to changes in workers' compensation compensability rules and administrative practices.

28. Leigh, Markowitz, Fahs, and Landrigan (2000, pp. 175–179) and Burton (2009, pp. 241–243) provide useful discussions of who pays for workers' compensation.

The adequacy of the benefits provided to those workers who actually qualify for benefits has been examined in important recent studies. Hunt (2004) provides a comprehensive survey of the meaning of adequacy of benefits in the workers' compensation program. The generally accepted standard is that workers' compensation benefits should replace two-thirds of the wages lost because of the work injuries. However, Boden, Reville, and Biddle (2005) found that in the five jurisdictions they examined (California, New Mexico, Oregon, Washington, and Wisconsin) permanent partial disability benefits replaced between 16 and 26 percent of earnings losses in the ten years after the workers' were injured, which meant the "replacement rates do not approach the two-thirds benchmark for adequacy."

The consequences of the tightening eligibility standards in workers' compensation may have another consequence that is troublesome for the future of the program. As the number of workers' compensation cases and costs of the program dropped in the 1990s, due in part to tighter eligibility standards for qualifying for benefits, the number of former workers qualifying for Disability Insurance (DI) under the Social Security program increased. Some commentators, such as Sengupta, Reno, and Burton (2010, pp. 43–44) have raised the possibility that some disabled persons are being shifted from workers' compensation to the DI program. This perception is reinforced because, according to Burton and Spieler (2001), the changes in eligibility rules for workers' compensation benefits that took place in the 1990s had a particularly adverse effect on older workers, who are the predominant source of applicants for DI benefits. In preliminary results from an ongoing study, Guo and Burton (2008) found that states in which workers' compensation compensability rules were tightened and cash benefits were reduced there were increases in applications for DI benefits between 1985 and 1999.

A final challenge to workers' compensation worth noting is the medical benefits provided by the program.[29] These benefits accounted for 50.4 percent of all benefit payments in 2008, up from 36.3 percent in 1987 (Sengupta, Reno, and Burton 2010, Table 4). Medical benefits in workers' compensation are also important because in many ways they are more generous than other medical benefits provided by employers.

With rare exceptions, medical care through workers' compensation is provided without deductibles, coinsurance, or premiums paid for by workers,

29. Burton (2009, 260–65) reviews studies of medical care and rehabilitation services in workers' compensation.

while these attributes are lacking in health care benefits for nonoccupational conditions paid for by employers. Indeed, many employers do not provide any health care benefits for their workers—other than the medical care mandated for work-related injuries. This provides a glaring contrast between two health care systems for workers, and provides incentives for workers (and often providers and sometimes even employers) to shift conditions that are arguably work-related, such as back injuries, into workers' compensation.

The disparity between these two systems has led many employers who do provide nonoccupational health insurance to integrate the administration of all their programs for disabled workers, regardless of the origins of the disability. Some commentators have even suggested that the medical benefits (and perhaps the cash benefits) provided for work-related and nonwork-related disabilities should be combined into a 24-hour coverage program.[30]

The most controversial aspect of the medical benefits provided by workers' compensation that has emerged in recent years concerns the relationship between workers' compensation and Medicare, which is the federal program that provides medical benefits to individuals who are at least 65 years old or who have received Social Security Disability Insurance benefits for more than two years. Since the mid-1980s, the Medicare as Secondary Payer (MSP) Act has provided that if medical expenses could be covered by either workers' compensation or Medicare, then workers' compensation, and not Medicare, should pay for the benefits. Medicare is administered by the Centers for Medicare & Medicaid Services (CMS), which started to vigorously enforce the MSP Act in 2001 by requiring certain workers' compensation settlements to be preapproved before they can be paid. The MSP Act has been amended to further protect the federal interest in the Medicare program, including a requirement effective in 2009 increasing the reporting requirements under the act for employers and carriers.

This final section has identified some tensions and challenges for the workers' compensation program that may suggest the program may not survive far into the 21st century. It is thus worth remembering that the premier study of workers' compensation published over a half-century ago (Somers and Somers, 1954) concluded with a chapter entitled "Workmen's Compensation at the Crossroads." The thrust of the chapter was that the problems of the program threatened its future unless fundamental changes were made. The program's name may have changed and the problems may

30. Several variants of 24-hour coverage are examined by Burton (1997).

be somewhat different than in 1954. But the experience of the intervening years suggests that the fundamental attributes of workers' compensation—a system confined to work-related injuries that provides limited benefits on a no-fault basis—are hard to successfully challenge and may be immutable.

BIBLIOGRAPHY

Aurbach, Robert, 2003, "*Delgado* v. *Phelps Dodge Chino, Inc.*: A Case Study in Judicial Legislation," *Workers' Compensation Policy Review*, Vol. 3, No. 3 (May/June), pp. 9–12 (can be downloaded from www.workerscompresources.com).

Barth, Peter S. and H. Allan Hunt, 1980, *Workers' Compensation and Work-Related Illnesses and Diseases*, Cambridge, MA: The MIT Press.

Boden, Leslie I., 1995, "Creating Economic Incentives: Lessons from Workers' Compensation Systems," in *Proceedings of the Forty-Seventh Annual Meeting of the Industrial Relations Research Association*, Madison, WI: Industrial Relations Research Association.

Boden, Leslie I., Robert T. Reville, and Jeff Biddle, 2005, "The Adequacy of Workers' Compensation Cash Benefits," in *Prevention and Compensation of Workplace Injuries and Diseases: Essays in Honor of Terry Thomason*, eds. Karen Roberts, John F. Burton, Jr., and Matthew M. Bodah, Kalamazoo, MI: W. E. Upjohn Institute for Employment Relations.

Burton, John F., Jr., 1997, "Workers' Compensation, Twenty-Four-Hour Coverage, and Managed Care," in *Disability: Challenges for Social Insurance, Health Care Financing, and Labor Market Policy*, eds. Virginia P. Reno, Jerry L. Mashaw, and Bill Gradison, Washington, DC: National Academy of Social Insurance.

Burton, John F., Jr., 2002, "The Intentional Injury Exception to the Exclusive Remedy Provision," *Workers' Compensation Policy Review*, Vol. 2, No. 4 (July/August), pp. 23–27 (can be downloaded from www.workerscompresources.com).

Burton, John F., Jr., 2004, "The National Commission on State Workmen's Compensation Laws," *Workers' Compensation Policy Review*, Vol. 4, No. 4 (July/August), pp. 13–20 (can be downloaded from www.workerscompresources.com).

Burton, John F., Jr., 2005, "Permanent Partial Disability Benefits," in *Prevention and Compensation of Workplace Injuries and Diseases: Essays in Honor of Terry Thomason*, eds. Karen Roberts, John F. Burton, Jr., and Matthew M. Bodah, Kalamazoo, MI: W. E. Upjohn Institute for Employment Relations, 2005.

Burton, John F., Jr., 2008a, "Workers' Compensation Insurance Industry Profits Remain High in 2007," *Workers' Compensation Policy Review*, Vol. 8, No. 5 (September/October), pp. 24–31 (can be downloaded from www.workerscompresources.com).

Burton, John F., Jr., 2008b, "Workers' Compensation Temporary Disability Cash Benefits," *Workers' Compensation Policy Review*, Vol. 8, No. 6 (November/December), pp. 3–12 (can be downloaded from www.workerscompresources.com).

Burton, John F., Jr., 2009, "Workers' Compensation," in *Labor and Employment Law and Economics*, eds. Kenneth G. Dau-Schmidt, Seth D. Harris, and Orley Lobel, Northhampton, MA: Edward Elgar.

Burton, John F., Jr., 2010, "National Averages of Employee Benefits and Employer Costs for Workers' Compensation," in *Use of Workers' Compensation Data for Occupational Injury and Illness Prevention—Proceedings from 2009 Workshop*, eds. David Utterback and Teresa M. Schnorr, Washington, DC: Department of Health and Human Services, National Institute of Occupational Safety and Health, NIOSH Document No. 2010-152.

Burton, John F., Jr. and James R. Chelius, 2007, "Workplace Safety and Health Regulations: Rationale and Results," in *Government Regulation of the Employment Relationship*, ed. Bruce E. Kaufman, Madison, WI: Industrial Relations Research Association.

Burton, John F., Jr. and Daniel J.B. Mitchell, 2003, "Employee Benefits and Social Insurance: The Welfare Side of Employee Relations," in *Industrial Relations to Human Resources and Beyond*, eds. Bruce E. Kaufman, Richard A. Beaumont, and Roy B. Helfgott, Armonk, NY: M. E. Sharpe.

Burton, John F., Jr. and Emily A. Spieler, 2001, "Workers' Compensation and Older Workers," in *Ensuring Health and Income Security for an Aging Workforce*, eds. Peter P. Burdetti, Richard V. Burkhauser, Janice M. Gregory, and H. Allan Hunt, Kalamazoo, MI: W.E. Upjohn Institute for Employment Research.

Durbin, David and Richard J. Butler, 1998, "Prevention of Disability from Work Related Source: The Roles of Risk Management, Government Intervention, and Insurance," in *New Approaches to Disability in the Workplace*, eds. Terry Thomason, John F. Burton, Jr., and Douglas E, Hyatt, Madison, WI: Industrial Relations Research Association.

Guo, Xuguang (Steve) and John F. Burton Jr., 2008, "The Relationship between Workers' Compensation and Disability Insurance," in *Proceedings of the 60th Annual Meeting of the Labor and Employment Relations Association*, ed. Adrienne Eaton, Champaign, IL: Labor and Employment Relations Association.

Guo, Xuguang (Steve) and John F. Burton Jr., 2010, "Workers' Compensation: Recent Developments in Moral Hazard and Benefits Payments," *Industrial and Labor Relations Review*, Vol. 63, No. 2 (January).

Hunt, Allan H., 2004, *Adequacy of Earnings Replacement in Workers' Compensation Programs*, Kalamazoo, MI: W.E. Upjohn Institute for Employment Research.

Larson, Arthur and Lex K. Larson, 2010, *Larson's Workers' Compensation, Desk Edition*, Newark, NJ: LexisNexis. (The legal treatise in a Desk Edition with three volumes, updated biannually. Also available as a 12-volume treatise.)

Leigh, J. Paul, Steven Markowitz, Marianne Fahs, and Philip Landrigan, 2000, *Costs of Occupational Injuries and Illnesses*, Ann Arbor, MI: The University of Michigan Press.

Neumark, David, Peter S. Barth, and Richard Victor, 2007, "The Impact of Provider Choice on Workers' Compensation Costs and Outcomes," *Industrial and Labor Relations Review*, Vol. 61, No. 1 (April).

Sengupta, Ishita, Virginia P. Reno, and John F. Burton, Jr., 2010, *Workers' Compensation: Benefits, Coverage, and Costs, 2008*. Washington, DC: National Academy of Social Insurance. (Annual publication with national and state information. Can be downloaded from www.nasi.org.)

Somers, Herman Miles and Anne Ramsay Somers, 1954, *Workmen's Compensation: Prevention, Insurance, and Rehabilitation of Occupational Disability*, New York, NY: Wiley.

Spieler, Emily A. and John F. Burton, Jr., 1998, "Compensation for Disabled Workers: Workers' Compensation," in *New Approaches to Disability in the Workplace*, eds. Terry Thomason, John F. Burton, Jr. and Douglas E. Hyatt, Madison, WI: Industrial Relations Research Association.

Thomason, Terry, 2005, "Economic Incentives and Workplace Safety," in *Prevention and Compensation of Workplace Injuries and Diseases: Essays in Honor of Terry Thomason*, eds. Karen Roberts, John F. Burton, Jr., and Matthew M. Bodah, Kalamazoo, MI: W. E. Upjohn Institute for Employment Relations.

Thomason, Terry and John F. Burton, Jr., 1993, "Economic Effects of Workers' Compensation in the United States: Private Insurance and the Administration of Compensation Claims," *Journal of Labor Economics*, Vol. 11, No. 1, Part 2, pp. S1–S37.

Thomason, Terry and John F. Burton, Jr., 2001, "The Effects of Changes in the Oregon Workers' Compensation Program on Employees' Benefits and Employers' Costs," *Workers' Compensation Policy Review*, Vol. 1,

No. 4 (July/August), pp. 7–23 (can be downloaded from www.workers compresources.com).

Thomason, Terry, Timothy P. Schmidle, and John F. Burton, Jr., 2001, *Workers' Compensation: Benefits, Costs, and Safety under Alternative Insurance Arrangements*, Kalamazoo, MI: W.E. Upjohn Institute for Employment Research.

Tompa, Emile, S. Trevithick, and C. McLeod, 2007, "Systematic Review of Preventions Activities and Regulatory Mechanisms for Occupational Health and Safety," *Scandinavian Journal of Work, Environment, and Health*, Vol. 33, No. 2.

Torrey, David B., 2007, "Compromise Settlements Under State Workers' Compensation Acts: Law, Policy, Practice, and Ten years of the Pennsylvania Experience (An Abridgement)," *Workers' Compensation Policy Review*, Vol. 7, No. 6 (November/December), pp. 13–25 (can be downloaded from www.workerscompresources.com).

U.S. Chamber of Commerce, 2010, *2010 Analysis of Workers' Compensation Laws*, Washington, DC: U.S. Chamber of Commerce. (Annual publication with charts providing information on various aspects of U.S. and Canadian workers' compensation programs.)

Williams, C. Arthur, Jr., 1969, *Insurance Arrangements under Workmen's Compensation*, Washington, DC: U.S. Department of Labor, Wage and Labor Standards Administration, Bureau of Labor Standards.

Willborn, Steven L, Stewart J. Schwab, John F. Burton, Jr., and Gillian L.L. Lester, 2007, *Employment Law: Cases and Materials*, 4th ed., Newark, NJ: LexisNexis.

APPENDIX 22.1

CALCULATING INSURANCE PREMIUMS

Workers' compensation insurance premiums are determined by a multi-step process. Table A22.1-1 shows the "traditional" procedure used in states that rely on the National Council on Compensation Insurance (NCCI) for actuarial assistance.[31] The following discussion indicates some of the recent changes in the process.[32]

Each employer who purchases insurance is assigned to a particular insurance classification (e.g., a bakery is assigned to class 2003). The first step shown in Table A22.1-1 is to determine the initial insurance rate by looking in an insurance manual that specifies the "manual rate" for each insurance classification.

Manual rates have two components: pure premiums and an expense loading. The pure premiums cover expected payments for cash benefits, medical care, and (in most jurisdictions) loss-adjustment expenses. The expense-loading factor provides an allowance for other insurance carrier expenses, such as general administrative expenses, taxes, licenses, fees, commissions, profits, and contingencies. In most states using manual rates, the loading factor is usually 35 to 40 percent of the manual rates.

Manual rates are specified as dollars per hundred dollars of payroll. The manual rates vary substantially within each state, reflecting the previous experience with benefit payments for all the employers in that classification. Manual rates in a particular state might range from $40 per $100 of payroll for logging to $0.75 per $100 of payroll for clerical workers.

Manual rates (line 1) multiplied by the employer's total payroll (line 2) equals manual premium without constants (line 3). In practice, few employers pay such a premium, because of several modifications. The first modification arises from the firm-level experience rating that is permitted for medium and large employers. Experience rating uses the employer's

31. Table A22.1-1 and the description of the procedure used to determine premium are based on Thomason, Schmidle, and Burton (2001, pp. 326–331).

32. This appendix is based in part on very helpful comments provided by Barry Llewellyn, Senior Divisional Executive for Regulatory Services, National Council on Compensation Insurance.

TABLE A22.1-1

Calculation of Net Workers' Compensation Costs to Policyholders

1.		Manual rates (MR)
2.	×	Payroll
3.	=	Manual premium without constants
4.	×	Experience-rating modification
5.	=	Standard earned premium excluding constants
6.	÷	Adjustment for expense constants
7.	=	Standard earned premium at bureau rates (DSR)
8.	×	Adjustment for deviations
9.	=	Standard earned premium at company level
10.	×	Adjustment for premium discounts, retrospective rating, and schedule rating
11.	=	Net earned premium
12.	×	Dividends adjustment
13.	=	Net cost to policyholders

Source: Based on Thomason, Schmidle, and Burton (2001, Table C.5).

own past record of benefit payments to modify the manual rates that would otherwise apply. If, for example, the employer's record is worse than the experience of the average employer in its classification, then its actual premium for the current policy period is larger than its manual premium. The product of the manual premium without constants (line 3) and the experience-rating modification (line 4) is line 5, the standard earned premium excluding constants.

The standard earned premium excluding constants is also modified for most employers, although the form of this modification depends on the size of the employer's premium. Employers in almost every state are assessed a flat charge, termed an "expense constant," to cover the minimum costs of issuing and servicing a policy. In addition, prior to recent years, employers in some states were assessed another flat charge, termed a "loss constant," because of the generally inferior safety record of small businesses. When the standard earned premium excluding constants (line 5) is divided by line 6, the adjustment for the expense constants), the result is the standard earned premium at bureau rates (DSR) (line 7), also termed the "standard earned premium at the designated statistical reporting (DSR) level."

The standard earned premium at bureau rates is further adjusted for many employers. Deviations are a competitive pricing device that has been in active use in many jurisdictions since the 1980s. In a state allowing deviations, individual carriers may use the manual rates promulgated by the rating organization or may deviate from those rates. The carrier might, for example, use manual rates that are 10 percent less than those issued by the rating organization. The deviations offered by a particular carrier must be uniform for all policyholders in the state in a particular insurance class (although different deviations for different classes are sometimes possible). If the standard earned premium at bureau rates (line 7) is multiplied by the adjustment for deviations (line 8), the result is the standard earned premium at company level (line 9).

There are several additional factors that may reduce workers' compensation insurance premiums. Premium discounts apply to employers with annual premiums in excess of a specified amount ($5,000 was a typical figure in the 1980s, while $10,000 is now used in most NCCI states), which basically reflect reductions in carrier expenses for larger policies because of economies of scale. The discounts based on a specified schedule are compulsory in the NCCI states, unless both the insurance carrier and the employer agree to substitute "retrospective rating" for the premium discounts. Although these retrospective rating plans vary among the NCCI states, they are basically similar in that they allow the employer to increase the effect of its own claims experience on the published manual rates.

The main difference between experience rating and retrospective rating is that the former uses the employer's experience from previous periods to modify the premium for the current policy period rate, whereas the retrospective plan uses experience from the current policy period to determine the current premium on an ex post facto basis. The same expense gradation (reduction in premiums for the employer) provided by the premium discount is built into the retrospective rating plans.

Schedule-rating plans have also been actively used in many jurisdictions since the 1980s. Under these plans, insurers can change (usually decrease) the insurance rate the employer would otherwise pay through debits or credits based on a subjective evaluation of factors such as the employer's loss-control program. There are two types of schedule rating. In states with uniform schedule-rating plans, regulators authorize all carriers to use identical schedule-rating plans. If all carriers are not given this permission, then individual carriers can apply for approval of their own schedule-rating plans.

The result of multiplying the standard earned premium at company level (line 9) by the adjustment for premium discounts, retrospective rating, and schedule rating (line 10) is the net earned premium (line 11). One final adjustment factor, a policyholder dividends adjustment (line 12), needs to be used to compute the premiums actually paid by employers. Mutual companies or stock companies with participating policies write a substantial portion of the workers' compensation insurance. While these companies normally use a quantity discount schedule less steeply graded than that of the nonparticipating stock companies, they pay dividends that usually decrease policyholders' net costs to levels below that charged by nonparticipating stock companies, especially for large employers. The product of the net earned premium (line 11) and the dividends adjustment is the net cost to policyholders (line 13), which is the premium actually paid by employers purchasing workers' compensation insurance.

As complicated as the process in Table A22.1-1 appears, there are actually additional charges that many if not most employers are assessed in determining their premiums. For example, an employer with a limited payroll may be required to make an additional payment in order to achieve a minimum amount of standard earned premium at step 5 of the process. And, depending on the state, there may be surcharges for the uninsured employers' fund, for terrorism, for catastrophes, for the second injury fund, and for the operating expenses of the state's workers' compensation agency.

The multistep process summarized in Table A22.1-1 is also inapplicable under several circumstances. First, in a number of states, the starting point for calculating the employer's premium is pure premium rates (or loss costs), rather than manual rates.[33] In these states, carriers add their own expense loadings to cover expenses, such as administrative expenses and commissions, rather than relying on the expense loadings built into manual rates.

Second, most workers' compensation insurance is provided in the voluntary insurance market. However, because the employers who cannot purchase policies in the voluntary market must still have insurance, all

33. The calculation of premiums when the starting point is pure premiums is discussed by Thomason, Schmidle, and Burton (2001, pp. 331–333).

states that do not have state funds have established assigned-risk plans.[34] The national average for the assigned-risk (or residual) market share in NCCI states ranged between 3.2 percent and 28.5 percent between 1975 and 2004. Recently, the share has declined from 12.7 percent in 2004 to 6.2 percent in 2008.[35] There are several types of residual market pricing plans used in various states, including those that use different manual rate (or loss costs) in the voluntary and residual markets and those that eliminate or modify premium discounts for large policyholders.

Third, the four states with exclusive state funds determine premiums using state-specific procedures. For example, each fund has a unique set of insurance classifications and experience rating formula, and Washington bases premiums on hours worked rather than payroll (as in all states with private carriers).

Employers that self-insure—that is, pay benefits to their own employees without use of an insurance carrier—represent a "pure" form of experience rating in which an employer's costs are solely determined by the benefits to that firm's employees. This characterization needs to be qualified to some degree because self-insuring employers generally purchase excess risk policies that protect them against unusually adverse experience; have administrative expenses that may not vary in proportion to benefit payments; and may be subject to assessments to support state workers' agencies or other purposes that are not solely based on benefit payments.

BIBLIOGRAPHY

National Council on Compensation Insurance, 2010, *Annual Statistical Bulletin: 2010 Edition*, Boca Raton, FL: National Council on Compensation Insurance. (Annual publication with underwriting data from all states with private carriers.)

Thomason, Terry, Timothy P. Schmidle, and John F. Burton, Jr., 2001, *Workers' Compensation: Benefits, Costs, and Safety under Alternative Insurance Arrangements*, Kalamazoo, MI: W.E. Upjohn Institute for Employment Research.

34. The calculation of premiums for employers who purchase insurance in the assigned risk market is discussed by Thomason, Schmidle, and Burton (2001, pp. 333–339).
35. Recent data on the national and state shares of premiums in residual markets are included in National Council on Compensation Insurance (2010, Exhibit XIII).

CHAPTER 23

Unemployment Compensation

US Department of Labor

The federal-state unemployment compensation (UC) program, created by the Social Security Act (SSA) of 1935, offers the first economic line of defense against the ripple effects of unemployment. Through payments made directly to eligible, unemployed workers, it ensures that at least a significant proportion of the necessities of life, most notably food, shelter, and clothing, can be met on a week-to-week basis while a search for work takes place. As temporary, partial wage replacement to the unemployed, UC is of vital importance in maintaining purchasing power and in stabilizing the economy.

Unemployment compensation is a social insurance program. It is designed to provide benefits to most individuals out of work, generally through no fault of their own, for periods between jobs. In order to be eligible for benefits, jobless workers must demonstrate workforce attachment, usually measured by amount of wages and/or weeks of work, and must be able and available for work.

The UC program is a federal-state partnership based upon federal law, but administered by state employees under state law. Because of this structure, the program is unique among the country's social insurance

This chapter was reprinted in its entirety from *Unemployment Compensation, Federal State Partnership*, US Department of Labor, Office of Unemployment Insurance, Division of Legislation, April 2010.

Note: This document was prepared for informational purposes only. Explanations should not be considered as official interpretation of law.

programs. The UC program is also unique in that it is almost totally funded by employer taxes, either federal or state—only three states collect taxes from employees.

Federal law defines certain requirements for the program. The SSA and the Federal Unemployment Tax Act (FUTA) set forth broad coverage provisions, some benefit provisions, the federal tax base and rate, and administrative requirements. The major functions of the federal government are to

- Ensure conformity and substantial compliance of state law, regulations, rules, and operations with federal law.
- Determine administrative fund requirements and provide money to states for proper and efficient administration.
- Set broad overall policy for administration of the program, monitor state performance, and provide technical assistance as necessary.
- Hold and invest all money in the unemployment trust fund until drawn down by states for the payment of compensation.

Each state designs its own UC program within the framework of the federal requirements. The state statute sets forth the benefit structure (e.g., eligibility/disqualification provisions, benefit amount) and the state tax structure (e.g., state taxable wage base and tax rates). The primary functions of the state are to

- Determine operation methods and directly administer the program.
- Take claims from individuals, determine eligibility, and ensure timely payment of benefits to workers.
- Determine employer liability, and assess and collect contributions.

Originally, most states paid benefits for a maximum duration of 13 to 16 weeks. Most states currently pay a maximum of 26 weeks, although Massachusetts and under certain conditions Washington pay 30 weeks. In periods of very high and rising unemployment in individual states, benefits are payable for up to 13 additional weeks (20 in some cases), up to a maximum of 39 weeks (or 46). These "extended benefits" are funded on a shared basis—approximately half from state funds and half from federal sources. The federal government will pay for 100 percent of most EB costs (where EB costs are typically shared with the federal government) for weeks of unemployment beginning after February 9, 2009, and before June 2, 2010. (This information was current at the time of writing.)

In periods of national recession, when all states are impacted by high and sustained unemployment, federally funded programs of supplemental benefits have been adopted occasionally. There were two such programs during the 1970s, one during the early 1980s, one during the 1990s, and one during the early 2000s. Currently, the Emergency Unemployment Compensation program of 2008 (EUC08) is effective from July 2008 through June 2, 2010, and the Federal Additional Compensation (FAC) program, which provides a $25 supplement to weekly benefits, is effective from February 9, 2009 through June 2, 2010, with a phase-out through December 7, 2010. (This information was current at the time of writing.)

The UC program operates counter-cyclically, paying out benefits during recessionary times and collecting revenue during recovery periods. The following are estimates of program activity for the fiscal year 2010:

- Number of workers covered 127.0 million
- Number of beneficiaries (all programs) 16.3 million
- Benefits paid (all programs) $157.1 billion
- Subject employers 7.6 million
- Administrative costs (total) $5.9 billion
    - State UC only $4.4 billion
- Payroll taxes—FUTA $6.8 billion
- Payroll taxes—State $44.5 billion

THE BASIC SYSTEM

Almost all wage and salary workers are now covered by the federal-state UC program. Railroad workers are covered by a separate federal program. Ex-service members with recent service in the Armed Forces and civilian federal employees are covered by a federal program, with the states paying benefits from federal funds as agents of the federal government.

If a state law meets minimum federal requirements under FUTA and Title III of the SSA:

- Employers receive up to a 5.4 percent basic and additional tax credit against the 6.2 percent federal unemployment tax.
- The state is entitled to federal grants to cover all the necessary costs of administering the program.

Approval for Tax Credit

Sections 3303 and 3304 of the Internal Revenue Code of 1986 (created by the law known as FUTA) represent some of the minimum federal requirements and provide that the Secretary of Labor shall approve a state law for basic and additional tax credit if under the state law:

- Compensation is paid through public employment offices or other approved agencies.
- All of the funds collected under the state program are deposited in the federal UTF (Title IX of the SSA prescribes the distribution of the tax revenue among the various accounts of the trust fund).
- All of the money withdrawn from the state trust fund account is used to pay compensation, to refund amounts erroneously paid into the fund, or for other specified activities.
- Compensation is not denied to anyone who refuses to accept work because the job is vacant as the direct result of a labor dispute, or because the wages, hours, or conditions of work are substandard, or if, as a condition of employment, the individual would have to join a company union or resign from or refrain from joining any bona fide labor organization.
- Compensation is paid to employees of state and local governments and Indian tribes.
- Compensation is paid to employees of FUTA tax-exempt nonprofit organizations, including schools and colleges, who employ four or more workers in each of 20 weeks in the calendar year.
- Payment of compensation to certain employees of educational institutions operated by state and local governments, nonprofit organizations, and Indian tribes is limited during periods between and within academic terms.
- State and local governments, nonprofit organizations, and Indian tribes are permitted to elect to pay regular employer contributions or finance benefit costs by the reimbursement method.
- Compensation is not payable in two successive benefit years to an individual who has not worked after the beginning of the first benefit year.
- Compensation is not denied to anyone solely because the individual is taking part in an approved training program.

- Compensation is not denied or reduced because an individual's claim for benefits was filed in another state or Canada and the state participates in arrangements for combining wages earned in more than one state for eligibility and benefit purposes.
- Compensation is not denied by reason of cancellation of wage credits or total benefit rights for any cause other than discharge for work-connected misconduct, fraud, or receipt of disqualifying income.
- Extended compensation is payable under the provisions of the Federal-State Extended Unemployment Compensation Act of 1970 (federal-state extended benefits program).
- Compensation is not denied solely on the basis of pregnancy or termination of pregnancy.
- Compensation is not payable to a professional athlete, between seasons, who has a reasonable assurance of resuming employment when the new season begins.
- Compensation is not payable to an alien unless the alien was in a specified state—such as legally authorized to work—at the time services were performed.
- The benefit amount of an individual is reduced, under certain conditions, by that portion of a pension or other retirement income (including Social Security and Railroad Retirement income) that is funded by a base period employer.
- Wage information in the agency files is made available, upon request and on a reimbursable basis, to the state agency administering Temporary Assistance to Needy Families; and wage and UC information to the Secretary of Health and Human Services for the purposes of the National Directory of New Hires.
- Any interest required to be paid on advances is paid in a timely manner and is not paid, directly or indirectly (by an equivalent tax reduction in such state), from amounts in such state's trust fund account. (Note that the Recovery Act waived interest payments and accruals through December 31, 2010.) (See also the subsection "Interest on Loans" in the section "Financing The Program" below).
- Federal individual income tax is deducted and withheld if a claimant so requests. (Note that in 2009, the first $2,400 in UC received by an individual is not subject to federal income tax.)

- Reduced tax rates for employers are permitted only on the basis of their experience with respect to unemployment.

Approval for Grants for Costs of Administration

Title III of the SSA provides for payments from the federal UTF to the states to meet the necessary costs of administering the UC programs in the states. (The major proportion of the cost (97%) of operating their public employment offices is provided for by the Wagner-Peyser Act.) Under Title III, the grants are restricted to those states that have a UC law approved under FUTA and have been certified by the Secretary of Labor as providing the following (some of these provisions are also included in FUTA):

- Methods of administration (including a state merit system) which will insure full payment of UC when due.
- Payment of UC through public employment offices or through other approved agencies.
- For fair, impartial hearings to individuals whose claims for UC have been denied.
- All of the funds collected under the state program are deposited in the federal UTF (Title IX of the SSA prescribes the distribution of the tax revenue among the various accounts of the trust fund).
- That all of the money withdrawn from the state trust fund account will be used either to pay UC, exclusive of administrative expenses, to refund amounts erroneously paid into the fund, or for other specified activities.
- Reports required by the Secretary of Labor.
- Information to federal agencies administering public works programs or assistance through public employment.
- For limitation of expenditures to the purpose and amounts found necessary by the Secretary of Labor for proper and efficient administration of the state UC law.
- For repayment of any funds the Secretary of Labor determines were not spent for UC purposes or exceeded the amounts necessary for proper administration of the state UC law.
- That as a condition of eligibility, any claimant referred to reemployment services pursuant to the profiling system, participate in such services.

- Information to the Railroad Retirement Board as the Board deems necessary.
- Reasonable cooperation with every agency of the United States charged with the administration of any UC law.
- That any interest on advances be paid by the date on which it is required to be paid or is not paid, directly or indirectly (by an equivalent reduction in state unemployment taxes or otherwise), by such state from amounts in the state's trust fund account.
- Information to the Department of Agriculture and state food stamp agencies with respect to employee wages, UC benefits, home address, and job offers.
- Information to any state or local child support enforcement agency with respect to employee wages.
- That a claimant disclose whether or not he or she owes child support obligations; deductions from benefits shall be made for any such child support obligations, and the amount of such deduction paid by the state UC agency to the appropriate child support agency.
- Information be requested and exchanged for purposes of income and eligibility verification in accordance with a state system meeting the requirements of Title XI of the SSA; the UC wage record system may, but need not, be the required state system.
- Information to the Secretary of Health and Human Services on a reimbursable basis, with respect to employee wages, UC benefits, and home address for the purpose of establishing a National Directory of New Hires.
- Information to officers and employees of the Department of Housing and Urban Development and to representatives of public housing agency with respect to employee wages and UC benefits.
- For establishment and use of a system of profiling new claimants of regular compensation to identify those likely to exhaust such compensation and need reemployment services.
- Requirement that, as a condition of eligibility for regular UC, claimants participate (unless exempt) in reemployment services if referred under the profiling system.
- Mandatory transfer of unemployment experience whenever there is substantially common ownership, management, or control of two employers, and one of these employers transfers its trade or business (including its workforce), or portion thereof, to the other

employer (applies to total and partial transfers); and, under certain conditions, prohibition of transfer when a person who is not an employer acquires the trade or business of an existing employer.

FINANCING THE PROGRAM

Pursuant to the provisions of the FUTA, a federal tax is levied on covered employers at a current rate of 6.2 percent on wages up to $7,000 a year paid to an employee. The law, however, provides a credit against federal tax liability of up to 5.4 percent to employers who pay state taxes timely under an approved state UC program. This credit is allowed regardless of the amount of the tax paid to the state by the employer. Accordingly, in states meeting the specified requirements, employers pay an effective federal tax of 0.8 percent, or a maximum $56 per covered employee, per year. Under current law, the 6.2 percent federal tax is scheduled to drop to 6.0 percent beginning with calendar year 2010, and the effective tax to 0.6 percent.

This federal tax is used to fund a number of different UC related expenditures:

- All federal and state administrative costs associated with UC programs
- The federal share of benefits paid under the federal-state Extended Unemployment Compensation Act of 1970
- The loan fund from which an individual state may borrow (Title XII of the SSA) whenever it lacks funds to pay UC due for any month
- Benefits under some of the federal supplemental and emergency programs

In addition, the FUTA tax is used to fund labor exchange services, employment and training services for veterans and disabled veterans, and some labor market information program activities. See Figure 23-1.

Provisions Relating to Loans

If it is anticipated that the balance in a state's unemployment fund is insufficient to pay expected benefit claims during a specified period of time, the state's Governor may request a loan from the Secretary of Labor. Such loans are made from the Federal Unemployment Account (FUA) in the UTF, in accordance with Title XII of the SSA.

FIGURE 23-1

Federal/State Unemployment Compensation (UC) Program—Federal Unemployment Trust Fund Flow of Funds

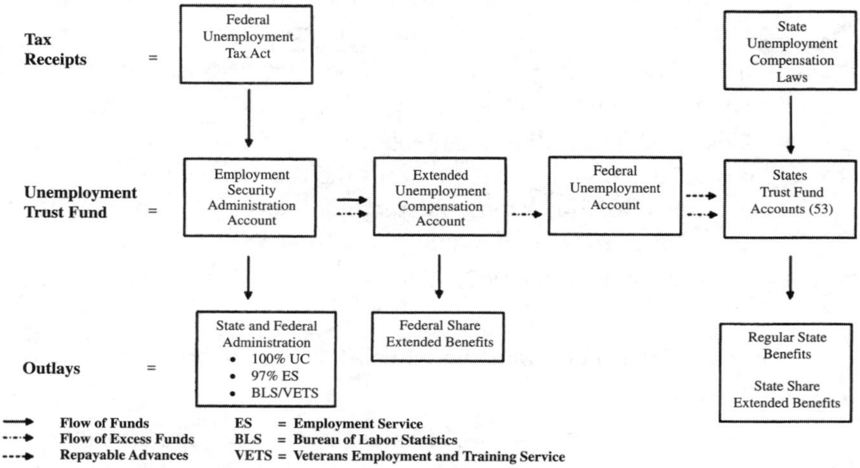

In order to assure that a state will repay any loans it secures from the fund, the law provides that when a state has an outstanding loan balance on January 1 for two consecutive years, the full amount of the loan must be repaid before November 10 of the second year, or the federal tax on employers in that state will be increased for that year and further increased for each subsequent year that the loan has not been repaid.

Specifically, the 5.4 percent credit is reduced in successive increments of a minimum 0.3 percent for each year in which a loan or loans remain unpaid (reducing the overall credit from 5.4 to 5.1, to 4.8, to 4.5 percent, etc.). Additional offset credit reductions may apply to a state beginning with the third and fifth taxable years if a loan balance is still outstanding and certain criteria are not met.

Cap on Loan Repayment Requirements

States with outstanding loans may seek relief from the automatic loan repayment provisions. If specific requirements are met, a cap (or limit) is provided on the reduction in offset credit at the higher of 0.6 percent or the federal tax rate in effect in the state for the previous year. These requirements are as follows:

- The state did not take any action (in the prior year) that would diminish the solvency of the state fund.
- The state did not take any action (in the prior year) that would decrease the state's unemployment tax effort.
- The average tax rate for the taxable year exceeds the 5-year average benefit cost rate.
- The state's outstanding loan balance as of September 30 of the tax year is not greater than that for the third preceding September 30. States with outstanding loans may also avoid the automatic increase in the federal tax by transferring, on or before November 9, money from their unemployment accounts to the FUA.

The following criteria must be met by the state in order to avoid the offset credit reduction:

- Repay all loans for the 1-year period ending November 9, plus any additional tax due by reason of the reduced credit amount.
- Have sufficient funds remaining after the transfer to pay benefits for at least 3 months after November 1 of the same year without receiving another loan under Title XII, SSA.
- Have taken action to increase the solvency of its UC system so that the increase at least equals the potential additional taxes that would otherwise be payable.

Interest on Loans

Except for cash flow loans (loans obtained and repaid January through September) interest is charged on all loans made on or after April 1, 1982. The rate is the lesser of 10 percent or the rate at which interest was paid on the state reserve balance in the federal UTF for the last quarter of the preceding calendar year. Interest paid by states is credited to the FUA in the UTF.

Interest is due and payable on the last day (September 30) of the fiscal year in which the loans were made. If a state borrows after September 30 in a calendar year in which any cash flow loans had been repaid earlier in the year without interest, then interest will be charged retroactively for the period that the state had held any earlier loans.

Interest may be deferred, to December 31 of the following calendar year, for loans made in the last five months of the federal fiscal year (May to September). Interest accrues on the delayed interest payment.

States with an average total unemployment rate of 13.5 percent or greater for the most recent 12-month period for which data are available may delay payment of interest for a grace period not to exceed 9 months. Interest does not accrue on the delayed interest payment.

States with an average insured unemployment rate of 7.5 percent or greater during the first 6 months of the preceding calendar year may pay interest in four annual installments of 25 percent per year. Interest does not accrue on the deferred interest payments.

Currently, interest accrual and payments on Federal loans to states to pay state unemployment benefits is waived through the end of 2010.

Penalty for Failure to Pay Interest

A state will lose all offset credit (5.4 percent) for any year in which all interest due under law is not paid by the date on which such interest is required to be paid. The state would also lose all grants for costs of administration until interest due has been paid.

Limitation on Source of Interest Payments

Interest payments may not be made from the state UC fund (directly or indirectly, by diverting some part of UC taxes). Violations of this requirement will lead to decertification of the state law and loss of all employer tax credits and of grants for costs of administration.

Liable Employers

An employer is subject to the federal unemployment tax if, during the current or preceding calendar year, he or she employed one or more individuals in each of at least 20 calendar weeks, or if he or she paid wages of $1,500 or more during any calendar quarter of either such year. Variations on these requirements relate to employers in agriculture and domestic service:

- In agriculture, employers who have at least 10 or more workers in each of at least 20 calendar weeks in the current or preceding calendar year or a cash payroll of at least $20,000 during any calendar quarter in either such year are subject to the tax.

- In domestic service, employers who have a cash payroll of at least $1,000 in any calendar quarter in the current or preceding calendar year are subject to the tax.

Taxable wages are defined as all remuneration from employment in cash or in kind with certain exceptions. The exceptions include earnings in excess of $7,000 in a year, and payments related to retirement, disability, hospital insurance, or similar fringe benefits.

State Taxes

All states finance UC primarily through contributions from subject employers on the wages of their covered workers. In addition, three states (Alaska, New Jersey, and Pennsylvania) collect contributions from employees. These taxes are deposited by the state to its account in the UTF in the Federal Treasury, and are withdrawn as needed to pay benefits. As of December 2009, aggregate state trust fund accounts had reserves of approximately $11.1 billion.

Experience Rating and the Federal Requirements

The system under which employers are assigned tax rates in accordance with their individual experience with unemployment (and subject to the needs of the state program) is referred to as experience rating. Within the confines of the general federal requirements, the experience rating provisions of state laws vary greatly. Though provisions have changed over the years, present federal law permits:

- Reduced rates (rates below the 5.4 standard or basic rate) for employers with at least 1 year of experience with respect to unemployment or other factors bearing a direct relation to unemployment risk.
- Reduced rates (but not less than 1.0 percent) for newly subject employers on a reasonable basis. Additional credit is allowed only with respect to a year in which the rate of the taxpayers in the state with the least favorable experience is at least 5.4 percent.

State Requirements for Experience Rating

All state laws provide for a system of experience rating under which individual employers' contribution rates vary from the standard rate on the basis of their experience with the amount of unemployment encountered by their employees. In most states, three years of experience with unemployment means more than three years of coverage and contribution experience.

As noted earlier, the experience-rating provisions of state laws vary considerably, and the number of variations increases with each legislative year. The most significant variations arise from differences in the formulas used for rate determination. The factor used to measure experience with unemployment is the basic variable that makes it possible to establish the relative incidence of unemployment among the workers of different employers. Differences in such experience represent the major justification for differences in tax rates, either to provide incentives for stabilization of employment or to allocate the cost of unemployment. At present, there are four distinct systems, usually identified as reserve-ratio, benefit-ratio, benefit-wage-ratio, and payroll-decline formulas. A few states have combinations of the systems.

In spite of significant differences, all systems have certain common characteristics. All formulas are devised to establish the relative experience of individual employers with unemployment or with benefit costs. To this end, all have factors for measuring each employer's experience with unemployment or benefit expenditures, and all compare this experience with a measure of exposure (i.e., payrolls) to establish the relative experience of large and small employers.

State Taxable Wage Base and Rates

Forty-six states have adopted a higher taxable wage base than the $7,000 now provided in FUTA. For 2010, Washington's taxable wage base is the highest at $36,800. In all states, an employer pays a tax on wages paid to each worker within a calendar year up to the amount specified in state law. In addition, most of the states provide an automatic adjustment of the wage base if federal law is amended to apply to a higher wage base than that specified under state law.

As a result of the many variables in states' taxable wage bases and rates, benefit formulas, and economic conditions, actual tax rates vary greatly among the states and among individual employers within a state. For the latest year available (2009), the preliminary estimated U.S. average tax rate is 0.6 percent of total wages, ranging from a high of 1.3 percent in Rhode Island (taxable wage base of $18,000) to a low of 0.08 percent in the Virgin Islands (taxable wage base of $22,100).

COVERAGE

As indicated previously, FUTA applies to employers who employ one or more employees in covered employment in at least 20 weeks in the current or preceding calendar year or who pay wages of $1,500 or more during any calendar quarter of the current or preceding calendar year. Also included are large employers of agricultural labor and some employment in domestic service. State legislatures tend to cover employers or employment subject to the federal tax because, while there is no compulsion to do so, failure to do so is of no advantage to the state and a disadvantage to the employers involved in terms of FUTA taxes due. While states generally cover all employment that is subject to the federal tax, they also may cover some employment that is exempt from the tax, such as smaller employers of agricultural labor and domestic service. Employers who do not meet the specific monetary or number of employee requirements are excluded from liability.

Although the extent of state coverage is greatly influenced by the federal statute, each state is, with a single exception, free to determine the employers who are liable for contributions and the workers who accrue rights under the laws. The exception is the federal requirement that states provide coverage for employees of nonprofit organizations, services performed for Indian tribes, and employees of state and local governments, even though such employment is exempt from FUTA.

BENEFIT RIGHTS

There are no federal standards for benefits in terms of qualifying requirements, benefit amounts, or duration of regular benefits. Hence, there is no common pattern of benefit provisions comparable to that in coverage and financing. The states have developed diverse and complex formulas for determining workers' benefit rights.

Under all state UC laws, a worker's benefit rights depend on his or her experience in covered employment in a past period of time, called the base period. The time period during which the weekly rate and the duration of benefits determined for a given worker apply to such worker is called the benefit year.

The qualifying wage or employment provisions attempt to measure the worker's attachment to the labor force. An insured worker must also be free from disqualification for causes that vary among the states. All but a few states require a claimant to serve a waiting period before his or her unemployment may be compensable.

All states determine an amount payable for a week of total unemployment as defined in the state law. Usually, a week of total unemployment is a week in which the claimant performs no work and receives no pay. In most states, a worker is partially unemployed in a week of less than full-time work when he or she earns less than his or her weekly benefit amount. The benefit payment for such a week is the difference between the weekly benefit amount and the part-time earnings, usually with a small disregard as a financial inducement to take part-time work.

Qualifying Wages and Employment

All states require that a claimant must have earned a specified amount of wages or must have worked a certain number of weeks or calendar quarters in covered employment, or must have met some combination of the wage and employment requirements within his or her base period, to qualify for benefits. The purpose of such qualifying requirements is to restrict benefits to covered workers who are genuinely attached to the labor force.

Benefit Eligibility and Disqualification

All state laws provide that, to receive benefits, a claimant must be able to work and available for work. Also, he or she must be free from disqualification for such acts as voluntary leaving without good cause, discharge for misconduct connected with the work, and refusal of suitable work. The purpose of these provisions is to limit payments to workers unemployed primarily as a result of economic causes.

In all states, claimants who are held ineligible for benefits because of inability to work, unavailability for work, refusal of suitable work, or any other disqualification are entitled to a notice of determination and an appeal of the determination.

Benefit Computation

Most states measure unemployment in terms of calendar weeks. Under all state laws, a weekly benefit amount—that is, the amount payable for a week of total unemployment—varies with the worker's past wages within certain minimum and maximum limits. The period of past wages used and the formulas for computing benefits from these past wages vary greatly among the states.

OTHER BENEFIT PROGRAMS

Other benefit programs are federal-state extended benefits, EB triggers, emergency unemployment compensation, unemployment compensation for federal civilian employees, disaster unemployment assistance, trade adjustment assistance, self-employment assistance, and short-time compensation.

Federal-State Extended Benefits

Since 1970, federal law has provided for the extension of the duration of benefits in periods of high and rising unemployment. When the insured unemployment rate in a state reaches certain specified levels, states must extend by 50 percent the benefit duration normally allowed up to a combined overall maximum of 39 weeks. There are also optional provisions for payment of extended benefits (EB). The federal government finances from federal revenue approximately half of the cost of EB paid during EB periods, including any state benefits paid in excess of 26 weeks. Currently, the federal government will pay 100 percent of most EB benefit costs for weeks of unemployment beginning after February 17, 2009, and before April 5, 2010.

EB Triggers

- Mandatory—A state must pay EB (13 weeks duration) if the insured unemployment rate (IUR) for the previous 13 weeks is at least 5 percent and is 120 percent of the rate for the same 13-week period in the two previous years.
- Optional—At its option, a state may pay EB (13 weeks) if the IUR for the previous 13 weeks is at least 6 percent, regardless of the experience in the previous years.

- Optional—At its option, a state may pay EB (13 weeks) if the average total unemployment rate (TUR), seasonally adjusted, for the most recent three months is at least 6.5 percent and is 110 percent of the rate for the same three-month period in either of the two previous years. If this rate is at least 8.0 percent and is 110 percent of the rate for the same three-month period in either of the two previous years, the duration increases from 13 to 20 weeks.

Emergency Unemployment Compensation

The emergency unemployment compensation (EUC08) program provides up to 34 weeks of benefits to eligible jobless workers in every state, and up to 19 additional weeks in states with "high unemployment" (for a maximum of 53). The federal government will pay for 100 percent of EUC08 costs. The EUC08 program is effective from July 2008 through June 2, 2010. (This information was current at the time of writing.)

Unemployment Compensation for Federal Civilian Employees

The unemployment compensation for federal civilian employees (UCFE) program provides unemployment benefits to federal civilian workers in the same amount and under the same general conditions as relate to UC for other workers. The program is administered on behalf of the federal government by the state UC agencies. Costs of UCFE benefits are charged to the federal agencies where the workers earned their base period wages.

Unemployment Compensation for Ex-Service members

Unemployment compensation for ex-service members (UCX) is a subsidiary program to UCFE. To qualify for UCX, an ex-service member separated from military service on or after July 1, 1981, must have completed a full term of active service in the armed forces or in the commissioned corps of the National Oceanic and Atmospheric Administration or in the commissioned corps of the U.S. Public Health Service, and must have been discharged or released under honorable conditions; and, if an officer, the individual must not have resigned for the good of the service. In addition, ex-service members discharged or released before completing their first full term of active service will nevertheless have a period of federal service if separated for one of the following reasons:

- The convenience of the government under an early release program
- Medical disqualifications, pregnancy, parenthood, or service-incurred injury or disability,
- Hardship
- Personality disorders or inaptitude, but only if the service was continuous for 365 days or more

Continuous active duty in reserve status may be counted in determining if an individual has federal service, but only if such active duty is continuous for 90 days or longer.

Disaster Unemployment Assistance

The Disaster Relief Act of 1974 authorizes the President to provide to any individual unemployed as a result of a major natural disaster such assistance as deemed appropriate while the individual is unemployed. In general, individuals living or working in those areas affected by a major natural disaster, who are unemployed because of the disaster, are eligible for disaster unemployment assistance (DUA) if they are not eligible for UC or other wage replacement payments and meet certain requirements. Assistance is available for a maximum of 26 weeks after the major natural disaster is declared. In some cases, this maximum has been increased to 39 weeks.

Trade Adjustment Assistance

The Trade Act of 1974 was reformed in 2002 to consolidate two separate programs, expand eligibility to more worker groups, increase timeliness for benefit receipt, training and rapid response assistance, legislate specific waiver provisions, and establish other trade adjustment assistance (TAA). The reform of the Trade Act in 2009 overhauls the TAA program and substantially expands TAA coverage to more workers and firms, including workers and firms in the service sector, and improves workers' opportuni ties for training, health insurance coverage, and reemployment. TAA includes a variety of reemployment services and benefits to workers who have lost their jobs or suffered a reduction of hours and wages as a result of increased imports or shifts in production outside the United States. Overall, the TAA program aims to help program participants obtain new jobs, ensuring they retain employment and earn wages comparable to their prior jobs.

To obtain TAA benefits and services, a group of workers must first file a petition with the Department of Labor requesting certification as workers adversely affected by foreign trade. A petition may be filed by a group of three or more workers, by a company official, by One Stop operators or partners (including state workforce agencies and dislocated worker units), or by a union or other duly authorized representative of such workers. The workers on whose behalf a petition is filed must be, or have been, employed at the firm or subdivision identified in the petition. Workers' employment must be, or have been, related to the production of articles (products) described in the petition.

If certified, each worker in the group must apply for individual services and benefits through his or her local One Stop Career Center to determine individual eligibility. Such services and benefits include reemployment services, job search allowances, relocation allowances, trade readjustment allowances, health insurance coverage assistance, and job training.

Self-Employment Assistance

States are given the option to establish self-employment assistance (SEA) programs to help unemployed workers to create their own jobs by starting small businesses. To be eligible for the program, an individual must be eligible for unemployment compensation, have been permanently laid off from his or her previous job, and been identified through the profiling system as likely to exhaust his or her benefits, and must participate in self-employment activities, including entrepreneurial training and business counseling. Weekly SEA allowances are funded out of each state's account in the UTF at no additional cost to the UC program. No more than 5 percent of claimants may be part of a SEA program.

Currently, there are ten states that have adopted SEA programs.

Short-Time Compensation

The short-time compensation (STC) program—commonly known as work-sharing—provides partial UC benefits to individuals whose work hours are reduced from full-time to part-time on the same job. STC is a program that allows an employer, faced with the need for layoffs because of reduced workload, to reduce the number of regularly scheduled hours of work for all employees rather than incur layoffs. Benefits are payable to workers for the hours of work lost, as a proportion of the benefit amount for a full week of unemployment. The STC program currently has 18 states participating.

PART SIX

Employee Benefit Plan Administration

Employee benefit plan administration has changed substantially in the last 30 years evolving into a multifaceted discipline requiring a combination of both general managerial skills and technical proficiencies. An overview of the principles of administration of employee benefit plans is presented in the first chapter of this part, Chapter 24.

The presence of flexible benefit plans or so-called cafeteria plans in employee benefits programs adds another level of complexity to employee benefit plan administration. Chapter 25 provides a historical overview of the development of flexible benefit plans and also discusses the advantages and limitations associated with flexible benefit plans and the regulatory structure of Internal Revenue Code Section 125 in which they operate. In addition, this chapter describes the various types of cafeteria plans, the use of flexible spending accounts by the plans, and the impact of a host of employment and benefit laws on the plans.

The fiduciary liability that the Employee Retirement Income Security Act (ERISA) imposes on benefits professionals is examined in Chapter 26, as well as the additional requirements required under the Patient Protection and Affordable Care Act (PPACA).

The last chapter of this part, Chapter 27, discusses the critical role of employee benefit communications in plan administration.

CHAPTER 24

Strategic Benefit Plan Management

Dennis F. Mahoney

Administering employee benefit plans has changed substantially in the last 35 years and has evolved into a multifaceted discipline. It requires a combination of both general managerial skills and deep technical proficiencies in select areas. It entails coordinating a team of internal and external specialists from the following diverse disciplines: human resources, law, tax, finance, medical care, risk management, information systems and Internet web services. And it is best accomplished by an individual skilled in leadership, project management, and general management principles.

The level of complexity in administering an employee benefits program is contingent on a number of factors. Among these are the complexity and comprehensiveness of the benefits design and coverages, the size of the employee group covered, the uniformity of the program for different categories of employees, the geographic dispersion of employees, and the existence of self-funded or self-administered arrangements. Multiple service providers can add to the complexity of plan administration and have become exceedingly prevalent as more organizations have proceeded to outsource the administration of employee benefits.

An employee benefits program is of strategic importance to an organization both from a human resource (HR) perspective and from a risk-management perspective. From an HR perspective, the program itself is instrumental in attracting and retaining a skilled workforce, which allows the firm to be competitive within its industry. Design of a retirement plan can affect retirement patterns and have a direct impact on the replenishment of the workforce. Equally important are risk management issues. Because of the significant costs involved and the potential to manage risks in various ways, a firm that effectively manages its employee benefits program risks can have a competitive advantage in terms of product and service pricing. Control over potential risks should be fully considered when evaluating the scope and nature of administrative activities.

The nature and scope of benefits administration activities will be based on the organization's philosophy about a benefits program, risk-management activities, the availability of various service providers with expertise in relationship to the organization's benefits offerings, and the ability of these service providers to administer the benefits program in the way that meets the organization's preferences. In addition, today's employee benefits management function is profoundly affected by the extent to which the administration is retained in house or outsourced to various administrators. When outsourced, a plan sponsor can opt for a "bundled solution" dealing with a single overseeing vendor, or alternatively through an "unbundled solution" where the plan sponsor must interact with and manage multiple service providers.

FOCUS OF BENEFITS MANAGEMENT ACTIVITY

Recognizing that scope and function of employee benefits administration differs within organizations, there are a number of core activities and common functions that universally apply to virtually every plan sponsorship situation. As a result, certain core competencies are inherent in plan management. The benefits director must be proficient in a variety of competencies to deal with a range of issues:

1. Benefits plan design
2. Benefits plan delivery
3. Benefits policy formulation
4. Communications
5. Applying technology
6. Cost management and resource controls
7. Management reporting
8. Legal and regulatory compliance
9. Monitoring the external environment

Benefits Plan Design

A critical function within the purview of employee benefits administration is the initial design and ongoing modification of the employee benefits program to meet changing market conditions, new regulatory requirements, or changing organizational and/or human resource objectives. Often, the benefits manager is not operating completely free of constraints in the design of employee benefit plans. Cost considerations, the culture of the organization, employee needs, and the historical development of benefit programs affect benefits design. Industry trends and competition as well as local market conditions concerning service providers also have a bearing on the design process. Collective bargaining agreements and benefit plan design changes that are negotiated between union and management are another determinant. Even when collective bargaining agreements do not exist, many employers will try to build employee consensus around benefit plan changes, especially if a plan change may be perceived as a "take-away."

At the time that this chapter was revised for publication, most organizations were actively engaged in redesigning their health benefits programs resulting from enactment of the Patient Protection and Affordable Care Act (PPACA) as amended by the Health Care and Education Reconciliation Act of 2010. Passage of these complementary acts represented a monumental legislative initiative whose intent was to effectuate comprehensive health care reform. Not only would this legislation mandate that individuals attain health coverage, but its far-reaching provisions, if fully carried out according to enactment, will fundamentally restructure the plan offerings offered by many commercial insurers and health plan providers, and will offer tax incentives and governmental subsidies to make health coverage more affordable. At this point, the effects of these comprehensive provisions are still evolving, with many years of clarifying regulatory pronouncements to be forthcoming. However, if fully enacted, the provisions will allow individuals to select plan offerings through state exchanges if these offerings are more attractive when compared to an employer's plan. Such alternatives will make the design of employer plans more involved, since employers will need to consider the ability of their workforce to opt out of their employer plan offerings. In essence, employers will now need to incorporate health care reform's "pay-or-play" provisions and the effects of plan departures and governmental excise taxes on their plan pricing and demographic assumptions.

Benefits design entails making structural decisions at a macro level as well as at a more micro level. Whether an organization uses a noncontributory defined benefit plan or a contributory 401(k) defined contribution plan as its primary retirement program can result in very different outcomes from a financial, human resources, and risk-management perspective. Use of a defined benefit plan means the organization commits to a pension formula and retains the risk for investing plan assets. In a defined contribution plan, the organization's responsibility to plan participants is largely fulfilled when assets are transferred to the investment custodian and investment risk is shifted to plan participants. These alternate pension forms may affect recruitment and retention as they present different opportunities for plan participant cash flow assurance and capital accumulation that ultimately affect retirement income. The choice of retirement plan forms also can have major impact on the administrative and communication activities associated with each plan. Inclusion of a loan feature with a 401(k) program can lead to more costly administrative and systems support but may result in greater plan participation, which could be necessary to pass plan nondiscrimination tests.

Successful plan design occurs when a benefits program properly addresses the needs of the organization and can be effectively administered and communicated to employees. Any design effort therefore starts with an understanding of the organization's underlying compensation and benefits program and philosophy and the specific objectives that the benefits plan is intended to address.

The plan should also be considered within the wider tax and marketplace contexts to determine whether it is achieving optimal efficiencies. Plans should be considered from a risk-management perspective to determine whether they are subjecting the organization to any special liabilities or creating a situation where the organization is exceeding the level of risk exposure that it is willing to bear. All of these considerations should help in refining the ultimate benefits program approach.

Benefits design is an ongoing and continual process. It is not generally performed once. Organizations often review their plans and make modifications after significant company events, market changes, and technology improvements. A good plan design will take into consideration short-term, intermediate, and long-term objectives and conditions, such as the maturing of a workforce. However, the benefits environment changes so rapidly, these long-term (and even intermediate) objectives can easily become obsolete. Changes in Medicare policy or other social insurance programs could alter long-term (and short-term) objectives of organizations' retiree medical plans.

As indicated earlier, passage of the Patient Protection and Affordable Care Act as amended by the Health Care and Education Reconciliation Act of 2010 required most organizations to reconsider and modify or redesign their existing health plan offerings, both to active employees and retirees. Particularly because of the extended period within which various provisions were phased in, benefits redesign would be an ongoing process for a number of years. The period of time in which its changes occurred began on March 23, 2010 and would not be fully operational until December 31, 2018. Such a protracted period of phase-in for a single legislative effort underscores the ongoing nature of benefits redesign in assuring compliance with legal requirements.

Though all future events impacting on plan design will not be known with certainty, management should be aware of possible longer-term impacts to the firm and balance these possible contingencies against the rationale for plan creation. Many times, a benefit plan can be justified on economic grounds when one examines some of the hidden costs in the absence of a plan, such as the continued service of employees who are not operating at a high level of productivity in the absence of a retirement plan or disability plan.[1]

Benefits Plan Delivery

Employee benefits administration is a customer service business with employees and management as the "clients." Serving plan participants can encompass a variety of activities, which again will dramatically vary depending on the scope of the benefits program, the nature of the organization, and the characteristics of the employee workforce. There are certain critical activities that will nevertheless be required, though the scope of activity and emphasis will vary:

- New employee benefits orientation
- Policy clarification on benefits eligibility, coverage, and applicability of plan provisions
- Dealing with exceptional circumstances and unusual cases
- Collection and processing of enrollment data, claims information, and requests for plan distributions either via the Internet or through submission of paper forms
- Benefits counseling and response to employee inquiries for active employees

1. Everett T. Allen, Jr., Joseph J. Melone, Jerry S. Rosenbloom, and Dennis Mahoney, *Retirement Plans*, 10th ed., New York: McGraw-Hill/Irwin, 2008, p. 10.

- Benefits counseling for terminating and retiring employees and employees with disabilities or on some form of leave

The scope of these activities will be affected by the characteristics of the organization. For instance, an employer that experiences high employee turnover will have to devote more resources to the new employee benefits orientation and to activities resolving benefits issues for terminating employees. Employers in mature industries are more likely to have a retiree population that exceeds the number of currently employed active workers. In such a situation, the benefits department may find itself routinely handling a greater number of inquiries from retirees on issues such as how the corporate health plan benefits are integrated with Medicare or how outside earnings will impact benefits provided from Social Security. In this instance, the mode of communication selected for disseminating plan information might be different than in other organizations. For example, use of certain technologies such as the Internet may be ineffective because some retirees may not have familiarity using this medium, nor view it as a preferred method for procuring information. If many retirees have relocated to Sunbelt states, the network of managed care providers would need concentrations of providers in these areas.

As is true in any customer service endeavor, the organization will attempt to achieve excellent customer service results meeting the valid requirements of the customer base with the given resources allocated for this purpose. Management must make determinations on the appropriate amount of resources to allocate to this endeavor given resource constraints. Management must ultimately seek the strategic deployment of all organizational resources.

There are two quality standards that generally are used to evaluate customer service satisfaction. One would be the desired outcome in terms of quality as determined by management, given resource allocations to the benefits administrative function. This targeted level of quality would be the maximum level targeted by management. The other standard would involve the minimum customer service standards that must be met to ensure a benefits program is in compliance with federal and state legal requirements. The special tax preferences that have historically been afforded to benefit programs also encompass certain required obligations that plan sponsors have to plan participants. Management should be aware that some of these legal obligations entail certain levels of customer service quality, which are legally mandated and which might result in severe penalties if not met. Though certainly not exhaustive, the following are some of the customer service requirements that must be met in sponsoring an employee benefits plan:

1. Requirement to provide a personal benefits statement at least annually if requested by an employee.
2. Employee Retirement Income Security Act (ERISA) mandated standards for responding to requests for benefits and stipulated time periods to deny claims and respond to appeals.
3. Requirements to make plan financial information available to participants and disclosure mandates for certain plan information.
4. Standards imposed by the Consolidated Omnibus Budget Reconciliation Act of 1985 (COBRA) regarding notification requirements to terminating employees on rights to coverage continuation under various plan sponsor health offerings.[2]
5. Provision of certificates of creditable coverage to those losing coverage under a group health plan or those requesting a certificate of creditable coverage as mandated by the Health Insurance Portability and Accountability Act (HIPAA).[3]

Benefits Policy Formulation

As part of the benefits management function, there are continuously arising human resource questions and issues that must be resolved. These include issues such as denial of claims by a carrier, confusion over waiting periods, service areas of a managed care network, and whether or not a new medical procedure will be covered by a benefit plan. Many of these must be codified in the form of policy to avoid future problems. Management may take either a proactive or reactive role in formulating policies related to the benefit plans.

---

2. As health care reform was being phased in, some health plan experts postulated what effects would result on certain previously enacted legislation. For instance, some practitioners suggested that COBRA coverage continuation features would be unnecessary with guaranteed access to affordable universal coverage. However, other practitioners suggest that COBRA continuation of health care coverage provisions will still be relevant for those types of plans (such as vision care, dental care, and hearing care) that are not required under the universal health care mandates. In effect, COBRA will still be relevant, but to a more limited subset of benefit offerings.
3. Similar to the preceding footnote, HIPAA's requirement to provide certificates of creditable coverage may still be necessary but to a more limited range of benefit plan offerings.

Although this component of benefit plan administration has always existed, it assumes a more significant role when benefit programs are modified or there is substantial change in the contextual environment. Adaptations in technology, plan design, compliance requirements, outsourcing, and the restructuring of the medical delivery system have forced a new emphasis on the policy formulation aspect of benefits management. Given the extensive anticipated changes in health plan offerings associated with the enactment of health care reform, there will likely be increased emphasis on benefits policy formulation during the foreseeable future.

Because many benefit functions are contracted out to insurance carriers, mutual fund companies, and third-party administrators, policy issues surface as these entities provide administrative services. For these issues, policy formulation takes the form of a vendor liaison role. The benefits director must be continually apprised of issues that surface, give direction for resolution, seek consistency among multiple providers, and at times exert pressure and negotiate to ensure these third parties are administering the benefit programs as the plan sponsor intends. Because these third parties are performing functions such as claims payment, deciding on adequate claims documentation, and monitoring appeal processes for claims denial, there are many areas requiring sound judgment and policy development. As some organizations have outsourced employee benefit call centers to international locations, managing the policy formulation function can involve cultural and communication nuances.

Many plan sponsors have found the practice of convening "vendor summits" as a valuable practice in facilitating communication with vendors, assuring consistency, and maintaining a rapport with those entities providing administrative support. "Vendor summits" involve periodic meetings, perhaps on an annual basis, where all of the various service providers assisting in plan administration attend a common meeting where they can discuss both administrative processes and client policies. These convocations serve several purposes. First, they allow the various providers to meet each other and form a personal relationship; they provide education on the entire administrative process, not just the unique area of specialty served by a single vendor; and finally they provide a forum in which the plan sponsor can explain its underlying benefit's philosophy, customer service expectations, and specific policy clarifications. Essentially, "vendor forums" promote good communication between the various vendors involved in the administrative process.

Communications

A principal activity in benefits plan management is to effectively communicate employee benefit programs, their plan provisions, and proper procedures to access these programs. A number of characteristics make the communication of benefit programs challenging. First, within many organizations, the workforce is diverse in composition, with various levels of education, financial sophistication, and interest in understanding plan provisions. The global nature of some organizations also raises issues of language and cultural diversity. Second, some benefits are of little interest to a majority of employees until point of use or access. For instance, there may be little interest in knowing much about a disability income plan until an individual contracts an illness that could result in a disabling condition; then there will be an intense desire to learn about and understand the plan. Similarly, many of the fine points associated with medical plan coverages are not completely understood until the onset of a particular health condition. Third, multiple regulatory requirements often affect plan features and lead to confusion. For the global organization, this entails integrating the laws of multiple national jurisdictions. Even in a single country, like the United States, the layers of plan stipulations can be confusing. Sometimes it is difficult for employees to distinguish between plan stipulations imposed by the Internal Revenue Service (IRS), a plan custodian, and the employer sponsoring a given plan. An employee may believe he or she has certain flexibilities permitted by law, while the plan sponsor may be more restrictive, not permitting these plan features; or, federal law may impose limits on highly compensated employees that are more restrictive than those of the employer. This is often particularly true in the realm of retirement and capital accumulation plans. For instance, the includable cap of compensation for computing pension contributions under Internal Revenue Code (IRC) Section 401(a)(17) may cause an employer to curtail the employer matching contributions an employee is expecting based upon the plan's standard contribution formula. Another example may be the ability to access loans from a 401(k) plan. Although there are restrictions on these loans, governmental rules allow for such plan provisions. A particular investment custodian may not offer that feature on a particular product, or the plan sponsor may choose not to offer such a plan feature, finding it contrary to its plan objectives. The potential for confusion is exacerbated when an employer offers multiple mutual funds or insurance companies as investment custodians with differing features.

Plan complexity also makes communicating benefits a challenge. Increased investment choices with participant-directed accounts; multiple program choices in flexible benefits programs; corporate mergers; and continuing market, technology, and legal changes contribute to the complexity.

Changing technologies, in particular, have and continue to dramatically alter employers' communications choices. In addition to written materials, employers have multiple alternatives: audio, video, interactive voice response (IVR), and the Internet. Some vendors have offered creative new technology features. One vendor was reported to be experimenting with "benefit specialist avatars." These various types of media allow employees to procure information on their personal benefits situation and direct changes in such areas as investment allocations and withholding amounts. Increasingly, benefit plan information is displayed in multiple media to provide increased awareness of benefit programs.

As with customer service quality, there are dual standards to meet in benefits communications—the maximum standards, i.e., those the company sets for creating a proper understanding and use of the plans, and a minimum standard specified by ERISA for meeting the legal compliance requirements for disclosure to plan participants. Use of electronic communications is increasing along with traditional standard print materials. Though not exhaustive, the following list delineates some of the most common communication requirements that a plan must meet to be in compliance with federal law:

1. *Summary plan descriptions (SPDs).* These are communication materials that provide a summary of the benefit plan's provisions in language that is supposed to be understandable to the average plan participant. In order to be considered a bona fide SPD, certain information must be included:
   - *a.* The requirement to describe how a participant covered by the plan can make a claim for benefits.
   - *b.* The procedure for appeal if a participant's claim for benefits is denied.
   - *c.* The name and address of the person or persons to be served with legal process should a legal action be instituted against the plan.

   It is important to note that there are precise time frames for making SPDs available to employees initially when a plan becomes subject to Title I of ERISA, and on an ongoing basis. New participants must receive an SPD 90 days after beginning plan participation. Subsequently, the SPDs must be revised every five years if the plan or information requirements have changed; otherwise, an SPD must be reissued every 10 years.

2. *Summary of material modification (SMM).* This is a written document that describes any "material" change that has occurred in the plan and must be issued if the plan sponsor has not issued an updated SPD describing the plan change. Like the SPD, there is a prescribed time frame for the issuance of this document. It must be issued within 210 days after the plan year in which the material modification was adopted. HIPAA reduced this 210-day period to 60 days for group health plans that make changes of "material reductions in covered services or benefits."
3. *Summary annual report (SAR).* This is a summary of the latest annual report for a benefit plan, in other words, a summary of the data reported to the IRS on Form 5500. Although the IRS has statutory oversight for 5500s, the Department of Labor (DOL) serves as a contractor to the IRS for processing Form 5500s under the ERISA Filing Acceptance System (EFAST). Unless an extension was granted for the filing of the Form 5500, the SAR must be distributed by the last day of the ninth month after the end of the plan year.

In addition to the required reporting and disclosure about general plan provisions, a number of targeted communication messages must be provided by the benefits administrator when specific events occur or certain conditions are met:

1. *Benefit statement to terminated vested participants.* Any terminated employee who is entitled to a benefit under a pension benefit plan must be advised of this entitlement by the time this information is reported to the IRS as part of the Form 5500 reporting.
2. *COBRA rights.* The Consolidated Omnibus Budget Reconciliation Act of 1985 requires employers with 20 or more employees to offer continued health care coverage to employees and their dependents who are losing their health coverage under the employer plan. There is an initial notification requirement at the time that an employee first becomes covered by the health plan

and a requirement to notify eligible participants of a 60-day election period when they experience a qualifying event such as termination of employment. As indicated earlier, the advent of easier access to health coverage under the enacted health care reform legislation is likely to diminish the importance of COBRA as it relates to basic health care coverage. Nevertheless, eligibility for COBRA continuation coverage will still have relevance to health-related coverage that is not specifically required under the law. This would include supplemental benefits exceeding health care requirements in areas such as vision care and hearing care.

3. *Explanation of tax withholding for rollover distributions.* The Unemployment Compensation Amendments of 1992 imposed a 20 percent mandatory withholding tax on pension plan distributions that are not directly transferred to another eligible plan. Generally, employers are to notify employees no earlier than 30 days and no later than 90 days before the eligible rollover distribution.
4. *Joint and survivor information.* Most pension plans must correspond with their participants between the plan year in which the participant first reaches age 32 and the plan year preceding the plan year in which the participant attains age 35, to advise the pension participant of the rules concerning death benefits for a spouse and the rules regarding survivor annuities and waiver of survivorship rights.
5. *Certificates of creditable coverage.* These must be provided automatically by the sponsor of a group health plan when an individual loses coverage under the plan, exhausts COBRA continuation coverage, or is requested by an individual before losing coverage or within 24 months of losing coverage. The requirement to provide certificates of creditable coverage was instituted by the Health Insurance Portability and Accountability Act of 1996. As with COBRA continuation coverage, this requirement will likely have varying importance depending on type of health-related plan as the provisions of health care reform are phased into practice.

Both the general and targeted communications are prescribed by law and must occur within noted time periods for the benefit plan to be in compliance. Failure to provide such communications within the mandated time requirements can subject the plan to financial penalties or result in other legal remedies against a plan. These financial penalties are by no means insignificant. For instance, failure to provide information on COBRA rights can result in a penalty equal to $110 per day, while willful violations of ERISA reporting and disclosure provisions can result in criminal prosecution carrying prison terms and fines up to $500,000 for a corporation.

Applying Technology

New technological applications are constantly emerging and have direct impact on the means to handle information, interface with customers, and enhance service.[4] In recent times, benefits administrators have been dramatically affected by technological innovations and will continue to be dramatically impacted as other innovations emerge, especially continuing dramatic advances in communications and record-keeping functions. Many innovations that did not exist in widespread commercial use 20 or more years ago have become commonplace in administering benefit plans. Among these would be voicemail, electronic mail, podcasts, and interactive Internet applications such as self-service enrollment and social networking sites. Implementing state-of-the-art administrative technology in benefits management has transformed the service delivery benefits function and revolutionized the way benefits directors monitor the effectiveness of their programs.

By way of historical perspective, the growth of flexible benefits programs during the 1980s and early 1990s spurred advanced record-keeping systems and communication technology. These more complex plans required the functionality of modern technology, which required an employee benefits information system that integrated participant demographic characteristics, cost data, and plan information into one source. The goal was to consolidate information that may need to be cross-referenced into one integrated source with easy access for multiple users. Such an approach made employee self-service the next progressive step as access to the Internet became commonplace.

---

4. The author gratefully acknowledges the extensive and comprehensive use of internal memos and explanations provided by Gary Truhlar, Director of Human Resources: Information Management at the University of Pennsylvania, in categorizing and describing information management principles and tools. Any errors in description are entirely the responsibility of the author.

The power of information technology is rooted in the way data is retained and stored (informational architecture), the expanded ability to retrieve relevant information (data-accessing capabilities), the development of features allowing nontechnical persons to easily extract the information they need (end-user tools), and a realization that this repository of data can be used by both plan administrators for plan management functions and by plan participants for customer service needs.

Informational Architecture

A common relational database is at the heart of the informational architecture and becomes the centralized repository of information for census, demographic characteristics, eligibility, and plan information for multiple benefit plans. The goal is to avoid the fragmentation of information that prevents an integrated and complete analysis when viewing benefits coverages by organizational unit, by individual employee, or by various employee types or certain demographic stratas such as geographic location or age. When effectively designed, a common relational database eliminates information "silos" where information is housed in one location and is inaccessible to decision-makers because of organizational, database, or benefit plan boundaries. A common relational database creates a universal repository of information that can be accessed directly by the plan participant on an as-needed basis to engage in financial planning, check balances in capital accumulation accounts, or monitor the status of coverages or pending claims made against a benefit plan. Such an approach also helps the plan administrator in the numerical analysis for nondiscrimination requirements and actuarial valuations.

Data-Accessing Capabilities

The way individuals work and the way customers receive service has changed. Information technology allows self-service, and customers want the freedom of easy access. Customer-driven processes enable applications that can be initiated by plan participants. Plan participants are empowered to access individualized benefits information from a common relational database without requiring the intervention of a human benefits specialist. Creating a customer-driven process results in a paradigm shift for servicing employees and becomes the primary, as opposed to secondary, means by which employees access information. The human benefits specialist adds specialized value, counseling, and training but should not be supplying answers related to eligibility, account balances, or standard available information such as claims procedures. Such generic, objective inquiries are more efficiently obtained through automated access.

The newly hired employee without specialized computer training should be able to obtain benefit plan information from the benefits information system. This occurs when user presentation has a reasonably consistent "look and feel." Data to the system is entered once, from the source, and appropriate edits and verification are performed throughout the initiation, review, approval, and submission processes. Access to the data is always available, and the data is always current and consistent when accessed by multiple users.

Security

Security is important because the same database is used for administrative processing as well as communications to plan participants. Information security is important to protect against fraudulent plan disbursements; unauthorized access to proprietary plan participant information; and entry into other proprietary and protected information, such as medical records or defined contribution investment selections.

The issue of privacy regarding medical records took on greater prominence following passage of HIPAA in 1996. Privacy of medical records continues to be an important issue. On July 14, 2010, the U.S. Department of Health and Human Services published proposed regulations modifying the privacy, security, and enforcement rules issued under HIPAA. These regulations implemented the statutory amendments made to HIPAA by the Health Information Technology for Economic and Clinical Health Act (HITECH) enacted as part of the American Recovery and Reinvestment Act of 2009 (ARRA).

HITECH was generally effective on February 18, 2010, although there were a number of statutory exceptions to this general effective date. HITECH extended the HIPAA privacy, security, and enforcement rules to apply not only to covered entities but also to entities assisting covered entities, known as business associates. The definition of business associate includes entities or persons that provide data transmission services to a covered entity and require routine access to protected health information (PHI); subcontractors that create, receive, maintain or transmit PHI on behalf of a business associate; and vendors that offer personal health records to one or more individuals on behalf of a covered entity.

HITECH strengthened an individual's right to access PHI. The individual has the right to a copy of PHI in an electronic format and can also direct the covered entity to transmit a copy directly to the individual's designee. The request to forward PHI to an individual's designee; however, must be clear, conspicuous and specific. Furthermore, a covered entity is required to provide the individual with an electronic copy of PHI in the electronic format requested. A covered entity may disclose a decedent's PHI to family members and others involved in the care of the individual unless doing so is inconsistent with the prior expressed preference of the individual. Also, a covered entity is permitted to provide proof of immunizations to schools without a written authorization required by the rules, provided the covered entity obtains an agreement to the disclosure from a parent, guardian or, if the individual is an adult or emancipated, the individual.

Unleashing Information Technology Potential

Today's benefits director can apply a variety of information tools on this landscape of an on-line, relational database supporting customer-driven processes:

- Executive information systems (EIS) are powerful end-user tools that provide management information in summary format. The user can immediately access "portraits" that summarize, analyze, and present in graphical display the information from the database that the benefits director routinely needs to understand and manage the firm's benefit plans. EIS can be designed to profile utilization patterns, risk exposures, and factors driving benefit plan costs.
- Imaging and optical storage eliminates paper records and creates "virtual records" (sharing of documents over a network). Use of this technology can improve customer access; eliminate misfiles attendant with manual record sorting; provide more efficient and timely data storage; and, through efficient electronic duplicative backup, reduce the potential for data loss in the event of a disaster, such as a fire or flood.
- Access to information over the Internet facilitates communication from the plan sponsor to insurance carriers, investment custodians, and third-party administrators without the physical exchange of paper files or computer tapes. This greatly reduces the amount of time required to access data, which improves efficiency. Given the decision by many organizations to outsource some component of benefits administration and the necessity to share plan data with specialized experts, such as consultants and actuaries, to monitor compliance and construct asset and liability

valuations, such methods greatly enhance the ability of plan sponsors to share information in "real time."

- Client-server technology integrates networked applications with desktop and mobile tools that are familiar to the user (windows, mouse, drag and drop, etc.). Laptops, portable mobile devices, and cellphones allow connection to a virtually unlimited array of resources, including electronic mail, the Internet, intranets, commercial databases, and vendor systems. Such technology opens tremendous opportunities to support decentralized management of various programs, distill information throughout the organization, and provide plan information through customer-driven processes supporting a more empowered and self-sufficient plan participant.
- Employee self-service allows customer-driven updating of personal data, benefits modeling, retirement planning, and so on. Ideally, applications are delivered directly to each employee's computer workstation, laptop and/or personal technology devices.

Cost Management and Resource Controls

Increasingly, cost management has become a critical issue for benefit plan administration as the costs of benefit programs have risen. What was sometimes viewed as a purely financial function handled by an organization's finance department is now more often viewed as a partnership with a finance department and an area where benefit plan management can significantly add value to decisions. There are various reasons for an expanded benefits management role in fiscal accountability. Beyond the obvious recognition that plan costs represent a significant operating expenditure as a component cost of total compensation, there are other environmental factors that have expanded the role of benefits management in this area. Many of these trends had their inception in the 1980s and 1990s. Among them were some of the compliance issues that arose during the late 1980s and early 1990s. Issuance of FAS 106 by the Financial Accounting Standards Board on December 21, 1990, meant that companies had to show on their balance sheets the liabilities associated with their retiree health plan programs. For most organizations, compliance was required in 1993. Because most organizations had not previously shown these liabilities and were accounting for their retiree health care costs on a pay-as-you-go basis, recognition of these liabilities was a major disclosure event for most organizations. Although some organizations chose to terminate their retiree health programs at that time, many other organizations tried to balance the financial (and shareholder) impact of the accounting recognition with their human resource considerations. Those involved in benefits management were able to add value to the decision process because of detailed knowledge on compliance with FAS 106 requirements and because some of the means to decrease plan liabilities could occur through plan design modification.

Similarly, failure to comply with the nondiscrimination tests of the Tax Reform Act of 1986 could have severe financial impacts. Again, many of the remedies available involved balancing plan design modifications with cost issues. Hence, the benefits management knowledge and expertise in plan design was required to find the optimal financial solutions for the firm. What is significant about both FAS 106 and many of the nondiscrimination requirements of the Tax Reform Act of 1986 is that there are very real and very substantial financial impacts to an organization related to the firm's knowledge of demographics, health trends, and utilization patterns within benefit programs. Those responsible for the benefits management and plan administration are often best positioned to have knowledge of these nuances and impact the firm in a significant financial way. As firms progress through the current millennium, this knowledge of demographics, health trends, and utilization is being used to develop consumer-driven health plans (CDHPs) that best serve participants and efficiently use organizational resources.

Benefits directors have special expertise and knowledge, not only of the cost experience of the firm's employee group, but also of insurance arrangements and the pricing of these risk-shifting devices in the marketplace. This knowledge of insurance pricing is useful in evaluating proposals from insurers and in developing the firm's risk-management approach. On insured products, a benefits director should carefully evaluate the underlying actuarial assumptions and reserve requirements, and compare these underlying cost determinants with plan experience. Actuarial assumptions that vary substantially from plan experience should be questioned. Even if a plan is being administered on a cost-plus basis, actuarial assumptions can be important. Reserve requirements or a stop-loss fee can be computed based upon expected claims experience. Retention, interest, and penalty charges should be thoroughly understood and negotiated. Some carriers include interest and penalty charges in retention. Because these computation methods may not be clearly elaborated in a contract, analysis of complete computation methodology is required.

As companies have attempted to compete more effectively in a technologically changing world, labor shortages can be a threat to some organizations. Design of compensation programs capable of recruiting and retaining the best workers has been viewed as a strategic imperative. Use of stock options in the total compensation package had been a widely used device to attract these workers. A less robust economy and lethargic stock market moved some companies away from a heavy emphasis on stock options in compensation programs. The expensing of options on corporate income statements also moved some companies to be more selective in awarding large stock option grants.

Management Reporting

Since the benefits program is a major consumer of firm resources and its effective design can contribute to strategic success, management reporting responsibilities have expanded for benefits staff. It is important for those responsible for benefits management to have the management information systems in place that will allow them to monitor financial results, track program utilization, assess risk exposures, note deviations from compliance targets, and measure progress toward overall human resource objectives. Such metrics go beyond traditional financial measures of plan costs. The management information component of benefits administration has expanded and requires ongoing refinement as new requirements are mandated and other environmental changes occur. Passage of PPACA has heightened management reporting responsibilities as plan sponsors need to compile significant actuarial data to determine whether their health plans comply with affordability measures under the "pay or play" requirement on employers.

Program Costs

Measuring direct program costs is necessary, but a wide array of other metrics are also necessary to fully understand the forces that are driving benefits costs. To understand hospitalization expenses, for instance, it is necessary to know the various medical procedures that are frequently used and the utilization patterns for hospitalizations and lengths of stay. As health costs have risen; health insurers, managed care companies, and health care coalitions have built community databases to better measure costs and quality. They look at physician practice patterns, and treatment regimens and outcomes. The measures permit benefit directors to benchmark their own plan performance with norms and will ultimately help in purchasing better-value health care.

To effectively manage health plan costs, the benefits director must understand the demographic characteristics of the company's covered population and establish a context for comparison. Even relative pricing between multiple plan offerings can be deceptive if pricing of options is viewed in isolation without adjusting for age and geographic selection patterns since these factors are highly correlated with the cost of health care. If a plan attracts a certain population cohort, its higher cost may reflect this dominant demographic feature and may not be indicative of truly higher cost relative to other plans if adjustments are made for population characteristics. For example, health maintenance organizations (HMOs) have often attracted younger employees for various reasons. Even though a health maintenance organization's premium may be lower than a preferred provider option, the HMO may not look as attractive if the employer makes an adjustment for this demographic characteristic and recompares relative pricing with expected pricing given uniform demographic assumptions.

Demographic and utilization patterns are necessary components for computing program liabilities and testing plan compliance. Though the requirement to book defined benefit pension obligations had been in use for some time, FAS 106 established similar financial reporting requirements for retiree health plans. The Tax Reform Act of 1986 ushered in specific numerical testing to determine whether highly compensated employees were being advantaged under retirement programs. Because of the adverse consequences resulting from failing the nondiscrimination tests, testing must be conducted regularly and be included in a management reporting system. The reports will identify any divergence from expected results and give lead time for remedial action such as additional contributions to the accounts of nonhighly compensated employees or redesign of benefit plan structures.

Comparison with the Competition

In order to judge the competitive position of a total compensation program, employers often seek to compare their benefits programs with those of similar employers. This endeavor is often difficult because the many plan provisions of benefit programs do not make for a homogeneous commodity that is directly comparable. Also, because an employer may have a geographically dispersed workforce and attract some employees from a local labor market and other employees from either a national or international labor pool, the relevant survey group can vary with type of employee. Often, employers find it necessary to segment their employee populations and compare both for their local marketplace and within their particular industry for professional and management personnel.

Survey data are often used, and some benefits consulting firms have attempted to develop comparative databases that give overall comparability ratings for benefit programs. Online databases allow employees to easily compare their own pay components with others in the talent marketplace. Various approaches can be used to make benefit plan comparisons more relevant, depending on the particular objective for undertaking the analysis. Some experts have identified various comparative methodologies, including the following[5]:

1. Compare the benefits actually payable to representative employees under different circumstances.
2. Compare actual costs to the employer for different benefit plans.
3. Measure plans on a basis that uses uniform actuarial methods and assumptions and focuses on the relative value of the different benefits provided.
4. Compare benefit plans feature by feature to isolate specific plan provisions that may be appealing to certain employee groups and offer a competitive advantage. Such a comparison may result in amending plan provisions or highlighting specific plan provisions in communication materials in order to attract and retain employees.

Measuring Achievement of Human Resource Objectives

Management will often be interested in knowing whether benefit plans are successfully achieving their objectives. As with conducting benefit plan comparisons, various approaches can be used, depending on the particular evaluative objective. Surveys of the industry can be a starting point to assess overall competitive standing. Employee surveys may be conducted to determine satisfaction levels with the current program and what particular modifications could be implemented to enhance existing programs. Focus groups can be conducted to receive more detailed explanations on how programs meet employee needs. Other approaches use actuarial calculations. For instance, an employer attempting to assess the adequacy of a retirement program can compute income-replacement ratios for

5. Everett T. Allen, Jr., Joseph J. Melone, Jerry S. Rosenbloom, and Dennis Mahoney, *Retirement Plans*, 10th ed., New York: McGraw-Hill/Irwin, 2008, pp. 34–36.

representative groups of employees at varied income levels and with various lengths of service. These determinations can then be balanced against target replacement ratios. Alternatively, retirement patterns could be examined to determine whether the employer is achieving desired results in replenishing its workforce.

At times, a purely quantitative measure of human resource objectives may not be available. Nevertheless, the benefits director must be cognizant of the rationale for plan sponsorship and monitor on an ongoing basis the effectiveness of the plans in meeting strategic organizational objectives.

Assessing and Managing Program Risks

Benefit directors should have a clear understanding of the risks the organization is assuming, the costs involved, and a means for managing them. This assessment can only be completed by understanding the characteristics of the benefits program, its historical experience, the demographic characteristics of the employee group, and the alternative risk-management techniques that are available in the marketplace. Risk-management techniques must be understood in terms of how they operate and how they are priced. Only with this information can the benefits director prudently assess whether the selected strategy is attuned to the organization's needs.

A benefits director must evaluate program risk by comparing past plan outcomes or modeling possible future outcomes under various risk-management techniques. For instance, a benefits director could model life insurance claims experience over various time intervals, comparing insured approaches to a cost-plus approach. The benefits director may alter the cost-plus approach by adding either an individual or aggregate stop-loss reinsurance feature. Even putting an existing insured benefit plan out for bid can result in compelling plan savings. Many plan sponsors will develop a cycle for rebidding their benefit plans, although this cycle will be modified if marketplace conditions are known to be changing, creating favorable pricing opportunities.

Another possibility for managing risk could be creation of a captive insurance company to handle employee benefit risks. Although more extensively considered for property and casualty risks, some employers are giving greater consideration to managing their employee-benefit plan risks through captive insurance arrangements today. When they pursue such an arrangement, employers will generally obtain prior approval from the Department of Labor (DOL). This approval is sought since the payment of premium to a captive insurer could constitute a "prohibited transaction" under the Employee Retirement Income Security Act of 1974 (ERISA). Specifically ERISA Section 406(a)(1)(D) prohibits the "transfer to, or use by or for the benefit of, a party in interest, of any assets of the plan." An entity owned by the employer, such as a captive, is considered to be a party in interest with respect to the employee benefit plan under ERISA Sections 3(14)(C) and 3(14)(G). The penalty for such a prohibited transaction is 5 percent of the amount involved in the transaction and would be assessed each year that the prohibited transaction is outstanding and owed by the party in interest. Under ERISA Section 408 and administrative related guidance, the DOL is permitted to grant exemptions to the prohibited transaction requirements and has established an expedited process, which it calls EXPRO, for handling routine transactions. Depending upon the nature of the captive arrangement, sometimes EXPRO can be utilized to be exempted from consideration as a "prohibited transaction."[6] A detailed explanation of the use of captive insurers in managing employee benefit risks can be found in Chapter 30.

Legal and Regulatory Compliance

Benefit programs must comply with a number of requirements. These include reporting and disclosure requirements (as discussed earlier in the "Communications" section); certain performance requirements in connection with claims for benefits (as discussed in the "Benefit Plan Delivery" section above); and fiduciary, funding, and other requirements as prescribed by various pieces of legislation that have been passed over the years. Many compliance standards, particularly for retirement plans, were codified with the passage of the Employee Retirement Income Security Act of 1974. ERISA set the framework for employer responsibilities in sponsoring a benefit plan; establishing broad and extensive funding requirements; and actuarial, fiduciary, and reporting and disclosure mandates. Since its initial passage, ERISA has been amended on an ongoing basis, incorporating new public policy initiatives into this important legislative framework.

A number of benefits compliance issues stem from the fact that benefit plans enjoy preferential treatment under the tax code. Such preferential tax treatment seems constantly to be reevaluated as the legislatures change. An examination of benefits legislation will indicate that almost every budget act for a number of prior years has had a number of benefits-related provisions. This was especially true during the 1980s and

6. "The 'Captivation' of Employee Benefits," June 2010, p. 10.

early 1990s in light of the large federal deficits. Benefit plans were seen as a potential source of federal revenue generation, and the preferential tax treatment was especially in jeopardy if the benefit plans were not seen to be benefiting a substantial segment of an employer's workforce. Hence, a fair amount of regulatory activity and compliance testing revolves around the issue of ascertaining who "benefits" under a plan and whether highly compensated employees are unduly advantaged.

The Tax Reform Act of 1986 was especially significant in that it instituted rigorous mathematical testing to ascertain whether a benefit plan is nondiscriminatory. Although the Section 89 testing requirements for health and welfare plans were subsequently repealed, as discussed later, rigorous mathematical testing to ensure nondiscrimination is required for tax-qualified pension and profit-sharing plans. This testing has become a major ongoing benefits administrative function since passage of this legislation. Subsequently, the Small Business Job Protection Act of 1996 saw an initiative to simplify some of these testing procedures in the hope of encouraging small employers to extend pension coverage.

Enactment of the PPACA and its related amending legislation in March of 2010 marked a new era in legal compliance for employers. In addition to major and immediate insurance-related reforms, this watershed legislation required that individuals obtain health coverage for themselves and their dependents. Coupled with the mandate for individual health insurance, employers were integrally linked to this public policy objective by so-called "pay-or-play" provisions in the law. Essentially, employers were required to provide affordable minimum essential health benefits to their employees or were required to pay employee subsidies or penalty taxes to advance attainment of universal health care. The employer role in achieving universal health care meant extensive compliance issues for virtually all plan sponsors. The full cost component of this transformational legislation is not yet fully known since phase-in occurs over a multi-year period of time. The onset again of significant federal budget deficits could mean governmental policy regarding employee benefits resorting to a more revenue-driven basis in the future.

Adhering to legal requirements involves not only compliance with federal legislation, but also attention to state and local statutes and requirements. Since insurance regulation has historically been an area for state oversight with limited federal mandates beyond those originating from ERISA, the federally imposed PPACA requirements create new dimensions involving integration and institutional change. Legal compliance also involves ongoing monitoring of pronouncements from regulatory agencies and the judicial review of the courts, which rule on many of the intricacies that federal and state statutes fail to address. PPACA means extensive compliance regulatory monitoring for the foreseeable future. Benefits directors must continually review benefits trade periodicals, e-zines, and specialized compliance publications to remain current on benefit plan legal requirements.

Monitoring the External Environment

As with any type of business activity, employee benefits management is affected by the larger business context in which these programs operate. Recently, the environmental context in which benefits programs operate has experienced significant change and has been a major determinant in setting the agenda for benefits plan design and other aspects of the benefits management activity. A review of some of these environmental factors helps illustrate the myriad factors a benefits director must monitor and gives a sense of some emerging trends that are likely to impact the benefits management activity in future years:

- General business and competitive conditions
- Governmental policy
- Workforce demographic shifts
- New product development
- New organizational structures
- Technological enhancement and innovation

General Business and Competitive Conditions

In the current millennium, the emergence of a more integrated world economy exerted influence on benefit programs in a number of different ways. First and foremost, benefit costs were a major component of labor cost and accordingly had a direct impact on the competitiveness of industries in the global marketplace. After a reprieve of a few years, the health care industry began to experience significant cost escalation once again. Accordingly, the price rise in this single benefit program brought a need for action to control costs, as these programs not only outpaced the general price level but were increasing more quickly than many companies' direct compensation costs. This extreme cost pressure resulted in a number of changes in the medical and health benefits offerings of companies culminating with passage of major health care reform legislation in the United States in 2010. Companies redesigned their medical benefit programs, introducing new ways of delivering care and changed pricing strategies for these benefits both before, and following passage of the health care reform legislation.

An integrated global marketplace also means that companies must attract and retain employees to remain competitive. Employee benefits are playing an increasingly important role in this endeavor. To remain competitive, firms must offer benefits plans that are competitive in design and in ease of access, utilizing state-of-the-art technology.

The growth of benefits consulting firms has been instrumental in bringing technological enhancements to the marketplace. The existence of these firms and their state-of-the-art capabilities have accelerated the trend towards benefits outsourcing. Interesting business combinations have emerged as some larger benefits consulting firms have merged with investment custodians, creating expanded record-keeping and financial services capabilities to plan sponsors. There are also other entrants in the marketplace with innovative services being offered by e-health providers.

Governmental Policy

During the 1980s and 1990s, benefit programs were the subject of intense scrutiny as policymakers concentrated on reducing the federal budget deficit. Because many benefit programs are designed to coordinate with social insurance programs such as Social Security, Medicare, and Workers Compensation, benefit plans are affected not only by direct statutory and regulatory pronouncements, but also by any alteration in governmental social insurance.

Policymakers also have become involved in benefit "protection" issues, such as employment nondiscrimination for persons with disabilities, required leave time for employees when they or family members are ill, legislation protecting employment rights for military personnel called into active service, further protections for employees covered by pensions, nondiscrimination issues related to age, and safeguards on the collection and use of genetic information for insurance enrollment and underwriting purposes. Many of these protections have been codified into law.[7] PPACA

7. For a more comprehensive explanation of benefit protection issues, consult the following laws: Consolidated Omnibus Budget Reconciliation Act of 1985, American with Disabilities Act of 1990, Older Workers Benefit Protection Act of 1990, Family Medical Leave Act of 1993, Uniformed Services Employment and Reemployment Rights Act of 1993, General Agreement on Tariffs and Trade of 1994, Mental Health Parity Act of 1996, Health Insurance Portability and Accountability Act of 1996, Working Families Tax Relief Act of 2004, American Jobs Creation Act of 2004, the Mental Health Parity and Addiction Equity Act (MHPAEA) of 2008, and the Genetic Information Nondiscrimination Act (GINA) of 2008. Both of the last two Acts from 2008 saw detailed regulations issued in 2010.

contained many insurance-related reforms that could be categorized as "protection" issues. Among these were prohibitions on lifetime and annual limits on essential benefits; stipulations against rescissions of coverage unless there was fraud or misrepresentation by an employee; prohibitions on the dropping of coverage for adult children (up to age 26), regardless of the adult child's student or marital status; and the stipulation against preexisting condition exclusions on enrollees who are under the age of 19.

Since most legislative initiatives that become law require subsequent clarifying regulations, the complete impact of the law unfolds over a period of years. Hence, those responsible for monitoring the external environment for benefit plans must be attuned to continuing regulatory pronouncements and judicial case determinations. At times, the necessity for clarification of the law is so pervasive that a second major law is required merely to fully implement the first measure. Such was the case with the Technical and Miscellaneous Revenue Act of 1988, which clarified many of the changes instituted by the Tax Reform Act of 1986 (TRA '86). So pervasive were the changes applicable to tax-qualified retirement plans originally instituted by TRA '86 that it was not until five years later, on September 12, 1991, that the Treasury Department and the IRS issued the long-awaited, final regulations for qualified pension and profit-sharing plans. These final regulations amounted to a 600-page document. This same sort of exhaustive, but necessary, need for clarifying regulatory pronouncements is occurring for the health care reform legislation. Given the scope and breadth of the health reform legislation, it is possible that its clarifying regulatory pronouncements may dwarf the 600-page document issued in 1991!

At times, some of the policy initiatives of major regulatory bodies will directly conflict with each other. An example includes the requirement to make contributions into retirement accounts of the working aged to avoid age discrimination in employment and the Treasury Department's requirements to make mandatory distributions from these same retirement accounts in pursuit of tax revenues.

Beyond the need to conform to benefits laws, benefits directors must constantly monitor proposed benefits legislation. Numerous benefits measures were passed in the past that were significantly modified, retroactively amended, or repealed outright before full compliance was required. The scuttled initiatives are still important because the deadline for original compliance often necessitates that organizations make an investment in systems modifications, data collection and strategic planning in order to comply. Many of these initiatives have been far-reaching in their intents and effects. These initiatives have included proposals for expansive benefit plan compliance testing,[8] modifications in social insurance programs and their coordination with employer plans,[9] very substantial additions to federal annual reporting requirements on plan participant dependents,[10] and a previously proposed fundamental reorganization of the U.S. health care delivery system that occurred prior to the landmark 2010 legislation.[11]

Passage and repeal of benefits legislation before implementation because of public outcry, inability to cost-effectively administer, or an

8. The Tax Reform Act of 1986 instituted comprehensive nondiscrimination testing for health and welfare plans, commonly referred to as Section 89. Originally, compliance was to occur for plan years beginning after the earlier of December 31, 1988, or three months after regulations were issued unless regulations were issued in 1987. Subsequently, President Bush signed a law on November 8, 1989, that abolished Section 89.
9. The Medicare Catastrophic Coverage Act of 1988 provided catastrophic benefits coverage through the Medicare program. Benefits under Part A of Medicare went into effect in 1989, while benefits under Part B were scheduled to commence in 1990. Congress approved the Medicare Catastrophic Coverage Repeal Act in November of 1989. Accordingly, Medicare participants were not required to pay an income surtax for 1989, and a supplemental Part B premium was repealed prospectively. Employers had to maintain Maintenance of Effort (MOE) provisions for 1989, whereby either additional benefits were provided to Medicare eligible retirees and their spouses or cash payments of up to $65 were provided to these same retirees. Compliance with the original legislation meant actuarial calculations for MOE and affected the calculation of FAS 106 liabilities. It was not until the repeal legislation was passed that Congress clarified the FICA and FUTA exclusion of MOE payments.
10. The Omnibus Budget Reconciliation Act of 1993 (OBRA '93) required employers to annually report individuals covered by an employer's health plan (both employees and dependents), starting with the 1994 calendar year by February 28, 1995, to the Medicare/Medicaid Coverage Data Bank. This was particularly onerous to many employers who did not keep detailed electronic records of employee dependents within their human resource databases. On May 10, 1994, the Health Care Financing Administration (HCFA) published preliminary guidance on the employer reporting requirements. Near the time of issuance, HCFA and President Clinton's administration recommended that Congress pass legislation giving an 18-month delay on implementation of the requirement. The Labor/Health and Human Services/Education appropriations bill for fiscal year 1995 spending, approved by Congress in the last week of September 1994, prohibited the Department of Health and Human Services from using federal funds in fiscal 1995 to implement the databank. Then HCFA announced in the first week of October 1994 that it was formally putting the requirements on hold.
11. President Clinton's health care plan was formally proposed in 1993. This legislative initiative would have resulted in a dramatic overhaul of the employer-sponsored health insurance system. Provisions included (1) creating a series of regional cooperatives, (2) assessing 1 percent of continued payroll assessment in 1996 unless the employer irrevocably waived its right to sponsor a corporate alliance, and (3) prohibiting the purchase of health coverage on a pretax basis through cafeteria plans or flexible spending accounts beginning January 1, 1997. Employers spent much of 1994 analyzing potential impacts to their plans and developing strategic responses, while alternate bills were proposed by Congressional leaders. It was not until late 1994 that it was evident that this legislative initiative had stalled and that passage of health care legislation seemed unlikely in either 1994 or 1995.

immediate policy reversal creates an onerous responsibility for the director of benefits programs because compliance activities and their attendant resource commitments must be approached as uncertain eventualities addressed in a prudent and discerning way, balancing the risks of immediate noncompliance with the costs of compliance. Some practitioners have noted the dangerous situation that the flurry of legislative reversals has caused, in that some practitioners will now refrain from immediate compliance and take a "wait and see" approach to see if the law will simply "go away."

Workforce Demographic Shifts

Demographic changes in the composition of the workforce have a profound impact on employee benefits plans. Transition from a homogeneous workforce primarily dominated by men with nonworking spouses to a workforce with a greater concentration of working mothers and nontraditional families has changed the nature of benefit plan offerings. Also, the increased presence of immigrants, expatriate workers, and third-country nationals in the global workforce has changed employee benefit offerings. A homogeneous workforce generally translated to "one size fits all" in benefits programs. These plans included less choice and were designed around needs of the traditional family model. Changing workforce demographics, coupled with advances in record-keeping technology and new product offerings, have spawned flexible benefit plan offerings that allow workers to customize their benefits program. The very framework of the health care reform legislation allows for choice in health care selection. Dependent care benefits also have become more important with more dual working couples, more single parents, and more aging parents.

Flexible benefits and work/life benefits often result in employee self-selection that affects the actuarial assumptions of programs and their cost underpinnings. Allowing employees to trade various benefit options results in the necessity to impute costs on an individual basis, and the pricing of plan offerings becomes an important exercise for the benefits director. Benefits pricing will affect selection patterns by employees and hence will impact the risks attracted to a particular plan and, in the longer term, will impact ultimate costs. Pricing policies of other employers now have become important, too, as employees sometimes choose medical coverage on the basis of whether one employer provides cash payments for opting out of coverage. Beginning in 2014, the presence of health exchanges expands opportunities for certain employees to seek alternative health coverage. These opportunities combined with the employer "pay-or-play" rules further enhance the importance of pricing employer-sponsored plan benefit options by those overseeing benefit plans.

The aging of the workforce has created greater interest in retiree health, capital accumulation, and retirement programs. Because the aging of the workforce has important implications for social insurance programs such as Medicare and Social Security, the benefits director must consider the impact to private employer-sponsored programs as the government modifies these social insurance programs. Health care reform with subsidies and excise taxes directly impacts plan design for private employers. Many employer programs were designed previously to coordinate with Medicare and Social Security. Thus, any reduction in social insurance programs affects the adequacy of employer programs and is likely to erode targeted benefit levels or increase the costs of employer plans if the employer programs absorb the impacts of government retrenchment.

New Product Development

Innovation in a global systems economy means a more rapid introduction of new products and services in the marketplace. This creates opportunities for the benefits director to better serve plan participant customers and more effectively administer benefit programs. An important aspect of a benefit director's job involves developing a means to evaluate these new product and service offerings and to determine capabilities to integrate these products and services into existing plan offerings or administrative structures. This is often difficult to accomplish in practice. For instance, a benefits director may identify substantial benefits to incorporating a disease-management program into an existing medical plan. A prescription benefits management (PBM) firm may have the expertise and systems to provide monitoring of drug use, increase greater utilization of generic drugs, and ensure greater quality control of the drug-dispensing system through computer linkage to network pharmacies. While achieving these advantages, the benefits director may need to integrate systems to ensure deductibles and coinsurance are merged and tracked for the dual systems; compare definitional differences between the old and new programs to ensure that discrepancies do not emerge when the program is introduced; and communicate changes in the way benefits will be accessed for plan participants. Dislocations that may occur may not be readily apparent, and often surface as the new plan is introduced. For instance, certain drug therapies with inpatient hospitalizations or supplied with home health care visits could be potential areas where dislocations can surface.

The timing of new product and service introductions can be critical. Because plan modifications necessitate a strategy for communicating changes to participants, they are typically introduced on plan-year anniversary dates and communicated to plan participants in advance of open enrollment periods. This timing allows plan participants to make informed benefit selections coordinating elections under the medical plan, health savings accounts (HSAs) or flexible spending accounts (FSAs), and so on. Plan anniversary dates often make the most sense, because deductibles and copayment schedules often run on plan anniversary dates. However, sometimes when a plan year is not the calendar year, there can be arguments for transitioning on the calendar year. This becomes compelling when the plan change will impact a tax limitation that is measured on the calendar year. This would be the case for an amount that can be contributed to a dependent care expense account. It should be noted that the phase-in of health care reform necessitated careful coordination particularly during key years when many provisions first became effective. This was particularly true leading up to 2014.

Benefits directors must often schedule reviews of programs and rebid plan offerings on a cyclical schedule and synchronize the benefits-program-planning function with the overall business planning cycle of the organization.

New Organizational Structures

Major transformations of organizational structures have occurred in the workplace, often with significant downsizings of the workforce. The elimination of various managerial levels within organizations, the flattening of hierarchical structures, the move toward decentralized organizations, the outsourcing of noncore activities, and greater use of specialized consulting services are among the trends shaping organizations. These changes, many of which are facilitated by evolving technology and the more integrated global economy, have important implications for the benefits management function. Many plan designs were crafted with a very different workforce in mind. Therefore, benefits directors are called upon to redesign plans that are appropriate to the "new economy" organization. Benefits programs are now called upon to represent the strategic direction of the organization, to contribute to the firm's bottom line, and to achieve certain goals, such as retention, team performance, and so on. For instance, a retirement plan where the benefit is significantly affected by years of service can be a retention incentive. Profit-sharing plans can be designed to reward accomplishment of team-based goals.

As a firm is redesigned, benefits directors need to be involved in a variety of ways. Benefit directors can craft early retirement options such as window plans when downsizing occurs, and assess the cost shifts that occur in other benefit plans with organizational transition. For example, offering an early retirement window plan could have multiple effects on other benefit plans. More retirees could mean greater expense for a retiree health plan and shifts in the FAS 106 liability, which must be shown on the balance sheet. If a retirement plan is on the margin with passing nondiscrimination tests, a shift in the workforce may cause noncompliance, necessitating a redesign of the existing core pension benefit for the remaining active workforce.

Technological Enhancement and Innovation

As noted earlier, technological enhancement and innovation in plan administration play an important role in benefits management. Clearly, these are environmental factors that need to be monitored by the benefits director. Ideally, the benefits director is keeping abreast of this technological change and proactively planning its introduction in administrative and communication activities. At times, the pace of environmental technological change may surpass existing modes of doing business within the organization. Because many benefits programs require exchange of data with insurance carriers, third-party administrators, and consultants, the necessity to interface has major implications for the pace at which advanced technology must be introduced into the host company if it is to remain compatible with marketplace products. The use of compatible technology has profound effects on the efficiency with which programs can be run, the amount of rework that must be done in monitoring and processing transactions, and the level of timely and useful management information that can be made available to plan administrators and top executives. In short, the ability to keep pace with technological change and rapidly integrate advanced technology into an organization's administration and culture can significantly impact its efficiency and effectiveness in meeting customer satisfaction and valid needs.

THE OUTSOURCING ALTERNATIVE

Many organizations, both large and small, have explored the issue of whether to outsource benefits administration or retain this function as an internal human resource activity. Depending on the scope and complexity of the organization's benefits program, the outsourcing decision can be a complex one. Outsourcing can involve whole programs or certain functions within benefits programs. The director of employee benefits is faced with some critical tradeoffs when it comes to an outsourcing decision, particularly if only portions of the benefits administration are outsourced. Outsourcing certain functions to third parties can result in fragmentation and lack of integration in the benefits information database. The procedures to access benefits and the manner in which benefits are communicated also can vary, causing confusion for plan participants. If outsourcing is chosen, the organization retains an oversight and supervisory role as well as the coordinating role to ensure benefits programs serve larger human resource and organizational objectives.

Outsourcing has become a very attractive alternative as organizations have downsized their workforces and jettisoned noncore business activities. Benefits administration has been a prime candidate for outsourcing because of the complexity of the function; the efficiencies attendant with specialized service providers; the ability of these specialized service providers to achieve beneficial pricing because of their business volume; and the ability of the service providers to more readily implement technological applications and to monitor the regulatory and market trends that occur within the employee benefits field. Some observers have noted that outsourcing has been especially attractive to organizations that have been faced with the necessity to upgrade their systems capabilities and make significant investments in advanced record-keeping and communications technology.[12] Because many of these technological innovations have occurred within the last 25 or more years, most organizations have been confronted with the decision to retain or outsource benefits administration. Health care reform and its multiple systemic- and compliance-related mandates have caused many organizations to revisit and further outsource emerging administrative requirements.

Introduction of new technology has affected the organizational design for employee benefits service delivery, whether retained in-house or outsourced. Many organizations have created employee benefits service centers where benefits specialists equipped with the latest technology facilitate access to customer-driven processes and handle nonroutine queries accessing computer menus that summarize plan policies and provisions. This automated environment can electronically monitor telephone volume so that managers can reallocate service center human resources at

12. Rod Zolkos, "System Update Costs Overwhelm Benefit Departments," *Business Insurance*, Vol. 29, No. 10, March 6, 1995, pp. 3, 6.

high-volume times. This customer service delivery approach is the model used by consulting firms to administer a variety of plans that have been outsourced from multiple firms.

Despite the level of administrative delegation, the employer providing the benefits program is still considered the plan sponsor and will continue to retain the legal responsibilities related to plan sponsorship under federal law. Application of state insurance laws can vary, depending on whether a program is being provided as an insured arrangement through an insurance company, is self-funded, or is a contracted administrative-services type of contract. Therefore, selection of a service provider and whether the organization retains or outsources administration can determine regulatory requirements and jurisdiction. This should be considered when choosing the appropriate administrative alternative. These issues are more complex within the multinational and truly global organization because of varied national insurance regulations, the ability to leverage financial and underwriting approaches across national boundaries, and the human resource issues of staff transfers between operating companies within different countries and the extent to which similar benefit structures will encourage or impede workforce mobility. In short, larger organizations have more alternatives, and often these alternatives have implications that are interwoven with other strategic considerations for the firm.

Decisions on whether to outsource the employee benefits administrative function can be quite different across various benefit programs as well. For instance, a national organization with a geographically dispersed workforce may find it advantageous to contract with a large managed care provider who in turn contracts with local and regional medical care providers. However, the same employer may find that it is more efficient to retain as an internal function the administration of a defined benefit pension plan because it is not subject to the same degree of regional difference and local market specialization.

SUMMARY AND CONCLUSIONS

Administering employee benefit plans is a multifaceted discipline that integrates broad managerial skills and thinking with a high level of technical expertise in a variety of specialty areas. Whether the majority of benefits management activities are retained within the organization or outsourced, benefits management almost always includes coordinating with other departments and groups, necessitating leadership, team-building, and project management skills. The scope and nature of the internal organizational benefits plan function is contingent on both the organization's internal capabilities and the availability of external services. There are certain core activities and compliance requirements inherent in plan sponsorship. Management should clearly understand how these activities are affected by the rapidly changing and dynamic environmental context in which benefits plan management operates.

BIBLIOGRAPHY

Allen, Everett T., Jr., Joseph J. Melone, Jerry S. Rosenbloom, and Dennis Mahoney, *Retirement Plans*, 10th ed., New York: McGraw-Hill/Irwin, 2008.

Aon Consulting, "The 'Captivation' of Employee Benefits," June 2010.

APPWP, Health Notes, September 15, 2000.

APPWP, Pension Notes, September 15, 2000.

Cheiron Consulting, "Healthcare Reform: The New Paradigm for America's Healthcare Financing," Summer 2010.

Frost, Karen, Dale Gifford, Christine Seltz, and Ken Sperling, *Fundamentals of Flexible Compensation*, New York: Wiley, 1993.

Hewitt Associates, "Employers to Face Double Digit Health Care Cost Increases for Third Consecutive Year," October 23, 2000.

Hewitt Associates, "On Flexible Compensation," January–February 1993.

Hewitt Associates, *Washington Status Report*, Vol. 10, No. 41, October 10, 1994.

Morgan Lewis, "Interim Final Rules Released on Preexisting Condition Exclusions, Lifetime and Annual Limits, Rescissions, Patient Protections, and Preventive Care," *Washington Government Relations and Public Policy Lawflash*, July 23, 2010.

Patterson Belknap Webb & Tyler, "Navigating National Health Care Reform: What Every Employer Should Know," *Employee Benefits and Executive Compensation Alert*, April 2010.

Pemberton, Carolyn and Deborah Holmes, eds., *EBRI Databook on Employee Benefits*, 3rd ed., Washington, DC: Education and Research Fund, 1995.

Schultz, Ellen E., "State Street Enters the Benefits Business," *Wall Street Journal*, December 7, 1995.

Seyfarth Shaw LLP, "HIPPAA HITECH Regulations Proposed," *Management Alert*, July 29, 2010.

Shutan, Bruce, "Fidelity Pursuit Changing Face of 'Total' Benefits Outsourcing," *Employee Benefit News*, Vol. 9, No. 5, May 1995.

Stright, Jay F., Jr., "The Revolution in Benefit Technology," Presentation at Employee Benefits Symposium, San Francisco, October 8–11, 1995.

Towers Perrin, "Congress Home for the Holidays—Wraps Up Budget Bill and Catastrophic Repeal; IRS Extends Qualified Plan Relief," *TPF&C Update*, November 1989.

Towers Perrin, "Employers Seeking People Strategies for Their E-Business," April 2000.

Towers Perrin, "The Nondiscrimination Rules: They're Finally Final," *TPF&C Update*, September 1991.

Truhlar, Gary, "Information Management Principles and Tools," Internal Memos, University of Pennsylvania, 1994–1995.

U.S. Department of Labor, *General Facts on Women & Job-Based Health Benefits*, April 2000.

U.S. Department of Labor, In Brief: 1999 Form 5500, February 2000.

Zolkos, Rod, "System Update Costs Overwhelm Benefit Departments," *Business Insurance*, Vol. 29, No. 10, March 6, 1995.

CHAPTER 25

Cafeteria Plan Design and Administration

Amy L. Cavanaugh

With the ever-increasing costs of benefits requiring employers to pass more of the benefit expense to employees, some form of cafeteria plan has become a standard benefit offering to today's employees. Through a cafeteria plan an employer can offer employees with vastly differing benefits needs some flexibility with respect to optional or supplemental benefit choices in addition to enabling them to pay for the benefits with pre-tax dollars. Allowing employees to select the benefits most appropriate to their personal needs and financial circumstances makes good sense for employers because it assures that the employer maximizes the value of its benefit dollars and avoids spending money on duplicated of unneeded benefits.

Billions of dollars are spent annually through flexible spending accounts (FSAs) funded through a combination of employer contributions and employee pretax contributions. In 2009, 20.4 percent of workers with employer-sponsored health insurance had health care FSAs for medical expenses, according to the Centers for Disease Control and Prevention (CDC), and even more pay for employee-paid health insurance expense on a tax-favored basis via participation in a full-flex cafeteria plan.

Cafeteria plans operate as an exception to the tax doctrine of constructive receipt. Usually, when an individual has control over how his or her money is spent, it becomes taxable to that individual. However, provided a cafeteria plan is designed in accordance with all applicable tax laws, a plan participant can avoid taxation and instead receive tax-free benefits. This concept is addressed in more detail later in the chapter.

With respect to plan design, cafeteria plans are as diverse as today's workforce. Plan design ranges from employee-pay-all/premium conversion plans, where the only benefit offered under the plan is the ability to pay employee-pay-all premium expense on a pretax basis, to full-flex arrangements where employees are offered a full range of benefit modules and credits from which to select. Regardless of whether a plan is a simple premium conversion plan or a more complex full-flex plan, all cafeteria plans are governed by the same general set of rules. These rules are set forth under Internal Revenue Code (IRC, or Code) Section 125 and the regulations promulgated thereunder. In addition, certain benefit offerings are subject to the Code sections applicable to the specific benefit.

The larger the employer, the more likely it is that it will sponsor a cafeteria plan and will select a sophisticated design. Recent studies have shown that almost one-third of employers with 1,000 or more employees offer a cafeteria plan that includes various benefit offerings including FSAs. Many more employers make available cafeteria plans offering premium conversion. While the smallest of employers can face significant constraints when they try to implement a traditional cafeteria plan because of nondiscrimination testing requirements as well as certain expense exposure, most can still benefit from establishing such a program. (The simple cafeteria plan that the Patient Protection and Affordable Care Act of 2010 established for small employers is discussed in detail starting on page 714.)

The purpose of this chapter is to provide a historical overview of the evolution of cafeteria plans as well as a general overview of the rules under which all cafeteria plans must operate. Understanding the history of cafeteria plans from a legislative and regulatory perspective is essential to being able to properly design and administer cafeteria plans.

CAFETERIA PLANS IN GENERAL

The first concept essential to understanding the overall operation of a cafeteria plan is that the plan is really an umbrella plan under which other tax-favored employee benefits are offered. A cafeteria plan is merely a mechanism to pay for employee benefits that ultimately provides tax savings. For this reason, Code Section 125 and the regulations related thereto govern cafeteria plan arrangements, and other Code sections apply to the underlying benefits funded within a cafeteria plan.

Code Section 125 was added to the IRC by the Revenue Act of 1978. Prior to the enactment of Code Section 125, if a participant had any type of choice with respect to available benefits, the tax doctrine of constructive receipt mandated that the participant be taxed as if he or she had elected the maximum available taxable benefits. The rationale was that since participants could elect these amounts in cash, they should be taxed as if they had elected the cash. This was the case even if the participants elected benefits that, if paid for by the employer, could be offered to participants on a tax-free basis.

The addition of Code Section 125 significantly changed this tax treatment by providing favorable tax treatment to certain benefits funded through a cafeteria plan. Code Section 125 specifically defines a cafeteria plan to mean a plan under which all participants are employees and under which all participants may choose among two or more benefits consisting of a combination of qualified benefits and cash. It is important to note that only certain employee benefits can be offered under a cafeteria plan. Long-term care, whole-life insurance, transportation benefits, and education reimbursement plans are not permissible benefits under a cafeteria plan. There is also a special rule under Code Section 125 that prohibits the deferral of compensation using a cafeteria plan with a very few exceptions. Among the permissible contributions are those to a 401(k) plan and a health savings account (HSA).

ADVANTAGES AND DISADVANTAGES OF CAFETERIA PLANS

Cafeteria plans offer significant benefits to employers and employees alike. These benefits include significant tax savings as well as maximizing the overall value of employer and employee benefit dollars. There are also certain considerations that could be perceived as disadvantages. It is important to review the disadvantages of plan sponsorship both in the decision of whether or not to sponsor a cafeteria plan as well as in what benefits to offer under the plan. Specific advantages and disadvantages are discussed below.

Advantages and Disadvantages to the Employee

Employees who participate in a cafeteria plan directly save money because they can pay for their share of benefit expenses on a tax-favored basis. The contributions to a cafeteria plan are exempt from federal income tax, and they are not subject to the Federal Insurance Contribution Act (FICA) or the Federal Unemployment Tax Act (FUTA) taxes. Most state and local tax laws follow the federal tax treatment, but this is not always the case. For this reason, the plan sponsor will have to make a determination as to whether or not contributions are exempt from state and local taxes.

From an employee perspective, the primary disadvantage of a cafeteria plan is the requirement that all benefit elections must be made prior to the beginning of the plan year and, with limited exception, the elections are irrevocable during the entire period of coverage. Another significant disadvantage that applies to FSAs is the "use lose it" rule. This means benefit dollars unused at the end of the plan year, with limited exception, are forfeited. However, proper planning and education can reduce the probability that an employee will forfeit contributions at the end of the year.

Another potential disadvantage of cafeteria plans exists when an employee may be better off financially by taking the tax credit on his or her personal tax return as opposed to contributing to a cafeteria plan with respect to certain benefits offered under the plan. Lastly, since there is no FICA tax on cafeteria plan benefit dollars, an employee who participates in a cafeteria plan may realize a slight reduction in Social Security benefits or in the accumulation for his or her employer-sponsored retirement plan.

Advantages and Disadvantages to the Employer

There are also advantages and disadvantages to sponsoring a cafeteria plan for the employer. First, there are significant financial incentives because of the payroll cost savings realized from the employer not paying FICA or FUTA tax on amounts contributed to the cafeteria plan. Additionally, deferral amounts are not considered wages for purposes of determining workers' compensation premiums and other payroll-based expenses. State and local tax treatment varies from state to state, with most states mirroring the federal treatment. Qualified retirement plans can be designed to either consider or not consider cafeteria plan contributions for purposes of contributions to the plan.

From an employee relations perspective, the required involvement in selecting benefits under a cafeteria plans helps employees conceptualize the overall value of their benefits. It is difficult for employees to fully appreciate the value of benefits when benefits are delivered in a traditional manner (i.e., employer-paid-all plans); benefits become an entitlement as opposed to a component of a total compensation package. A cafeteria plan also serves as a mechanism to contain health care costs and prevent squandering benefit dollars on duplicate or unneeded benefits.

For example, an employee who is single may have little need for life insurance, and in dual-income couples there is often duplication in benefit coverage. Given the exorbitant costs of health care, it is important to assure that benefit dollars reap maximum value. Because of cost increases, more and more employers continue to shift some or all of these cost increases to employees. At the same time, workers have varying needs, and a one-size-fits-all approach to benefits is no longer acceptable. A cafeteria plan offers a mechanism to address both cost containment and benefit optimization.

In recent years, there has been a shift towards consumer-driven or consumer-directed health care. This is the concept of making benefit consumers (insured employees) take a more active role in controlling benefit costs by offering options. In a traditional health care environment, employees are not offered any incentive to make wise consumer-based benefit decisions—the more they use their health care coverage, the more value they perceive to receive for their investment. A cafeteria plan is a form of consumer-driven health care; employees invest and make choices based on their expected needs. To the extent an employer is considering implementing benefit changes that will result in employees sharing more of the cost, a cafeteria plan is an excellent tool to minimize the financial impact of that shift.

Despite the many advantages of sponsoring a cafeteria plan, employers should be aware of the potential disadvantages. First, there are ongoing costs associated with the administration and operation of the plan. In many cases, the payroll-tax savings the employer gains will far outweigh the plan's operational costs. Nevertheless, an employer must be aware that there are costs involved in establishing and operating the plan. Also, a cafeteria plan is required to be operated in accordance with strict adherence to federal tax law through a written plan document.

In addition, if the cafeteria plan includes a medical reimbursement feature (a health care FSA), the uniform coverage rules require the full amount of benefit elected to be available during the entire plan year regardless of how much an employee has actually contributed to date. This means that the employer assumes a certain degree of financial risk with respect to elected benefits. For example, if an employee elects $1,000 of coverage in his or her medical reimbursement account, this total amount is typically contributed ratably over the period of coverage, but if the employee incurs a medical expense of $600 at the time there is only $400 in the participant's account, the employer would need to pay the employee the full $600, which means it would need to pay $200 of this $600 claim out of employer assets.

Also, there are potential problems associated with adverse selection on the part of plan participants. This adverse selection could result in underwriting problems. For example, if all the unhealthy participants select the best insurance and all the healthy participants select minimum or no health coverage, the overall employer cost of coverage may increase since utilization will increase in certain health plans. Also, employees may view with negativity and scepticism a shift to using a cafeteria plan as a mechanism for benefit delivery, especially if it is introduced at the same time as benefit cutbacks or cost increases.

Lastly, cafeteria plans are subject to complex coverage and nondiscrimination testing; some of these tests apply to the cafeteria plan as a whole, while others apply to the underlying benefits. Depending on the demographics of the workforce, some of these tests may be difficult to pass, in which case the favorable tax treatment could be sacrificed with respect to owners and other highly paid employees.

TYPES OF CAFETERIA PLANS

There are several different types of cafeteria plans. Code Section 125 uses the term "cafeteria plan" to describe all of these types of arrangements. Cafeteria plans were given their name because benefits are offered up cafeteria style and plan participants select the benefits they need. These optional benefits are purchased with dollars or credits given to the participant as part of a benefit package. In some instances, employees are not given any employer money to spend, but can enhance their overall benefit package by making tax-favored contributions to the cafeteria plan that can be spent on additional benefits that are tax-free when paid out to the participant. Benefit selection becomes a combination of need and budget.

Cafeteria plans are also referred to as flexible benefit programs, flexible compensation, choice plans, and flex plans. A plan that includes only pretax premium conversion is generally referred to as a premium conversion plan or premium-only plan (POP). While the many different types of cafeteria plans differ in complexity, at their core they are similar in that employees use the plan as a vehicle for obtaining selected employee benefits on a tax-favored basis.

Premium Conversion Plans

A premium conversion plan is a cafeteria plan in its simplest form. Generally, in this type of cafeteria plan, there are no employer contributions and the plan is offered to employees so that they may pay for their employee-paid insurance costs on a tax-favored basis. A cafeteria plan is the only mechanism that can be used to accomplish this. In the absence of a written cafeteria plan, the tax-free treatment of premium payments paid by the employee will be disallowed.

For example, an employer may pay the full cost of single medical insurance coverage but nothing for family medical insurance coverage or dental insurance. Assume that family medical insurance coverage and dental coverage costs $400 a month. If the employer did not have a cafeteria plan, the employee would have to pay that $400 a month on an after-tax basis. In a cafeteria plan, the employee would elect to reduce his or her salary by $400 a month that would be contributed to a cafeteria plan and used to pay for the employee's share of the overall premium expense.

If an employer is going to offer employees the ability to opt out of employer-paid insurance coverage, this must also be done through a cash option within a cafeteria plan. In a case like this, the employer would contribute to the cafeteria plan the employer cost of insured benefits. Employees would then elect whether or not they want coverage. To the extent they elect coverage, their salary would be deferred to the extent the employer contribution is insufficient to fund the benefits elected.

For the employee who does not want or need insurance coverage, he or she would elect the cash benefit, in which case the employer's contribution would be paid to the employee as cash compensation (at which point any favorable tax treatment is lost). The employer does not need to offer a dollar-for-dollar cash option.

For example, assume that the employer wants employees to have the ability to opt out of medical insurance coverage if the employees do not need the coverage. If the employer does not want to offer a big incentive, it could offer employees a stated percentage of the cost of benefits or some lesser dollar value to the extent employees elect not to take the insurance coverage.

As a general rule, a premium conversion feature is used only for medical insurance (including dental, vision, and other types of health care coverage) and group term life insurance not in excess of $50,000. In some instances, the plan may provide that outside, employee-owned policies can be paid for through the premium conversion feature provided that the insurance is not from another employer-sponsored plan (such as one provided by the spouse's employer). While disability income premiums can by law be paid through a premium conversion feature, it is important to note that if the premium payments are tax-free, any disability income benefits will be taxed when they are received. Considering the relatively low cost of disability income coverage, most employees prefer to pay disability income premiums with after-tax dollars and receive any benefits they may receive on a tax-free basis.

Flexible Spending Accounts

Another type of cafeteria plan is one that includes flexible spending accounts (FSAs). FSAs are also referred to as reimbursement accounts. Generally, these accounts are bookkeeping accounts, with the funds remaining part of the employer's general assets. Records are maintained to show each participant's account activity. When an FSA is funded purely by salary deferrals, the participant effectively exercises a choice between two or more benefits consisting of cash and qualified benefits.

FSAs are permitted for medical reimbursements, dependent care assistance and adoption assistance. While cafeteria plans covering these types of expenses generally include a premium conversion feature, they may also include FSAs to deal with them. FSAs offer an employee the ability to fund certain qualified benefits on a pretax basis through a salary-reduction agreement or a combination of salary reductions and employer contributions. The participant must specifically earmark how much will go towards the health care FSA and how much to the dependent care assistance. (Adoption-assistance programs are employer-paid plans.) Throughout the plan year, as the participant or his or her dependents incur covered expenses, he or she submits to the plan claims for reimbursement. The period of coverage for an FSA is 12 months, except when a short plan year is permitted in the first plan year or when the plan is being changed. A short plan year (or a change in plan year resulting in a short plan year) is permitted only for a valid business purpose. A change in plan year resulting in a short plan year, for other than a valid business purpose, is disregarded. If a principal purpose of a change in plan year is to circumvent the rules of Section 125, the change in plan year is ineffective. (Employers are permitted to adopt a grace period of up to two-and-a-half months after the end of the plan year for employees to access FSA funds unused during the plan year.)

The source of funding in a cafeteria plan with FSAs is usually salary reductions. In a salary-reduction FSA, a participant's salary reductions are credited to a reimbursement account, and benefits are paid from this account. The specific operation of cafeteria plans that include FSAs will be discussed later in the chapter.

Full-flex Plans

The final category of cafeteria plan is a full-flex plan. These plans are also known as a full-choice plans. As the name implies, this type of plan gives participants the opportunity to select from among a full range of benefits.

In a full-flex plan, the employer determines a dollar value it wishes to earmark for benefits, which is in addition to any employee salary reductions made by the participants. Based on that election, either the cash is contributed to the cafeteria plan or a credit system is established and used to fund the cost of benefits.

The key to developing a credit methodology is understanding the appropriate pricing parameters of the benefits offered under the plan and developing a pricing matrix. The pricing matrix is designed to take into consideration a number of factors, including the number of credits a participant will be given, the acceptable level of employee contribution, the number of participants expected to select each benefit offered, the number of credits expected to be paid in the form of cash, the purchase price of benefit options, and the hidden employer subsidies and the total premium cost.

Generally it is advantageous for an employer to express its contribution toward benefits as credits rather than dollars. The credit system can serve to smooth out perceived benefit inequities, and not divulging the true benefit costs makes it possible for the employer to offer a cash option that is not a dollar-for-dollar value, making the benefits more attractive than the cash. It is rare that an employer will want to give a participant who is electing cash an amount equal to the full cash value of the benefits, because it will be too attractive to the participant and result in employees being underinsured. Once the credits have been established, a participant shops for the benefits he or she needs, supplementing the credits with salary deferrals. Some full-flex plans are designed to offer participants different packages of benefits. There may be a core level of benefits offered to all participants plus a second layer of optional benefits from which participants have a choice. The core benefits may require that the participant select some form of basic health coverage where there is no cash incentive for opting out.

Depending on the plan design, there could be a traditional indemnity policy, a preferred provider organization (PPO), a health maintenance organization (HMO), or a high-deductible plan. Another variation of this type of plan would be a modular plan where there are several predesigned packages of benefits. Typically, at least one of the packages involves no additional participant cost. Through salary reductions, the participant can buy additional benefits that may be needed or desired.

PLAN DESIGN

It is important that the design of a cafeteria plan reflect the demographics of the employer and the corporate culture with respect to benefits and that the benefits be financially suited to the employer and the employees. Because success of a cafeteria plan depends on participation, it may be useful to survey employees before establishing one. This is especially true if the plan is going to include spending accounts in addition to premium conversion. Low levels of participation will defeat the purpose of establishing the plan and perhaps cause the plan to not pass required nondiscrimination testing. Therefore, educating employees to make reasonable elections is important. The type of cafeteria plan an employer offers depends on the employees who will participate. Lower-paid employees are not that interested in tax savings; rather, they like to maximize their weekly take-home pay. If an employer's demographics consist largely of low-paid workers, a full-flex plan with a generous cash option might probably result in employees not being adequately protected. The organization will need to come to terms with the level of moral and legal obligation they feel comfortable with, recognizing that some employees could face serious financial injury as a result of a decision in favor of immediate cash payment.

To address these types of issues, employers may wish to minimize the available cash, or mandate certain core levels of benefits. When designing a cafeteria plan, it is often prudent to start with a basic premium conversion feature and then add more sophisticated plan designs such as FSAs and eventually a full-flex type of design as employees become more comfortable with the concept. This type of plan design approach assures a basic level of coverage with the opportunity for additional tax savings and protection.

When establishing a cafeteria plan, the employer must be prepared for negative employee reactions. Employees may be skeptical of the real reason behind the implementation of this new benefit. The idea of reducing current pay in anticipation of benefits payable in the future can be unsettling to some employees, especially since these assets are not held in trust as are those in a retirement plan. Without proper communication including adequate time for questions and answers, the employees could view the cafeteria plan as a way for their employer to pay them less. The key to overcoming this potential adversity is a carefully crafted communication program that includes both the positives and negatives of plan participation. However, if during the implementation phase, employee input is solicited, the plan should be tailored to meet the needs of the employees and reflect their suggestions and input.

GOVERNING LAW

Because of the special tax treatment given to the contributions made to and the benefits paid from a cafeteria plan, the Internal Revenue Service (IRS) governs cafeteria plans. In general, cafeteria plans are classified as specified fringe benefit plans under Code Section 6039D and must meet specific requirements of that section in order that plan contributions and distributions are tax favored.

A cafeteria plan itself is not governed by the Employee Retirement Income Security Act (ERISA), because it is not classified as a welfare benefit plan under ERISA Section 3. However, some of the underlying benefits that are funded through a cafeteria plan may be subject to ERISA because they are considered to be welfare benefit plans. ERISA Section 3 defines a welfare benefit plan as any plan, fund, or program that is established or maintained by an employer or employee organization for the purposes of providing participants' or beneficiaries' medical, surgical, or hospital care or benefits in the event of sickness, accident, disability, death, or unemployment.

In addition, benefits for vacation, apprenticeship or other training programs, daycare centers, scholarship funds, or prepaid legal services are considered welfare benefits. As mentioned earlier, not all welfare benefit plans can be funded through a cafeteria plan.

For this reason, cafeteria plans that include welfare benefits are subject to ERISA. In addition to complying with applicable sections of the IRC and ERISA, certain benefits funded through a cafeteria plan are subject to other employment laws, specifically the following:

- The Consolidated Omnibus Budget Reconciliation Act of 1985 (COBRA)
- The Family and Medical Leave Act of 1993 (FMLA)
- The Health Insurance Portability and Accountability Act of 1996 (HIPAA)
- The Mental Health Parity Act of 1996 (MHPA)
- The Newborns' and Mothers' Health Protection Act of 1996 (NMHPA)
- The Women's Health and Cancer Rights Act of 1998 (WHCRA)
- The Medicare Prescription Drug, Improvement, and Modernization Act of 2003 (MPDIMA)
- The Working Families Tax Relief Act of 2004 (WFTRA)
- Heroes Earnings Assistance and Relief Tax Act of 2008 (HEART Act)
- Michelle's Law (H.R. 2851)
- Mental Health Parity and Addiction Equity Act of 2008

- Genetic Information Nondiscrimination Act of 2008 (GINA)
- Patient Protection and Affordable Care Act of 2010 (PPACA)

The specific application of these other benefit laws depends on what benefits are funded through the cafeteria plan. For example, if a cafeteria plan offers only premium conversion, these other benefit laws will not apply directly to the cafeteria plan but rather to the policies purchased with the cafeteria plan dollars. In other words, the cafeteria plan will not need to conform to these rules but the policies paid for from the plan will need to be in compliance.

For example, because of new Federal Trade Commission (FTC) Red Flag Rules, cafeteria plans that issue a debit card to pay for medical expenses should adopt policies and procedures to identify and prevent instances of identity theft. In general, the plan administrator should make sure that the business that issues the debit card account complies with these rules. Companies subject to the Red Flag Rules were required to comply by November 1, 2009.

FTC guidelines set forth four specific areas of compliance. The issuing agency must establish reasonable policies and procedures first to identify the "red flags" of identity theft that the entity may come across during the entity's day-to-day operations. Red flags are specific activities, patterns, or practices that indicate the possibility of identity theft. For example, the entity may identify the use of a fake ID by a customer as a red flag. In addition, the identification program must be designed to detect the red flags that the entity has identified. For example, the entity may have a procedure in place to detect possible fake IDs. Then, the entity must set forth the actions that will be taken when red flags are detected. Lastly, these policies and procedures should be periodically reviewed and modified as appropriate.

Both the IRS and the Department of Labor (DOL) periodically release regulations that offer specific guidance as to how to design and operate cafeteria plans. These regulations come in a number of formats, including temporary regulations, proposed regulations, and final regulations.

Temporary regulations are designed to address specific issues and are generally short in duration. Proposed regulations are released in order to give practitioners a good indication as to how the agency intends to govern a specific situation. Proposed regulations are usually released with the intent that they are commented on by the industry. Based on those comments, changes may be made, at which point final regulations are issued.

Additionally, from time to time, the IRS releases Revenue Rulings, Revenue Procedures, Announcements, and Notices, each designed to address specific matters of plan design or operation.

If an employer has a specific issue that is not addressed by the regulations or other IRS releases, the employer can apply for a Private Letter Ruling. The IRS charges a fee for a Private Letter Ruling and the ruling is only valid for the party that requested it. Nonetheless, the rulings are usually published so that other employers may get a general idea how the IRS would rule under similar circumstances.

Lastly, an important component with respect to operational guidance for cafeteria plans is case law. To the extent there is a dispute between an employer and the IRS or DOL, the result may be litigation in either the tax court or the federal district court. The outcome of a trial forms another body of law that can be relied on not just by the party involved, but by other employers as well.

HISTORICAL EVOLUTION OF CAFETERIA PLANS

In order to understand how cafeteria plans operate, it is essential to be familiar with the historical evolution of the laws that apply to them. In 1978, Code Section 125 was added to the IRC and amended many times over the years as summarized in the next section. There are other Code sections that apply to cafeteria plans. These include the following:

- Code Section 79—Group Term Life Insurance
- Code Section 105—Accident and Health Insurance
- Code Section 129—Dependent care assistance
- Code Section 151—Deductions of Personal Exemptions
- Code Section 152—Definition of Dependent
- Code Section 223—Health Savings Accounts
- Code Section 318—Constructive Ownership of Stock
- Code Section 414—Controlled Group Definitions
- Code Section 1372—Partnership Rules to Apply for Fringe Benefit Purposes
- Code Section 3121—Definition of FICA
- Code Section 3306—Definition of FUTA
- Code Section 3401(a)—Definition of Income Subject to Withholding
- Code Section 5000—Certain Group Health Plans

Regulatory History

Over the years, the Treasury Department, in conjunction with the IRS, has issued proposed, temporary, and final regulations that interpret the provisions of Code Section 125. The following is a general overview of the regulations released with respect to Code Section 125 since it was enacted in 1978:

- On May 7, 1984, Proposed Regulations 1.125-1 were published in question and answer format. The primary concept set forth in these initial regulations was "use it or lose it." This means that a participant could not carry forward unused cafeteria plan benefit dollars from one plan year to the next. This was the first indication from the IRS that in order to be entitled to favorable tax treatment, there needed to be a certain elements of risk, similar to what could be found in an insured benefit.
- Certain corrections were made to the original proposed regulations on December 31, 1984. These were released in proposed form.
- Temporary Regulations were issued on February 4, 1986 that specifically defined the benefits that could be offered under a cafeteria plan (Temp. Treas. Reg. Section 1.125-2T).
- On March 7, 1989, more proposed regulations were published (Prop. Treas. Reg 1. 125-2). These regulations went one step further by requiring that cafeteria plan spending accounts operate in a manner similar to insurance coverage in that the regulations introduced the concept of "uniform coverage" for health care FSAs. In addition, they added new claims substantiation requirements.
- On November 7, 1997, Temporary Regulation 1.125-4T was issued addressing the mechanics of changing benefit elections due to certain changes in status.
- On March 23, 2000, the temporary regulations issued in 1997 were revised, expanded, and finalized. Simultaneously, proposed regulations were released that expanded changes in cost and coverage rules.
- On January 10, 2001, final guidance was issued with respect to changes to benefit elections outside of the open enrollment period.
- On October 17, 2001, final regulations were issued with respect to the correlation between cafeteria plans and the Family and

Medical Leave Act that provide specific guidance with respect to cafeteria plan administration during a period of approved family leave.

- Released on May 6, 2003, Revenue Ruling 2003-43 stated that, to the extent an FSA issued a debit card to pay for medical expenses, all over-the-counter (OTC) medicines and drugs to the extent reimbursable would need to be purchased at a pharmacy as opposed to a nonpharmacy retailer such as a grocery store. In addition, all such purchases would require a paper receipt.
- On June 6, 2005, IRS Notice 2005-42 modified the application of the rule prohibiting deferred compensation after the end of a plan year under a Section 125 plan by permitting a plan to be designed to include a grace period immediately following the end of each plan year during which unused benefits or contributions remaining at the end of the plan year may be used to pay qualified expenses incurred during the grace period. For purposes of applying this rule, the grace period can be no longer than 2 1/2 months after the close of the plan year.
- On November 22, 2005, IRS Notice 2005-86 allowed for the coordination of the grace period discussed in Notice 2005-42 with the eligibility to participate in an HSA during the grace period.
- Enacted on December 20, 2006, the Health Opportunity Patient Empowerment Act of 2006, Public Law 109-432 (120 Stat. 2922 (2006) allowed "qualified health savings account distributions" to be made from health FSAs to HSAs.
- In July 2006, IRS Notice 2006-69 established a procedure for using debit cards for health care expenses at any nonpharmacy retailer selling over-the-counter medications using the Inventory Information Approval System (IIAS).
- In 2007, the IRS issued Proposed Regulations on Section 125 plans. It was expected that the proposed regulations would be finalized in 2008. However, they were delayed by the health care debate and the proposed regulations may be relied upon for now.
- On September 29, 2008, the IRS released Notice 2008-82 which provides guidance allowing qualified reservists distributions (QRDs) of unused amounts in a health care FSA to reservists ordered or called to active duty.

- In 2010, the PPACA revised the definition of medical expense. The details are discussed in the Health Care Flexible Spending Account section later in this chapter.
- On December 27, 2010, the IRS released Notice 2011-5 which offers additional circumstances under which health FSA and HRA debit cards can be used to purchase over-the-counter (OTC) medicines or drugs obtained with a prescription, as required under PPACA.
- Issued on April 22, 2010, IRS Notice 2010-38 states that the IRS is amending the change-of-election regulations to allow changes in elections for events affecting adult children's eligibility, whether or not they are tax dependents. The IRS also allowed amendments to cafeteria plans to allow such changes of election, retroactive to when the plan started, allowing such changes as long as the amendment was adopted by December 31, 2010.

GENERAL LEGAL REQUIREMENTS

In order for a cafeteria plan to be afforded favorable tax treatment, the plan must be operated in accordance with a written benefit plan maintained by an employer primarily for the benefit of its employees. The plan must allow participants to choose between two or more benefits consisting of cash (or a taxable benefit that is treated as cash) and qualified benefits. A plan cannot be designed to offer only a choice among qualified benefits, without the cash or cash-equivalent component. Without the cash component, the plan is not a cafeteria plan. A salary-reduction agreement is sufficient to satisfy the cash requirement. If a participant wanted to elect cash in a salary-reduction-only cafeteria plan, he or she would elect not to reduce his or her salary, thus receiving his or her total compensation in cash. The proposed cafeteria plan regulations provide that, while a choice between taxable and nontaxable benefits is permitted under cafeteria plans, plans may not offer taxable benefits other than those explicitly defined in the regulations; nor may they offer nonqualified benefits (such as dependent group term life insurance or education assistance). The proposed regulations are clear that plan designs that combine a cafeteria plan with elements of other health and welfare benefits should not be offered in a single document.

In order for the plan to be considered qualified with respect to its written form, certain requirements must be satisfied. A new plan must be adopted and effective *on or before* the first day of the cafeteria plan year. The written plan must include the following provisions:

1. A specific description of each benefit available under the plan and the period of coverage applicable to each. This description is not required to be within the cafeteria plan; rather, the cafeteria plan could make reference to other documents.
2. The rules governing employees' eligibility and participation. The proposed regulations provide an extensive definition of "employee" and only permit nonemployee participants in limited circumstances.
3. The procedures for making participant elections under the plan, including when elections may be made, rules governing the irrevocability of elections, and the period of coverage for which elections are effective.
4. The manner in which contributions may be made, such as via a salary reduction agreement between the employer and employee, nonelective employer contributions, or a combination of both
5. The maximum amount of employer contributions available to any participant. To meet this requirement, the plan must describe the maximum amount of elective contributions available to any participant either by stating the maximum dollar amount or the maximum percentage of compensation that may be contributed as elective contributions or by stating the method for determining the maximum amount or percentage of elective contributions that a participant may make.
6. The plan year.

Under a new rule set forth in the proposed regulations, the *nondiscrimination testing rules* must be described in the plan, as must any optional administrative features utilized by sponsoring employers, such as grace periods or run-out periods. In addition, cafeteria plans that offer FSAs or the purchase or sale of paid time off have additional documentation requirements under the proposed regulations. Additionally, if a cafeteria plan is considered to have welfare benefit plans, a claims provision that satisfies ERISA must be included. For such a purpose, underlying welfare benefits include medical, disability, death, and vacation benefits.

If the plan includes a health care reimbursement account, the plan must include specific language addressing the uniform-coverage rule and the use-it-or-lose-it-rule. Under the 2007 proposed regulations, a cafeteria plan must make specific reference to the fact that only employees may participate in the cafeteria plan and that all provisions of the written plan apply uniformly to all participants.

From time to time, plan amendments may be needed. Plan amendments are either required by law or a result of desired plan redesign or additional benefit offerings. The amendments must be in writing and may only be effective for periods *after the later of* the adoption date or the effective date of the amendment. If an amendment adds a new benefit, the plan can only reimburse expenses for the new benefit incurred after the later of the amendment's adoption or effective date.

Qualified Benefits in a Cafeteria Plan

Qualified benefits that can be offered in a cafeteria plan include the following:

1. Employer-provided accident or health coverage under Sections 105 and 106. This includes health, medical, hospitalization coverage, prescription plans, drugs, dental and vision programs, disability income insurance, and coverage under an accidental death and dismemberment policy. In addition, business travel accident plan, hospital indemnity or cancer policies, and Medicare supplements can be funded, as can short- and long-term disability (although, as already discussed, there are good reasons to fund disability policies outside of the cafeteria plan). It also includes reimbursement for health care expenses under a health care FSA. Looking ahead, health plans offered through an exchange are not a qualified benefit in a cafeteria plan. These rules are expected to apply starting in 2014 once the PPACA is fully implemented.
2. Individually owned accident or health insurance policies may be offered under a cafeteria plan, provided that the employer requires an accounting to insure that the health insurance is in force and is being paid by the employees. The plan may not reimburse the health insurance premiums under a health care FSA, nor may it reimburse policies maintained by another employer.
3. Employer-provided group term life insurance coverage excludable from income under Section 79 or includible in income

solely because the benefit exceeds the $50,000 limit of Section 79. Only the first $50,000 of coverage is nontaxable; income is imputed on amounts in excess of $50,000. Dependent group term life insurance may not be included in a cafeteria plan if the benefit is eligible for exclusion under Code Section 132.

4. Employer-provided dependent care assistance under Code Section 129.
5. Employer-provided adoption assistance under Code Section 137.
6. A 401(k) plan or purchase of retiree group term life insurance by participants employed by certain educational institutions described in Code Section 170(b)(l)(A)(ii).
7. Contributions to an HSA under Code Section 223.

Some benefits paid through a cafeteria plan are taxable benefits. A taxable benefit is a benefit that results in taxable income for the employee when it is received and a tax deduction for the employer when it is paid. The most common taxable benefit is cash; however, paid time off and group term life insurance in excess of $50,000 are examples of taxable benefits that can be paid from a cafeteria plan.

The 2007 proposed regulations allow a cafeteria plan to offer after-tax employee contributions for qualified benefits or paid time off. A cafeteria plan may only offer the taxable benefits specifically permitted in the new proposed regulations. A cafeteria plan is not required to allow employees to pay for any qualified benefit with after-tax employee contributions. Nonqualified benefits as described below may not be offered through a cafeteria plan, even if paid with after-tax employee contributions:

1. Contributions to medical savings accounts under Code Section 106(b)
2. Qualified scholarships under Code Section 117
3. Educational assistance programs under Code Section 127
4. Certain fringe benefits under Code Section 132
5. Qualified long-term care insurance under Code Section 7702B. (An HSA funded through a cafeteria plan may, however, be used to pay premiums for long-term care insurance or long-term care services.)
6. Archer medical savings accounts

7. Athletic facilities
8. *De minimis* (minimal) benefits
9. Dependent life insurance
10. Employee discounts
11. Lodging on the business premises
12. Meals
13. Moving expense reimbursements
14. No-additional-cost services
15. Parking and mass transit reimbursement
16. Contributions to a Code Section 529 college savings account
17. Legal assistance
18. Financial assistance
19. 403(b) plans

As already mentioned, cafeteria plan must offer a cash option (this is usually in the form of a salary-reduction agreement). Cash benefits include not only cash, but also benefits that may be purchased with after-tax dollars, or the value of which is generally treated as taxable compensation to the employee.

Eligible Employers

Basically, any employer with employees who are subject to taxation under U.S. tax law is eligible to sponsor a cafeteria plan. Self-employed individuals described in Section 401(c), including sole proprietors, partners in a partnership, and 2 percent or greater shareholders in an S-corporation are ineligible to participate in a cafeteria plan; however, they may sponsor a Section 125 plan for their bona fide employees. A spouse or other beneficiary of a plan participant may receive benefits under a cafeteria plan; however, only the plan participant may make the election of benefits under the plan.

Cafeteria plans are subject to a battery of coverage and nondiscrimination testing. It is important to note that very small employers may have a hard time passing these required tests, thus diminishing the overall value of plan sponsorship. The mechanics of these tests are discussed later in the chapter.

The IRC sets forth specific rules with respect to the aggregation of related employers. These "controlled group" rules apply with respect to cafeteria plans. All employers that are required to be aggregated under Code Sections 414(b), 414(v), or 414(m) relating to controlled groups of corporations, trades, or businesses under common control or affiliated service groups are treated as a single employer for cafeteria plan purposes. This means that all employees of the aggregated group of employers must be eligible to participate or, if they are not, the plans need to pass the coverage and nondiscrimination tests considering all members of the controlled group when performing the tests.

Eligible Employees

Eligible employees are defined to include present or former employees. The 2007 proposed regulations provide that employees include common law employees, leased employees described in Section 414(n), and full-time life insurance salesmen (as defined in Section 7701(a)(20)). However, the IRC restricts the participation of certain individuals who are considered to be self-employed. Treasury regulations clarify that while former employees can participate in a cafeteria plan, a cafeteria plan cannot be established primarily for the benefit of former employees. In addition, spouses and dependents of employees cannot participate in a cafeteria plan; however, the plan can be designed to provide benefits to family members via family coverage elected by the employee. Care must be taken if an employer provides health coverage to domestic partners—a growing trend—because cafeteria plan rules do not permit the benefits of nonspouse partners to be paid on a tax-favored basis. When coverage under an underlying benefit of a cafeteria plan includes coverage for a nonspouse domestic partner, the cost attributable to the domestic partner must be parsed out of the overall cost and paid outside of the plan, that is, paid on an after-tax basis. (There is also imputed income on any employer contribution for the nonspouse coverage.)

As mentioned earlier, self-employed individuals cannot participate in a cafeteria plan. This restriction does not preclude a sole proprietor or partnership from sponsoring a cafeteria plan for its common law employees. With respect to the spouse of a self-employed individual, the attribution rules set forth in Code Section 318 do not apply to cafeteria plans in the same manner as they apply to qualified plans. That is, to the extent a spouse of a self-employed individual is a bona fide employee in his or her own right and has no ownership interest (including ownership interest created under state community property law), he or she can participate in the cafeteria plan as an employee.

Leased employees are treated as employees of the employer and may be included in an employer's cafeteria plan. Regardless of whether leased employees are included in the plan, they must be considered with respect to all applicable coverage and nondiscrimination tests that apply to a cafeteria plan. The specifics of performing these tests are addressed later in the chapter.

Retirees are not permitted to pay for medical coverage on a pretax basis through a cafeteria plan using qualified retirement plan contributions.

No outside directors and no employees of marketing partners or any other company not within the controlled group can participate in the cafeteria plan unless the cafeteria plan is structured as a multiple-employer welfare plan (MEWA). MEWAs are subject to state insurance laws.

Certain employees can be excluded. These include employees who have not completed three years of employment and may be excluded as long as participation begins no later than the first day of the first plan year beginning after the three-year requirement has been satisfied. The plan may also be designed to exclude other categories of employees, as long as it does not discriminate in favor of a prohibited group of employees that includes owners and highly paid individuals.

Allowing ineligible individuals to participate or benefit in a cafeteria plan can taint the favorable tax treatment afforded the cafeteria plan as a whole and could result in taxation of all benefits to all participants, not just those who are ineligible to participate.

The term "employee" should be carefully defined in the cafeteria plan to make sure that independent contractors are excluded from participation even if the IRS or DOL later reclassifies them as employees.

CONTRIBUTIONS AND BENEFIT ELECTIONS

For participants to avoid constructive receipt of taxable benefits, the plan must require employees to elect annually between taxable benefits and qualified benefits. Elections must be made before the earlier of the first day of the period of coverage or when benefits first become available.

Most cafeteria plans have an open enrollment period once a year prior to the beginning of a new period of coverage during which participants must elect the amounts and types of benefits to be received. Annual elections generally must be irrevocable and may not be changed during the plan year. There are, however, certain special enrollment periods that may apply based on certain events and circumstances. These special enrollment rights are discussed later in the chapter.

Generally, the plan may not permit participants to elect their benefit coverage, benefit reimbursement, or salary reduction for less than 12 months. However, this does not prohibit new employees from electing benefits for a part of the cafeteria plan year or from a plan having an initial short plan year.

Contributions to a cafeteria plan are usually made pursuant to a salary-reduction agreement between the employer and the employee in which the employee agrees to contribute a portion of his or her salary on a pretax basis to pay for qualified benefits. Salary-reduction contributions may be made at whatever interval the employer selects, including ratably over the plan year based on the employer's payroll periods or in equal installments at other regular intervals (e.g., quarterly installments). These rules must apply uniformly to all participants. A salary reduction agreement is sufficient to satisfy the "cash" requirement of a cafeteria plan. Thus, a cafeteria plan need only offer a choice between one qualified benefit and salary reduction.

To the extent the cafeteria plan offers only premium conversion, it is quite likely that the only contributions will be employee salary deferrals. In order to avoid constructive receipt of the compensation, a salary-reduction agreement is entered into between the employer and the employee prior to the beginning of the period of coverage, which is usually the plan year. Under a salary-deferral agreement, the employee agrees to forgo a portion of his or her salary. In lieu of the compensation, the employer contributes this amount towards the cost of certain benefits, which the employer can pay for on a tax-favored basis, and which employees can buy on a pretax basis without the monies being considered constructively received by the participant. Because the participant has entered into an agreement to forgo salary in lieu of benefits, the amounts that are deferred as contributions to the cafeteria plan are not considered wages for federal income tax purposes. In addition, those sums are generally not subject to FICA and FUTA taxes, although in some cases, some state or local taxes may apply.

Employees may also be able to sell vacation days and turn the cash equivalent of these days off into other qualified benefits or cash. Some plans are designed to convert unused vacation days into cafeteria plan benefits in order to eliminate the carry forward of unused vacation days to the next plan year.

With respect to employer contributions, the employer could decide to contribute all employee benefit costs to the cafeteria plan and then let employees shop for benefits, or it may continue to pay for certain core benefits outside the cafeteria plan and then make a lesser contribution to the cafeteria plan with which participants will have the ability to shop for benefits they choose.

Negative and Evergreen Elections

Revenue Ruling 98-30 as amplified by Revenue Ruling 2002-27 introduced the concept of automatic enrollment. The 2007 proposed regulations permit a cafeteria plan to provide an optional election for new employees between cash and qualified benefits. New employees avoid gross income inclusion if they make an election within 30 days after the date of hire, even if benefits provided pursuant to the election relate back to the date of hire.

Employees must receive reasonable notice of the automatic deferral and have the option to decline coverage each plan year. A problem with negative elections is that they can violate state withholding laws or the Fair Labor Standards Act (FLSA) that sets the minimum wage and prohibits involuntary assignment or reduction in pay that would reduce a workers pay below the minimum wage.

A plan can also be designed with an evergreen election, whereby a participant makes a one-time election with respect to insured benefits, and that election stays in force from plan year to plan year unless the participant elects to make a change during the applicable election period. While technically this could be offered with respect to all benefits under a cafeteria plan, rarely is it used for dependent care assistance or medical reimbursement, since those types of expenses tend to change from year to year.

Changes in Coverage

Again, as a general rule, after a participant has elected a level of benefits for a period of coverage (the plan year), the plan may not permit the participant to revoke the benefit election during the period of coverage unless the revocation is because of certain permitted events. There are some notable exceptions to this rule.

If HSA contributions are made through salary reduction under a cafeteria plan, employees may prospectively elect, revoke, or change salary-reduction elections for HSA contributions at any time during the plan year with respect to salary that has not become currently available at the time of the election.

The Health Insurance Portability and Accountability Act (HIPAA) sets forth special enrollment rights. HIPAA requires group health plans (including those offered under a cafeteria plan) to permit individuals to make mid-year changes with respect to enrollment for coverage following the loss of other health coverage, or, if a person becomes the spouse or dependent of an employee through birth, marriage, adoption, or placement for adoption. If a participant has a right to enroll in an employer's group health plan or to add coverage for a family member under HIPAA, the participant can revoke an existing election and make a new election under the cafeteria plan that conforms to the special enrollment right.

Within the Section 125 regulations, there are special change-in-status rules, under which a plan may permit participants to revoke an election and make a new election with respect to accident and health coverage, dependent care expenses, group term life insurance, or adoption assistance if a permissible change in status occurs and the election change is "consistent" with the change in status. In order to make a mid-year change of election in a participant's medical account, the qualifying event must fall into one of the following categories:

- Changes in legal marital status
- Changes in number of dependents
- Changes in employment status
- Changes in the place of work or residence
- Significant change in the participant's or the participant's spouse's health coverage as a result of the spouse's employment status
- The dependent satisfies or ceases to satisfy the dependent-eligibility requirements for a particular benefit

With respect to adoption assistance benefits, the commencement or termination of adoption proceedings is considered a change in status.

In order to make a mid-year change of election in or termination of a participant's dependent care account, the participant must have a change in family status falling into one of the following categories:

- Changes in legal married status
- Changes in the number of dependents
- Changes in the work schedule of the participant or the participant's spouse
- Termination or commencement of employment of the participant's spouse

- An unpaid leave of absence taken by either the participant or the participant's spouse

Further, an election change is considered "consistent" if that change is on account of and corresponds with a change-in-status event that affects eligibility for coverage. In the case of accident or health coverage (such as a health care FSA), if a change in status results in an increase or decrease in the number of an employee's family members or dependents who may benefit from coverage under the plan, the eligibility requirement is satisfied. Election changes must be on a prospective basis only.

A plan may permit a participant to revoke and change an election if a judgment, decree, or order resulting from a divorce, legal separation, annulment, or change in legal custody requires accident and health coverage for a participant's child, and that coverage is actually obtained.

A plan may permit a participant to revoke an election for accident or health coverage if the participant, spouse, or dependent becomes entitled to Medicare or Medicaid.

A plan may permit an employee to modify or revoke elections in accordance with Code Sections 401(k) and 401(m) and the regulations thereunder. If the costs under a health plan increase or decrease during the plan year, the plan may automatically increase or decrease all affected participant contributions to it. Alternatively, if the cost significantly increases or decreases, the plan may permit participants to (1) make a corresponding change in their premium payments, (2) commence participation (in the case of a premium decrease), or (3) revoke their elections and, in lieu thereof, receive coverage under another health plan with similar coverage. If the cost significantly increases and there is no similar coverage, participants may drop coverage. These rules do not apply to health flexible spending arrangements.

If the coverage provided ceases or is significantly curtailed, the plan may permit participants to revoke their elections of the health plan and, in lieu thereof, to receive prospective coverage under another health plan with similar coverage. A significant curtailment is defined as an overall reduction in coverage provided under the plan so as to constitute reduced coverage generally. If a significant curtailment amounts to a loss of coverage and no similar coverage is available, participants may drop coverage. A loss of coverage means a complete loss of available benefits and includes the elimination of a benefits package option, an HMO ceasing to be available in the area where the individual resides, or the individual losing all coverage under a benefit option by reason of an overall lifetime or annual limitation.

In addition, the cafeteria plan has discretion to treat other similar events as a loss of coverage.

Under the PPACA, dependent coverage is extended through the end of the calendar year in which the child turns 26. This change in the law can result in a mid-year change in the health care FSA. In Notice 2010-38, the IRS stated that it will formally amend the change-of-election regulations to allow changes in elections for events affecting adult children's eligibility, regardless of whether the adult children are actually tax dependents. Not all plans are required to expand their dependent-child coverage to include children up to the age of 26. The new rule only applies to plans that are subject to the HIPAA Portability rules. Non-HIPAA portability plans have the option to extend health coverage for children or to continue covering children as provided under the definition of dependent in Code Section 152 (as many plans traditionally defined dependent). A plan must allow a participant who takes unpaid Family and Medical Leave Act (FMLA) leave to revoke an existing election for all health-plan coverage for the remainder of the coverage period (notwithstanding any contrary rules stated in the cafeteria plan document). A participant who takes FMLA leave may revoke elections for nonhealth benefits only under the same rules that apply to participants taking non-FMLA leave. In either case, the participant may choose to be reinstated in the plan upon return from FMLA leave on the same terms and conditions as prior to taking FMLA leave. In addition, it is the DOL's opinion that employees taking unpaid FMLA leave must have the portion of their cafeteria plan allotment allocated to group health insurance premiums paid by their employers in the same amounts as paid prior to the start of FMLA leave.

A participant who takes a leave of absence under the Uniformed Services Employment and Reemployment Rights Act (USERRA) may elect to continue participation in the plan during the period of the leave. Amounts previously deferred that would otherwise continue to be deferred under this section if the participant were still employed may be paid to the plan as a single lump sum at the beginning of each year (or at the beginning of the expected leave of absence period), or in the form of monthly payments.

The Heroes Earnings Assistance and Relief Tax Act of 2008 enhanced the protections set forth in USERRA. The most notable aspect of HEART as it relates to cafeteria plans is that plan sponsors are permitted to design their cafeteria plans to provide for "qualified reservist distributions." This means that an employee called to active duty for a period of at least 179 days, or for an indefinite period, who participates in a cafeteria plan may elect to receive a distribution of the unused balance of his or her health FSA. The distribution must be made by the deadline for making reimbursements under a health care FSA that applies to the year in which the employee was called to active duty, which presumably includes any applicable grace period set forth in the plan. The right to a qualified reservist distribution is only available from plans that provide for such distributions and only from the participant's health care reimbursement account, not from the dependent care or other plan accounts. Qualified reservist distributions are included in the employee's gross income and are subject to employment taxes.

With respect to rehires, a former participant will become a participant again if and when the eligibility requirements of the plan are met, but such an employee cannot commence participation until the first day of the plan year following the plan year in which the employee is rehired. However, if the former participant returns to employment with the employer within 30 days of his or her cessation of employment, the employee's prior elections will be reinstated.

EMPLOYER-PROVIDED ACCIDENT AND HEALTH PLAN

Coverage under an employer-provided accident and health plan that satisfies the requirements of Section 105(b) may be provided as a qualified benefit through a cafeteria plan. Prior to the enactment of the PPACA, the nondiscrimination rules under Section 105(h) generally applied only to self-insured medical plans. Under the Act, insured group health plans that do not qualify for grandfathered status as defined by the Act are also required to comply with Section 105(h). The compliance effective date is dependent on the release date of IRS guidelines which have not been issued as of the writing of this text.

The 2007 regulations specifically permit a cafeteria plan to pay or reimburse substantiated individual accident and health insurance premiums. In addition, a cafeteria plan may provide for payment of COBRA premiums for an employee.

GROUP TERM LIFE INSURANCE

Generally, under Section 79(a), the cost of $50,000 or less of group term life insurance on the life of an employee provided under a policy (or policies) carried directly or indirectly by an employer is excludible from the employee's gross income. Special rules apply to key employees if the group term life insurance plan does not satisfy the nondiscrimination rules in Section 79(d). However, if the group term life insurance exceeds $50,000 (taking into account all coverage provided both through a cafeteria plan and outside a cafeteria plan), the cost of coverage exceeding coverage of $50,000 is includible in the employee's gross income. For this purpose, the cost of group term life insurance is shown in Section 1.79-3(d)(2), Table 1. The 2007 proposed regulations provide that the cost of group term life insurance on the life of an employee that is either less than or equal to the amount excludible from gross income under Section 79(a) or provides coverage in excess of that amount, but not combined with any permanent benefit, is a qualified benefit that may be offered in a cafeteria plan. The new proposed regulations also provide that the entire amount of salary reduction and employer flex-credits for group term life insurance coverage on the life of an employee is excludible from an employee's gross income. For example, life insurance with a cash-value build-up or group term life insurance with a permanent benefit (within the meaning of Section 1.79-0) defers the receipt of compensation and thus is not a qualified benefit.

HEALTH CARE FLEXIBLE SPENDING ACCOUNT

A health care FSA is a plan that meets the qualification requirements set forth under Code Section 105. If the plan is maintained as part of a cafeteria plan, additional requirements set forth in the regulations must also be satisfied. Expenses reimbursed under the health care FSA must be for qualified medical expenses incurred during the participant's period of coverage. Only employees participating in the plan may submit claims for reimbursement. These include hospital expenses, physician or registered nurse services, dental services, prescriptions, eyeglasses, contact lenses or prescription sunglasses, psychiatric and psychological care, special education for the handicapped, and other therapy, as well as travel expenses to receive medical treatment and miscellaneous expenses such as hearing aids, prosthetics, and guide dogs.

Under PPACA, the definition of medical expense was revised. Under the new definition, expenses incurred for medicines and drugs may only be reimbursed under a health care FSA if (1) the medicine or drug is prescribed by a doctor with a formal prescription, (2) the medicine or drug is available without a prescription (i.e., it is an over-the-counter medicine or drug) and the individual obtains a prescription for the medicine or drug, or (3) the medicine or drug is insulin. (Note that without a doctor's order, an over-the-counter medicine or drug is not an eligible FSA expense.) To further clarify these new rules, the IRS released Notice 2010-59, Revenue Ruling 2010-23 and Notice 2011-5.

A health care FSA may be an HSA-compatible limited-purpose health care FSA. A health FSA may not reimburse premiums for accident and health insurance or long-term care insurance.

The maximum amount of reimbursement reasonably available must be less than five times the value of the coverage. Expenses are treated as having been incurred when the participant or his or her dependent is provided with the care or service that gives rise to the expense, as opposed to when the expense is formally billed or charged. Some health care FSAs provide plan participants with debit cards. These debit cards can be used to pay for qualifying medical expenses, thus eliminating the need for claims reimbursement. With respect to the amount available for reimbursement, a health care FSA must follow the uniform coverage requirements set forth in the regulations. This means that the maximum amount a participant has elected for the period of coverage must be available at all times during that period of coverage.

For example, assume a participant has earmarked $1,200 towards the health care FSA, but has only contributed $100 to the plan to date. This participant incurs a medical expense equal to $800. If the participant submits a claim, he or she would be entitled to a reimbursement for the full $800 even though the level of funding is only $100. The employer would be forced to prefund the additional $700 needed to pay the claim. Participants can submit claims at any time during the plan year and for a specified period after the close of the plan year referred to as the run-out period, which is generally 30–90 days after the close of the plan year.

For a health care FSA to qualify for special tax treatment under a cafeteria plan, it must meet all of the requirements of Code Sections 105 and 106 that apply to accident and health plans as well as the requirements of Code Section 125 and the regulations thereunder. To qualify as an accident or health plan, a health care FSA must exhibit the risk-shifting and risk distribution characteristics of medical insurance.

In addition, in a health care FSA participants must be reimbursed specifically for medical expenses they have already incurred during the period of coverage. The health care FSA cannot operate in a manner that allows participants to receive coverage only for periods in which the participants expect to incur medical expenses if such period is less than one plan year unless the plan is new or terminating on a short plan year because of an administrative change in the plan year.

The health care FSA cannot eliminate all or substantially all risk of loss to the employer maintaining the plan. The maximum contribution and reimbursement amounts available in a given year must be set forth in the plan document, or alternatively, there must be a method of determining the maximum available during a period of coverage.

Participants cannot receive payment from any other source for expenses reimbursed by the plan and must certify (by signing the claim voucher) that they are not eligible to bill any other source for the expense submitted. Before a plan reimburses an expense under a health care FSA, the participant must provide the FSA with a written statement from an independent third party stating that the medical expense has been incurred and the amount of the expense. The substantiation may take the form of an explanation of benefits certificate or receipt from the doctor's office. Documentation of expenses submitted for reimbursement must accompany the claim form and include the following information: (1) the provider's name and address; (2) the patient's name; (3) the date of service; (4) a description of services; and (5) the amount charged. Expenses reimbursed by the plan cannot be claimed for income tax purposes.

Among the other permissible substantiation methods are copayment matches, recurring expenses, and real-time substantiation. The 2007 proposed regulations also allow point-of-sale substantiation through matching inventory information with a list of Section 213(d) medical expenses. The employer is responsible for ensuring that the inventory information approval system complies with the proposed regulations and the recordkeeping requirements.

The funds in a health care FSA that are not used during the plan year (or applicable grace period, if one is so provided) are forfeited and belong to the employer. Some employers keep the money, while others use it to pay plan expenses or give it to charity. In no event can it be returned to the participant who incurred the forfeiture. So, while the employer could elect to divide it equally among all employees, it could not be given only to employees who incurred forfeitures. These amounts cannot be carried forward or returned, nor can any unused funds in an account be used for expenses eligible for reimbursement in another account. To reduce the risk of forfeiture, during the enrollment process, participants should be instructed to make realistic projections as to their medical expenses for the upcoming year.

Effective January 1, 2013, health care flexible spending account contributions are capped at $2,500, and thereafter, the cap will be adjusted annually for inflation.

MICHELLE'S LAW

Michelle's law applies to group health plans for plan years beginning after October 9, 2009. This includes health care FSAs offered through a cafeteria plan. In general, group health plans that provide dependent coverage for college-age students under their parents' coverage must continue coverage for such dependents that leave school due to a medically necessary leave from school. For this purpose, a "medically necessary leave of absence" means a leave of absence (or any other change in enrollment) for a child from a postsecondary educational institution, that

- Commences while the child is suffering from a serious illness or injury (as certified by a physician).
- Is medically necessary (as certified by a physician).
- Causes the child to lose student status for purposes of coverage under the terms of the plan or coverage.

Cafeteria plans offering health care FSAs must provide for continuing coverage to dependents who are under age 24 and who leave school due to a medically necessary leave of absence for a period of up to one year. Certain cafeteria plans are not subject to Michelle's Law—specifically, cafeteria plans that do not include health care FSAs and plans that are not subject to the HIPAA Portability rules. In general, this means cafeteria plans with fewer than two participants who are current employees as of the first day of the plan year; plans that provide coverage (reimbursements) for benefits that are limited to dental, vision, and long-term-care benefits that are not an integral part of a group health plan; or plans where the employer offers other group health plan coverage (that is not just dental, vision, or long-term-care coverage) but where the maximum benefit payable to a participant under the health care FSA is less than or equal to the greater of (1) $500 (plus any participant contribution) or (2) two times the participant's salary reduction election for the year.

Interestingly, because Michelle's Law did not amend Code Section 152, reimbursements for eligible expenses of dependents covered under Michelle's Law but who do not meet the definition of dependent under Code Section 152 may be subject to income tax. In addition, it is unclear whether COBRA coverage for Michelle's Law dependents is measured from the loss of student status or the loss of extended coverage provided by Michelle's Law.

DEPENDENT CARE ASSISTANCE

A dependent care assistance plan is a plan that meets the qualification requirements set forth under Code Section 129. Dependent care assistance is defined as the payment for or provision of services that, if paid for by the participant, would be considered employment-related expenses.

A participant is only eligible to claim benefits under a dependent care assistance plan if he or she pays dependent care expenses in order to be able to work. If married, the participant's spouse must also work, go to school full time, or be incapable of self-care. A spouse is considered incapable of self-care if he or she is not able to dress, clean, or feed him or herself. A spouse is considered a full-time student if he or she is enrolled at and attends a school for the number of hours the school considers to be full-time for some part of each of five months during the plan year. Only care of dependents under the age of 13 or dependent adults or children over the age of 13 who are incapable of self-care can be reimbursed under a dependent care assistance plan

Dependent care assistance plans can be offered either on a standalone basis or as part of a cafeteria plan. To the extent they are offered under a cafeteria plan, they must meet all the requirements of both Code Sections 125 and 129. A dependent care assistance plan offers participants the ability to pay for the first $5,000 of dependent care assistance on a tax-free basis. While the Economic Growth and Tax Relief Reconciliation Act (EGTRRA) increased the tax credit for eligible dependent care from $2,400 to $3,000 for one qualifying dependent and from $4,800 to $6,000 for two or more qualifying dependents, it did not raise the maximum for dependent care assistance under a dependent care assistance plan, which remains at $5,000.

It is important to note that employees have a choice of taking advantage of the dependent care assistance program or the dependent care tax credit on their tax returns. They cannot use both. Some employees will fare better taking the tax credit as opposed to taking advantage of dependent care assistance. Current law does not require an employer to help employees determine which tax benefit is more advantageous; however, most employers provide their employees with worksheets to help them make a fair comparison of the tax consequences of each.

The $5,000 limit is reduced by other dependent care assistance provided by the employer. Examples of this would include on-site day care that is offered at a reduced rate or otherwise subsidized. There is also a dollar-for-dollar offset for any tax credit a participant takes on his or her income tax return.

Eligible reimbursement expenses under a dependent care assistance plan are defined as those that enable the participant and the participant's spouse to work or look for work. Eligible expenses include child-care centers that care for six or more children, caregivers for a disabled spouse, babysitters, nursery schools, day camps, and household expenses provided that a portion of these expenses are incurred to ensure a qualifying dependent's well-being and protection. Dependent care services may take place either inside or outside the home. Care cannot be provided by a person for whom a personal tax exemption is taken on the participant's tax return. If the caregiver is a child or stepchild of the participant, he or she must be at least age 19. Expenses cannot be submitted for babysitting for social events, educational expenses, overnight camp, or expenses that the participant will claim on his or her tax return. In addition to the documentation required for all reimbursable expenses, dependent care claim submissions must include (1) the provider's Taxpayer Identification Number (TIN) or Social Security Number (SSN), (2) the dependent's age, and (3) the signature of the provider

Unlike the health care FSA, dependent care expenses need only be reimbursed to the extent funded. For example, if a participant submits a claim for $600 of dependent care expenses at a time when the level of funding is only $400, the plan is only required to reimburse $400.

In order to be reimbursed, the participant must provide a written statement signed by an independent third party (e.g., the service provider) confirming that the dependent care expense has been incurred and citing the amount of the expense. Also, the participant must declare that the expense has not been and will not be reimbursed under any other coverage. Reimbursement cannot be made in advance of the expense being incurred. The name, address and employer identification number of the service provider must also be provided. The 2007 proposed regulations also provide rules under which a dependent care assistance plan may pay or reimburse dependent care expenses using debit cards.

A new optional rule set forth in the 2007 proposed regulations permits an employer to reimburse a terminated employee's qualified dependent care expenses incurred after termination through a dependent care assistance plan.

A dependent care assistance plan must be in writing. The plan must disclose its availability and terms. To claim the expense as an exclusion from income, the participant must report to the plan administrator the name, address and TIN of the dependent care provider. Lastly, on or before each January 31, the expenses incurred by the employee for dependent care assistance benefits in the preceding calendar year must be reported on the employee's Form W-2. This is a calendar-year requirement, regardless of the plan year under which the dependent care assistance plan operates. For a detailed discussion of dependent care programs, see Chapter 17.

PAID TIME OFF

The 2007 proposed regulations replace the term "vacation days" with "paid time off" to reflect combined vacation, sick leave and personal days. A participant in a cafeteria plan may be offered an option to buy or sell paid time off. A cafeteria plan that offers paid time off must make a distinction between elective and nonelective options. Nonelective paid time off is those days that are not subject to an election by the employee. For example, if an employee's total paid time off is two weeks but he or she can sell back only one week, this employee has one week of nonelective paid time off and one week of elective paid time off. A plan offering an election solely between paid time off and taxable benefits is not a cafeteria plan.

401(K) CONTRIBUTIONS

A cafeteria plan may provide for contributions to a Section 401(k) plan. The 2007 proposed regulations clarify the interactions between Sections 125 and 401(k). Contributions to a Section 401(k) plan expressed as a percentage of compensation are permitted. Elective contributions to a Section 401(k) plan may be made through automatic enrollment (i.e., when the employee does not affirmatively elect cash, the employee's compensation is reduced by a fixed percentage, which is contributed to a Section 401(k) plan).

ADOPTION ASSISTANCE

A cafeteria plan may offer an adoption assistance FSA. The uniform-coverage rule does not apply to adoption assistance. Under such a provision, a participant may elect to receive an exclusion from gross income for employer payments for qualifying adoption assistance. For plan years beginning in 2010, the dollar limit is $13,170. This limit applies per adoption, not on a year-by-year basis. These benefits are subject to an income limit. The maximum amount begins to be reduced at $150,000 and is eliminated at $190,000. Qualifying adoption expenses are those expenses that are reasonable and necessary adoption fees, including attorney fees, travel expense, and other expenses directly related to a legal adoption. An eligible adopted child is either under age 18 or physically or mentally incapable of caring for itself. All adoption assistance programs must meet certain requirements, including that the program be set forth in writing. In addition, the plan must be nondiscriminatory and maintained for the exclusive benefit of employees. The employees must be given reasonable notice of the plan.

HEALTH SAVINGS ACCOUNTS

HSAs are employee-owned trust or custodial accounts for reimbursement of medical expenses. As with 401(k) plans, HSAs may be funded with employee salary deferrals or employer contributions through a cafeteria plan. The Medicare Prescription Drug, Improvement, and Modernization Act of 2003 added the concept of HSAs to the IRC. Employers may contribute to HSAs, but may be limited by the cafeteria plan nondiscrimination rules that are discussed later in this chapter.

Contributions to an HSA are only permitted in months that the participant has as his or her only health coverage a qualified high-deductible health insurance coverage in place.

A plan qualifies as qualified high-deductible health insurance coverage only if it has, among other things, a minimum deductible of $1,200 for self-coverage and $2,400 for family coverage and an out-of-pocket maximum of $5,950 for self-only coverage and $11,900 for family coverage (2011 amounts). Preventive care may be covered without regard to the minimum deductible. A qualified high-deductible health insurance policy may coexist with certain permitted insurance such as workers compensation and certain specific disease insurance. There can also be other coverage, including a health care FSA, as long as there are no overlapping benefits. This would include a limited-purpose health care FSA that does not reimburse expenses that are not reimbursable under the qualified high-deductible health insurance coverage.

The overall limits are the same whether or not the HSA is funded inside or outside the cafeteria plan. The participant's maximum annual HSA contribution from any source is equal to the deductible amount under the qualified high-deductible health insurance coverage up to $3,050 for self-only coverage and $6,150 for family coverage in 2011. These amounts are indexed annually. In addition, eligible individuals age 55 or over may make catch-up contributions up to $1,000.

CASH

The term "cash" is used rather broadly for purposes of a cafeteria plan. Cash is not limited to the actual receipt of dollars. Two conditions must be met in order for a payment to be considered cash. First, the benefit must be one that is not specifically prohibited by Section 125. Second, the benefit must be provided on a taxable basis. This can be accomplished in one of two ways: either the participant can pay for the benefit on an after-tax basis or the employer can pay for the benefit and report the cost of the benefit as taxable income to the employee.

PLAN ADMINISTRATION

Once a cafeteria plan has been implemented, policies and procedures must be established with respect to the plan's ongoing operation. Employee needs may change from year to year; as a result, each plan year, participants must be given an opportunity to make adjustments to their elections. The plan must be properly communicated to participants. Detailed administrative procedures must be implemented to address the ongoing operation of the program. Issues to address include coordination of benefits during periods of unpaid leave, treatment of new hires, addressing permitted mid-year benefit election changes, claims adjudication, and payment of reimbursements.

A cafeteria plan may also impose reasonable fees to administer the plan, which may be paid through salary reduction.

The most important administrative task is annual enrollment. However, before the enrollment process can commence, participants must have all the information needed to make informed choices. In addition, it will be necessary to have basic employee data on participants. New elections and revocations or changes in elections can be made electronically. Only an employee can make an election or revoke or change his or her election. An employee's spouse or dependent may not make an election under a cafeteria plan and may not revoke or change an employee's election. The more choices available, the more complex the enrollment process becomes. Most premium conversion plans do not have annual enrollment. Rather, the amount that is withheld from payroll is directly related to the employee-paid premium expense, and, as costs change, adjustments are made automatically. A procedure must be implemented for setting up default elections to the extent the election forms are not returned; generally, this is set forth in the plan document.

Payroll and accounting issues must be addressed. Decisions need to be made with respect to how the various salary-reduction amounts will be reflected on a participant's paycheck. Since cafeteria plan assets remain the general assets of the employer, some plans use the existing payroll system to pay claim reimbursements. This means that a paycheck is going to show money being withheld and reimbursed. Care must be taken to properly code these contributions and disbursements to assure proper tax withholding and reporting. Most payroll providers are well versed in cafeteria plan issues and can assist with respect to the coordination.

Grace Periods

Revenue Procedures issued in 2005 and 2007 introduced the concept of a grace period immediately following the end of each plan year, extending the period for incurring expenses for qualified benefits. A grace period may apply to the health care FSA or the dependent care assistance program, but in no event does it apply to paid time off or contributions to Section 401(k) plans.

The amount of unused benefits and contributions available during the grace period may be limited by the employer. A grace period may extend up to $2\frac{1}{2}$ months after the close of the plan year to which it related, but can be a shorter period. Benefits or contributions not used as of the end of the grace period are forfeited under the use-it-or-lose-it rule. The grace period applies to all employees who are participants (including through COBRA), as of the last day of the plan year. Grace period rules must apply uniformly to all participants.

Coverage and Nondiscrimination Testing

As already mentioned, cafeteria plans are subject to a battery of coverage and nondiscrimination testing. Some of these tests apply to the cafeteria plan as a whole, others to certain underlying benefits funded by the cafeteria plan. The tests were clarified as part of the 2007 proposed regulations. The changes in the rules provided certain defined terms that until then had been arbitrarily defined. The 2007 proposed regulations also provide that a cafeteria plan must give each similarly situated participant a uniform opportunity to elect qualified benefits, and that highly compensated participants must not actually disproportionately elect qualified benefits. This means that benefits cannot discriminate with respect to availability or utilization.

The 2007 proposed regulations provide a uniform definition of compensation to use for all testing purposes. For purposes of all cafeteria plan coverage and nondiscrimination tests, the term "compensation" means compensation as defined in Section 415(c)(3).

Cafeteria Plan Tests

There are three general tests that apply to the cafeteria plan as a whole. These include (1) an eligibility test, (2) a contributions and benefits test, and (3) the key employee concentration test. In order for a cafeteria plan to be deemed nondiscriminatory, it must pass all three of these tests.

The *eligibility test* consists of two parts. Included in this test are a classification test and a length-of-services test as well as a participation test. The test collectively is designed to measure whether or not a cafeteria plan discriminates in favor of highly compensated individuals or their dependents with regard to their ability to participate in the plan.

Part one requires that no employee be required to complete more than three years of employment as a condition of eligibility and all employees be subject to a uniform eligibility requirement. All eligible employees who satisfy the eligibility requirements must enter the plan by the first day of the plan year following the completion of the eligibility requirements unless they have separated from service before such date.

The second part of the eligibility test is a facts and circumstances determination. The cafeteria plan may not discriminate in favor of highly compensated individuals. A cafeteria plan does not discriminate in favor of highly compensated individuals if the plan benefits a group of employees who qualify under a reasonable classification established by the employer, as defined in Section 1.410(b)-4(b) and the group of employees included in the classification satisfies the safe harbor percentage test or the unsafe harbor percentage component of the facts and circumstances test in Section 1.410(b)-4(c). For this purpose, a highly compensated individual means an officer, a 5 percent owner, a highly compensated employee, or a spouse or dependent of an employee meeting one of these criteria. The term "highly compensated" means any individual or participant who for the preceding plan year (or the current plan year in the case of the first year of employment) had compensation from the employer in excess of the compensation amount specified in Section 414(q)(1)(B), and, if elected by the employer, was also in the top-paid group of employees (determined by reference to Section 414(q)(3)) for that preceding plan year (or for the current plan year in the case of the first year of employment).

Any employee who has completed three years of employment (and who satisfies any conditions for participation in the cafeteria plan that are not related to completion of a requisite length of employment) must be permitted to elect to participate in the cafeteria plan no later than the first day of the first plan year beginning after the date the employee completed three years of employment (unless the employee separates from service before the first day of that plan year).

For purposes of the safe harbor percentage test and the unsafe harbor percentage component of the facts and circumstances test described above, if the cafeteria plan provides that only employees who have completed three years of employment are permitted to participate in the plan, employees who have not completed three years of employment may be excluded from consideration. However, if the cafeteria plan provides that employees are allowed to participate before completing three years of employment, all employees with less than three years of employment must be included in applying the safe harbor percentage test and the unsafe harbor percentage component of the facts and circumstances test. In addition, for purposes of the safe harbor percentage test and the unsafe harbor percentage component of the facts and circumstances test, the following employees are excluded from consideration: (1) employees (except key employees) covered by a collectively bargained plan; (2) employees who are nonresident aliens and receive no earned income (within the meaning of Section 911(d)(2)) from the employer that constitutes income from sources within the United States (within the meaning of Section 861(a)(3)); and (3) employees participating in the cafeteria plan under a COBRA continuation provision.

The *contributions and benefits test* must also be satisfied. This test involves mathematical testing as well as general nondiscrimination with respect to benefits. This test uses the same definition of highly compensated as applied for qualified plan purposes, which means an individual is considered to be a highly compensated employee if he or she is a greater than 5 percent owner (either directly or through attribution) or earned more than the applicable dollar amount in the prior year (for 2011, this amount is $110,000).

A cafeteria plan must provide nondiscriminatory contributions and benefits with respect to both benefit availability and benefit utilization. A Section 125 plan must give all similarly situated participants the same opportunity to elect qualified benefits, and the actual selection of benefits through the plan must not be disproportionately elected by highly compensated participants. Qualified benefits are disproportionately elected by highly compensated participants if the aggregate qualified benefits elected by such participants, measured as a percentage of the aggregate compensation of such participants, exceed the aggregate qualified benefits elected by nonhighly compensated participants measured as a percentage of the aggregate compensation of nonhighly compensated participants.

A plan must also give each similarly situated participant a uniform election with respect to employer contributions, and the actual election with respect to employer contributions for qualified benefits through the plan must not be disproportionately utilized by highly compensated participants (while other participants elect to receive employer contributions as permitted taxable benefits). Employer contributions are disproportionately utilized by highly compensated participants if the aggregate contributions utilized by such participants, measured as a percentage of the aggregate compensation of such participants, exceed the aggregate contributions utilized by nonhighly compensated participants measured as a percentage of the aggregate compensation of nonhighly compensated participants.

There is an additional rule that applies if the plan is providing health benefits. If a cafeteria plan provides health benefits, the plan will not be discriminatory provided that any contributions made on behalf of a participant are equal to one of the following:

1. 100 percent of the cost of health benefits coverage under the plan of the majority of highly compensated participants who are similarly situated.
2. 75 percent of the cost of the most expensive health benefits coverage elected by any similarly situated participant.

Lastly, the plan must pass the *key employee concentration test.* This test requires that nontaxable benefits provided to key employees do not exceed 25 percent of the aggregate benefits provided to all employees. For this purpose, the term "key employee" must be defined. This is the same definition that is used for qualified plan purposes with respect to the top-heavy determination. A key employee is defined to include all employees who are

1. An officer having annual pay of more than $160,000
2. A 5 percent owner of the business
3. A 1 percent owner of the business whose annual pay was more than $150,000

A key employee covered by a collective bargaining agreement is a key employee.

In determining whether the nontaxable benefits provided to key employees exceed the 25 percent threshold, the test is based on the level of coverage as opposed to the level of reimbursements. This means that even if dollars are left over at the end of the year because they are not used to pay for qualified benefits, they are considered for purposes of applying this test.

If a cafeteria plan fails the required nondiscrimination testing, the highly compensated and key employees are taxed based on the value of their benefits. There are no negative tax consequences for nonhighly compensated participants or nonkey employees who participate in a cafeteria plan that is deemed to be discriminatory. A plan maintained pursuant to a collective bargaining agreement does not favor highly compensated employees and mathematical testing is not required.

A cafeteria plan must also test some of its underlying benefits for nondiscrimination. These tests include testing the following:

- With respect to benefits, a health care FSA will not be considered discriminatory if the same benefits are available to all participants on the same basis. For testing purposes, the same dollar amount of benefits (rather than the same percentage of pay) must be available.
- Certain employees may be excluded from a health care FSA with no negative impact on the applicable nondiscrimination tests. They include employees who have completed less than three years of service, employees who have not yet attained age 25, seasonal employees, part-time employees who work fewer than 35 hours per week, and union employees represented by a collective bargaining unit where health benefits have been the subject of good-faith collective bargaining.
- The prohibited group with respect to a dependent care assistance plan is highly compensated employees as defined in Code Section 414(q). There are several tests that apply to a dependent care assistance plan. First, the plan must not discriminate in favor of highly compensated employees with respect to contributions and benefits. The plan must benefit all employees or a classification of employees that is found by the IRS to be nondiscriminatory, no more than 25 percent of the dependent care assistance benefits

may be payable to 5 percent owners, and no more than 55 percent of the benefits payable under the plan can be payable to highly compensated employees.

- In applying the 55 percent test certain employees can be excluded. They include employees who earn less than $25,000, union employees provided that there is evidence that the dependent care benefits were the subject of good-faith collective bargaining, employees who have not completed at least one year of service, and employees who have not attained age 21. If a dependent care assistance plan fails to meet all of the nondiscrimination requirements, the plan benefits become taxable to highly compensated employees.
- With respect to group term life insurance features offered under a cafeteria plan, there are coverage and benefits discrimination tests that must be satisfied. The coverage rules are deemed to be automatically satisfied if the group term life insurance is offered under a plan that meets all the nondiscrimination requirements applicable to a cafeteria plan as a whole. The prohibited group in this case is *key employees*. There is also a group term life insurance coverage test that must be satisfied. There are four options with respect to passing this test:

  1. The plan must benefit at least 70 percent of all employees.
  2. The plan must benefit a group of employees of which at least 85 percent are not key employees.
  3. The plan must benefit a nondiscriminatory classification of employees as determined by the IRS.
  4. If the plan is part of a cafeteria plan, the cafeteria plan must meet all the nondiscrimination rules with respect to cafeteria plans.

In applying these tests, employees who have not yet completed three years of service, part-time or seasonal employees, and employees who are part of a collective bargaining unit can be disregarded.

Accident and health-plan coverage, group term life insurance coverage, and benefits under a dependent care assistance program or adoption-assistance program do not fail to be qualified benefits under a cafeteria plan merely because they are includible in gross income because of applicable nondiscrimination requirements.

Simple Cafeteria Plans

The health care reform bill (PPACA) amended Section 125 to allow small employers to establish "simple cafeteria plans." These special plans can be established for plan years beginning after December 31, 2010 and are similar to safe harbor Section 401(k) plans. In general, the employer must qualify as an eligible small employer. In addition, the plan must be designed with specific eligibility and contribution requirements. In exchange, the plan is exempt from the otherwise-applicable nondiscrimination testing that applies to cafeteria plans. In order to sponsor a simple cafeteria plan, the sponsoring employer cannot employ more than 100 employees during either of the two preceding years (or, if the employer has not been in existence for two years, based on the average number of employees it reasonably expects to employ in the current year). Employers that satisfy this eligibility requirement and establish a simple cafeteria plan for any year will continue to be treated as eligible employers in all future plan years, until its average number of employees equals or exceeds 200.

Simple cafeteria plans are subject to more stringent plan eligibility requirements. Specifically, eligible employees include all employees who were credited with at least 1,000 hours of service for the preceding year. That said, the plan may be designed to exclude certain classes of employees, including those who will not have attained age 21 before the close of the plan year; those who will not have completed at least one year of service as of any day during the plan year; those who are covered under a collective bargaining agreement in which cafeteria plan benefits were the subject of good faith bargaining; and nonresident aliens working outside the United States.

It is important to note that these age and service exclusions differ from the eligibility requirements that are commonly used in a cafeteria plan because they are applied throughout the plan year, as opposed to requirements that are met before the initial plan year of participation.

Simple cafeteria plans have specific contribution requirements that include employer contributions. Employer contributions are required regardless of whether or not the participant enters into a salary deferral election. Participants entitled to employer contributions are referred to as qualified employees. A "qualified employee" is defined to mean any employee who is eligible to participate in the plan except a highly compensated employee or a key employee.

There are two contribution options. The employer may design the plan to make a contribution equal to at least 2 percent of each qualified employee's compensation; or an amount equal to at least 6 percent of the qualified employee's compensation for the plan year; or, if less, a matching contribution equal to twice the amount of the salary-reduction contributions of each qualified employee. The rate of matching contribution to highly compensated or key employees cannot result in a rate greater than the matching contribution it provides to all other employees. In addition, the same method must be applied to all nonhighly compensated employees.

The contribution requirements set forth above are expressed as minimum requirements. This means that an employer may provide additional qualified benefits under the plan over and above the safe harbor contributions described above. If an eligible employer satisfies both the eligibility and contribution requirements applicable to a safe harbor cafeteria plan, the plan is exempt from the eligibility, contributions and benefits, and key employee concentration testing requirements of Sections 125(b)(1)(A), 125(b)(1)(B), and 125(b)(2). In addition, the nondiscrimination requirements for group term life insurance in Section 79(d), the requirements for self-insured medical expense reimbursement plans in Section 105(h), and the dependent care assistance requirements in Section 129(d) (2), (3), (4), and (8) also are treated as satisfied. There are several benefits to establishing a safe harbor cafeteria plan. The plan design should result in lower administration costs, and plans where benefit utilization negatively impacts discrimination test results will be able to avoid the unwanted consequence of taxing plan benefits.

Taxation

Cafeteria plans that comply with all of the rules and regulations set forth in the IRC are protected from the doctrine of constructive receipt. This means that when participants make a selection between cash or benefits, to the extent that they select qualified benefits, these amounts are not taxable. In the absence of this special treatment, the participant would be taxed on the value since he or she had the right to take the cash.

Because of the special tax treatment afforded qualified benefits under a cafeteria plan, deferral amounts are not subject to FICA, FUTA, or income tax withholding. It is important to note that group term life insurance that exceeds $50,000 of coverage is subject to Social Security and Medicare taxes, but not FUTA tax or income tax withholding, even when provided as a qualified benefit in a cafeteria plan. Adoption-assistance benefits provided in a cafeteria plan are subject to Social Security, Medicare, and FUTA taxes, but not income tax withholding.

Cafeteria plans provide tax savings to employers as well. The employer reduces its overall payroll tax expense since it does not have to pay the employer-paid FICA, FUTA or other state payroll taxes such as state unemployment and workers' compensation premiums. If a participant elects to receive cash instead of any qualified benefit, it is treated as wages subject to all employment taxes, both employer-paid and employee-paid.

Trust Requirements

Under current law, cafeteria plans are exempt from the requirement that plan assets be held in trust until such time as the IRS releases final regulations with respect to contributory welfare benefit plans. On May 17, 1988, the DOL announced that participant contributions to a cafeteria plan are to be considered plan assets within the meaning of ERISA Section 403(a). This means that salary reduction contributions must be segregated from the employer's general assets as soon as administratively feasible but in no event later than 90 days after the payroll deduction or the date the participant would have received the amount in cash.

On August 12, 1988, the DOL announced that it would not enforce the trust requirement for cafeteria plans. However, the DOL did not exempt cafeteria plans from the requirement that plans that hold assets in trust and cover 100 or more employees be audited. While this trust moratorium was intended to be temporary, it has been extended several times. As a practical matter, few cafeteria plans hold the assets in trust, thus avoiding the need for an audit.

ERISA

As mentioned earlier, not all cafeteria plans are subject to ERISA. However, the employer-provided welfare plans funded with cafeteria plan dollars are generally subject to ERISA. In general, only health care FSAs are subject to ERISA, while premium conversion features and dependent care assistance are not subject to ERISA. The ERISA requirements with regard to health care FSAs and ERISA-covered cafeteria plans include reporting and disclosure and fiduciary requirements.

Reporting and Disclosure

In 2002, the IRS released Notice 2002-24 announcing the suspension of the filing requirement of the Form 5500 and Schedule F imposed on (1) cafeteria plans under Section 125 of the Internal Revenue Code of 1986, as amended, (2) educational assistance plans under Section 127, and (3) adoption assistance plans under Section 137.

The Notice was effective "upon publication" (April 22, 2002) and applied to all plan years for which any such Form 5500 and Schedule F had not been filed. This retroactive relief came as a pleasant surprise for employers who may have overlooked the filing requirements for past years.

The Form 5500 and Schedule F filing requirement derives from Section 6039D, which also imposes the requirement on other employee benefit programs, including group term life insurance plans under Section 79, accident and health plans under Sections 105 and 106, and dependent care assistance programs under Section 129. IRS Notice 90-24 previously suspended the filing requirements for all of these types of plans as well. This Notice does not relieve employers of the Form 5500 filing requirement on most other welfare benefit plans, including medical, dental, and disability insurance plans, even if such plans are component plans offered under a Section 125 cafeteria plan.

A dependent care assistance plan is required to report to each participant the expenses incurred each plan year. Generally, that report is made on Form W-2. There are no Form 5500 filing requirements for a dependent care assistance plan.

Fiduciary Requirements

ERISA's fiduciary requirements address both the establishment and the operation of the cafeteria plan. With respect to the establishment of the plan, the plan must be in writing and have a plan administrator and a named fiduciary. The plan must also have a funding policy and describe the allocation of responsibilities for the operation and administration of the plan. There must also be provisions relating to the amendment of the plan and the basis on which payments are made to and from the plan.

HIPAA COORDINATION

Health care FSAs are considered to be limited-scope benefits under the terms of HIPAA. As such, they are not subject to HIPAA certification requirements and in many cases are exempt from coverage under COBRA. If an employer provides health coverage that is subject to HIPAA, the maximum amount that the health care FSA could require a former participant to pay for a full plan year of COBRA continuation coverage equals or exceeds the maximum benefit available under the health care FSA for the year. The health care FSA maximum benefit is the lesser of

1. Two times the salary reduction amount.
2. The salary reduction amount plus $500.

In the plan year after the qualifying event occurs, HIPAA does not apply; therefore, the health care FSA is exempt from COBRA in the year following the year of the qualifying event. If, however, as of the date of the qualifying event, the maximum benefit available under the health care FSA is less than the maximum amount that the plan could require payment for the remainder of that year to maintain coverage under the plan, then the health care FSA is exempt from COBRA in the year of the qualifying event.

Certain plans are not subject to HIPAA portability—specifically, plans that have less than two participants who are current employees as of the first day of the plan year; plans that provide coverage (reimbursements) limited to dental, vision, and long-term care benefits that are not an integral part of a group health plan; and plans in which the employer offers other group health plan coverage (i.e., not just dental, vision or long-term care coverage) and the maximum benefit payable to a participant under the health care FSA is less than or equal to the limit set forth above.

This means that HIPAA portability does not apply to most Section 125 plans. As long as the employer offers other group health plan coverage, the cafeteria plan will not be subject to HIPAA portability.

SUMMARY PLAN DESCRIPTION AND PLAN COMMUNICATION

All plans subject to ERISA must provide a summary plan description (SPD). If the plan does not include welfare benefit plans such as a health care FSA, SPD is not required. However, many plans sponsors still distribute an SPD in order to properly communicate the benefits offered under the plan.

Even if an SPD is not required, it is important to adequately communicate available benefits. Communication can be classified into four primary categories: plan announcement, education, enrollment, and ongoing continuation communication.

DOL Regulations (Regs. Sec. 2520.104-1(c)) allow for electronic distribution of ERISA-required documents even to nonemployees. However, these final regulations impose relatively significant paperwork burdens in connection with electronic disclosures to nonemployees as well as to employees who do not have work-related computer access. Employees are treated as having work-related computer access if they have the ability to access documents at any location where they reasonably could be expected to perform employment duties; in addition, access to the employer's electronic information system must be an integral part of their employment duties. It should be remembered that not all cafeteria plans are subject to ERISA. Nonetheless, it may be wise to follow these guidelines to assure that benefits are properly communicated via electronic means.

The final regulations significantly expand the class of documents that may be distributed electronically to include all ERISA Title I disclosures. This covers any Qualified Medical Child Support Orders (QMCSO) notices, COBRA notices, HIPAA certificates of creditable coverage, and documents that must be provided to participants and beneficiaries after written request under ERISA Section 104(b). Even if a company decides in principle to use electronic communications for employees and former employees, for various reasons, some types of notices (e.g., COBRA election notices) are not well suited for electronic transmission.

The PPACA refines the appeal processes for health care claims. Certain grandfathered plans in existence on March 23, 2010 are not required to comply with these rules. However, one of the requirements of a plan to be considered grandfathered is that notices must be distributed to participants stating that they are a grandfathered plan. PPACA adds some new requirements to the internal appeals procedures, as well as a new external appeals process. The external health care appeals process will follow federal requirements for the external appeals process. Non-ERISA-covered plans will likely be required to meet the applicable external state appeal process. This will require updates to both plan documents and summary plan descriptions and arrangements with an independent review organization to review the external claims.

The PPACA also creates some new notice requirements with respect to non-English-speaking employees. For plans with fewer than 100 participants, if 25 percent or more of participants are literate in the same non-English language, the plan's appeals procedures notices must be made available in that language. For plans with 100 or more participants, if the lesser of 10 percent of participants or 500 participants or more are literate only in the same non-English language, relevant appeals procedures notices must be made available in that language.

CONCLUSION

A cafeteria plan is an important vehicle in providing employee benefits to a diverse workforce and through which employers can construct programs that permit employees to have more control over their compensation packages. However, in order to protect the tax-favored status of contributions made to the plan and benefit payments paid from it, the plan must be carefully drafted, properly tested for nondiscrimination, and operated in accordance with all of the applicable guidance. It involves coordination with payroll providers, and it is essential that the plan's operation be clearly communicated to employees.

CHAPTER 26

Fiduciary Liability Issues Under ERISA

Alan P. Cleveland

An appreciation of the legal duties and responsibilities of a fiduciary to the participants and beneficiaries of a trusteed employee benefit plan is both fundamentally simple and exceptionally difficult. Legal definitions and statements of basic principles that seem straightforward in concept often prove elusive when applied in real situations. A plan fiduciary in the discharge of his or her duties under the Employee Retirement Income Security Act of 1974 (ERISA) is well advised to err on the side of caution, to resolve doubt in favor of a liberal interpretation of plan benefits, to be well informed at all times of the duties and responsibilities of all the fiduciaries of the plan, and to act uniformly and in strict accordance with the plan document but with a broad reading given to the fiduciary responsibilities and standards of the Act.

FIDUCIARY DUTIES UNDER THE COMMON LAW OF TRUSTS

In the employee benefits area, fiduciary relationships are fundamental to the administration and investment of employee benefit trusts. When does a fiduciary relationship exist? Under the common law of trusts, it is said that a person is in a fiduciary relationship with another if the person who receives certain powers or property does so on the condition that with such receipt is the corollary duty to utilize that conferred power or property for the benefit of that other. A trust is recognized as a formal fiduciary relationship concerning property and imposing on the person (the trustee) who holds title to that property (trust assets) certain fiduciary duties to deal with that property for the benefit of another (the beneficiary). When a person as trustee accepts ownership of such property "in trust" for a beneficiary, the trustee at the same time accepts the fiduciary responsibility and duty to use the power over trust assets for the benefit of the beneficiary of that trust.

Under the common law of trusts, a trustee has several basic fiduciary duties to the beneficiaries of the trust: a duty to see that the property of the trust is legally designated as trust property; a duty not to delegate to others trustee powers over trust property; a duty of undivided loyalty to the beneficiaries of the trust; and a duty to invest prudently by maximizing return on and ensuring the safety of trust assets. Primary among these trustee responsibilities are the duties of loyalty and prudence.

Duty of Loyalty

A trustee's duty of loyalty is the duty to act in the interest of the trust as if the trustee had no other competing interests to protect, especially his or her own. The trustee must resolve all conflicts between his or her personal or other interests and those of the trust and its beneficiaries in favor of the trust beneficiaries. This duty of loyalty is a component of all fiduciary relationships, but is particularly important in the case of a trust created to provide economic support or benefits for a specific beneficiary. A much-cited court opinion by Justice Benjamin Cardozo articulates this high standard of loyalty, and warrants quoting at length:

> Many forms of conduct permissible in a workaday world for those acting at arm's length are forbidden to those bound by fiduciary ties. A trustee is held to something stricter than the morals of the marketplace. Not honesty alone, but the punctilio of an honor the most sensitive, is then the standard of behavior. As to this there has developed a tradition that is unbending and inveterate. Uncompromising rigidity has been the attitude of courts of equity when petitioned to undermine the rule of undivided loyalty by the "disintegrating erosion" of particular exceptions. Only thus has the level of conduct for fiduciaries been kept at a level higher than that trodden by the crowd.[1]

This extreme expression of singular loyalty under the common law of trusts sets out that strict prohibition against fiduciary conflicts of interest

1. Meinhard v. Salmon, 294 N.Y. 458, 464, 164 N.E. 545, 546 (1928).

that has been the hallmark of subsequent legislation and judicial law under ERISA in regulating the fiduciary management of employee benefit plans.

Duty of Prudence: The Prudent Man Rule

In addition to the duty of undivided loyalty to the beneficiaries of a trust, a trustee under the common law of trusts has the duty of prudence in managing trust assets. This duty of prudence established a standard of performance in managing trust assets measured as equivalent to that care exercised by a person of ordinary prudence in dealing with the fiduciary's own personal property. The standard of skill and care established under traditional American trust law—that of a person of ordinary prudence, or the prudent man rule—is largely derived from a decision of the Supreme Judicial Court of Massachusetts in 1830, which held:

> All that can be required of a trustee to invest is that he shall conduct himself faithfully and exercise a sound discretion. He is to observe how men of prudence, discretion, and intelligence manage their own affairs, not in regard to speculation, but in regard to the permanent disposition of their funds, considering the probable income, as well as the probable safety of the capital to be invested.[2]

This flexible standard under the common law later proved so vague that trustees, including the fiduciaries of employee pension plans, found little comfort in making individual investment choices on behalf of the trust. Likewise, beneficiaries who were disappointed in the investment of a trust often found it difficult to maintain a legal action in proving a fiduciary's lack of prudence and breach of trust. The prudent man rule was also applied on an investment-by-investment basis rather than looking to the overall performance of the trust's portfolio of assets as a whole. All in all, the common law of trusts ultimately proved a poorly stocked toolbox in meeting the special requirements of employee pension plans.

EXCLUSIVE BENEFIT RULE UNDER THE INTERNAL REVENUE CODE

As a precondition for the substantial tax advantages afforded contributing employer sponsors and the participants and beneficiaries of qualified pension plans as tax-exempt organizations, Congress had long included

2. Harvard College v. Amory, 26 Mass. (9 Pick.) 446, 461 (1830).

in the Internal Revenue Code (IRC, or Code) certain limitations and safeguards analogous to those provided under the common law of trusts. The code provisions were intended to ensure that a pension plan in fact was operated for the exclusive benefit of its members. This intent is codified as the exclusive benefit rule. A key provision under Section 401(a) of the IRC, which enumerates the general qualification requirements for a pension plan's tax-exempt status, mandates that a trust created by an employer as part of a pension or profit-sharing plan must be "for the exclusive benefit" of the plan's covered employees and their beneficiaries, and that it must be "impossible ... for any part of the corpus or income ... to be ... used for or diverted to, purposes other than for the exclusive benefit" of the employees or their beneficiaries. The duty of loyalty of the trustee of a pension plan qualified under Code Section 401(a) is, therefore, threefold:

- To be qualified as tax-exempt, a plan must be established for the "exclusive benefit" of the covered employees and their beneficiaries.
- All contributions received by the plan must be "for the purpose of distributing to such employees or their beneficiaries the corpus and income of the fund accumulated by the trust."
- And, under the express terms of the trust, it must be impossible for trust assets to be diverted to purposes "other than for the exclusive benefit of [the] employees or their beneficiaries" prior to the satisfaction of benefits due under the plan.

Failure of an employee benefit pension plan to operate in accordance with the exclusive benefit rule would cause it to lose its tax-exempt status under the Code, further resulting in a loss of deductibility of employer contributions to the plan as well as loss of the tax-preferred treatment enjoyed by the plan's participants and beneficiaries.

FIDUCIARY STANDARDS UNDER ERISA

Immediately prior to the passage of ERISA, it was estimated that more than 35 million employees were dependent for their retirement benefits on a private pension system whose noninsured trust assets then exceeded $130 billion. Congress determined that the rapid and substantial growth in size and scope of hundreds of thousands of pension plans had such economic impact on the continued well-being and security of their millions of covered employees that it was in the national public interest to establish under

ERISA adequate safeguards to ensure the adequacy of funds to pay the retirement benefits promised under those pension plans. Toward these ends, ERISA mandated national standards of conduct, responsibility, and obligation for the fiduciaries of employee benefit plans, and further provided appropriate remedies, sanctions, and access to the federal courts for the enforcement of such fiduciary standards.

Before ERISA, pension plan fiduciaries were largely subject to the common law of trusts, the principles of which were developed and refined primarily during the 19th century to order personal trust relationships between private parties. Unfortunately, traditional trust law proved inapposite to the special purposes of pension plans, which had evolved to such a massive scale in the postindustrial period. Before ERISA, the only real sanction under federal law for fiduciary breaches involving an employee pension plan was revocation of the plan's tax-exempt status for violation of the exclusive benefit rule under the IRC. However, it was realized early that the adverse consequences of withdrawal of a plan's tax preferences would bear most heavily on innocent employees as the plan's beneficiaries, and the sanction was rarely applied in practice.

Under ERISA, Congress intended to establish a comprehensive federal regulatory scheme for the operation of pension and other employee benefit plans based on new and unwavering principles of fiduciary duty to be enforced with uncompromised rigidity. This new federal law of employee benefit trusts had four main objectives:

- A uniform legal culture of fiduciary duties would be developed incrementally by the federal courts to define further the statutory standards of ERISA on a case-by-case basis that would supersede the traditional common law of trusts unevenly applied and interpreted under the individual laws of each state.
- Those fiduciary standards developed under ERISA would be clarified and modified purposely to accommodate the special needs and purposes of pension funds.
- Employee pension plan beneficiaries would have liberal access to the federal courts in enforcing the fiduciary standards of ERISA, and those plan fiduciaries found to have breached their duties could be held personally liable for resulting plan losses.
- Fiduciaries of employee benefit plans not utilizing the trust form as a funding vehicle would still be subject to the fiduciary standards of the Act.

ERISA in a number of important respects went beyond the common law of trusts in establishing or extending new legal standards of conduct for plan fiduciaries:

- By combining the exclusive benefit rule under the IRC with the "sole benefit standard" as stated under the Labor Management Relations Act, ERISA now required plan fiduciaries to act solely in the interest of the plan's participants and beneficiaries for the exclusive purpose of providing plan benefits or defraying the reasonable administrative expenses of the plan. This established the sole benefit standard of fiduciary conduct under ERISA.
- For the future, a plan fiduciary could take little comfort in acting for a plan with only the ordinary prudence required under the traditional prudent man rule. Instead, a fiduciary needed to act under ERISA with the care, skill, prudence, and diligence under the circumstances then prevailing that a prudent man acting in a like capacity and familiar with such matters would use in the conduct of an enterprise of a like character and with like aims. This established the prudent expert rule of ERISA.
- A fiduciary was still required to diversify the investments of a plan portfolio so as to minimize the risk of large losses unless under the circumstances it was clearly prudent not to do so. This closely resembled the fiduciary principle well known under the common law of trusts as the diversification rule.
- A fiduciary needed to follow strictly the terms of the written plan document (unless otherwise in violation of ERISA) and to administer the plan in a fair, uniform, and nondiscriminatory manner. This principle has come to be called the plan document rule.
- Unless otherwise exempted, a fiduciary could not allow the plan to engage directly or indirectly in transactions prohibited under ERISA, a caveat known as the prohibited transactions rule.

The Sole Benefit Standard

The sole benefit standard of ERISA borrows from the previously discussed exclusive benefit rule of Section 401(a) of the IRC and also in large part from Section 302(c)(5) of the Labor Management Relations Act (LMRA). The LMRA had long required that a collectively bargained employee benefit trust fund be maintained "for the sole and exclusive benefit of the employees . . . and their families and dependents."

The United States Supreme Court stressed the legislative intent of ERISA as designed to prevent a fiduciary "from being put into a position where he has dual loyalties, and, therefore, he cannot act exclusively for the benefit of a plan's participants and beneficiaries."[3] The federal courts have continued to strengthen this fiduciary duty of unwavering loyalty under ERISA to require a fiduciary to act with an "eye single to the interests of the participants and beneficiaries" and to impose liability against plan fiduciaries "at the slightest suggestion that any action taken was with other than the beneficiaries in mind." At this point in the evolution of the national fiduciary law of pension trusts under ERISA, the sole benefit standard should be understood as imposing on the fiduciary a rigid, complete, and undivided loyalty to act for the beneficiaries of the employee benefit trust devoid of any other motivating considerations by the fiduciary.

The Prudent Expert Rule

In an effort to draw attention to the distinction between the standard of ordinary prudence under the common law of trusts and the prudent expert standard contemplated under ERISA as particular to pension plans, the U.S. Department of Labor promulgated prudency regulations in 1979 that introduced the new ERISA standard as one "built upon, but that should and does depart from, traditional trust law in certain respects." For example, unlike traditional trust law, the degree of riskiness of a specific investment would not render that investment per se prudent or imprudent. Rather, the prudence of the investment decision would be judged under ERISA in the context of the plan's overall portfolio.

The prudent expert standard of ERISA is an objective one, and the mere good faith of an inattentive or unknowledgeable fiduciary is not a viable defense. The prudent expert standard differs from the traditional prudent man rule under the common law of trusts in several important respects. First, the plan fiduciary under ERISA must invest plan assets not in the same way as he or she would handle his or her personal estate but must look to how similar pension plans under similar circumstances are being invested. Second, it is not enough for an ERISA fiduciary to be merely "prudent," but he or she additionally must exercise the skill of a

3. NLRB v. Amax Coal Company, 453 U.S. 322, 335 (1981).

prudent person especially knowledgeable and experienced—that is, an expert—in the management of pension plans. Third, the focus is not to be on the performance of the individual plan investment but on how the investment contributes to the net performance of the pension portfolio as a whole, which assumes the conceptual framework of modern portfolio theory in its broadest terms. In investing a pension plan portfolio under the prudent expert rule, the fiduciary should weigh the risk of loss against the opportunity for gain, taking into consideration the following elements: (1) the liquidity and current return of the portfolio relative to the liquidity requirements of the plan; (2) the projected return of the portfolio relative to the funding objectives of the plan; and (3) the composition of the portfolio with regard to diversification.

The Diversification Rule

Consistent with the traditional common law of trusts, an ERISA fiduciary is required to diversify plan investments "so as to minimize the risk of large losses, unless under the circumstances it is clearly prudent not to do so." The legislative history of ERISA suggests that the elements a fiduciary should consider in diversifying a plan's portfolio include the purposes of the plan, the amount of plan assets, the overall financial and industrial conditions of the economy, the special characteristics of the particular type of investment (e.g., mortgages, bonds, and shares of stock), distribution as to geographic location, distribution as to industries, and dates of maturity. There are, unfortunately, no clear-cut tests under the statute on what would constitute a plan's lack of diversity or undue concentration in any particular investment.

During the legislative hearings leading to the enactment of ERISA, Congress heard testimony that under the common law of trusts, fiduciaries had rarely been held liable for investment losses unless trust holdings in a single investment exceeded 50 percent. Also under the pre-ERISA common law of trusts, a plan's concentration of investments of 25 percent or less of portfolio assets in an individual security or geographic locale did not ordinarily result in sanctions by the courts. However, since passage of ERISA, fiduciary liability has been imposed by the courts in a case where 23 percent of a plan's assets were invested in a single real estate loan. In a separate case, the investment of 85 percent of a profit-sharing plan's assets in long-term government bonds without the fiduciary having first adequately investigated the plan's liquidity needs was found to be a breach of the fiduciary duty to diversify plan assets.

The Plan Document Rule and Benefit Claims Administration

Plan fiduciaries are required to act in strict accordance with the documents and instruments governing the plan insofar as such documentation is consistent with the provisions of ERISA. As a corollary to this statutory mandate, and in part a derivative of the sole benefit standard, the federal courts are now developing a growing body of fiduciary law under ERISA relating specifically to fiduciary conduct in the administration of plans, especially concerning the role of the plan administrator as a fiduciary in the disposition of participant claims under health and other employee welfare benefit plans.

Plan fiduciaries are generally required to uniformly follow the express, written terms of the plan's documents. However, fiduciaries are not relieved of their fiduciary responsibilities by sole reliance on the plan instrument as dictating their actions. The written terms of a plan can only be relied upon by a fiduciary to the extent they are consistent with the fiduciary requirements of ERISA, including the duties of loyalty and prudence.

A plan administrator's decisions on benefits claims are normally accorded deference by the courts unless there is a substantive issue raised on whether (1) the relevant terms of the plan are overly vague or ambiguous, (2) the plan document fails to expressly include a provision that the courts should defer to the administrative decisions of the plan's fiduciaries, or (3) there is an apparent conflict of interest and the fiduciary would be personally or institutionally affected by the benefit decision. The holding of the United States Supreme Court in *Firestone v. Bruch*[4] is significant for its apparent rejection of the judicial deference normally accorded administrative benefit decisions under case law decided under the Labor Management Relations Act and, instead, has substituted those governing principles developed under the law of trusts in cases involving abusive discretion by plan fiduciaries in deciding benefit claims. Still, the decision of an administrator with discretionary authority to interpret a plan is given deference by the courts, and will be upheld, unless the denied claimant on appeal can prove the decision to be arbitrary, capricious or an abuse of discretion.

However, the administrator of a plan, such as the employer sponsor or plan insurer, often determines whether a claimant should be paid and acts against its financial interests when directly or indirectly paying benefits out

4. Firestone v. Bruch, 109 S. Ct. 948 (1989).

of its own pocket. This dual role creates a structural conflict of interest for the administrator, and its presence weighed as an important factor in determining whether there was an abuse of discretion. The United States Supreme Court has held that such a conflict of interest would be of great importance "where circumstances suggest a higher likelihood that it affected the benefits decision" and "should prove less important (perhaps to the vanishing point) where the administrator has taken active steps to reduce potential bias and to promote accuracy, for example, by walling off claims administrators from those interested in firm finances, or by imposing management checks that penalize inaccurate decision making irrespective of whom the inaccuracy benefits."[5]

The external review process for appeals from denials of claims has been materially changed for many health benefit plans and their insurers under the reform provisions of the Patient Protection and Affordable Care Act (the Act). Under the Act and its regulations, all "nongrandfathered plans," including nonERISA church and governmental health plans, must comply with the new corrective claims and appeals procedures under the Act as of the first plan year beginning on or after September 23, 2010. In general, those health benefit plans in existence on March 23, 2010, the date of the Act, are considered "grandfathered plans," and exempt from the external appeal processes provided under the Act. Regulations issued under the Act provide that "grandfathered plan" status may be lost by materially changing certain features of the plan in existence as of March 23, 2010—for example, by significantly reducing benefits, raising coinsurance charges, significantly raising deductibles, significantly raising copayment charges, or significantly lowering employer contributions by more than 5%.

If a benefit claim appeal is denied under an insured nongrandfathered plan's internal appeals process, under the Act and its regulations, there is a right to an external appeal to an independent reviewer in compliance with the laws of the applicable state's external review process. If a state's external review process does not meet the minimum standards and procedures of the Uniform Health Carrier External Review Model Act (NAIC Model Act), and noncompliant states are encouraged to adopt these standards before July 1, 2011, then the Federal government will establish external appeals standards comparable to the NAIC Model Act.

If a nongrandfathered plan is self-insured, and not subject to, or elects not to voluntarily comply with, a state's external review process, then the

5. Metropolitan Life Insurance Co. v. Glenn, 128 S. Ct. 2343 (2008).

plan will be required to implement an external review process that meets those standards to be established by the U.S. Departments of Labor, Health and Human Services (HHS), and Treasury.

Prohibited Transactions Rule

Arising from yet going well beyond the common trust law duty of loyalty, ERISA prohibits a fiduciary from causing a plan to directly or indirectly enter into transactions with certain persons defined as "parties-in-interest." This group is similar to but more narrowly defined than the class of "disqualified persons" identified under companion provisions of the IRC. A fiduciary may not cause the plan to directly or indirectly engage in a transaction with a party-in-interest—as either buyer or seller—that would constitute any of the following:

- A sale or exchange, or leasing, of any property between the plan and a party-in-interest
- Lending of money or other extension of credit between the plan and a party-in-interest
- Furnishing of goods, services, or facilities between the plan and a party-in-interest
- Transfer to or use by or for the benefit of a party-in-interest of any assets of the plan
- The acquisition, on behalf of the plan, of any employer security or employer real property not otherwise specifically exempted by law or regulation

Congress recognized the great potential for abuse in self-dealing with plan assets, and so made fiduciaries liable for any losses sustained by a plan resulting from a prohibited transaction. Under ERISA, the fiduciary has a duty to make a thorough investigation of any party's relationship to the plan to determine if that person is a party-in-interest with respect to the plan. The term "party-in-interest" is broadly defined as including nearly everyone who has a direct or indirect association with a plan, and specifically includes, but is not limited to, the following persons listed under Section 3(14) of ERISA:

1. A plan fiduciary (such as an administrator, officer, trustee, or custodian of the plan)
2. The legal counsel or employee of the plan

3. Any other person providing services to the plan
4. An employer whose employees are covered by the plan
5. An employee organization (such as a union) any of whose members are covered by the plan
6. A direct or indirect 50 percent or more owner of an employer sponsor of the plan
7. Certain relatives of the foregoing persons
8. The employees, officers, directors, and 10 percent shareholders of certain other parties-in-interest
9. Certain persons having a statutorily defined direct or indirect relationship with other parties-in-interest

Even as the prohibited transaction provisions of ERISA precisely codify what would in many instances be considered only a possible conflict of interest under the common law of trusts, the ERISA rules in this area are less tolerant and more strictly applied than those of the traditional law of trusts. For example, a plan's engaging in a prohibited transaction would still result in a fiduciary breach even if the plan profited by the prohibited transaction.

Under Section 408(b)(2) of ERISA, however, statutory exemption from the prohibited transaction rules is conditionally available for certain arrangements between plans and their service providers if (1) the contract or arrangement is reasonable; (2) the legal, accounting, record-keeping, or other services are necessary for the operation or establishment of the plan; and (3) no more than reasonable compensation is paid for the services provided.

But this exemption may be lost, and so become a nonexempt prohibited transaction, if the contract or arrangement between a service provider and an ERISA-covered defined benefit or defined contribution pension plan (including 401(k) and 403(b) plans) is not considered "reasonable" because of the failure of covered service providers and responsible plan fiduciaries to make those disclosures required under ERISA regulations effective July 16, 2011. The information required to be disclosed by plan service providers must be in writing to the plan fiduciary, and include (1) a description of the services to be provided and all direct and indirect compensation to be received by the service provider, its affiliates, or subcontractors for each service to the plan, without regard to whether the service is contracted separately or furnished as part of a bundle or package of services; (2) a statement whether the service provider is providing any service as a fiduciary of the plan; and (3) full disclosure of the circumstances where a service provider is to be compensated by someone other than the plan or plan sponsor, the identity of such third person, and the compensation to be received.

Upon application to the Secretary of Labor, a plan fiduciary may also request an individual exemption enabling a plan to be allowed to prospectively enter into what otherwise would be deemed a prohibited transaction upon the secretary's finding that granting such an exemption would be administratively feasible, demonstrably in the interests of the plan and of its participants and beneficiaries, and otherwise protective of the rights of the plan's participants and beneficiaries. Administrative exemptions may be granted for specific transactions on an individual plan basis or as a class exemption for certain categories of transactions typical of the industry for a substantial number of unrelated plans. Under a 1978 accord between the two agencies, administrative exemptions from the prohibited transaction rules granted by the Department of Labor are also binding upon the Internal Revenue Service. But a prohibited transaction exemption does not relieve a plan fiduciary from the continued responsibility under ERISA to act solely in the interests of the plan's participants and beneficiaries in accordance with the prudent expert standard.

The comprehensive definitional scope of what would constitute a "prohibited transaction" as defined under ERISA, the exacting conditionality of available regulatory exemptions, the involved attribution rules identifying persons as "parties in interest" (many of whom may themselves have no personal knowledge of the plan), the broad regulatory definition about what property constitutes "assets" of the plan for purposes of applying the prohibited transaction rules, and the severe sanctions and excise taxes assessed for such prohibited transactions dictate that a fiduciary should approach this area with great caution, be well counseled, and seek an administrative exemption in questionable cases before causing the plan to enter into a questionable arrangement or transaction.

WHO IS A FIDUCIARY?

ERISA defines a plan fiduciary as any person who (1) exercises any discretionary authority or control over the management of a plan, (2) exercises any authority or control concerning the management or disposition of its assets, or (3) has any discretionary authority or responsibility in the administration of the plan. Fiduciary status extends not only to those persons named in the plan documents as having express authority and responsibility in the plan's investment or management, but also covers those persons who undertake to exercise any discretion or control over the plan regardless of their formal title.

Fiduciary status under ERISA depends on a person's function, authority, and responsibility, and does not rest merely on title or label. To illustrate: a person who exercises discretion in the administration of a plan by making the final decision on a participant's appeal of a denial of a benefit claim would be considered a plan fiduciary under ERISA, even if the plan document makes no express provision authorizing such person's discretionary responsibility. However, those persons simply performing ministerial functions for a plan under administrative procedures established by others would not be considered fiduciaries. Professional service providers to a plan, such as attorneys, accountants, actuaries, and consultants, acting strictly within their professional roles and not exercising discretionary authority or control over the plan or providing investment advice for fees or other compensation, are not ordinarily to be considered fiduciaries of the plan. Anyone exercising sufficient authority or control over an employee benefit plan can be deemed a fiduciary under the broad interpretation often applied by the courts concerning ERISA as remedial legislation. Plan trustees and administrators, by the very nature of their functions and authority, would be considered fiduciaries. Corporate officers and directors of an employer plan sponsor, if found to have exercised sufficient discretionary authority or control over plan assets, or over the appointment, retention and removal of plan fiduciaries, may themselves be deemed fiduciaries and held personally liable under ERISA after a fact-specific inquiry by the courts.[6] Following the notorious collapse of the Enron and WorldCom corporations in 2002, and the resulting destruction of their employee pension plans, the courts have demonstrated a new willingness to expand the universe of plan fiduciaries, and to broaden the fiduciary obligations under ERISA to include the duty not to misinform participants through material misrepresentations, or incomplete, inconsistent or contradictory disclosure.

A written plan document is required to provide for "named fiduciaries" having authority to control and manage the plan so that employees may know who is responsible for its operation. A named fiduciary may in fact manage or control the plan, or merely be identified in the document by name or office as the person authorized to appoint those fiduciaries who actually will exercise discretion and control in administering the plan or investing its assets. Only the named fiduciary may appoint a plan's

6. In re Enron Corp. Securities, Derivative & ERISA Litigation, 284 F. Supp. 2d 511 (S.D. Texas, 2003).

investment manager and allocate investment responsibility to such manager as to make him or her a plan fiduciary.

ERISA forbids persons convicted of any of a wide variety of specified felonies from serving as a fiduciary, adviser, consultant, or employee of a plan for a period of the later of five years after conviction or five years after the end of imprisonment for such crime. A fine of up to $10,000 or imprisonment for not more than one year may be imposed against the named fiduciary and others for an intentional violation of this prohibition.

LIABILITY FOR FIDUCIARY BREACHES UNDER ERISA

A plan fiduciary breaching the fiduciary requirements of ERISA is to be held personally liable for any losses sustained by the plan resulting from the breach. The fiduciary is further liable to restore to the plan any profits realized by the fiduciary through the improper use of the plan assets. Additionally, the fiduciary is subject to a broad panoply of other equitable relief, including removal, as may be ordered by the courts.

If found to have engaged in a prohibited transaction with a plan, a disqualified person may be subject to an excise tax payable to the U.S. Treasury equal to 15 percent of the amount involved in the transaction occurring after August 5, 1997, for each year the prohibited transaction was outstanding, plus interest and penalties on the excise tax. (different rates of excise tax apply before that date). This excise tax increases to 100 percent of the amount involved upon failure to remedy the transaction upon notification. A fiduciary acting solely in such capacity with a plan, however, is not liable for the tax. The Secretary of Labor may separately assess a civil penalty under ERISA of up to 5 percent of the amount involved in a prohibited transaction for each year in which it continues, or 100 percent of the amount involved if not corrected within 90 days of notice from the Secretary. The Department of Labor has also established a Voluntary Fiduciary Correction program for certain fiduciary violations of ERISA, such as an employer's delinquent payment to a plan of employee 401(k) contributions. Under the program, a fiduciary may voluntarily make application to correct a fiduciary breach by restoring lost profits to the plan and taking such other action as the Department of Labor may require.

Co-Fiduciary Liability

A plan fiduciary, moreover, is liable for the fiduciary breaches of other fiduciaries for the same plan if such fiduciary participates knowingly in or knowingly undertakes to conceal an act or omission of a cofiduciary knowing such action constitutes a breach; imprudently fails to discharge his or her own fiduciary duties under the plan (and thereby enables the cofiduciary to commit the breach); or has knowledge of the cofiduciary's breach and makes no reasonable effort under the circumstances to remedy the breach.

Enforcement

Enforcement of the fiduciary provisions of ERISA may be by civil action brought in federal or state court by a plan participant or beneficiary (individually or on behalf of a class of plan participants and beneficiaries), by the Secretary of Labor, or by another plan fiduciary.

Exculpatory Provisions

Exculpatory provisions written into a plan document or other instrument to relieve a fiduciary from liability for fiduciary breaches against the plan are void and to be given no effect under ERISA. A plan may purchase liability insurance for itself and for its fiduciaries to cover losses resulting from their acts or omissions if the insurance policy permits recourse by the insurer against the fiduciaries in case of a breach of fiduciary responsibility.

Bonding and Fiduciary Insurance

Every fiduciary of an employee benefit plan and every other person who handles plan funds or property is required to be bonded, naming the plan as the insured, in an amount fixed at the beginning of each plan year as not less than 10 percent of the amount of funds handled, but in no event less than $1,000. Certain insurance companies, banks, and other financial institutions handling plan assets may be relieved of the bonding requirement if such institutions meet certain capital and other regulatory criteria established by the Secretary of Labor.

Further Sanctions for Breaches of Fiduciary Responsibility

In addition to a fiduciary's personal liability to restore losses sustained by the plan as a result of a breach of the fiduciary's responsibilities, the fiduciary also may be liable for (1) court-ordered attorneys' fees and costs incurred to remedy the breach, (2) punitive damages awarded by a court against the fiduciary, (3) special damages in an amount equal to the profits received by a fiduciary resulting from the wrongful use of plan assets, and (4) mandatory assessment of a civil penalty equal to 20 percent of the amount recovered by the Secretary of Labor on account of a fiduciary breach.

- *Attorneys' fees.* Under ERISA, a court in its discretion may award attorneys' fees to a prevailing plaintiff against a plan fiduciary by taking into account certain factors, including the degree of the fiduciary's culpability or bad faith, the offending party's ability to satisfy the award of attorneys' fees, whether its award would deter other fiduciaries from acting similarly under like circumstances, the relative merits of the parties' positions in the litigation, and whether the action conferred a common benefit on the plan's participants and beneficiaries.
- *Punitive damages.* The courts have broad discretion under ERISA to award punitive damages to a plan for fiduciary breaches in cases where it is found a fiduciary acted with malice or wanton indifference. On awarding such damages, a court would take into consideration (1) the trust and pension laws as developed by the state and federal courts in a particular jurisdiction, (2) whether the allowance of such relief would conflict with other public-policy objectives under ERISA, and (3) whether granting such relief would best effectuate the underlying purposes of ERISA.
- *Restitution for wrongful profits.* Where a fiduciary has personally profited by wrongfully using plan assets for the fiduciary's own account, even where the plan itself has sustained no direct loss and may actually have gained by the transaction, the fiduciary will likely be required by the courts to disgorge to the plan the full amount of those personally realized profits. And if there is any commingling of plan assets with the fiduciary's personal property, all issues of apportionment of the wrongful profit will be resolved against the fiduciary and in favor of the plan. The purpose of this disgorgement requirement is to remove any incentive for the fiduciary to misuse plan assets whether or not the plan sustains a loss by the fiduciary breach. As a matter of equity, the fiduciary will not be permitted to gain by his or her wrongful acts.
- *Twenty percent civil penalty.* Added by the Omnibus Budget Reconciliation Act of 1989 (OBRA '89), ERISA was amended to require the Secretary of Labor to assess a civil penalty against

fiduciaries who breach their fiduciary responsibilities under ERISA and also to make such assessments against any nonfiduciary who knowingly participates in such breach. The amount of civil penalty is equal to 20 percent of the amount of applicable recovery obtained pursuant to any settlement agreement with the Secretary of Labor or ordered by a court to be paid in a judicial proceeding instituted by the Department of Labor. The 20 percent civil penalty assessment is to be reduced by the amount of any excise tax payable to the U.S. Treasury on account of a prohibited transaction. In the Secretary of Labor's sole discretion, the civil penalty may be waived or reduced if the secretary determines in writing that the fiduciary or other person so assessed acted reasonably and in good faith, or that it is reasonable to expect that as a consequence of the penalty's assessment it would not be possible to restore all losses to the plan without severe financial hardship unless the waiver or reduction were granted.

ALLOCATION OF FIDUCIARY RESPONSIBILITIES

Plan documents may provide that specific duties may be allocated by agreement among the fiduciaries, provided those duties are specifically delineated in writing, the procedures for such allocations are sufficiently detailed, and the fiduciaries act prudently in implementing the established allocation procedure. If fiduciary responsibilities are allocated in accordance with the plan documentation, the fiduciary will not be held liable for any plan loss arising from the acts or omissions of those other fiduciaries to whom such responsibilities had been properly delegated. Regardless, a plan fiduciary will remain fiduciarily responsible if he or she does not act in general accordance with the prudency requirements of ERISA in making the delegation, or if the fiduciary had knowledge of another's fiduciary breach and yet failed to make reasonable efforts to remedy the breach.

Only the named fiduciary of a plan may allocate or delegate duties involving the management and control of plan assets. In duly appointing an investment manager in writing and in accordance with the procedural requirements of ERISA, the fiduciary responsibility of investing or otherwise managing the assets of the plan may be transferred to the manager within the terms of the delegation. Yet, the named fiduciary would still be held liable for imprudently selecting or retaining the manager or for permitting, concealing, or failing to remedy a known breach of that fiduciary's responsibility to the plan.

A fiduciary also must demonstrate procedural prudence in the management of the plan's affairs and must be able to show that the fiduciary's reliance on the plan's advisers and other fiduciaries was reasonable and informed. As fiduciary status is functionally determined; so, too, is prudency measured by conduct no less than result. The court in a lead ERISA case aptly summarized the fiduciary obligation of affirmative vigilance in holding that "a pure heart and an empty head are not enough" to avoid liability for a breach of fiduciary responsibility under the Act.[7]

SUMMARY

This brief survey has reviewed the changing course of the fiduciary standards of employee pension plans from their traditional meaning under the common law of trusts to the passage of the broad statutory standards set out under ERISA. The national fiduciary law of pension trusts is continuously shifted by the decisions of the federal courts and by administrative rule making. For example, the Department of Labor by interpretive bulletin and administrative announcement has established a fiduciary duty of plan trustees to cause the proxies of plan-owned stock to be voted solely in the interests of the participants and beneficiaries without regard to the interests of the plan sponsor.

This chapter has merely touched the surface of the deep, swift-running, and ever-wandering stream that plan fiduciaries must negotiate. Knowing its ways and understanding their own roles, fiduciaries may guide the plan and its beneficiaries to their intended destination in trust without upset or misadventure.

7. Donovan v. Cunningham, 716 F.2d 1455, 1467 (5th Cir. 1983).

CHAPTER 27

Employee Benefits Communications

Serafina Maniaci

OBJECTIVES OF EMPLOYEE BENEFITS COMMUNICATIONS

The Internet has spawned a new generation of communication applications in employee self-service. Web-based applications have all but replaced interactive voice-response (IVR) systems in human resources (HR) administration. At work or at home, at the click of a mouse, employees are accessing information on provider networks, modeling plan costs, enrolling in health plans, and changing retirement plan allocations. Government policies such as the Electronic Signatures in Global and National Commerce Act of 2000 and Department of Labor favorable regulations on the use of electronic communication have advanced the progress toward a paperless HR department. Yet, regardless of the technological advancements, the fundamental nature of benefits communications remains the same. Whether print or nonprint media are used, benefits communication objectives do not change and can be classified into three areas:

1. Adhere to statutory reporting and disclosure requirements.
2. Support employee benefits cost-containment strategies.
3. Support HR recruitment and retention objectives.

MANDATORY DISCLOSURE REQUIREMENTS

In general, an employer[1] in the private sector that voluntarily sponsors an employee benefit plan is required to meet disclosure requirements. The basic requirements were established by Title I of the Employee Retirement Income Security Act of 1974 (ERISA) and since then other legislation has expanded and/or amended the ERISA provisions. Until the passage of the Patient Protection and Affordable Care Act of 2010 (PPACA), two major acts that have had impact on disclosure requirements, among other requirements, are the Consolidated Omnibus Budget Reconciliation Act of 1985 (COBRA) and the Health Insurance Portability and Accountability Act of 1996 (HIPAA). It is expected that in the coming decade, as the provisions of the PPACA take effect, the structure and compliance landscape of health care plans will dramatically change as the insurance market, plan sponsors, and workers react to the Act's requirements. As of the writing of this chapter, much uncertainty exists regarding how these requirements will be interpreted by federal agencies tasked with writing interim and final regulations. Appendix 27.1 highlights some of the key PPACA provisions related to health-plan communications.

The government agency that has principal jurisdiction over the reporting and disclosure requirements of Title I of ERISA is the Department of Labor (DOL). The Department of the Treasury, through its bureau of the Internal Revenue Service (IRS), and the Department of Health and Human Services (DHHS) are the other government agencies that have regulatory and interpretive responsibility for legislation related to employee benefits plans. The focus of the chapter is on employer disclosure requirements and not on DOL or IRS reporting requirements.

An employer that sponsors an employee benefit plan is required to provide to participants and beneficiaries a summary plan description (SPD) that describes in "understandable terms" the participants' and beneficiaries' rights as well as the benefits and responsibilities under the plan. For health plans, among the new reporting requirements that the PPACA created is a mini-SPD called a uniform Summary of Benefits (see Appendix 27.1). The employer must also provide participants with a summary of any material modifications (SMM) to the plan or changes to the information

1. An "employer" is any person acting directly as an employer, or indirectly in the interest of an employer, in relation to an employee benefit plan, and includes a group or association of employers acting for an employer in such capacity. See Frank J. Bitzer and Nicholas W. Ferrigno, Jr., *2010 ERISAFacts*, The National Underwriter Company, 2010, p. 3.

contained in the summary plan description. In addition, plan administrators must furnish participants and beneficiaries with a summary of the annual report (IRS Form 5500 Series). Table 27-1 shows selected documents that must be provided to participants at various times and upon the occurrence

TABLE 27-1

Selected Documents Required by ERISA for Plan Participants of Welfare and Pension Benefits Plans

1. Statement of ERISA Rights (to be included in the SPD)
2. Summary Plan Description (SPD)
3. Summary of Material Modifications (SMM)
4. Summary Annual Report (SAR) (PBGC-covered defined benefit plans must file Annual Funding Notice in lieu of SAR)
5. Notification of Benefit Determination
Additional Disclosure for Group Health Plans
6. Summary of Material Reduction in Covered Services or Benefits
7. COBRA Notices
8. HIPAA Notices
9. Wellness Program Disclosure
10. Women's Health and Cancer Rights Act Notices
11. Medical Child Support Order Notices
Additional Disclosure for Pension Plans
12. Periodic Pension Benefit Statement
13. Statement of Accrued and Nonforfeitable Benefits
14. Suspension of Benefits Notice
15. Domestic Relations Order (DRO) and Qualified Domestic Relations Order (QDRO) Notices
16. Notice of Failure to Meet Minimum Funding Standards
17. Section 404(c) Plan Disclosures
18. Notice of Blackout Period for Individual Account Plans
19. Qualified Default Investment Alternative Notice
20. Notice of Funding-based Limitation
21. Notice of Right to Divest

of specific events.[2] (Starting with plan years beginning in 2008, Pension Benefit Guaranty Corporation (PBGC)-covered defined benefit plans must provide an Annual Funding Notice rather than a Summary Annual Report.[3]) Table 27-2 shows items reported in the Summary Annual Report which is a narrative of the plan's annual return/report, the IRS Form 5500.

Timing and Methods of Distribution Requirements for Key Documents

In general, the Statement of ERISA rights (often included in the SPD) and the SPD must be provided within 90 days after the person becomes a participant (or a beneficiary) in the plan or within 120 days after the plan becomes subject to the reporting and disclosure provisions of ERISA.[4] The Summary Annual Report (SAR) must be provided no later than nine months after the close of the plan year. If a change is made to the plan that affects information contained in the SPD, an SMM must be provided within 210 days after the close of the plan year in which the modification was adopted. HIPAA reduced the 210-day period to 60 days for group health plans that make changes of "material reductions in covered services or benefits" and PPACA went a step further, requiring a notice to be sent at least 60 days before the effective date of the group health plan's modification.

As for the method of distribution, the general disclosure requirements by the DOL's Employee Benefits Security Administration state that "the plan administrator shall use measures reasonably calculated to ensure the actual receipt of the material by plan participants and beneficiaries."[5] The regulation states that materials such as SPDs and SMMs that are required to be furnished to all plan participants must be sent by a method or methods of delivery likely to result in full distribution. The regulation

2. For a complete list of the Disclosure Requirements, see *Reporting and Disclosure Guide for Employee Benefit Plans*, Employee Benefits Security Administration, U.S. Department of Labor, Revised October 2008.
3. See Pension Protection Act of 2006 Section 503(c) and ERISA Section 104(b)(3). This Notice is due 120 days after the plan year ends for large plan filers. Small plans have until the date that the annual report (Form 5500) is filed to issue the notice.
4. An updated SPD must be issued every five years integrating all plan amendments or 10 years if no changes are made to the plan during that period.
5. 29CFR 2520.104b-1.

TABLE 27-2

Items from IRS Form 5500s that must be included in Summary Annual Reports (SARs) of Pension Plans and Welfare Plans

Pension Plans	Welfare Plans
1. Funding arrangement	1. Name of insurance carrier
2. Total plan expenses	2. Total (experience-rated and nonexperienced-rated) insurance premiums
3. Administrative expenses	3. Experience-rated premiums
4. Benefits paid	4. Experience-rated claims
5. Other expenses	5. Value of plan assets (net):
6. Total participants	*a.* End of plan year
7. Value of plan assets (net):	*b.* Beginning of plan year
a. End of plan year	6. Change in net assets
b. Beginning of plan year	7. Total income
8. Change in net assets	*a.* Employer contributions
9. Total income	*b.* Employee contributions
a. Employer contributions	*c.* Gains (losses) from sale of assets
b. Employee contributions	*d.* Earnings from investments
c. Gains (losses) from sale of assets	8. Total plan expenses
d. Earnings from investments	9. Administrative expenses
10. Total insurance premiums	10. Benefits paid
11. Funding deficiency:	11. Other expenses
a. Defined benefit plans	
b. Defined contribution plans	

Source: Electronic Code of Federal Regulations, e-CFR. Title 29: Labor, Part 2520-Rules and Regulations for Reporting and Disclosure, Appendix to 2520.104-10. August 27, 2010, www.gpoaccess.gov.

states that it is not acceptable to merely place copies in locations that are frequented by participants.

In April 2002, the DOL issued final regulations on the use of electronic communication (and record-keeping) technologies by employee pension and welfare benefit plans.

The safe harbor rules cover "documents required to be furnished or made available under Title I of ERISA and regulations issued thereunder that are within the jurisdiction of the DOL."[6] Under the rules, besides SPDs, SMMs, and SARs, other documents that may be provided electronically to participants include COBRA notices, qualified domestic relations order notices, and decisions on benefit claims.

The safe harbor permits the electronic delivery of plan information beyond the workplace to participants, beneficiaries, and other persons entitled to disclosures under ERISA, as amended, where certain conditions designed to protect these individuals are satisfied. The following highlights those conditions:[7]

- The plan administrator must take appropriate and necessary measures to ensure that the system for furnishing documents results in actual receipt by participants, such as the use of a return-receipt electronic mail feature or periodic reviews or surveys by the plan administrator to confirm the integrity of the delivery system.
- The plan administrator must protect the confidentiality of personal information relating to an individual's account and benefits.
- Electronically delivered documents must be prepared and furnished in a manner consistent with the style, format, and content requirements applicable to the disclosure. These requirements will be satisfied where the electronic and paper versions of a disclosure document, albeit different, each satisfy the style, format, and content requirements of the specific document when viewed independently.
- The plan administrator must notify each participant and beneficiary, through electronic means or in writing, of the disclosure documents that are furnished electronically and the significance of the documents. The requirement applies only where the significance of the document may not be reasonably

6. L. Lemel Hoseman and Russell Greenblatt, "Bush Administration Saves Trees: DOL Expands Electronic Communication and Recordkeeping Safe Harbors," *Benefits Law Journal*, Vol. 15, No. 3, Autumn 2002, pp. 71–75. For more information, see Jonathan J. Boyles, "Practical Advice for Using Electronic Media to Disseminate Participant Notices, Disclosures, Elections, and Consents," *Benefits Law Journal*, Vol. 20, No. 4, Winter 2007.

7. www.gpoaccess.gov/fr/index.html; *Federal Register*, Tuesday April 9, 2002, Part V, Department of Labor, Pension and Welfare Benefits Administration, 29 CFR Part 2520, Final Rules Relating to Use of Electronic Communication and Recordkeeping Technologies by Employee Pension and Welfare Benefit Plans; Final Rule.

evident from the transmittal, such as where it is an attachment to an e-mail.

- The plan administrator must notify the individuals of their right to request and receive a paper copy of each such document. If the document is required by ERISA, as amended, to be furnished free of charge, then, under the safe harbor rules, it must be furnished without any charges to participants and beneficiaries; otherwise, the administrator may charge a fee for a paper version of the document.

The safe harbor explicitly states that it is not acceptable merely to make documents available in a location frequented by participants (e.g., kiosk). However, it is acceptable to use a company's Web site as a method of "furnishing" disclosures. The method is deemed similar to using an insert to a company publication. That is permissible provided the distribution list for the periodical is comprehensive and up to date and a prominent notice appears on the front page of the publication advising readers that the publication contains important information about rights under the plan.[8] In addition, the IRS has its own E-SIGN regulations that apply when IRS rules require that employee benefits communications to and from plan participants must be in writing. The IRS rules allow some flexibility of what is deemed "written consent" or "notice."

Information Mandated for SPDs

The original regulations governing the required content for Summary Plan Descriptions were issued in 1977. On September 9, 1998, the DOL proposed new regulations affecting mostly health-plan SPDs, and on November 21, 2000, it published amended final regulations that took effect on the first day of the second plan year beginning on or after January 22, 2001. A plan administrator must file a copy of an SPD with the DOL only if it is requested by the DOL. An SPD must contain information on

1. Plan administration
2. Plan eligibility requirements
3. Summary of benefits, rights, and obligations
4. The Pension Benefit Guaranty Corporation (PBGC) for pension plans

8. Ibid.

5. Claims and appeals processes
6. ERISA rights

Selected detailed items that fall into these categories are

1. The plan sponsor's name and address and the employer identification number (EIN)
2. A statement clearly identifying circumstances that may result in disqualification, ineligibility, denial, loss, forfeiture, or suspension of any benefits that a participant or beneficiary might otherwise reasonably expect the plan to provide on the basis of other information provided in the SPD
3. For an employee pension benefit plan, information about whether the plan is insured with the PBGC and, if not, the reason for the lack of insurance
4. For an employee welfare benefit plan that is a group health plan, any cost-sharing provisions, including premiums, deductibles, coinsurance, and copayment amounts for which the participant or beneficiary will be responsible
5. For an employee welfare plan that is a group health plan, provisions governing the use of network providers, the composition of the provider network, and whether, and under what circumstances, coverage is provided for out-of-network services
6. The identity of any funding medium used for the accumulation of assets through which benefits are provided
7. The procedures to be followed in presenting claims for benefits under the plan and the remedies available under the plan for the redress of claims that are denied in whole or in part

To draft an SPD, there are various sources of expertise available. There are employee benefits consultant firms that specialize in writing SPDs; some of these firms also offer software programs that require the plan sponsor to simply insert plan-specific information to generate customized SPDs. Also, some insurance carriers and other third-party administrators are willing to assist employers in drafting these documents.

However, before these documents are distributed to plan participants, an attorney who specializes in employee benefits should review the documents to ensure compliance and limit litigation risk. It is important to remember that courts generally follow the legal principle of interpreting unclear or confusing SPD language in favor of the "nondrafting party," that is, employees and their beneficiaries.

EDUCATING EMPLOYEES

Plan sponsors offering the most basic employee benefits program have to concern themselves with ERISA, COBRA rights, HIPAA provisions, and other legislation while striving to merge business needs with employee needs. The programs offered must be communicated to new hires, workers experiencing life changes, terminating individuals, and retirees. Not only does the content differ for each of the groups, but so does the delivery.

New-Hire Communication Objectives

Newly hired employees are an important audience because their initial exposure to communication materials can affect overall employee morale. In most companies, the benefits communication materials and media used for this group are usually the best of whatever the companies can provide. For the new-hire process, HR departments have developed communication tools that incorporate notification and disclosure requirements and present their benefits program with its most advantageous aspects. In most cases, the new-hire processes in place are capable of delivering the benefits package, providing counseling services, and enrolling a new hire with remarkable efficiency. Whether the processes are through a one-on-one contact or a Web application, they communicate the benefits program, provide the means for the new hire to perform the required actions (select plans, authorize payroll deductions, and designate beneficiaries), and confirm participant choices in the program.

Common problems that can arise are misunderstandings about actual benefits offered, missing applications, vendor enrollment delays, and employee challenges to mandatory benefits. A good communication process will anticipate and thus reduce some of these problems. For instance, communication materials can be used to educate hiring officers on the pitfalls of miscommunicating benefits to prospective employees. System-generated notifications to new employees on the types of vendor confirmations to expect can reduce interfacing vendor problems.

Annual Open Enrollment Communication Process

Once the new-hire process has been established, it requires periodic attention for maintenance and potential modification when plan changes occur. These changes are often easier to communicate if they are adopted during the open enrollment period. In general, the open enrollment communication process requires a major commitment of HR resources. Four to six months prior to the effective date of a new plan year, HR professionals begin to work on the open enrollment process. Much effort is devoted to updating and revising personal data reports, printed materials, and Web-application programs. All available communications media are employed to communicate plan design modifications, revisions related to new legislation, and vendor administration updates. Other changes that must be communicated each year are plan cost increases, changes in family members' eligibility statuses, and personal savings accounts notifications. However, with the exception of communicating benefits cutbacks when applicable, the most challenging task of open enrollment communications is securing employee participation. Best practices entail a communication campaign that motivates employees to take the time to understand the plan changes and their impact, get their questions answered, and make informed decisions on next year's choices. The campaign should aim for a high employee participation rate to increase the number of benefits-knowledgeable employees. Employees who take the time to study and make informed decisions during the open enrollment period are less likely to need assistance or misinterpret plan provisions. Thus, designing the best open enrollment Web application or the most comprehensive open enrollment brochure is not enough—the communication campaign must attract employees' attention and then convince them that access to the information is easy and the information is relevant to them. Benefits fairs, newsletters, e-mails, and memos from senior management and employee representatives are examples of actions needed to boost employee participation.

Communications Throughout the Year

Today, many HR offices, benefits call centers, and Web applications are using the "life-events approach" to communicate with employees who experience life changes mid-year. Using this approach, the plan sponsor extracts from each of its benefits plans applicable information for a specific event (e.g., marriage, adoption, or divorce) and then in one place the sponsor communicates step by step the options available and actions required to make benefits changes as a result of the particular life-event. For example, acquiring a new dependent has an impact on medical, dental, and life plans; flexible spending accounts; and even pension contributions. Selecting or clicking on the "Adding A New Dependent" button would show all benefits affected by the event, the options available to the employee, and the actions required to make any change. The communication medium can also provide educational materials on child safety precautions, child-care facilities, and tax-advantaged savings plans for college tuition. Although the life-events approach in communications materials is not new, intranet and Internet technology are enabling plan sponsors to standardize and integrate the approach into their communication function with modest investment. Without this technology, the life-events based approach could not be as effectively employed.

An employee who has access to a fully interactive HR Web site that uses a life-event approach is an empowered individual. The employee can now maximize his or her benefits with minimal transactional cost to the plan sponsor. And, with the linking capability of the Web, an employee's opportunities expand beyond what the employer has to offer. An employer can link to various external informational resources. The employer's overall employee benefits' cost may actually increase from such enhancements in benefits communication. Still, plan savings can be derived from effective benefits communications as discussed later in the "Employer Objectives" section.

Communications to Retirees

In the days of free, lifetime retiree medical benefits, periodic mass communications were unnecessary once an employee retired. The records of those who retired before age 65 and their dependents were monitored, and retirees were notified when they or their dependents became Medicare-eligible. The other contact occurred, if applicable, when a life insurance policy claim was filed. Defined benefit pension payments were routinely processed each month. Retiree communications dealt with operational matters such as maintaining current addresses. That is no longer possible. The adoption of Financial Accounting Standard 106, which achieved its objective of having employers recognize their retiree medical expenses on an accrual basis; the need to communicate managed and, in some cases, consumer-driven health care benefits in the retiree population; and the continuing double-digit increases in health care costs—particularly in prescription drug costs—are factors for today's frequent design and pricing changes in those dwindling number of retiree medical plans still being offered. Consequently, employers committed to these benefits are expending more resources on retiree communications, including, in many cases, holding open enrollment periods for this population.

The mode of communication for the retiree group has been traditionally predominantly printed materials. However, the use of Web-based programs is gaining ground with newly retired workers and older retirees having greater access to computers and more familiarity with the e-world. Regardless of the medium, communication to retirees should state clearly what has not changed, be very specific of how a change will affect the recipient, if possible include personalized materials, and give step-by-step instructions on the actions that the retiree must take and by when. Again, as with any other employee communications, the literature should use short sentences, avoid jargon (include a glossary of terms if necessary), refrain from using the passive voice, whenever possible give examples, and, of course, avoid small font sizes. If feasible, materials should be tested first with a subset of the group. A phone number should be prominently displayed on all communications to facilitate inquiries ideally handled by dedicated HR or call center representatives. Also, employers with retirees living nearby may find that some retirees still prefer face-to-face communications. The cost of offering this type of service should be measured against the value placed on maintaining good relations with retirees and its effect on employee morale.

Retiree communication needs have also changed because of changes in pension benefits. As more individuals retire with defined contribution plan accumulations, more educational programs are needed to assist retirees not only upon retirement but also throughout their retirement years. HR offices and their third-party administrators are learning that retirees who continue to keep balances in their 401(k) and other similar accounts expect their former employer to provide investment and financial planning advice. Web-based education applications are being utilized for this younger retiree group. However, investment education poses unique communication challenges to employers, as discussed in the following section.

Investment Education

Section 404(c) of ERISA states that sponsors of participant-directed plans can avoid responsibility for investment decisions made by a participant with respect to his or her own account if the participant "exercises control."[9]

9. 29 CFR 2550.404(c). Under these regulations, however, the DOL states that "a fiduciary is not relieved by the 404(c) from the liability for plan losses resulting from the imprudent selection and monitoring of an investment option offered by the plan . . . ."

Participant-directed accounts include those from 401(k), money purchase, profit sharing, or 403(b) plans. A plan is deemed to allow exercise of control by participants or beneficiaries if participants are provided with the opportunity to[10]

1. Choose from a broad range of investment alternatives, which consist of at least three diversified investment alternatives, each of which has materially different risk and return characteristics.
2. Give investment instructions with a frequency that is appropriate in light of the market volatility of the investment alternatives, but no less frequently than once within any three-month period. (The plan must allow transfers among investment options at least quarterly.)
3. Diversify investments within and among investment alternatives.
4. Obtain sufficient information to make informed investment decisions with respect to investment alternatives available under the plan.

To avail themselves of Section 404(c) protection, plan sponsors must provide certain information automatically to participants. One required disclosure is an explanation that the plan intends to comply with Section 404(c), which limits the liability of plan fiduciaries. Other items of disclosure include the following:[11,12]

1. A description of the investment alternatives under the plan and a general description of the investment objectives and risk/return characteristics of each alternative, including information relating to the type and diversification of assets comprising that portfolio.
2. Identification of any designated investment managers the plan might provide for the participants.
3. An explanation of how to give investment instructions, any limits or restrictions on giving instructions (including information of

10. Frank J. Bitzer and Nicholas W. Ferrigno, Jr., *2010 ERISAFacts*, The National Underwriter Company, 2010, p. 323.
11. Bitzer and Ferrigno, pp. 334–335.
12. In addition, the Pension Protection Act of 2006 (PPA 2006) provides protection to those plan sponsors of a participant-directed individual account pension plan that select default investments for employees who fail to direct their own investments. Under certain DOL conditions, participant assets invested in a "qualified default investment alternative (QDIA)" can obtain safe harbor relief from fiduciary liability for investment outcomes. This protection is not contingent on a plan being fully ERISA 404(c) compliant.

withdrawal penalties and valuation adjustments), as well as any restrictions on the exercise of voting, tender, or similar rights.

4. A description of transaction fees or expenses that are charged to the participant's account (e.g., commissions).
5. If the plan provides for investment in employer securities, a description of those procedures established to provide for confidentiality to participants regarding their transactions in those securities. This requirement includes the name, address, and telephone number of any fiduciary in charge of maintaining such confidentiality and information on independent fiduciaries that are required in transactions that involve employer securities where there is a high potential for a conflict of interest.
6. Shareholder information, subsequent to a specific investment, including any material the plan receives regarding the exercise of voting and ownership rights to the extent such rights are passed through to the participant, along with any references to any plan provisions regarding the exercise of these rights.
7. A copy of the most recent prospectus must be provided to participants immediately after they have made an initial purchase of an investment that is subject to the Securities Act of 1933. (In 2009, the Securities and Exchange Commission published rules for an enhanced disclosure framework for mutual funds, including a new Summary Prospectus rule. Under this rule, the delivery obligation may be satisfied by providing the statutory prospectus online at a specified Web-site address and providing the prospectus free of charge to any individual requesting the document in paper or by email.)
8. A description of those materials available only upon request and the identification of the person responsible for providing that information.

Yet, despite the issuance of these final 404(c) regulations in 1992, a number of employers still refrained from offering investment education because of fears of widening their fiduciary liability. In 1996, hoping to encourage more employer-sponsored financial education, the DOL issued Interpretive Bulletin (IB) 96-1, which established guidelines on what constitutes investment education versus advice. Although perfectly legal and offered by some plan sponsors, investment advice has fiduciary implications that can weaken Section 404(c) protection. The DOL's IB 96-1 stated that benefits communications comprising general plan information, general financial and investment information, asset allocation models that follow generally accepted investment theories, and interactive investment material are providing investment education, not advice. Many plan sponsors today do offer investment education, and the Internet is the ideal vehicle for the delivery of this service.

With just a few clicks of the mouse, participants can learn about general investment principles, read about the investment objectives of particular funds, request prospectuses, and obtain current benchmark performance data, as well as compare fund fees and expenses and their ultimate impact on earnings. Participants can also access interactive tools and financial calculators to guide them on asset allocation decisions to meet specific financial goals, such as buying a home or saving for retirement. Not many years ago, HR professionals were demonstrating the power of compounding by using brochures with cardboard slides that allowed for several different assumptions on retirement age, inflation, and interest rates. Today, the number of permutations that Internet investment models can accommodate is limitless.

However, offering employees financial and retirement planning services via the most innovative medium is not enough. Similar to open enrollment communication, a communication campaign is needed for financial education. The services that are offered only on the Internet must be publicized through other media and supplemented with other activities. General financial planning seminars should be offered throughout the year, as well as other sessions targeting specific groups. Those sessions targeting groups near retirement age should include topics such as Social Security benefits, retiree medical insurance, and long-term care. One-on-one counseling sessions could be offered by contracting with independent financial planners when employers are willing to augment investment education with investment advice.

EMPLOYER OBJECTIVES

The common employer objectives of benefits communications are to meet statutory requirements, educate plan participants on the provisions of programs, and demonstrate the value of benefits to the employee's total compensation package. But another critical objective is to support employers' efforts in managing employee benefits program costs. As discussed, effective employee communication can do much to assist employers in averting plan administration problems and lowering administrative costs.

Well-developed benefits communications can also assist in managing direct benefits costs. Employers have successfully utilized benefits communications tools to increase employee participation in defined contribution plans such as 401(k) plans in order to pass nondiscrimination test requirements. Another area where employers have used effective benefits communication tools in controlling costs has been in workers' compensation programs. The capacity of occupational safety training programs to reduce job injuries increases when their messages are reinforced through employee-supervisor communication campaigns.

Similarly, dynamic benefits communication programs are supporting health care cost-containment efforts of employers that attack the problem via managed care and consumer-driven products. These employers' plans require more than a description of the medical plan benefits. As employers continue to shift cost increases to employees and larger portions to those whom they consider unwise consumers of health care, the role of the communication program expands. It must compare and contrast medical plans, detail the advantages of in-network providers, promote the benefits of preventive care, and emphasize healthy lifestyles; its objective is to influence the behavior of plan participants. Ultimately, effective benefits communication tools can contribute toward increasing the number of visits to primary care physicians and decreasing those to specialists, increasing mammogram screenings, and increasing smoking-cessation enrollment. All are outcomes proven to have a positive impact on health-care costs.

SUMMARY

As companies continue to reduce paper-based processes and empower employees with Web-based self-service applications, HR departments are diverting resources from transactional activities to value-added strategic activities. HR professionals have begun to devote their energies to (1) designing plans that reduce the risk of moral hazard in group plans; (2) improving the quality of health care by interpreting data on providers, utilization, and outcomes; and (3) developing financial planning education that assists plan participants in balancing current needs with future ones.

Today, the challenge for HR professionals is to sift through mounds of data and design applications with information technology (IT) specialists that convert this mass of information into a knowledge base. Using this knowledge base, HR professionals can then continue to enrich employee benefit programs both for employees and for employers.

APPENDIX 27.1

KEY REPORTING AND DISCLOSURE REQUIREMENTS OF THE PATIENT PROTECTION AND AFFORDABLE CARE ACT OF 2010

The chart on the following pages provides an informal explanation of the 2010 health care reform legislation and has been adapted from the Affordable Care Act Regulations and Guidance, Provision Summary Chart, of the Employee Benefits Security Administration, Department of Labor, August 2010, www.dol.gov/ebsa/pdf/grandfatherregtable.pdf.

Selected Reporting and Disclosure Provisions of PPACA 2010

Provision (Effective date)	Summary of Provision	Application to Grandfathered Plans*
1. Advance notice of material notification. (Plan Years beginning on or after March 23, 2010 for grandfathered plans and Plan Years beginning on or after September 23, 2010 for new plans.)	Requires a group health plan to provide advance notice of a material plan modification at least 60 days prior to the effective date of the change. This is a change to the current ERISA requirement, which does not require that notice of health-plan changes be delivered in advance of such changes.	Applicable
2. Development and utilization of uniform explanation of coverage documents and standardized definitions. (Department of Health and Human Services develops rules by March 23, 2011, and group health plans provide the Summary of Benefits for Plan Years beginning on or after March 23, 2012.)	Requires the Federal government to develop standards for use by group health plans and by health insurance issuers in compiling and providing an accurate summary of benefits and explanation of coverage for applicants, policyholders or certificate holders, and enrollees. The explanation of coverage must describe any cost sharing, exceptions, reductions, and limitations on coverage, and give examples to illustrate common benefits scenarios. (The Uniform Explanation of Coverage Summaries is in addition to the summary plan descriptions (SPDs) ERISA requires to be provided to plan participants.)	Applicable
3. Additional information provision (transparency requirements). (Plan Years beginning on or after September 23, 2010.)	Requires group health plans and health insurance issuers offering group or individual health insurance coverage to disclose, to the Federal government and the State insurance commissioner, certain enrollee information such as claims payment policies and practices and enrollee rights. Requires such plans and issuers to provide information to enrollees on the amount of cost sharing for a specific item or service.	Not applicable

(continued)

4. Ensuring quality of care. (Department of Health and Human Services develops rules by March 23, 2012, and group health plans provide the Summary of Quality of Care for Plan Years beginning on or after March 23, 2013.)	Requires the Federal government to develop guidelines for use by health insurance issuers to report information on initiatives and programs that improve health outcomes. Prohibits a wellness program from requiring the disclosure or collection of any information relating to the presence or storage of a lawfully possessed firearm or ammunition in the residence or the lawful use, possession, or storage of a firearm or ammunition by an individual.	Not applicable
5. Bringing down cost of health care coverage (medical loss ratio provisions). (Plan Years beginning on or after January 1, 2011.)	Requires health insurance issuers offering group or individual health insurance coverage to submit annual reports to the Federal government on the percentages of premiums that the coverage spends on reimbursement for clinical services and activities that improve health care quality, and to provide rebates to enrollees if this spending does not meet minimum standards for a given plan year.	Applicable to insured grandfathered plans
6. Appeals process (for Plan Years beginning on or after September 23, 2010).	Requires group health plans and health insurance issuers offering group or individual health insurance coverage to provide an effective internal appeals process of coverage determinations and claims and comply with any applicable State external review process. If the State has not an established external review process that meets minimum standards or the plan is self-insured, the plan or issuer must implement an external review process that meets standards established by the Federal government.	Not applicable
7. W-2 reporting (not required for tax year 2011 as originally mandated; deferred until tax year 2012).	Requires employers to report the aggregate cost of employer-sponsored health coverage (determined on a basis similar to that under COBRA). FSAs, HSA contributions of the employee or the employee's spouse, and Archer medical savings accounts are excluded from the cost analysis.	Applicable

(continued)

Provision (Effective date)	Summary of Provision	Application to Grandfathered Plans*
8. Provide employee notices regarding Exchange Program.	By 2014, requires each state to establish one or more American Health Benefit Exchanges through which individuals and small employers can purchase health insurance, with states being allowed to opt out under certain circumstances. Beginning in 2017, states can allow large employers to purchase group health coverage as well. Requires an employer to provide the employee, at the time of hire, information regarding the existence of the Exchange, eligibility for premium tax credits and cost-sharing reductions. Requires employers that offer coverage and make a contribution to provide free-choice vouchers to qualified employees for the purchase of qualified health plans through exchanges.	Applicable
9. Automatic enrollment (effective date is unclear but the intent appears to be 2014).	Requires an employer subject to the Fair Labor Standards Act with more than 200 full-time employees that offers health-plan coverage to automatically enroll new full-time employees in the plan, subject to any allowed waiting periods and give employees notice of automatic enrollment program and the opportunity to opt-out of such health coverage.	Applicable
10. Special Internal Revenue Service (IRS) reporting requirements to demonstrate minimum essential coverage (effective January 31, 2015 for 2014 taxable year).	Requires health insurance and issuers or group health plans that provide minimum essential coverage to an individual to report the coverage to the IRS, including any portion of premium paid by the employer, and provide a statement to the individual. Large employers and employers required to provide free choice vouchers† are subject to expanded reporting requirements.	Applicable

*The Act established two different types of health care plans: (1) new plans (those established after March 23, 2010) and (2) grandfathered plans, which are any group health plans that were in effect on March 23, 2010. Certain changes to a grandfathered plan can result in loss of grandfathered status and certain plans may elect to opt out of the status. Some the new health reform rules do not apply to grandfathered plans and some of the rules do apply but at later dates than they do to nongrandfathered plans.

†The legislation includes an employer mandate that all employers that offer minimum essential coverage through a group plan and pay any portion of the costs of coverage are required to provide vouchers to certain employees who opt out of the employer's coverage.

PART SEVEN

Group and Health Benefit Plan Financial Management

Part Seven covers the crucial areas of taxation of group welfare benefit plans and the funding of health benefits.

Chapter 28 examines the federal tax law requirements in place for group welfare plans.

This is followed by two funding chapters: Chapter 29, which concentrates on insured funding arrangements from full insurance to administrative-services-only type approaches, and Chapter 30, which deals with self-funding techniques and captive arrangements.

CHAPTER 28

Federal Tax Law Requirements for Group Welfare Benefit Plans

Everett T. Allen, Jr.

At one time, group welfare benefit plans were mostly free of significant regulation by federal authorities. Employer contributions for these benefits were tax-deductible and, other than for group life insurance in excess of $50,000, were income tax free to employees. Benefits paid, for the most part, were also income tax free, the only notable exception being employer-provided disability income benefits. Nondiscrimination requirements were generally nonexistent and, in addition, employers had much latitude in prefunding future plan liabilities.

The first major legislation relating to group welfare benefit plans was the Employee Retirement Income Security Act of 1974 (ERISA), and even this law had limited application—the plans were subject only to its reporting, disclosure, and fiduciary requirements. Legislative activity in more recent times, however, along with regulatory interpretation, has brought these plans under an increasing amount of federal regulation. Age and sex discrimination laws and, in particular, tax law now impose significant restraints on group welfare plans and the benefits they provide.

This chapter reviews the federal tax law requirements applicable to the major employer-provided group welfare plan benefits—group life insurance, health care and disability income, as well as flexible benefit plans. The bulk of the tax issues relate to a plan's meeting of nondiscrimination requirements. These are addressed in the first section of the chapter. The discussion then moves to the taxation of contributions and benefits, how taxation varies when the nondiscrimination requirements are not met, and highlights key tax provisions of the Patient Protection and Affordable Care Act of 2010 (PPACA). Detailed coverage is beyond the scope of this chapter; additional information may be found in other chapters of the *Handbook* that deal with specific group and flexible benefit plans.

GENERAL TAX LAW REQUIREMENTS

Group welfare benefit plans must comply with a number of tax law provisions in order to receive favorable tax treatment. Some of the major nondiscrimination requirements are found in Internal Revenue Code (IRC, or Code) Sections 79 (group life insurance), 105 (employer health plans), 125 (cafeteria plans), 505 (voluntary employees' beneficiary associations (VEBAs) that utilize a tax-exempt trust), and 4980B (the so-called Consolidated Omnibus Budget Reconciliation Act (COBRA) requirements for the continued availability of health care coverage in certain situations). The PPACA amended Title I of ERISA by adding a new Section 715 which encompasses various health reform provisions of the Public Health Services Act (PHS). A conforming amendment (Section 1562(e)) applied the PHS Act provisions as if they were also included in ERISA and the IRC. The following subsections review the general concepts of these key provisions of the law.

SECTION 79—GROUP LIFE INSURANCE

Employee-pay-all group life insurance plans—in which all employees contribute, at all ages, either less or more than the imputed income rates published by the Internal Revenue Service (IRS), and in which there is no significant employer involvement—are not subject to Section 79 requirements. Employer-provided group life insurance benefits, however, must meet the nondiscrimination requirements of this section of the Code if key employees are to enjoy the tax advantages normally associated with these benefits.

In general, Section 79 requires that a group life insurance plan not discriminate in favor of key employees as to eligibility to participate and the type and amount of benefits available.

Eligibility Test

To satisfy the eligibility test, a group life insurance plan must meet one of four requirements: (1) the plan must cover at least 70 percent of all employees; (2) at least 85 percent of the participants must not be key employees; (3) the employees covered must qualify under a classification set up by the employer and found by the Department of the Treasury (the Treasury) not to discriminate in favor of key employees; or (4) if the plan is part of a flexible benefit plan, it must meet the requirements of Section 125. Although this is called an eligibility test, it is in fact a coverage test.

Some employees may be excluded when applying the eligibility test. These are employees who (1) have not completed three years of service, (2) are part time or seasonal, and (3) are covered by a collective bargaining agreement.

Benefits Test

Assuming one of the four eligibility tests is met, it is also necessary that the plan meet a benefits test. This test is not met unless all benefits available to participants who are key employees are also available to all other participants. A plan will meet this test if the amount of coverage provided bears a uniform relationship to employee compensation. Also, the IRS has informally indicated that the use of reasonable compensation brackets in a benefit schedule will be acceptable. On the other hand, the IRS has indicated that coverage based on job classifications will be acceptable only if it can be shown that their use does not discriminate in favor of key employees.

Section 79 Testing in General

The regulations require that all policies carried directly or indirectly by an employer that provides group life insurance to a common key employee are to be considered a plan (i.e., aggregated) for purposes of these tests. The employer also has the option of treating two or more policies that do not provide coverage to a common key employee as a single plan. This allows an employer to treat a plan for key employees and a separate plan for non-key employees as one plan, thus increasing the likelihood that the tests will be met for the combined plan.

In all cases, coverage is tested separately for active and retired employees. The regulations also provide that a plan will not be discriminatory as to the amount of coverage available if (1) the coverage group consists of a key employee and all other participants who receive an amount of insurance, as a multiple of compensation, that is equal to or greater than the coverage of the key employee; and (2) the plan, if tested separately, will pass one of the four parts of the eligibility test. For example, assume that an employer has a total of 500 participants, 10 of whom are key employees. Assume further that 400 nonkey employees have coverage equal to 100 percent of compensation and that the 10 key employees and 90 non-key employees have coverage equal to 200 percent of compensation. The plan will not be discriminatory, because 90 percent (i.e., more than 85 percent) of the participants in the group with 200 percent coverage are not key employees. In determining the groups that may be tested separately under this rule, allowances may be made for reasonable differences due to rounding, the use of compensation brackets or other similar factors. Section 79 uses the same definition of a "key" employee as for the retirement plan top-heavy rules (Section 416(i)). Under those rules, a "key" employee is one who, at any time during the plan year or any of the four preceding plan years, is (1) an officer with annual compensation in excess of an indexed amount ($160,000 for 2011), (2) a 5 percent owner, or (3) a 1 percent owner with annual compensation greater than $150,000. Section 79 adds retired employees to the Section 416(i) definition if any retiree was a key employee when he or she retired or separated from service.

There are certain qualifications about who should be counted as a key employee. First, there is an overall limit on the number of employees who are considered officers. The limit is 50, or, if fewer, the greater of three or 10 percent of the employees. This rule is particularly important for large employers, since it effectively caps the prohibited group at 50 employees. Also, the definition of officer is limited to executive officers; those with limited authority, such as bank loan officers, are not key employees under this rule. Certain other individuals are excluded as officers: (1) those who have not completed six months of service; (2) those who normally work fewer than $17\frac{1}{2}$ hours per week or six months or less per year; (3) those who have not attained age 21; and (4) those who are covered by a collective bargaining agreement.

SECTION 105(h)—EMPLOYER HEALTH PLANS

Before the passage of the PPACA, employer health plans that were insured were not subject to nondiscrimination standards. By contrast, self-insured employer health plans were subject to nondiscrimination rules under Section 105(h). Under the PPACA, group health plans that do not qualify for grandfather status as defined by the Act are required to comply with Section 105(h). The Department of Treasury and IRS requested public comments on what additional guidance would be helpful when they issued Notice

2010-63. This Notice indicated that a plan failing to comply with the 105(h) rules will be subject to a $100 per day penalty "per individual discriminated against." Hence, the penalty for noncompliance is based on the number of nonhighly compensated individuals that are discriminated against under the discriminatory health plan. Subsequently, Notice 2011-1 announced that compliance for insured health plans would not be required until guidance was issued. Furthermore, the eventual effective date was expected to occur with plan years beginning a yet-to-be-determined amount of time after the issuance of this guidance. Notice 2011-1 sought public comments on 13 specific issues to be submitted by March 11, 2011. Acccordingly, earliest compliance is unlikely before the latter part of 2011.

An interesting example of grandfathered plans that apparently would be excepted from the 105(h) rules would be certain previously established retiree only executive medical plans. Prior to enactment of PPACA, the 105(h) rules applied only to self-insured plans, which is why executive medical plans were created on a fully insured basis. Note however that such plans, although exempt from the 105(h) rules, would be subject to other provisions of PPACA such as the insurance market reforms prohibiting lifetime and annual dollar limits.

Employer health plans provided through a tax-exempt trust under Section 501(c)(9) of the IRC are also subject to nondiscrimination rules.

Going forward health plans subject to nondiscrimination testing, both self-insured and insured (once guidance is issued), include medical, dental, vision, and health care spending accounts. Disability income, business travel accident, and accidental death and dismemberment (AD&D) plans are not subject to the Section 105(h) nondiscrimination requirements.

The nondiscrimination standards of Section 105(h) require that the plan meet both an eligibility and a benefits test.

Eligibility Test

A health plan does not meet the eligibility test unless it covers (1) 70 percent or more of all employees, (2) 80 percent or more of all eligible employees if at least 70 percent of all employees are eligible, or (3) such employees as qualify under a classification set up by the employer and found by the Treasury not to discriminate in favor of highly compensated individuals. (The third alternative is often referred to as the fair cross-section test, because this requirement is satisfied if the covered group represents a fair cross section of all employees.)

For all three alternatives, the eligibility test is based upon the employees actually covered by the plan, not just those who are eligible for coverage. Also, each individual plan of the employer must meet one of these alternative eligibility tests. As will be noted later, however, aggregation of plans is permitted for testing purposes.

In applying these eligibility tests (as of 2011 before guidance issuance), an employer is allowed to exclude the following employees: (1) those who have not completed three years of service; (2) those who have not attained age 25; (3) part-time or seasonal employees; (4) those covered by a collective bargaining agreement; and (5) nonresident aliens who receive no earned income from the employer that is income from sources within the United States.

Benefits Test

A health plan does not meet the benefits test unless all benefits provided under the plan to highly compensated participants are provided to all other participants. This includes benefits provided to dependents as well as to employees.

In general, each individual plan of the employer must meet the benefits test, although, as will be noted later, aggregation of plans is permitted for testing purposes. A plan that provides optional benefits will be treated as providing a single benefit as to the benefits covered by the option if (1) all eligible participants may elect any of the benefits covered by the options and (2) there are either no required employee contributions, or the required employee contributions are the same amount for all participants.

The benefits test is applied to the benefits eligible for reimbursement under the plan, rather than to actual benefit payments, and all benefits are considered both as to the type of benefit and the amounts reimbursable.

An employer is not allowed to combine benefits available to highly compensated participants, determine the value of the combined benefits, and then compare that value with the value of benefits available to the other participants. Each benefit available under the plan must be considered separately.

If the difference in benefits is based on different waiting periods for employees in different subsidiaries or divisions, the problem of providing different benefits may be avoided if separate plans are actually created for the different subsidiaries or divisions. Each separate plan would then have to pass the discrimination tests on its own, using all of the employees in the controlled group for the eligibility test and the covered employees for the benefits test.

A plan is permitted to integrate with benefits paid under another plan or with benefits paid under Medicare or other federal or state laws.

Other Considerations in Section 105(h) Testing

Not only must a plan not discriminate on its face in providing benefits, it also must not discriminate in actual operation, based on the facts and circumstances of each case. A plan is not considered discriminatory, however, simply because highly compensated individuals utilize plan benefits to a greater extent than do the other employees.

The Section 105(h) regulations (issued prior to the enactment of PPACA) say that benefits provided to a retired employee who was a highly compensated individual will not be considered discriminatory if the type and dollar limitations of benefits provided to retired employees who were highly compensated individuals are the same as for all other retired participants. This rule could affect plans in which benefits differ by reason of employees' length of service—an approach that became more popular as employers sought ways to limit their liability for postretirement health care coverage. Technically, each service bracket represents a plan, and that plan is nondiscriminatory only if it satisfies the fair cross-section requirement.

Some additional matters under Section 105(h) requirements include the following:

- *Aggregation.* An employer may designate two or more plans as constituting a single plan for purposes of determining whether the nondiscrimination requirements are met. In the absence of comparability standards for aggregating plans, however, this rule is unclear. All employees under an aggregation of plans would probably not be eligible to receive the same benefits. If the combined plans fail the tests, the income of highly compensated individuals will be determined using the benefits paid under the combined plan.
- *Cafeteria plans.* If a health plan subject to Section 105(h) is included in a cafeteria plan, Section 105(h) determines the status of the benefit as being discriminatory or nondiscriminatory—that is, as being taxable or nontaxable—and Section 125 determines whether an employee is taxed as though he or she elected taxable benefits.
- *Definition of highly compensated.* For purposes of Section 105(h), a highly compensated individual is (1) one of the five highest-paid officers, (2) a 10 percent owner, or (3) an employee who is among the highest-paid 25 percent of all employees (other than the 10 percent owners who are not participants).

- *Exception for physical examinations.* The regulations provide an important exception from discrimination testing for reimbursements paid under a plan for "medical diagnostic procedures" for employees. Such procedures include routine medical examinations, blood tests, and x-rays. They do not include expenses incurred for the treatment, cure, or testing of a known illness or disability or for the treatment or testing for a physical injury, complaint, or specific symptom of a bodily malfunction. In addition, the procedures do not include any activities undertaken for exercise, fitness, nutrition, recreation, or the general improvement of health, unless they are for medical care. The procedure may only be for employees, not dependents, and it must be performed at a facility that provides no other services than medical and ancillary services. An employee's annual physical examination conducted at the employee's personal physician's office under a health plan is not subject to the Section 105(h) nondiscrimination tests and may be excluded from the employee's income if the requirements of Section 105(h) are met. If the examination is conducted at a resort, however, it will be subject to the Section 105(h) nondiscrimination tests, with the taxation of the benefit being based on whether the plan passes the tests.

SECTION 125—CAFETERIA PLANS

Under normal tax law rules, an employee who has a choice of receiving an element of compensation either in the form of cash or as a nontaxable benefit would have to consider this element of compensation as currently taxable income even if he or she chose the nontaxable benefit. This "doctrine of constructive receipt" is waived, however, if the choice is made under a cafeteria plan that meets the requirements of Section 125.

A cafeteria plan is defined by Section 125 as one that permits such a choice. A plan that permits a choice between only two nontaxable benefits (e.g., a choice between two medical expense plans or between group life insurance of less than $50,000 and disability income coverage) is not a "cafeteria" plan within the meaning of Section 125 and not subject to the requirements of this section or to the doctrine of constructive receipt.

A cafeteria plan may involve full choice making, may be limited to a flexible spending account (FSA), or might simply involve an arrangement whereby employees contribute for nontaxable benefits on a before-tax basis by taking pay reductions. Even this latter arrangement constitutes a cafeteria plan and must meet the requirements of Section 125. Section 125 imposes three nondiscrimination tests on any cafeteria plan: an eligibility test; a contributions and benefits test; and a concentration test.

Eligibility Test

The eligibility test requires that the plan be available to a nondiscriminatory classification of employees. The requirements for this test are generally the same as those that apply to qualified pension and profit-sharing plans. If the percentage of nonhighly compensated employees covered by the plan is at least 50 percent of the percentage of highly compensated employees covered, the test will be passed. On the other hand, if the percentage of nonhighly compensated employees covered is 40 percent or less of the percentage of highly compensated employees covered, the test will be failed. (Where the nonhighly compensated employees make up 60 percent or more of the total workforce, both of these percentages are reduced.) If the coverage ratio is between these two levels, a subjective facts and circumstances standard will be applied to determine whether the test is met. Employees with fewer than three years of service may be disregarded for testing purposes.

The regulations issued on August 6, 2007, modified the eligibility test by adding a benefits component. This change requires that benefits and employer flex credits be made equally available to highly compensated participants and to nonhighly compensated participants. Previously, plans were not required to look at benefits or contributions in conducting the eligibility test—these items were only important for purposes of passing the contributions and benefits test and the key employee concentration test.

Contributions and Benefits Test

The second test requires that contributions and benefits under the cafeteria plan not favor highly compensated participants. The "contributions and benefits test" consists of a "benefits" component that determines whether benefits and contributions are equally available to employees and a "utilization" component that determines whether highly compensated individuals are disproportionately utilizing plan benefits. The August 6, 2007, regulations clarified the utilization component of the test by requiring that plans show that all eligible employees have a uniform opportunity to make elections and that the actual elections of qualified benefits and the actual elections of qualified benefits with employer contributions are not disproportionately made by highly compensated participants. To demonstrate this, the regulations require plan sponsors to show that neither the aggregate qualified benefits nor the aggregate contributions elected and utilized by highly compensated participants exceed the aggregate benefits and contributions elected and utilized by nonhighly compensated participants. Plans must measure these aggregate amounts as a percentage of the respective group's compensation. However, a cafeteria plan providing health benefits can elect to satisfy a "safe harbor" provision if the contribution for all participants is either (1) the same as the cost of the health coverage chosen by the majority of highly compensated participants (similarly situated) or (2) at least 75 percent of the highest cost health coverage chosen by any similarly situated participant. Benefits or contributions in excess of these amounts must be uniformly proportional to compensation. Also, for these two tests a highly compensated employee is (1) an officer of the employer, (2) a 5 percent owner, and (3) any employee who is "highly compensated."

The August 6, 2007 regulations provide some measure of relief to plans that cannot pass testing when the plan population is tested as a whole. These rules permit such a plan to be disaggregated into two plans: one plan that benefits employees who have completed up to three years of employment and another plan that benefits employees who have completed at least three years of employment. Each of these component "plans" must be tested separately for both the "eligibility test" and the "contributions and benefits test."

Concentration Test

The third test, known as the concentration test, limits the benefits actually provided to "key" employees to no more than 25 percent of the aggregate benefits provided to all employees under the plan. For this test, "key" employees include (1) 5 percent owners, (2) officers earning more than an indexed amount ($160,000 in 2011), and (3) 1 percent owners earning more than $150,000. (The Economic Growth and Tax Relief Reconciliation Act of 2001 (EGTRRA) changed the definition of key employees.)

Additional Requirements

Other Section 125 requirements are the following:

- *Permissible benefits.* Only qualified benefits, as defined in Section 125 and regulations, may be included in a cafeteria arrangement. Permissible benefits include cash, Section 401(k) deferrals, medical expense benefits, dental expense benefits, employee group life insurance, disability income, time off, dependent care, and any other benefit permitted under regulations. Taxable benefits (e.g., financial counseling) are considered to be the equivalent of cash and may be included in the arrangement if such benefits are either purchased with after-tax employee contributions or are included in the gross income of the employees who elect the coverage.

- *Excluded benefits.* Benefits that are not permissible include any other form of deferred compensation, educational assistance, statutory fringe benefits, scholarships, and fellowships.
- *Participant elections.* A participant's choice must be made before the beginning of the plan year and must be irrevocable for the year unless the plan permits changes in the case of a "change in family status," such as marriage, separation, divorce, death, birth or adoption of a child, loss or commencement of employment by a spouse, change in job status of the employee or spouse, and any significant change in health care coverage of the employee or spouse by reason of change in employment. Any change must be consistent with the event that permits the change to be made. Change may also be made if a third party, such as an insurer, significantly changes the cost of the plan or if an insurer terminates or significantly cuts back benefits.
- *Spending account rules.* If a flexible spending account is maintained (for health care or dependent care expenses), additional rules must be observed. A separate account must be maintained for each eligible benefit and there can be no commingling of assets, nor can there be a transfer of assets from one account to another. Amounts not utilized by the end of the plan year[1] must be forfeited by employees, although they are permitted to share in a per capita reallocation of such forfeitures among all employees. Except for dependent care, the full amount of coverage chosen must be available for reimbursement to the employees from the beginning of the plan year even though not yet contributed. Any claims against a spending account must be substantiated by a provider statement, and the employee must verify that the expense involved has not been otherwise reimbursed.

1. For health care flexible spending accounts, employers are permitted to adopt a grace period of up to $2\frac{1}{2}$ months after the end of the plan year for employees to use flexible spending account funds that were unused during the plan year.

- *Health savings accounts.* If an employer makes contributions to employees' health savings accounts through a cafeteria plan, those contributions are subject to the nondiscrimination rules under Section 125 and not to the health savings account comparability rules under IRC Section 4980G. Outside Section 125 plans, employer contributions must be "comparable"; that is, they must be in the same dollar amount or the same percentage of the employee's deductible for all employees with the same category of coverage. The comparable requirements were liberalized in 2006 permitting employers to make larger contributions to the health savings accounts of the rank-and-file employees than to those of the highly compensated employees.

PPACA's Special Cafeteria Plan for Small Employers

The PPACA amended Section 125 to allow small (as defined by the Act) employers to establish "simple cafeteria plans." If an eligible small employer satisfies certain minimum eligibility and contribution requirements, the employer can take advantage of a safe harbor from the nondiscrimination rules of Section 125. That is, the small employer does not have to satisfy the "eligibility," "contributions and benefits," and "concentration" tests discussed above.

SECTION 505—VOLUNTARY EMPLOYEES' BENEFICIARY ASSOCIATIONS

In order for a voluntary employees' beneficiary association (VEBA) to retain its tax exemption under Section 501(c)(9), any plan of which it is a part must comply with the nondiscrimination provisions of Section 505. (An exception from this requirement exists for a VEBA that is part of a plan maintained pursuant to a collective bargaining agreement.)

A plan meets the requirements of Section 505 only if (1) each class of benefits under the plan is provided for a classification of employees that is set forth in the plan and found by the Treasury not to be discriminatory in favor of highly compensated employees and (2) no class of benefits discriminates in favor of highly compensated employees. The employer may elect to treat two or more plans as one plan for testing purposes.

In the case of any benefit that has its own statutory nondiscrimination rules, the above discrimination rules do not apply. The nondiscrimination requirements of the VEBA for such benefit will be treated as having been met only if the nondiscrimination rules applicable to that benefit are satisfied. Thus, for example, it will be necessary for Section 79 to be met with respect to group life insurance and for Section 105 to be met with respect to a medical reimbursement plan included in the VEBA if the VEBA is to enjoy a tax-exempt status.

An additional requirement is that a VEBA is discriminatory if any benefit provided through it (other than group life insurance) is based on compensation above an indexed amount. As a result of this provision, many employers have elected to exclude long-term disability and AD&D coverage from their VEBAs.

The definition of highly compensated employee for Section 505 is the same as the one used for qualified pension and profit-sharing plans—that is, any employee who (1) is a 5 percent owner or (2) receives annual compensation in excess of an indexed amount and is in the group consisting of the top 20 percent of employees when ranked by compensation.

The excludable employees for purposes of the Section 505 nondiscrimination rules (as of 2011) are (1) employees who have not completed three years of service, (2) employees who have not attained age 21, (3) seasonal employees or less-than-half-time employees, (4) employees covered by a collective bargaining agreement, and (5) nonresident aliens with no earned income from the employer that is income from sources within the United States.

SECTION 4980B—COBRA HEALTH CARE COVERAGE CONTINUATION

The Consolidated Omnibus Budget Reconciliation Act of 1985 amended the IRC and ERISA to require that health care coverage be available to employees (and their dependents) under employer-sponsored plans for a limited time after the coverage might otherwise terminate. These requirements generally apply to all employers with 20 or more employees.

In general, each "qualified beneficiary" who would otherwise lose health care coverage caused by a "qualifying event" must be given the opportunity to continue coverage during the applicable "continuation periods." A "qualified beneficiary" is the employee, the employee's spouse and the employee's children if they were covered by the plan immediately prior to the qualifying event. A "qualifying event" is

- Death of the employee
- Employee's termination of employment (except for gross misconduct)

- A reduction in the employee's hours
- Divorce or legal separation of the employee and his or her spouse
- Eligibility for Medicare coverage
- Cessation of a child's eligibility as a dependent
- Reduction, loss or subsequent elimination of retiree medical coverage one year before or after the beginning of an employer's bankruptcy proceeding

The "continuation period" is 18 months if the qualifying event is termination of employment or reduction in hours; otherwise, it is 36 months. In addition, coverage must be available for up to 29 months for individuals determined by Social Security to be disabled at the time of the employee's termination of employment or reduction in hours.

The coverage provided must be identical to the coverage provided for active employees who have not had a qualifying event. The election period during which a qualified beneficiary may elect to continue coverage is the 60-day period following the day coverage is terminated or the day notification of eligibility is received, whichever is later. The beneficiary may be charged up to 102 percent of the cost of the coverage. This limit is raised to 150 percent of the cost for certain disabled individuals for months 19 through 29. A plan administrator who fails to give proper notice may be subject to a penalty of up to $110 a day for each day of the failure.

TAXATION OF CONTRIBUTIONS AND BENEFITS

In understanding the federal tax law as it relates to the taxation of welfare plans, it is helpful to consider several aspects:

- Taxation of employer contributions
- Taxation of benefit payments
- Taxation of income on reserves held under the plan
- Deductibility of employer contributions
- Treatment of employee contributions
- Imposition of excise taxes

It is also helpful to consider most of these aspects in terms of the type of benefit, and this is the approach in the following discussion. It should be noted that, for some aspects, the tax treatment depends on whether the plan meets the qualification or nondiscrimination requirements, or both, of various IRC sections.

Taxation of Employer Contributions

The taxation of employer contributions for welfare plan benefits is quite favorable to employees. Employer contributions for health care coverage are not taxable to employees regardless of whether the plan is insured or self-insured. Nor are employer contributions for disability income and accidental death and dismemberment coverage taxable to employees, even for plans that discriminate in favor of key or highly compensated employees.

The major exception is that employer contributions for group life insurance in excess of $50,000 are taxable to the employee (or retiree). The amount that is reportable as income is determined under Section 79 of the IRC and under a table prepared by the IRS (see Table 28-1), but the amount otherwise reportable is reduced by any after-tax employee contributions—including amounts the employee might have contributed for the first $50,000 of term coverage. An exception to this occurs if the employee has named a tax-exempt charity as beneficiary. In this case, the employee is not taxed.

TABLE 28-1

Reportable Income per $1,000 of Coverage under Nondiscriminatory Group Life Insurance

Age Bracket	Reportable Income (Monthly) per $1,000 of coverage
Under 25	$0.05
25–29	$0.06
30–34	$0.08
35–39	$0.09
40–44	$0.10
45–49	$0.15
50–54	$0.23
55–59	$0.43
60–64	$0.66
65–69	$1.27
70 and above	$2.06

If a group life insurance plan is discriminatory, all key employees lose the $50,000 exclusion and have imputed income for all employer-provided coverage. Nonkey employees, however, are not affected if a group life insurance plan is discriminatory. They continue to have the $50,000 exclusion, and any imputed income is determined under the IRS rates.

If a cafeteria plan fails to meet the nondiscrimination requirement tests of Section 125, "highly compensated" or "key" employees, as the case may be, will have to include as taxable income the value of all benefits they could have received in taxable form. No other employees, however, will be affected by a plan's failure to meet these tests. Also, if a cafeteria plan fails to comply with the Section 125 requirements (other than the nondiscrimination rules), the doctrine of constructive receipt will apply, and all employees will have to include as taxable income the amounts they could have received in cash—even if their choices were for "nontaxable" benefits.

Taxation of Benefit Payments

Whether a group life insurance plan meets or fails to meet the nondiscrimination tests has no effect on how the actual benefits paid are taxed. Group life insurance proceeds that are received in a lump sum are free of income tax. If paid in installments, the portion of each payment representing interest paid by the insurer is taxable under the annuity rules of Section 72. Also, the proceeds are included in the employee's gross estate for federal estate tax purposes unless the employee assigned all incidents of ownership at least three years prior to death.

All insured health plan benefits are income tax-free. The same is true for self-insured employer health plan benefits if the plan is nondiscriminatory. If a self-insured employer health plan is discriminatory, benefits received by nonhighly compensated individuals are income tax free, but some or all of the reimbursements received by highly compensated individuals may be included in their gross income. If the plan fails the eligibility test, the amount that is counted as income to a highly compensated employee is the amount he or she received under the plan that is attributable to employer contributions, multiplied by a fraction, the numerator of which is the total amount reimbursed during that plan year to all highly compensated participants and the denominator of which is the total amount reimbursed during the plan year to all participants. If the plan fails the benefits test, all amounts received under the discriminatory features of the plan that are attributable to employer contributions are included in the income of highly compensated participants. In any event, benefits attributable to an employee's contributions are not included in the employee's income.

Employer-provided disability income benefits are taxable as income. Benefits attributable to after-tax employee contributions are income tax free. It should be noted, however, that before-tax employee contributions—through salary reduction—are considered employer contributions and will result in the disability income benefit being taxable.

Taxation of Income on Plan Reserves

Some welfare plans hold assets or reserves to pay for future benefits. These reserves may be held for a number of purposes, such as incurred but unreported claims, claims in process, and the like. Amounts so held are credited with investment income (either interest declared by an insurance company or actual income earned by assets held in trust). Provided that the reserves do not exceed a prescribed level and that certain other requirements are met, this investment income is generally free from income tax to the employer (or to the trust). Otherwise, it is taxed as unrelated business income.

Reserves that are actuarially reasonable are acceptable. An actuarial certification is required by the IRS if reserves exceed certain safe harbor limits. In determining safe harbor limits, reserves for benefits that exceed certain amounts are excluded, even though the higher benefits may be included in the plan. The safe harbor limits and the excluded benefits are shown in Table 28-2.

Additional amounts may be held for life insurance and medical expense benefits for retirees if additional requirements are met. These requirements are that separate accounts must be maintained for key employees, and that their benefits must be paid from such accounts. Furthermore, no amounts may be reserved in these accounts for discriminatory benefits

TABLE 28-2

IRS Limits on Welfare Plan Reserves

Type of Benefit	Reserve Limit	Excluded Benefit
Life insurance	To be determined by IRS under regulations	Taxable benefits (in excess of $50,000) for retirees
Disability income	Short-term plans: 17.5% of last year's claims Long-term plans: to be determined by IRS under regulations	Excess of the benefit over the lesser of 75% of the highest three-year average pay or Section 415 limit for defined benefit plans
Medical	35% of last year's costs	None

or for group life insurance in excess of $50,000, and funding of these accounts must be on a level basis, with no assumptions as to future increases in health care costs. Finally, and most importantly, income on reserves held for postretirement health care (but not life insurance) is taxable to the employer or trust, even when the above requirements are met and the coverage is nondiscriminatory. In recent years, the number of employers offering postretirement health care benefits has declined dramatically.

Deductibility of Employer Contributions

Employer contributions to a welfare plan are generally deductible if they do not result in the payment of unreasonable compensation. An exception is that contributions to a special reserve for life insurance or medical benefits for retirees are not deductible if the plan is discriminatory.

The general rule for deductibility is that contributions cannot exceed (1) benefits actually paid plus (2) additions to a reserve within the limits previously described minus (3) after-tax income on plan assets, including employee contributions. Contributions within this limit are deductible in the tax year in which the contribution is made. Excess contributions are deductible in subsequent years.

Treatment of Employee Contributions

Employees may make contributions to welfare plans on an after-tax basis. As previously noted, such contributions for group life insurance reduce the amounts otherwise taxable under Section 79 and, in the case of disability income benefits, provide a benefit that is free of income tax.

If a cafeteria plan meets the requirements of Section 125, employee contributions for group life insurance, health expense benefits and disability income may also be made through pay reduction—that is, on a before-tax basis. This is particularly advantageous for health expense coverage since otherwise taxable income is converted into tax-exempt income, thus saving the employee an amount equal to his or her marginal tax rate on the amount involved.

The following are some additional comments concerning before-tax employee contributions:

- Unlike the pay reductions permitted for Section 401(k) savings plans, amounts contributed on a pay-reduction basis for welfare plan benefits are not subject to FICA taxes by the employee, nor are they taken into account when determining the employee's Social Security benefits. For most employees, however, the value of the tax savings will more than offset any loss of Social Security benefits.

- The employer also receives a tax advantage for such before-tax employee contributions in that it, too, does not pay FICA (or FUTA) taxes on the amount involved.
- It rarely makes sense to make before-tax contributions for group life insurance in excess of $50,000.
- Disability income benefits attributable to after-tax employee contributions are free from income tax. If these contributions are made on a before-tax basis, the benefits are taxable.
- Even though an employee reduces his or her pay to make contributions under Section 125, other employee benefits may be based on gross compensation prior to the pay reduction. However, the employee's net pay, after the reduction, is used to determine contribution and benefit limitations for qualified pension and profit-sharing plans under Section 415 of the IRC.

Excise Taxes

A means of ensuring compliance with the tax law in the field of employee benefits has been the imposition of excise taxes on employers (and sometimes employees). Most of these excise taxes are associated with pension and profit-sharing plans qualified under Section 401 of the IRC. A few also apply to welfare benefit plans.

A 100 percent employer excise tax will be imposed on

- The value of medical or life insurance benefits paid to a retired key employee unless paid from a separate account as required by law
- The value of medical or life insurance benefits paid under a discriminatory plan funded through a welfare benefit fund, such as a tax-exempt trust under Section 501(c)(9) of the IRC
- Amounts reverting to the benefit of an employer from a welfare benefit fund.

A second area where an excise tax may be imposed on an employer concerns the COBRA requirements for the availability of continued health expense coverage in certain situations. An employer may face an excise tax of $110 per day for each beneficiary for whom there is a failure to comply with this law. The maximum excise tax under this provision for a year is the lesser of (a) $500,000 or (b) 10 percent of the employer's group health plan expenses for the prior year.

A third area where an excise tax may be imposed involves employer plans that fail to pay their benefits (as primary payers), before Medicare pays, for certain active and disabled individuals who are also entitled to Medicare benefits. This tax is set at 25 percent of the employer's expenses for all group health plans to which the employer contributes.

A fourth area where an excise tax may be imposed is on an employer that fails to make "comparable" contributions to employees' HSAs during a calendar year. A 35 percent excise tax is applied to the employer's aggregate contributions to its employees' HSAs during the calendar year. (Employees incur an additional tax on distributions from an HSA that are not used for qualified medical expenses.)

Additional Tax Provisions Under the Patient Protection and Affordable Care Act of 2010

Additional tax provisions under the Patient Protection and Affordable Care Act of 2010 include employer "Free-rider" penalties and small business health care tax credit.

Employer "Free-Rider" Penalties

Effective 2014, employers with at least 50 employees that do not offer minimum essential health coverage must pay a penalty in any month during which a full-time employee receives coverage through a state insurance exchange.

Effective 2014, a penalty is also imposed on large employers when certain employees choose not to enroll in the employer-sponsored plan and receive a federal subsidy to enroll in certain other insurance coverage.

Small Business Health Care Tax Credit

Effective 2014, the PPACA provides a tax credit to small businesses and small tax-exempt organizations that pay employee health insurance premiums. The credit is designed to encourage employers with 25 or fewer full-time workers to offer health insurance coverage for the first time or maintain coverage they already have. The credit is specifically targeted for employers with low- and moderate-income workers and that pay at least half the cost of single coverage. The credit is available only as an offset to tax liabilities.

CHAPTER 29

Funding Health Benefits: Insured Arrangements

Richard L. Tewksbury, Jr.

The cost of health and welfare benefit plans has become a substantial budget item for employers, causing them to take steps that control plan cost and liabilities. Employers—particularly large ones—are demanding that conventional insurance products become funding arrangements that are used as corporate financing tools. In response, insurance companies and third-party administrators have designed a number of alternative funding arrangements for group insurance programs. This chapter first explains a conventional insurance arrangement, then highlights the development of alternative funding arrangements and describes each in detail.

CONVENTIONAL INSURANCE ARRANGEMENTS

This section considers conventional insurance arrangements.

Definition

In a conventional insurance arrangement, an employer purchases a group insurance contract and agrees to pay premiums to an insurance company. In return, the insurance company agrees to pay specific benefit amounts for such events as death, medical care expenses, or disability. The employer's annual premium is based on historic claims cost experience of employers of similar size and characteristics and the underwriting factors and administrative expenses of the insurance company.

The insurance company uses the premiums paid by all employers to pay the claims incurred under its group insurance plans. Employers whose actual claims costs are less than their premium payments subsidize employers whose claims costs exceed their premium payments. In a conventional insurance arrangement, there is no reconciliation of an employer's premium payments to its actual plan expenses. Instead, any adjustment of premium charges reflects the loss experience of all employers.

Premium Cost Factors

The insurance company considers a number of factors in determining the total cost of insuring a risk.

Paid Claims

This is the total benefits paid to insured employees or their dependents during the policy period.

Reserves

This cost reflects the insurance company's liability to pay benefits in the future for a loss incurred during the policy year. The most common reserve is the incurred but unreported claim reserve established to pay losses incurred during the policy year but not reported for payment until after the policy year has ended. Reserves are also established for deferred benefit payment liabilities such as reserves for the life insurance waiver of premium, retiree life insurance, and future disability benefit payments.

Other Claim Charges

Several additional costs are assumed by the insurance company for providing special benefit coverages such as extended liability coverage and conversion to an individual insurance policy when a participant terminates employment.

Administrative Charges

Although the terminology and allocation of administrative expenses vary by insurance company, there are six main cost categories:

1. *Commissions.* This is the payment to a licensed insurance agent or broker for helping the employer obtain the insurance coverage and administer the plan. The commission amount is normally determined as a percentage of the premium paid, with the percentage either remaining level or declining as the premium increases.

2. *Premium taxes.* A state tax is levied on the premiums received by insurance companies in the resident states of insured employees. This tax expense is passed directly to the employer, normally as a percentage of premium paid. The current tax rate averages about 2 percent of premium, but varies from state to state.
3. *Risk charge.* Each insured employer contributes to the insurance company's contingency reserve for unexpected, catastrophic claims. The risk charge is normally determined by a formula based on the premium amount.
4. *Claims administration expenses.* These are the expenses incurred by the insurance company to investigate claims and calculate and pay the appropriate benefits. These expenses are normally fixed per claim, with the per-claim cost varying by the type of benefits paid. For example, life insurance benefits are relatively simple and quick to administer and have a low administrative cost per claim compared with disability and medical claims, which often require medical review and more difficult benefit calculations.
5. *Other administrative expenses.* Charges for actuarial, legal, accounting, and other such services plus overhead expenses are shared by all contract holders. These expenses are determined as a percentage of the premium amount, as a fixed charge, or as a variable charge based on the insurance company's actual services provided to the employer.
6. *Insurance company profit (stock company) or contribution to surplus (mutual company).*

ALTERNATIVE FUNDING ARRANGEMENTS

This section considers alternative funding arrangements.

Definition

An alternative funding arrangement defers, reduces, or eliminates the premium paid by the employer to an insurance company to transfer risk and receive plan administration services. This change in premium is accomplished in various ways that affect the standard reserves, claim charges, and administrative costs of a conventional insurance arrangement.

The deferral, reduction, or elimination of the premium provides an employer direct and indirect savings. Direct savings result from the reduction or elimination of specific insurance and administration charges.

Indirect savings are gained through the more profitable employer use of monies that otherwise are held and invested by the insurance company.

The trade-off for these savings is the employer's assumption of some insurance company functions and/or risk. For example, the employer might assume all or part of the financial liability—that is, benefit payments to employees—and therefore reduce the necessary premium paid to the insurance company to pay benefit claims. Similarly, an employer might agree to administer all or part of the plan to reduce the insurance company's administrative charges, or to purchase administration services at a lesser cost from an independent service firm, typically referred to as a third-party administrator.

Reasons for Alternative Arrangements

Reasons for alternative funding arrangements include premium charges, corporate value of money, and competition.

Premium Charges

An employer's main reason for purchasing group insurance is to transfer a personnel risk that has unpredictable occurrence and potentially greater costs than the insurance company's premium charge. If a substantial loss occurs, the insurance is a valuable investment. But if losses over a period of time are less than the premium charges, employers begin to analyze the insured risk and the conventional insurance arrangement for ways to reduce or eliminate the fixed cost of premium charges.

Employers with large insured employee groups have more predictable loss experience. They can reasonably project the expected claims costs of their employee groups over time and determine the expected annual cost to provide health and welfare benefits. The value of the conventional insurance arrangement then becomes protecting against unexpected catastrophic losses.

Because large employers can reasonably project their future benefit costs, they can determine the financial advantages and trade-offs of participating in the assumption of the risk. This participation reduces the premium paid to the insurer and potentially reduces the overall cost to the employer through reduced claims charges, premium tax, risk charge, and other administrative charges. These financial advantages have been the impetus to such alternative insured arrangements as participating and experience-rated contracts.

In some cases, employers are willing to assume total financial responsibility for providing health and welfare benefits to employees. This arrangement, called self-funding, eliminates premium payments to an insurance company and potentially reduces overall plan costs through reduced reserves and the elimination of premium tax, risk charge, and other claims and administration expenses. In addition, a self-funding arrangement may enable the multistate employer to lower plan costs by avoiding different state-mandated benefits and administrative regulations through the preemption clause of the Employee Retirement Income Security Act of 1974 (ERISA).[1] Self-funding is covered in detail in Chapter 30.

Corporate Value of Money

The significance of corporate value of money increases when premium costs and interest rates are rising. Under a conventional insurance arrangement, the insurance company invests the excess premiums when the paid premium exceeds plan costs. The insurance company also invests the various claim reserves it maintains for each group insurance plan.

Some of this investment income is credited to the employer. However, if the employer can earn more than this interest credit, it is advantageous to minimize the transfer of funds to the insurer. This factor has encouraged the development of deferred premium arrangements, reduction or waiver of accumulated reserves, and various self-funding arrangements.

Competition

There is intense competition among insurance companies for insuring "good" risks. As already mentioned, under the conventional insurance arrangement, employers have similar premium charges, which means that employers with favorable loss experience (premiums exceed plan costs) subsidize employers with unfavorable loss experience (plan costs exceed premiums). Employers with favorable loss experience—the "good" risks—will look for funding alternatives that better reflect their actual costs. The availability of alternative funding and administration arrangements is often the key factor in an employer selecting and continuing with an insurance company. This shift to alternative funding arrangements is especially true for medical expense and short-term disability plans. One survey reports that on average 75 percent of large employers and 15% of small employers currently self-fund one or more of their health plans.[2]

1. ERISA Sec. 514.
2. Mercer, *National Survey of Employer-Sponsored Health Plans*, 2009.

INSURED ALTERNATIVE FUNDING ARRANGEMENTS

There are a number of ways an employer may potentially reduce total plan costs and still remain in an insured arrangement that transfers the underlying benefit plan risk and plan administration to the insurance company. These alternatives can be classified in three ways, based on the employer objective(s) for the arrangement: (Note: While some of these methods have lost popularity in the recent past, they are included here for historical perspective and because they are still being used in some existing plans.)

1. Sharing year-end plan financial results:
    a. Participating arrangement
    b. Experience-rating arrangement
2. Minimizing plan assets held by the insurer:
    a. Deferred premium arrangement
    b. Annual retrospective premium arrangement
    c. Terminal retrospective premium arrangement
    d. Extended plan-year accounting
    e. Exclusion of the waiver of premium provision (life insurance)
3. Minimizing premium payments during the plan year:
    a. Claims-plus premium arrangement (life insurance)
    b. Partial self-funding arrangement (long-term disability)
    c. Large-deductible arrangement (medical)
    d. Minimum premium arrangement (health care, short-term disability)

The prevalence and importance of managed care plans in today's health care benefits programs have caused employers to expect similar alternative funding arrangements for these plans. The insurers, including health maintenance organizations (HMOs), have adopted some of the arrangements that share year-end results or minimize annual premium payments. However, the details often differ because managed care plans must also satisfy provider reimbursement contracts and unique state regulations.

Each insured alternative funding arrangement is described in the following sections.

Participating Arrangement

In a participating insurance arrangement, the employer shares in its favorable or unfavorable financial experience during the policy period. If the financial experience is favorable—that is, the claims and administrative costs are less than the premium paid during the policy period—the employer receives the surplus premium from the insurance company at the end of the policy year. If the financial experience is unfavorable—that is, the claims and administrative costs are greater than the premium paid during the policy period—the plan is considered to be in a deficit balance equal to the difference between total plan costs and paid premium. In most instances, this deficit balance is carried forward by the insurance company to be recovered from the employer in future years of favorable experience.

Therefore, in a participating insurance arrangement, the true cost, or net cost, of a group insurance plan is the premium paid during the policy year, adjusted for the balance remaining at year end.

Underwriting Factors

Because the insurance company shares with each employer in the net cost of its group insurance plans, several underwriting factors are included in a participating insurance arrangement that are unnecessary in a conventional insurance arrangement.

Employer Participation

An insurance company will vary the percentage of employer participation in the actual financial experience depending on two key factors: the "spread" of risk and the predictability of losses.

Spread of risk refers to the ability of the employer's benefit plan to absorb a major, catastrophic loss relative to its paid premium base. The larger the employee group, the easier it becomes to incur a major loss from one or a few plan participants without substantially affecting the year-end actual financial experience. The reason is that the total paid premium is large enough to pay the infrequent major losses as well as the expected plan benefit and administration costs. The risk is effectively "spread" across the premium base of the insured employee group. For health care plans, employee groups of more than 100 employees typically are considered large enough for a participating insurance arrangement. For life insurance and disability plans, the insured employee groups typically must be much larger—at least 250 employees—for a participating contract.

Predictability of losses is the most important factor in determining the percentage of participation. Essentially, the more predictable the total losses for each year, the greater the percentage of employer participation. Plans such as medical care, dental care, and short-term disability cover risks in which losses normally occur frequently and at relatively low benefit costs per occurrence. The predictability of loss experience for these plans is much better than for life insurance and long-term disability plans that cover risks with less frequent losses and normally much higher total benefit costs per loss. For this reason, participating insurance arrangements are more common in indemnity and preferred provider organization (PPO) medical care, dental, and short-term disability plans. Point of service (POS) and HMO managed medical care plans are less likely to offer participating arrangements due to the prefunding and incentive provisions of their provider reimbursement contracts.

To control the employer's percentage of participation in the plan's actual financial experience, the insurance company sets individual pooling points for each plan. A pooling point is the annual dollar limit of individual benefit costs that will be included in the actual financial experience of the participating insurance arrangement. Any individual benefit costs in excess of the pooling point will not be included in the plan's financial experience. Instead, this excess amount is included in the insurance company's "pool" of conventional insurance arrangements for the same risk. For example, a medical insurance plan could insure employees with unlimited lifetime medical care benefits but have an annual pooling point of $50,000. This means that an individual's benefits claims costs up to $50,000 are included in the plan's actual financial experience, and any benefit amounts in excess of $50,000 are assumed by the insurance company.

The employer pays an additional premium charge, called a pooling charge, for the exclusion of benefits amounts in excess of the individual pooling point. This charge is based on the loss experience of the conventional insurance "pool" and reflects the type of risk and expected average benefit costs that each employer will have in excess of the pooling point. For instance, a life insurance plan pooling charge normally equals the volume of life insurance in excess of the pooling point, multiplied by the insurance company's conventional premium rate. The medical care plan pooling charge is normally determined as a percentage of annual paid claims or a fixed fee per employee.

Table 29-1 illustrates a typical schedule of pooling point levels for medical care and life insurance plans, which are the most common participating insurance arrangements requiring pooling points.

Underwriting Margin

The premium paid under a participating insurance arrangement includes a charge for the possible fluctuation of actual costs in excess of the expected total plan costs during the policy year. This charge is commonly called the insurance company's underwriting margin.

TABLE 29-1

Pooling Points

Life Insurance Plan	
Volume of Insurance ($)	**Pooling Point ($)**
5 million	40,000
10 million	60,000
25 million	85,000
50 million	135,000
Medical Care Insurance Plan	
Annual Claims ($000s)	**Annual Benefit Pooling Point ($)**
500–2,000	50,000
2,000–4,000	75,000
4,000–8,000	100,000
Over 8,000	150,000 or more

Underwriting margin reflects the normal range of deviation of the plan's actual loss experience in any year from the expected loss experience. The underwriting margin is determined from actuarial studies on the fluctuation of actual claims experience relative to insurance company norms for similar employee groups and types of insurance coverage. In general, the underwriting margin decreases as the predictability of the plan's expected claims experience increases.

The underwriting margin for a basic group life insurance plan varies between 10 percent and 20 percent of premium, depending on the size of the employee group and volume of life insurance. As the number of employees and volume of insurance increases, the underwriting margin decreases. Table 29-2 illustrates the typical level of underwriting margins for medical care plans. It should be kept in mind, however, that these margins may vary substantially for similar employer groups, depending on employer-specific historical claims experience and market competition for the employer's business.

Eligible Employee Participation

Many employers have employees pay some or all of the benefit plan premium, especially for medical, dental, long-term disability, and supplemental

TABLE 29-2

Underwriting Margin for Medical Care Plans

Number of Covered Employees	Percent of Premium
Fewer than 500	10–15
500–1,000	7–12
Over 1,000	5–10

life insurance programs. A part of the eligible employee group typically will not pay this premium because they can obtain the benefits through their spouse or other sources at a lesser cost, or they do not feel the value of benefits coverage is worth the premium expense. Insurers are concerned that those nonparticipating employees are the "better risks" and the participating employee group is more likely to incur benefits claims costs. To mitigate this concern, insurers often require that a minimum percentage of eligible employees participate in the plan for the employer to receive the best premium rates, to be able to participate in alternative insured funding arrangements, or even to offer the benefit plan to employees. The typical percentage participation requirements differ by benefit plan (Table 29-3).

Determining the Year-End Balance

The underlying principle in a participating insurance arrangement is that the employer's final or net cost equals paid premiums adjusted for the year-end balance (surplus or deficit). The year-end balance is determined by the actual plan costs in relation to the paid premium.

TABLE 29-3

Percentage Participation Requirements for Different Types of Benefit Plan

Medical—75% participation*
Dental—50% participation
Long-term disability—35% participation
Supplemental life insurance—25% participation

*The 75% includes employees who pay the medical plan premium or waive coverage because they are enrolled in their spouse's benefit plan.

Basic Formula

The determination of a surplus or deficit year-end balance for group insurance plans is straightforward:

Paid premium – Claims costs – Administrative costs = Balance

Paid premium refers to the employer's total payments to the insurance company during the plan year, plus any fund transfers from a premium stabilization reserve or surplus carry-forward account.

The claims costs factor is made up of various charges:

1. Paid claims: the actual benefit payments during the policy year.
2. Reserve charge: the establishment of or adjustment to claims reserves held for incurred but unreported claims and any other specific pending liabilities, such as waiver of premium life insurance claims and unsettled claims payments at year-end.
3. Pooling charge: the additional cost for having large individual claims "pooled" in excess of a specific pooling point.
4. Other claim charges: the most common charge is a penalty charge levied against the employer when a terminated employee converts from a group to an individual insurance policy.

The administrative costs are essentially the same six expense categories mentioned previously for a conventional insurance arrangement.

Surplus Balance

If the year-end balance is positive, there will be surplus premiums available to be returned to the employer. The following example illustrates how a surplus year-end balance is determined. During the policy year, the employer pays $500,000 of group insurance premiums to the insurance company. Claims paid during the year are $375,000, reserve charges are $10,000, pooling charges are $20,000, and other claim charges are $5,000, for a total of $410,000 in claims costs. Total administrative costs equal $60,000. These total costs subtracted from the paid premium result in a year-end balance of $30,000 surplus premium.

Surplus premium that accumulates with the insurance company during the plan year is normally credited with interest earnings that are used to reduce the insurance company's administrative costs. The credited interest rate is based on the investment performance of the insurance company's general assets.

The insurance company can return the surplus balance by issuing a dividend check equal to the surplus amount. This dividend reduces the year-end employer-paid premium total that is tax deductible as an ordinary business expense under Section 162 of the Internal Revenue Code (IRC). Alternatively, the insurance company deposits the surplus balance in a special reserve, normally called a premium stabilization reserve. The major advantages of a premium stabilization reserve are as follows:

- It avoids a reduction in the tax-deductible paid premium amount at year end.
- It helps stabilize the future budget and cash-flow requirements of the plan by supplementing future premium rate increases with funds from the special reserve.
- It receives tax-free investment earnings on the reserve balances held for active employees' benefit plans.

A disadvantage of a premium stabilization reserve is the low interest rate typically credited by the insurance company on the reserve amount. Also, an insurance company may be able to retain and use these funds after contract termination to pay unexpected plan costs.

Another disadvantage of premium stabilization reserves is the potential tax implications if the reserve amount does not meet specific definitions of a "welfare benefit fund." The "fund" definitions were established in the 1984 Deficit Reduction Act (DEFRA) under Section 419 of the IRC. The principal purpose of this law is to prevent employers from taking premature deductions for expenses that have not yet been incurred. In essence, a premium stabilization reserve is considered reasonable, and deposits to the reserve tax-deductible, if there is no guarantee of renewal of the insurance contract and the reserve amount is subject to "significant current risk of economic loss," as defined under Section 419.

Deficit Balance

A negative year-end balance, or deficit balance, occurs when the employer's premium paid during the policy year is insufficient to pay the plan's total costs during the year. Such a situation is illustrated in the following example. Suppose that the premium and plan costs are the same as in the previous example, except paid claims during the year are $425,000, and the total administrative costs are $70,000. The total plan expenses now result in a year-end premium deficit balance of $30,000.

The deficit balance is offset during the policy year from the insurance company's corporate surplus to pay all claims and other immediate costs of the plan. In a sense, these insurance company funds act as a "loan" to the employer. While a plan deficit exists, the outstanding balance is charged with an interest expense similar to the interest credited on surplus premiums of other policyholders.

An employer's deficit balance will be carried forward and will be repaid by the employer through surplus premium balances that may result in future policy years. However, the employer normally is not contractually required to repay this insurance company "loan" and can switch insurance companies while a plan deficit is outstanding. This is a risk assumed by the insurance company and is reflected in the risk charge and the underwriting margins of the insurer.

Instead of repaying the deficit balance through future surplus premium, the employer can negotiate with the insurance company to repay the "loan" in a lump sum or in installments over a specified period. However, the insurance company interest charge on the outstanding deficit balance is often less than the interest charge if the employer were to borrow monies from another financial institution. In these instances, it is more cost-effective to repay the outstanding deficit balance through future surplus premiums.

In some participating insurance arrangements, the insurance company contractually cannot recover deficit balances from future employer surplus balances but still shares annual surplus balances with the employer. This type of arrangement reduces the insurance company's risk of an employer switching insurance companies before repaying a deficit balance. Also, this type of participating insurance arrangement may be more favorable for the employer because it participates only in years of positive financial results. The trade-off will be a higher annual risk charge or underwriting margin compared to an arrangement that participates in both year-end surplus and deficit-balance situations.

Employer Advantages

The advantage of a participating insurance arrangement is that the employer pays its "net" insurance cost and is rewarded for favorable financial experience by the return of year-end surplus premium. During a policy year of favorable experience, cost savings can be gained in two additional ways:

1. Premium tax is reduced because it is based on the net premium received by an insurance company; that is, the employer's premium paid during the policy year less the surplus balance returned at year end.

2. Administrative costs are reduced by lower general overhead charges based on net premium paid and by interest income earned on the surplus premium during the policy year.

The financial trade-off to the employer of a participating insurance arrangement is a higher-risk charge and underwriting margin in comparison with a conventional insurance arrangement. Also, the carryover of deficit balances will increase the future years' plan costs due to interest charges on the outstanding deficit balance and possibly additional underwriting margins required by the insurance company.

Experience-Rating Arrangement

Whereas a participating insurance arrangement lets the employer share in year-end surplus or deficit balances, an experience-rating insurance arrangement enables the actual financial experience of previous policy years to affect the employer's future premium charges. If the employer's actual financial experience has been favorable in the past, the future premium rates will be less than the conventional premium rate of other similar employers. If the historic financial experience has been unfavorable, future premium rates will be greater than the conventional insurance rates for similar employers.

An experience-rating arrangement can be included with either a participating or a conventional insurance arrangement. In either case, the actual historic financial experience of the employer's plan is the basis for determining the future plan year's premium rates.

Underwriting Factors

If an employer's actual loss experience has fluctuated significantly in the past, substantial changes can occur in the experience-rated premium charges from year to year. For example, a plan year with favorable loss experience will reduce the next year's premium charges. If unfavorable experience actually occurs during that next year, subsequent premium charges will increase to reflect this unfavorable year. Such annual swings in premium costs usually disturb employers and hinder their ability to budget future costs and control cash-flow needs. Similarly, the insurance company usually finds it more difficult to satisfy the employer when the required premium charges vary significantly from year to year.

To minimize this problem, the insurance company controls the significance of an employer's historic loss experience in determining premium charges. This is done through underwriting factors based on the statistical credibility of the actual paid claims experience and the type of risk.

Statistical Credibility

Statistical credibility refers to the validity of an employee group's actual paid claims experience representing the expected loss experience for such a group. The greater the statistical credibility, the greater the significance given to the group's historic financial results in determining future premium rates.

Statistical credibility is based on the applicability of the law of large numbers, which states that the larger the number of separate risks of a like nature combined into one group, the less uncertainty there will be as to the relative amount of loss that will be incurred within a given period.[3]

Statistical credibility is determined by the size of the employee group and number of years of actual paid claims experience that can be analyzed. Theoretically, the statistical credibility of cumulative years of actual experience for a smaller employee group will be similar to the one-year historic results of a much larger employee group. For example, the cumulative five-year life insurance experience of a 350- to 400-employee group has similar statistical credibility to the one-year experience of a 1,750- to 2,000-employee group.

The importance of the type of risk is similar to the underwriting of a participating insurance arrangement. Statistical credibility of actual loss experience is greater for risks that occur more frequently and have a lesser average cost per occurrence, such as medical care and short-term disability. Therefore, greater significance can be given to the actual paid claims experience for these types of risks. For instance, only one to three years of loss experience are normally necessary to determine the experience-rated premium charges of medical care, dental, or short-term disability coverages.

On the other hand, the insurance company applies statistical credibility to the employer's life insurance and long-term disability loss experience only if three to five years of paid claims experience are available for review. This caution is due to the greater volatility of loss experience (lesser frequency, greater cost per occurrence) from year to year for these types of risk. By analyzing three to five years' loss experience, individual years of unusually favorable or unfavorable loss experience are blended into a more typical historic trend of claims costs.

---

3. For a good explanation of the law of large numbers, see S.S. Huebner and K. Black, *Life Insurance*, 10th ed., Englewood Cliffs, NJ: Prentice-Hall, 1982, p. 3.

Credibility Factors

There are several ways an insurance company values the statistical credibility of historic loss experience in an experience-rating arrangement. The most common method is to use a weighted average of the employer's actual claims experience and the insurance company's standard loss factors for a similar conventional insurance arrangement. The percentage weighting given to the employer's actual paid claims experience is called the credibility factor. The greater the statistical credibility of the risk, the closer the credibility factor is to 100 percent—in which case the employer's prior loss experience is wholly representative of future loss experience.

Table 29-4 shows typical credibility factors applied to life insurance and medical care plans. The life insurance factors are determined by the number of covered employees and the number of available years of actual claims experience. The factors for a medical plan are typically based on the number of employees covered by the plan.

For example, if an employer's medical plan covers 200 employees and incurred $1 million of paid claims last year, a 50 percent credibility factor may be applied to this loss experience. If the insurance company's

TABLE 29-4

Credibility Factors (in percent)

Life Insurance Plan	Number of Years of Experience		
Number of Covered Employees	**1**	**3**	**5**
250–500	10%	25%	35%
500–1,000	20	55	75
1,000–2,500	40	65	85
2,500–5,000	65	85	100
5,000–10,000	75	100	100
Over 10,000	85	100	100

Medical Care Insurance Plan Number of Covered Employees	Credibility Factors
100–250	15%–50%
250–500	50–100
Over 500	100

expected losses for a similar size and type of employee group are $900,000, the expected paid claims for this employee group would be $950,000:

Employer's past year's actual claims ($1,000,000)

× Credibility factor (0.50) = $500,000

Plus

Insurer's expected losses ($900,000)

× Noncredible factor (0.50) = $450,000

Equals

Expected claims cost = $950,000

Pooling Points

A second method of controlling loss experience volatility is to establish pooling points, as described previously in the section on participating insurance arrangements. By placing dollar maximums on the individual and total plan claim costs that will be included in each plan year's actual financial experience, the volatility of losses in any year is limited. The insurance company levies a fixed annual charge, or pooling charge, for providing this limitation on the employer's "experience-rated" losses.

With a life insurance plan, the pooling charge is added to the average of the prior years' experience-rated paid claims to determine the expected claims costs for the next policy year. For example, if the average experience-rated claims cost over the last five plan years is $100,000, the life insurance volume in excess of the pooling point is $2,500,000, and the monthly pooling charge is $.60 per $1,000 of life insurance, then the expected claims costs for the next policy year are $118,000, as calculated here:

Average annual experience-rated claims = $100,000

Plus

Monthly pooling charge ($0.60)

× Excess insurance volume ($2,500)

× 12 months = $18,000

Equals

Expected claims cost = $118,000

The medical insurance pooling charge is normally stated as a percentage of annual paid claims or a fixed fee per employee. For instance, if the annual paid claims are $2,500,000, the pooling point is $75,000 per individual, and the pooling charge is 6 percent of claims, a charge of $150,000 would be included in determining the necessary premium charges for the next year.

Determining the Experience-Rated Premium

The exact method for determining the experience-rated premium charges varies by the type of insurance coverage and the insurance company. The following description covers the common principles for life insurance and medical care coverages.

Life Insurance

The life insurance premium charge is based on the expected paid claims, underwriting margin, reserve adjustment, pooling charge, and administrative costs.

- *Expected paid claims.* Determining the next year's expected paid claims depends on the credibility factor given to the employer's historic actual loss experience. The credibility factor is applied to the average actual paid claims total for a three- to five-year period. This average actual annual paid claims total should also reflect annual changes in the volume of life insurance and plan design changes during this period to provide a meaningful comparison of year-to-year claims experience. If the credibility factor is less than 100 percent, the insurance company's actuarial estimate of paid claims is used for the "noncredible" part of the expected paid claims. This actuarial estimate of paid claims is affected by insurance volume, covered employee demographics, industry, and other job-related factors.
- *Reserve adjustment.* The incurred but unreported reserve is initially established as a percentage of premium or paid claims and is adjusted each year thereafter to reflect changes in these factors. An estimate of the next year's adjustment is included in the premium-charge calculation based on expected paid claims or premium.
- *Underwriting margin.* This charge is normally stated as a percentage of expected paid claims and reserve adjustments. If a

participating insurance arrangement is included with the experience-rated arrangement, additional underwriting margin is added.

- *Pooling charge.* An annual charge is included based on the volume of "pooled" life insurance and premium rate for the employee group.
- *Administrative costs.* These costs are normally determined as a percentage of the experience-rated premium charges.

The sum of these factors determines the experience-rated life-insurance-premium charge for the next policy year. An example of calculating a required premium rate is illustrated in Table 29-5.

Medical Care Insurance

The medical care insurance premium charge for traditional indemnity plans and for preferred provider organization (PPO) and point of service (POS) managed care plans is based on expected paid claims, inflation/utilization trend, underwriting margin, reserve adjustments, pooling

TABLE 29-5

Life Insurance Experience-Rating Calculation

Assumptions: Five-year average actual paid claims	$100,000
Expected annual losses*	80,000
Credibility factor	.60
Underwriting margin	10% of incurred claims
Reserve adjustment	2,000
Pooling charges	6,600
Administrative costs	10,000
Example:	
1. Expected paid claims: ($100,000 × .6) + ($80,000 × .4)	$ 92,000
2. Reserve adjustment	2,000
3. Incurred claims	94,000
4. Margin: 10% of incurred claims	9,400
5. Pooling charges	6,600
6. Administrative costs	10,000
Required premium: (3) + (4) + (5) + (6)	$120,000

*Based on insurance company's actuarial statistics.

charge, and administrative costs. These factors are applied similarly to the life insurance premium charges, with the following exceptions.

- *Expected paid claims.* Two years' historic loss experience typically is evaluated, with much greater credibility given to the historic loss experience of the most recent plan year. For PPO and POS plans, total claims charges often include fixed costs for delivery of specific services, such as a capitated professional charge or a per-claim or per-case hospital facility fee arrangement, plus variable costs for all other services based on a negotiated discounted fee per transaction.
- *Inflation/utilization trend.* Rising medical care prices (inflation) and utilization of services are the primary economic factors that will increase the next year's paid claims; therefore, the expected paid claims are increased by a trend factor projected for the next policy year. This factor will vary by the type of medical care plan, the typical plan design, the medical risk of plan participants and the included cost-management features, such as preauthorization of hospital admissions and care management of high-cost individual medical care cases. For example, the national average rates of cost increase (trend) applied to health care plans in 2009 are as follows:[4]

Plan type	Trend factors
HMO	9.1 percent
CDHP[5]	6.1 percent
PPO	6.6 percent

It also is important to consider the variance in cost trend by employee location (geography factor) when determining the appropriate trend factor. The following chart is an example of the trend factor by geographic region.

4. Mercer, *National Survey of Employer-Sponsored Health Plans*, 2009.
5. Consumer-driven health plan.

Plan Type	Geographic Region			
	West	Midwest	Northeast	South
HMO	7.6	11.7	14.2	4.6
PPO	13.2	9.3	4.4	4.0

- *Pooling charge.* This charge is typically stated as a percentage of expected paid claims or a fixed monthly fee per covered employee.
- *Administrative costs.* For PPO and POS plans, these costs include an access fee expense to pay for the initial development and ongoing management of the provider network. This cost is typically set as a cost per covered employee per month or a percentage of the provider discount passed on to the plan sponsor.

The sum of these factors determines the experience-rated medical premium charge, as illustrated in Table 29-6.

The experience-rated premium calculation for an HMO is based on these same factors, but typically has less impact on future premium rates than the other types of health care plans, for several reasons:

1. The HMO rate-setting process is more closely regulated by the licensing states. The states often limit the weighting given to an employer's actual loss experience in determining future rates.
2. Compared with the other plans, HMO claims costs are influenced more by the service fees and fixed-cost reimbursement arrangements negotiated with hospitals, physicians, and other health care providers. These arrangements tend to be one- to three-year contracts that become "fixed" claims costs in calculating the next year's premium. The "variable" claims costs—which drive the experience-rated premium calculation—become a smaller part of total plan costs.

A variety of experience-rating methods are used by HMOs. For example, some HMOs apply the same methodology as previously described, but place a limit—such as 15 percent of current premium—on the annual change in rates. In other words, if the current experience-rated monthly premium rate for a single employee is $500, the maximum rate reduction or increase for the next year can be 15 percent, that is, $425 or $575 respectively. Another common technique is to use several years—typically three years—of claims cost experience in calculating the next year's rates.

TABLE 29-6

Medical Care Experience-Rating Calculation

Assumptions:	Prior year's paid claims		$2,000,000
	Expected annual losses*		2,200,000
	Credibility factor		.50
	Pooling charge		6% of expected paid claims
	Inflation/utilization trend		10% of expected claims costs
	Underwriting margin		7% of trended losses
	Reserve adjustment		50,000
	Administrative costs		125,000
Calculation:			
1. Expected paid claims			$2,100,000
Actual experience factor	($2,000,000 × .50)	$1,000,000	
Insurance company factor	($2,200,000 × .50)	1,100,000	
2. Pooling charge: (1) × .06			126,000
3. Inflation/utilization trend: [(1) + (2)] × .10			222,600
4. Trended claims cost: (1) + (2) + (3)			2,448,600
5. Underwriting margin: (4) × .07			171,402
6. Reserve adjustment			50,000
7. Administrative costs			125,000
Required premium: (4) + (5) + (6) + (7)			$2,795,002

*Based on insurance company's actuarial statistics.

Employer Advantage

An experience-rated insurance arrangement is much more a financing method for the employer's actual plan costs than a true insurance arrangement in which employers collectively share in the loss experience and have a common premium rate. With the experience-rating arrangement, the primary insurance protection is against the unexpected catastrophic losses in one plan year that might severely affect the ongoing financial condition of the plan. To the employer with favorable and predictable claims experience, this arrangement is a cost-effective way to share the plan's financial gains without assuming substantial financial risks.

Deferred Premium Arrangement

In a deferred premium arrangement, one to three months' premium payments to the insurance company can be deferred and used more advantageously by the employer. If and when the insurance contract terminates, the deferred premium must be paid to the insurance company.

In essence, this arrangement allows the employer to retain an amount similar to the plan's incurred but unreported reserves until it is actually needed by the insurance company at contract termination. The necessary amount of reserve varies by the type of coverage, with life insurance plan reserves equaling one to two months' premium, and disability and medical plan reserves equaling two to four months' premium. These reserves are part of the insurance company's total corporate assets and typically earn investment income that either reduces the employer's administrative charges or reduces the reserve amount held by the insurer. The interest credit is related to the insurance company's after-tax investment return on its general assets, which is often significantly less than an employer's after-tax rate of return earned on assets.

If this is the case, the deferred premium arrangement allows an employer to more effectively invest the reserve amount otherwise held by the insurer and thus enhance its cash flow and year-end earnings level.

To illustrate this advantage, assume an employer normally pays monthly premiums of $200,000 and has an after-tax employer value of money of 10 percent. The insurance company currently credits 5 percent interest on incurred but unreported reserves. If the employer and insurer agree to a three-month deferred premium arrangement, the financial advantage is the annual additional investment earnings the employer earns on the three-month deferred premium amount. In this case, the employer would earn an additional 5 percent return on each of the $200,000 monthly premium deferrals for the remainder of the policy year, which provides an annual cash flow advantage of $27,500. This is shown in Table 29-7.

TABLE 29-7

Example of Savings to Employer under a Three-Month Deferred Premium Arrangement

Month	Deferred Premium		Additional Interest Credit		Duration of Policy Year		Savings
1	$200,000	×	5%	×	1 year	=	$10,000
2	$200,000	×	5%	×	11/12 year	=	$9,167
3	$200,000	×	5%	×	10/12 year	=	$8,333
					Total	=	$27,500

The loss of the interest credits from the insurance company is reflected in higher annual administrative or reserve charges. However, these increases should be more than offset by the additional employer investment earnings.

Deferred premium arrangements are most common in health care plans that have substantial reserve requirements. Managed medical care plans typically offer only a one-month premium deferral if they have capitated or prefunded financing arrangements in their provider contracts.

Annual Retrospective Premium Arrangement

An annual retrospective premium arrangement reduces the employer's monthly premium payments by a specified percentage, with the understanding that this percentage of premium will be paid to the insurance company at year end if the plan's actual claims and administrative costs exceed the actual paid premium. The specific percentage reduction of premium normally relates to the insurance company's underwriting margin. The employer gains a cash-flow advantage through its use of this premium amount during the plan year if the employer value of money exceeds the insurance company's interest credit on surplus premium.

Underwriting margin provides the insurer with premium in excess of the funds necessary to pay expected claims and administrative charges, as illustrated below. During the plan year, any surplus premiums held by the insurance company are credited with interest based on the investment return of the insurance company's general corporate assets. In a participating insurance arrangement, this surplus premium is returned to the employer at the end of the plan year.

If the insurance company's interest credit is less than the employer's value of money, an annual retrospective premium arrangement is advantageous. By investing during the plan year the premium amount otherwise held by the insurer as underwriting margin, the employer can improve its current cash flow and its year-end earnings level through the additional investment income earned.

For example, assume an employer's annual premium cost is $3 million, or $250,000 per month, and the plan's underwriting margin is 10 percent of premium. A 10 percent annual retrospective premium arrangement would reduce the premium payments to $2.7 million per year and provide $300,000 of reduced premium to be invested by the employer during the plan year. The financial advantage is the additional investment earnings the employer can earn on the $300,000 of reduced premium amount. If the employer after-tax value of money is 10 percent and the insurance company interest credit is 5 percent, the additional investment income to the employer is approximately $7,500. (This value assumes premiums are paid monthly and that the additional investment earnings equal the monthly interest rate multiplied by the remaining months of the plan year.)

As part of the annual retrospective premium arrangement, the employer agrees to pay to the insurance company at the end of the policy year a part or all of the reduced premium amount if the actual claims and administrative charges exceed the actual premium paid during the plan year. The insurance company pays charges in excess of paid premium during the year from its capital or surplus accounts. An interest charge is applied to these excess charges that represents the insurance company's lost investment earnings.

Terminal Retrospective Premium Arrangement

With a terminal retrospective premium arrangement, the employer agrees to pay the outstanding deficit that may exist at the time the insurance contract is terminated with the insurance company. The agreement usually specifies a maximum percentage of premium or dollar amount up to which the employer will indemnify the insurance company at contract termination.

In this arrangement, the insurance company substantially reduces the annual risk charge and the underwriting margin. The terminal retrospective premium arrangement transfers some or all of the unexpected claims cost risk to the employer; therefore, these charges can be reduced. This reduction is reflected in lower monthly premium costs and gives the employer use of this reduced premium amount for potentially more profitable investment.

Also, this arrangement offers more underwriting flexibility for insuring high benefit limits and special plan design features that otherwise pose a potentially greater financial risk to the insurance company. Because some of the risk of underestimating the losses from these special benefit arrangements is transferred to the employer, the insurance company is more apt to underwrite the coverage to satisfy the employer's needs.

Both annual and terminal retrospective premium arrangements can be included to maximize the reduction of the risk charge and underwriting margin and the potential cash flow savings. However, the terminal retrospective premium arrangement is less common than the annual arrangement. Insurance companies are less apt to offer a terminal retrospective premium arrangement because its long-term nature makes it difficult to determine a reasonable value to the insurer. Secondly, its attractiveness is limited to the very large employer that is willing to assume a potential long-term liability and that is considered a good long-term credit risk by the insurance company. Therefore, the applicability and current use of this alternative insurance arrangement is limited.

Extended Plan-Year Accounting

Some insurance companies extend the plan year's accounting of claims paid as a means of reducing or eliminating the necessary incurred but unreported claims reserves. These insurers record the claims incurred before the end of the plan year but paid after the plan year as actual paid claims during that plan year. This extended accounting period, which is normally an additional one- to three-month period, allows the actual incurred but unreported claims to be more accurately accounted to the appropriate plan year and substantially reduces or even eliminates the incurred but unreported claims reserves maintained by the insurance company.

For example, if the accounting period for a life insurance plan is extended an additional month, the incurred but unreported reserve, which is normally about 10 percent of premium, is often reduced to 2 to 3 percent of premium. Similarly, extending by two months the plan year accounting for a traditional indemnity or PPO medical care plan may reduce the incurred but unreported reserve by 50 percent or more.

This financial alternative is normally available only to large employers with predictable monthly claims experience. For such employers, this arrangement provides a more accurate accounting of incurred but unreported claims during each plan year. To the extent these actual claims are less than the insurance company's normal reserve factors, the employer gains a direct savings and cash-flow advantage. In addition, the insurance company substantially reduces the required reserve levels held during the contract period. The employer gains a cash-flow advantage on the reserve difference equal to the additional investment income earned by the employer using these funds in its business compared to receiving an interest credit from the insurance company.

Exclusion of the Waiver-of-Premium Provision (Life Insurance)

The waiver-of-premium provision is common in a group life insurance program. It continues coverage for a totally and permanently disabled employee without continued premium payments by the employer for the employee's coverage. Although such a provision sounds attractive, the additional cost of including it in the life insurance plan is often greater than its actual value, especially for large employers.

Monthly premium costs typically increase 10 to 15 percent due to the increase in incurred but unreported claims reserves and the additional risk of the waiver-of-premium provision. The additional monthly cost of this provision can be avoided in large part by the employer eliminating the waiver-of-premium provision and continuing to pay monthly premiums for the disabled employees. The total cost of these continued premium payments after the disability date may be substantially less than the additional 10 to 15 percent monthly premium charge for all employees.

A potential disadvantage to excluding the waiver-of-premium provision occurs if the employer changes insurance companies. There can be a problem continuing life insurance coverage for previously disabled employees with the new insurer because most contracts only insure employees actively at work as of the effective date of the new life insurance coverage. Insurance companies often waive this provision for large employers, but they may hesitate to do so for smaller employers if the inclusion of disabled employees' coverage could adversely distort the expected loss experience. Therefore, excluding the waiver-of-premium provision is often suggested only for larger employers.

Claims-Plus Premium Arrangement (Life Insurance)

A claims-plus premium arrangement bases the employer's monthly life insurance premium on the actual loss experience of previous months plus fixed monthly administrative and reserve charges. To the extent that actual monthly loss experience is less than the level monthly premium payments normally paid during the plan year, this difference can remain with the employer as additional cash flow. If the employer's value of money is greater than the insurer's interest credit on surplus premium, the employer gains additional investment income on this difference during the plan year.

To limit the cash flow risk of the employer incurring monthly benefit claim payments in excess of the level monthly premium amount, insurance companies set the maximum monthly employer cost at the level monthly premium amount plus any "surplus" accumulated from prior months. Also, the maximum annual claims cost assumed by the employer is the same as the annual premium cost determined by the insurer. In this way, the employer still is fully insured against unexpected or catastrophic loss experience that may occur during any policy year.

To illustrate how this claims-plus premium arrangement works, assume the employer's annual life insurance premium cost is $360,000, or a level monthly premium payment of $30,000. This $30,000 monthly premium payment is based on $27,000 of expected losses per month and a standard monthly administrative and reserve charge of $3,000. Table 29-8 shows the actual monthly premium costs under a claims-plus arrangement given the above assumptions and assumed actual loss experience during the plan year.

The typical administration of the claims-plus arrangement is for the first month's premium payment to equal the level monthly premium payment amount and thereafter to equal the actual loss experience of the previous month plus the standard administrative and reserve charge. In the example illustrated in Table 29-8, the employer pays the monthly premium payment of $30,000 in month 1 and from then on pays the actual losses of the previous month plus the standard monthly administrative and reserve charge of $3,000. For instance, the premium payment for month 2 is $23,000; that is, $20,000 of actual losses in month 1 plus the $3,000 administrative charge. The cumulative balance for month 2 and thereafter equals the cumulative difference between actual monthly payments and the normal monthly premium payments. In months 5, 9, and 11, the employer pays substantially more than the normal premium payment, reflecting the previous months' high actual losses. This can occur under

TABLE 29-8

Life Insurance Claims-Plus Arrangement ($thousands)

	Months												
	1	2	3	4	5	6	7	8	9	10	11	12	Total
Normal premium	30	30	30	30	30	30	30	30	30	30	30	30	360
Actual losses	20	0	20	50	10	0	0	70	20	50	30	20	290
Administrative/ reserve	3	3	3	3	3	3	3	3	3	3	3	3	36
Actual monthly payment	30	23	3	23	53	13	3	3	73	23	53	26	326
Cumulative balance	–	7	34	41	18	35	62	89	46	53	30	34	34

this arrangement as long as any actual monthly payment does not exceed the typical monthly premium payment plus the cumulative claims balance as of that date. At the end of the plan year, a reconciliation occurs between the actual annual plan expenses and the year-to-date (11 months) actual monthly payments. In month 12, the employer pays the reconciling balance required to cover actual annual plan expenses, subject to the maximum annual plan premium of $360,000. In the example, the employer pays a reconciling balance of $26,000:

Actual annual plan expenses:		$326,000
• Actual losses:	$290,000	
• Administrative/reserve:	$36,000	
Actual monthly payments (11 months)		$300,000
Month 12 reconciling balance		$26,000

Insurance companies have various trade names for this arrangement, the most common being flexible funding or minimum premium arrangement. Normally, such an arrangement is offered only to large employers that have substantial monthly life insurance premiums. Normally, for employers with less than a $30,000 monthly life insurance premium, this arrangement is not advantageous, because of the increased internal administration and administrative costs, the volatile fluctuation in monthly claims, and limited potential financial gain.

Partial Self-Funding Arrangement

Long-term disability (LTD) insurance promises to pay a significant percentage of an employee's income for the duration of his or her total and permanent disability. Typically, the number of claims incurred by an employer is few, but the total cost per claim is quite large because of the duration of benefit payments. In the plan year that an LTD claim is incurred, a reserve is charged to that year's financial experience equal to the discounted expected cost of all future benefit payments. Often, the reserve charge of a new claim equals a majority of the annual paid premium. However, the limited number of claims over a three- to five-year period allows the insurance company to set the premium rate at the expected average annual cost over this time period, thereby keeping it relatively stable and affordable for the employer.

The employer can partially self-fund its group LTD plan by assuming the financial liability of any claim for a specific duration and transferring the remaining liability to the insurance company. This arrangement reduces the monthly premium payments to the insurance company, provides potential cash-flow savings through increased investment earnings on the premium difference, and still provides the employer substantial insurance protection against a catastrophic claim situation. Two other financial advantages to a partial self-funding arrangement are (1) the incurred but unreported reserve requirement is normally reduced and (2) the premium tax liability is reduced.

There are two ways this arrangement can be designed. The more common method is for the insurer to assume the benefit payment liability for the first two to five years and the employer to continue benefit payments beyond this specific time period. There are several advantages of this plan design:

1. The average duration for an LTD claim is less than two years, so the long-term financial liability and administration assumed by the employer is limited.
2. The insurance company establishes minimal reserves for future benefit payments in comparison with a fully insured arrangement, which reduces the required premium payment and offers cash-flow savings to the employer.
3. Because an extended period exists before the employer assumes financial liability and begins periodic benefit payments, the employer typically prefunds its liability only when the disability actually occurs.

The second plan design option is for the employer to pay the LTD benefits for the initial two to five years and the insurance company to assume the risk thereafter. The main employer advantage is that premiums are substantially reduced because the employer is assuming the full liability of most LTD claims.

As a general rule, this alternative insurance arrangement is offered only to employers with at least 1,500 to 2,000 insured employees. For smaller plans, typically the claim occurrence is too volatile and the potential long-term financial liability normally too large for the employer to effectively self-insure the risk.

High-Deductible Arrangement (Medical)

Like the partial self-funding arrangement for LTD plans, the high-deductible arrangement for medical care plans has been designed for the employee and employer to assume the financial liability for a substantial part of each medical plan participant's initial annual covered medical expenses and transfer only the excess claims costs to the insurance company. This arrangement substantially reduces the monthly premium payments to the insurance company, provides potential cash-flow savings through additional investment earnings on the unused premium difference, and still provides the employee and employer substantial insurance protection against a catastrophic individual claim situation.

Other potential advantages of this arrangement are (1) the incurred but unreported reserve requirement is typically reduced, (2) the premium tax liability is reduced, (3) it facilitates the employee sharing some of the assumed claims costs, and (4) tax-favored employee health accounts can be used (for a more detailed description, see below). A high-deductible arrangement typically is used with traditional indemnity or PPO plans.

The typical design of this arrangement is illustrated below and shows the three parties—the employee, employer, and insurance company—assuming some of the annual benefits cost.

The employer typically assumes the financial liability for the initial \$1,000 to \$5,000 of annual medical plan benefit payments per participant, which is called the self-funded risk. In turn, the employer typically requires the employee (and dependents) to assume the financial liability for a budgetable amount of the self-funded risk—typically the initial \$500 to \$1,500 of covered expenses per year per family member (referred to as the individual deductible) and 10 or 20 percent of the remaining self-funded risk. Usually, there is a family maximum annual expense, defined either as a dollar limit or when two or three family members have each reached the individual deductible limit.

The financial liability in excess of the self-funded risk level is transferred to the insurance company, which also serves as plan and claims administrator for the total program.

This arrangement is of greatest interest to employers that want to manage utilization, assume financial responsibility for the high-frequency, relatively low-cost health care services, and be protected from the infrequent and unbudgetable high-cost individual medical episodes. High-deductible arrangements have also been an outgrowth of the popularity of flexible spending accounts, medical savings accounts, and similar employee-funded medical reimbursement accounts.

Recent legislation has encouraged the use of health savings accounts (HSAs) for eligible individuals participating in a high-deductible health plan.[5] HSAs are the most recent form of tax-favored medical reimbursement accounts created through federal legislation, the others being medical savings accounts (MSAs), health reimbursement accounts (HRAs), and flexible spending accounts (FSAs). Each account type was created at a point in time for a specific employer-employee need, and each has many similarities but also several significant legislated differences from the others. The intent of each account type is the same—to offer tax-favored health savings arrangements for employees that relieve employers of some health benefit expense and provide employees access to affordable employer-sponsored health benefits.

Minimum Premium Arrangement (Health Care, Short-Term Disability)

In a minimum premium arrangement, the employer pays the health care and/or short-term disability benefits directly from its general assets instead of transferring funds in the form of premium payments to the insurance company. The employer essentially self-funds the payment of benefits up to the expected loss level for the plan year, with the insurance company assuming the financial liability for any claims costs in excess of the expected loss level. The only premium paid to the insurer is for the normal administrative, risk, and reserve charges.

This arrangement is typically used for traditional indemnity or PPO medical plans, dental plans, and short-term disability plans.

The primary advantages of this arrangement are reduced premium tax liability and potential cash-flow savings. The payment of benefits from general assets is not considered an insurance arrangement in most states;[6] therefore, no premium tax liability is incurred. This offers a direct average annual savings of 2 percent of the normal premium amount used to pay benefits. Typically, a minimum premium arrangement is suggested only for employers with at least $5 million in premiums. At this minimum level of premium, approximately 90 percent of premium, or $4.5 million, is used to pay benefits. This implies the annual savings from reduced premium tax liability are approximately $90,000 (2 percent of $4.5 million).

6. IRC Section 223 defines a "high-deductible health plan" as having, for tax years beginning in 2011, an individual-coverage annual deductible of at least $1,200 and a family-coverage annual deductible of at least $2,400.

7. California assesses a premium tax on all benefits paid through a minimum premium arrangement.

As the premium size increases, the percentage of premium used to pay benefits similarly increases and the premium tax savings become more substantial. For instance, an employer paying $8 million in annual medical premium may use 93 percent of the normal premium to pay benefits, or $7.44 million. At this level, the annual premium tax savings would be $148,800.

The second advantage is potential cash-flow savings gained by the employer having the use of "surplus" funds during the plan year. Minimum premium arrangements are generally designed so the employer pays benefit claims during the plan year up to the annual expected loss level determined by the insurance company. This limit is often called the employer maximum liability. The employer pays benefits periodically from a separate cash account[7] to meet the plan's claims liability. If the actual claims paid during the initial months of the plan year are less than the expected monthly claims costs, a "surplus" develops in the cash account. To the extent the investment return earned by the corporation on this "surplus" is greater than the insurance company's interest credit on surplus premium, the employer gains additional investment earnings and a cash-flow advantage.

By paying benefit claims as they are reported during the plan year, the employer also can have a cash flow loss if claims in the initial months are greater than the expected monthly claims costs. To avoid this possibility, a minimum premium arrangement can be designed to limit the maximum monthly payment of claims from the employer cash account equal to the monthly level of expected claims costs plus any "surplus" funds accumulated during the plan year. If the actual claims costs in a month exceed this limit, the insurance company pays all excess benefit claims from its funds. If "surplus" funds develop in future months, the insurer immediately uses these funds to recoup its payment amount of prior months. The insurance company normally increases its administrative and risk charges to reflect the potential additional monthly liability it assumes in this specific case.

In a minimum premium arrangement, the insurance company administers all claims payments and assumes the risk of claims costs in excess of the annual expected loss level, just as in conventional or other alternative insurance arrangements. Figure 29-1 illustrates the flow of a benefit claim from its initial receipt, review, and benefit determination by the insurance

8. This corporate cash account typically is either a wire transfer institutional account or a 501(c)(9) trust.

FIGURE 29-1

Claim Flow of Minimum Premium Arrangement

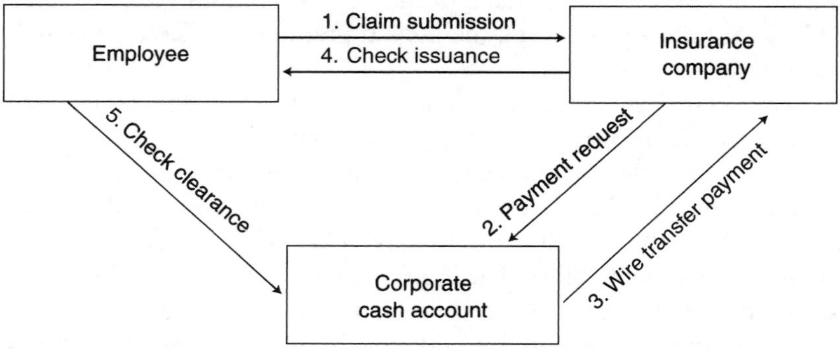

company to the issuing and clearing of a corporate check through the corporate account.

The insurance company typically has similar administrative, risk, and reserve charges as in a conventional or other alternative insurance arrangement. The employer pays a monthly premium to the insurer equal to the expected annual cost of these charges. Premium taxes must be paid by the employer on these monthly premium amounts. In the previous examples, where 90 and 93 percent of normal premium are deposited into the employer cash account to pay expected claims costs, the remaining 10 and 7 percent of normal premium, respectively, reflect the monthly premium charge for administrative, risk, and reserve costs.

Minimum Premium–No-Reserve Arrangement

A significant difference between a minimum premium arrangement and self-funding (described in Chapter 30) is that the insurance company still maintains a substantial reserve for incurred but unreported claims in the minimum premium arrangement. As in other alternative insurance arrangements, the employer can potentially gain a cash-flow savings by gaining the employer use of the reserves. To meet this employer demand, the insurance companies offer a minimum premium–no-reserve arrangement.

The employer gains the use of these reserves by the insurance company returning the incurred but unreported reserves it has been holding and reducing the future premium charges paid to the insurance company. This arrangement allows the employer to use the reserve funds until they are required to pay incurred but unreported claims at the time of plan or contract termination. Because of state insurance regulations, insurance companies cannot fully release to the employer the financial liability for incurred but unreported claims at termination of its insurance contract with the employer. Therefore, the employer must either repay the reserve amount to the insurer at time of termination, or specifically pay the incurred but unreported claims up to the insurer's contract reserve amount for a similar medical and/or short-term disability plan.

The minimum premium–no-reserve arrangement offers most of the financial advantages of self-funding, and it limits the employer's liability for benefit payments in excess of the expected annual loss level. The liability for these possible unexpected costs is still assumed by the insurance company. A disadvantage of the minimum premium–no-reserve arrangement is that administrative costs will be higher than in the minimum premium arrangement because the interest credited by the insurance company on reserves, which is applied to reduce the administrative charges, no longer exists. However, the additional investment income gained through the corporate use of these funds offsets this disadvantage.

Multi-Option Arrangements

HMO, PPO, and/or POS plans are now included in most employers' health care programs. These managed care plans are designed to control costs by steering patients to hospitals and physicians that have agreed to a reduced or fixed payment, and by managing utilization of services. Employees often choose between these managed care options and employers often establish separate benefit, funding, administration, and insurance arrangements to manage each plan.

While a multi-option benefit program helps control total claim costs, the additional plan administration and separate funding arrangements can cause problems. Plan administration is more complex due to the additional reporting, employee communication, and tracking of eligibility, payments, and expenses. This complexity increases internal and third-party administration costs. When employee participation is spread among several plans, the previously discussed alternative insured arrangements may have less impact or even be inappropriate. For instance, the employer's credibility factor may be substantially less in an experience-rating arrangement if the number of participants in the PPO significantly decreases. And if this insured group becomes too small, cash-flow arrangements such as minimum premium may not be feasible.

In addition, the separate financial arrangements can limit the employer's ability to share in the overall claims cost savings. HMO coverage often is provided through a fully insured arrangement, with premium rates often based on the average community costs of all HMO participants and the employer being unable to participate in the year-end financial settlement. If the actual claims costs of the employer's HMO participants are less than the overall community costs, the employer is subsidizing the plan and not gaining the total savings of the HMO option.

In response, insurance and managed care companies are offering employers the managed care options as one funding, administration, and insurance arrangement. After the employees make their plan choices, a multi-option arrangement essentially works as if it is one plan. The enrollment, reporting, and communications activities are consolidated, typically reducing both internal and third-party administration expenses. The financial results of each plan option are combined to determine the year-end balance, which enables the employer to fully share in any plan savings. And the insurance or managed care company may offer the alternative funding arrangements previously discussed in this chapter.

Table 29-9 illustrates the potential financial advantages of a multi-option arrangement. Assume there are three plans—indemnity, PPO, and

TABLE 29-9

Multi-Option Arrangement Financial Advantages ($thousands)

	Indemnity	PPO	HMO	Separate Plan Total	Multi-Option Total
Employees	1,000	1,000	1,000	3,000	3,000
Premiums	$8,500	$7,800	$7,700	$24,000	$24,000
Actual Expenses					
Claims	$8,150	$6,820	$6,230	$21,900	$21,200
Administration	$850	$780	$770	$2,400	$2,400
Total	$9,000	$7,600	$7,000	$24,300	$23,600
Balance	($500)	$200	$700	($300)	$400

HMO—with 1,000 employees covered in each plan. The indemnity and PPO plans are separate, participating insurance arrangements, whereas the HMO is conventionally insured, which means the employer doesn't participate in a year-end surplus balance. The premiums and total expenses for each plan are different, resulting in a $500,000 deficit balance for the indemnity plan, a $200,000 surplus balance for the PPO, and a $700,000 surplus balance for the HMO. The balance in the Separate Plan Totals column is a $300,000 deficit balance because the employer doesn't collect the $700,000 surplus balance from the conventionally insured HMO plan. However, with a multi-option funding arrangement, the employer has a $400,000 surplus balance total at year-end. This favorable result is due to the favorable HMO claims cost being included in the total balance of the multi-option arrangement.

The multi-option arrangement is available primarily to large employers—typically those with at least 1,000 employees—whose employee locations match the locations of the insurer's managed care networks. Also, some states limit the scope of this arrangement by restricting the consolidation of actual HMO financial results with the other employer-sponsored plans.

SHORT- AND LONG-TERM IMPLICATIONS OF 2010 HEALTH CARE REFORM LEGISLATION

Health care for all US citizens, especially those who receive health care insurance through their employers, likely will be significantly impacted by the 2010 health care reform legislation—formally the Patient Protection and Affordable Care Act (PPACA)—which was signed into law on March 23, 2010, by President Obama. This landmark legislation has three primary goals:

1. Increase access to health care—about three-fourths of the current uninsured are expected to have access to health care benefits through expansion of Medicaid eligibility, premium subsidies and credits, market reform provisions, state-based health insurance exchanges, and coverage mandates.
2. Improve affordability—this aspect is primarily focused on low- and middle-income individuals and on small employers that find health care insurance unaffordable.
3. Control long-term health care costs—the decrease in uninsured costs and cost-shifting to private insurance, and improved

private and public insurance marketplace risk, efficiencies, and quality of care are the primary drivers for achieving this goal.

However, there are uncertainties and challenges in how this legislation will ultimately be implemented, as would be expected of a law trying to change such a dynamic marketplace. For example, the law was written as a framework with many of the details to be defined by regulation; there are 1,045 references in the law that state "the Secretary of Health and Human Services shall determine . . ." the rules and specifics of the legislation's provisions—and it likely will be many months and even years before all of these regulations are issued. Also, at the time of writing of this chapter, legal action by a number of states challenging the constitutionality of a federal law mandating individual health coverage is moving through the federal court system and likely will be decided by the U.S. Supreme Court.

In the meantime, employers offering employee health benefits must implement short-term market reform provisions and assess the long-term implications of the PPACA, and their covered employees must understand the changes and new provisions of this law.

Short-Term Market Reform Provisions

Short-term market reform provisions include general provisions, those effective from September 23, 2010, and January 1, 2011, and provisions that impact insured plans.

General Provisions

Many market reform provisions apply to all employers sponsoring health benefits plans for their employees, regardless of whether the plans are insured or self-funded. The primary intent of these provisions is to expand access to coverage and eliminate or modify certain restrictive insurance provisions tied to underwriting requirements, medical history, and plan administration processes.

The key provisions, based on the implementation effective date, are provided below. The applicability of the provisions is complicated by whether the employer's benefits plan is a "grandfathered plan," which is defined as a plan in existence as of March 23, 2010 and that remains relatively unchanged after that date in its benefits and employee cost-sharing levels.

Effective Date: First Plan Year Following September 23, 2010

- Uninsured adult children are covered under the parent's benefits plan up to age 26.

- Lifetime benefit maximums are prohibited for essential health benefits, which include coverage for ambulatory, emergency, hospitalization, surgery, maternity and newborn care, mental health and substance abuse, prescription drug, laboratory, and rehabilitation services.
- Annual benefits maximums for essential health benefits are phased out over the next three years and prohibited in 2014.
- Exclusion from coverage due to preexisting health conditions is prohibited immediately for children under age 19 and for all plan participants in 2014.
- Rescission of coverage is prohibited except for fraudulent actions.
- Preventive services benefits are paid in full (nongrandfathered plans only).
- There is automatic enrollment of new hires (applies to employers with more than 200 full-time employees). The Department of Labor (DOL) has postponed compliance with this mandate until it issues implementing regulations. The DOL expects to complete the rulemaking process by 2014.
- For nongrandfathered plans, the employee has the right to designate a primary care provider and select a pediatrician and obstetrician/gynecologist even for HMO and POS managed care plans, and in- and out-of-network benefits for emergency room services must be similar.

Effective Date: January 1, 2011

- Over-the-counter medicines are not covered in flexible spending and health reimbursement or individual savings accounts.
- Nonmedical withdrawals from Health Savings Accounts incur a 20 percent penalty.
- Employers must prepare to report the value of employees' health care benefits on 2011 tax year W-2 forms.[8]

9. However, the IRS has stated in Notice 2010-69 that the reporting requirement is not mandatory for Forms W-2 issued for 2011.

Provisions Impacting Insured Plans

The PPACA has provisions that immediately affect only insured health benefits plans:

- *Minimum medical loss ratio* (effective January 2011). The intent of this provision is to limit insurance company administrative costs and profits. An insurance company must use at least 80 percent (for small employers with fewer than 100 employees) or 85 percent (for large employers with 100 or more employees) of insurance premium to pay health benefits and services that improve the quality of care, such as medical management services. If the insurance company does not meet this minimum, e.g., it spends only 83 percent of premium on benefits reimbursement and care improvements for large employers, the "excess amount" (2 percent in this example) must be rebated to all covered employees.
- *Review of premium rate increases* (effective 2011). The Secretary of Health and Human Services (HHS) will set up a process for health plan insurers to report and justify their annual premium increases by state.
- *Ban on discrimination favoring highly compensated employees* (plan year following September 23, 2010, only for nongrandfathered plans).[9] Similar to the current nondiscrimination rules for self-funded plans under IRC Section 105(h), insurers cannot offer plans that favor highly compensated employees in eligibility for coverage or benefits provided. There are specific rules and calculations to determine discriminatory provisions.

Long-Term Market Reform and Other Employer Provisions

Long-term market reform and other employer provisions include general provisions and those that impact insured plans.

---

10. IRS Notice 2011-1, released December 22, 2010, provides that fully insured plans do not have to comply with the nondiscrimination rules until the IRS issues guidance.

General Provisions

Regardless of employer plans being insured or self-funded, they must comply with several market reform provisions as of January 1, 2014:

- For all plans, the waiting period for eligibility to participate in the health plan cannot exceed 90 days from date of hire.
- Small-employer and new nongrandfathered plans have limits on out-of-pocket (deductible, copay, coinsurance expenses) maximums similar to the high-deductible health plan maximums on health savings accounts.
- For nongrandfathered plans, coverage for clinical trials must be provided.

In addition, employers will be able to offer wellness program incentives up to 30 percent and possibly 50 percent of individual premium costs (the current limit is 20 percent of costs). The most significant provision, however, is that each employer with at least 50 full-time employee equivalents is mandated to provide health benefits to employees or pay a $2,000 annual penalty per full-time employee (net of the first 30 full-time employees). And, if the employer's plan does not satisfy minimum benefits or affordability requirements for employees earning less than 400 percent of the federal poverty levels and at least one of these employees selects to participate in the Health Exchanges instead of the employer plan, the employer either pays a $3,000 per employee penalty to the government (if employee contributions exceed 9.5 percent of household income) or makes monthly voucher payments to the employee (if employee contributions are between 8 and 9.5 percent of household income).

Provisions Impacting Insured Plans

The PPACA has provisions that affect only insured health benefits plans in 2014.

- *Ban on coverage denials.* Insured plans must provide guaranteed issue and guaranteed renewal policies.
- *Rate reform.* For small-group (fewer than 100 employees) plans and in the Health Exchanges, there will be caps on the rating variation for age, geography, family composition, and tobacco use; premiums cannot vary based on health or gender.
- *Health Exchange participation.* Insurers of small-group plans, and possibly large-group plans, will be allowed to compete in the state-based Health Exchanges.

- *Annual health insurer fees.* To finance the health reform law, an annual fee will be imposed on health insurance companies ranging from $8 billion in 2014 to $14.3 billion in 2018 and more in subsequent years. This fee can be passed through to employer plan costs, so employers are likely to see higher premiums in 2014 due to these fees.

CONCLUSION

This chapter has described a number of creative solutions for reducing or, at least, controlling the employer costs of health and welfare benefit plans. However, as these costs continue to increase, employers and the insurers and other third-party service firms supporting their plans will be designing additional alternative funding arrangements to meet employers' needs. This trend will be most prevalent in funding HMOs and other managed care plans. At the same time, federal and state regulatory and legislative branches are increasingly interested in how employers finance and administer their benefit plans. This oversight will add another dimension to designing and administering alternative funding arrangements in the future. These dynamic market forces ensure continued activity and creativity in the funding of employee benefit programs.

CHAPTER 30

Funding Health Benefits: Self-Funded and Captive Arrangements

Richard L. Tewksbury

Timothy J. Luedtke

As health care expenses increasingly became a bigger and bigger portion of a business' cost structure during the late 1970s and early 1980s, business owners sought ways to retain greater control and flexibility with the working capital associated with their health insurance programs. Initially, as discussed in Chapter 29, they sought control over claim costs and any associated investment income by delaying premium and claim payment through retrospective premium, minimum premium, experience-rated, and other alternative insured programs.

As business owners become ever more comfortable with the potential volatility associated with health care claims, they increasingly seek to retain control over not only the health care claims but also over the risk capital associated with their plans. Such risk capital may be retained either implicitly with a self-insured arrangement or more explicitly with the creation of an insurance captive. This chapter discusses these more advanced risk retention approaches and the related implications of the Patient Protection and Affordable Care Act of 2010 (PPACA).

NONINSURED (SELF-FUNDING) ARRANGEMENTS

The final step in potentially reducing total plan costs is for the employer to assume essentially the total financial risk of the benefit plan, which is called self-funding. In this arrangement, the only plan costs are the actual paid claims, claims administration and other administrative expenses, and, in some cases, excess loss premium expense. By eliminating the other insurance-related expenses, the employer is in a position to pay only the basic administration expenses and fully capture favorable loss experience. Of course, the employer is also responsible for all unfavorable loss experience, because there is little or no transfer of risk to an insurance company.

The most common benefits plans being self-funded are medical, dental, and other health care plans, and short-term disability benefits. The same self-funding principles apply to managed care plans (including HMO and POS plans) as to traditional indemnity and PPO health care plans, except where noted in this section. Life insurance benefits plans seldom are self-funded because only insured death benefits are tax advantageous to the beneficiary. And, the number of employers self-funding long-term disability benefits has decreased because of a competitive insurance market and 1993 federal tax law changes that limit self-funded coverage for compensated employees using a tax-exempt trust.

Corporate employers have been self-funding benefits plans for many years, especially after the courts clarified in 1974 that self-funding should not be construed as doing an insurance business and therefore does not subject these plans to state insurance laws. Government and not-for-profit employers and Taft-Hartley welfare plans have lagged behind corporate employers in implementing self-funding arrangements, due in part to unique legislation authorizing this alternative funding arrangement and in part to their greater hesitancy to assume total financial risk. However, at this point, self-funding is applicable and common for all types of employers and benefit plan sponsors (see Table 30-1).

Definitions

Self-funding refers to a funding arrangement in which the ultimate financial and legal responsibility for providing the plan benefits is assumed by the employer. These arrangements typically must comply with federal disclosure, documentation, and fiduciary requirements under the Employee Income Retirement Security Act (ERISA).

Although the "payor of last resort" in this type of funding arrangement is the employer, the risk of losses exceeding an affordable threshold is often transferred to an insurance company through the purchase of excess loss insurance. This insurance coverage is also referred to as stop-loss insurance or reinsurance.

TABLE 30-1

Percentage and Type of Employees with Self-Funded PPO and HMO Medical Plans

	PPO/POS	HMO
Manufacturing	82%	20%
Wholesale and retail trade	75%	15%
Finance	56%	26%
Services	55%	13%
Government	77%	68%
Total large employers	75%	24%
Small employers	15%	7%

Source: Mercer, *National Survey of Employer-Sponsored Health Plans*, 2009.

There are two types of excess loss insurance: individual and aggregate. Individual excess loss insurance covers the claims costs incurred by and/or paid for an individual during a specified time period (typically a 12-month plan year) that exceed a specific threshold. For example, an employer may purchase medical plan individual excess loss insurance that applies to any plan participant's medical benefits claims costs exceeding $100,000 (the typical threshold ranges from $50,000 to $200,000) that are incurred and paid during a calendar year. Aggregate excess loss insurance protects an employer from total plan claims costs exceeding a specified threshold during a specific time period. For example, if medical plan paid claims exceed 125 percent (the typical range is 110 to 130 percent) of an agreed-upon, expected cost threshold (e.g., $5 million) during the calendar year, all costs in excess of $6.25 million are reimbursed by the aggregate insurance coverage.

The claims and other plan administration services for a self-funded arrangement can be performed by the employer or, more often, by a third-party administrator (TPA) or an insurance company as part of an administrative-services-only (ASO) contract. No risk is assumed by the TPA or insurance company, so the contract charges are related only to claims payment transactions and other plan administration processes. Typical administrative charges of an insured funding arrangement, such as premium tax, risk charge, commissions, and general administrative and underwriting expenses, are not included in an administrative services contract.

Advantages of Self-Funding

Self-funding arrangements can provide employers both financial and plan-management advantages. The primary advantages include capturing favorable claims experience, reducing administrative and other claims expenses, avoiding state-mandated benefits, and having greater flexibility in managing the benefit plans.

Capturing Favorable Claims Experience

Self-funding is most effective for group insurance plans with a substantial number of claims transactions and a relatively low cost per transaction, such as medical, dental, and short-term disability benefit plans. The expected financial result for these types of plans is more predictable. This predictability helps an employer project its expected annual claims costs and assess whether these costs are less than similar costs in an insured arrangement. If the employer is confident its actual plan costs will be less than the insurance company's premium charges and the potential savings outweigh taking the risk, the employer should consider self-funding.

For example, to calculate future premium charges, insurance companies often use factors in addition to historical claims experience, such as demographics of the insured group, industry-specific actuarial factors, and the average claims experience of other similar employers. Let us say that, looking at these factors, the insurance company determines an employer's short-term disability claims costs for next year will be $500,000. The employer knows that actual claims costs for the last two years have been 15 to 20 percent less than the insurance company's projections. If the employer is confident this historical experience should repeat itself, this situation is appropriate for self-funding.

Reducing Administrative and Other Claims Expenses

While capturing favorable claims experience offers the greatest potential savings, the more certain savings of self-funding come from lower "fixed" plan costs—that is, administration, reserves, and other claims charges.

Because the employer assumes the financial risk, the types of administrative services and charges of an insurance company or TPA differ in several ways from an insured arrangement:

1. No premium tax liability is incurred by the insurance company or TPA, so no premium tax charges are transferred to the employer.

2. There is no risk charge, because the insurance company or TPA assumes no financial liability for benefit payments.
3. Typically, no commission payments are included in a self-funding arrangement.
4. General administrative and underwriting services performed by the insurance company or TPA typically are much less than in an insured arrangement, so the charges for these activities are comparatively much less.

The insurance company or TPA administers the plan and determines the benefit payments under a self-funded arrangement in the same way as in a conventional insured arrangement. The typical services provided under this arrangement include the following:

- Claims processing
- Financial and administrative reports
- Plan descriptions for employees
- Banking arrangements
- Government reporting and compliance
- Basic underwriting and actuarial services
- Individual conversion policies
- COBRA administration
- Legal, clinical, and other professional services

By performing these services, the insurance company or TPA accepts the fiduciary responsibilities and powers necessary to administer the plan. However, they do not assume financial responsibility for the plan. The benefit payment checks are drawn against the employer's general assets or assets deposited into an employer-sponsored trust (see "Funding and Accounting Considerations" later in this chapter). Often, the insurance company or TPA is not even identified on these checks.

Many employers also consider internally administering the plan to further reduce their administrative costs. However, there are a number of reasons why purchasing administrative services from a third party may be more cost-effective:

1. The initial investment expense and ongoing operating costs of computer hardware and storage can be spread over a larger customer base.
2. Typically, it is more economical to purchase rather than internally develop the computer software for a health care

claims payment system, because the details of the system are complex and unfamiliar to the employer's computer programmers.

3. The ongoing employee training to stay current with legal, clinical, and operating changes can be costly and time-consuming to the employer.
4. The insurance company or TPA can achieve greater economies of scale for standard operating procedures.
5. It is more economical for the insurance company or TPA to be staffed with legal, clinical, and other technical expertise necessary to administer health care and disability plans.
6. The employer maintains a third-party "buffer" in disputing or denying benefit payments.

Avoiding State-Mandated Benefits

ERISA preempts self-funded employee benefits programs from state laws that mandate minimum benefits coverage, regulate financial management of the plans, or assess taxes on "insured" arrangements. This preemption gives the employer greater authority and flexibility in designing and funding the benefits programs. This advantage of self-funding is especially important to multistate employers, which can establish a similar benefits program for all employees and avoid the expense and complexity of meeting the unique benefits and financial requirements of each state.

Almost every state currently has some state-mandated benefits, typically involving minimum benefit levels of specific health care services, such as physical therapy or mental health/substance abuse, or minimum coverage requirements, such as preexisting-condition or surviving-spouse coverage provisions. The ability of self-funded benefit plans to avoid these mandates has been continually tested by state and federal legal actions. However, the courts have been relatively consistent in upholding the ERISA preemption.

Greater Flexibility and Control

In addition to the legal requirements avoided or at least simplified by self-funding, employers have greater authority on plan design, financing, and administration than in an insured arrangement. Because the financial risk is assumed by the employer, the insurance company or TPA is not as restricted by state or federal insurance laws and is less concerned with the underlying benefit levels and cost of the health care plan. Therefore, their underwriting, funding, contractual, and operational requirements are relatively minor in a self-funded arrangement.

The employer has greater flexibility to design and finance a benefits plan that fits its business, human resources, and benefits strategies and meets the needs of its workforce. With the dynamic changes in managed care and cost-containment options, self-funding can help employers change their health care plans quickly and creatively in response to savings and quality of care opportunities. These advantages do not lessen the need to follow prudent underwriting, plan design, and administrative principles—they give the employer greater control in implementing them.

Potential Disadvantages of Self-Funding

As noted earlier, a recent survey found that 75 percent of large employers currently self-fund their PPO or POS medical plans, compared with only 15 percent of small employers (fewer than 500 employees).[1] One of the primary reasons small employers use an insured arrangement is a concern over the predictability of annual plan costs and the ultimate financial responsibility that comes with self-funding. Most of these employers weigh the availability, security, cost, and financial protection of an insured arrangement with a self-funded plan and excess loss insurance—and decide on the insured arrangement.

The following are other reasons an employer may decide not to self-fund health care benefits:

- To gain the additional underwriting, legal, and administrative services available through an insured arrangement.
- To avoid potential employee concerns about the financial security of their health care benefits.
- To respond to specific collective-bargaining negotiations and stipulations.
- To have a financial and administrative third-party buffer with employees.
- To avoid the additional financial risk of numerous Consolidated Omnibus Budget Reconciliation Act (COBRA) participants.

1. Mercer, *National Survey of Employer-Sponsored Health Plans*, 2009.

- To gain the cost advantages of HMOs and other managed care plans that are limited or prohibited from self-funding by state insurance laws.
- To capture the lower costs of a community-rated, insured arrangement compared to the expected actual costs of an employee group based on its demographics, health status, and/or previous claims experience.

During the late nineties a concern arose as to whether self-funding medical plans could subject employers to increased liability for medical malpractice and third-party denial of employees' medical care claims. Several legislative measures were considered in Congress that would impose responsibility on the health care plan sponsor for medical benefit and coverage decisions. Yet, to date, ERISA's preemption protections have largely stood with the Supreme Court's *Pegram v. Herdrich* providing much greater clarity regarding the line between benefit administration and the practice of medicine. The Court "adopted a distinction between benefit coverage (eligibility) decisions—for which there was no remedy under state law—and medical treatment decisions—which were subject to state malpractice suits."[2,3] "Acknowledging that HMO determinations often cannot be simply characterized as purely eligibility or treatment decisions, the *Pegram* Court recognized a new category of "mixed eligibility and treatment decisions," which decided whether a particular service would be covered, but made this determination based on medical judgment."[4]

An employer, as a plan sponsor, can be protected where they contract with an HMO and do not participate in 'mixed medical decisions'. "Thus, when an employer contracts with an HMO to provide benefits to employees subject to ERISA, the provisions of documents that set up the HMO are not, as such, an ERISA plan; but the agreement between an HMO and an employer who pays the premiums may, as here, provide elements of a plan by setting out rules under which beneficiaries will be entitled to care."[5] If this increased liability is placed on the employer, employers may move away from sponsorship and management of medical care benefit plans for their employees.

---

2. 530 U.S. 211, 223 (2000), *Pegram v. Herdrich.*
3. Timothy S. Jost, J.D., "Pegram v. Herdrich: The Supreme Court Confronts Managed Care".
4. Timothy S. Jost, ibid.
5. Pegram et al. v. Herdrich—530 U.S. 211, http://supreme.justia.com/us/530/211/case.html.

Implications of 2010 Health Care Reform Legislation

As mentioned in Chapter 29, health care for all US citizens, especially those who receive health care insurance through their employers, likely will be significantly impacted by the 2010 health care reform legislation—formally the Patient Protection and Affordable Care Act (PPACA)—which was signed into law on March 23, 2010, by President Obama.[6] All employers offering employee health benefits must implement short-term market reform provisions and assess the long-term implications of PPACA, and their covered employees must understand the changes and new provisions of this law. The following short- and long-term provisions apply specifically to employer-sponsored self-insured plans. More general provisions and those impacting insured plans are covered in Chapter 29. Captive arrangements are likely to be impacted both by the provisions outlined in Chapter 29 and, depending upon how the plans are structured, by the provisions outlined here.

Short-Term Market Reform Provisions Impacting Self-Funded Plans

The PPACA has several provisions that immediately affect self-funded health benefits plans.

- *Elimination of lifetime maximums.* The prohibition of lifetime maximums in employee health benefit plans affects stop-loss insurance protection. Until now, most self-funded plans purchased individual claimant, also called specific, stop-loss insurance that has individual lifetime maximums typically in the $2 million to $5 million range. Because the PPACA lifetime maximum prohibition does not apply to this specific insurance coverage, there is now a potential employer risk if a high-cost claimant exceeds the stop-loss insurance lifetime maximum. However, most stop-loss insurers are adding a no-lifetime-maximum-option to their policies that can eliminate the employer risk—at an expected premium increase of 5 percent or more.
- *New reporting requirements.* The law requires that in 2011 self-funded plans submit to Health and Human Services (HHS)

6. See "Chart of Key PPACA Provisions", April 21, 2010, *Groom Law Group* (www.groom.com) for a detailed listing of PPACA including the provisions impacting self-insured plans.

and employees a new annual report describing their claims and coverage history and current rate-setting, plan administration, and claims payment practices. In addition, these plans must complete an informational report to HHS on the percentage of total annual plan cost used for benefits reimbursement and quality-of-care improvements, similar to the 85 percent minimum medical loss ratio provisions for health insurance companies. In subsequent years, nongrandfathered self-funded plans must add to their annual report information about quality-of-care improvements, medical management, patient safety, and wellness programs. Finally, to satisfy the reporting requirements, these plans will have to adopt health information technology standards to communicate with providers and participants.

- *Appeals and external review.* For nongrandfathered plans, enhanced internal claims appeals processes and more extensive and expedient federal external review practices are required as of the first plan year following September 23, 2010.
- *Comparative effectiveness fee.* Beginning in 2012, self-funded plans must pay a $2 fee per covered participant to fund comparative effectiveness research initiatives.

Long-Term Market Reform Provisions Impacting Self-Funded Plans

While there are no specific PPACA provisions that affect only self-funded health benefits plans in 2013 or later, there are a few important long-term considerations.

- *Plan administration complexity and cost.* The additional administration demands on self-funded plans are substantial, especially those involving reporting and disclosure to employees and regulators, and management of the voucher provision under the employer mandate responsibilities. As plan sponsor, the employer is responsible for the timeliness and accuracy of these processes and reports. TPAs, including the administrative-services-only division of insurance companies, will support most, if not all, of the additional processes, but for additional administration fees.
- *Uncertain plan cost trends and marketplace dynamics.* The sweeping changes driven by the PPACA legislation and regulations will likely take several years to show favorable or

unfavorable impact. The employers sponsoring self-funded plans will need to closely monitor plan costs and use of health care services relative to historic patterns to determine if PPACA market reform provisions, the Health Exchanges and other dynamics are uniquely changing the health care marketplace and the employer's ability to manage future health-plan costs, quality of care, employee health improvement, and medical outcomes.

- *Three-year health industry fee.* To finance a transitional reinsurance program, TPAs and health insurers will pay a pro-rata share of a $12 billion assessment in 2014, $8 billion in 2015 and $5 billion in 2016. TPAs will pass this fee to self-funded plans through additional administration costs.

Funding and Accounting Considerations

Because the employer assumes ultimate financial and fiduciary responsibility, specific attention should be given to how a self-funded plan is structured to hold and invest assets (funding) and how the plan accounts for plan expenses and liabilities.

The expenses of a self-funded plan are typically paid from one of three employer funding sources: the general assets of the organization, a tax-favored trust, or a captive insurance company. The differences between these funding vehicles center on security and use of assets, tax treatment of fund deposits and investment income, and employer access to surplus assets.

General Assets of the Organization

Plan expenses are paid directly from the general assets of the organization, similar to the payment of any other general expenses. Assets to pay plan costs are commingled with all other assets. Employee contributions withheld through payroll deduction can be reported as specific plan assets but also are commingled with the general assets of the organization. The plan liabilities and expenses are recognized as a general operating expense, and the claimant is a general creditor of the organization.

Self-funded short-term disability and wage continuation plans are typically funded on this basis. If there is no insurance involved, the benefit payments are considered and administered much like a payroll expense. Payments are drawn from general assets but reported as a separate benefit plan expense. The employer recognizes the benefit payments as a general operating expense for tax purposes, and any additional funding of plan liabilities is tax-deductible only when the liability has been incurred and can be determined. The benefit payments for these wage continuation and disability plans are typically ordinary taxable income to the employee, excluding any portion of the benefit attributable to employee contributions.

The advantages of this funding arrangement are primarily administrative. Initial qualification filings are avoided, and annual government reporting is simplified. General plan administration is typically included with the daily payroll and treasury functions.

The primary disadvantages involve the tax treatment of plan assets and the security of future benefit payments. As mentioned before, the accumulation of plan assets in a general-asset funding arrangement are tax-deductible only if the liability has been incurred and can be determined. This tax treatment limits the applicability of general asset funding to pay-as-you-go benefit plans, such as self-funded paid-time-off plans and health care plans. In addition, the promise to pay benefits in the future is only as good as the financial condition of the organization. For this reason, most organizations are encouraged by their employees and financial advisers to use another funding source for a benefit plan with any extended liabilities.

Tax-Exempt Trust

If any plan assets are accumulated to pay extended plan benefit liabilities, a special trust is typically used that exempts from federal tax the investment income earned on these assets. This special tax-exempt entity is technically called a voluntary employees' beneficiary association (VEBA), but is better known as a 501(c)(9) trust.

A VEBA can be created to fund "for the payment of life, sick, accident or other benefits" to the members, and their designated dependents and beneficiaries, participating in the trust. Medical, other health care, and disability benefits for active employees are the most common plans funded through a VEBA. Benefits payments for retiree plans, such as post-retirement life insurance and medical and other benefit plans can be funded through a VEBA in a limited manner if specific regulations are followed.

To qualify for this special tax status, the VEBA must satisfy several requirements:

1. Membership eligibility essentially is limited to employees with an employment-related common bond, such as common employer or employers in the same line of business in the "same geographic locale."

2. The eligibility for benefits provided through the trust cannot discriminate in favor of officers, shareholders, or highly compensated employees.
3. The VEBA must be controlled by the participating members or trustees designated by the members.
4. The assets or earnings of the VEBA can be used only to pay permissible benefits (including specified insurance premiums). At plan termination, the contributing employers can receive any remaining assets only after all plan liabilities have been satisfied.
5. The VEBA must apply to the Internal Revenue Service (IRS) and receive approval of its tax-exempt status.

In addition, there are detailed regulations limiting the tax-deductible annual contributions and the accumulated assets in a VEBA, referred to as the trust's "qualified cost." Basically, this "qualified cost" is the actual annual cash payments for benefits, administration, and other reasonable direct plan costs, and the annual additions to actuarially reasonable accumulated assets held in the trust to pay incurred but unpaid claims liabilities.

A VEBA operates as an independent entity with financial reporting and auditing requirements. The participating employers and/or employees make periodic contributions into the trust to fund current and accrued liabilities. A VEBA is common when employee contributions are required, especially after-tax contributions or substantial contribution amounts that need to be segregated from the general assets of the organization. Assets are distributed from the trust as required to meet the plan's financial obligations. The federal income tax treatment of employer contributions into the trust and of benefit payments from the trust follows the applicable tax rules of any qualified employee benefit program.

The primary advantages of a VEBA are the tax-exempt treatment of investment income (except for retiree health care reserves) and the increased security of benefit payment for employees. Standard accounting rules and reporting requirements serve as a monitor of the financial integrity of the plan. The trustees have fiduciary responsibilities for the appropriate management of the VEBA. And plan assets can only be used for the payment of plan benefits and expenses.

The primary disadvantages are the compliance requirements and related expenses to operate the trust. The regulations are complex and often require professional advice and technical support. And, the IRS is stepping up its auditing activity of VEBAs to ensure excess assets are not accumulating on a tax-favored basis. This interest has increased the scope and expense of actuarial and auditing services required to manage plan funding.

CAPTIVE INSURANCE

Self-insurance is rewarding where a business owner's claim experience is better than that anticipated by an insurer's premium underwriting class.[7] When self-insured, the employer reaps the benefits that otherwise would inure to the insurance company. Yet, one drawback of self-insurance is that the business owner may only deduct claims as paid and cannot receive any tax benefit for prefunding reserves. Under certain circumstances captive insurance companies may give business owners the best of both worlds: retention of excess insurance profits and the tax advantages of an insured plan.

A captive insurance company is an insurance company, licensed under the legal statutes of the insurer's place of domicile, that provides insurance coverage to the operations and entities of the captive insurance owners. The owners may be a single owner or multiple owners. Additionally, the insurance may be offered exclusively to businesses within the same ownership group or may offer insurance outside the corporate family.

Captive Advantages

Captives offer business owners many opportunities for improving their business management practices.[8] Captives offer numerous advantages that larger companies have taken advantage of, and are increasingly becoming available to mid-size and smaller companies. The following are some of these advantages:

- *Freedom.* Captives provide business owners with much greater flexibility in how to manage their business risks. By owning a captive, the business owner may gain access to insurance coverage when the traditional insurance market becomes tight with higher insurance premiums and reduced availability of desired coverages. While the business owner may still need to

7. Special thanks to Randall Beckie for his review of the captive insurance section of this chapter.
8. Tim Luedtke, "You Are Your Own Boss … You Take The Risk … Now Protect Your Business and Be Rewarded," *Navigator Benefit Solutions LLC, The Actuarial View*, June 2010.

pay premiums at market prices, any "excess profits" built into the market premium will be retained in the captive insurance company and by the captive's owner.

- *Access to reinsurance.* By owning an insurance company, the business owner gains access to reinsurers and surplus lines carriers that were previously unavailable. Such access fosters increased competition and ultimately an improved, more accurate market pricing mechanism.
- *Enhanced discipline in risk management.* A captive insurance company must comply with the insurance regulations of the domicile government (country, state, etc.) where it is established. To effectively meet these requirements, a disciplined framework is followed to measure, monitor, and price the risks accepted by the captive. Such discipline is instilled through the assistance of professional advisers and the captive's reinsurers, and by meeting the domicile's regulatory capitalization and reserving requirements.
- *Reward favorable loss experience.* Any successful insurance company succeeds because it is able to attract sufficient numbers of good risks to offset any losses suffered from bad risks. Characteristically, good risks follow risk management practices that represent industry best practice. As an example, for those in the medical and dental profession, such practices would include continual learning, following standards of care, keeping good medical records, and practicing confidentiality on a need-to-know basis. Where one owns its own captive, the benefits associated with process improvement and lowering claim costs directly rewards the good risks and are not shared with the bad risks.
- *Lower costs.* Direct rewards associated with owning a captive include reduced premiums for those having lower claims due to following good risk management practices, lower premium taxes, reduced premiums due to lower insurer profit margins (as captives generally have lower capital requirements versus traditional insurers), and access to a broader array of insurance options. Additionally, where captives are utilized to insure an employer's employee health plan, with careful design the captive arrangement may qualify as part of a self-funded plan for ERISA purposes and enable the employer to avoid state-mandated coverage requirements.

- *Enhance the business owner's supply chain.* Captives may be used by a business owner to insure third-party risks. While generally a riskier proposition than insuring one's own risks, insuring third-party risks may be attractive where the business owner is intimately familiar with the third-party risks being accepted. For example, if a manufacturer has a long-standing business relationship with a component supplier known to establish and follow best industry practices, the manufacturer may wish to insure some aspects of the component supplier's business.

Captives–Background

Businesses use captives to enhance their enterprise risk management practices. Historically, captives see rapid growth during periods when the traditional insurance markets become tight with higher premiums and/or unavailable coverage. As many business owners are required to have insurance to operate, for example, directors and officer liability, workers' compensation, commercial automobile liability and product liability, oftentimes establishing their own captive insurer might be the only economically viable outlet available. Several hurdles exist for using a captive for employee benefits, and, as such, most captive insurance companies are utilized primarily for property and casualty risks.

According to *Business Insurance*'s annual captive survey,[9] there were 5,390 captives at the end of 2009, of which almost all were created for property and casualty risks. Most of these are single-company-owned captives, though recently many captive jurisdictions have established legislation that encourages development of group, protected cell, or "rent-a-" captives. Other forms of captives include association captives (owned by a trade group or other association), agency captives (a captive formed by a brokerage firm or agency), Series LLC, or a risk retention group (RRG). RRGs are often formed by a common profession to share regularly recurring risks—for example, physicians might form an RRG to pool medical malpractice insurance risk. Some captives are the direct writers and primary insurers that issue the policy, while others are reinsurers of the risk, which is placed through a fronting company that acts as the primary insurer.

Captives are domiciled in many jurisdictions around the world. The top five domiciles are home to over half of the existing captives. These

9. Rodd Zolkos, "Leveled by the Economy: Cost-Conscious Parent Companies Tap Their Captives to Enhance Corporate Capital", *Business Insurance*, March 8, 2010.

include Bermuda, Cayman Islands, Vermont, Guernsey, and the British Virgin Islands. Where foreign insurers and reinsurers are engaged, the captive owner should carefully consider and discuss with their tax advisers the application of any excise taxes that may apply.[10] While, historically, there has been primary interest in off-shore (outside of the United States) locations, recent growth has been centered in the United States[11] in Vermont (33), Utah (54), South Carolina (9), Montana (26), Hawaii (12), Nevada, Arizona (8), Missouri (6), and Delaware (48). Delaware, in particular, has experienced rapid growth, doubling its number of captives during 2010, and celebrating the license of its one hundredth captive in early 2011.[12]

Over the past two decades, there has been increasing interest in utilizing captives for employee benefits. To that end, there are several issues that companies and plan sponsors must consider before using a captive for employee benefits.

Employee Benefit Captives—Issues to Consider

Insuring employee benefit risks through a captive insurance company may raise federal tax, state insurance regulatory, and prohibited transaction issues under the Employees Retirement Income Security Act.[13]

Federal Tax Issues

Captive sponsors who pay taxes strive to structure captive insurance programs so as to receive current period tax deductions for premiums paid to their captives. Court rulings and recent revenue rulings outline several key provisions for receiving a tax deduction for premiums paid to a captive insurance company.

Key questions include:

1. Is the transaction a sham? To meet this test the transaction must provide a nontax business purpose.
2. Does the transaction meet traditional insurance standards? Elements considered for determining whether insurance standards are met include whether an insurable risk exists that is

10. Revenue Ruling 2008-15.
11. New licenses for 2010 are listed in the parentheses and come from Business Insurance publications; note there may be other states, yet these are the primary issuing states.
12. Jerry Geisel, "Delaware issues 48 captive licenses in 2010", Business Insurance, February 2, 2011.
13. Tim Luedtke, "Considering Insuring Employee Benefits With Your Captive?" *Navigator Benefit Solutions LLC, The Actuarial View*, September 2010.

shifted from one party to another and whether there exists an insurer having sufficient risk distribution.

Revenue Ruling 2005-40 stated "risk shifting occurs if a person facing the possibility of an economic loss transfers some or all of the financial consequences of the potential loss to the insurer, such that a loss by the insured does not affect the insured because the loss is offset by a payment from the insurer." Further, the ruling stated "risk distribution incorporates the statistical phenomenon known as the law of large numbers." The ruling is consistent with the findings of the United States Supreme Court in *Helvering vs. Le Gierse* (1941).

Theories on both "risk shifting" and "risk distribution" continue to develop, with numerous revenue rulings and court decisions impacting how the concepts apply to a specific situation. As such, it is important that a qualified tax advisor be engaged to assess the specifics of any particular situation. Over time, some safe harbors have developed. It is generally held that a captive that accepts a threshold level of unrelated third-party business (sometimes viewed to be as little as 29 percent) will provide support for sufficient "risk distribution"[14] and that captives that are "brother-sister" organizations are supportive of "risk shifting".[15]

While premium deductibility is important, this is only because insurance companies are subject to different accounting and tax rules that enable them to deduct claim reserves for anticipated losses. The captive and the insured party are generally part of the same consolidated tax return. In the absence of different accounting and tax treatments, the deductibility of insurance premiums would be negated by the income generated by the insurance premiums received in the captive. Without the added benefit that insurance companies receive for the deduction of their reserves, a captive insurance owner would receive no tax benefit from essentially paying a premium to themselves. But insurance companies are entitled to tax deductions for their reserves and thus business owners which insure a risk with a captive are entitled to accelerate tax deductions for prefunding expected losses.

ERISA Concerns

Under ERISA, transactions involving plan assets among parties in interest are generally prohibited without an applicable exemption. Employer-owned

14. *Harper Group* vs. *Commissioner*, 979 F.2d 1341 (9th Circuit 1992).
15. *Humana* vs. *Commissioner*, 881 F.2d 247, (6th Circuit 1989). This ruling overturned "economic family doctrine."

captives are considered a party in interest with respect to the employer's employee benefit plan. The prohibition is designed to protect plan assets against self-dealing that could conflict with the interests of plan participants. Available exemptions include the following:

1. *Statutory exemption.* Although a transaction involving plan assets of an employee benefit plan would be prohibited, the prohibition does not apply where benefit premiums account for less than 5 percent of affiliated insurance companies' aggregate premiums.
2. *Class exemption.* The Department of Labor (DOL) automatically provides a class exemption for any prohibited transaction if certain criteria are met as outlined in PTE 79-41. Generally, the PTE 79-41 criterion that is most difficult to meet is that at least 50 percent of the captive's premiums must come from unrelated business.
3. *Individual exemption.* This is an exemption provided specifically to a plan sponsor for its specified transaction.

For years, plan sponsors sought individual exemptions to permit the use of captives for employee benefit plans. A watershed event occurred with the DOL's exemption approval given to Columbia Energy Corporation in 2000. PTE 2000-48 permitted Columbia Energy to reinsure its long-term disability plan with its captive, Columbia Insurance Corporation LTD. Subsequent to this approval, the DOL approved Archer Daniels Midland Company's use of their captive to provide life insurance benefits (PTE 2003-07) and approved SCA's use of their captive for accidental death and dismemberment, long-term disability, and life insurance (PTE 2004-12).

These early approvals gave rise to an expedited process (ExPro) for new individual exemption requests by other captive owners. Under the ExPro process, the DOL will fast-track approval for any request where there are at least two substantially similar approvals within the prior 18-month period. The accelerated process can provide an exemption within 75 to 90 days of an application. To achieve such approval, the DOL outlined several criteria that must be met, including:

- The captive (or a branch thereof) is licensed and authorized in the United States or a U.S. territory.
- No sales commissions are paid.
- At least one year of audited financials for the captive must exist.

- There must be an independent third-party fiduciary.
- The plan cannot pay more than adequate consideration for insurance.
- The insurance is with a fronting company that is rated 'A' or better by A.M. Best.
- Plan participants must receive enhanced benefits.
- Premiums are computed within industry standards and comparable to other insurers.

Since installing the ExPro process for individual captive exemptions, nearly 20 prohibited transaction exemptions have been granted. Most have been for life insurance and long-term disability benefits. A recent approval that was granted to Coca-Cola is interesting in that the approval (PTE 2010-11) allowed Coca-Cola to fund retiree health benefits and pay premiums with assets contained in an existing VEBA. A key challenge for Coca-Cola was to prove that its proposal was substantially similar to previous ExPro approved situations and initially was denied by the DOL.

State Insurance Requirements

As already stated, the process of insuring employee benefits within a captive is streamlined under an ExPro process where the captive is licensed and authorized in the United States or a U.S. territory. To meet this licensing requirement, captive sponsors are required to choose a domicile and meet the licensing, operating, and financial requirements of that domicile.

When implementing a captive insurance company, a captive owner generally engages a captive manager whose primary responsibilities include ensuring that the captive meets minimum capitalization requirements, establishing and receiving approval for its business plan, engaging an actuary, completing a feasibility study, determining what services to perform in-house or finding out-sourced service providers, enlisting a fronting company or reinsurers, and meeting with regulators to have its plan approved. On an on-going basis, the captive must be continuously monitored to assure that the risks are appropriately managed with reinsurance and the company is appropriately capitalized.

Captives—Future

The future for captives looks bright. The recent financial challenges experienced around the world make the need for creative financing mechanisms vitally important. Captives help to reduce the frictional costs of financing and could help free up capital. In particular, the opportunities to reduce costs, lower taxes, and improve economic management of all of a company's risks are promising opportunities for captives to improve company operations. Additionally, utilizing independent, external captive managers to measure and manage company risks may be a welcome addition to a company's CEO and CFO during this post–Sarbanes-Oxley era.

PPACA also significantly changes the health care landscape and creates new opportunities for employers, payors, health care providers, and individuals. PPACA sought to make health care accessible and affordable for all Americans. It introduced individual and employer coverage mandates, penalties for noncompliance, and new markets for accessing coverage. And, it created new regulatory agencies.

Evolving accounting pronouncements and the Pension Protection Acts of 2006, 2008, and 2010 could also encourage the use of captive insurance. Benefit plan designs, too, are changing with several newer approaches perhaps further simplifying the use of a captive and increasing the potential for a complete retirement, health care, and long-term care security solution.[16] The addition of a captive insurer to a company's financing suite will provide company leadership with a useful tool to manage through what is certain to be an uncertain period.

CONCLUSION

Business owners continue to seek greater and greater control over all aspects of their businesses, from the cost of raw materials to the cost of labor. To attain this control, business owners must be flexible as they operate within an environment that continues to evolve as federal and state legislation and regulation change. And, with enterprise risk-management principles gaining greater traction with business owners and executive leadership, there likely will be continued creativity and growth in alternative approaches to funding employee health care benefits.

16. Tim Luedtke, "Considering Insuring Employee Benefits With Your Captive?", *Navigator Benefit Solutions LLC, The Actuarial View*, September 2010.

PART EIGHT

Employee Benefit Plan Issues

The final part of the *Handbook* is devoted to issues of special interest in employee benefit planning and begins with Chapter 31 on welfare benefits for retirees, a topic that will continue to have major implications for employer plan sponsors as long as health care cost increases continue to escalate.

Chapter 32 introduces the subject of benefits for small companies and examines the particular issues faced by the small-company employer in providing benefits to its employees.

As the name suggests, a multiemployer plan is an employee benefit plan to which two or more unrelated companies contribute under the terms of a collective bargaining agreement between them and one or more labor organizations. These plans are discussed in Chapter 33.

In our global economy, international employee benefit planning has assumed a much greater role in corporate planning. This topic is explored in Chapter 34.

CHAPTER 31

Welfare Benefits for Retirees

Richard Ostuw

Stuart H. Alden

Most large companies provide life insurance and health care benefits for their retired employees. However, because most of the U.S. workforce is employed by small to medium-sized companies, only a minority of workers are currently eligible for employer-sponsored postretirement welfare benefits. Nonetheless, these benefits are an important component of retiree income and a significant cost to the employers providing them.

Many employers began providing postretirement benefits when their retiree populations were small and the cash costs of the benefits were low. Also, the introduction of Medicare in 1966 encouraged the installation of supplemental medical benefits for retirees. Costs have grown tremendously since then because of growing numbers of retirees, increases in health care costs, cost-shifting from governmental plans, and changes in the accounting for the benefits. As a result, companies are paying close attention to their retiree benefit programs and are attempting to ensure that they meet specific objectives, including the following:

- Protecting retirees against the cost of unbudgetable medical expenses and providing a modest life insurance benefit to cover burial expenses.
- Providing retirees access to coverage not otherwise available or affordable to them as individuals.
- Promoting cost-effective use of medical care and discouraging the use of unnecessary care.

- Ensuring that employer contributions make the program competitive with those of other companies and that the employee contributions are affordable.
- Attracting and retaining experienced workers.

The following pages review current practices with respect to retiree benefits, starting with an overview of trends and issues affecting these benefits. After a brief discussion of life insurance, the remainder of the chapter focuses primarily on health care benefits.

CURRENT TRENDS AND ISSUES

Employers have made major changes to their retiree welfare benefit programs over the years. Continued fine-tuning and occasional major changes are necessary to maintain a suitable balance between cost control and employee relations in a dynamic environment. A study by the Financial Accounting Standards Board (FASB) of possible changes in the accounting rules for postretirement benefit obligations prompted many companies to make significant changes in the late 1980s and early 1990s. New rules were published in December 1990 as *Financial Accounting Standard No. 106* (FAS 106). Subsequent amendments and extensions to FAS 106 have now been "codified" under the heading ASC (Accounting Standards Codification) 715-60.

Under ASC 715-60, the company's actuary determines the expected postretirement benefit obligation (EPBO), which represents the current value of employer payments for current and future retirees and their dependents. The calculation of the EPBO reflects facts and assumptions such as

- The provisions of the "substantive plan," including the benefit payable and the retirees' share of the contribution toward the premium
- The per capita cost for the plan
- The percentage of eligible retirees and dependents who enroll in each plan
- The mortality rate of the plan participants
- The age at retirement for future retirees
- The rate of termination of employment

The accumulated postretirement benefit obligation (APBO) represents the portion of the EPBO attributable to past service. This represents the full value of benefits for current retirees and a prorated portion for future retirees. The APBO is the key measure of the employer's obligation earned to date.

The annual expense for postretirement benefits includes the following components

- The service cost, or the value of future benefits attributable to the current year of employee service
- The interest cost, or the growth in the APBO due to the change in the interest discount for future payments
- Amortization of the initial transition obligation (unless the employer recognized the entire APBO as a one-time charge when adopting FAS 106—as most did)
- Adjustments to amortize the effect of (1) actuarial gains and losses and (2) plan changes

FASB is currently revisiting all benefits accounting issues in an effort to better align U.S. generally accepted accounting principles (GAAP) accounting with international accounting standards.

Companies will continue to modify their retiree benefits to reflect changes in the environment, such as general pressure on the cost of business operations, changes in health care benefits for active employees, increases in plan costs for retirees, and the availability of alternatives to employer-sponsored coverage in the individual market. Most employers have focused on health care benefits rather than life insurance benefits. The specific steps vary from employer to employer, but often include the following:

- Revisions in the definition of covered expenses and/or their reimbursement
- Restrictions in the group eligible for employer subsidies and/or benefits
- Increases in employee contribution, especially for short-service retirees and for dependent coverage, including "access-only" coverage where the retiree pays the entire cost
- Limits on the dollar amount of employer contribution
- Greater use of managed care techniques where feasible

In their ongoing efforts to balance cost concerns with the specific program objectives cited earlier, employers have to address the following issues in their decision to retain or modify their current plans:

- Should we continue to offer a plan to retirees? Can they secure coverage elsewhere on favorable terms?
- What benefits provisions should the plans include? Should the medical plan, for example, have a low deductible and high coinsurance or vice versa?
- How should the premium cost be shared between the company and employees for each optional plan?
- How should retiree welfare benefits be integrated with other components of the retirement program?
- What special grandfather or transition rules, if any, should apply?
- What are the appropriate elements of the expensing policy?
- How should the plan cost be funded?

LIFE INSURANCE

In general, retirees' death benefit needs are less than those of active employees and are met to some extent by survivor-income benefits under a pension plan and Social Security or by significant savings or profit-sharing balances at retirement. Many employers also provide some form of retiree life insurance and some provide a modest death benefit through their pension plans.

Benefit Design

Life insurance for active employees typically takes the form of a basic employer-paid benefit amount that can be supplemented with optional employee-paid insurance. For retirees, the life insurance benefit is usually a flat dollar amount—generally in the range of $5,000 to $20,000—that the employer may update from time to time for new retirees. Ad hoc increases for current retirees are unusual. Another common approach, particularly for salaried employees, is to express the postretirement life insurance schedule as a percentage of the employee's final preretirement life insurance amount or final preretirement salary. Most employers then reduce the benefit amount during retirement. They might, for example, reduce life insurance of one times salary for active employees by 20 percent per year during retirement to an ultimate level of 20 percent of the preretirement benefit, that is, 20 percent of final pay. Such benefit formulas also frequently have a postretirement coverage maximum (such as $20,000 or $50,000) and a minimum (such as $5,000).

Group universal life programs (GULP) are common for salaried employees. They provide a flexible vehicle for employees to tailor the amount of insurance to their needs, reflect changes in their needs over time, and prefund postretirement costs as desired. For a detailed discussion of group universal life programs, see Chapter 15.

Cost

Growth in the size of the retiree population—exacerbated in many companies by downsizing—has increased the cost of postretirement benefits substantially. As discussed above, ASC 715-60 requires that employers recognize the cost of these benefits on a pension-style expensing basis over the working lifetime of employees.

On such an advance-expensing basis, the cost of postretirement life insurance is typically about 0.5 percent or less of the active employee payroll—typically quite small relative to the cost of postretirement health care benefits.

HEALTH CARE BENEFITS

Few employers provided medical coverage to retirees before 1965, because the cost of doing so was prohibitive. However, when Medicare became effective in 1966, companies realized they could supplement Medicare coverage for their retirees at a modest cost. Although Medicare is still the primary payer for retirees, over the years, the share of medical expenses covered by Medicare has diminished, requiring increased outlays from the employer plan and/or retirees themselves. Thus, what was once a low-cost postretirement benefit has become enormously expensive.

Medical Plan Design Elements

Medical plan design elements are generally the same for retirees and active employees, but there are key differences between the two groups. For example,

- Age differences make retiree medical costs substantially higher than those of active employees. The average annual cost per person for retirees under age 65 is commonly one-and-a-half to two times the average cost for active employees. Both the frequency and intensity of health care (including hospitalization, physician visits, and use of prescription drugs) increase with age.

- Certain health conditions, such as hearing impairments and the need for various prostheses, are more common among the elderly.
- Elderly individuals require more time to recover from serious medical conditions and therefore are likely to require longer hospital stays and more care after a hospital discharge.

Medicare assumes the bulk of the cost of hospital and physician services after age 65. The relative share of employer plan costs by type of expense for retirees over 65 thus differs from the cost share for active employees. For example, prescription drugs might represent 15 to 20 percent of the plan cost for active employees but 60 to 80 percent for Medicare-eligible retirees.

Covered Services

As with active-employee plans, retiree medical plans generally cover a wide range of care and treatment, including hospital care, surgery, doctors' visits, therapy, and prescription drugs. Typically excluded from coverage are cosmetic surgery, experimental procedures, and hearing and vision care (although sometimes vision may be covered by a separate plan). Frequently, routine physical examinations are covered in today's plan designs.

New developments in technology will have a substantial impact on medical costs for retirees. How the plan defines experimental procedures and how the administrator updates the rules can have significant cost consequences.

Coordination with Medicare

Retirees usually receive medical benefits similar to those for active employees and often have the same or similar array in choice of plans. When they reach age 65 and become eligible for Medicare, their employer-provided benefits are coordinated with Medicare in one of two ways:

- Offset—the employer plan continues to provide the same benefits structure, but those benefits are offset by Medicare payments. This can be structured in a way that preserves cost sharing by the retiree.

- Medigap—plan coverage is limited to specific expenses that are not paid by Medicare. Under this approach, the plan fills in the gaps (wholly or in part) in Medicare's coverage.

There are three general forms of the offset approach:

- Under "Medicare carve-out," the net benefit is the regular plan benefit less the amount paid by Medicare.
- Under "government exclusion" (sometimes referred to as "maintenance of benefits"), the Medicare benefits are subtracted from covered expenses before calculating the plan benefits.
- Under traditional "coordination of benefits" (COB), the net benefit is the amount of covered expenses less the amount paid by Medicare but not more than the regular plan benefit.

In general, COB is the richest offset method (most costly for the plan), carveout is the leanest, and exclusion is somewhere in between.

Under the Medigap approach, the employer plan might pay all or part of the following hospital expenses for its retirees:

- The first level of expenses for each hospital admission, that is, the Medicare Part A deductible ($1,100 in 2010).
- The Medicare copayment amounts beginning on the 61st day of hospitalization ($275 in 2010).
- Copayment amounts during the lifetime reserve days ($550 in 2010).
- The cost of hospital care extending beyond the period covered by Medicare.

Similarly, the employer plan may pay all or part of the expenses for physician and other nonhospital services not reimbursed by Medicare Part B. It may also cover all or part of the expenses commonly excluded by Parts A and B of Medicare, such as prescription drugs and private nursing. Few employer-sponsored plans cover long-term custodial care in a nursing home. Some employers offer separate long-term care insurance, usually on an employee-pay-all basis, to address the cost of such care. See Chapter 12 for a discussion of long-term care insurance.

We can use the Medicare Part A deductible to illustrate two methods of updating retiree medical coverage. Under one approach, the employer plan defines covered expense as the Medicare Part A deductible. When the Part A deductible amount increases, the employer plan automatically fills the gap. Under the other approach, the employer specifies a coverage amount (such as $700) and increases that amount only by plan amendment. The latter approach gives the employer the ability to control the impact of inflation and Medicare changes on its plan and its costs.

Liberal Medigap plans virtually eliminate out-of-pocket medical expenses for retirees; more restrictive plans may provide only modest benefits. For example, some plans do not cover hospital stays beyond the Medicare limit, Medicare's coinsurance for physicians' fees, prescription drugs, or nursing care.

The Medicare program theoretically reimburses 80 percent of physicians' fees after a modest deductible. Since 1989, the basis for Medicare's fees has been the resource-based relative value scale (RBRVS). Medicare limits "balance billing" by physicians to contain cost shifting to the patient. By limiting the physicians' fees, these rules significantly reduce the retiree's share of the cost and therefore the cost under the employer's medical plan. Because of Medicare's restrictions on balance billing, an increasing number of physicians choose not to participate in the Medicare program.

Medicare Part D Prescription Drug Benefit

The Medicare Modernization Act of 2003 (MMA) established a prescription drug benefit under the new Medicare Part D program, beginning in 2006. The provisions of the standard Part D benefit for 2011 are as follows, with indexing of the dollar amounts in the future:

- A $310 annual deductible.
- Coverage of 75 percent of drug costs between $310 and $2,840.
- No coverage for drug costs between $2,840 and $6,448 (known as the "donut hole").[1]
- After reaching the $6,448 threshold ($4,550 in out-of-pocket spending), beneficiaries reach a "catastrophic" level of coverage and will only be required to pay the greater of a copayment ($2.50 for generic drugs or $6.30 for brand name drugs) or coinsurance of 5 percent.

The Medicare Part D benefit is provided through prescription drug plans (PDPs). The PDPs offer benefits to Medicare-eligible individuals in their regions with a federal subsidy for the cost.

1. PPACA gradually phases down the coverage gap from 2010 through 2020.

Employers that continue to provide qualifying drug coverage for Medicare-eligible individuals can receive a federal retiree drug subsidy (RDS) for each covered person of 28 percent of the individual's eligible drug expenses between $310 and $6,300 (for 2011, indexed thereafter).[2] Employers have several alternative approaches available to them. They can provide drug benefits and receive the federal subsidy. They can facilitate coverage through a PDP, with or without an employer subsidy or supplemental benefit. Or they can exclude drug coverage and allow retirees to navigate the public PDP system on their own. (Chapter 21 provides a detailed discussion of Medicare Part D.)

Patient Protection and Affordable Care Act of 2010

The Patient Protection and Affordable Care Act (PPACA) legislated sweeping changes in the way health insurance will be provided and financed in the United States. The following are some of the items most likely to impact retiree health plans

- Mandated plan provisions and eligibility rules
- Loss of the previous tax-free status of payments received through the retiree drug subsidy program as of 2013
- Closing of the Medicare Part D "donut hole"
- Early retiree reinsurance program which provides reimbursement to employment-based health plans for a portion of the health benefit costs for early retirees and their dependents
- Changes in the reimbursement formulas for Medicare Advantage plans (discussed later)
- State-run "exchanges" established (beginning in 2014) as marketplaces for individual insurance coverage for pre-Medicare individuals (retirees as well as actives), with restrictions on plan design and underwriting and federal subsidies provided for lower-income participants
- An excise tax on "high-cost" plans (those with per-capita costs exceeding a CPI-indexed threshold) beginning in 2018

2. The PPACA eliminates the employer tax deduction for the subsidy as of 2013.

Eligibility

In the typical retiree benefit program, eligibility rules for postretirement health care and life insurance benefits follow the employer's pension plan definition of retirement. The most common definition specifies termination of employment after attainment of age 55 and 10 years of active service. Some plans impose no minimum-service requirement for employees who terminate employment at or after age 65.

Employees may also be eligible for retirement after 30 years of service regardless of age, or upon attaining a specified number of years of age plus service. The "Rule of 80," for example, would be satisfied by any combination of age plus service that equals or exceeds 80. The latter approach is common for both unionized and salaried employees in industries with a strong union presence.

Many retiree medical plans extend coverage to the spouses and children of retirees, as those relationships are defined in the active employee plan. Some plans are more restrictive, however, and may, for example, exclude the spouses and children of marriages that occur after employees retire.

Employee Contributions

The level and nature of retiree contributions varies significantly among large employers. For some current retirees, the plans are noncontributory because of grandfathering provisions. But nearly all employers require contributions for new retirees. Retirees' contributions may be based on a percentage of plan cost, a flat dollar amount, or the excess of the plan premium over a fixed employer contribution.

In general, required contributions for retirees represent a greater percentage of premium costs than for active employees. Post-age-65 retiree contributions typically represent a greater percentage of total plan cost than do contributions by pre-age-65 retirees. Employee pay-all coverage is rare for active employees but not for retirees over age 65. Often called "access only," retiree-pay-all coverage has become more common.

Under a percentage-of-cost approach, retirees are required to contribute a specified percentage of the expected plan cost for the coming year. If a plan requires a 25 percent employee contribution and plan costs are expected to be $300 per month per covered person, for example, retirees would have to contribute $75 per month. As the plan cost increases due to inflation and utilization changes, the retirees' contribution increases proportionately in subsequent years.

It is also common for employers to require specified dollar contributions. Although such an approach may reflect a cost-sharing policy, the underlying percentage of plan cost is not necessarily disclosed to employees or retirees. Employers using this approach usually update dollar amounts every few years. Nonetheless, such updates have generally failed to keep pace with increases in plan costs. Employers often procrastinate in making changes that employees and retirees will view as benefit reductions. Further, planning for and implementing such updates can be time consuming.

The percentage approach has become more popular because it allows employers to update contribution amounts without creating the perception of a benefit take-away. By indicating that retiree contributions will increase as plan premiums increase, retirees accept the year-to-year changes, the courts accept the employer's right to change the amounts, and ASC 715-60 allows the employer to anticipate future increases in retiree contributions.

Retiree contributions are generally payable by deduction from the retiree's pension check, although sometimes retirees send a monthly check to the employer or a third-party administrator. Coverage is terminated if payment is not made on a timely basis.

Plan Types and Benefit Levels

Managed care plans now dominate as the standard type of health care benefit plans offered, although indemnity plans are still found on a limited basis. Under indemnity plans, the benefit represents reimbursement of eligible expenses for use of any health care provider. Under network or managed care plans, the program administrator contracts with selected providers, and benefits are more liberal when the participant uses a network or preferred provider.

During the 1980s, many employers changed from "basic plus major medical" programs to comprehensive plans for both active employees and retirees. In the 1990s, employers shifted to network-based plans. In some cases, the change applied only to future retirees. The first decade of the 21st century has seen increased movement toward managed care plans such as preferred provider organizations (PPOs), point of service (POS) plans and, most recently, consumer-driven health plans (CDHPs).

The goal of network-based and managed care plans is to reduce the fees and cost of health care services while enhancing quality of care. To achieve these results, a plan will sometimes incur some added cost in the form of administration expenses and commonly more liberal benefits for selected services such as preventive care. For active employees and retirees who are not eligible for Medicare, though, the employer will experience a net cost reduction.

The various types of managed care plans are summarized below.

Preferred Provider Organizations

A PPO contracts with a network of physicians and health care facilities to provide services to members at a reduced cost. PPOs do not require members to name a primary care physician, and members are free to select a specialist from the network without first obtaining a referral. Because PPO networks are not subject to the same regulations as health maintenance organizations (HMOs), employers generally have greater flexibility with PPOs than with HMOs in plan design and financing. PPO plans offer benefits for using nonnetwork providers, but generally on a less favorable basis than for network providers. Most often, the base offering for pre-65 retirees is a PPO.

Point of Service Managed Care

During the late 1980s and the 1990s, many companies implemented POS managed care programs for employees and retirees. Each time the employee or retiree needs health care, he or she chooses among hospitals and physicians who participate in the managed care network or choose nonnetwork providers. When they use in-network services, the benefits are more liberal than those applicable to nonnetwork services. Because of negotiated fee discounts and managed care techniques, the networks reduce the cost of care for employees and retirees not yet eligible for Medicare. Since about 2000, POS plans have become more like PPO plans in the way they operate. In particular, the member can commonly use a specialist without prior referral from a primary care physician.

Health Maintenance Organizations

As the first form of managed care plan, employers began offering HMOs to active employees as an alternative to their traditional medical plans. Most employers also offer the same HMOs to their retirees. Because retirees are more geographically dispersed than active employees, some employers offer additional HMOs to retirees in retirement destinations such as Florida and Arizona.

The HMO offering for retirees under age 65 is generally the same as for active employees. Many employers self-insure HMOs for actives and pre-65 retirees. The offering is often labeled an exclusive provider organization (EPO). The nature of the arrangement differs, however, for Medicare-eligible retirees. Medicare pays a fixed monthly premium, and the HMO takes the risk for the cost of providing the care on a fully insured basis. Because of HMO efficiencies in many parts of the country, the amount paid by Medicare is more than enough to cover the HMO's cost of providing the Medicare level of benefits, allowing the HMO to offer supplemental benefits and charge a small premium for them.

Medicare HMOs

Three key federal laws have changed the way HMOs operate under Medicare. The Balanced Budget Act of 1997 (BBA '97) ushered in a major change in Medicare—perhaps the most important revisions since Medicare's inception some 32 years earlier. By authorizing the development of new Medicare plans (known as Medicare + Choice), the bill was intended to expand competition in the delivery of medical services and, consequently, the choices for all Medicare enrollees.

Initially, there was a significant growth in Medicare HMO enrollment. However, the payment by Medicare failed to keep pace with health care cost increases, which led to reduced HMO attractiveness and enrollment.

The Medicare Modernization Act was enacted in 2003. In addition to providing a Medicare drug benefit, it changed the name for Medicare HMOs to Medicare Advantage and increased federal premium subsidies. The increased federal financial support reinvigorated HMO enrollment for a period of time.

Most recently, PPACA provisions will reduce the growth in reimbursement for Medicare Advantage plans, and this is expected to significantly reduce Medicare Advantage participation in the future, as plans pull out of certain markets and higher premiums cause individuals to drop out and seek alternative coverage.

Account Based Plans

Two account-based plan types have shown rapid growth since their relatively recent introduction. The health reimbursement arrangement (HRA), first offered in 2001, involves an employer-funded account plus a high-deductible health plan (HDHP). The health plan may, for example, have an annual deductible of $1,000. The employer may contribute, for example,

$500 per year into the account. The account balance may be used to pay for expenses during the year not reimbursed by the health plan, with any remainder available for future years. Such programs often are called consumer-driven health plans (CDHPs) since the intent is to provide financial incentives for the employee to be a more prudent buyer of health services. These plans are still more common for active employees than for retirees. See Chapter 7 for a detailed discussion of CDHPs.

Health savings accounts (HSAs) were authorized by the Medicare Modernization Act of 2003, and are growing in popularity. An HSA is somewhat similar to an HRA except that employee pretax contributions are permitted and account balances are always portable. A key difference is that, to qualify for contributions to an HSA, the employee must be covered by an HDHP—and only by an HDHP. An HDHP must have a deductible of at least $1,200 for single coverage and $2,400 for family coverage (2011 values, indexed thereafter), with an exception for preventive care services. Contributions may continue to be made to the HSA until Medicare eligibility. If significant balances accumulate during employment, they could be put toward medical expenses incurred during retirement.

THE CHANGING NATURE OF THE PROMISE

Under a traditional retiree medical plan, the employer "promises" to provide a stated level of benefits (with the possibility of changes in the benefit provisions). The key element is the benefits level.

Defined Dollar Benefit Approach

Under a newer approach, the key element is the dollar amount the employer will pay toward the cost of the benefits. The employer contribution is the defined dollar benefit (DDB). Many large companies have implemented this approach since the late 1980s or early 1990s. Here is an illustration of how the DDB approach works:

- The employer offers retirees a medical plan with benefit features comparable to those offered to active employees.
- The employer contributes up to $200 per month per person for coverage until age 65 and $100 per month thereafter. The retiree must pay the balance of the plan cost. The employer contribution is available only as a subsidy toward the cost of the medical plan.

- The employer updates benefit features from time to time and will consider ad hoc increases in the DDB.

The DDB approach has the following advantages:

- The employer has full control over future increases in its benefit costs because it determines the amount and timing of any increases in its contributions. (However, employee concern about benefit adequacy and competition may create pressure for ad hoc increases.)
- Benefit features can be updated more easily than in traditional programs. This is because the employer's promise involves its contribution—not the benefits themselves—and any reduction in the benefit level will directly reduce retiree contributions.
- Because benefit costs are communicated, employees will better understand the substantial value of the benefits they receive.
- The approach facilitates service-related benefit coverage. In the above illustration, for example, the $200 and $100 employer contribution amounts could be prorated for service of less than 25 years.
- If desired, retirees can be offered choices in how to apply their defined dollar benefit—for example, toward premiums for employer-sponsored or individual market coverage, or for direct reimbursement of out-of-pocket expenses.

Retiree Health Accounts

One of the problems with retiree health programs is that employees frequently do not understand the value of the employer's contributions. To raise the level of understanding, some companies have introduced retiree health accounts, a nontraditional approach similar to cash balance and pension equity pension plans. Under a retiree health account program, the employer makes an annual "contribution" to an account for each employee. The account may grow with interest, depending on provisions established by the employer. During the individual's retirement, the account can be used to pay for medical premiums. If the account runs out, the retiree becomes fully responsible for the premiums. The appeal of this approach is that the employee is made more aware of the value of the employer contributions. Moreover, the program is more equitable with reference to employees who retire at different ages, as well as to those who enroll their dependents and those who do not. By contrast, under traditional programs, the employer typically contributes much more for employees who retire early and for those who enroll dependents.

Most retiree health accounts limit the use of the account balance to payment of premiums (for employer-sponsored or individual market coverage). In some cases, the programs operate as HRAs and allow the account balance to be used for premiums and/or direct reimbursement of the expenses for medical services.

FINANCING

The three key considerations in financing retiree benefits are expense recognition, level of cost, and the funding vehicle.

Expense Recognition

Nearly all employers initially recognized the cost of retiree welfare benefits on a pay-as-you-go basis. In a sense, this is an historical accident. When employers began providing these benefits, they believed they were making a year-by-year commitment rather than a lifetime promise. They did not consider postretirement welfare benefits to be a form of deferred compensation earned during an employee's working career. This was in sharp contrast to prevailing views applicable to postretirement income benefits, that is, those provided by pension plans. Court decisions have prompted many employers to change their views on the nature of their commitment, and accounting rules now require most employers to recognize these costs during the working years of employees.

During the 1980s, the FASB considered the issue of how retiree welfare benefits should be expensed. The key question is this: Should companies be required to recognize the expense of postretirement welfare benefits during the working careers of employees and charge such amounts against current earnings? As a first step, FASB Statement 81 required the disclosure of the amount expensed for these benefits and the basis for expensing. Pay-as-you-go cost recognition was still permitted.

The FASB subsequently published new accounting rules (FAS 106, now codified as ASC 715-60), effective December 15, 1992, that require a pension-type expensing approach for life insurance and medical benefits on the grounds that such benefits represent a form of deferred compensation whose cost should be charged against earnings during the period when employees are productive. Under ASC 715-60, companies must recognize the accruing cost of postretirement coverage during the working years of employees and must disclose specific information about the plan, the aggregate value of accrued benefits, and the actuarial assumptions used to calculate the results.

Cost

On a pay-as-you-go basis, retiree medical plan costs typically average about $14,000 per year per retiree (including costs for any dependent(s)) until age 65 and $6,200 per year thereafter (based on Towers Watson's 2010 Health Care Cost Survey). The cost varies significantly among employers. The present value of these costs depends on employee age at retirement and, of course, on the assumptions for the interest discount rate, mortality rates, and increases in health care costs. Representative amounts are shown in Table 31-1.

Typically, about 60 percent of the cost is attributable to retired employees and 40 percent to their dependents. By comparison, the cost commonly is split 50-50 between active employees and their dependents, reflecting the larger average family size of these employees. Relatively few retirees have children who are still eligible under the medical plan.

Pay-as-you-go costs will rise in the future as a result of the following

- Price increases measured by the consumer price index (CPI)
- The introduction of new medical technology and new procedures
- Changes in the frequency or utilization of health care or in the mix of services

TABLE 31-1

Present Value of Medical Benefits (Per Retiree)

Age at Retirement	Single Coverage	Family Coverage
55	$150,000	$300,000
60	$100,000	$200,000
65	$70,000	$140,000

TABLE 31-2

Retiree Benefit Costs as Percentage of Payroll

Normal cost	3–5%
Amortization of unrecognized past service liability	1–3%
Interest on past service liability	4–6%
Total expense	8–14%

The health care share of the gross domestic product (GDP) was 17.3 percent in 2009, up from 12.0 percent in 1990, 9.1 percent in 1980 and 7.3 percent in 1970. While the growth of national health care costs in the last 20 years has been significant, the rates of change have been quite variable. There is no consensus on the rate of future growth, or on whether there is some maximum or limiting value to the health care share percentage.

Expensing annual retiree benefit costs on a pension-type basis during the working years of employees under ASC 715-60 has the results shown in Table 31-2 for representative groups of employees.

Funding

Several funding alternatives are available to employers. These include the following:

- *Book reserve/"pay as you go" funding.* The employer accrues the cost on its financial statement and retains the assets within the organization. ASC 715-60 requires pension-type expensing, but there are no requirements that assets be maintained in a separate trust.
- *Voluntary employees' beneficiary association (VEBA).* Under Section 501(c)(9) of the Internal Revenue Code (IRC), the employer contributes funds to an independent trust, from which benefits subsequently are paid. Section 419 of the IRC severely restricts the use of VEBAs for retiree health plans by limiting the amount of tax-deductible contributions to such trusts and subjecting the investment income to the unrelated business income tax. Neither of these problems applies to prefunding of

retiree life insurance, the welfare plans of a not-for-profit organization, or health benefits provided through collective-bargaining agreements.

- *Pension plans.* A special account for medical benefits may be maintained as part of a pension plan under Section 401(h) of the IRC. Within limits, contributions to the account are deductible when made and investment income is exempt from tax. Because benefits represent health care cost reimbursement, payments from the 401(h) account are tax-free.
- *Insurance contracts.* Insurance contracts can be used in either of two ways to prefund retiree welfare benefits. Assets can be accumulated in an insurance continuation fund for subsequent payment of pay-as-you go costs. Paid-up insurance may also be used. Under the latter approach, a one-time premium is paid to fund benefits for the lifetime of the retirees. These insurance approaches may be used for either life or medical insurance, but are much more common for the former. The life insurance contracts are issued to the employer, and the arrangement is often labeled corporate owned life insurance (COLI). If issued to the trust, the arrangement may be labeled trust owned life insurance (TOLI). The use of captive insurance companies is sometimes optimal.
- *Union funds.* Under many multiple-employer union-negotiated plans, contributions are made to a Taft-Hartley fund. The fund is responsible for the benefits to retirees.

LEGAL ISSUES

Unlike with pension benefits, The Employee Income Retirement Security Act (ERISA) does not provide for the statutory vesting of retiree medical benefits. As such, employee communication materials usually describe the employer's right to modify or terminate the overall benefit plan. Without such effective disclaimers, employers may be accused of having voluntarily offered lifetime medical benefits.

Employer attempts to reduce or eliminate medical benefits in the 1990s sometimes resulted in significant litigation, and, since that time, most employers have instituted and successfully relied on clearly worded communication materials.

CHAPTER 32

Employee Benefit Plans for Small Companies

Ronald I. Woodmansee

Designing and implementing competitive employee benefit plans for small companies[1] can be challenging. While many similarities exist between benefit programs for large and small companies, there also are many differences, including a smaller and sometimes more regional market from which to choose potential vendors. In the case of insured plans, once a company grows beyond 10 employees, insurance carriers and vendors that offer certain pricing breakpoints and increased opportunities for plan design and product flexibility become available to them.

The first stage of the planning process for small-company benefits includes clearly defined goals, desires, and, of course, a budget. With these factors in mind and with intelligent plan designs, a small company can provide a package of basic core benefits that can compete readily with those of larger companies. This is important as the small company attempts to recruit and retain employees from a talent pool that is accustomed to the wide variety of benefit options typically provided by larger firms. Surprisingly, there are even some areas of benefit planning that allow smaller companies to be more competitive than larger ones. These are discussed later in the chapter.

1. For the purposes of this chapter, small companies range from start-up mode of fewer than 10 employees to approximately 200 employees.

Although small companies typically do not have the same level of human resources (HR) support staff as larger ones, they can and should be able to get expert help and support from the vendors with whom they choose to do business, particularly as it pertains to issues of plan design, employee communication, trouble shooting, and the like. The benefit plans in general (and particularly the insured ones) of a small company in a high-growth mode need more constant and ongoing review, requiring a closely aligned working relationship with its outside advisors, brokers, and HR consultants among others.

With this background, the core components and planning nuances that small companies should consider in their employee benefit packages will be considered here. The chapter discusses health and welfare benefit plans, including medical insurance, short- and long-term disability income coverage, group life and accidental death and dismemberment (AD&D) insurance, dental insurance, and IRS Code Section 125 flexible spending accounts (FSA's).

MEDICAL INSURANCE

Usually, the first and most important benefit that small companies implement is a group medical insurance plan.

Special Considerations for Small Companies

Group medical insurance can be particularly challenging for small companies, and even more so for new start-up companies, for the following reasons:

1. Because they are most often fully insured[2] (instead of being either partially or fully self-insured as they are in many of their larger company counterparts), they are subject to state-mandated plan design options.
2. Because the employees of most small companies are in a relatively small geographic area, the plans must be designed using options available in that area. Most regions typically have only a local Blue Cross-type option and perhaps one or two national carriers operating in the small-group marketplace.

---

2. Insurance carriers generally define a small-group medical plan as one with 50 or fewer employees.

While additional regional and local carriers may exist, depending on the geographic areas involved, these carriers may provide only in-network coverage. Because of their limited network of local area hospital and physician providers, companies may be restricted in their plan design options.

3. Small companies in general, and start-up companies in particular, may have to provide additional documentation not required for larger companies in order to put a new plan in place so that insurance carriers can verify the existence of an actual company, and not just a banding together of people solely for the purpose of obtaining insurance. This documentation may include such items as payroll verification to be sure that employees actually work for the firm, articles of incorporation or other state-filed documents to verify the legal status of the business.
4. As of this writing, most states do not allow companies and organizations to join forces to form larger purchasing pools in order to get group discounts. That is scheduled to change in 2014 when state-based "insurance exchanges" and multistate and cooperative plans are to be established under the Patient Protection and Affordable Care Act of 2010 (PPACA) discussed later in the chapter. Even if these purchasing pools were currently allowed, there is no way of knowing what effect, if any, they would have on plan cost or availability.

Type of Plan

Although carriers in most geographic areas offer the entire current range of plan designs, this may not be true everywhere. It is very rare to see an old-style indemnity plan; that is, one that does not have some form of managed care. Available plan design options include

1. Health maintenance organizations (HMOs)
2. Preferred provider organizations (PPOs)
3. point of service (POS) plans
4. Direct access point of service plans (DPOS, open access, or nongated POS plans)
5. Consumer-driven health plans (CDHPs)

The choice of plan depends on what the company's business decision makers and/or its employees want. Many small company decision makers came from large companies, and what they were accustomed to in their prior organizations is often reflected in their choice of plan design. Also, they may believe that certain choices are necessary in order to attract a high caliber of employee. For example, a start-up biotechnology company trying to hire employees away from large pharmaceutical companies may have no choice for competitive and recruiting reasons but to offer a rich PPO plan instead of a basic HMO. Many times, senior executive decision makers themselves want plans similar to what they had at their prior companies. Conversely, a small company with young employees may be able to offer an inexpensive HMO plan, on the theory that the younger employees will focus more on preventive-type care and lower premiums at least initially and in the early parts of their careers before they have families.

Three trends in the small-group marketplace regarding pricing and plan design that a small company might want to consider are the following:

1. The marginal cost difference between offering a POS plan and an HMO plan may be small in some geographic areas. Therefore, some carriers in certain areas are choosing to offer only POS plans and have stopped offering HMO plans altogether.
2. Some smaller employers are "downgrading" from higher-cost PPO options to a DPOS plan. HMO and POS plans are similar in that each requires a referral from a primary care physician (PCP) to see a specialist inside the network. The DPOS plan is generally less restrictive in this area and therefore becoming more popular. Even though some DPOS plans may require an insured and/or his or her family to pick a PCP at time of enrollment, generally these plans do not require a referral from that PCP in order to see a specialist in the network. However, there may be certain areas of coverage that still do require a referral. Implementing a DPOS plan can sometimes cost significantly less than a standard PPO plan, and it is worthy of consideration for a small business trying to manage its health care budget.
3. Many small employers are turning to CDHPs as a way to control medical costs. These plans include a high-deductible medical plan combined with a tax-favored medical reimbursement account, either in the form of a health savings account (HSA) or a health reimbursement arrangement (HRA).

Because these plans require a great deal of employee involvement, employee understanding and the communication process are critical. A hastily implemented plan, or one that is not well understood by employees, risks not meeting employer objectives or employee needs. In order to work optimally, there needs to be transparency in costs and quality for hospital, physician, medical, and pharmacy services available. As this information becomes more readily available and accessible, the value to employees and cost savings potential will further increase. Consumer-driven health plans are discussed more fully in Chapter 7.

Dual-Option Plans

For many years, large companies have offered dual-option plans that include a lower-cost plan such as an HMO and one or more higher-cost options, such as a POS or PPO. This is done to give the employees choices and flexibility and, perhaps more importantly, because the employer is trying to fix its medical plan costs as best it can. To do this, the employer may peg its contribution to the premium of the lower-cost plan. Then, employees who choose a more costly plan must also pay the difference in cost between the two plans.

For the past several years, small employers have increasingly been offering dual-option plans when practical and allowed. Truly small companies (those with fewer than 10 employees) may be able to offer only one plan, but carriers are increasingly allowing small groups with fewer than ten employees to offer at least two options. Although they are getting more flexible, small market carriers may impose restrictions on available options. Consideration of dual-option offerings requires sound advice and counsel regarding the available options that are specific to a company's local geographic area.

Employee Contributions

Understandably, small companies sometimes cannot offer as generous a compensation and benefits package as large employers. This may lead decision makers to the mistaken conclusion that they should counterbalance this by offering fully paid health insurance with no employee contributions. There are several reasons why a small company, particularly a start-up one, usually should require employee contributions for medical care insurance coverage:

1. In today's benefit climate, most employees are accustomed to paying some level of contribution. This may range from 10 to 20 percent or more for single employees to a larger percentage for employees with dependents—sometimes including the full cost difference. Paying the entire difference for dependents is often the case with very small and particularly start-up companies, simply because of budgetary constraints.
2. Requiring a contribution usually motivates or forces employees who have coverage, or the option to get coverage elsewhere—typically through a spouse's employer plan—to decline the coverage under their small employer's plan. Without the contribution requirement, employees will enroll in the fully paid coverage simply because it is there at no cost to them.
3. It is much easier to set policy and precedent, and plan for future growth, by introducing the concept of contributions at the inception of the plan when there are only a few employees. Changing from a noncontributory to a contributory plan at a later date when the company is substantially larger can be viewed as a reduction in benefits and can create employee anxiety and ill will.
4. Having a contribution also can help to avoid potential legal problems. A risk issue might arise, for example, if a medical provider attempts to get payment from an employer for the bills incurred by one of its employees who was allowed to opt out of a noncontributory plan. To minimize this risk, employees may be required to apply for a formal exception. Waivers may only be granted for religious reasons or where the employee has other coverage, such as through a spouse.

The Patient Protection and Affordable Care Act

On March 23, 2010, President Obama signed the Patient Protection and Affordable Care Act (PPACA) into law, the most comprehensive and controversial health insurance reform act in over 50 years. Basically, the law applies only to medical insurance. Ancillary services such as dental insurance are not affected. As of this writing, much of the law still needs to be clarified, and there are many unanswered questions regarding the practical applications of many of its provisions. Keeping this in mind and understanding that many of the new regulations apply to all companies, the following are some of the PPACA's key provisions that apply exclusively to small companies.

Small employers are eligible for tax credits beginning in 2010. To be eligible, employers must have no more than 25 full-time equivalent (FTE) employees (as defined in the law), have average annual wages of $50,000 or less per employee, and pay at least 50 percent of the insurance premiums (not including dependents) for employees. From 2010 through 2013, the credit can be as high as 35 percent of employer-paid insurance premiums, going up to a possible 50 percent credit in 2014. Beginning in 2014, the credit can be taken for up to two consecutive years, but only if employees are covered under a state-based insurance exchange. The credit is on a sliding scale. For a small employer to get the maximum credit, it must have fewer than 10 FTE employees with average annual wages of less than $25,000.

Simple cafeteria plans are available to promote the use of tax-free health benefits to employees beginning in 2011. A small employer for these plans is defined as having an average of 100 or fewer employees on business days during either of the two preceding years. However, if the plan is maintained without interruption, the employee limit can go up to 200 employees. If this requirement is met, a safe harbor from nondiscrimination testing is available, similar to the SIMPLE 401(K) rules. The safe harbor rules can be met with minimum employer contributions for all nonhighly compensated employees of either

1. A uniform percentage of at least 2 percent of the employee's compensation whether or not the employee makes salary reduction contributions to the plan; or
2. A matching contribution of the lesser of the 200 percent of the employee's contribution or 6 percent of the employee's compensation.

The same calculation method must be used for all nonhighly compensated employees. The impact of this should be an improvement in the utilization rates by all employees of these pretax accounts. However, that remains to be seen, given all of the other simultaneous and numerous changes to medical plans in general.

Beginning in 2012, all group plans, including those of small businesses, will be required to provide a summary of benefits and a coverage explanation that meets specific criteria set out by the Department of Health and Human Services (HHS) to all enrollees when they apply for coverage, enroll, or reenroll, at policy delivery, and when any material coverage modifications are made. The required information will be substantially more than what is in a current summary plan description (SPD) and will have very specific format and layout requirements. It is not yet known whether this new communication will be the employer's responsibility or if the insurance companies will be required to produce and provide it.

Additionally, all group plans will have to annually submit reports to HHS on whether or not the benefits provided under their plans meet HHS-established criteria on improving health outcomes, improving patient safety, and the like. The report must also be provided to all plan participants during the annual open enrollment period, and HHS will make the reports publicly available through the Internet. Fines and penalties can also be levied by HHS.

Beginning in 2013, all employers must provide notices to their employees informing them of the existence of the state-based insurance exchanges. State-based health insurance exchanges are scheduled to become operational in 2014 to assist individuals and small employers (generally defined as 1 to 50 employees, but including up to 100 employees beginning in 2016) purchase qualified health care that complies with new federal standards for "essential health benefits," the specifics of which are yet to be defined. The exchanges will offer four levels of benefits: bronze at 60 percent of the benefit costs of the plan, silver at 70 percent, gold at 80 percent, and platinum at 90 percent of the benefit costs of the plan. Cooperative plans and multistate national plans will be offered to individuals and small employers through these state-based exchanges.

Employer "pay or play" responsibility—that is, offer minimum essential coverage to full-time employees or make nondeductible payments to the government—begins in 2014 for employers with 50 or more employees.[3]

Depending on the cost of individual and small-group plans, some people, especially younger ones, may be more inclined to pay the penalties at these levels instead of purchasing insurance. The new "large employer" (defined as having had an average of 50 employees during the preceding calendar year) "pay or play" rules further complicate this issue. They do so by penalizing what are really small employers who either do not offer medical insurance to their employees or have employees that opt out of the

3. Part-time employees are counted for purposes of reaching the 50-employee threshold but not for purposes of applying any penalties.

employer plans and enroll in one of the state-based insurance exchange plans.

This presents a real dilemma for a small firm, having to design a medical plan such that all employees are able to afford their contributions and stay in the plan, while needing to meet government-mandated plan designs that include lower copays, new and lower out-of-pocket maximums, and the like. Some companies may try to stay below 50 total employees to avoid these potential penalties. This raises the additional question of the viability of using subcontractors instead of employees in order to stay below the 50-employee threshold.

2014 also brings modified community rating in the individual and small-group markets and the exchange. Small employers are defined as those with up to 100 employees (although some states may elect to keep this threshold at 50 employees until 2016). This means that premium band variations are only allowed for age (with a 3-to-1 ratio), tobacco use, family composition, and geographic regions and that experience rating is prohibited. The main impact of this is likely to be less price competition between carriers for the same risk, since one of the only differentiators may be administrative costs.

DISABILITY INCOME INSURANCE

Although they do not always think of it as such, arguably the most important protection for employees is disability income insurance. Often, this coverage is neglected even in large firms, and, in far too many small companies it is not addressed or even considered at all. Employees at all levels rarely realize that their biggest asset is not their homes, bank accounts, or retirement plans. Rather, it is their ability to earn a lifetime of income.

Generally speaking, there are two types of employer-sponsored group disability options: short-term disability (STD) and long-term disability (LTD). Although employees typically ask for the STD benefits first, LTD is by far the more important of the two, covering a much larger and more catastrophic risk, by providing more income for a much longer period of time.

STD plans typically begin after one or two weeks of disability and last for as long as 13 or 26 weeks. These plans are perfect for the short-term illnesses, maternities, and other noncatastrophic events for which they were designed. With 10 or more insured employees, STD plans also have no preexisting-condition limitations and need no underwriting to implement. LTD benefits typically begin at the cessation of any short-term benefits, and, when implemented together, the long-term plan dovetails with the short-term plan so that as one plan benefit ends the other begins. Interestingly, the cost of the insured STD plan may be close to the cost of the LTD plan for a given group of employees. Actuarially, this illustrates the fact that long-term disabilities are fewer in occurrence than STD claims but are far more catastrophic.

A typical plan design for an STD program might be for an employer to provide 60 percent of an employee's base salary, although insured benefits can go as high as 70 percent. When insured, maximum weekly benefits typically range between $500 and $2,000. It is also more efficient to insure the STD claim with a two-week waiting period before the insurance begins, thereby allowing the employer to self-insure the first two calendar weeks of claims (10 business days), also known as the elimination period. Employees can also then use sick and vacation days to fill that gap, sometimes as part of a paid time-off (PTO) policy. Starting insured benefits after two weeks, instead of after day one or one week, can yield significant savings on the cost of the insured program. Unfortunately, many employers, particularly small companies, are not aware of the cost saving involved by looking at this longer waiting period before STD benefits begin. That being said, this is one of the plan design options mentioned earlier that may not be available to plans covering fewer than 10 employees because of plan design inflexibility at that size.

Insuring an STD plan may be more efficient than self-insuring the risk, especially for a small company, for several reasons:

1. When intelligently designed, the cost is not expensive.
2. It takes the employer out of the role of having to deal with privacy issues and claim adjudication, especially since small employers have few, if any, human resource professionals on staff on a full-time basis.
3. Just one claim per year, with a maternity claim being the most common, could pay for the cost of the annual premium.

The most cost-efficient combination of an STD and LTD plan is to structure the benefit period of the STD plan to last for 13 weeks and the LTD plan to begin after 90 days. The reason for the choice of a 90-day rather than a 180-day elimination period is that the nominal cost savings is often far exceeded by the cost of the additional three months of covered compensation. This is especially true for small companies that do not have the cash flow and claim adjudication resources to self-fund the benefits for the first 180 days, something that large companies often do.

Again, for very small companies of fewer than 10 employees, insured plan designs available in the marketplace for STD and LTD coverage are not as flexible as they are once the 10-employee threshold is met. Therefore, once a small employer reaches 10 employees, it could benefit from repricing its STD and LTD coverage, not only because there is generally a large price break point beginning at 10 covered employees, but, and perhaps more importantly, because of the already-mentioned increased plan flexibility, which also helps directly with the pricing. Because of insurance company underwriting guidelines, the maximum monthly LTD benefit will typically correspond to the average incomes of the three highest-compensated individuals. Although there generally is no underwriting necessary to implement a group LTD plan, there is a preexisting-condition clause invoked by the insurance carrier to prevent adverse selection. That clause needs to be communicated to, and understood by, the employees, especially for a new plan that is not a takeover of a prior plan.

The following important contractual features should be considered and addressed in any LTD plan design:

1. The definition of total disability is an area where small companies can provide benefits that are much better than their large-company counterparts. A typical group contract for large companies says that an employee is disabled if he or she cannot do the main duties, or perhaps every duty, of his or her own occupation, but only for the first 24 months of a claim. Sometimes large companies, particularly self-insured ones, may even use the most rigid Social Security definition of total disability—expected to be out of work for at least one year or to die. After 24 months of claim payments, the definition of total disability for large company plans almost always becomes more rigid and normally states that an employee will then be paid only if he or she cannot do the duties of any gainful occupation by reason of education, training, or experience. This is the classic "own occupation" definition versus the "any occupation" definition of total disability. Once a small company reaches 10 employees, if it has a workforce that consists fully or partially of white-collar or professional workers, it would be able to have an own-occupation definition of total disability throughout the entire claim maximum benefit period, typically to age 65 or more commonly the Social Security normal retirement age (SSNRA). The cost to improve this definition of total disability

is nominal, is a substantial benefit upgrade in this market, and is one that is seldom discussed. A small company also often creates two or more classes of employees for the application of the own-occupation definition of total disability if it has a mix of white-collar and blue-collar employees. This is one area in which employers can and should legally discriminate between classes of employees. Lastly, the newer contracts in the market use the SSNRA benefit period, which can provide benefits for younger employees out to age 67 for those born after 1960.

2. Whenever possible, contracts should be written to cover a partial disability from the first day of disability, meaning that a partial disability benefit can be paid without first having to have a total disability benefit. Given that the incidence of partial disabilities is far greater than that of total disabilities, this is an extremely important feature, as it encourages the employee to return to work on a part-time or limited basis while receiving a partial benefit. In many older LTD contracts, and many times in the large-company marketplace, this provision is not automatic. Contracts as such are counter productive as they encourage an employee to remain totally disabled, instead of being productive. In most partial disability claims, the benefits from all sources, including partial employment earnings and group benefits combined, may exceed a total disability benefit that may be paid when the employee is not working at all. Also, it is commonly known by disability claims people that the best way to get an employee off of a disability claim is to motivate him or her to return to work. A properly designed LTD contract can help provide that financial motivation in addition to providing vocational and rehabilitation resources to aid in the return-to-work process.

Another virtually unknown and available feature in a group LTD plan, and one that will make a small-company LTD plan far more competitive than one of a larger firm, is the addition of a cost-of-living adjustment (COLA).

It is easy to see what would happen to a monthly benefit for, let us say, a 30-year old employee who is disabled for 10 or 20 years. Using the Rule of 72 (a basic rule used to calculate the rate at which money doubles by dividing the number 72 by the interest rate) and assuming a 4 percent inflation factor, we find that the disabled employee's benefits essentially would be cut in half in about 18 years.

A COLA simply compounds a monthly benefit by an inflation factor if someone is disabled. The compounding normally occurs after every 12 months of a disability claim and is typically in the 3 percent range, although it may be tied to the consumer price index (CPI). Many LTD carriers also allow the compounding to last as long as the claim lasts, even until age 65 or the SSNRA if needed.

While the cost for a COLA option may seem large as a percentage of premium, from an absolute dollar standpoint it is not costly at all. However, it is rare to find a large-company LTD plan with a COLA feature.

Supplemental Long-Term Disability Insurance

One of the more neglected areas that should be considered, particularly for senior and highly paid executives and business owners, is the concept of supplemental LTD insurance. Generally, this is accomplished by using individual high quality noncancelable policies, also known as "noncan" policies. Noncan means that the premiums and the contracts, once underwritten and issued, are guaranteed until age 65, or perhaps age 67 under the newer market contracts.

This concept should be considered for several reasons. First, it is important because of the tax ramifications of an employer-paid group LTD plan. Since many LTD plans are fully, or at least partially, paid for by the employer, under long-standing income tax law, this makes the benefits either fully or partially taxable to the employee in the same proportion as the premium payment. That is, if the employer pays 100 percent of the cost, the benefits in the event of disability are 100 percent income-taxable. When the after-tax replacement of income is considered, employees generally have a much lower percentage of income replaced than expected. There are many times when highly paid executives are replacing only 20 to 30 percent of their take-home pay and not even realizing it. Because of the sometimes fairly low and limited maximum benefit on small group LTD plans, senior executives are reversely discriminated against, meaning that as they receive higher and higher compensation, they also receive less of their total compensation in the event of a disability. This problem is often more pronounced in a small company, where one or two of the top-paid executives may have only $5000 per month of group LTD benefits, because of an insurance company underwriting limitation under which it insures only the average incomes of the top three highest earners.

Also, group LTD policies are not guaranteed. Either party to the contract—the insurance company or the employer—can terminate the policy at any time. This is even more important in small companies, where the livelihood of the company is more dependent on the senior executives, and reallocating company resources to pay their salaries could be catastrophic.

Bonuses and other incentive compensation paid in addition to base salary generally are not covered by group LTD contracts, although the contracts can be designed to do so. With the trend towards more variable and incentive compensation in today's compensation systems, this important fact should not be overlooked or neglected.

When multiple individual contracts are issued to individuals in the same company, there can be substantial policy price discounts, as well as underwriting concessions. Permanent and portable discounts depend on the number of people who are issued contracts and who pays the premium. Women in these groups also get the additional advantage of a unisex price, which can further reduce the cost by 30 percent or more.

GROUP LIFE AND AD&D INSURANCE

Although group life insurance, particularly for small companies, may not be perceived as an important benefit by employees, especially when compared with other benefits such as group dental or STD income coverage, it can be a high-visibility and low-cost benefit. When designing group life insurance plans, it is important to make a distinction between small companies of fewer than 10 employees and those having more than 10 employees.

Generally speaking, true group life contracts for companies of fewer than 10 employees are neither price competitive nor cost effective because there are low limits on what is called guaranteed issue (GI) coverage, meaning amounts of coverage that can be issued without medical underwriting—typically between $10,000 and $50,000 maximum per employee. Benefits in excess of these amounts require additional medical underwriting, which can be cumbersome for a small company. Therefore, if life insurance is really needed or wanted, a very small company might be better off issuing and paying for individual term insurance policies, especially if it is going to remain under 10 employees for a reasonably long period of time. This approach also provides the employees the added advantage of owning an individual and portable contract that might have a rate guarantee for 10, 15, or 20 years. Assuming the employees are reasonably healthy, the combined cost for the individual policies in most cases is actually cheaper than the total cost for group term life insurance for the same group. Otherwise, waiting until the company reaches the 10-employee threshold might be a better strategy.

Once a company reaches 10 employees, true group term life policies become much more cost effective and can be an important part of the overall benefits package. Group term life insurance for small companies can provide multiples-of-salary plan designs, with reasonably high maximum benefits, all for literally pennies per thousand dollars of coverage per month. It is not uncommon to see benefits of one to two times compensation with maximum benefits per person of between $100,000 and $400,000 of coverage. The monthly cost for such a benefit for a small company depends on the demographic make up of the group, employee occupations, industry and the like.

Although not required, these life insurance benefits generally include accidental death and dismemberment (AD&D) coverage, which simply doubles the life insurance benefits in the event of an accident. The cost of the AD&D benefit for almost any company is generally very small with the exception being one that performs hazardous occupations.

The only slightly negative consequence to employees having larger amounts of group life insurance is that, under Internal Revenue Code (IRC) Section 79 rules, the employees pay federal income tax on any employer-provided amounts in excess of $50,000 of coverage. Even with the taxable income, the after-tax cost for the employees is still normally cheaper than the cost for personal and individually owned term insurance, making this coverage a valuable part of the employees' total personal life insurance portfolio. Because of Section 79 taxation, some companies cap the group life amounts at $50,000 per employee. However, in many cases, as the overall total company life insurance volume increases, particularly in small companies, the unit costs per thousand dollars of coverage decrease, making the higher benefits even more cost effective.

An employer might also offer a voluntary group term life insurance plan in addition to the company-paid base benefit described above. A voluntary group term life plan for a small company may have some limited and small amount of guaranteed issue benefits (such as $25,000 to $50,000), depending on the percentage of the population enrolled. However, unless the company is substantially large (generally 250 or more employees) and/or the employer subsidizes the cost, the voluntary group term life rates usually do not represent any price or underwriting bargain for the employees when compared with individual marketplace term insurance rates. This is generally because individual term insurance policy rates have come down substantially in the last several years.

An employer-sponsored product that has become more popular in smaller companies in the last several years is the group universal life (GUL) contract—although it typically is offered by only the largest of small companies (perhaps 100 or more employees). This product is a hybrid of an individual and a group life product. It offers some of the underwriting concessions such as guaranteed issue coverage and price breaks of group life insurance while having the portability and flexibility of an individual product. Although group universal life contracts have an option to be funded as long-term permanent policies, with the attendant tax-deferred cash values of such a contract, most times they are funded as term policies. Because group universal life contracts do have premium loads for adverse selection, and sometimes are based on a "unismoke" rate—one that does not differentiate between males and females, and smokers and nonsmokers—they may not be any cheaper than quality and fully underwritten term insurance policies that employees can acquire on their own.

GROUP DENTAL INSURANCE

Although group dental coverage may be a popular request by employees of small firms—often because they have come from larger companies and have been accustomed to having it—it is not the most cost-effective benefit, especially for the smallest of employers. It is not that dental coverage is unimportant, but that if a start-up company is just beginning its benefit package and has a very limited budget, it is not as important as the other coverages already described.

For especially small companies of under 10 employees, dental insurance has often been referred to as "dollar trading" with the insurance company. This means that the value of claims paid about equals the total premiums paid over the course of the year. For example, if coverage for a single employee costs $25 to $30 per month, and the employee has no major dental work done during the year, this premium equals the yearly cost of routine semiannual cleanings.

However, the coverage can be more cost effective for employees for two reasons. First, the employer may be paying for some of the cost on behalf of the employee and/or the employee's family. Second, if an employee pays all or part of the cost of the dental program, the true after-tax cost to the employee is substantially discounted when an employer also implements a Section 125 pretax spending account. This planning tool, which is discussed later in the chapter, is quite simple and very cost effective even for the smallest of employers.

Larger-company plans usually have some level of orthodontia coverage. However, smaller companies, depending upon the size of the group (and certainly those of fewer than 10 employees), may not be able to offer orthodontia coverage as an option. Additionally, smaller companies, particularly very small or new firms, may consider offering only a "starter plan" that would include basic and preventive coverage only, with the option to add major restorative and perhaps orthodontia at a later date. Certainly this approach, which obviously is less expensive, would be preferred to offering no coverage at all.

As with the group life and disability plans discussed above, small-company dental plans do have price break points and some additional plan design and flexibility options when an employer has 10 covered employees. When a small employer is on the cusp of 10 employees, it might try to "incent" employees, who might otherwise opt out of coverage for any number of reasons, to be in the plan, simply to reach the price break point, and also increase the design flexibility. Unlike medical plans, which may be more regional in scope regarding network coverage, insured dental plans, even for small companies, tend to be available with more national carriers, meaning those that have networks of dentists throughout most parts of the country.

There are a handful of large specialty dental carriers that also provide for competitively priced comprehensive dental plans, including major work, and without preexisting-condition limitations, for even the smallest of companies, starting at only two employees. Often, a good strategy for very small companies, or those with limited budgets, might be to initially use a vendor such as that and later upgrade and review the coverage and cost options once the 10-employee break point is reached.

Many small-group dental plans are written as a PPO-type of coverage in which an employee can choose to use an in-network dentist or a dentist not in the network. Some PPO plans provide the same reimbursement percentage for both in- and out-of-network claims, while others attempt to "steer" employees into the network by paying a higher reimbursement percentage for using in-network dentists. Although not readily apparent when the same percentage reimbursement applies to in- and out-of-network claims, the use of an in-network dentist will lower the out-of-pocket costs for the employees because they will not be subject to the usual and customary rate (UCR) restrictions that insurance carriers apply to nonnetwork claims, thereby providing more discounted value to the plan users.

Some small-company dental plans are written as a "passive PPO" plan design in which design and reimbursement levels work the same as in an active PPO plan but in which there are potentially more UCR reductions because the reimbursement levels for the out-of-network dentists are applied at the discounted in-network reimbursement levels. It is important that employees understand this in detail, lest they become surprised or sometimes disappointed at some of the larger UCR reductions at claim time.

As with the medical insurance plans described above, and for all the same reasons, it is recommended that the employees contribute some portion of the cost for dental insurance both for themselves and for dependents. The one short-term exception may be where, as mentioned above, a small employer needs to have 10 employees in the plan in order for price break points and enhanced plan designs to be available.

CAFETERIA PLANS

Cafeteria plans come in many forms and are governed by IRC Section 125. They are also known as Section 125 plans, flexible benefits programs, and flex plans. In its simplest form, a Section 125 plan would include only pretax premium payments and is known as a premium-only plan (POP). As one of the lowest-cost benefits, and sometimes even a no-cost benefit, a POP plan can be provided by even the smallest of companies. Only a large company can provide a full-range cafeteria plan, which may offer as many as three or four options in each benefit area. It can do so because of the large numbers of employees across its entire population. Small companies do not have that luxury, from either a cost or an administration standpoint and, as already mentioned, the insurance carriers in the small-company marketplace typically do not offer as much flexibility or as many plan design options to small companies because of the smaller number of employees covered and the attendant risk of creating excessive adverse selection.

However even the very smallest of companies can easily establish POP plans for their employees. This is very inexpensive and can be done either through a payroll company or an outside vendor. The Internal Revenue Service (IRS) requirement to allow pretax premiums simply requires having a Section 125 plan document in place. Once the plan is established, the employee contributions for medical and dental insurance, and sometimes disability income and other insurance, can all be made on a pretax basis. Because in the eyes of the IRS a Section 125 election is a salary reduction plan, the employee saves federal income taxes and FICA (Social Security), Medicare, and FUTA (federal unemployment) taxes, as well as state and local income taxes in most states and localities. Therefore, employees should think of this as an approximate 20 to 35 percent discount on the cost of whatever contributions they are required to make for medical and/or dental insurance premiums.

The employer can also take into account the employees' personal tax savings when establishing employee contributions for medical and dental insurance, since the employee's after-tax costs are now lower. It might also be wise to have employee contributions as a fixed percentage of the premium instead of a fixed dollar amount. In doing so, employees realize that, at rate renewal time each year, they will share in the premium increase in the same percentage. Using this strategy the employer does not have to "renegotiate" the employee contributions each year.

The employer gets a tax advantage on this benefit as well, of the matching FICA/Medicare and FUTA insurance tax savings on any salary reduction based on the employee contributions rates. Based on the 2010 FICA wage base limit, this is a savings of 7.65 percent of payroll up to $106,800 of salary and a 1.45 percent Medicare tax savings on the excess on compensation above that. This is where the small employer can recoup the administration cost and provide this plan as a no-cost or at least low-cost benefit. The cost recovery, or payback, to the employer of implementing just this pretax premium portion of the Section 125 plan is typically 12 to 24 months at most.

The other two parts of Section 125 plans are health care and dependent care reimbursement accounts. These reimbursement accounts are also called flexible spending accounts (FSAs). Although a company can implement one or the other, these are rarely done separately. Most employers offer both spending accounts at once because the fixed pricing or administration cost for most third-party administrators (TPAs) in this marketplace do not separately break out the cost of administering each account.

The administration cost to a small company for adding the two spending accounts is a little bit higher than what it would be for having only the pretax premium account. Again, the employer saves the matching FICA/Medicare and FUTA taxes on the employee contributions, thus making the net out-of-pocket cost to administer the plan very low, especially when compared with the value that is gained by the employees and the good will that is established in the process.

Generally speaking, smaller employers limit the employee elections in the medical expense account to somewhere between $2,000 and $5,000 per year, although it can be higher, based on specific company and employee needs. There is no IRS limit here through 2012 and the maximum is dictated only by the firm's plan document. Under the new PPACA law the annual election for medical expenses is capped at $2,500 per employee for plan years beginning January 1, 2013. There is a rudimentary discrimination test that the firm must pass, not unlike that for a 401(K) plan. Generally, no more than 25 percent of all the salary deferrals, including premiums, can be attributed to highly compensated employees as defined by the IRS.

Because the IRS rules concerning health care expense reimbursement accounts require that an employee's entire annual election must be made available to him or her at any point during the plan year, there is the risk to the small employer that an employee who makes a large annual election may get over-reimbursed early in the plan year and terminate employment, in which case the employer loses the chance to recoup that money from the employee's paycheck over the balance of the year. As a trade-off or "premium" for this risk, any unused employee balances at the end of the plan year revert back to the employer under IRS regulations.

There is also a minor risk to the small employer of having to temporarily "front" money in the early part of the plan year, if there are not enough early plan-year receipts to cover early plan-year claims. If this happens, it is only temporary and can easily be repaid as plan assets are recouped through each payroll cycle.

Neither of these two risks applies to a dependent care reimbursement account, which reimburses expenses only up to the amount currently in the account.

Over the last several years, virtually all TPAs in this market have provided debit cards for employees to use to pay for approved services and items, both minimizing the paperwork and making administration much easier. With automated claim adjudication, there is no manual claim intervention in many cases. This feature has increased the ease of use for all employees and therefore lowered the complaint from small employers that setting up a Section 125 plan is not advantageous because of low employee utilization. The one caveat, however, is that, under strict IRS rules, employees need to keep detailed copies of their debit card transactions. If the TPA is not able to determine what item was purchased, the employee must document the items through the TPA within the required amount of time or the debit card will be deactivated until the appropriate documentation has been provided. It is important to note that nonprescription over-the-counter items will no longer be eligible for reimbursement after December 31, 2010 under the PPACA, except in very well-defined and limited circumstances.

For a dependent care spending account, there is a somewhat complicated 55 percent benefits discrimination test that must be performed—ideally before the plan is fully implemented, to ensure that the plan is in compliance with the IRS testing rules. In general, this means that if only one employee uses the plan and that employee is "highly compensated," the plan will likely not pass the test, and that employee will be very limited in the amount of the annual election, if it is allowed at all. This is why employee education is needed on these plans to ensure they work properly and as intended. Chapter 25 provides a more detailed discussion of cafeteria plans.

COMMUNICATION OF SMALL-PLAN BENEFITS

The implementation of a Section 125 plan is a great tool for a small employer to use in communicating all of its benefit plans. What is very helpful, but very often not or poorly done in small companies, is the education of employees regarding what coverages they do and do not have under their entire benefit plan package. It may be recommended that the employer ask its providers—including consultants, brokers, human resources professionals and the like—to develop education and communication pieces and hold employee communication meetings, perhaps in small groups, to explain the details and nuances of all the benefits. This may even be followed up with one-on-one consultative meetings with employees to help them answer questions, especially very personal ones, that the employer may not and need not know. A Section 125 plan can truly augment the entire benefits package. Therefore, in order to implement one properly so that employees can maximize their tax savings, the employer should take advantage of this time and use the education process to fully explain all the benefits to the employees. For example, many times the employee tax savings can be used to enhance or increase an employee's 401(K) election, and perhaps help a small 401(K) plan meet or improve its discrimination testing results by doing so.

CONCLUSION

Designing a competitive benefits package for a small firm is not an easy task, nor is it a static process. Although small companies generally cannot replicate what can be done in large companies, when properly designed and communicated, their benefit plans should be able to compete very well with the offerings of large companies. This requires constant review, especially as small companies grow and reach certain thresholds of employees, and particularly in the light of ever-changing laws and government regulations.

CHAPTER 33

Multiemployer Plans

David Blumenstein

As the name suggests, a multiemployer plan is an employee benefit plan to which two or more unrelated companies contribute in accordance with a collective bargaining agreement (CBA) between them and one or more labor organizations. These types of plans are also commonly called "Taft-Hartley" plans. Multiemployer plans make it possible for small employers and large employers alike to come together and use their group purchasing power to offer their workers affordable benefits on a group basis, which enables them to remain competitive with other employers in their industry. Moreover, multiemployer plans permit portability of benefits across many employers. This makes it possible for workers who work for many employers due to the nature of their jobs (e.g., jobs in the construction and entertainment industries) and who otherwise might not be able to accumulate enough tenure with any one employer to earn credits under one plan and often to qualify for benefits based on the total credits earned from all the plan's contributing employers. Typically, employer contributions are paid based on an amount per hour, day or week worked, but the contributions could be based on other negotiated formulas such as dollars per ton of coal mined or per loaf of bread baked. The money for the benefits is held in a trust fund administered by a board of trustees that includes both labor and management representatives.

There are two broad types of multiemployer plans:

- Retirement plans, both defined benefit (DB) plans which provide retirement income benefits through a pension, and defined contribution (DC) plans, which many sponsors also offer as a supplement to pension coverage.

- Health and welfare plans which can provide a wide variety of benefits, including group health coverage for medical, hospital, and health care costs (including prescription drug, dental and vision), unemployment subsidies, vacation pay, life insurance, dependent care, apprenticeship training and prepaid legal services.

Multiemployer plans can be local, regional or national. In most cases, the plan participants are engaged in the same kind of employment (e.g., truck drivers, carpenters or retail food workers).

ORIGINS AND PHILOSOPHY

The first multiemployer plan[1] was an employer-funded pension plan started in 1929 by Local 3 of the Brotherhood of Electrical Workers and the Electrical Contractors Association of New York City. Subsequently, certain negotiated plans were developed in the 1930s and 1940s in industries such as the needle trades and coal mining to provide benefits for two often-overlapping segments of the unionized workforce:

- Workers whose employment was transitory due to the nature of their work and who otherwise would not have been able to accumulate enough tenure with any one employer to earn eligibility for benefits, and
- Workers employed by small employers that did not have adequate resources to provide benefits.

Two important events laid the groundwork for the further development of multiemployer plans. The first was the enactment of the Labor-Management Relations Act of 1947, the Taft-Hartley Act. The second was the *Inland Steel* decision of 1949,[2] which held that federal labor law requires

1. There are also non-negotiated multiemployer plans, which have been established by certain employers that have chosen, on their own initiative, to provide their employees with a benefit package. Non-negotiated plans are common in the nonprofit area among religious, charitable, and educational institutions. They are categorized as multiple-employer plans under the Employee Retirement Income Security Act of 1974 (ERISA) and the Internal Revenue Code (IRC) and are generally subject to the same legal rules as single-employer plans.
2. Inland Steel Co., 77 NLRB 1, enforced, 170 F.2d 247 (7th Cir. 1948), cert. denied 336 U.S. 960 (1949).

an employer to negotiate pensions if the union representing the workers requests bargaining over pensions. Section 302(c)(5) of the Taft-Hartley Act established the rules for employer-funded employee benefit trusts in which the union plays an oversight role. It requires separate trusts for pension and health and welfare plans. It also stipulates that the plans must be governed by a board of trustees (who act as fiduciaries) on which employer and union representatives have equal power, with a procedure to resolve a deadlock. There must be at least two companies contributing to a multiemployer plan pursuant to collective bargaining agreements, but there is no maximum.

The labor movement, particularly the part of it organized by craft rather than by industry, was the driving force behind the creation of multiemployer plans. This group believed that workers could be best protected through using risk pooling and economies of scale spreading the risk and costs of benefits as well as the associated administrative expense over a large population. Risk pooling means that if one employer has adverse experience (e.g., a disproportionate number of long-lived workers or surviving spouses whose pension benefits continue longer than the actuaries would have projected), that higher cost is spread over the pool of participating employers. Risk pooling also means that any financial difficulties experienced by an individual employer in the pool would not be as threatening to the benefits of its employees as they would be if those participants were in a plan sponsored solely by that employer.

The philosophical underpinning of today's multiemployer plans is collective bargaining for wages and benefits and shared labor-management responsibility for the stewardship of the plan. Typically, the collective bargaining takes into account tradeoffs between investing more of a finite "supply" of dollars into one form of compensation, such as wages, versus pensions and health care. The result is an explicit trade-off of current compensation (wages) for retirement and health benefits. The collaborative labor-management structure at the heart of multiemployer plans assures that the interests of all stakeholders are taken into account.

GROWTH AND PREVALENCE

Little reliable data on the prevalence of multiemployer plans is available prior to 1958, when the Federal Welfare and Pension Plans Disclosure Act was passed. In 1960, the Bureau of Labor Statistics (BLS) reported that 798 multiemployer DB retirement plans covering approximately 3.3 million active and retired workers had filed reports by the spring of that year and that more than 92 percent of those plans were less than 10 years old. The primary growth period for DB retirement plans was between 1955 and 1963.

In 1974, the Employee Retirement Income Security Act of 1974 (ERISA) created the Pension Benefit Guaranty Corporation (PBGC) which began collecting premiums from and data on multiemployer DB retirement plans the following year. It has reported consistent data on the number of plans and participants since 1980. In 2009, the PBGC insured nearly 1,500 insured plans with almost 10.5 million participants, 30 percent more than the total number of participants covered in 1980. This total includes active participants, retired participants and separated vested participants (see Table 33-1).

The total number of PBGC-insured plans has slowly declined since 1980, primarily due to plan mergers. This change mostly reflects the loss of plans with fewer than 1,000 participants. For example, the number of PBGC-insured plans with fewer than 500 participants fell from 910 in 1980 to 335 in 2009, while the number of multiemployer pension plans with 10,000 or more participants rose from 120 to 171 (see Table 33-2).

Data for multiemployer health and welfare plans is very hard to come by, but according to a search of Form 5500 filings in 2008, there were approximately 2,000 plans with close to four million active participants.

INDUSTRIES

Multiemployer plans are typically found in unionized industries that have mobile workforces because of seasonal, irregular or project-based employment and/or many small companies where few workers would qualify under an individual plan if one were established. For example, many construction jobs are for short durations and workers may be hired by a contractor for only a few weeks or months. When the job is completed, the worker may be unemployed until another contractor needs his or her particular skills.

The construction trades account for more than one-third of all multiemployer DB retirement plans covered by the PBGC. Such plans also are common in the service, retail trade, manufacturing and trucking industries (see Figure 33-1). Multiemployer health and welfare plans tend to be concentrated in the same industries.

Most large industries have more than one multiemployer plan. Some plans cover people working in several industries in one geographic area. Many plans cover a trade or craft rather than an entire industry. The key common link is that in most cases, the participants are represented by the

TABLE 33-1

PBGC-Insured Plans, Participants and Participant Status (1980–2009) Multiemployer Program

Year	Total Insured Plans	Total Insured Participants	Participant Status*		
			Active Participants	Retired Participants	Separated Vested Participants
1980	2,244	7,997,000	75.9%	17.7%	6.5%
1985	2,188	8,209,000	66.1%	22.6%	11.4%
1990	1,983	8,534,000	58.6%	25.2%	16.2%
1995	1,879	8,632,000	52.4%	28.9%	18.7%
1996	1,876	8,649,000	52.1%	29.1%	18.8%
1997	1,846	8,740,000	52.2%	28.9%	18.9%
1998	1,817	8,876,000	51.2%	30.4%	18.3%
1999	1,800	8,991,000	50.9%	30.5%	18.6%
2000	1,744	9,132,000	51.1%	30.1%	18.7%
2001	1,707	9,423,000	49.5%	29.6%	20.9%
2002	1,671	9,630,000	48.1%	29.7%	22.2%
2003	1,612	9,699,000	47.1%	30.2%	22.8%
2004	1,586	9,829,000	46.0%	30.8%	23.2%
2005	1,571	9,887,000	45.7%	30.8%	23.5%
2006	1,538	9,911,000	45.3%	30.9%	23.8%
2007	1,522	10,032,000	44.6%	31.0%	24.4%
2008	1,517	10,170,000	NA	NA	NA
2009	1,495	10,417,000	NA	NA	NA

**Source:* Internal Revenue Service Form 5500 Series Filings for multiemployer plans. Data for plan years prior to 1999 include only plans with 100 or more participants. Due to rounding of individual items, percentages may not add up to 100%. 2007 figures are estimates from PBGC internal calculations.

Source: PBGC *Pension Insurance Data Book 2009.*

TABLE 33-2

PBGC-Insured Plans, 1980–2009, by Number of Participants

Year	10,000 or more participants	5,000–9,999 participants	2,500–4,999 participants	1,000–2,499 participants	500–999 participants	250–499 participants	Fewer than 250 participants
1980	120	131	211	452	420	404	506
1985	137	124	216	459	402	376	474
1990	140	127	214	428	402	332	340
1995	144	123	205	409	368	303	327
1996	143	132	206	400	373	287	335
1997	145	131	206	401	365	296	302
1998	147	136	193	400	357	290	294
1999	149	137	189	403	357	279	286
2000	152	138	197	388	357	258	254
2001	159	133	210	377	327	254	247
2002	163	133	212	397	316	233	217
2003	166	129	206	391	321	202	197
2004	166	129	208	393	305	198	187
2005	164	134	204	381	309	195	184
2006	162	132	203	380	305	184	172
2007	167	124	197	388	293	177	176
2008	167	130	205	308	283	176	168
2009	171	128	203	380	278	170	165

Source: PBGC *Pension Insurance Data Book*, 2009.

FIGURE 33-1

PBGC Insurance Plans by Industry

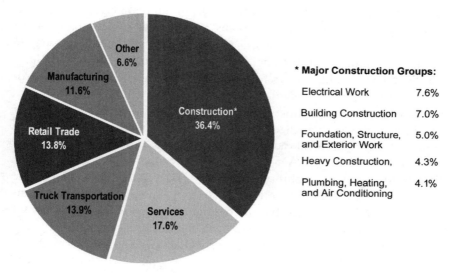

* **Major Construction Groups:**

Electrical Work	7.6%
Building Construction	7.0%
Foundation, Structure, and Exterior Work	5.0%
Heavy Construction,	4.3%
Plumbing, Heating, and Air Conditioning	4.1%

Source: PBGC *Pension Insurance Data Book*, 2009

same union, or locals of the same international union. (Workers in industries like the automotive or steel industries, where workers have been organized vertically rather than by trade or craft, are often covered by single-employer negotiated plans rather than by multiemployer plans.)

REGULATION AND OVERSIGHT

In addition to Taft-Hartley, the primary rules that multiemployer DB and DC retirement plans must follow are set out in the Internal Revenue Code (IRC) and ERISA.

IRC—To obtain the benefits of being treated as a "tax qualified" plan, a multiemployer DB or DC pension or profit-sharing plan must meet the qualification standards and related requirements set out in the IRC and enforced by the Internal Revenue Service (IRS). These standards include rules related to virtually every aspect of plan design and administration including eligibility, participation, vesting, benefit accrual, benefit limitations, nondiscrimination testing, distributions and funding.[3] While most

3. Many of these tax rules also appear in Title II of ERISA.

of the tax rules that govern multiemployer plans also apply to single employer plans, the IRC also contains certain special provisions that reflect the unique nature of multiemployer plans. For example, benefits provided to union-represented participants in multiemployer DB and DC pension plans and profit-sharing plans are deemed to meet many of the IRC's nondiscrimination standards automatically, and there are separate minimum funding rules for single employer and multiemployer DB plans. Multiemployer health and welfare plans are generally subject to IRC provisions that govern voluntary employees' beneficiary associations (VEBAs) and labor organizations, as well as the provisions that cover specific benefits such as medical coverage, including the health coverage continuation requirements added to the IRC by the Consolidated Omnibus Budget Reconciliation Act of 1985 (COBRA), the Health Insurance Portability and Accountability Act of 1996 (HIPAA), the new Affordable Care Act[4] and others. These rules also apply to single employer plans providing similar benefits, but the regulations often include features for multiemployer plans that recognize their unique characteristics.

ERISA—Title I of ERISA imposes additional requirements on multiemployer DB and DC pension and profit-sharing plans which are enforced by the Department of Labor (DOL). The most important of these requirements are the fiduciary duties imposed on those responsible for administering plans in order to protect the benefits of participants. In addition, ERISA requires compliance with numerous reporting and disclosure requirements[5] also intended to further the goal of protecting participant benefits and informing them and the government about the plans.

As with the IRC provisions, above, multiemployer health and welfare plans generally are also subject to the same ERISA provisions as any other health and welfare plan subject to ERISA, including COBRA, HIPAA and the ACA. Multiemployer DB retirement plans are also subject to various requirements under Title IV of ERISA, which is administered by the PBGC. These include the multiemployer benefit guarantee provisions and the withdrawal liability provisions. The withdrawal liability provisions were added to ERISA in 1980 by the Multiemployer Pension Plan Amendments Act (MPPAA). This effort to protect worker pensions in

4. The Patient Protection and Affordable Care Act (PPACA) was enacted on March 23, 2010. The Health Care and Education Reconciliation Act (Reconciliation Act) was enacted on March 30, 2010. The Reconciliation Act contains a package of significant changes to the PPACA. Together, the two laws are referred to as the Affordable Care Act (ACA).
5. See, e.g., ERISA Sec. 101(a)–(m).

multiemployer DB retirement plans makes most employers who withdraw from a multiemployer plan liable for their share of unfunded plan benefits with exceptions for certain industries and types of withdrawals.

In recent years, Congress has passed numerous laws that make further changes to both the IRC and ERISA rules that govern multiemployer pension and profit-sharing plans, particularly with respect to funding. The Pension Protection Act of 2006 (PPA'06) is the most significant piece of pension legislation since ERISA, and, among its many other changes, it established new funding and disclosure requirements for multiemployer DB plans. An actuary must certify a plan's funding status within 90 days of the start of the plan year. Plans that are in endangered status (less than 80 percent funded, colloquially referred to as being in the "yellow zone") or critical status (in the "red zone") must take specific actions to improve their financial status and notify plan participants.

PPA'06 was followed by the Worker, Retiree and Employer Recovery Act of 2008 (WRERA), which gave multiemployer DB retirement plans temporary relief from PPA'06 requirements by allowing them to temporarily freeze their zone status at the previous year's level or extend the time to improve the plan's financial status. This relief was designed to give those plans time to recover from the economic downturn at the end of 2008. However, more time was needed, and in June 2010, Congress passed short-term pension funding relief as part of the Preservation of Access to Care for Medicare Beneficiaries and Pension Relief Act of 2010 (PRA). The PRA offers eligible multiemployer plans the opportunity to use any or all of three different funding adjustments that would provide the plans more time to make up for 2008–2009 investment losses.

Legislation has been proposed with respect to severely underfunded multiemployer DB plans, which would, among other things, increase the PBGC guaranty for multiemployer benefits and enable certain deeply troubled plans to shed liabilities attributable to bankrupt employers, through a process known as partition. Future legislative activity on multiemployer funding seems inevitable, because the PPA'06 multiemployer funding rules are set to expire on December 31, 2014.[6] The DOL, IRS and PBGC are charged with the task of conducting a study of the impact of the PPA'06 funding rules on multiemployer plans and reporting the results to Congress not later than December 31, 2011.[7]

6. PPA'06 Sec. 221(c).
7. PPA'06 Sec. 221(a)–(b).

Congress also has passed numerous laws that make further changes to both the IRC and ERISA rules that govern multiemployer health and welfare plans. For example, under the American Recovery and Reinvestment Act of 2009 (ARRA), the HIPAA privacy rules were strengthened and temporary reimbursement of COBRA premiums was provided to involuntarily terminated individuals. Most recently, Congress passed a sweeping overhaul of the health care system, the ACA. The centerpieces of this reform—the individual mandate, subsidies, health insurance exchanges and employer free rider penalty—become effective in 2014. However, important changes to plan benefit design rules, certain tax rules and the Medicare program are effective either in the near future or over the next four years. Multiemployer health plans are subject to the same rules as single employer health plans under the ACA except for a special grandfathering rule for insured collectively bargained plans.[8]

Finally, virtually every federal law and regulation concerning employee benefit plans affects multiemployer plans, including those relating to age discrimination, equal employment opportunity, veterans' rights, labor-management relations and labor standards.

ESTABLISHING A MULTIEMPLOYER PLAN

In most cases, a union and various employers will agree to set up a multiemployer plan under the terms of a CBA. In many cases, they may agree to establish a DB retirement plan and oftentimes a group of companion plans such as a health and welfare benefit plan, a DC plan and an apprenticeship trust fund. The first step in establishing a multiemployer DB retirement plan is usually to negotiate how much each employer will contribute. Employer and union representatives then adopt a trust agreement that establishes a board of trustees that sets overall plan policy, establishes the benefits to be provided, directs plan activities, and is responsible for proper fund management. Related multiemployer plans may have the same or different trustees.

The trustees typically hire a group of specialists to help run the plan. This may include an attorney and an accountant to assist in establishing a trust fund to accept employer contributions, benefits and actuarial consultants to help work out plan details and determine a supportable benefit level, and a professional investment consultant and portfolio

8. As guidance is issued under the new law, there may be areas in which special rules are provided for multiemployer plans, but no such rules have yet been issued.

manager to ensure competent asset management. The board also hires a salaried plan administrator and staff or retains an outside administration firm to manage the plan and handle day-to-day details such as the collection of employer contributions and employee claims, payments, recordkeeping, and inquiries. (All costs of administration are paid from plan assets.) Finally, the trustees must adopt a formal plan document and publish a summary plan description in layman's language informing participants of plan benefits, eligibility rules, and procedures for filing benefit claims.

Although the trustees may delegate certain of their duties and functions, including the management of plan funds, they bear ultimate responsibility for all actions taken in their names. Fund management is a serious responsibility, since vast sums of money may be involved and the pensions and/or other benefits of hundreds, thousands or tens of thousands of people are at stake. The trustees are bound by strict fiduciary rules of integrity and performance and are required by both ERISA and the Taft-Hartley Act to act solely in the interests of plan participants and as a prudent person familiar with such matters (i.e., financial affairs) would act.

FUNDING

Multiemployer plans are funded by contributions by the employers that are signatory to the CBA and income from investment of the plan's assets. The employer's contribution amount is determined through negotiations and fixed in the CBA, which is typically renegotiated on a periodic basis. Two, three or even five years are common bargaining cycles. The contribution amount is usually based on a measure of the covered participant's work (e.g., $5 for each hour worked by each employee). All contributions are pooled in a common fund that pays for plan benefits and operating expenses. Plan assets must be used for the sole and exclusive benefit of the plan's participants and beneficiaries. They cannot be returned to employers or paid to the union.

Most companies participating in the same multiemployer plan pay contributions at the same rate. However, large national or regional multiemployer plans often provide several levels of benefits based on different levels of employer contributions, to accommodate the greater variety of economic conditions in different labor markets.

An increasing number of DC retirement plans have been adapted to permit participants to defer a portion of their wages for retirement.

Occasionally, employees may also be required or permitted to make additional contributions to welfare plans (e.g., during short unemployment periods) and it is not uncommon for health and welfare plans that offer retiree coverage to require contributions from retirees to cover all or a portion of the benefit cost.

BENEFITS DETERMINATIONS

Benefit formulas under multiemployer DB retirement plans vary widely. The most common are a flat-dollar amount for each year of service or a percentage of contributions required on the individual's covered service. Most plans base benefits on length of service and not on earnings level. Not only is this consistent with the egalitarian philosophy of the sponsoring unions, it simplifies administration. The need to collect and keep individual earnings records is eliminated; the contribution rate for all participants at a given benefit level is usually identical.

Most multiemployer DB retirement plans suspend benefit payments to retirees who work in the same trade or industry in their jurisdictions after having started to receive their pensions. This discourages retirees from competing for jobs with active workers or practicing their skills in the nonunion sector of the industry with a subsidy from the multiemployer plan.

In most cases, a multiemployer health and welfare plan's board of trustees determines what kinds and levels of benefits will be provided. They take into account the needs and wishes of the covered workers, the plan's financial condition and prospects, industry conditions, claims experience, plan costs, employment patterns and other factors. The trustees also set eligibility rules for workers, usually based on hours worked. Everyone who is eligible tends to receive the same benefits, although benefit levels may differ for full-time and part-time workers. All of these decisions must be made within the legal and regulatory framework discussed above.

Multiemployer health plans may self-insure, purchase policies from commercial insurers or use a combination approach. The insurance premiums are paid by plan assets. Many plans that self-insure carry some form of "stop loss insurance" under which an insurance company assumes the benefit liability above a certain amount to protect the plan against unforeseen catastrophic claims. Many other plans create and maintain financial reserves for this reason. The added coverage requirements of the ACA are expected to increase the incentives for self-insured plans to increase their stop-loss insurance coverage.

ADVANTAGES FOR EMPLOYERS

There are many advantages for employers that participate in multiemployer plans. These include the following:

- *Efficient management.* Contributing employers are freed from managing (or hiring someone to manage) the day-to-day operations of a DB and/or a health and welfare plan. Their administrative obligations are limited to filing monthly remittance reports and making payments to the fund. In certain circumstances and using special participation agreements, non-bargained staff can participate in the plan to benefit from the economies of scale.
- *Legal and regulatory oversight.* Multiemployer plans take over the burden of complying with legal and regulatory requirements from the individual employer. Employers do not need to worry about pension, health care, and/or other benefits legislation in order to make decisions.
- *Cost-effectiveness.* As with all benefit plans qualified under the IRC, employer contributions to a multiemployer plan are generally tax deductible when paid to a trust. Because they tend to be large, multiemployer plans benefit from significant economies of scale, which can reduce administrative, investment, and other professional fees on a per-capita basis. For example, the large number of participants can help plans command better prices in the market, negotiate lower administration costs from vendors and improve their purchasing power. The large risk pool allows multiemployer plans to take advantage of self-insurance options, build adequate reserves and, as a result, reduce the relative amount of stop-loss coverage needed, thereby lowering costs. In addition, at $9 per participant per year in 2010, multiemployer plan PBGC termination insurance premiums are a bargain compared with the minimum $35 rate for single-employer plans. Of course, the PBGC guarantees are lower for multiemployer plans than for single-employer plans.[9]
- *Predictable labor costs.* Because of CBAs, benefit costs are standardized and generally not subject to wild short-term swings. Although health care costs continue to rise employer

9. The PBGC's maximum annual benefit guarantee for multiemployer plan participants with 30 years of service has been $12,870 since December 2000. In contrast, the guarantee for single-employer beneficiaries is up to $54,000 per year for a retiree at age 65.

costs are generally fixed for the length of a CBA. As a result, the burden of health care inflation shifts from the employer to the plan. Predictable labor costs are easy to insert into a contract estimate.

- *Standardized labor costs.* Contributing at a uniform rate to a multiemployer plan standardizes benefits costs throughout a region or an industry. This means that health care costs for a particular employer's workforce are not a factor in pricing work (which eliminates undermining) if all those competing for the work have union contracts. It also can help reduce employee turnover, since workers will not be attracted to other jobs by the promise of better benefits.
- *Coverage flexibility.* In addition to deciding to offer different tiers or benefit schedules to new participating groups, multiemployer plans can tailor the plan design to reflect such special programs as job-sharing, reciprocity agreements,[10] flexible benefit suspension rules and hour banks to bridge service during periods of temporary unemployment. The design can accommodate the provision of early retirement incentives, self-funded disability coverage, and self-funded death benefits.
- *Protection from unanticipated expenses: withdrawal liability.* While sometimes viewed negatively, the purpose of withdrawal liability—the assessment levied on employers that pull out of a multiemployer pension plan that is not "fully funded" with respect to its vested benefits—is to be a financial safeguard for the ongoing employers as well as the participants. Withdrawal liability provides a measure of protection for the plan and the ongoing contributors from terminating employers "dumping" vested liabilities on the remaining pool of contributing employers. The purpose of withdrawal liability is to protect the financial integrity of multiemployer plans by eliminating the incentive for employers to "bail out" during a downturn, leaving remaining employers with a disproportionate share of the plan's financial obligations.

10. Under a reciprocity agreement, a worker can move among employers, contributing to different plans that are signatory to the agreement without impairing the value of his or her pension credits. Reciprocity agreements are common in the construction industry, and a number of multiemployer plans in other industries, such as trucking, also have industry-wide reciprocity agreements.

- *Recruitment and retention.* In a healthy economy, offering a health and welfare and/or a pension plan will help organizations attract the best employees by demonstrating that they value their workforce.

ADVANTAGES FOR WORKERS

Several features of multiemployer plans add to their general appeal for workers. These include the following:

- *Accessibility of coverage.* Employers that offer DB retirement plans are increasingly rare. Most workers understand the value of a good health and welfare plan. Organizations that offer these plans are often identified as being among the best places to work. Multiemployer plans also provide an incalculable advantage to employees of small companies, who might not receive benefits if multiemployer plans did not make benefit programs more affordable for their employers.
- *Portability.* In most cases, workers may carry health and welfare plan coverage and pension credits with them as they move from one contributing employer to another within the same industry. This means workers receive a continuity of coverage for benefits, such as medical insurance, when they move from project to project. In addition, employees can earn pensions based on all accumulated credits, even if some of their former employers have gone out of business or stopped making plan contributions. In order for pension credits to transfer from one multiemployer plan to another, the trustees of the various plans must have negotiated reciprocity agreements. As international unions continue to encourage plan consolidation for greater efficiencies, multiemployer plans are merging or joining larger funds, which expands the reach of their internal portability.
- *Plan design and plan offerings.* Because of their structure, multiemployer plans make more comprehensive plan designs possible. Many health and welfare plans offer ancillary coverages, such as dental and vision, that might not be offered by smaller group plans. Eligibility rules are also more flexible. Typically, workers are able to become eligible for health care benefits in less than three months and generally have coverage for one to six months after they stop working. In an industry with a high rate of turnover, the plan may offer first-day eligibility for

coverage. In addition, many multiemployer plans continue to offer retirees comprehensive health coverage.

- *Fiduciary responsibility and labor-management cooperation.* Management of multiemployer plans by a joint labor-management board of trustees consisting of an equal number of union and management representatives assures that the interests of the participants will be protected. Since the passage of ERISA in 1974, trustees have had a well-defined fiduciary responsibility to act in the best interest of plan participants—a responsibility they take very seriously. In establishing special rules for multiemployer plans as part of PPA'06, Congress recognized and built on the tradition of labor and management working together to manage their benefit plans.
- *Fairness.* Multiemployer plan benefits are considered equitable because employers contribute a fixed amount per employee, regardless of the employee's age or length of service in an industry. Workers also know that a uniform contribution structure precludes any incentive for employers to hire workers based on age or length of service. (These plans are flexible enough to provide increased credit accruals for those who are able to work more hours.)
- *Stability.* Because they do not depend on the fortunes of a single company, multiemployer plans are often more secure and stable than corporate plans. On the DB side, funding levels have historically been high and very few multiemployer plans have been terminated. Moreover, withdrawal liability ensures that plans and participants have some measure of protection when an employer withdraws from the plan. PPA'06 improved the stability of multiemployer plans by creating consequences and requiring funding improvement for underfunded plans.
- *Flexibility.* Multiemployer plans offer special provisions to preserve coverage during periods of temporary unemployment, whether it is seasonal or the result of the economy. Many multiemployer DB retirement plans provide ancillary benefits, such as disability and death benefits. Some are considering new features, including auto-enrollment, lifecycle funds,[11]

11. A lifecycle fund is a mutual fund that maintains a certain mix of stocks and bonds to attract investors of a given age and risk preference. Different lifecycle funds with various asset allocations are designed to appeal to investors of different ages.

sophisticated investment alternatives with floors, and insurance products that guarantee a stream of income.

THE FUTURE OF MULTIEMPLOYER PLANS

For both pension and health and welfare plans, it is clear that there is a trend to consolidate plans into fewer, larger entities. This is being driven by many of the issues discussed in this chapter, and has been adopted as an explicit goal by labor and management in many industries. Consolidation enables plans to have greater leverage in purchasing services in the marketplace, allows them to add and improve service to participants and, generally, to capture greater economies of scale. In addition, the affordability of DB plans and health and welfare plans will continue to be an issue. Almost all plans are facing demographic issues such as the relationship of actives to retirees and the overall aging of the workforce.

DB plans and health and welfare plans will face separate and distinct issues as well. For DB plans, all pension plans—single and multiemployer—have been hard hit by the two market downturns and this has left them less well funded. These plans will need to do well from an investment perspective to improve their funded status to historical levels. Because these plans are relatively mature (more retirees and steady or declining numbers of actives), they can rely less on active contributions and must rely more on investments to remain well funded. This creates challenges for plan sponsors with respect to volatility of funding. The plans are looking for ways to address this through new pension plan designs and investment policies that decrease risk for the plan sponsors and for the participants.

Beyond these structural and economic issues and the new pension plan design and investments solutions, which will be developed over time, perhaps the biggest impact will be the regulatory environment. The sunset of PPA'06 in 2014 means that legislators may address fundamental issues regarding the funding and structure of DB plans. Perhaps more than anything else, this will determine the future of the existing plans and the kinds of plans that will emerge in the future.

At the time of this writing, the Financial Accounting Standards Board (FASB) had recently introduced an exposure draft regarding the accounting obligations of employers contributing to multiemployer DB pension plans. If adopted as proposed in the form of a revised accounting standard, the changes would expand the amount of information that employers would have to disclose about the multiemployer plans to which they contribute and about their relationship to those plans. While the proposed changes would only appear in footnotes to financial statements, it is unclear what the final requirements will be and what impact, if any, these requirements will have on the employers who contribute to multiemployer plans.

For health and welfare plans, the ACA will have significant and not yet completely clear impact. Currently, multiemployer plans are assimilating the changes required for compliance in 2010 through 2014 determining whether it is possible to maintain grandfather status, applying for the Early Retirement Reinsurance Program (ERRP) funding, adding adult children to age 26, making necessary plan changes to annual and lifetime limits and adding preventive care with no cost sharing. These are relatively straightforward, but they have added costs to plans, many of which were already struggling in the current economic environment.

The changes to annual and lifetime limits will have an impact on part-time workers and workers in low-wage industries where the annual and lifetime limits are often $100,000 or less and focus mainly on "first dollar" coverage. Many of these plans have filed for waivers to be allowed to continue coverage at the current levels. Failing the receipt of these waivers, the plans may have to fold and the plan sponsors will be forced to look for other coverage solutions for participants.

One of the most important features of the ACA is the creation of the state-based exchanges. While they will start accepting individuals beginning in 2014 and larger groups in subsequent years, the picture is unclear as to when and how they will interact with multiemployer plans.

Other large questions that must be worked through relate to the subsidies that will be offered in the exchanges for low-income individuals and the so-called "free rider penalty" that requires employers of a certain size the offer benefits of a certain value to their employees or be required to pay a penalty. The interaction of all these elements further complicates the ability to predict how multiemployer plans will respond to these changes.

One of the main issues that all health plan sponsors including multiemployer plans have been facing for years is high medical inflation. For multiemployer plans, this has been handled by a combination of strategies designed to hold down costs, including discounted networks, care and utilization management, disease management and wellness programs. In addition, the share that plans have been asking participants to contribute through deductibles and copayments has also increased. More recently, especially with health care reform's requirement to cover adult children, plans are examining their eligibility provisions much more closely and performing eligibility audits to assure that only valid dependents are covered. While this has always been the case in some industries, a broader array of industries are beginning to discuss the need for the introduction of contributions for dependents.

While not universal, it is not uncommon for multiemployer plans to offer coverage to both pre-Medicare and Medicare retirees for no cost or at significantly subsidized rates. As cost pressures increase, plans are stepping up their review in this area and introducing novel and traditional benefit design and eligibility changes. This more often than not means that a greater burden of the cost will be shouldered by the retirees.

CONCLUSION

All sponsors of DB and health and welfare plans—multiemployer, corporate and public sector—are being challenged by the recent legislation affecting them and the difficult economic environment. The unique characteristics and strengths of multiemployer plans are, however, often overlooked because they are not well understood, and they are often lumped together with better known corporate or public sector plans.

Multiemployer plans have a decades long proven track record of adapting successfully to a variety of economic and political environments as well as legislative and regulatory changes. Indeed, the factors that first made them appealing to workers and employers still apply.

- The cooperative approach between labor and management that underlies the establishment of the benefits and the stewardship of the benefit plans.
- Risk pooling
- Relative administrative convenience
- Simplicity and flexibility for small and large employers alike
- The ability for employers to reasonably predict and manage costs, and
- True portability for employees who work for many employers during the course of a single year.

The enduring importance and appeal of multiemployer plans comes from their many strengths.

History has shown that—except in the most extreme economic conditions, such as a disappearing industry—multiemployer plan trustees and bargaining parties have an excellent track record in funding and supporting these unique programs. The inherent strengths of multiemployer plans have enabled them to adapt and endure. Because of their proven resilience, it is likely that multiemployer plans will continue to play an important role in providing health and retirement security for millions of American workers, retirees and dependents.

BIBLIOGRAPHY

Employee Benefit Research Institute, *EBRI Quarterly Pension Investment Report*, Washington, DC: Employee Benefit Research Institute, 1986–2010.

Employee Benefit Research Institute, *Databook on Employee Benefits*, Washington, DC: Employee Benefit Research Institute, 1990–2010.

National Coordinating Committee for Multiemployer Plans, *A Basic Guide to Multiemployer Plans*, Washington, DC: National Coordinating Committee for Multiemployer Plans, January 2005.

Pension Benefit Guaranty Corporation, *Annual Report to the Congress*, Washington, DC: Pension Benefit Guaranty Corporation, 1993–2009.

Pension Benefit Guaranty Corporation, *Pension Insurance Data Book*, 2009, 2010.

Harriet Weinstein and William J. Wiatrowski, "Multiemployer Pension Plans," *Compensation and Working Conditions*, Spring 1999, pp. 19–23.

The Segal Company, *Viewpoint*, "The Enduring Importance and Appeal of Multiemployer Defined Benefit Plans," New York: The Segal Company, 2007, www.segalco.com/publications/2007viewpoint.pdf.

The Segal Company, *2010 Survey of Withdrawal Liability Funded Ratios*, New York: The Segal Company, Spring 2010, www.segalco.com/publications/surveysandstudies/spring2010wdfrsurvey.pdf.

The Segal Company, *Survey of Calendar-Year Plans' 2010 Zone Status*, New York, The Segal Company, Spring 2010, www.segalco.com/publications/surveysandstudies/spring2010zonestatus2010.pdf.

U.S. Department of Labor, Employee Benefits Security Administration, *Private Pension Plan Bulletin: Abstract of the 2005 Form 5500 Annual Reports*, Washington, DC: U.S. Department of Labor, 2008.

U.S. Department of Labor, Employee Benefits Security Administration, *Private Pension Plan Bulletin Historical Tables*, Washington, DC: U.S. Department of Labor, February 2008.

CHAPTER 34

Global Employee Benefits

Mark S. Allen

Tony R. Broomhead

Around the world, the rationale for supplemental or occupational employee benefits is pretty much the same in each country regardless of its legislative environment. They generally are provided to protect employees in the event of retirement, death, disability, and accident or illness to the extent these are not covered by the government. But for most countries, this is where the similarities end. The framework in which these benefits are provided varies significantly from country to country, ranging from comprehensive government programs ("cradle-to-grave" coverage provided by the government) to partnership arrangements (combinations of employer, employee, and government benefits, with many options from which to choose). But one of the noticeable shifts in recent years has been for some governments to pull back on the level of coverage they provide, with some employers starting to pick up this gap in coverage.

The challenge for multinational organizations is to manage the design, delivery, and financing of these benefits from both a global and a local perspective. This process entails a balancing act among:

- Local benefits objectives with local and global business objectives and philosophies
- Differing competitive environments and economic realities
- The cost and benefits available from old age, survivors, and disability programs with supplemental retirement and capital accumulation plans

- The cost, quality, and availability of national health insurance programs with emerging private medical practices in many countries
- Changing regulatory environments that impact the design, delivery, and cost of supplemental benefits plans with local and global benefits objectives

In order to be effective in this process, most managers will need to gain an understanding of the local environment; assist in establishing global benefits objectives and in designing local plans; and, to the extent required, help in the administration and cost management of local plans.

This chapter will review each of these issues from a macro or global perspective. The reader should realize that the benefits environment in many countries is very complex, and that each country and situation needs to be very carefully evaluated on an individual basis.

BACKGROUND CONSIDERATIONS

Benefits for individuals in international operations are often affected by where they were hired and the location of their assignment. For clarification, the main situations are described below:

- *Expatriates or international assignees.* These are employees who are currently on temporary assignment overseas. Often, these employees are paid on terms and conditions that are representative of their home country and not their country of assignment. For U.S. companies, for example, expatriates are normally paid a U.S. base salary and are generally entitled to U.S. benefits.
- *Local nationals.* This group comprises individuals employed, working, and residing on a long-term basis in a particular country, regardless of the country of which they are citizens. Compensation and benefits programs are usually based on local practices, although there are some exceptions to this as companies attempt to globalize their compensation and benefits. These exceptions are usually found at the executive level.
- *Locally hired foreigners.* This group comprises nonlocal individuals employed on local terms and conditions, for example a Singaporean hired to work full time in China. In many emerging market countries, local terms and conditions would

represent a significant reduction in pay and benefits to these individuals, not to mention living and working conditions. Often these employees will enjoy "extra" compensation and benefits, such as educational and housing allowances and enhanced medical benefits, in order to attract them to and retain them in the country.

- *Third-country nationals (TCNs).* TCNs normally are individuals working for a foreign company on assignment outside of their home country. "True" TCNs will serve in at least two, but usually more, countries during their career. They can be employees of the corporate office, the subsidiary at which they were hired, or the subsidiary where they are working. Consequently, pay and benefits might be provided on a home-country, a host-country, or some special basis designed to suit operational needs. Usually, the duration and number of foreign assignments are key considerations when establishing benefit packages for TCNs. Sometimes these employees are referred to as "career expatriates" or "internationally mobile employees."

UNDERSTANDING THE LOCAL ENVIRONMENT

The local issues that need to be understood are

1. Statutory and government-provided benefits.
2. Regulatory environment and taxation of employee benefits.
3. Economic and labor environment.

Statutory and Government-Provided Benefits

These benefits generally include retirement, death, disability, severance, and medical plans, and the amount and type of coverage will vary significantly from country to country. Some countries, such as Italy and France, have fairly comprehensive government systems that mitigate to some extent the need for supplemental plans. Other countries, such as Brazil and Hong Kong, have basic benefits that give employers the choice, usually for competitive reasons, to offer supplemental benefits, while others—usually impoverished or developing countries—offer minimal benefits that provide for only the very basic needs. The way in which these benefits are financed also will differ. Most are financed by employer and employee taxes on pay, while some countries fund the benefits from general revenues. Most countries fund the benefits on a "pay-as-you-go" basis, although there has been a trend among newly established programs to be funded (as in Chile and much of Eastern Europe).

Retirement and Old-Age Benefits

With respect to retirement, most social security systems provide an income benefit for the life of the individual with reduced benefits to survivors. Benefit formulas range from final pay plans (Ukraine and Pakistan) to career-average plans (Germany, Belgium, and the United States—although Germany and Belgium adjust career-average pay for inflation). Some countries, such as Australia and Hong Kong, provide flat-rate benefits. The most common defined benefit plan is a final average pay plan with the averaging period ranging from one to 10 years. Table 34-1 provides an example of the approximate level of final pay replaced by some countries in Europe, Latin America, and the Pacific region for an employee earning the equivalent of US$25,000, US$50,000, and US$100,000 after 30 years of coverage. As the table indicates, the level of pay replacement by social security is very high in some countries, while in others social security provides only a limited benefit, leaving sufficient scope for supplemental or private retirement plans.

Social security benefit levels correlate closely to the level of contribution. Table 34-2 shows a comparison of the employee and employer contribution rates and applicable contribution ceilings for the retirement portion of social security for each of these countries. Total contributions range from a high of 33 percent in Italy (which provides a generous benefit) to less than 6 percent in Taiwan (where benefit levels are not as high).

Some social security systems provide a two-tier benefit, where the first part is a flat benefit for all eligible employees and the second is an earnings-related benefit, which is provided in addition to the flat benefit. The United Kingdom and Japan have this type of system. In both, companies may be able to "contract out" of the earnings-related portion of social security if a private plan that produces equal or greater benefits is provided to all employees. "Contracting out" simply means that companies can divert the contributions earmarked for that part of the social security system to a private plan if certain conditions are met.

In an increasing number of countries, social security retirement benefits are provided in the form of a defined contribution plan. This is most common in Asian, Central and Eastern European, South American, and

TABLE 34-1

Social Security Pay Replacement: Approximate Percentage of Final Pay Replaced for Workers Earning Various US$ Equivalents

	Worker Earning Equivalent of:		
	$25,000	**$50,000**	**$100,000**
Belgium	43	36	20
Canada	61	34	17
Germany	61	34	27
Italy	54	54	54
Japan	39	29	18
Mexico	22	11	6
Netherlands	59	30	15
Spain	81	70	35
Taiwan	22	11	6
United Kingdom	45	26	14

Notes:
- These figures are for a worker whose career starts in 2006 and are based on provisions in effect in 2006; workers retiring currently will often receive a different benefit from what is shown because many systems have changed their provisions prospectively.
- They assume that the worker is single; many systems offer significant additional benefits if the retired worker has a dependent spouse or other dependents.
- They assume retirement at normal retirement age.
- Exchange rates are effective as of June 30, 2010.

Source: Organization for Economic Cooperation and Development, (OECD) Pension Calculator, http://www.oecd.org/document/12/0,3746,en_2649_34757_43024076_1_1_1_1,00.html, with adjustments.

African countries. Singapore, Malaysia, India, Indonesia, Poland, Chile, Egypt, and Nigeria all have a defined contribution arrangement, usually called a "provident fund," from which benefits are generally paid out in a lump sum. In Central and Eastern Europe, the emerging model is to provide a modest first pillar on a defined benefit pay-as-you-go basis, supplemented by a second pillar on a defined contribution basis. This approach has been taken in Hungary, Russia, and Slovakia. One exception to this is France, which has a complicated system of social security and mandatory complementary plans funded on a quasi-defined contribution basis—similar to cash balance plans in the United States. However, in France, benefits are paid out in the form of an annuity.

TABLE 34-2

Social Security Contribution Levels: Maximum Employee and Employer Contribution Rates for Old-Age and Survivor Benefits

Country	Percent Employee	Percent Employer	Ceiling on Covered Pay	US$ Equivalent
Belgium	7.50	8.86	None	None
Canada	4.95	4.95	C$46,300	$44,700
Germany	9.95	9.95	€66,000*	$81,300
Italy	9.19†	23.81	€92,147‡	$113,600
Japan	7.68	7.68	¥7,440,000	$82,500
Mexico	1.75	6.90	MXP356,200	$28,100
Netherlands	19.00	0.00	€31,589	$38,900
Spain	4.70	23.60	€36,889	$45,500
Taiwan	NT$674§	5.25	NT$526,800	$16,400
United Kingdom	11.00	12.80	£40,400¶	$60,500

Exchange rates were effective as of June 30, 2010.
* The ceiling shown is for the former West Germany; in the former East Germany, the ceiling is €55,800.
† The rate on pay above €42,364 is 10.19%.
‡ The ceiling applies only to workers whose career started in 1996 or later.
§ The employee contribution is a fixed amount, not a percentage of pay.
¶ Contributions are only levied on annual pay in excess of £5,480, and the ceiling only applies to employee contributions; there is no ceiling for employer contributions.

Source: *Social Security Programs Throughout the World*, U.S. Social Security Administration, http://www.ssa.gov/policy/docs/progdesc/ssptw/. This publication appears in four volumes covering Europe, Asia and the Pacific, Africa, and the Americas and is published on a rolling basis every six months. The information here is the latest available from these volumes; generally the ceilings are adjusted annually for inflation, so the amounts shown may have increased.

Eligibility conditions for qualifying for and receiving benefits also vary from country to country. In some countries, residency is the only requirement, whereas in others, 10 years or more of coverage is needed to qualify for benefit payments. The age at which these benefits commence has generally been different for men and women, but there is a gradual worldwide trend to equalize and increase the retirement age. This trend is perhaps more apparent in Europe, where legislation now requires equalization of retirement ages, than it is in other parts of the world. Table 34-3 shows the age at which normal retirement benefits can commence for men and women in several countries, with a brief description of the plan type.

TABLE 34-3

Social Security Normal Retirement Age, Required Service or Years of Contributions, and Plan Type

Country	Normal Retirement Ages for:		Service or Contribution Requirement for a Benefit*	Plan Type
	Men	Women		
Argentina	65	60	30 years	Final 10-year average plus flat amount
Australia	65	65	Means-tested	Fixed amount
Belgium	65	65	45 years	Adjusted career average
Canada	65	65	10 years	Adjusted career average plus flat amount
Colombia	60†	55†	25 years	Final 10-year average or defined contribution
Egypt	60	60	10 years	Final 2-year average
France	65	65	40 years	Adjusted 25-year average
Germany	65	65	5 years	Adjusted career average
Greece	65	60	15 years	Final 5-year average adjusted
Hong Kong	65‡	65‡	7 years of residency	Fixed amount
Ireland	66	66	5 years	Fixed amount
Italy	65	65	5 years	Adjusted career average
Japan	60§	60§	25 years	Adjusted career average plus flat amount
Korea	60§	60§	20 years	Career average plus flat amount
Mexico	65	65	25 years	Defined contribution
Netherlands	65	65	None	Fixed amount
Pakistan	60	55	15 years	Final year's pay
Portugal	65	65	15 years	Adjusted career average
Saudi Arabia	60	55	10 years	Final 2-year average
United Kingdom	65	60	30 years	Adjusted career average plus flat amount

* Under many countries' systems, reduced benefits are payable to retirees with less than the required service period.
† If paid under the defined contribution portion, the retirement age is two years later than what is shown.
‡ The benefit is means-tested between ages 65 and 70.
§ The benefit is means-tested between ages 60 and 65.

Source: *Social Security Programs Throughout the World*, U.S. Social Security Administration, http://www.ssa.gov/policy/docs/progdesc/ssptw/. This publication appears in four volumes covering Europe, Asia and the Pacific, Africa, and the Americas and is published on a rolling basis every six months. The information here is the latest available from these volumes.

Death and Disability Benefits

Salary continuation, workers' compensation, survivor benefits, and long-term disability benefits are commonly mandated by most countries, although the amount of benefit and the length of payment vary considerably. Long-term disability benefits and survivor benefits are often related to the retirement benefits provided through social security.

Medical

Some form of national health insurance for all ages is provided by most countries. Argentina, Brazil, Canada, Mexico, Australia, Japan, Italy, and the United Kingdom are some examples of countries providing comprehensive coverage. Although this would appear to eliminate the need for supplemental medical plans, these plans are common practice in many countries with national health insurance programs. The reasons range from necessity (the poor quality of service from national health providers) to executive compensation (perquisites given to executives but not other employees). Table 34-4 provides a brief description of the environment for supplemental medical coverage in a few countries.

The reasons for supplemental medical benefits range from providing executive and management-level benefits in order to attract and retain key employees to simply filling the gap from governments that can no longer bear the increasing costs of medical. Table 34-5 shows the levels of health care spend in 2007, while Figure 34-1 depicts the trend in spend since 1990. While the United States still spends the most on health care, the spend trend as a percentage of gross domestic product (GDP) is increasing faster in many other countries.

Wellness

The importance of promoting wellness among the workforce is growing globally. In the United States, the growth is fueled by an interest in lowering health care costs, as well as driving engagement in employees. Outside the United States, the objective is more related to employee engagement, as supplemental health care costs are not yet at levels that create concern with employers. The concept is that a healthier employee is more engaged, and therefore more productive. There are emerging studies that suggest a strong correlation between these factors; however, hard metrics are not yet available to prove this relationship.

Wellness programs can be comprehensive and include on-site gyms, annual physical examinations, health fairs and screenings, and training and education, as well as global and local portals dedicated to wellness.

TABLE 34-4

Environment for Supplemental Medical Coverage

Australia	▪ Self-insurance of employer-provided health benefits for employees is prohibited (except for small top-up amounts). ▪ Premium rates for private health insurance cannot be experience-based (community rating is required by legislation). ▪ Insurers are able to charge a premium loading of 2% for every year over age 30 when a new member is taking out coverage (up to a maximum loading of 70%). ▪ Employer-provided insurance premiums are subject to Fringe Benefits Tax. ▪ Main benefits of private health insurance are the avoidance of public hospital waiting lists, and patient's ability to choose his or her medical practitioner for in-hospital services.
Brazil	▪ Supplemental coverage is commonly provided to employees and often extended to part-time workers, with many companies varying the benefits by employee seniority. ▪ Dental care is often included. ▪ Average cost sharing is 86% for employers versus 14% for employees. ▪ Average plan cost measured as a percentage of payroll is 8%. ▪ A law enacted in 1998 specifies minimum benefit levels of coverage for private plans. ▪ This law also establishes that employees who contribute to plan cost through a fixed monthly contribution are eligible to maintain their affiliation to the plan upon retirement or dismissal. Employer contributions are not required in these cases. ▪ Plans vary from the pure indemnity plan to an HMO style with restricted access or networks.
China	▪ Health infrastructure development is prominent in cities such as Beijing and Shanghai on the coast. Western-style hospitals and medical staff are common in cities. ▪ Wholly owned foreign enterprises are not required by law to pay all employees' medical expenses; it is a common practice to provide private insurance or a self-funded arrangement. ▪ For outpatient and inpatient benefits, employers typically provide 90–100% reimbursement to employees and 50% reimbursement to children. ▪ According to a regulation issued in June 2009 retroactive to January 1, 2008, total employer premiums for supplementary medical insurance plans are tax-deductible to the employer up to 5% of total payroll. ▪ Annual medical check-ups are common and typically provided to all employees.
Hong Kong	▪ It is typical to provide group medical insurance for all employees and their dependents. ▪ Benefits offered cover basic medical expenses for hospitalization and outpatient treatment. ▪ Hospitalization benefits are geared to the private, semiprivate, and ward accommodations of private hospitals, with itemized limits for daily room and board, in-hospital doctors' visits, surgeons' fees, etc. ▪ Supplemental major medical benefits are provided by over 60% of employers, with 80% reimbursement and up-to-maximum ranges from HK$100,000 to HK$200,000 (about US$12,886 to US$25,773) per disability. ▪ Deductibles vary from HK$500 to HK$1,000 (about US$64.43 to US$128.87)

(*continued*)

TABLE 34-4 (continued)

India	▪ Large employers typically provide private medical coverage to all employees and their dependents. Some employers, however, restrict the coverage to management employees. Private medical plans are usually noncontributory and provide hospitalization coverage. These private plans are either self-financed or insured. ▪ Benefit limits usually vary depending on the employee category. ▪ Many policies specify up to four family members, and the employee can choose who is covered. ▪ Most employers in the private sector also provide a cash medical benefit to cover outpatient expenses. This benefit is usually fully paid by the employer. The employer will reimburse the employee and their dependents for medical day-to-day expenses, up to a maximum annual limit. The typical benefit level ranges from one month's salary to Rs. 15,000, which is the maximum tax-free benefit allowable per year. ▪ Dental coverage is not typically provided except as part of outpatient medical. ▪ Additional insurance plans covering critical illness such as cancer, bypass surgery, and dialysis are now offered.
Mexico	▪ There is a focus on companies sharing managed care and medical benefit costs with employees. ○ There is a trend toward higher benefits and employee contributions, especially for dependents. ○ In cases where employees share costs, the average contribution is approximately 20%. ▪ There is typically a deductible of 3 times monthly minimum wage per event and coinsurance of 10–20%. ▪ Typical benefits include hospital expenses, physician charges, surgeon charges, specialist fees, operating room, outpatient care, X-rays, and laboratory results. ▪ Dental and vision care are becoming more prevalent, whether as part of the general coverage or as additional riders. ▪ Annual check-ups are usually granted to executives only.
Russia	▪ It is common practice for large Russian companies and subsidiaries of multinationals to offer private health care, as state-provided health care is seen to be of a poor standard. ▪ Private health care plans give access to better medical facilities, as well as inpatient and outpatient benefits and ambulance services. ▪ Many companies require employee contributions for dependent coverage. ▪ Large companies often have their own medical centers, while foreign companies use private insurance. ▪ Employers providing their own private arrangements must still contribute to the Social Security Medical Insurance Fund.
United Kingdom	▪ Professionals, lower management, and up tend to be offered private company plans. The current trend is to offer it further down the organization to all employees. In some industries, such as financial services and high-tech, private medical care is already offered to all employees in most firms. ▪ Plans are on an indemnity basis as a supplement to the National Health Service (NHS), covering specialist and hospital visits and surgeries. Managed care is starting to emerge due to cost-containment issues. ▪ Many companies require employee contributions for dependent coverage, although some companies pay for spouse and family coverage. Executive-level employees are more likely to have employer-paid family coverage, although the trend towards more extensive coverage for all employees is seeing family coverage for executives scaled back. ▪ Plans are typically fully insured, although some large employers do self-insure.

Source: Towers Watson internal document.

TABLE 34-5

Level of Health care Spend as a Percentage of GDP in 2007

Country	% of GDP, 2007	Country	% of GDP, 2007
Australia	8.5	Mexico	5.8
Austria	10.3	Netherlands	9.7
Belgium	10.0	New Zealand	9.1
Canada	10.1	Norway	8.9
Czech Republic	6.8	Poland	6.4
France	11.0	Spain	8.4
Germany	10.4	Sweden	9.1
Ireland	7.5	Switzerland	10.6
Italy	8.7	United Kingdom	8.4
Japan	8.1	United States	15.7
Korea	6.3		

Source: Organization for Economic Cooperation and Development (OECD) oecd iLibrary, http://www.oecd-ilibrary.org/statistics.

FIGURE 34-1

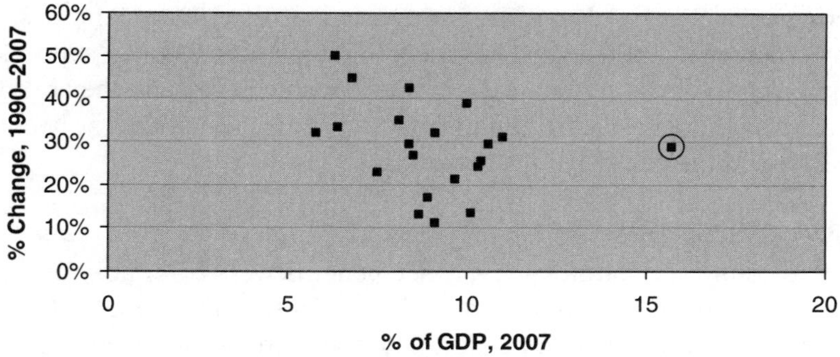

Source: *Source*: Organization for Economic Cooperation and Development (OECD) oecd iLibrary, http://www.oecd-ilibrary.org/statistics.

TABLE 34-6

Top Health Risks and Issues Driving Wellness Strategies–2009

Priority	Africa	Asia	Australia	Canada	Europe	Latin America	United States
1	Stress	Stress	Stress	Stress	Stress	Physical activity/ exercise	Physical activity/ exercise
2	Infectious diseases/ AIDS/HIV	Physical activity/ exercise	Physical activity/ exercise	Work/life issues	Physical activity/ exercise	Nutrition/ healthy eating	Nutrition/ healthy eating
3	Work/life issues	Nutrition/ healthy eating	Work/ life Issues	Depression	Work/ life issues	Stress	Chronic disease (e.g., heart disease, diabetes)

Source: *2009 Global Wellness Survey*, Buck Consultants, LLC.

Or they can be as simple as a program dedicated to reducing stress and improving the work/life balance for employees, or making available annual flu immunizations. Table 34-6 shows the top health risks and issues driving wellness strategies, by region, while Table 34-7 shows the most common elements of the wellness programs.

Implementing a global wellness program can be a challenge for many reasons, but the keys to success include conducting a needs assessment in each country, developing appropriate metrics to measure success, obtaining both executive and local management support for the programs, and creating annual plans that address the needs of the local operations. For many companies, the greatest hurdle is to obtain management support for the programs (including any upfront and ongoing costs) and the ability of the organization to sustain the effort over many years–until it becomes embedded in the culture of the company.

Severance Benefits

In some countries, statutory severance benefits were originally designed to force employers to provide some form of retirement benefit. In these countries, the amounts can be significant and are an important factor in supplemental plan design. As an example, in some Latin American

TABLE 34-7

Top Wellness Program Elements by Region—2009

Africa	Asia	Canada	Europe	Latin America	United States
Biometric health screening	Biometric health screening	Immunizations/ flu shots	Gym/fitness club membership discount	Immunizations/ flu shots	Immunizations/ flu shots
Executive screening program	On-site health classes	Gym/fitness club membership discount	Biometric health screening	Biometric health screening	Health risk appraisal
Health portal/ Web site	Company-sponsored sports teams	Executive screening program	Immunizations/ flu shots	On-site health classes	Gym/fitness club membership discount
Employee health fairs	Executive screening program	Health portal/ Web site	Employee health fairs	Health risk appraisal	Employee health fairs
Health risk appraisal	Health risk appraisal	On-site health classes	On-site health classes	Gym/fitness club membership discount	Health portal/ Web site

Source: *2009 Global Wellness Survey*, Buck Consultants, LLC.

countries, the statutory severance benefit can be as high as two months' pay times years of service, where the definition of pay includes all components of compensation, including benefits in kind such as company cars, ancillary benefits, nonaccountable cash payments and expense accounts (representation allowances), and the like. For some positions, particularly in those countries where there is a confiscatory tax environment, the value of the benefits in kind can exceed 50 percent of base salary.

In some countries, severance benefits are the main form of retirement for employees. This is the case in Mexico, where the statutory severance benefit for involuntary termination of employment is three months' pay plus 20 days for each year of service. A long-service employee can realize a lump sum in excess of two times final annual pay from this benefit. In Korea, there is a similar severance benefit known as the SPS, which provides a lump sum of one month's pay for each year of service.

A number of countries have begun to require this benefit to be provided by a funded individual account, effectively turning the severance benefits into defined contribution arrangements. Brazil's FGTS and Italy's TFR are programs that have taken this step.

Bilateral Social Security Treaties for Expatriates and TCNs

Many countries have bilateral social security agreements that enable expatriates, including TCNs, to avoid making simultaneous contributions to both their native and host countries' social security systems. The agreements also permit employees to combine periods of coverage under foreign systems for the purpose of determining eligibility in their home country programs (totalization). Currently, the United States has agreements with the following 24 countries:

Australia	Denmark	Italy	Portugal
Austria	Finland	Japan	South Korea
Belgium	France	Luxembourg	Spain
Canada	Germany	Netherlands	Sweden
Chile	Greece	Norway	Switzerland
Czech Republic	Ireland	Poland	United Kingdom

The specific provisions regarding coverage and totalization of benefits will vary among the individual agreements. For U.S. expatriates, most agreements provide that work performed abroad on a permanent basis be covered under the system in the country in which the employee is working. For temporary assignments—generally less than five years—it is usually possible to remain in the U.S. system and not make duplicate contributions.

The European Union (EU) has a special totalization agreement created by the Treaty of Rome. It has three main features:

1. It allows nationals of EU countries to combine their years of participation under the social security systems of all EU countries to establish eligibility for benefits. Each country then pays proportionate benefits for the years of coverage under its own system.
2. It allows employees on temporary assignment to another EU country to remain in their home-country system for pension benefits and to participate in the host-country system for other benefits. "Temporary" is defined as 12 months, with the possibility of one 12-month extension.

3. It provides for equal, nondiscriminatory treatment of all EU nationals under the systems of member countries.

In a move to modernize its administration, the Electronic Exchange of Social Security Information will be implemented by May 2012, and EU citizens will be issued portable documents, including the European Health Insurance Card, to verify the social security system under which they are covered.

Regulatory Environment

The regulatory environment includes taxation of benefit plans, financing and funding restrictions, and other issues.

Taxation of Benefit Plans

In most countries, employer and employee contributions and pension plan assets receive some form of tax relief. Benefits are commonly taxed as ordinary income, although some countries tax either lump-sum or income benefits on a more advantageous basis. The requirements for this tax relief will differ from country to country, but generally they include provisions similar to those in the United States. However, the requirements are usually not as comprehensive.

Not all countries offer complete tax relief on pension plans. In Australia, employer contributions (and certain employee contributions) to approved plans are partially taxed, as are the plan assets. In New Zealand, pension plans are tax-neutral. Here, employer and employee contributions to pension plans, and the assets, are fully taxed, but benefit payments are generally tax-free.

In many countries, discrimination is not such a concern as it is in the United States. In those countries where it is not, benefit programs can often discriminate by using different

- Retirement ages for males and females
- Required levels of employee contributions
- Eligibility requirements
- Benefit formulas for classes of employees

There are many other ways in which employers may discriminate. What is permitted will depend on the country, and for some countries the ability to discriminate is beginning to disappear. In 1990, in the case of *Barber* v. *the Guardian Royal Exchange*, the European Court of Justice ruled that occupational pension schemes are considered as pay, and, therefore, must be equal between the sexes. It cited the nondiscrimination clause of the Treaty of Rome as the basis for its decision. This case had implications for all companies with operations in the European Community.

Financing and Funding Restrictions

Often, the requirements for an approved plan will include restrictions on the funding of the plan or on where the plan assets may be invested.

In Germany, employers have several choices for the funding of retirement plans, which include a form of trust fund (support fund or pension funds), book reserves, and direct insurance, but only plans that are book-reserved are free from restriction. Tax-free contributions to direct insurance, pensionfonds, and support funds are limited.

Many other countries have restrictions. Currently, companies subject to the Labor Standards Law in Taiwan are required to fund a portion of the retirement benefits with the Central Trust of China, while trustee-managed provident funds in India must be invested 15 percent in specified government securities and government-approved securities, and 25 percent in bonds and securities of public sector companies and financial institutions. In Mexico and Switzerland, the restrictions are less onerous, but are still there and include limitations on the amounts that can be invested outside the country and in certain asset classes like real estate and equities.

Other Issues

There are numerous other regulatory issues particular to each country that need to be understood. The principal ones include mandatory indexation of benefits, works councils and employee representation, and accounting and reporting requirements.

Mandatory Indexation of Benefits

Typically, most countries do not require that pension payments be indexed to inflation (although it may be customary practice to provide such protection), but this may be changing. Inflation is a worldwide concern, and its effect on the erosion of pension benefits is being addressed by some countries. The United Kingdom enacted the Pensions Act of 1995, which mandates limited indexation of pensions in payment for service after April 1997. Similar legislation exists in Germany.

Works Councils and Employee Representation

Many countries, particularly those in Europe, require that employees have a say in the management of a company's activities, and this generally

TABLE 34-8

Minimum Number of Employees Before a Works Council is Required

	Number of Employees in Company
Belgium	100
Denmark	35
France	50
Germany	5
Netherlands	50

includes issues relating to pay systems (which include employee benefits), dismissals, recruitment, and working hours. The forms that this role takes vary, but the most common are Works Councils. The degree of authority and control will be different for each country, but these councils almost always cover employee benefit plans. Table 34-8 indicates the minimum number of employees in a company before a Works Council is required in five European countries.

Employee representation may take other forms, such as direct representation on pension committees or boards. For example, in Spain, there is legislation permitting pension funds on a tax-advantaged basis. However, one of the requirements for achieving the tax-qualified status is that each company must establish a committee to oversee the plan and fund management, and employees must represent at least one half of that committee.

Accounting and Reporting Requirements

U.S. multinationals must be concerned with both local and U.S. reporting requirements. Local accounting and reporting requirements are not usually as onerous as the requirements in the United States for domestic plans, although that is beginning to change. In the United States, most of the requirements for foreign plans relate to Financial Accounting Standards Board (FASB) Statements No. 87 (FAS 87), No. 106 (FAS 106), No. 112 (FAS 112), and No. 158 (FAS 158), which have now been consolidated under Accounting Standards Codification (ASC) 715.

FAS 87 requires U.S. companies to calculate and report pension costs using explicit assumptions and also requires (via FAS 158) expanded disclosure in financial statements; FAS 106 has similar requirements for other postemployment costs, such as life insurance and medical coverage; FAS

112 covers other postemployment costs, including severance payments and continued medical coverage while disabled. Most non-U.S. plans must be included on a basis similar to U.S. plans.

All companies listed in the Economic Union, as well as in Brazil (from 2010) and Canada (from 2011), have to follow International Accounting Standard 19 (IAS 19). Australia, Japan, Mexico, and Taiwan have similar rules that deal with accounting and reporting requirements.

There are projects in progress looking at revising IAS 19, which will likely change the way in which postretirement and postemployment benefits are treated and reported. In addition, the International Accounting Standards Board and the FASB have been meeting regularly with a stated goal of developing a common set of accounting standards.

Economic and Labor Environment

Prevailing economic conditions can be an influencing factor in the design of international benefit plans and can have a significant impact on plan costs. However, rarely will they dictate the final plan design. The more important factors are inflation and interest rates, but exchange-rate manipulation or currency controls can also have an impact—particularly in countries with high inflation. Normally, currencies appreciate or depreciate in line with inflation, but some countries (e.g., Mexico and Brazil) have previously manipulated exchange rates to further other economic goals. In these instances, costs in U.S. dollar terms can be affected. Table 34-9 shows inflation and interest rates in selected countries.

With respect to labor, it is important to have an understanding of the following:

1. The prevalence and types of labor unions—whether they are local or national in scope.
2. The depth of the labor movement—does it encompass management as well as hourly employees?
3. The local supply of and demand for labor.

The makeup of the labor movement will vary significantly in each country. In some, most of the workforce may not be unionized, and those workers that are generally are concentrated in small, loosely organized local unions. In others, most of the country may belong to one union or another, as in Belgium, where more than 80 percent of the workforce is unionized—including white-collar or management employees. Unions may operate at the local or national level. In Italy, management employees,

TABLE 34-9

Inflation and Interest Rates–June 2010

Country (%)	Inflation (%)	Yield on 10-Year Government Bonds
Argentina	2.0	13.07* (5-year bond)
Australia	2.5	5.09*
Belgium	2.0	3.45
Canada	2.0	3.09*
Chile	3.0	NA
China	4.0	3.31*
Colombia	NA	3.69 (5-year bond)
Denmark	1.8	2.68
Egypt	NA	5.61*
France	1.9	3.05
Germany	1.6	2.57
Hong Kong	2.8	2.29
India	4.7	7.57*
Japan	1.1	1.09*
Korea (South)	2.5	4.96*
Mexico	3.4	6.85*
Netherlands	1.8	2.81
Russia	NA	6.37* (9-year bond)
Sweden	2.4	2.57
Turkey	4.1	9.62
United Kingdom	3.3	3.31*
Venezuela	NA	15.15*

- Government bond yields were obtained from Datastream.
- Inflation rates are 10-year forecasts from the Economist Intelligence Unit or Consensus Economics.
- Bond yields with an asterisk are based on semiannual coupons; in most cases, the effective annual yield is close to the rate shown.
- Data effective June 2010.
- NA, not available.

or dirigenti, generally belong to one of two trade unions, which negotiate on their behalf on a national basis.

Obviously, the supply of and demand for labor can also affect the design and costs of benefit plans. As an example, countries with younger populations generally might find defined contribution plans more acceptable than defined benefit plans. Similarly, older populations would probably prefer the security of a defined benefit plan. Around the industrialized world there is a trend for governments to shift a greater burden of their benefit costs to the private sector. As in the United States, the population in these countries is growing older, and there are fewer workers to contribute to programs such as social security. Table 34-10 shows the population of people under age 15 and over age 64 as a percentage of the population between ages 15 and 64 in ten countries. It shows that the number of older people is steadily increasing (rapidly in Italy and Japan), while the number of young people entering the workforce is stable or declining.

But, this is not the case in every country. Many Latin American countries, as well as some of the developing countries, are currently enjoying a "baby boom" period, and the number of eligible workers far outnumbers older workers and retired employees. For example, in India and Mexico, more than 30 percent of the population is under age 15, which contrasts with only 14 percent in Japan and Italy. However, the problem in some of these countries may not be the quantity of labor, but the quality.

GLOBAL BENEFIT OBJECTIVES AND PLAN DESIGN

Most employers recognize the importance of rewarding their employees for their contributions to growth and profits without regard to whether they are domestic or international employees. One of the ways in which employers balance the need for employee reward and business objectives (including sound governance) is to develop a statement of policy and objectives that acts as a guide to the establishment, modification, and administration of benefit plans. Usually, this statement is an expression of the employer's preferences as opposed to rigid instructions.

Establishing international benefit programs takes place at two levels—determining global objectives, and designing plans for local nationals, expatriates, and TCNs that meet these objectives.

Global Benefit Objectives

Global policy statements and objectives generally state the company's philosophy and overall attitude for employee benefits, as well as outlining

TABLE 34-10

Population Projections (Data Updated 2010)

	1965	1995	2010	2030	2050
Age < 15 as Percentage of Age 15–64					
United States	51	33	30	32	32
Japan	38	23	21	18	21
Germany	35	24	21	21	23
France	41	30	29	27	27
Italy		22	21	18	22
United Kingdom	36	30	26	27	26
Canada	57	30	23	25	25
Mexico		60	44	34	30
China		41	24	23	21
India		59	47	35	34
Age ≥ 65 as Percentage of Age 15–64					
United States	16	19	19	32	33
Japan	9	21	35	51	71
Germany	18	23	31	45	52
France	19	23	25	37	44
Italy		24	30	44	62
United Kingdom	19	24	24	35	39
Canada	13	18	27	43	45
Mexico		7	10	18	31
China		9	12	25	40
India		8	8	13	25

Source: U.S. Bureau of the Census, International Data Base, http://www.census.gov/ipc/www/idb/informationGateway.php

the process to receive approval for new programs or plan changes. The documents also include broad policy statements on total remuneration; definition of competitive practice; uniformity of treatment and internal equity; mergers and acquisitions; costs; and employee communications.

Global objectives rarely get into specifics on the type of benefits for each country, because the variations are likely to be too great. The following is a synopsis of the elements in a global policy.

Total Remuneration

This part of the policy encompasses the overall level of competitiveness for each element of pay, including employee benefits. The total package (base pay, regular bonus, incentive bonus, perquisites, allowances, and employee benefits), as well as each individual component of pay, is usually addressed. Such items as tax effectiveness and the state of the business (e.g., startup situations require different rewards than mature, stable operations) are also covered.

Preferences for specific levels and types of benefits are included. For example, a policy for retirement plans might state the following:

- Defined contribution plans are preferred to defined benefit plans.
- For defined benefit plans, career-average formulas are preferred to final-pay plans.
- Where possible, employees should share in the cost of funding the plans.
- Benefits should be at the 60th percentile of comparable companies for management employees, and the 50th percentile for all other employees.
- Plans should take into account social security benefits wherever possible, but not through a direct offset.
- Trust arrangements are preferred to insurance.
- Insurance contracts should be experience-rated where possible by using a multinational pooling arrangement (discussed in detail later in the chapter).
- Actuarial valuations should be performed for defined benefit plans no less frequently than every three years.

Similar information should be recorded for each benefit area—retirement, death, disability, and medical.

Definition of Competitive Practice

While actual competitive practice is likely to differ from country to country, it is helpful to have some broad guidelines for each local operation to follow. In some countries, it may be appropriate to limit the definition to only those companies that are direct competitors in a specific industry. In other countries, it may make sense to expand to other industries. Much will depend on the state of the business in a particular country—for example, a manufacturer may not want to limit the definition to only those companies in its industry when the competition operates principally sales and distribution facilities and does little or no manufacturing. Similarly, a startup operation in a mature market environment will want to include relatively stable and long-standing companies in its definition. The definition does not have to be limited to industry alone, nor does one standard have to apply for all groups of employees. Many companies expand it to include geographic location (city, suburb, or country location), ownership (U.S. multinational, foreign multinational, or indigenous), type of activity (sales or manufacturing), and size, and also will have different definitions for different groups of employees. Table 34-11 is a useful guideline for determining appropriate comparator groups and companies for different categories of employee.

Uniformity of Treatment

In many countries, it is permissible to differentiate between groups of employees (e.g., senior management and other employees), although this differential treatment may not be considered appropriate by U.S. management, whether it is permissible or not. This section of the policy usually deals with these issues, and generally it is expanded to include matters concerning internal equity, particularly those that involve cross-border comparisons. Cross-border evaluations are difficult because many factors, such as exchange-rate fluctuations, local taxes, social security, and living standards are involved.

Mergers and Acquisitions

Typically, companies have three choices for dealing with mergers and acquisitions issues: (1) integrating immediately with corporate benefit programs and policies, (2) maintaining current arrangements without change, or (3) a gradual integration into corporate programs. To the extent a company's preference is articulated in a global policy statement, local managers will be better equipped to handle mergers and acquisitions situations. Many companies simply follow established U.S. company policy in these instances.

Costs

A global statement will outline how costs are to be budgeted and reported and also indicate the preferred level of employee cost sharing. There also

TABLE 34-11

Guidelines to Identification of Comparison Companies

Comparison Factor	Production	Clerical and Administrative	Professional and Technical Staff	Sales persons and Middle Managers	Senior Managers
Geographical location	City and Country				
Industry	Type of Industry(ies)				
Ownership of company	Locally Owned, Multinational Companies, U.S.-Owned Subsidiaries				
Type of activity	Manufacturing, Marketing, Sales, and Distribution				
Company size (sales)	Comparable, Smaller, Larger Than Operations				
Competitive level	Quartile Ranking—1st, Median, 3rd, Other				

may be sections outlining the company's policy relating to funding levels and types of investments.

Employee Communications

This section might indicate the information that employees are entitled to have on existing programs and the frequency with which it should be provided to the employees. It may also specify how the information might be made available to employees.

Local Benefit Plan Design

Local benefits should be determined for each country within the framework of the global policy, but this is not always possible. The employer must try to balance corporate policy against the local realities, which include the following:

- Legislative restrictions
- Tax implications
- Other liabilities, such as termination indemnities that are really delivering retirement income
- Different actuarial practices
- Smaller, more volatile local investment markets
- Cultural differences or preferences

The local programs can be designed by a corporate benefits manager, but more often they are developed locally for approval by the head office. Generally, it makes sense to involve local and corporate management in the decision-making process as early as possible.

Plan Design—U.S. Expatriates

The objective of the vast majority of U.S. employers with respect to benefit plans for expatriates is to keep the employee in the U.S. programs—but this is not always possible. Much will depend on whether the employee is working for a branch or foreign subsidiary of the U.S. company.

Employees working in a foreign branch of a U.S. corporation are automatically covered by their employer's U.S. qualified plan unless specifically excluded. Section 410(b)(3)(C) of the Internal Revenue Code (IRC) and Section 4(b) of the Employee Retirement Income Security Act (ERISA) allow a U.S. qualified plan to exclude nonresident aliens from plan coverage in cases where they do not receive any U.S. source income. This permits companies to cover only those employees of a foreign branch who are U.S. citizens or resident aliens (green card holders).

Any company considering this approach should note the following:

- The exclusion of nonresident aliens must be specifically written into the plan document.
- The law in some foreign jurisdictions may treat the accrual of benefits under a U.S. plan as a taxable event.
- The law in some countries may not allow a deduction, for foreign income tax purposes, to the foreign branch; a U.S. tax deduction is allowed, however.

Individuals working in a foreign subsidiary, unlike employees in a branch, are not employees of the U.S. corporation. As such, these employees are not legally entitled to participate in qualified plans maintained in the United States unless specific steps are taken. IRC Section 406 allows such employees to be deemed employees of the U.S. parent company, but, to qualify, companies must elect, under Section 3121(1), to provide U.S. Social Security coverage for all U.S. citizens and resident alien employees of the foreign subsidiary. This election can be made separately for each subsidiary and is irrevocable. The election is made by filing Form 2032 with the Internal Revenue Service (IRS).

Alternatively, if the subsidiary is part of the controlled group of the U.S. parent (requiring at least 80 percent ownership of the subsidiary by the U.S. parent), selected U.S. citizens and resident alien employees can be covered in U.S. qualified plans under IRC Section 414.

Plan Design—Third-Country Nationals

By definition, TCNs are expatriate employees, but for benefit purposes they are often treated differently. Few companies will try to maintain a TCN in his or her home-country benefit plan unless the assignment is temporary. If the transfer abroad is clearly denoted as temporary and if the employees can be classified as "on loan" to the foreign office, then it is usually possible to continue home-country coverage for periods up to two or three years. If this is not possible, then the employee is typically "made whole" on his or her return to the home country.

Other TCNs can be either permanent or mobile ("true TCNs"). Permanent TCNs are normally included in the host-country plan ("localized") and are not usually a problem. True TCNs, on the other hand, create problems because they are rarely in one country long enough to accrue any meaningful service for retirement benefits. For this reason, many companies design international retirement plans that cover this specific category of employee. These plans may provide a benefit based on home- or host-country programs, U.S. levels, or a special benefit formula designed for the TCNs. These plans are generally either book-reserved or funded offshore in order to minimize the tax implications. Many of the plans that have been in place for a number of years are umbrella plans, in which the actual benefit provided by the plan is generally offset by other retirement benefits accrued during the employee's career, including social security, termination indemnities, and any company-provided benefits. Newer TCN plans are much more likely to be developed on a defined contribution basis.

ADMINISTRATION AND FINANCIAL MANAGEMENT OF INTERNATIONAL BENEFIT PLANS

The administration and management of international plans, from the corporate perspective, typically involves two key areas: design and financial considerations. But before these can be examined, there will probably be a need to get information concerning the benefit programs at each foreign location.

Most companies conduct periodic audits of their international benefit plans. In the past, this process involved designing a questionnaire, getting the local operations to complete it, and analyzing the results. Nowadays, with the development of the Internet, there are a number of Web-based systems specifically developed to facilitate the data collection process. Table 34-12 provides a list of the items that are typically included on a questionnaire or within a Web-based system.

Once the data have been collected, it will be possible to determine the potential cost savings with respect to design considerations by evaluating the following:

1. The relative competitive position.
2. Whether the plans are properly integrated with statutory benefits.
3. Whether the program specifications, such as normal retirement age and employee contribution levels, are consistent with the global objectives.
4. The administration of the plans to see if there are more cost-effective methods.

TABLE 34-12

Data Collection Items for International Audit

Retirement Plans	Health Care Plans	Long-Term Disability Income Plans
Type of plan	Type of plan	Type of plan
Eligibility requirements	Eligibility requirements	Eligibility requirements
Definition of covered earnings	Hospital room & board	Benefit amount
Benefit formula	Hospital miscellaneous	Integration
Normal retirement	Surgical	Duration of benefit
Early retirement	Attending physician	Lump-sum benefits
Integration	In-Hospital	Employee contributions
Benefit payment form	Outpatient	Company contributions/cost
Vesting	Major medical	Claims history
Employee contributions	Deductible	Financing medium
Company contributions/cost	Coinsurance	
Financing medium	Maximum	
	Employee contributions	
	Company contributions/cost	
	Claims history	
	Financing medium	
	Dental	
	Vision/Hearing	**Severance**
	Maternity	Amount of payment
	Prescription drugs	Conditions of payment
	Psychiatric	Notice period

Salary Continuation	Preretirement Death Benefits	Perquisites
Type of plan	Eligibility requirements	Company cars
Eligibility requirements	Lump-sum amount	Driver
Benefit amount	AD&D	Club memberships
Integration	Business travel	Annual medical checkups
Duration of benefit	Survivor income	Subsidized meals
Lump-sum benefits	Employee contributions	Mobile telephones
Employee contributions	Company contributions/cost	Long-term incentives
	Claims history	Separate executive contracts
	Financing medium	

Financial considerations include accounting, funding, investment management, and risk management. With respect to funding and investment management, corporate managers need to focus on the issues in each country that are similar to those for their U.S. plans. These include determining the pace at which funding should occur; appropriate funding media; whether the plan should be funded at all, or book-reserved; the actuarial process (reporting, methodology, and assumptions); and investment management.

With funding media, some progressive multinational companies are also exploring the use of their captive insurance arrangements and cross-border (i.e., multiple-country) financing vehicles to further leverage their global purchasing power.

The investment management process probably has the most scope for controlling or reducing benefit costs. It has been estimated that a 1 percent per year improvement in return on plan assets can reduce costs by 10 percent or more per year. In the United States, this area gets considerable attention; but this is not so overseas, where the plans are generally smaller and encumbered with different types of legislation. However, in such countries as Australia, Canada, Japan, the Netherlands, Switzerland, and the United Kingdom, where trusts are common, or at least an acceptable alternative for pension investing, the same scope exists for managing the investment process, and generally the same principles used in the United States can be exported overseas, and even considered on a global basis.

The risk management aspect of international benefit plans generally revolves around the concept of multinational pooling.

Multinational Pooling

Insured employee benefits in a multinational company are generally undertaken through separate arrangements in each country. Thus, employees in each country will be covered for such benefits as life insurance, medical and dental coverage, disability, and retirement benefits through a local insurance company or financial organization in accordance with local conditions and practices. In the absence of multinational pooling, local insurance arrangements would not enjoy any economies of scale based on the worldwide size of the group.

Using group life insurance as an example, the insurance contract in each country involves a premium payment to the local insurance company in return for the agreed-upon coverage. Dividends may be paid out of the insurer's overall profits (if any) at the end of the contract year. A variation on this, known as "experience rating," involves the linking of either the dividend or the premium to the actual claims experience of the local subsidiary.

Experience rating is an advantage when claims are lower than the "average," because the cost of insurance is based partly on the company's own claims, rather than on the average level of claims. Experience rating can also reduce insurance costs by reducing the "risk charge" made by the insurer. In return, the company incurs an additional risk of loss when claims are high. This is generally more practical if the company has a large number of employees insured under the contract, because there is likely to be greater stability of total annual claim payments.

Multinational pooling enables the principles of experience rating to be applied to the worldwide insurance arrangements of a multinational company. If the subsidiary companies use insurers associated with an insurance "network," then a "multinational dividend" can be paid based on the actual combined experience of those subsidiaries. Thus, the group will benefit from favorable experience and also bear some of the risk of bad experience.

The multinational pooling arrangement consists of a contract between the parent company and the coordinating insurer of the network. It is thus independent of local practice governing payment of dividends on local contracts. In fact, the existence of the multinational contract has little effect on the premiums, dividends, and claim payments under the local contracts.

A multinational pooling arrangement operates on two levels. First, an employer contracts with an insurance network to share the profits and losses of the network's business with the subsidiaries of the parent company. Second, individual contracts are negotiated between the subsidiary and the local network insurer. These contracts conform with local laws, competitive practice, dividend payments, and the like. A multinational dividend is paid based on the sum total of experience under each of the individual contracts. In essence, this is the meaning of multinational pooling.

Advantages of Multinational Pooling

The primary objective of multinational pooling is a reduction in overall insurance costs, resulting from the receipt of multinational dividends. These dividends arise in years when experience is favorable. If experience is unfavorable, however, the worst that can happen is the cancellation of the dividend, perhaps for several years.

In a sense, an insurance network can afford to give "something for nothing."

Multinational dividends arise from the following factors:

- If a company has low claims, the experience rating approach enables that company to share in the savings.
- In a few countries, local regulations or gentlemen's agreements exist that limit the freedom of the insurers to compete on premiums and dividends. Pooling arrangements may provide a legal means of returning some of the profits resulting from these restrictions.
- Pooling reduces the risk faced by the local insurers, because heavy claims in one country can be met out of the multinational dividend earned from favorable experience in other countries. This can result in reduced "risk charges" by the local insurers.
- Membership in a multinational network offers competitive advantages to a local insurer. Therefore, an insurer may be willing to offer favorable terms to users of a network to become the network's associate insurer in the local country.

Reduced insurance costs are the main advantage of multinational pooling. However, there are a number of other benefits to be gained:

- *Annual accounting on a centralized basis.* More information is available on a company's group insurance costs around the globe and on how those costs are determined.
- *Centralized communication.* In dealing with one "group" office, rather than individual local insurance companies or branches in each country, a company can reduce administrative time and expense.
- *Relaxed underwriting limits.* Because insurance companies wish to protect themselves against high risks, group life and disability coverage for executives is typically subject to satisfactory medical examinations. By pooling lives in a number of locations, the risk of adverse experience is reduced substantially, and the insurance company is more willing to raise or eliminate the limits at which medical evidence is required. This can also be helpful if an executive transfers to a new country.

The Multinational Pooling Account

The multinational pooling account is sometimes known as a "second-stage account" because it is drawn up after all payments under the local contracts (e.g., premiums, claims, and dividends) have been made. Its principal advantage is that it provides financial information, normally not available from the local insurers, on the foreign benefit programs for each operation in the pooling program.

Although the actual format of a multinational pooling account (or experience statement) will vary from one carrier to the next, it will normally contain the following items:

- Credits:
  - Premiums paid by the company
  - Investment earnings on company-paid premiums
- Debits:
  - Claims
  - Risk charges
  - Insurer expenses
  - Commissions
  - Local dividend payments
- Funds retained:
  - Additions to reserves (most often for pensions but also occasionally for some risk benefits)
- Balance:
  - Multinational dividend

The multinational dividend is the balance of the account, and the anticipated result of a pooling program. Positive balances arising in countries where experience has been favorable are used to offset negative balances in countries where experience has been poor. Any remaining balance is paid by the network as a dividend to the multinational parent company. In some companies, this dividend is then distributed to the subsidiary companies that had positive balances.

Where Multinational Pooling May Not Work

Over recent years, many companies have established multinational pooling contracts for their overseas employee benefit coverage, and more can be expected to do so. However, pooling is not necessarily appropriate for every multinational organization or every situation. Examples of situations in which multinational pooling may not work include the following:

- Not enough employees are located overseas. Typically, an employer should have at least 500 employees in at least two countries outside the United States who are covered by group insurance, although some networks are now offering small-groups pools where less than 500 employees are involved.

- In some countries, the network's local insurer may not be competitive or the network may not have a local representative insurer.
- In a few countries, such as Brazil and India, some networks may experience difficulty in pooling or in paying dividends outside the country.
- Local management may refuse to change carriers. This could occur for a number of reasons, including excellent service from the existing carrier, long-standing personal relationships, or national pride.
- In some countries, such as the United Kingdom and the United States, premium rates are extremely low. This means that the insurer's profit margin is low and the risk of adverse claims experience might outweigh the expected additional multinational dividend.
- The employer's business is in an industry with above-average claims experience.

SUMMARY

There are several trends that are influencing the design and management of international employee benefits. These include the following:

- An emerging objective of "shared responsibility" where both employers and employees have roles in containing costs and providing for benefits
- A global shift from defined benefit plans to defined contribution
- Globalization of operations whereby the workforce demographics are becoming increasingly international and companies must balance local design with international expectations (and mobility)

In the United States, it has been common for years for employees to share in the costs for medical and retirement plans, and this is expanding quickly around the world. With respect to health and welfare benefits, employees share the costs through payment of premiums as well as deductibles and coinsurance. This responsibility has expanded beyond simple cost sharing, and, through education and plan design, employees are being encouraged to become active consumers of medical assistance to help control costs. Additionally, the emergence of wellness and disease management as key health and welfare objectives puts a greater obligation on employees to maintain their health and control costs. On the retirement side, defined contribution plans place a significant responsibility on employees to fund their own retirement.

The switch from defined benefit to defined contribution plans in the United States is well documented and understood, and many even think that the trend has slowed or perhaps reached a peak. But, outside the United States and particularly in Western Europe, the trend is still emerging and picking up speed. Defined contribution plans have been common in countries like the United Kingdom for years, but not in places like Germany or Spain, where traditional defined benefit plans that are integrated with social security have been the standard—until now. Recent legislation now permits defined contribution plans, albeit with local nuances (e.g., in Germany, benefits must still be paid out in an annuity instead of a lump sum to retain tax advantages), and many companies are taking a hard look at their old defined benefit plans to see what new, lower-cost, alternatives may be available.

Walk into any office of a multinational company outside the United States and you are now likely to see a very diverse and international workforce. Previously, the Country Manager and Head of Finance or Manufacturing may have been expatriates while the rest of the workforce were local nationals. But now there are expatriates on temporary assignments, former expatriates who have decided to stay on and have, localized nonlocals who have been recruited from competing companies, foreign students who have gained local employment, and so on. These diverse workforces are creating some very interesting challenges for benefits design, as the expectations of the nonlocals can be very different from what the local labor, accounting, and tax laws permit in terms of benefits design.

The challenge for employee benefit managers is to assist their companies in developing and maintaining their competitive edge while at the same time keeping an eye on issues such as internal equity and cost. In order to accomplish these tasks on a global basis, managers must have a thorough understanding of the employee benefits and related environments in the countries in which they operate, and must be satisfied that the programs they have in place are in compliance and have been appropriately reported.

INDEX

F

H

M

O

Z

ABOUT THE EDITOR

Jerry S. Rosenbloom, Ph.D., is the Frederick H. Ecker emeritus professor of insurance and risk management at the Wharton School of the University of Pennsylvania. His areas of research include employee benefits, financial planning, financial services, risk, and risk management. Dr. Rosenbloom resides in Broomall, PA.